Property in Land
and Other Resources

Property
in Land and Other
Resources

Edited by
Daniel H. Cole *and* **Elinor Ostrom**

LINCOLN INSTITUTE
OF LAND POLICY
CAMBRIDGE, MASSACHUSETTS

Library of Congress Cataloging-in-Publication Data

Property in land and other resources / edited by Daniel H. Cole and Elinor Ostrom.
    p.   cm.
Includes index.
   ISBN 978-1-55844-221-4
   1. Right of property.   2. Real property.   3. Natural resources.   I. Cole, Daniel H.   II. Ostrom, Elinor.
   HB701.P737 2012
   333.3—dc23   2011029993

Designed by Westchester Book Services

Composed in Minion Pro by Westchester Book Services in Danbury, Connecticut.
Printed and bound by Puritan Press Inc., in Hollis, New Hampshire.

♻ The paper is Rolland Enviro100, an acid-free, 100 percent PCW recycled sheet.

MANUFACTURED IN THE UNITED STATES OF AMERICA

Third Printing, May 2015

Contents

Illustrations

FIGURES

Foreword

As evidenced by the quality of the chapters in this volume, the study of property rights has come a long way in the past half century. The pioneering role of three major contributors to this progress should be acknowledged. Vincent Ostrom played a critical role in the development of property rights and institutions long before they were fashionable; he and Charles Tiebout did some spectacular early work on property rights. Herb Simon deserves acknowledgment as well because he forced economists to move beyond the narrow view and to think in broader terms about the issues that are of interest to us today.

Looking behind the issues and assumptions of the chapters that follow, we may consider some of the persistent and underlying problems that confront us: problems the basic sources of which underlie all explanations in the social sciences.

First our understanding of the external world is subjective. We have only our eyes, ears, nose, and feeling with which to interpret the world. Because our experiences are unique to each individual and only partially shared by others, the result is a complicated world. Our brains translate the communications from our senses and construct the elaborate framework that we use to interpret this world. This assertion is not unique or original to me. Friedrich Hayek said it in his book *The Sensory Order*, and one cannot help but be awed by his early understanding of the issues: he wrote the book as a graduate student in 1920, although it was not published until 1952. Hayek's intuitive understanding of how the mind and brain work in constructing an explanation of the external world has led to our evolving, but incomplete, explanations of the world around us. It is the cultural heritage of different societies that makes for the variety of explanations, and we have no simple way to resolve these differences. Conflicting understandings about the world around us, such as those between the Western world and the Islamic world, derive from the constructions of different cultures to account for the political/economic/social systems.

Second, the tools we use to translate understanding into a framework are institutions composed of formal rules, informal norms, and enforcement characteristics. Institutions are very blunt instruments to deal with very complex issues. Perhaps because the norms of behavior and the formal rules do not work or because enforcement is imperfect, the problems are still unresolved. Underlying the economic and social institutions must be a political framework. In order to understand that framework and how societies work, we need a theory of politics, which does not exist.

Third, time poses a thorny set of problems. It is necessary to take into account the culture of a society, including the beliefs and institutions that we inherit from the past that constrain our choice sets in the present and the future. Culture therefore embodies what we have brought up from the past that we build on in dealing with the present and the future. You must know where you have been in order to know where you are going. Another important aspect of time is that we are evolving, and that evolution poses serious limits on our understanding of the problems we will face in the future. In consequence, there are real limitations on the creation of a genuine dynamic theory of change because the problems down the road will be different from those we had in the past. We have only to look at the evolution of the financial structure in the crisis that began in 2007 to see how different that structure is from the past one. Financial theories inherited from earlier times cannot give us a complete understanding of future problems. One of the dilemmas that economists confront is that their models are derived from the past, but in many fundamental ways the future, while built on the past, is inherently new, unique, and different.

All of this makes for a real challenge in constructing explanations, and we have a long way to go to do better. The chapters that follow are a good beginning.

DOUGLASS C. NORTH
Professor
Washington University in St. Louis

Introduction

DANIEL H. COLE AND ELINOR OSTROM

This book stems from a conversation between the two editors in 2008 about a variety of new articles on the California gold rush that challenged or substantially revised the conventional economic history of the 49ers. According to that conventional history, the miners chose contracts over guns for organizing their camps and erected, through a kind of Hayekian spontaneous organization, efficient property institutions (Umbeck 1981). The new historical analyses revised or challenged this "naïve" theory by (1) positing that the miners shared mental models of the world based on similar legal-cultural backgrounds, which enabled them to solve collective-action problems in the mining camps (Zerbe and Anderson 2001); (2) claiming that the governance regimes of the mining camps were much more than simple systems of contractually agreed private ownership (Clay and Wright 2005); and (3) noting how egalitarian norms of fairness, as much as or more than commitments to property rights, explained the organization of the mining camps (McDowell 2002).

The editors initially contemplated organizing a small conference on these new theories and histories of the gold rush. Gregory Ingram, the president of the Lincoln Institute of Land Policy in Cambridge, Massachusetts, expressed interest in the conference idea, but thought the conference should be broader in conception. After further conversations and the Lincoln Institute's offer to sponsor the conference and this book, the editors, along with Gregory Ingram and Yu-Hung Hong of the Lincoln Institute, organized a broader conference exploring the variety of property systems around the world and their implications for property theory (or theories). The gold rush remained part of the program, but it was no longer the focal point.

The conference, entitled "Evolution of Property Rights Related to Land and Natural Resources," was held in Cambridge, Massachusetts, in September 2010. In addition to the panel on the gold rush, the conference featured an opening lecture by Douglass C. North; a keynote presentation by Thráinn Eggertsson; and panels on air, wildlife, land, water, and the global commons. In addition to the presenters and discussants represented in this volume, conference participants included Scott Barrett, Vicki Been, Lee Anne Fennell, the late David Getches, Gregory Ingram, Jan Laitos, and Thomas Schelling. The editors would like to thank all the participants for their enthusiastic discussions, as well as Yu-Hung Hong of the Lincoln Institute, who worked very hard to bring the conference and this book to fruition.

This book begins, like the conference, with two introductory chapters designed to set the stage for the contributions that follow. In chapter 1, Thráinn Eggertsson expands on his keynote address, "Opportunities and Limits for the Evolution of Property Rights Institutions." He examines how assumptions of costly information and rational politics yield valuable tools for exploring the logic of institutions and institutional changes. After introducing some basics of the economics of property rights, Eggertsson explores six case studies from his native Iceland, where relatively simple and transparent institutions are ideal for identifying social regularities with general applicability. Those six cases cover a broad range, from feudal-like institutional structures that obstructed modernization of fishing technologies and led to widespread starvation in premodern Iceland to communal pastures in Iceland's mountainous regions that still persist after more than one thousand years and to Iceland's ongoing financial crisis and the recent political controversy over property rights in health records. Each of these cases illustrates concepts and topics in the current mainstream of new institutional economics (NIE). Eggertsson moves beyond the NIE mainstream to explore new directions stemming from work on social-choice theory showing how uncertainty and competing mental models of the world affect individual and social choices. As an example, Eggertsson examines the evolution of Iceland's persistently controversial system of fisheries regulation based on individual transferable quotas (ITQs). This system has been highly influential around the world, but it seems to be on the brink of being dismantled in Iceland because of a lack of social fit, stemming in large part from its institutional design. That design (1) reflected a "hodgepodge of conflicting social theories," which left the property status of ITQs ambiguous; and (2) resulted in huge windfall profits for the original recipients of fishing quotas, many of whom subsequently left Iceland, taking their profits with them. The design issues created both legal problems—the United Nations Human Rights Committee ruled in 2000 that Iceland's method of initially allocating fishing quotas only to experienced vessels violated international human rights law— and large-scale public dissatisfaction with the system. Because of that dissatisfaction, the system is now in jeopardy, even though it produces wider social benefits and ecological benefits for fisheries, and despite the fact that current holders of quotas paid a great deal of money for them and are not reaping windfall profits. Eggertsson's chapter provides an eye-opening introduction to the complex array of institutional design and implementation problems that confront efforts to conserve natural resources.

In chapter 2, Daniel H. Cole and Elinor Ostrom examine the current state of property theory relative to the impressive range, scope, and depth of recent social-scientific investigations into real-existing property systems. Property theory remains dominated by what Thráinn Eggertsson (1990, ch. 8) has called the "naïve" theory, according to which private property rights emerge and proliferate at some stage in a society's socioeconomic development in order to reduce externalities, transaction costs, and overexploitation of scarce resources that otherwise would be subject to an inexorable "tragedy of the commons" (following Demsetz 1967; Hardin 1968). However attractive that naïve theory of property rights might be, the simplistic story it tells of a unilateral progression toward private property, resulting in optimal (or, at least, maximal) resource conservation, is not consistent with the empirical evidence. We do, of course, find a great deal of private property virtually everywhere. In many cases, private property does successfully conserve resources over long periods of time. However, when we examine property systems around the world we find an almost bewildering variety of property systems in use, often involving complex admixtures of private, common, and public rights (and duties), which sometimes fail but often succeed in conserving resources over long periods of time. Neither the naïve theory of property nor any other existing theory explains the wealth of property systems found in the world. Thus, chapter 2 concludes with a call for more complex and realistic theories of property to keep pace with lessons from the social sciences.

In chapter 3, Karen Clay and Gavin Wright argue that the gold-mining camps of California had a more complex governance structure than economic historians have supposed. In some respects, the mining camps were canonical examples of the emergence of private-order property regimes, key elements of which were eventually codified in state and federal law (Umbeck 1981). However, the property rights created pursuant to the mining contracts (or codes) were far less secure than most other types of real property rights. Indeed, claim jumping became the most common method of acquiring a claim because of rules that often favored claim jumpers who would put the claims to more immediate use. In addition, Clay and Wright explore how the evolution of mining in nineteenth-century America fostered features that today are associated with a knowledge economy, including synergies between higher education and industry, federal support for scientific research and infrastructure, diffusion of codified forms of useful knowledge, and economic progress based on extension of the knowledge frontier. Thus, the conventional property rights story of the California gold-mining camps is only part (and perhaps not the most important part) of a larger tale about innovative advances in resource discovery, extraction, and processing that together created the world's leading national mining sector. This and the remaining chapters in this book are followed by commentaries from the scholars who discussed them at the conference. In this case, the Clay and Wright chapter is discussed by Peter Z. Grossman.

Chapter 4 presents another take on the California gold rush. Andrea G. McDowell compares that gold rush with others around the world and finds important common traits. She finds that the governance structure of California mining claims has been replicated in gold rushes in Australia, West Africa, South America, and Southeast Asia. That governance structure, she argues (consistently with Clay and Wright), has never involved the simple imposition of secure private property rights. Rather, gold-mining claims throughout the world have provided limited use rights, codified in local regulations. In each case, individuals have held small mining claims on condition of active use. Larger investors stay out of the gold region until surface mining by individuals is no longer profitable, so that capital can take advantage of superior technology, economies of scale, and lower wages. McDowell suggests that a system of individual mining claims will generally emerge under circumstances like those in California, that is, where there is a lot of gold near the surface that individual miners can reach with little capital investment. As mining becomes more difficult—for example, when collective action is required to work deeper shafts or to reach gold underlying river bottoms—the internal organization of mining teams begins to vary from one gold rush to another. Indeed, from a comparative analysis, it appears that California mining companies were unusually democratic in their organization. However, surface mining claims at the height of gold rushes seem to be shaped less by local culture than by the physical proximity of gold to the surface. McDowell's chapter is discussed by Mark T. Kanazawa.

In chapter 5, Daniel H. Cole argues that, contrary to both the suppositions of some legal scholars and the theoretical underpinnings of regulatory takings doctrine, government regulations not only impose on existing private property rights but also vindicate and sometimes even create public, private, and/or common property rights. After examining conflicting common-law and Roman law rules relating to property rights in the atmosphere, Cole focuses on how assertions of state sovereignty and regulations combine to create Hohfeldian rights and duties respecting the atmosphere, where rights and duties were previously unclear or nonexistent. Cole's claim is supported by evidence from both civil aviation regulation and air-pollution control. Cole also addresses how regulations have created private property rights to pollute in emissions-trading programs (regardless of congressional assertions to the contrary). In some cases, assertions of public property via acts of sovereignty are a prerequisite for the allocation of private property rights, not just in the atmosphere, but also in other natural resources, such as marine fisheries. The chapter concludes with a discussion of normative implications for property theory generally and regulatory takings doctrine in particular. A more dignified treatment of public regulations that are designed to protect public rights would raise a serious question about which set of property rights should prevail in the several regulatory takings cases where privately owned lands meet publicly owned waters. That question cannot reasonably be answered, however, until more work is done on a theory (or multiple theories) of public property to complement existing theories of private and common property. Cole's chapter is discussed by Wallace E. Oates.

In chapter 6, Nives Dolšak examines the property-based approach to air-pollution control known as "cap-and-trade" and analyzes aspects of its institutional design and implementation, particularly monitoring and enforcement issues that determine its success or failure as an environmental protection tool. The first part of the chapter combines the institutional analysis and development (IAD) framework first developed by Elinor Ostrom (2011) with elements from the comparative transaction-cost literature. Dolšak derives a novel analytical framework consisting of three basic elements: (1) external factors, including biophysical characteristics of the resource, external regulatory environments, and characteristics of resource users; (2) rules regulating resource use and users; and (3) design features of the cap-and-trade market, including trading rules, permits, and transaction costs. External factors can easily affect the success of a cap-and-trade regime. For example, a large, highly dispersed resource may make it difficult (that is, costly) to monitor use and assess the effects of use on resource stock. Similarly, a cap-and-trade regime may be more easily monitored and enforced, when the number of resource users/permit holders is relatively small. Rules regulating resource use, in particular quota limits and the structure and security of permitting, can also affect the success of a cap-and-trade market. For example, if the allocation system is perceived as grossly unfair or permits are insecure, the market may not take off. Constraints on, or high costs of, transferability may also hamper emissions markets.

In the second part of the chapter, Dolšak applies her framework to analyze several cap-and-trade programs (all from the United States), including the phasedown of lead in gasoline, early EPA emissions-trading programs, the Southern California Air Quality Management District's Regional Clean Air Incentives Market (RECLAIM), and the phaseout of ozone-depleting substances. Somewhat surprisingly, she finds that neither the spatial extent of the resource nor nonuniform effects of resource flows on resource stocks have had a significant impact on market performance under those various regimes. Meanwhile, transaction costs tend to fall over time. Thus, Dolšak concludes (with some caveats) that cap-and-trade programs may be applicable to a larger number of environmental problems than some critics have argued. Shi-Ling Hsu follows with a discussion of Dolšak's chapter.

In chapter 7, Jason F. Shogren and Gregory M. Parkhurst raise the question, who owns endangered species? The simple answer is that we all do. However, the authors note, that answer does not help us resolve the practical problem of ensuring the preservation of endangered species, especially the approximately 90 percent of those species whose critical habitats are on privately owned lands. Publicly owned endangered species on privately owned lands inevitably create a property regime conflict that federal agencies have attempted to defuse, to some extent, with safe-harbor and habitat-conservation plans. In addition, federal and state agencies, as well as nongovernmental organizations, have offered funding in the form of grants, loans, case payments, and tax allowances to private landowners who engage in habitat-protection, enhancement, or restoration activities. Whether such funding constitutes implicit compensation for a taking of private land for endangered species preservation is not the central question for Shogren and Parkhurst. Instead, they are concerned with the quality of habitat for species preservation, stemming from uncoordinated land management decisions of multiple private owners when species require relatively large, contiguous parcels of land crossing multiple private boundaries. As the authors note, "voluntary compensation programs are not designed to address directly the biologist's concern that landowners may not coordinate conservation efforts to create a contiguous reserve that falls across property lines. . . ." What is required is an incentive mechanism that will induce voluntary participation in species preservation while, at the same time, creating the necessary spatial configuration for effective preservation. Shogren and Parkhurst offer, as a potential solution to this two-part problem, agglomeration bonuses (a.k.a., "smart subsidies"), which provide higher levels of compensation to private landowners who retire land adjacent to other parcels devoted to species habitat. An experimental test of the agglomeration bonus confirms that it is a potentially superior tool of habitat preservation. It is "more biologically efficient at creating contiguous conservation reserves than current status quo policies of compulsion and a simple flat fee subsidy." James Wilson comments on the Shogren and Parkhurst chapter.

In chapter 8, Bonnie J. McCay explores the privatization trend in marine fisheries policy and its implications for communities of fishers. After briefly discussing the larger framework of spatial enclosure, exemplified by expanded national jurisdiction, marine protected areas, and territorial fishing rights, she focuses on the trend toward the creation of exclusive, transferable fishing rights, as exemplified in the Atlantic surf-clam fishery and individual transferable quotas (ITQs). ITQs have been promoted as tools not only for economic rationalization in overcapitalized fisheries, but also for enhanced stewardship. McCay reviews the literature and selected cases to assess their performance in relation to economic, social, and conservation goals in marine fisheries management. She finds that concerns about equity, as well as recognition that ITQs alone are generally incapable of achieving fishery-conservation goals, are leading to increased interest in the place of "community" in marine fisheries. In the United States this has led to catch-share allocations to communities and community-oriented groups, such as cooperatives and fishing associations. McCay examines several cases of community-based allocations and considers their usefulness as a tool for equitable and sustainable management of the marine commons. Anthony Scott discusses McCay's chapter.

Chapter 9, by William A. Fischel, examines three broad themes in the evolution of zoning. The first theme is the persistence of localism in zoning despite numerous top-down attempts to reform zoning in the past three decades, including the affordable-housing movement, school-finance-equalization requirements, the environmental justice movement, "smart growth" initiatives, and regulatory takings litigation. Most state reform efforts have made nary a dent in local zoning. A few exceptional federal reform efforts, such as the Fair Housing Act and the Religious Land Use and Institutionalized Persons Act, are exceptions, but even their effects on local zoners have been modest. Indeed, Fischel argues that the chief consequence of all the reforms, taken together, has been to make local zoning more restrictive. The chapter's second theme is a more personal reflection on how the author's views of zoning have changed over the past quarter century, during which he has come to view zoning increasingly as a critical part of local government, and local government as an essential part of a federal system. His third and final theme is a "gingerly advanced" proposition that the evolution of zoning is comparable to that of the common law and thus deserves more serious attention from scholars than it has received. Robert C. Ellickson discusses Fischel's chapter.

In chapter 10, C. Leigh Anderson and Richard O. Zerbe examine psychological aspects of property rights in the context of Native American land ownership. Specifically, they posit that a relevant concept of ownership derives from a sense of psychological entitlement, which depends not only on legal rights, but also on cultural and historical norms and expectations that give rise to a moral claim. Thus, moral claims underlie psychological entitlements. Those psychological entitlements, in turn, affect reference levels (the set of perceived rights from which one measures gains and losses) and potentially create valuation disparities (differences between willingness to pay and willingness to accept) across individuals with different moral claims over resources. In the absence of differing moral claims, those individuals could well value the resource identically. Applying their hypothesis to historical valuations of real property among Native American tribes, Anderson and Zerbe find that treaties, which focused on operational-level rights and economic valuation, presupposed reference points that failed to recognize the psychological entitlements many Native Americans held over the lands that were the subject of those treaties. The Native Americans' psychological entitlement arose from complex entitlement structures with roots in spiritual and religious traditions that supported cooperative behavior on tribal lands, which were held as common property. The treaties imposed untimely transitions from common to private property that eroded psychological, and possibly economic, value through changes in the complexity of the structures that promoted cooperative behavior. John A. Baden comments on the Anderson and Zerbe chapter.

Richard A. Epstein, in chapter 11, examines the similarities and differences between the law of land and water in both private and constitutional law. He notes that the nature of the two resources differs such that exclusive rights for occupation usually constitute the best framework for analyzing land use disputes, while a system of shared, correlative duties works best for water. Once these baselines are established, an accurate rendition of the constitutional law issues requires the proper articulation of private law rules of adjudication to explain which government actions result simply in a "mere" loss of economic value and which government actions generate losses that require compensation. Epstein offers a two-step process for dealing with the private law issues: (1) developing principles of parity between private claimants, to the extent physically possible; and (2) picking the set of rules that maximizes the overall utility of all parties concerned, subject to the parity constraint. However, this system must yield to reasonableness considerations when the conditions of physical parity cannot be satisfied, as in all disputes between upper and lower owners of land, as well as upstream and downstream riparians. In such cases, the objective should be to create, when possible, rules that treat the last element of loss to one party as equal to the last element of gain of the next. Epstein argues that using these natural law baselines would produce, by and large, efficient results in private disputes, while their rejection in the takings context in both land and water cases would concede far too much power to state authorities in both land and water cases. He concludes that rationalizing both areas of law requires that the constitutional protection of private property start with the definitions of private property that have worked well in practice under the natural law traditions of private law. Epstein's chapter is discussed by Henry E. Smith.

Chapter 12, by William Blomquist, provides a positive political treatment of property rights. His approach supplements standard political-economic accounts of property rights that combine a simple story of property rights emerging from conditions of scarcity (rising demand relative to supply) with empirical assessments of why and how certain property rights regimes emerge at certain times and places, along with normative critiques of existing property structures based on public choice analysis. Blomquist endeavors to supplement political-economic explanations of property with a more realistic assessment of the role of politics in the evolution of private property. A political approach to property rights is concerned with, in an elaboration on Lasswell's (1958) famous phrase, who gets to decide (and according to what criteria) "who gets what, when, how." To resolve that issue, Blomquist focuses on how property rules are developed and changed over time in settings involving multiple actors, multiple resource use values, and multiple rule-making arenas. Empirical examples relating to water resources demonstrate how basic conceptions of specific property rights can be associated with various water resource uses, including, for example, navigation, hydropower, recreation, waste disposal, and aesthetics. He then explains the ways in which resource use issues (or conflicts) are framed in political situations to influence inclusion or exclusion of certain participants and the choice of decision-making arenas. In every case, however, the outcomes are contingent and subject to being recontested, overruled, or contradicted on appeal. One important implication is that property rights are never settled for once and for all. In other words, they are never completely "well-defined," which is a condition that much of the property rights literature presupposes as necessary to secure investment. Blomquist illustrates these points with a description of developments in Colorado water law, where traditional holders of water rights, including agriculture and municipal/industrial supply, have focused on protecting their interests in courts based on legal precedents, while proponents of legal recognition of recreational uses and instream flows have taken their case to other decision-making arenas, including the legislature, administrative agencies, and public referenda. Beyond the obvious point that water law is complex and dynamic, his analysis shows that (1) individuals compete not only for the same rights but for different rights in the same resource; (2) a multifunctional resource multiplies the types of use rights over which individuals compete; and (3) a multiorganizational policy arena not only multiplies the number of decision points but also affects the strategies of interested parties. He suggests that the quest for any kind of simple theory of property institutions is likely to be fruitless. After all, he asks, how often would we expect to find a resource that has only one dimension of value and only one use, entitlements to which are determined by a single decision-maker in a single forum for once and for all? A more realistic theory of property must account for the dynamic political nature of ongoing contests between competing users of multiple-use resources. Edella C. Schlager discusses this chapter.

In chapter 13, Gary D. Libecap explores water in the semiarid western United States—a region in which many of the intensifying demand and supply problems regarding fresh water are playing out—as a mixed private/public resource. The complex politics of water, as well as its physical characteristics, raise the resource and political costs of defining and enforcing property rights and complicate efforts to manage and allocate water in markets. Libecap finds major differences in water prices in 12 western U.S. states across agricultural, urban, and environmental uses. The persistence of those differences suggests that water markets have not developed enough to narrow the gaps. Considerable differences in the extent and nature of water trading across the western states indicate that water values and transaction costs of trading vary considerably across jurisdictions. Libecap then examines the resource and political costs of defining water rights and expanding the use of markets. In this discussion, efficiency and equity objectives often conflict. Public and private water uses are often substantially intertwined, generating public interest claims that, although legitimate, are susceptible to abuse by special interests to weaken private property rights and the efficiency-enhancing incentives those rights provide. Lee J. Alston discusses Libecap's chapter.

Jouni Paavola, in chapter 14, investigates the potential of institutional diversity and polycentric governance to deal effectively with climate change. Starting with the recognition that top-down governance solutions are a "false panacea," Paavola observes that although climate change is, indeed, a global commons problem, that does not necessarily mean global governance is the most effective or efficient way of dealing with it. Indeed, the global regimes that have been created so far—the United Nations Framework Convention on Climate Change and the Kyoto Protocol—have made scant progress in reducing emissions of greenhouse gases (GHGs). Consequently, Paavola considers the extent to which regional, local, sectoral, and other partial or smaller-scale approaches to climate governance might speed progress on reducing anthropogenic GHG emissions. He considers whether the best approach is not to set collective goals at a high level of governance, but to establish mechanisms for achieving such goals at lower levels. On the basis of two streams of the broader governance literature—new institutional economics (growing out of Coase's work [1937; 1960]) and polycentric governance (stemming from V. Ostrom, Tiebout, and Warren [1961])—Paavola suggests that smaller-scale efforts to reduce GHG emissions might prove more effective than global governance by minimizing the costs of achieving collective action, for example, by reducing incentives to free ride. He examines two small-scale, purely voluntary initiatives: Cities for Climate Protection and the Cement Sustainability Initiative. Although he finds such initiatives valuable, he admits that they are likely to realize only GHG emissions reductions that lead to (private) cost savings. Because GHG emissions need to be cut significantly by the middle of this century to stabilize the climate, he realistically notes that conventional state-based solutions retain a vital role. However, the contribution of voluntary, bottom-up, small-scale emissions-reduction programs should not be underestimated. Indeed, Paavola believes that such voluntary programs will proliferate as state-level climate regimes are implemented, suggesting a synergistic effect between levels of polycentric governance. Paavola's chapter is discussed by V. Kerry Smith.

In the final chapter, chapter 15, Katrina Miriam Wyman addresses a novel property problem stemming from climate change: the submergence of low-lying lands because of sea-level rise and the resultant damage to property rights and state sovereignty. Low-lying Pacific island nations, such as the Maldives, are already in the process of being submerged. Wyman notes that President Mohamed Nasheed of the Maldives has created a sovereign wealth fund to purchase new territory on which to resettle all 300,000 Maldivians, but she raises a profound question of international law: what if, instead of buying new land, the citizens of the Maldives and other submerged states claimed a legal right to resettle elsewhere? She assesses historical precedents and jurisprudential and moral arguments (by the likes of Kant, Puffendorf, and Grotius) that support such a claim of right to property in another sovereign territory. She also examines how such a right might be operationalized. The main historical precedent Wyman discusses is the right to safe haven, which is rooted in the age of discovery. That precedent is further supported by moral arguments from utilitarianism or a "cosmopolitan variant of liberal egalitarianism." An independent, nonmoral ground for the right may also stem from natural law arguments about collective ownership of the earth (Risse 2009). Even if such a right is supported and recognized, however, questions of implementation remain. To implement a right of relocation, Wyman first considers and rejects two simple principles for allocating duties to countries for resettling persons displaced by climate change:

(1) the proportion of their historical contribution to the existing stock of green-house gases in the atmosphere; and (2) availability of resources. Instead, Wyman proffers an allocation mechanism based on the average of three metrics: (1) population density (countries with lower population densities would have more responsibility to take climate refugees); (2) 2005 gross domestic product (GDP); and (3) 2005 GDP per capita, adjusted for purchasing power parity. Richard A. Barnes concludes the book with comments on this final chapter.

REFERENCES

Clay, Karen, and Gavin Wright. 2005. Order without law? Property rights during the California gold rush. *Explorations in Economic History* 42:155–183.
Coase, Ronald H. 1937. The theory of the firm. *Economica* 4:386–405.
———. 1960. The problem of social cost. *Journal of Law and Economics* 3:1–44.
Demsetz, Harold. 1967. Toward a theory of property rights. *American Economic Review* 57:347–359.
Eggertsson, Thráinn. 1990. *Economic behavior and institutions.* Cambridge, U.K.: Cambridge University Press.
Hardin, Garrett. 1968. The tragedy of the commons. *Science* 162:1243–1248.
Lasswell, Harold. 1958. *Politics: Who gets what, when, how.* New York: Meridian Books.
McDowell, Andrea. 2002. From commons to claims: Property rights in the California gold rush. *Yale Journal of Law and Humanities* 14:1–72.
Ostrom, Elinor. 2011. Background on the institutional analysis and development framework. *Policy Studies Journal* 39(1):7–27.
Ostrom, Vincent, Charles M. Tiebout, and Robert Warren. 1961. The organization of government in metropolitan areas: A theoretical inquiry. *American Political Science Review* 55:831–842.
Risse, Mathias. 2009. The right to relocation: Disappearing island nations and common ownership of the earth. *Ethics and International Affairs* 23:281–299.
Umbeck, John. 1981. *A theory of property rights, with application to the California gold rush.* Ames: Iowa State University Press.
Zerbe, Richard O., and C. Leigh Anderson. 2001. Culture and fairness in the development of institutions in the California gold fields. *Journal of Economic History* 61:114–143.

Property Systems

Opportunities and Limits for the Evolution of Property Rights Institutions

1

THRÁINN EGGERTSSON

The economics of property rights is concerned with explaining or predicting three types of social phenomena: (1) the allocation of resources within a particular framework of organization and property rights; (2) the logic of organization within a specific system of property rights; and (3) the emergence of a particular bundle of property rights.[1] In the 1960s, the assigned readings in economics courses dealt almost entirely with a subset of the first category: resource allocation in a well-defined market system, which sometimes suffered from impurities such as monopoly, spillovers, and business cycles. But already in the 1960s, two relatively minor changes within the rational-choice paradigm had sowed the seeds of a revolution that gradually pulled issues (2) and (3) into mainstream economic research: the extension of rational and strategic behavior into the political domain; and the formal recognition of information as a scarce resource (Alchian 1965; Buchanan and Tullock 1962). When information is scarce, search, measurement, and enforcement are costly activities, and it is important to know how various forms of organization and various bundles of property rights influence the costs of transacting.[2] The appearance of selfish maximizers in the political sphere spoils the traditional story of welfare economics about politicians whose goal is to maximize a social welfare function.[3]

The new institutionalism that emerged in the 1970s and 1980s relies not only on microeconomics extended in the direction of transaction costs and politics, but also on game theory.[4] The assumption of strict selfish rationality requires that all institutional arrangements be self-enforcing, and modern game theory provides

---

[1] Eggertsson's (1990a) survey of new institutional economics is organized around these three types of questions or dependent variables.

[2] Williamson (1985) and Barzel (1989) pioneered the transaction-costs approach to the economics of organization.

[3] See Mueller (2003) for a survey of the public choice literature. Olson's (1965) classic *The Logic of Collective Action* created a path for later work on group behavior. The transaction-costs approach to politics, however, indicates that agency problems limit the power even of absolute rulers (North 1979).

[4] The new literature on institutions, or "the literature," refers to "new institutional economics" (NIE). For more information about NIE, see the Web page of the International Society for New Institutional Economics, http://www. isnie.org.

tools for modeling self-enforcement.[5] As late as 1990, the research questions, tools, and findings of the new institutionalists appeared exotic. Twenty years later, this approach has entered the mainstream of economics and political science, and the typical young researcher seeks progress (and promotion) by refining existing research tools and data rather than struggling with methodology.

This overview pays special attention to the origins and evolution of institutions. The literature offers three explanations of the emergence of institutions: they appear spontaneously; they arise through self-governance; or a high authority hands them down. Social norms, which grow in a decentralized, spontaneous manner, not unlike coral reefs in marine waters, are to a large extent independent of deliberate policy making. Self-governance is often found in small groups, such as clubs, parliaments, and local resource users who set their own rules. Finally, high authority, such as a legislature or a government bureau, may create institutions and impose them on the ruled. Although the three types of institutions vary in origin, they are closely related. New formal laws are often based on prior social norms; formal laws may lose their effectiveness if they conflict with strongly held norms; and public law usually circumscribes the scope of self-governance by small groups.

Institutional policy involves the design of rules and methods of enforcement (social mechanisms) that channel individual and aggregate behavior in some desired direction. Social mechanisms are complex systems, and, except for minor reforms, institutional policy is a knowledge-intensive activity. The new literature usually simplifies by assuming that the makers of institutional policy know how to reach their goals. However, effectively accounting for incomplete knowledge is the most important and difficult problem facing the economics of institutions.

To illustrate the problem of knowledge, let us compare the builders of institutions to the builders of bridges. Imagine that the designers of bridges of a specific kind already know (or know where to access) the relevant and effective engineering technology.[6] There is no disagreement among experts about the construction technology, and carefully built bridges function as planned. Here we have no reason to look for a knowledge problem. There is no need to explore how competition among alternative models of bridge technology sometimes results in collapsing bridges. Instead, scholars study other more relevant issues. An economist might examine, for instance, how the cost of supervising builders is related to the quality of bridges, or how changes in relative price lead designers to adjust their use of various building materials marginally. The same reasoning applies to the study of institutional policy. When all players know the appropriate effective social technology, social scientists can forget about the problem of knowledge and can focus entirely on other issues, especially the role of power and preferences in shaping institutional change.

In reality, institutional policy is often plagued by serious knowledge problems, and the policy process is driven by competition among (mental) models of design

---

[5] See Greif (2006). The self-enforcement requirement arises because of the classic question: who monitors the monitors? In the literature on institutions, many scholars implicitly ignore the problem of self-enforcement by not modeling it.

[6] Note, however, that knowledge of bridge building is not a constant but changes over time, which is also true of knowledge of social mechanisms.

and social fit. Models of design involve such questions as the following: How do I design structures of incentives, planning methods, and enforcement mechanisms that produce my desired social outcome (regularity in social behavior)? And how do the planned institutions harmonize with existing structures of incentives, planning, and enforcement in the social system? Social fit models, on the other hand, focus on the compatibility of new social mechanisms with general social theories and worldviews, which are embodied in religion, ethics, political philosophy, legal systems, and cultural symbols. Design issues usually involve hypotheses that, in principle, are testable, but social fit theories are generally not testable.[7] Official policy makers are usually first movers in the game of public institutional policy, making the design decisions. Courts, public intellectuals, the media, various political and religious leaders, and the general public make the social fit decisions. The success of institutional policy initiatives depends on the distribution and nature of design and social fit models, as well as on the usual concerns of the new institutionalism, the distribution of power and material preferences.

The first part of this chapter examines how the assumptions that information is costly and that politics is rational yield useful tools for exploring the logic of institutions and the sources of institutional change. Six case studies of historical and modern institutions in Iceland present the various tools and techniques in action. Iceland's relatively simple and transparent institutions are ideal for identifying fundamental social regularities that have general application. The chapter's second part discusses new directions for the economics of institutions, in particular, competing mental models in the arenas of design (social technologies) and social fit. The confusing evolution of Iceland's fisheries regulations illustrates these issues.

Opportunities and Limits for Reform: The Traditional Approach

The modified neoclassical approach to institutions has provided economics and politics with useful new tools and concepts for studying organization and institutions (Furubotn and Richter 2005; North 1990). It is helpful to look at several theoretical constructs, beginning at the top of the social pyramid and descending to the local level. Table 1.1 lists these theoretical constructs and links each of them to a particular topic in Iceland's economic history. The linkage between a construct and particular case, however, is an artifact or a rhetorical device because several tools and concepts are necessary to analyze each historical case.

Social Equilibriums and Limits to Reform: Why Iceland Starved

Jagdish Bhagwati (1978) observed many years ago that the introduction of rational, selfish, and optimizing political actors creates a dilemma in the study of public policy. The design of top-down institutions is no longer a haphazard process where the authorities look to idealistic reformers, social scientists, or international aid agencies for advice on how to fix social dilemmas and reform inefficient

---

[7] Theories of the social fit of institutions are derived from beliefs in moral and other social principles that usually cannot be verfied scientifically. Consider, for instance, moral beliefs forbidding the use of interest in financial transactions.

TABLE 1.1
Testing the Economics of Institutions in Iceland

New Institutional Tool or Concept	Icelandic Topic
Social equilibriums and limits to reform	Starvation in Iceland
Shocks and institutional change	Modernization in the nineteenth century
Political logic of bad economics	Financial markets until the 1990s
Transaction costs and efficient organization	Historic mountain pastures
Spontaneous opposition to reform	Upholding the hay-sharing norm
Coase's theorem to the rescue	Property rights and Iceland's health records

arrangements.[8] Rather, current institutions embody the rulers' interests and power. Idealistic reforms come up against rock-solid social equilibriums, and only random exogenous events will upset the status quo.[9] In recent decades, the idea of a stable overall balance of interests has made economists rethink institutional reform, foreign aid, and historical and modern economic development (Easterly 2006).

In a study of economic decline in Iceland in the premodern period, Bhagwati's dilemma and the idea of social equilibrium can explain why Iceland starved (Eggertsson 1996; 2005). A particular question is why Icelanders did not develop a full-scale fishing industry until the nineteenth century. The fishing grounds around Iceland are among the richest in the world, whereas the country's farmland is of marginal quality. But in premodern times, fishing was strictly limited to small open rowboats that were staffed by farmworkers who usually returned to shore the same day and went fishing mostly in the winter season. From around 1400, the Icelandic fishing grounds attracted fleets from various European countries, and, theoretically, the Icelanders could have cooperated with some of these nations (for instance, the French, the English, the Spanish, and the Germans) to develop a strong export industry and transform their living conditions.

The solution to the puzzle proposed here rests on the notion of a two-tier social equilibrium that was held together by a domestic component and an external one. First, consider the local element. In historical times, a few wealthy owners possessed most of the country's farmland and rented it to poor tenant farmers, who typically employed even poorer farmworkers. The workers received only token compensation, in addition to food, clothing, and housing. A regulation from 1490 required all citizens to live on a farm, with the exception of a very small, restricted category of cottagers. In effect, social relationships in Iceland resembled serfdom, and tenants and farmworkers were trapped on the island.

The domestic equilibrium was fragile because a powerful landlord with a relative advantage in fishing and exporting had an incentive to defect from the coalition of landlords. A new fishing industry could easily attract necessary labor by offering a small margin on top of the rural subsistence pay. The landlords feared defections

---

[8] A useful role for economic advisers can be reestablished by making political leaders uncertain about how best to reach their goals.

[9] Unexpected and unwanted internal dynamics that undermine social systems also upset social equilibriums. A financial system that unexpectedly sets off wild speculative activities that end in general bankruptcies creates a policy vacuum, competition among mental models, and, possibly, opportunities for radical reform.

from the rural areas, believing that a full-time fishing industry would dramatically raise their labor costs.[10] The empirical evidence shows that landed interests tried to block expansion and modernization of the fisheries and even sought court orders to prevent introduction of new productive fishing gear. But the domestic element required a complementary foreign component to maintain the status quo.[11]

In the fifteenth and sixteenth centuries, when Iceland was a colony of Denmark, the island was overrun, first by English fishing and commercial interests and later by German fishers and merchants of the Hanseatic League. When the foreign incursions started, Denmark had not built a strong navy, and it never maintained a permanent military presence in Iceland. Instead, the Crown protected its interests in Iceland through cooperation with the powerful landowners.[12] Once the newly built Danish navy had driven English and German interests out of the country, the Danish Crown developed a strategy to solve its Iceland problem that would yield satisfactory benefits at low cost. Its solution included the following elements:

1. Isolate the island and establish an off-limits cordon of the ocean around it. Forbid all contacts between Icelanders and foreigners from outside the Kingdom, including all visits to the country and all forms of trade.
2. Establish a Danish trade monopoly that buys farm products and fish from the Icelanders and sells them essential imports, such as grain. Trade takes place in the summer; the monopoly traders are not allowed to winter in Iceland; the relative price of fish is kept artificially low.
3. Further strengthen the Danish navy.

The Danish trade monopoly lasted from 1602 to 1787. The Icelandic population nearly perished in a series of famines, the country's capital stock deteriorated, productivity declined, and in the eighteenth century, the mean stature of the population fell by an estimated five centimeters. Cooling temperatures, volcanic eruptions, and epidemics overwhelmed the primitive farming economy, but the social equilibrium was reform proof.

Shocks and Institutional Change: Impetus for Modernization in the Nineteenth Century

The *How the West Grew Rich* literature is probably the best-known strand of the new institutional economics, which should not come as a surprise.[13] Few, if any, topics in social science are of greater general interest than the origins of modern economic growth. In their accounts, the various scholars generally use exogenous events and conditions to explain critical turning points in the economic history of Europe—various impulses that upset the social equilibriums. The literature has few direct policy

---

[10] A robust fishing industry would have stimulated demand for farm outputs and would have increased prices. The analysis here assumes that the landlords were not able to formulate and test their hypothesis with the help of a global model (general equilibrium analysis) of supply and demand.

[11] See Eggertsson (1996; 2005) for references relevant to this subsection.

[12] The Icelandic fisheries did not attract the fishing fleets of the Danish kingdom, which had access to abundant fishing grounds nearer home.

[13] The title is that of a book by Rosenberg and Birdzell (1986). The topic has generated a thriving cottage industry. See North and Thomas (1973) for an early contribution.

implications for the poor countries of the world, except that they will remain stuck in a poverty trap until the right kinds of exogenous shocks release them.

The account of the origins of modern growth in Iceland falls squarely in the category of exogenous shocks (Eggertsson 1996; 2005). External events crushed the Danish element of the pernicious social equilibrium, and the local component was too weak to restrain public disobedience and control free riding. The external events that upset the equilibrium included the destruction of the Danish navy in 1807 during the Napoleonic Wars and the rise of British domination in the North Atlantic. Also, in the late eighteenth century and in the nineteenth century, some of Europe's leading powers adopted the free-trade model (an exogenous ideological impulse). When Denmark was at war, Iceland was virtually on its own, and later, in 1855, a much-weakened Denmark gave Iceland the right of free trade with all countries, which was the last step in a series of trade-liberalization measures.

In Iceland the landlords did not respond to the exogenous move of free trade by lifting domestic constraints on the labor force; on the contrary (and not surprisingly), they tried to tighten those constraints. Throughout the long process of liberalization, landed interests fought to control labor mobility and prevent the emergence of an independent fishing industry. The Crown abolished the Danish trade monopoly in 1787 and opened trade with Iceland to all subjects in the kingdom. Already in 1781 Iceland's landed interests had responded to Danish attempts to modernize the Icelandic fisheries and liberalize the local economy by introducing internal passports for people crossing county boundaries, and two years later they withdrew the occupational licenses of the very small, confined, but potentially dangerous group of independent workers. The ban against cottagers remained in effect. But the historical evidence clearly shows that with the external element gone, the devastating historical equilibrium broke down. Iceland modernized with the traditional formal domestic institutional framework still in place. Workers ignored formal restrictions on labor mobility and drifted into urban areas. Historians frequently date the advent in Iceland of a modern fishing industry around 1870, but the Althingi (Iceland's parliament) formally removed labor bondage in 1894 and restrictions on cottagers only in 1907.

Political Logic of Bad Economics: Financial Markets Until the 1990s

In an empirical study of endogenous ideology, Chai (1998) finds that leaders in former colonies, in the first decades of their independence, attempt homegrown economic policies to differentiate themselves from their former masters. These rulers embrace what Chai calls "opposition ideology" (1998, 263).[14] The leaders of third world countries with no colonial history usually lack these tendencies. In the modern era, Iceland has had close relations with the other Nordic countries; the country's institutions are, to large degree, copies of the Scandinavian system. But there are important differences because Iceland's governments have embraced opposition ideology. For example, consider the country's financial system.

---

[14] In terms used later in this chapter, Chai (1998) attempts to make endogenous a particular class of models of design and fit. Chai supports his theoretical claim concerning "opposition ideologies" with reference to well-known psychological processes.

In the decades after World War II, when the Scandinavian countries (and the countries of western Europe) gradually liberalized their financial systems, Iceland set up mechanisms of financial governance that more closely resembled the rules in use in Colombia than in western Europe. According to the well-known terminology of McKinnon (1981), and McKinnon and Mathieson (1981), financial repression can involve any of five ascending stages. A study of Iceland's post–World War II financial system found that it belonged to the fifth and highest stage in the 1970s (Eggertsson 1990b).[15] The perverse features of the system included a large inflation tax on currency and bank deposits, a requirement that commercial banks keep very large reserves (unprotected against inflation) in the central bank, the suppression of nonbank financial institutions, low ceilings on interest rates, and rationing of bank credit by the state.

In Iceland from the 1960s to the late 1980s, the only available financial instruments were bank deposits that yielded negative real interest rates, often in the double digits. There was no market in the country for bonds and stocks. The entire financial system was politicized, not obliquely but formally. All financial organizations had three directors who represented (and were selected by) the country's three largest political parties. Commercial banks were owned by the state, as were investment credit funds, which were financed through forced loans from the country's commercial banks and pension funds.[16] A political selection mechanism guided the granting of loans, both for commercial credit and long-term investment. The system favored borrowers with strong political connections, who usually dealt directly with financial managers who represented their political parties. The flow of credit also reflected the electoral overrepresentation of rural districts.

In the early 1970s, it was an odd experience to find a Colombian financial system in a Nordic country, one that violated nearly all the principles of good governance that textbooks had extolled. But the system met the needs of the political parties, which snoozed in a comfortable equilibrium and had no plans for a major overhaul of the system. The structure of the financial organizations was bad economics, but good politics. The financial institutions served the political parties well because regardless of whether they were in or out of power, they had secure property rights to one of the three managing positions in all financial organizations and control over the flow of credit. In the business community, major clients of the political parties were well supplied with loans that carried negative real interest rates.

McKinnon (1981) argues that the highest stage of financial repression is not sustainable in the long run, but lower stages of financial repression are more durable, and the experience in Iceland confirms this.[17] But the shock that compelled Iceland

---

[15] McKinnon (1981) uses the financial system of Colombia in 1972 to illustrate the institutional structure that characterizes the fifth and highest stage of financial repression.

[16] Special-interest groups, however, controlled a few investment credit funds. Eventually, the government decided to reduce pressure by tolerating small private banks that were associated with commercial and manufacturing interests that were dissatisfied with the services provided by the state banks. From 1975 to 1985, the private banks were allowed a share of about 20 percent of total commercial banking, and until 1984, they were not permitted to deal in foreign currency.

[17] According to McKinnon (1981), the highest state of financial repression is unsustainable because spontaneous internal dynamics undermine the system. Eventually, highly negative real interest rates will shrink real bank deposits and make the credit system unworkable. In Iceland, during the 1960s and 1970s, the public's avoidance of bank deposits effectively cut the banking system's holdings in half, as measured by the ratio of bank deposits to gross domestic product. The authorities responded to the ensuing credit crises with partial reforms, such as indexation of financial obligations, which lowered the stage of financial repression.

to introduce market-based financial organizations came from abroad. Iceland is not a member of the European Union (EU), which is the country's largest export market. Toward the end of the twentieth century, in order to maintain access to the EU's internal market, Iceland made an agreement with the EU to adopt virtually all regulations related to the EU's single market, including the European financial rules in use.[18] The old financial system thus came to an end, but it had two important long-term consequences. It preserved the country's post–World War II industrial structure, blocking modernization by providing credit primarily to traditional political supporters and industries. Second, at the time of the changeover to a market-based and open financial system, there were virtually no bankers and regulators in Iceland with substantial experience in international finance. The lack of experience and knowledge was an important factor contributing to the collapse of the country's financial system in 2008 (Eggertsson and Herbertsson 2009).

The Logic of Organization and Transaction Costs: The Historic Mountain Pastures

The structure of top-down institutions often seems illogical when the criterion of joint wealth maximization is used, but it makes better sense when it is evaluated in terms of the interests of the rule makers (the high authority). Private interests and social efficiency often overlap when small groups set their own rules. Self-governing groups often have detailed knowledge of relevant issues and receive feedback from their trials relatively rapidly, which encourages experimentation and trial by error. Elinor Ostrom's book *Governing the Commons* (1990) is the classic reference. Williamson's book *The Economic Institutions of Capitalism* (1985) also brims with examples of efficient solutions for economic governance.

Inspired by Ostrom (1990), Eggertsson (1992) studied the effectiveness of self-governance in Iceland's historical mountain pastures, which local farm communities have managed for more than a thousand years. The pastures are used for individually owned flocks of sheep (and sometimes horses), which graze the pastures unattended during the summer months.[19] The article examines whether the institutional arrangements (property rights) governing the pastures involve obvious unnecessary costs. Specifically, it uses an informal model borrowed from Field (1989) to analyze whether the pasture arrangements minimize the sum of three types of costs: regular production costs (transformation costs) and two types of transaction costs, the cost of exclusion and the cost of (internal) governance in the pastures. Exclusion costs arise when insiders invest in keeping outsiders from using a resource; governance costs arise from attempts to enforce cooperation and to make the insiders

---

[18] Iceland protected its European export market by joining the European Economic Area (EEA), which was established in 1994. EEA membership allows Iceland, as well as Liechtenstein and Norway, to participate in the EU's single market without conventional EU membership, provided the countries adopt all EU regulations related to the single market except those in fisheries and agriculture. Financial reform, therefore, was one of the conditions of access to European markets. Before the EU shock, those who preached fundamental financial reforms had little or no influence.

[19] Farms in Iceland usually are scattered through low-lying coastal areas. Huge mountain pastures belong to the farmers in each region.

maintain the resource and avoid overusing it. One implication of models that allow for exclusion and governance costs is that in some circumstances, communal ownership (rather than individual ownership) is the most efficient property rights arrangement.

Throughout most of Iceland's history, surprisingly sophisticated institutional arrangements protected the mountain pastures from overuse (Eggertsson 1992). The relative costs of enforcement and governance easily justify the communal nature of the pastures. Various ancient institutional arrangements lowered the cost of coordination among the insiders, took advantage of scale economies in monitoring, and limited spillover effects. It is surprising to learn that the communal system employed the price mechanism and relied on marginal analysis. The grazing quotas of each farmer were tradable, and the law recommended marginal analysis for estimating the total grazing capacity of the commons. Grágás, the law book of the Icelandic Commonwealth from 930–1262, establishes the following method for estimating total capacity: "Let them find the number [of grazing sheep] that does not give fatter sheep if reduced but also fills the pasture" (Eggertsson 1992, 433).

Spontaneous Opposition to Reform: Defending the Hay-Sharing Norm

In the new literature on institutions, reform failure is usually explained in terms of organized opposition by political groups and special interests or by spontaneous, norm-based opposition. Scholars tend to see social norms as slow-moving institutions that usually are beyond the reach of the makers of public policy (Roland 2004). The life cycle of social norms is poorly understood, and the phenomenon does not lend itself well to rational-choice analysis. Some of these truths can be found in a study of ancient hay-sharing practices in Icelandic farming and the failure of public policy makers to override the norm of sharing by public rules (Eggertsson 1998).

The following two statements about the traditional Icelandic farm economy are not in dispute. First, farmers did not practice systematic livestock management. They did not trim their stocks and store fodder (hay) in anticipation of exceptionally hard and long winters, which sometimes came two or more in a row. Instead, farmers took their chances. Second, as late as the early twentieth century, when the climate was harsh, a substantial part of the country's livestock starved to death. Eggertsson's study (1998) relates the farmers' high-risk strategy to uncertain individual property rights in hay and interprets the uncertain rights as side effects of the farm community's ancient social welfare system.

In historical Iceland, the farm community pooled specialized risks in each district (*hreppur*) by making farm households collectively responsible for helping members who were stricken by misfortune, such as fires, flooding, avalanches, or deaths of heads of households. When misfortune struck and support from wider family and kin was unavailable, either the stricken household received material help from the district, or its members were dispersed and placed with other farms. Ancient laws and social norms also required that farmers, when asked, always share their animal fodder (hay) with their neighbors.[20] Because a prudent farmer who tried to protect himself against random climatic downswings by storing extra supplies of hay would have his stores depleted by neighbors in a hard winter, it is not surprising that farmers typically did not prepare for such winters.

Given the difficult environment and the country's primitive technology, Iceland's traditional welfare system was relatively effective except when risks were general and affected whole regions or the whole country (Eggertsson 1998). In analyzing the system, one can speculate that psychological principles may have made it impossible to exempt the sharing of hay from the general principle of supporting needy neighbors. There are, of course, various counterarguments to this thesis. Perhaps practical factors ruled out large-scale storage of hay, or the most efficient strategy available to farmers was indeed the high-risk strategy of maximizing the size of livestock in each period and not storing emergency hay reserves. But, no matter whether the high-risk strategy was inefficient or efficient, hay sharing is a striking example of a slow-moving informal institution that was utterly resistant to reform.

The episodic mass starvation of farm animals had for centuries appalled the authorities in Iceland and Denmark, who saw the hay-sharing solution and the high-risk strategy as dangerously inefficient.[21] However, all their reforms failed. For more than 150 years, royal Danish decrees, legislation by the Althingi, and informal campaigns by private reformers had no effect. In 1806, for instance, the Danish Crown abolished by decree a hay-sharing law from 1281 that called for serious punishments of farmers who refused to share their fodder with neighbors.[22] The Danish decree had no influence on the farmers. The Icelanders were given home rule in 1874. In the next few years, the Althingi passed a series of laws aimed at dismantling the farmers' high-risk strategy, gradually raising the punishment for offenders. A law from 1889 even called for the imprisonment of farmers who starved their animals. But all these efforts were in vain. The farm community ignored the new laws, and the local authorities made no effort to enforce them. Mass starvation of farm animals continued intermittently into the early years of the twentieth century.[23] The phenomenon disappeared only when the national government organized a centralized system of relief, more or less at taxpayers' expense, and welfare-state social services and commercial insurance replaced the communal system of sharing as the main method of coping with specialized risks. In other words, the hay-sharing norm did not disappear until a fundamentally new social system (and new production and transportation technologies) had made the ancient hay-sharing norm irrelevant.

---

[20] Farmers could charge only a trivial or token price for their hay. The community forgave nonpayment or even theft of hay, but attempts to steal sheep would ruin reputations.

[21] Indeed, the storage problem spans the entire economic history of Iceland. It even helped give the country its name. The sagas record that Raven-Flóki, one of the first Norsemen to settle in Iceland (probably in the ninth century), neglected to make hay for his animals, which perished during his first winter in the country. Flóki then renamed the new country "Iceland" and returned to Norway.

[22] No records of court verdicts based on the hay-sharing law of 1281 have been found, but there is abundant evidence that the farm community informally enforced the norm of hay sharing.

[23] A cold spell in 1800 reduced the sheep population by three-fifths, or 171,000 animals. In the cold spell of 1881 to 1883, the loss was 187,000 sheep, and for the period 1881 to 1908, the loss of grown sheep, lambs, and horses and the reduction in quality of survivors was equivalent to 884,000 sheep, or an average of about 13 sheep for each person in the farm community (Eggertsson 1998, 18–19). Note that horses are counted as sheep in calculating this figure.

Coase to the Rescue: Property Rights and Iceland's Health Records

In the complex interactions among property rights and science and technology, three basic relationships can be discerned. First, advanced technology is a necessary condition for operating advanced forms of social organization and property rights, and, conversely, primitive physical technology can support only primitive social organization (Posner 1980). The causal link between the sophistication of property rights and the level of technology runs primarily through the dependence of methods of enforcement (communication, measurement, monitoring, and sanctioning) on physical technology. The second relationship between property rights and natural science concerns the important role of social organization in stimulating both scientific discovery and the application of science to practical uses. The third relationship arises because efficient use of new technology calls for complex adjustments in property rights. In fact, in modern high-income countries, the two key developments that create pressure for major adjustments in property rights are new technology and increasing scarcity of environmental resources. In recent decades, biotechnology, digitalization of data, the Internet, and new communication and computing technologies have altered the effectiveness of existing property rights and stimulated plans for various reforms.

New technology often raises the expected value of a resource that previously was in little demand and subject to uncertain ownership rights.[24] Unexpected increases in the value of resources can trigger ownership races among competing groups and sometimes among previous informal or de facto owners and new interests. Demsetz's (1967) well-known theory of property rights recognizes how rising values create demand for exclusive rights, but his theory does not consider how the new rights are supplied.

A recent study (Eggertsson 2011) examines the evolution since the mid-1990s of property rights to the records of Iceland's national health system. The curious case of the country's health records has several interesting features: The rule maker, the state, passes a new law that formally removes the informal ownership rights of the de facto owner (Iceland's medical research establishment) and gives a new right holder, a U.S.-registered biogenetics corporation, formal control rights of the health records. The informal owners, now formally the designated duty bearers, rebel. The state gives in and does not enforce the new law. The final act in the drama involves bargaining, whereby the de facto owners voluntarily transfer (sell) their informal property rights to the corporation.

The population of Iceland is about 300,000. The local medical research community is more sophisticated and better connected internationally than the size of the nation suggests. Local medical specialists are mostly educated at major foreign universities, especially in the United States, Sweden, and the United Kingdom. Iceland has had a unified health system since 1915, and comprehensive national health records are dispersed across the various health and research organizations. Icelanders

---

[24] Investment in the definition and enforcement of exclusive property rights is a costly activity that is not worthwhile for resources that have very low expected value (Demsetz 1967; Libecap 1989).

also possess unique genealogical records for almost the whole nation that span 300 to 400 years. In some instances, the records go back to the High Middle Ages. Finally, Icelanders have a relatively homogeneous genetic structure.[25]

The corporation Decode Genetics, which was registered in Delaware and mostly financed by international venture capital, was the brainchild of an Icelander, Kári Stefánsson, who in the mid-1990s served as a professor at Harvard Medical School. In the first years of the twenty-first century, Decode Genetics became a world leader in discovering relationships between genetic structures and major diseases.

The business model that inspired Decode Genetics rested on the belief that the Icelandic data were of unique value in hunting for the genetic roots of major diseases and finding their cures. The project drew international attention, and the media and scientific journals regularly reported the firm's latest discoveries.[26] In 1998 Decode Genetics persuaded the Icelandic government to pass a law that authorized a licensee to build a central electronic database containing the country's health records (health sector database, or HSD). As planned, Decode Genetics became the licensee. Scientists who did not work for the corporation would be allowed to use the HSD provided their projects did not conflict directly with those of the firm. The de facto owner of the health records, the local medical establishment, responded furiously: an international corporation was planning to make startling profits by using "its" health records.

According to the 1998 HSD Act, the country's health sector workers, in cooperation with Decode Genetics, were expected to transfer their data into the central database, but they rebelled and refused to cooperate. The refusals were usually oblique. Questions were raised about both procedures and techniques for encrypting the data (the law had required encryption). The Ministry of Health hesitated and decided not to quell the rebellion: An outright confrontation with the country's health workers was not attractive, and the use of compulsion to classify, encrypt, and transfer data from the health records to the HSD was unfeasible because the opportunities for sabotage were innumerable.

The designated duty bearers were successful; a central databank has not been set up. Decode Genetics responded to the failure of the HSD by switching to a decentralized strategy that involved the following steps. For each of its disease projects, the firm identified the de facto owners (medical specialists) of the relevant health records and, in step with Coase theorem, offered the owners a deal.[27] Decode Genetics would acquire the right to use the medical records in return for payments in cash and even in kind. Qualified de facto owners sometimes participated directly

---

[25] Historians claim that Iceland was settled by Nordic and Celtic groups in only a few decades around 900. Until the twentieth century, there was apparently only trivial migration into and out of the country. Almost all Icelanders are related if one goes back some six to eight generations.

[26] For instance, a search of the archives of the *New York Times* shows that the newspaper saw Decode Genetics as a world leader in its field and sometimes made the firm's discoveries front-page news.

[27] Coase's theorem states that the ultimate allocation of property rights is independent of their initial allocation, provided that the rights are clearly specified and the cost of transacting is zero (or neglible). According to the theorem, property rights will find their highest valued uses. In an unending debate, many theorists have argued that the validity of Coase's theorem depends on several strict assumptions that prevent its applicability to any real-world situation (Hahnel and Sheeran 2009). The use of the concept in the context here is more casual: when transaction costs are positive but relatively low, property rights are often transferred from low- to high-value uses. Coase (1959) uses a similar casual approach in discussing the allocation of radio frequencies among broadcasters in his article on the Federal Communications Commission.

in the projects and coauthored the resulting scientific papers. Decode Genetics declared bankruptcy in 2009. The bankruptcy was not caused by the failure of the database project, but by unexpected lags and high costs in the firm's drug development projects. New uncertainty about the genetic causes of disease has also emerged.

The Saga of Individual Transferable Quotas

Uncertainty and Model Competition: Design and Fit

Although the case studies discussed here have a narrow geographic focus, they employ the standard methodology of new institutional economics: microeconomics and game theory applied to both economics and politics, costly information, transaction costs, and social equilibriums. Has the paradigm reached an end point, and, if not, where is the new institutionalism heading? Many scholars are pleased to work within the current theoretical framework, but some exploration still continues, primarily on three margins that involve experimental game theory, behavioral economics, and the mental-models approach.[28] The following discussion is limited to the mental-models approach and its relation to uncertainty (Denzau and North 1994; North 2005). The basic idea is simple: In an uncertain world (one of incomplete knowledge), people rely on models and theories to make choices. The models are often incomplete or outright misleading, and not everyone uses the same model. After a general discussion of uncertainty and mental models, this argument will be illustrated with an Icelandic case study.

Uncertainty is a problem child in the family of modern economics. Economists usually try to avoid uncertainty by dressing it up in the clothes of its stepsister, risk (Hirshleifer and Riley 1992). They do this by assuming that decision makers accurately know all the elements in their choice sets, either with certainty or as empirical or subjective probabilities. The actors then choose among the various alternatives on the basis of their expected utility. The quality of their decisions depends on how accurately the relevant probabilities are known. The expected-utility approach does not recognize that in situations of deep uncertainty, the elements in the choice set are unknown. Consider an example from natural science: the discovery in the second half of the nineteenth century of the germ theory of disease, that is, the discovery of the relationship between bacteria and disease (Waller 2003). It is possible, of course, to say that in prior historical periods, people assigned zero probability to the bacteria-disease relationship, but that is a trivial statement about the behavior of people who cannot observe bacteria, do not know that bacteria exist, and, therefore, cannot imagine a relationship between bacteria and disease.

In the late nineteenth century, the germ theory of disease created a new paradigm, as well as corresponding programs of medical research and practice. For a short period, the germ theory competed with other paradigms, but efficient methods of measurement and testing, as well as relatively unambiguous feedback, created rapid support for the new theory. The convergence of mental models on a new paradigm,

---

[28] Only approaches that belong to some form of methodological individualism are considered here.

however, does not necessarily imply convergence on corresponding programs. For instance, there is room for disagreement on how to deal with bacterial infection, but now risk has (at least partly) replaced uncertainty. Empirical or subjective probabilities can be associated with specific methods to prevent bacterial infection.

Uncertainty and incomplete mental models affect institutional policy at two levels: (1) decisions concerning design and; (2) decisions concerning (social) fit. First, consider the design decision. An authority that seeks to change social behavior in a specific direction must design appropriate rules and methods of enforcement. The authority first formulates the problem in terms of its chosen paradigm and then selects an appropriate program (social technology) for creating the new social mechanism. Disagreements over how to proceed with institutional design involve both paradigms and programs. Note that an instrument-outcome relationship indicated by one paradigm may not exist in another paradigm.

Now consider decisions about the fit of new institutions. New social mechanisms (institutions) become part of a larger social system, which raises the question of how they fit the overall system according to general social theories that are prevalent in the community.[29] General social theories are made up of formal and informal beliefs concerning the social and natural order and the meaning of life—worldviews that are based on ideas about science, historical myths, legal theories, ethics, political philosophy, and religion. Actors apply general social theories when they evaluate the legitimacy of new institutions, that is, how the institutions fit in their worlds. In making its design decisions, a rational authority must also consider how the planned institutions will fit with prevailing general social theories and beliefs. Experts, such as lawyers, measure the fit of new social institutions in terms of theories rooted in sophisticated paradigms. Nonexperts usually frame the issues in terms of cultural symbols and informal beliefs.

Successful institutional policy requires that the policy authority correctly anticipate and overcome opposition based on (1) general disbelief about the operational quality of the design program; (2) material interests of prospective right holders and duty bearers; and (3) unfavorable interpretations by various parties of the social fit of the new institutions. As table 1.2 shows, the knowledge problem of successfully carrying through major structural changes in the social system is huge: the authority must design new mechanisms that in principle produce the desired results, and it must correctly anticipate the nature and strength of the opposition. The policy process usually involves campaigns where various groups promote their own models and criticize the models or beliefs of others. The outcome of such campaigns can make or mar planned institutional reform.

In economics and politics, the theory of interest groups has developed the useful concept of "rational ignorance" (Downs 1957, 139). Politicians and organized lobby groups often feed false data to the general voter, but the stakes for the average voter are too low to make it worthwhile for the voter to invest in finding the appropriate information (and to take action). The voters decide to be rationally ignorant. The

---

[29] A new social mechanism (a new institution) must also fit operationally with the system into which it is introduced. For instance, in designing housing regulations, changes on one margin can have repercussions throughout the system. Operational considerations are classified as design issues.

TABLE 1.2

Four Ways for Institutional Policy to Fail

Policy Authority Basic Design Failure	Right Holders and Duty Bearers		
	Source of Opposition		
Unworkable institutional design, even when there is no opposition	Material interests hurt by the new institution	Beliefs that the institutional design is operationally unworkable	Beliefs that the new institution is illegitimate because it does not fit general social theories

facts in question usually are easily measurable and known to the politicians and the lobbyists. Empirical work on interest groups has conclusively demonstrated that politicians and lobby groups frequently lie to voters, and voters remain rationally ignorant or fail to mobilize (Mueller 2003). But in situations of deep uncertainty, the story is more complicated. General social theories (of religion, law, ethics, or political philosophy) often involve beliefs or hypotheses that cannot be tested. Design programs aimed at substantially changing the structure of social systems typically generate noisy feedback, in part because in social experiments, other things usually are not equal. In social science, experts strongly disagree and, as is well known, have not converged on common paradigms and programs. An Icelandic case, the saga of the individual transferable quotas, illustrates some of these ideas.

Regulating Iceland's Fisheries

Social equilibriums, exogenous impulses, transaction costs, and Coasean bargaining are all essential tools for analyzing institutional change in Iceland's fisheries during the past 50 years. But there is more to the story. Ignoring the fierce competition among models of fit and design results in a saga with the plot missing.

Iceland depends on ocean fisheries to a greater extent than any other high-income country. In recent years, the fishing industry has accounted for about 30 to 40 percent of the country's exports.[30] In the twentieth century, property rights arrangements in the fisheries around Iceland went from essentially open access to a two-hundred-mile economic zone in 1975. Excessive harvesting by domestic and international fleets, which was already a serious issue before World War II, became a major problem in the first decades after the war.[31] The task of regulating Iceland's fisheries became heavier as the problem of overfishing grew larger and the country's fisheries jurisdiction expanded.

Initially, the Icelandic government relied on various methods of direct control to regulate the fisheries: aggregate quotas, which ignited races to be first; access licenses; fishing effort restrictions; investment controls; and vessel buyback programs.

---

[30] The direct share of the industry in gross domestic product (GDP) is 6 to 10 percent, but economists have estimated that the direct and indirect contribution of the fisheries to GDP is around 25 percent. The country's fishing fleet consists of about 1,300 vessels, of which 700 small vessels are of less than 15 register tons (Agnarsson and Arnason 2007). One register ton is equivalent to 100 cubic feet of cargo space.

[31] Paradoxically, World War II brought some peace to the fishing grounds.

In the mid-1970s the authorities began experimenting with individual nontransferable vessel quotas for specific species (initially, herring). In each instance, the quotas were eventually made transferable. These experiments culminated in a law of 1990 that set up a comprehensive system of individual transferable quotas (ITQs) for virtually all species in Iceland's fisheries (Arnason 1993; Fisheries and Agriculture Ministry, Iceland 2006). The reforms are consistent with the theory that major reforms usually are associated with severe unanticipated shocks, including unexpected institutional design failures. The startling collapse of the herring fisheries in the late 1960s, which threw the Icelandic economy into a depression, initiated the reform process. The subsequent expansion of ITQs to other species was propelled by unexpected reductions in their catches and dire warnings from marine biologists about the precarious state of valuable fish stocks, such as cod.

Model Competition: The Question of Design

An authority preparing to create a structure of rights to govern a valuable resource searches its social (and natural) science paradigms for a suitable program. At the most general level, social science paradigms can be divided into two categories that dominate economic history (Eggertsson 2005). These can be called the microparadigm and the macroparadigm. Put simply, the macroparadigm emphasizes spillover effects, the importance of seeing the whole picture, and central control. It deemphasizes the cost of information, agency problems, and the role of perverse incentives. The microparadigm focuses on the alignment of individual incentives with social goals, self-enforcing mechanisms, and monitoring costs. It deemphasizes spillover effects, the capacity to see the whole picture and manage it from the center, and systemic instability.[32]

After World War I, the policy orientation in the Western world drifted away from decentralization toward the macroparadigm. In the twentieth century's last quarter, policy makers returned to the microparadigm. The world financial crisis of 2008 may possibly have created another turning point toward the macroperspective. Although the paradigms toss and turn, the macromodel has, for some reason, kept a relatively strong and lasting hold over fisheries regulations. The EU, for example, has relied primarily on the macroparadigm to select its fisheries programs. Hannesson (2005), examining the perch fisheries of Soviet Estonia, concludes that the typical Western system of fisheries regulations is similar to the methods used by the Soviet Union in Estonia until the 1991 breakdown. The relatively new management system of ITQs, first introduced on a national scale in Iceland and New Zealand, is an attempt to apply programs based on the microparadigm to the regulation of fisheries (Yandle 2003). [33]

In the world's ocean fisheries, increasing demand and advances in fisheries technologies and in communications and transportation have in recent decades magnified

---

[32] The microparadigm deemphasizes externality problems (spillover effects) by assuming that low-level units are able to negotiate solutions to externality or scale problems with parallel and higher social units.

[33] In the former Soviet Union, the state dealt with the problem of enforcing fisheries regulations by directly taking over the industry and running it as a large firm. The Soviet planners faced countless agency problems and high production costs, but the system apparently removed at least some of the fishers' incentives to enrich themselves through overfishing (Hannesson 2005).

the problem of overfishing (FAO 2009). The prevailing view is that if government fisheries regulations throughout the world are evaluated by the criterion of efficiency, most of them have failed. One possible explanation of this general failure is that in most countries, especially high-income ones, fisheries are a relatively minor industry, and an efficient fisheries policy is not a major economic concern. In Iceland, on the other hand, self-preservation should (in theory) compel a rational government to give highest priority to sustainability and efficiency in the fisheries and, in case of conflicts, second place to narrow special interests.

In Iceland in the 1980s, a great many observers believed that the previous macro-oriented regulatory programs in the fisheries had failed and initially welcomed the new ITQ design. But early in the 1990s, a rowdy debate (which still continues) flared up over design issues and, especially, the social fit (legitimacy) of the new regulatory mechanism. This subsection looks at the conflict over design questions. The following subsection examines the social fit issues.

Critics of the ITQ design argue that it is counterproductive. Three points of criticism are probably most common: (1) the ITQ system is an ineffective tool for restoring and sustaining fish stocks; (2) the system is an ineffective method for increasing economic efficiency in the fisheries; and (3) windfall gains from the original free ITQs have contaminated the country's financial system. The following discussion does not attempt to evaluate the veracity of these charges. Instead, it outlines why the available empirical evidence has not produced clear-cut answers and silenced the debate.[34]

Consider the first point, the restoration of fish stocks. The development of fish stocks in Icelandic waters since the late 1980s has varied by species: some stocks have prospered, while other stocks have declined. Critics emphasize that the valuable cod stock has shrunk steadily, eventually to less than half its former size, but in 2010 a strong recovery was apparently under way.[35] In essence, the aggregate data on fish stocks are not conclusive enough to silence supporters or critics. Two theoretical considerations further confuse the debate. First, fish stocks in the oceans depend on many factors other than the catch. Understanding of marine biological conditions is limited, and scientists cannot always accurately predict the evolution of fish stocks. Second, in virtually all known regulatory systems for fisheries, the regulator (the government) selects the total allowed catch for each species. To evaluate the impact of management systems on fish stocks, it is necessary to correctly establish the relationship between the government's choice of the total allowed catch, the resulting total catch, and the nature of the regulatory system.[36] But little is known about the subtle impact of management systems on the behavior of politicians, administrators, and fishers (Eagle and Thompson 2003). The answer is likely to depend on

---

[34] There has been relatively little discussion of the operational merits of alternative methods for regulating the fisheries. The critics are more unified in their rejection of the current system than in a choice of an alternative.

[35] Scientific reports in English on the state of marine stocks in Icelandic waters are available on the Web site of Iceland's Marine Research Institute, http://www.hafro.is. See, for instance, a report on the state of marine stocks in Icelandic waters, 2009, dated 2010.

[36] In Iceland, following the introduction of the ITQ system, the government's choice of the allowed catch was closer than before to the level recommended by government scientists. But other things were not equal. The introduction of ITQs in Iceland was correlated with scientific reports predicting that fish stocks were near collapse.

local conditions and idiosyncratic details of regulatory programs, rather than on general categories of regulatory systems.[37]

Next, consider the second point, the impact of an ITQ system on efficiency. Unlike the considerable theoretical uncertainty concerning the net impact of various public management systems on fish stocks, microeconomics and Coase's theorem tell a relatively unambiguous story about the impact of transferable quotas on operational efficiency. The following is a brief summary: The trade in quotas transfers fishing rights to the most efficient users. Relatively efficient and innovative operators put upward pressures on the price of quotas, which compels inefficient operators either to leave the industry or to reorganize. Reorganization involves lower costs (because of new technology, relocation, and horizontal and vertical integration) on the production side and various marketing innovations aimed at raising prices on the distribution side.

Empirical evidence indicates that the fishing industry has been transformed through location adjustments, takeovers, and mergers. Marketing of the product has been revolutionized. Most vessel owners strongly defend the ITQ system, and drastic reorganization may explain why the industry has operated with rising profits, even with the sharp reduction in the valuable cod catch. Again, other things have not been equal. The introduction of the ITQ system was correlated with two other variables, liberalization of the Icelandic economy and important technological change in the fisheries. Multicollinearity, therefore, interferes with attempts to measure the net economic impact of the ITQ system. Experts can also quibble over interpretation of data, for instance, whether the ITQs have reduced excess capacity in the industry. In the 1990s structural adjustment and new technology involved new investment. Therefore, there is some ambiguity concerning how to interpret aggregate data on the industry's capital stock.

Finally, consider the third point, the charge that the ITQs contaminated Iceland's financial system. The initial allocation of the quotas was based on a grandfathering rule that provided the original recipients of the fishing quotas with windfall gains, sometimes in the millions of dollars. Some expert and nonexpert critics claim that these gains triggered gamblers' instincts in unqualified or unsophisticated individuals, some of whom used their new wealth in financial speculations that in 2008 contributed to the collapse of Iceland's financial system. There appears to be no systematic theoretical and empirical evidence in support of these claims, but they have figured large in discussions of the ITQ system since 2008.

---

[37] The relative importance of bycatch and discards under various public fisheries management systems is not discussed here. ITQ systems (and other systems) can vary substantially in their use of built-in incentives aimed at reducing the extent and cost of bycatch and discards. In Iceland only indirect government estimates of discards are available, which apparently show that the problem is not serious. Critics, using informal evidence, such as hearsay, do not agree and see a large problem. There is no unique relationship between the use of an ITQ system and the fishers' incentives to preserve stocks. If the owners of fishing vessels overcome free riding and act collectively through their associations, their semipermanent property rights (quotas) might stimulate a long-term interest in preserving the resource. It is possible that individual fishers in ITQ systems will eventually develop proprietary instincts. Ownership norms are more likely to emerge when the fishers and their associations are made directly responsible to some degree for maintaining the resource, which has not been the case in Iceland. In 2010 the regulatory system appeared to be moving in the opposite direction through discussion of plans to switch to short-term fishing licenses.

In sum, the available theoretical and empirical evidence has not ended discussion of the design merits of the ITQ system. However, by itself, the stiff criticism involving the question of efficiency and sustainability does not pose a threat to the system, presumably because the system is correlated with rising profits, and most vessel owners are satisfied and are fighting hard to protect current arrangements. The real threat to the ITQ system comes from critical views regarding its fit in the general social fabric.

Model Competition: The Question of Fit

Few social institutions in Iceland stand out as examples for other OECD (Organisation for Economic Co-operation and Development) countries to follow. The country's welfare system is well liked in many quarters, but it is essentially a Scandinavian copy. The ITQ system is an exception. Iceland and New Zealand pioneered comprehensive ITQ systems, and many other countries have shown considerable interest in their experiments. There are reports, for instance, that the EU looks to Iceland's ITQ system when it is contemplating reforms of its lamentable fisheries regulations. However, as has already been noted, the design of the ITQ system has been criticized. There is also opposition to transferable quotas from fishers and fishing communities because the transfers have directly hurt their material interests. The real challenge, however, involves questions of fit. Criticism comes both from nonexperts (the general public) and from United Nations legal experts.

Already in the early 1990s, it was clear that the average voter did not favor the ITQ system, and the institution has not become more popular over time. In recent years, opinion polls have often registered that 65 to 75 percent of those responding in national samples oppose the system in its current form. The opposition has little to do with direct material incentives. People in small fishing communities that have lost their fishing quotas are only a small fraction of the electorate. The opposition is largely based on shared beliefs about the illegitimacy of windfall gains accruing to those who received the original quotas some 20 to 30 years ago.

The symbol that serves as a focal point for public opposition to the system is the first paragraph of the law from 1990 that set up the ITQ system (Fisheries and Agriculture Ministry, Iceland 2006). This paragraph states that all valuable species in Icelandic waters are the joint property of the nation. In brief, typical critics typically believe that the vessel owners stole the nation's family jewels when the government allocated the original quotas free of charge (on the basis of the recent catch history of each vessel). The critics demand that the government recall the fishing quotas without compensation. They do not understand, or do not care, that in 2010 the majority of vessel owners had bought their quotas at a high price from other operators in the industry.[38] Many of the original owners are gone. Recall and then resale literally implies that most operators will have to purchase the same fishing licenses twice.

---

[38] According to standard economic reasoning, the market price of a fishing quota equals the present value of the expected net income stream associated with the license to fish.

The eventual wealth consequences of the ITQ system caught most experts, the quota market, and the public by surprise. Initially, the price in the quota market was insignificant, but then it took off on a sharply rising trajectory. The industry claims that improved management has created the new wealth, but few members of the public seem to buy its argument. Although withdrawal of the quotas and the introduction of a license fee would have a trivial effect on the living conditions of the average household in terms of lower taxes or better public services, a large part of the public refuses to recognize the legitimacy of the current ITQ system. [39]

Experts, especially judges in Icelandic courts, have also evaluated the social fit of the ITQ system. But first it should be noted that the fingerprints of parliamentary compromise are clearly visible on the 1990 ITQ law, making the legislation a hodgepodge of conflicting social theories. The marine resource is said to be the property of the nation, which is not a recognized category in the law of property. There is also a hint of state property: the state, on behalf of the nation, is responsible for effective use of the fisheries. Elements of private property enter when the law grants experienced vessel owners free license to use the resource for an indefinite period or sell their quotas to qualified vessel owners. Exclusive private rights are then withdrawn in a clause that states that the allocation of use and transfer rights to vessel owners neither constitutes a transfer of property rights nor gives the holders irreversible control of the fishing licenses (Law No. 38/1990, sections 1 and 2). To top off the confusion, private property reappears in court rulings that recognize the valuable fishing quotas as collateral in financial markets and as part of the estate in divorce and inheritance cases.

The opponents of the system have appealed to Icelandic courts to remove barriers to entry in the fisheries (the requirement of possessing quotas) in the name of freedom of occupation and industry. These attempts have been fruitless, except that the Supreme Court in a 1998 judgment extended the right to buy quotas from the original recipients to all owners of fishing ships. According to the decision, all properly registered fishing vessels can buy (and sell) quotas. In another judgment, in 2000, the court confirmed that the fishery system's restrictions on individual freedom to engage in commercial fishing are compatible with the country's constitution. The system was not a misfit.

Finally, the United Nations Human Rights Committee has ruled on the human rights fit of the Icelandic ITQ system.[40] The case involved two Icelanders who in 2001 decided to test (by fishing without quotas) whether the Icelandic government had violated basic human rights by allocating the initial fishing quotas only to experienced vessel owners. In 2004 the enterprising fishers took their case to the United Nations Human Rights Committee. On 24 October 2007, the committee ruled that

---

[39] A previous government, trying to obtain public support for the ITQ system, introduced a small use fee on the industry, which was said to approximately cover the government's expenses of managing the fishing grounds and enforcing the ITQ system. However, the fishing industry that was originally glorified, for instance, during the so-called cod wars with Britain, is idealized no more. In heated public debates, not necessarily on fisheries management, it is not uncommon to declare that one's opponent is an agent of the Federation of Icelandic Vessel Owners.

[40] The case is available on the Web site of the Netherlands' Institute of Human Rights, http://sim.law.uu.nl /SIM/CaseLaw/CCPRcase.nsf/f4c4778b9e02a1b1c12567b70044cc03/88db4de3b85a7a48c12573f40049f19f ?OpenDocument. The case material provides a good description both of the ITQ system and of the two Supreme Court of Iceland cases mentioned in the text.

the Icelandic quota system violated basic human rights, or the International Covenant on Civil and Political Rights. In particular, the committee found that using grandfathering to allocate use rights to a natural resource violates basic human rights. Not all members of the committee agreed with this social theory. Four separate dissenting reports expressed some surprise at the majority views. The committee did not propose specific remedies but concluded that the state "is under an obligation to provide the authors [the two fishers] with an effective remedy, including adequate compensation and review of its fisheries management system."[41] In August 2011 the Icelandic government had not given a final response to the committee; the request, which is not binding, is still under consideration.

In 2009 the confluence of several developments made the removal of the current ITQ system a top priority for the Icelandic government. The financial collapse of the country in the fall of 2008 brought to power a coalition government of parties that oppose the fisheries management system. As previously mentioned, many voters link the 2008 financial tsunami in Iceland to the ITQ system. The 2007 verdict by the United Nations Human Rights Committee was for many Icelanders a final proof that the system was illegitimate—a misfit.

The coalition government of the Social Democratic and Left-Green parties that took office in February 2009 promised to begin recalling the fishing quotas on 1 September 2010, in 20 yearly installments of equal sizes. The quotas, the government stated, would be rented back to the industry, but they would also be used to support regional policy. The year 2010 was an extraordinary year in Iceland. The financial system was in ruins, and the government was close to defaulting, but the fishing industry was still going strong. It was a bright star on a dark night. Initially, the government moved slowly, only nibbling at the ITQ system. In July 2010 the fisheries minister, for instance, declared open access in the ocean shrimp fisheries but failed to introduce the promised structural reforms. In May 2011, the government finally presented in Althingi a major proposal for overhauling the country's fisheries institutions (bill no. 1475, 2010–2011).[42] Moreover, the fisheries minister appointed a committee of five economists to evaluate the economic and social consequences of the proposed structural changes. The committee presented their findings on 14 June, 2011.[43]

The new institutions proposed by the government indicate a move from the microparadigm toward the macroparadigm. The new social technology creates a large role for the fisheries minister in managing the industry and pays little attention to the incentives of individual operators. The reformers are not deterred by agency problems, transaction costs, rent seeking, or the knowledge problems of a central government minister who attempts to micromanage a complex industry that operates in an unstable environment and markets diverse products internationally.

---

[41] Internet access to the ruling of the committee is available on the Web site of the Netherlands' Institute of Human Rights. See note 39. The citation is found in Paragraph 12, "Remedy proposed" of the committtee's report: United Nations International Covenant on Civil and Political Rights. CCPR/C/91/D/1306/2004 14 December 2007.

[42] The bill is available in Icelandic on the Web site of the parliament, http://www.althingi.is.

[43] The report is available in Icelandic on the Web site of the Ministry of Fishieries and Agriculture, http://www .sjavarutvegsraduneyti.is.

The reform bill divides total allowed catch, TAC, into department 1 containing the ITQs of the current system, and department 2 containing six so-called "pots" or regulatory sub-systems. The long-term goal of the reformers is to increase the relative importance of the six pots. The new bill proposes a time limit of fifteen years on the possession of current ITQs. The limit can possibly be extended eight more years but the conditions for extension are unclear. The share of TAC going to department 1 will be gradually reduced, the right to transfer quotas will be limited, and the right to use ITQs as collateral will be reduced and eventually taken away. The micro-paradigm suggests that the reforms will interfere with long-term planning, raise the cost of financing in the industry, and create barriers to entry. The gradual reduction of the share of TAC in department 1 is a tax on ITQ owners, reducing quantity rather than lowering net price. The bill also proposes doubling the current resource tax paid by ITQ owners.

The obvious long-term goal of the reform bill is to shrink the current ITQ system and gradually replace it with the pot system. The largest of the six pots is one where fishers can rent ITQs for a period of one year. The rental market for ITQs will be dominated by the fisheries minister, who will decide how many ITQs are available for each category of boats, regions, equipment, and so on. The rental market for ITQs is intended in part to ease entry into the fisheries, but the one year limit on the rental agreements, and the ban against using ITQs as collateral makes entry difficult. The other five pots are designed to meet specific goals, such as the promotion of environmentally friendly fishing, regional policy, and labor-intensive fisheries technologies. Each pot gets a share of the TAC, and operators who qualify for pot fishing will compete—race to be first—to finish the total pot quota. There is, for instance, a special pot for boats that use set longlines—fishing lines with hundreds of baited hooks at regular intervals. In the spirit of the macroparadigm, the bill states that to qualify for the longline pot, fishers must manually bait the hooks and not use (existing) machines for baiting.

The committee of specialists that the fisheries minister appointed to evaluate the new regime unanimously objects to many features of the new institutions. They predict that the new system will be inefficient, introduce a framework for rent seeking, fail to achieve various desired social goals, and create severe financial problems in the industry.

In a survey of the Icelandic economy dated June 2011, the OECD (2011) fears that the proposed changes in the fisheries regime may hinder the country's recovery from the 2008 financial collapse. The OECD recognizes the importance of strengthening political consensus on the quota system but points out that "there is nothing that the government can do now to undo the perceived unfairness of the initial allocation as most current quota holders purchased their quotas" (OECD 2011, 3).

While waiting for the next chapter in the Icelandic ITQ saga, we have learned a few lessons. The ambiguous concept "property of the people" is a cover for the more conventional term "state property." Popular calls for distributive justice have given politicians the opportunity to attempt a switch to the macroparadigm and central management. And we have learned that in the middle of a severe economic crisis policy makers, applying to their ideas about design and fit, are ready to turn a successful industry upside down.[44] In most highly developed countries the fisheries sector is of trivial importance for the national economy. In Iceland of the modern era, the fisheries have been the prime engine of economic growth.

REFERENCES

Agnarsson, Sveinn, and Ragnar Arnason. 2007. The role of the fishing industry in the Icelandic economy. In *Advances in fisheries economics*, eds. Trond Bjørndal, Ragnar Arnason, and U. Rashid Sumalla, 237–256. Oxford: Blackwell Publishing.

Alchian, Armen A. 1965. Some economics of property rights. *Il Politico* 30(4):816–829.

Arnason, Ragnar. 1993. The Icelandic individual transferable quota system: A descriptive account. *Marine Resource Economics* 8(3):201–218.

Barzel, Yoram. 1989. *The economic analysis of property rights*. New York: Cambridge University Press.

Bhagwati, Jagdish. 1978. *Anatomy and consequences of exchange control regimes*. Cambridge, MA: Ballinger.

Buchanan, James M., and Gordon Tullock. 1962. *The calculus of consent: Logical foundations of constitutional democracy*. Ann Arbor: University of Michigan Press.

Chai, Sun-Ki. 1998. Endogenous ideology formation and economic policy in former colonies. *Economic Development and Cultural Change* 46:263–290.

Coase, Ronald H. 1959. The Federal Communications Commission. *Journal of Law and Economics* 2(Oct.):1–40.

Demsetz, Harold. 1967. Toward a theory of property rights. *American Economic Review* 57(2):347–359.

Denzau, Arthur T., and Douglass C. North. 1994. Shared mental models: Ideologies and institutions. *Kyklos* 47(1):3–31.

Downs, Anthony. 1957. An economic theory of political action in a democracy. *Journal of Political Economy* 65(2): 135–150.

Eagle, Josh, and Barton H. Thompson, Jr. 2003. Answering Lord Perry's question: Dissecting regulatory overfishing. *Ocean and Coastal Management* 46(6):649–679.

Easterly, William. 2006. *The white man's burden: Why the West's efforts to aid the rest have done so much ill and so little good*. London: Penguin Press.

Eggertsson, Thráinn. 1990a. *Economic behavior and institutions*. New York: Cambridge University Press.

——. 1990b. Repressed financial systems as instruments of taxation: Evidence from Iceland. *Finnish Economic Papers* 31(1):14–25.

——. 1992. Analyzing institutional successes and failures: A millennium of common mountain pastures in Iceland. *International Review of Law and Economics* 12:423–437.

——. 1996. No experiments, monumental disasters: Why it took a thousand years to develop a specialized fishing industry in Iceland. *Journal of Economic Behavior and Organization* 30(1):1–23.

——. 1998. Sources of risk, institutions for survival, and a game against nature in premodern Iceland. *Explorations in Economic History* 35(1):1–30.

——. 2005. *Imperfect institutions: Possibilities and limits of reform*. Ann Arbor: University of Michigan Press.

——. 2011. The evolution of property rights: The strange case of Iceland's health records. *International Journal of the Commons* 5(1):50–65.

---

[44] According to the OECD (2011, 28): "Iceland has managed its local fish stocks, i.e., stocks that are not shared with other countries, in a sustainable and profitable way."

Eggertsson, T., and Tryggvi T. Herbertsson. 2009. System failure in Iceland and the global financial crisis. Paper presented at the 2009 ISNIE Meeting, Berkeley. http://papers.isnie.org/berkeley.html.

FAO (Food and Agriculture Organization). 2009. *The state of world fisheries and aquaculture, 2008.* Rome: Food and Agriculture Organization of the United Nations.

Field, Barry C. 1989. The evolution of property rights. *Kyklos* 42(3):319–345.

Fisheries and Agriculture Ministry, Iceland. 2006. *The Fisheries Management Act of 1990, as amended.* Icelandic Fisheries (August 10). http://www.fisheries.is/management/fisheries-management/the-fisheries-management-act/.

Furubotn, Eirik G., and Rudolf Richter. 2005. *Institutions and economic theory: The contribution of new institutional economics.* 2nd ed. Ann Arbor: University of Michigan Press.

Greif, Avner. 2006. *Institutions and the path to the modern economy.* New York: Cambridge University Press.

Hahnel, Robin, and Kristen A. Sheeran. 2009. Misinterpreting the Coase theorem. *Journal of Economic Issues* 43(1):215–238.

Hannesson, Rögnvaldur. 2005. Rights based fishing: Use rights versus property rights to fish. *Reviews in Fish Biology and Fisheries* 15(3):231–241.

Hirshleifer, Jack, and John G. Riley. 1992. *The analytics of uncertainty and information.* New York: Cambridge University Press.

Libecap, Gary D. 1989. *Contracting for property rights.* New York: Cambridge University Press.

Marine Research Institute, Iceland. 2010. *State of marine stocks in Icelandic waters 2009* (June 4). http://www.hafro.is/undir_eng.php?ID=26&REF=4.

McKinnon, Ronald I. 1981. Financial repression and the liberalization problem within less-developed countries. In *The world economic order: Past and prospects,* eds. Sven Grassman and Erik Lundberg, 365–386. New York: St. Martin's Press.

McKinnon, Ronald I., and Donald Mathieson. 1981. How to manage a repressed economy. *Essays in International Finance,* Princeton University, No. 145.

Mueller, Dennis C. 2003. *Public choice III.* New York: Cambridge University Press.

North, Douglass C. 1979. A framework for analyzing the state in economic history. *Explorations in Economic History* 16:249–259.

——. 1990. *Institutions, institutional change and economic performance.* New York: Cambridge University Press.

——. 2005. *Understanding the process of economic change.* Princeton, NJ: Princeton University Press.

North, Douglass C., and Robert P. Thomas. 1973. *The rise of the Western world: A new economic history.* New York: Cambridge University Press.

OECD. 2011. *Economic Surveys: Iceland, June 2011.* Available at http://www.oecd.org/bookshop.

Olson, Mancur. 1965. *The logic of collective action.* Cambridge, MA: Harvard University Press.

Ostrom, Elinor. 1990. *Governing the commons: The evolution of institutions for collective action.* New York: Cambridge University Press.

Posner, Richard A. 1980. A theory of primitive society, with special reference to law. *Journal of Law and Economics* 23(1):1–53.

Roland, Gérard. 2004. Understanding institutional change: Fast-moving and slow-moving institutions. *Studies in Comparative International Development* 38(4):109–131.

Rosenberg, Nathan, and L. E. Birdzell. 1986. *How the West grew rich: The economic transformation of the Western world.* New York: Basic Books.

Waller, John. 2003. *The discovery of the germ: Twenty years that transformed the way we think about disease.* New York: Columbia University Press.

Williamson, Oliver E. 1985. *The economic institutions of capitalism: Firms, markets, and relational contracting.* New York: Free Press.

Yandle, Tracy. 2003. The challenge of building successful stakeholder organizations: New Zealand's experience in developing a successful fisheries co-management regime. *Marine Policy* 27:179–192.

The Variety of Property Systems and Rights in Natural Resources

2

DANIEL H. COLE AND ELINOR OSTROM

Property theory has not kept pace with the growth of empirical and historical data on property systems. Economists, legal scholars, and other social scientists continue to rely on simplistic, outmoded, and incomplete models that fail to capture the variety and complexity of property arrangements found throughout the world. Although one cannot deny the significance and continuing relevance of theories derived from Aristotle, Roman law, and more recent scholarly contributions from the likes of Garrett Hardin and Harold Demsetz, the time has come to move beyond simple models of property panaceas to develop a more descriptively accurate and analytically useful theory of property systems and rights in natural resources.

In 1968 Garrett Hardin used the memorable phrase "tragedy of the commons" to describe a phenomenon that fisheries economists had previously analyzed: natural resources not subject to institutional limitations on access and use would be overexploited, degraded, and eventually destroyed (Gordon 1954; Scott 1955; Warming 1911). The "commons" to which Hardin referred were open-access, common-pool resources where property rights had not been defined. The "tragedy" he described was the inexorable overexploitation and destruction of those resources resulting from the structure of incentives in which no one could exclude anyone else from accessing and using the resource (Hardin 1968).

A year before Hardin published "The Tragedy of the Commons," the economist Harold Demsetz (1967) published an almost equally famous article, "Toward a Theory of Property Rights," which sought to explain the rise of private-individual property rights as a natural, evolutionary response to increasing demand for scarce natural resources.[1] Demsetz's article gave rise to what Eggertsson (1990, 254) has called "the naïve theory of property rights," according to which the entire history of civilization is an inexorable, unidirectional movement toward private-individual ownership of land and other natural resources. In a kind of institution-free, Hayekian spontaneous generation, private-individual property is said to emerge at some point

---

[1] Demsetz (1967) differed from Hardin (1968) in one very important respect. Hardin was clearly describing a nonproperty/open-access system (a pasture open to all). Demsetz, by contrast, purported to describe an evolutionary shift from common property to private-individual property. His understanding of the common property regime he was purporting to describe was both anthropologically and theoretically flawed.

in the socioeconomic development of every culture in order to reduce externalities and transaction costs as demand for natural resources increases relative to supply. It is also said to increase gains from trade and to facilitate resource conservation (Demsetz 1967; Umbeck 1981).

As Eggertsson suggests, this theory is naïve because (1) it is oblivious to the failure of some private ownership regimes to conserve scarce resources over time (Clark 1973a; 1973b; Hurst 1984); (2) it neglects the effectiveness of alternative property/regulatory arrangements that have evolved to manage scarce natural resources successfully throughout the world (E. Ostrom 1990; Poteete, Janssen, and Ostrom 2010); and (3) it implausibly promotes private-individual ownership as an institutional panacea (E. Ostrom, Janssen, and Anderies 2007).

The history and evolution of actually existing property regimes applicable to natural resources do not support the naïve theory, even as a first approximation. Instead, there is a vast array of complex property systems, including various combinations of private-individual, common, and public property rights that apply differentially to various natural resources on the basis not only of supply relative to demand, but also of many other variables, including the structure of underlying institutions (both social norms and formal laws), ecological conditions, and culture. Moreover, specific property regimes that prove viable and sustainable in one set of social-ecological circumstances (or in a single case) may prove nonviable or unsustainable in another (or many others). Just as the ecology of natural resources is highly complex and still not fully understood, so too are the property/regulatory systems that human societies deploy to manage, with greater or lesser success, those resources.

Empirical property-systems research not only belies the naïve theory of property rights, but also exposes Hardin's binary solutions to the tragedy of open access (private ownership or government regulation) as overly simplistic. Both private ownership and government regulation of access and use have not always successfully conserved natural resources. Coase (1964) has shown that government failure is just as important a category as market failure. Moreover, governments and markets can fail together. The Deepwater Horizon oil spill, arguably the worst environmental disaster in U.S. history, is only the most recent example of a combined government and market failure. The Marine Minerals Service of the Department of the Interior failed to regulate British Petroleum (BP) adequately because it suffered from an inherent conflict of interest: the revenues BP brought into the federal government caused the service to neglect its regulatory function.[2] Meanwhile, BP's private cost-benefit calculations of precautionary measures did not account for potentially catastrophic externalities. Most important, Hardin neglected viable alternatives to both private-individual ownership and government regulation, including self-organization and self-management by the resource users themselves (E. Ostrom 1990). Field studies, laboratory experiments, and appropriately structured games (Cole and Grossman 2010; E. Ostrom, Gardner, and Walker 1994) confirm that common property regimes are often, though not always, able to avert the tragedy of open access and conserve scarce resources over long periods of time.

---

[2] On the general problem of regulatory conflicts of interest and their effects on administrative oversight, see Cohen-Tanugi (1985) and Cole (1998).

One important goal of this book is to move beyond naïve, simplistic theories of commons tragedies and solutions by considering (or reconsidering) the wide variety of actually existing property systems applicable to natural resources that have evolved over time in response to changing social-ecological circumstances and to derive from those observations some implications for a more complex, but also more realistic and robust theory of property rights. Admittedly, the effort is complicated by the availability of multiple interpretive lenses through which any existing set of property institutions or regulations might be described or explained. For example, did the miners' codes adopted during the California gold rush constitute spontaneously organized property regimes (Umbeck 1981), agreements based on shared mental models (Anderson and Zerbe 2001), governance regimes more complex than simple contracts for property rights (Clay and Wright 2005), or attempted solutions to coordination games based on a wider variety of norms, including norms of fairness, at least some of which deviated significantly from basic tenets of American property law (McDowell 2002; 2004)? Even such conceptual disputes about the nature of actually existing institutions may contribute to a fuller and more realistic understanding of the nature and meaning of "property" as that term is applied to natural resources.

Defining Property Systems and Rights

The social science literature is replete with discussions of property rights and systems. However, conceptions of property differ significantly across that literature, and the phrase "property rights" and the term "institutions" are used in a wide variety of ways that are sometimes inconsistent (Alston, Eggertsson, and North 1996; North 1990). This volume is intended to lead to a better working definition of "property" as a concept and an institution or collection of institutions, as well as improved understanding of how various property systems have emerged, evolved, and developed (and continue to do so).

During the twentieth century, legal scholars focused predominantly on private property rights in land and often treated the right to exclude as the "*sine qua non* of property" (Merrill 1998, 730). Resource economists were preoccupied with private-individual property rights and often equated ownership with the right to alienate (Becker 1977). The focus on just a few specific private property rights was, of course, myopic and limited understanding of the wide variety of existing property systems for a long time.

Scholars from several disciplines, including history, economics, political science, law, sociology, and anthropology, have studied cases from around the world that illustrate the diverse ways in which resource users and other stakeholders have developed and instituted property-based governance regimes to manage those resources successfully and sustainably (Deininger, Ali, and Yamano 2008). Empirical research has contributed to a greater recognition and understanding of the diversity of rights and "bundles" of rights (Bromley 1989; Ciriacy-Wantrup and Bishop 1975; Wilson 1990; 2002; Wilson, Yan, and Wilson 2007).

From that research, scholars have distilled sets of rights that regularly apply to specific kinds of natural resources. Honoré (1961), for example, identified nine distinct rights and two duties that are typically present in the case of full (fee-simple) ownership of land: (1) the right to exclusive possession; (2) the right to use; (3) the right to manage; (4) the right to the income; (5) the right to the capital; (6) the right to security; (7) transmissibility; (8) absence of term; (9) the prohibition of harmful use; (10) liability to execution; and (11) the right of residuary character. Of course, not all property is owned in fee simple. Lesser property interests would be categorized in Honoré's system by the absence of one or more distinct rights and duties. An owner of a conditional fee simple (such as fee simple to condition subsequent or fee simple determinable) would have only limited use and management rights; the term of his or her ownership interest could be cut short by a breach of the condition. A leasehold tenant would necessarily lack (5), (8), and (11). Mere licensees would have even fewer of the sticks from the full bundle of property rights.

Most property systems for water and other common-pool resources fail to exhibit many of Honoré's specific rights. Common-pool resources are large enough that it is costly to exclude potential beneficiaries, and they generate goods (resource units) whose extraction reduces the quantity of goods available to others (V. Ostrom and E. Ostrom 1977). Private rights to common-pool resources tend to be more limited, correlative, contingent, and attenuated than those applicable to land. Broadly considering ownership rights in common-pool resources, including many fishery and water resources, Schlager and Ostrom (1992) discerned five distinct property rights in use:

1. Entry: the right to enter a resource, which could be achieved by buying a ticket to enter a state park for a day or a month, by declaration of a national or state government that all citizens of the nation or state could enter footpaths or property of a wide diversity of kinds, or by inheritance of joint use rights.
2. Withdrawal: the right to harvest and take some resource units out of the resource system. Those who purchase a permit, for example, obtain a right to extract various kinds of resource units, including fish, nontimber forest products, firewood, timber, and diverse amounts of water.
3. Management: the right to change the physical structures in a resource system, such as building an irrigation system or a road, changing the shoreline of a fishery, or developing a variety of physical infrastructures for any particular resource.
4. Exclusion: the right to determine who else could use the resource and what their specific rights would be.
5. Alienation: the right to sell one or more of the first four rights permanently or for a given time period. Most attention has been given to the right to transfer full ownership of a segment of a resource that would involve having all four of the other rights. Some forms of alienation are not that general, but still assign the right to sell some meaningful subset of the rights that are held by a participant.

Schlager and Ostrom's list of property rights in common-pool resources significantly overlaps with Honoré's list of private property rights in land, but the differences between the two sets of rights may be more important than the commonalities. Moreover, one should not blithely assume that scholars mean the same thing by their designations and descriptions of various property rights. There is still no standard, cross-disciplinary agreement on a common set of names, contents, and meanings of the term "property right" (Cole and Grossman 2002). The problem, then, is how to define this term.

What makes a right a right? Must it be enforceable by a court of law? Does the term "right" incorporate lesser interests (or entitlements), such as licenses, permissions, or mere unimpeded uses? Nearly one hundred years ago, the legal scholar Wesley Newcomb Hohfeld designed a powerful analytic system for understanding the nature of various legal entitlements and burdens, including rights and duties (Hohfeld 1913; 1917) (see table 2.1). The most important aspect of that system for present purposes is Hohfeld's correlation of right and duty, according to which one cannot be said to possess a "right," including a "property right," unless one can identify at least one other person who possesses an enforceable, corresponding duty of noninterference. Unfortunately, Hohfeld's system has not been widely followed outside the legal academy and remains somewhat controversial within it (but see Singer 2006).[3] Some social scientists, including Barzel (1989), throw around the word "right" casually and without clear definition (Cole and Grossman 2002). In this chapter, the term "right" is used in Hohfeld's strict sense.

Similar problems attend the term "property," which, if anything, is even less well defined than the term "right." It is not clear, in the first place, what makes a certain right a "property right," as opposed to a "personal right," a "human right," or some other kind of right. Even if we assume that such distinctions make sense, on what basis do we distinguish these different types of rights? What, if anything, makes "property" special? Is it anything more than a descriptive appendage to the term "right," signifying that the right relates to things, including incorporeal things, such as shares of communal or corporate assets?[4]

When scholars have focused on parsing specific private property rights governing various resources under different systems, they have sometimes neglected higher-order categorizations of property systems, which have their roots (but not necessarily their modern understandings)[5] in Justinian's compilation of Roman law: *res privatae*

TABLE 2.1
Hohfeld's Jural Relations

Correlatives	Opposites
Right/duty	Right/no-right
Privilege/no-right	Privilege/duty
Power/liability	Power/disability
Immunity/disability	Immunity/liability

SOURCE: Hohfeld (1913; 1917).

---

[3] For a description of legal/jurisprudential critiques of Hohfeld's jural relations and a strong defense of Hohfeld's system, see Lazarev (2005). V. Ostrom and E. Ostrom (1972) analyze the work of Hohfeld (1917) and Commons (1959) as a foundation for analyzing water rights and water development.

[4] In Hohfeld's system of jural relations, "all legal interests are 'incorporeal,' consisting, as they do, of more or less limited aggregates of *abstract* legal relations" (1913, 24; emphasis in original).

[5] It needs to be stressed that the conventional typology of property systems sketched here reflects modern understandings of the Roman law property categories, rather than the original Roman conceptions. Significant differences include the treatment of *res nullius* and *res communes*. At Roman law, *res nullius* or nonproperty was capable of

(private property), *res publicae* (public property), *res communes* (common property), and *res nullius* (nonproperty) (see table 2.2).

These Roman law categories arguably are incoherent or at least incomplete. Few, if any, real-existing property arrangements fit within a single category. Is a corporation, for example, better described as private property or common property? When is local self-government public, as opposed to common, property? Might not common property resources be described as the private property of each individual member of the common ownership group? Because of the lack of coherence and completeness in the description of property systems, scholars have sometimes confused or conflated Roman law property types, but they can take solace in the fact that the Roman lawyers who first developed them also did so. Consider the following sections from Justinian's *Institutes*:

TABLE 2.2

Conventional Typology of Property Systems

State/public property	The state or its agencies have the right to determine rules of access and use, but a duty (at least in theory) to manage publicly owned resources for the public welfare. Individual members of the public do not necessarily have a right of access or use, but they have a duty to observe access and use rules promulgated by the controlling/managing agency.
Private property	Owners have the exclusive right to undertake socially acceptable uses to the exclusion of nonowners, and they have a duty to refrain from socially unacceptable uses. Nonowners have a duty to refrain from preventing owners' socially acceptable uses, but they have the right to prevent or be compensated for socially unacceptable uses.
Common property	Each member of the ownership group has the right to access and use group-owned resources in accordance with access and use rules established collectively by the group, and a duty not to violate access and use rules. Each member also has the right to exclude nonmembers of the ownership group, but no right to exclude other members of the ownership group. Nonmembers of the ownership group have a duty not to access and use the resource except in accordance with rules adopted collectively by the ownership group.
Nonproperty/open access	No individual has a duty to refrain from accessing and using a resource. No individual or group has the right to prevent any other individual or group from accessing and using the resource as they choose.

SOURCE: Adapted from Bromley (1991).

appropriation, that is, conversion to *res privatae* through acts of possession and occupation; and *res communes* referred to things not susceptible to private or state ownership, such as the open seas. *Res communes* originally designated open-access resources (Rose 2003; Sohm [1907] 1994). Today, however, most scholars treat the Roman category of *res nullius* or nonproperty as synonymous with open access; it is unowned by anyone and open to all users. The term *res communes*, by contrast, now denotes property co-owned by one group to the exclusion of others (E. Ostrom 1990). However, some scholars (e.g., Freyfogle 2002; Platt 2004) distinguish "open-access commons" from "closed-access commons."

Section I.—These things are, by the Law of Nature, common to all mankind,—air, running water, the sea, and consequently the shores of the sea. No one, therefore, is forbidden to approach the shore of the sea, providing he abstain from injuring houses, monuments and buildings, for these are not of common right, as is the sea.

Section II—All rivers, also, and ports are public property, therefore all men have a common right to fish in a port, or in rivers.

. . .

Section V. —The use of the shores of the sea is as public, and common to all men as is the sea itself; therefore any person is permitted to build a house there, for his habitation, or to dry his nets, and draw up anything from the sea upon the shore. The property of the shore, however, must be understood to be vested in no individual, but to partake of the same legal nature as the sea itself, and the soil or sand which is beneath it. (Grapel 1994 [1855], 50)

Nearly all property scholars are familiar with section I, but few have paid due attention to sections II and V, which confirm that Roman lawyers failed to delineate clearly the content of the property categories they established. In asserting that the air and waters are "common to all mankind" and constitute "public property," so that "all men have a common right to fish in a port, or in rivers," Justinian's lawyers conflated common property with public property and both of those property categories with open access. A similar problem arises from the assertion that "any person is permitted to build a house" on the seashores because they are "public" property and "common to all men."[6] Conceptual confusions over property systems are not a modern invention, but seemingly date back to the very Roman lawyers who first described them.

Figure 2.1 provides a graphic representation of the Roman law property systems (plus hybrids) in a way that illustrates the conceptual problems they generate. The nonproperty/property and public/private property dichotomies seem clear enough, but once common property and hybrid systems are added, distinctions become blurred. In a more realistic depiction of actual property relations, the category "hybrid property" would probably blot out all other systems. Virtually all real-existing property systems contain admixtures of private, public, and common rights. There is no such thing as purely private or purely public property (Cole 2002).

The old Roman law property categories seem increasingly obsolete in a world of mixed, hybrid, and nested property systems. Nevertheless, they continue to serve as the conventional types for purposes of description, comparison, and analysis. Is it finally time to replace them?

More important, perhaps, than improving or replacing the conventional typology of property systems passed down from Roman lawyers is learning about the specific rights and duties meant by the phrases "private property," "public property," and "common property" as applied in particular locations. Bromley observed that

---

[6] A different translation of the *Institutes* refers to "hut" instead of "house" and to "shelter" rather than "habitation" (Birks and McLeod 1987, 55). This alternative translation suggests a more temporary arrangement, rather than permanent occupancy. We are grateful to Richard Epstein for directing us to this alternative translation.

FIGURE 2.1

Relations of Property Systems

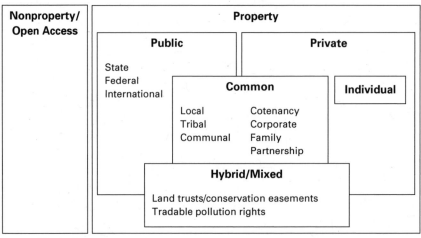

SOURCE: Cole (2002).

those who write about property systems and rights are only rarely "specific about the content of those terms" (1989, 187). When someone uses the phrase "private property," it is often difficult to tell whether that person means something like Blackstonian absolute dominion (Blackstone 1979 [1766]), which did not really exist even in Blackstone's time (Rose 1998), or something more like modern real estate ownership, which is subject both to the correlative rights of neighbors and to substantial government control.

Roman Law Conceptions of Property and the Sustainability of Natural Resources

Even though the broad types of property rights as traditionally defined are characterized by conceptual problems, one or another of them is frequently recommended as the best way to manage natural resources in a sustainable manner. Advocacy for idealized types of property rights relies on a widely accepted view in the environmental management literature that property rights over land or other natural resources are required in order to provide the appropriate incentives for conservation to users (Hanna and Munasinghe 1995). It is presumed that if someone does not "own" a resource, that person does not have long-term interests in sustaining that resource and thus cannot be expected to act beneficially toward it. Without property rights, open-access conditions prevail, which frequently do lead to environmental destruction when users are located near a resource and are interested in harvesting from it.

Instead of recognizing the diversity of rules actually used in the governance of resources that are sustained over long periods of time, much of the policy literature strongly recommends private or government ownership, with a strong bias for governmental property rights systems. One important example is the repeated recommendation of protected areas and national parks. Public ownership with stringent formal regulations regarding use patterns is recommended by some as the silver bullet to achieve biodiversity conservation (Lovejoy 2006; Terborgh 1999; Dowie

2010 [on observing that formal institutions designed to protect biodiversity sometimes harm indigenous cultures]). Empirical studies are uncovering a diversity of institutions, however, that achieve sustainable development, as well as those that do not (E. Ostrom 2005). Many factors beyond the generalized names associated with the idealized property rights systems discussed earlier are associated with achievements in the field (Grafton 2000). What are some of the attributes of resources in the field that are conducive to private property, and why have some of the heralded policies not performed as recommended in the policy literature?

Attributes of Resources Conducive to Individual Ownership

The advantage of individual ownership of strictly private goods, where the cost of exclusion is relatively low and one person's consumption subtracts from what is available to others, is so well established that it does not merit attention here. Industrial and agricultural commodities clearly fit the definition of private goods. Individual rights to exclusion and to transfer of control over these goods generate incentives that tend to lead to higher levels of productivity than other forms of property arrangements.

It has frequently been assumed that land is also best thought of as a private good and therefore is most efficiently allocated by using market mechanisms based on individual ownership rights. Gaining formal title to land, however, may or may not increase efficiency. Feder et al. (1988) conducted an important econometric study that showed that agricultural land in Thailand without a formal title was worth only one-half to two-thirds as much as land with a formal title. Further, increasing the security of private property rights also led to an increased value of the crops produced (between one-tenth and one-fourth higher than the value of those from land without a secure title). More secure titling also provided better access to credit and led to greater investments in improved land productivity (see also Feder and Feeny 1991).

Title insurance is one mechanism used to reduce the risk of challenges to ownership of land. Registering brands is another technique used to increase the security of ownership over resource units in the form of cattle that may range freely over a large area until there is a communal effort to undertake a roundup. Gaining formal titles, however, is costly. In societies that do not yet have high population densities and in which customary rights are still commonly understood and accepted, formal titling may be an expensive method of increasing the security of a title that is not associated with a sufficiently higher return to be worth the economic investment (Migot-Adholla et al. 1991). In addition, the cost of fencing land by physical and/or institutional means is nontrivial, and there are types of land and land uses that may be more efficiently governed by groups of individuals than by single individuals.

A commonly recommended solution to problems associated with the governance and management of mobile resources units, such as water and fish, is their privatization (Christy 1973; Clark 1980). What private ownership usually means in regard to mobile resource units, however, is ownership of the rights to withdraw a quantity of a resource unit and the right to alienate this harvesting right. Water rights are normally associated with the allocation of a particular quantity of water per unit of time or the allocation of a right to take water for a particular period of time or at a particular location. Fishing rights are similarly associated with quantity, time, or location. These rights are typically withdrawal rights that are tied to resource units and not to a resource system.

Some coastal fisheries in Canada, New Zealand, and Iceland have been able to develop individual transferable quota (ITQ) systems that have reduced the level of harvesting. In British Columbia, early governmental policies trying to control over-fishing of the trawl fishery for groundfish included restricting the number of fishing vehicles and the equipment that could be used and assigning quotas of total allowable catch and fishing trips. In 1995 the fishery was closed, however, because of a major collapse. The government reopened the fishery several years later with new regulations, including an annual ITQ system (Clark 2006). In addition, it established a rigorous monitoring program in which onboard observers record all catches. The ITQ system has collected more valid data, decreased fleet overcapacity, recorded catch levels that are close to the allocated quotas, and reduced discard of unwanted species. Thus, the British Columbia ITQ system has had positive impacts on the fishery. In addition to the allocation of fishing rights each year, an effective and costly monitoring system has also been an essential aspect of this success. ITQ systems that do not have an effective monitoring system have suffered from considerable under-reporting of catch levels.

New Zealand declared its two-hundred-mile Exclusive Economic Zone in 1983. In 1986 New Zealand became one of the first countries to adopt a market-based fishery regulation when it adopted its Quota Management System and allocated ITQs to a subset of domestic fisheries (Yandle and Dewees 2003). New Zealand authorities found that the biological models underlying the initial assignment of permanent allocations of fixed quotas needed to be adjusted over time in light of further evidence. As a result, in 1990 the commercial fishers received a revised ITQ based on a proportion of the total catch assigned annually (Yandle 2007). Over time, the original ITQ system has evolved into a comanagement system in which the fishers participate in gathering data and making policies. The system is still evolving and faces problems related to mismatches among the temporary and spatial dimensions of the property rights assigned to diverse groups (Yandle 2007).

In 1990 Iceland also introduced an ITQ system that is similar to the evolved New Zealand ITQ system. Quotas are not fixed quantities, but rather a share of the annual authorized catch level set by the government (Arnason 1993). Iceland's ITQ system appears to have averted the collapse of many valuable species for the Iceland fishery, but it has been less successful in restoring Icelandic cod stocks. In his analysis of the long and conflict-ridden road to the Icelandic ITQ system, Eggertsson (2004; 2005) reflects that introducing major institutional changes is a subtle art compared with using a simpler one-size-fits-all formula. Designing a top-down system and imposing it on the harvesters is not as successful as working with the users of a resource over time to develop a system that is well matched to the ecological system, as well as to the practices, norms, and long-term economic welfare of the participants, as was eventually accomplished in New Zealand.

Although the fishers have rights to the quotas or "fishing units," they do not own the fishing stock. Governmental units exercise various types of management rights in relationship to these stocks, which thus constitute public or state property before private allocation or appropriation. In groundwater basins that have been successfully litigated, individual pumpers own a defined quantity of water that they can produce, rent, or sell, but the groundwater basins themselves may be managed by a combination of general-purpose and special-purpose governmental units and private associations (Blomquist 1992; Steed 2010).

Implementing operational and efficient individual withdrawal rights to mobile resources is far more difficult in practice than demonstrating the economic efficiency of hypothetical systems (Yandle 2001). Simply gaining valid and accurate measurements of "sustainable yield" is a scientifically difficult task. In systems where resource units are stored naturally or by constructing facilities such as a dam, the availability of a defined quantity of the resource units can be ascertained with considerable accuracy, and buying, selling, and leasing rights to known quantities are relatively easy to achieve in practice. Many mobile resource systems do not have natural or constructed storage facilities, and gaining accurate information about the stock and reproduction rates is costly and involves considerable uncertainty (Allen and McGlade 1987; Wilson et al. 1991). Further, as Copes (1986) has clearly articulated, appropriators from such resources can engage in a wide diversity of evasive strategies that can destabilize the efforts of government agencies trying to manage these systems. Once such systems have allocated individual withdrawal rights, efforts to regulate patterns of withdrawal further may be difficult and involve expensive buyback schemes. Experience with these individual withdrawal rights systems has varied greatly in practice (McCay 1992; McCay et al. 1996; Pinkerton 1992; 1994; Wilson et al. 1994). Further, efficiency is not the only criterion that should be taken into account in analyzing the effect of privatizing essential goods, such as water (Frohlich and Oppenheimer 1995).

Exactly which attributes of both physical and social systems are most important to the success of individual withdrawal rights from common-pool resources is not as well established as the attributes of common-pool resource systems conducive to group proprietorship or ownership. On the physical side, gaining accurate measurements of the key variables (quantity, space, technology) that are to be involved in management efforts is essential. Resource systems that are naturally well bounded facilitate measurement, as well as ease of observing appropriation behavior. Storage also facilitates measurement. Where resource units move over vast terrains, the cost of measurement is higher than when they are contained. For example, it is easier to develop effective withdrawal rights systems for lobsters than for whales.

Considerable recent research has also stressed the importance of involving participants in the design and implementation of individual withdrawal rights systems (Yandle and Dewees 2003). When participants do not look on such rules as legitimate, effective, and fair, the incentive to invent evasive strategies is substantial (Seabright 1993; Wilson 1995). The very process of allocating quantitative and transferable rights to resource units may, in fact, undo some of the common understandings and norms that allowed communal ownership systems to operate at lower day-to-day administrative costs.

Finally, even where the costs of establishing, implementing, and monitoring private property rights in resource systems are manageable, sustainable levels of resource extraction are not guaranteed. Clark, for example, observes that the "extermination of an entire [whale] population may appear as an attractive policy, even to an individual resource owner," when "(a) the discount (or time preference) rate sufficiently exceeds the maximum reproductive potential of the population, and (b) an immediate profit can be made from harvesting the last remaining animals" (1973b, 950–951; also see Clark [1973a]; Cole [2002]; Larson and Bromley [1990]; Schlager and Ostrom [1992]). Clark's findings are supported by other empirical studies, including Fidzani's (2000) investigation of the effects of privatization on pastureland degradation in Botswana and Hurst's (1984) study of deforestation of private timberlands in Wisconsin. Even when individual private ownership is practicable, then, it is not a panacea for resource conservation.

Comparing Farmer-Managed and Agency-Managed Irrigation Systems in Nepal

Although the evidence regarding the use of private property for sustainable resource use is not generally positive, some very creative common property regimes have a higher success rate. A brief description of research findings related to irrigation systems and forests illustrates the importance of unpacking broad property concepts to understand why some work effectively in some settings but are not universally applicable.

Rice farmers are highly dependent on how effectively the irrigation systems serving their land work. No irrigation system works well, however, without agreed-on rules for allocating both water and responsibilities to provide the needed labor, materials, and money to build the system and maintain it over time. Until the 1950s, farmers in Nepal built all the farmer-managed irrigation systems (FMISs) that they used to supply water to irrigate paddy rice fields because the central government did not take any responsibility for planning, building, or maintaining these systems. In the mid-1950s a Department of Irrigation was established that articulated and developed a series of five-year plans to add new systems to the many FMISs that the farmers had established. Since then, international development agencies (including the Asian Development Bank and the World Bank) have invested large sums in designing and constructing large-scale irrigation systems that were turned over to the national government to be agency-managed irrigation systems (AMISs). The existence of two broad ownership patterns for irrigation systems has provided an excellent opportunity to compare the performance of systems built and organized by farmers with that of systems designed by engineers and then owned by a national government.

Researchers associated with the Institute of Agriculture and Animal Science at Tribhuvan University in Nepal have been working with colleagues at Indiana University since the early 1990s (Benjamin et al. 1994; Lam, Lee, and Ostrom 1997). They jointly developed the Nepal Irrigation Institutions and Systems (NIIS) database that now has information on more than 225 irrigation systems located in 29 of the 75 districts in Nepal (Joshi et al. 2000).[7] The consistent finding is that on average, FMISs

---

[7] The findings discussed in this chapter are based on data that were mostly collected in earlier peaceful times.

TABLE 2.3

Relationships Between Governance Structure and Physical Condition of Irrigation Systems

Physical Condition of Irrigation Systems		Type of Governance Structure		Chi-Square Value	Significance
		FMIS (%)	AMIS (%)		
Overall condition	Excellent [37]	18.2	8.4	23.02	.00
	Moderately good [144]	67.4	45.8		
	Poor [48]	14.4	45.8		
Technical efficiency	Highly efficient [58]	28.9	12.5	27.30	.00
	Moderately efficient [137]	62.8	50.0		
	Inefficient [33]	8.3	37.5		
Economic efficiency	Highly efficient [66]	33.2	12.5	45.35	.00
	Moderately efficient [140]	63.5	52.1		
	Inefficient [23]	3.3	35.4		

SOURCE: Joshi et al. (2000).

NOTE: Numbers of irrigation systems are in brackets.

outperform AMISs on multiple dimensions. A very brief overview of these findings is presented here.

In regard to the physical condition of the irrigation system at the time of data collection, as shown in table 2.3, a larger proportion of FMISs than of AMISs are able to maintain the overall physical condition of a system in excellent or moderately good condition and to achieve higher technical and economic efficiency (see Lam 1998 for definitions of these terms as used in the NIIS database). The better physical condition of the canals enables FMISs to achieve increased levels of cropping intensity (the number of crops grown during a year) at both the head end and the tail end of a canal, as shown in table 2.4. Thus, the investment of farmers in keeping their systems in good physical condition pays off in significantly more agricultural productivity.

Approximately two-thirds of both the FMISs and AMISs have formal written rules that include provisions for imposing fines on farmers who do not contribute resources to operate and manage the systems (Joshi et al. 2000). In eight out of ten AMISs, an official guard is hired to monitor the system, while only six out of ten FMISs rely on an official guard. The presence of an official guard, however, does not increase the likelihood that fines are actually imposed. On 75 percent of the FMISs, fines are reliably imposed if farmers are observed to break a rule, while fines are imposed on only 38 percent of the AMISs (Joshi et al. 2000). Farmers follow the rules of their system to a greater extent on FMISs than on AMISs, and they also tend to achieve a higher level of mutual trust.

The specific rules that farmers use in governing their systems on a day-to-day basis vary substantially from one system to another (Shivakoti and Ostrom 2002). Some FMISs use a rotational system where each farmer has a right to extract water from the canal at a particular time during a week. Others located in zones of abundant

TABLE 2.4

Relationships Between Governance Structure and Cropping Intensity of Irrigation Systems

Cropping Intensity		Type of Governance Structure		Chi-Square Value	Significance
		FMIS (%)	AMIS (%)		
Intensity at head end	High [142]	70.2	52.2	5.27	.02
	Low [72]	29.8	47.8		
Intensity at tail end	High [123]	65.1	34.1	13.74	.00
	Low [87]	34.9	65.9		

SOURCE: Joshi et al. (2000).

NOTE: Numbers of irrigation systems are in brackets.

water allow authorized farmers to extract any amount of water they need from a continuous supply in the canal. Most systems change the rules in use during the monsoon season, as contrasted with the drier periods of the year (Shukla 2002). The rules specifying water allocation, as well as responsibilities to monitor and to impose sanctions for rule breaking, are thus not consistent from one system to the next. The "official" guard on many of the FMISs is one of the farmers who rotates into this position on a regular basis. Thus, the monitoring of water allocation and contributions to maintenance is largely performed by farmers who have participated in the crafting of the specific rules of their system and have a strong interest in seeing their system perform well and ensuring that others on the system are not free riding or taking more water than their official share (E. Ostrom, Lam, et al. 2011).

Comparing Government, Private, and Community-Owned Forests Around the World

In the early 1990s, Dr. Marilyn Hoskins at the Food and Agriculture Organization of the United Nations asked colleagues at the Workshop in Political Theory and Policy Analysis at Indiana University to initiate an extensive multicountry research program to study the impact of diverse institutional arrangements on forests and the people relying on forests in Africa, Asia, Latin America, and the United States. Colleagues at the Workshop drew on their general research on institutional diversity and their research on Nepal irrigation systems to develop the International Forestry Resources and Institutions (IFRI) research program and an extensive database (Gibson, McKean, and Ostrom 2000). The purpose of the study was to gain a scientifically rigorous understanding of the variety of factors that affect forest sustainability. The desire was to develop a network of collaborating centers located in many countries around the world that would conduct comparable studies in each of their countries. At the present time, Arun Agrawal of the University of Michigan is coordinating the IFRI research program and working with collaborating research centers in Bolivia, Colombia, Guatemala, India, Kenya, Mexico, Nepal, Tanzania, Thailand, Uganda, and the United States (http://www.sitemaker.umich.edu/ifri/home).

As mentioned earlier, government-owned protected areas are frequently recommended as the way to preserve the ecosystem services generated by forests (Terborgh 1999), but they are also criticized for having few effective rules (Busch 2008; Sheil et al. 2006). Given the repeated recommendations that government-owned protected areas are the way to sustain forest ecosystems, it is not surprising that national governments own roughly 86 percent of the world's forests. Further, protected areas have grown to cover approximately 6.4 million square kilometers of forest globally (Agrawal, Chhatre, and Hardin 2008). Formal ownership of forest resources by itself, however, is not strongly related to their sustainability. Agrawal, Chhatre, and Hardin conclude that "the effectiveness of forest governance is only partly explained by who owns forests. At the local level, existing research finds only a limited association between whether forests are under private, public, or common ownership and changes in forest cover or sustainability of forest management" (2008, 1462).

In an effort to examine whether government ownership of protected areas is a necessary condition for improving forest density, Hayes (2006) used IFRI data to compare broad forest governance types via a rating of forest density (on a five-point scale) assigned to a forest by the forester or ecologist who supervised the forest mensuration of trees, shrubs, and ground cover in a random sample of forest plots.[8] Of the 163 forests included in the analysis, 76 were government-owned forests legally designated as protected forests, and 87 were public, private, or communally owned forested lands used for a wide diversity of purposes. No statistical difference was found between the forest densities in officially designated protected areas and in all other forested areas.

Robbins et al. (2007) reported on a study of the spatial distribution of vegetation change over time at the Kumbhalgarh Wildlife Sanctuary in the Aravalli range of Rajasthan in India. Instead of no change, as hoped for by proponents of protected areas, their results showed that 28 percent of the study area was undergoing change, although in multiple trajectories, with both increasing and decreasing density of vegetation in discrete patches. Areas closer to entrance points had a higher level of change than areas located within the reserve. They concluded that the patchiness resulted from the complex challenges faced by middle- and lower-level officials in the Forest Department's bureaucracy. The rules are the same, but the results differ across space. Thus, even in one reserve, using a frequently recommended general property right does not have uniform results.

Although scholars do not find a consistent relationship between forest conditions and the very broad terms used to describe property regimes for forests, activities related to monitoring and rule enforcement are generally important. Gibson,

---

[8] Extensive forest mensuration is conducted at every IFRI site at the same time at which information is obtained about forest users, their activities and organization, and governance arrangements. Comparing forest measures across ecological zones is misleading because the average diameter at breast height in a forest is strongly affected by precipitation, soils, elevation, and other factors that vary dramatically across ecological zones. Thus, the forester or ecologist who has just supervised the collection of forest data is asked to rate the forest on a five-point scale from very sparse to very abundant.

Williams, and Ostrom (2005) examined the monitoring behavior of 178 forest user groups and found a strong and statistically significant correlation between the level of monitoring and a forester's assessment of forest density when they controlled for many other variables. Chhatre and Agrawal (2008) examined the changes in the condition of 152 forests under diverse governance arrangements as affected by the size of the forest, collective action in forests related to improvement activities, size of the user group, and the dependence of local users on a forest. "Forests with a higher probability of regeneration are likely to be small to medium in size with low levels of subsistence dependence, low commercial value, high levels of local enforcement, and strong collective action for improving the quality of the forest" (Chhatre and Agrawal 2008, 13287). Studies by Coleman (2009) and Coleman and Steed (2009) also find that a major variable affecting forest conditions is investment by local users in monitoring. Further, when local users are allocated harvesting rights, they are more likely to monitor illegal uses themselves. Other focused studies also stress the relationship between local monitoring and better forest conditions (Banana and Gombya-Ssembajjwe 2000; Ghate and Nagendra 2005; E. Ostrom and Nagendra 2006; Webb and Shivakoti 2008).

IFRI research shows that forests under different property regimes (government, private, or communal) sometimes meet enhanced social goals, such as biodiversity protection, carbon storage, or improved livelihoods. At other times, any of these general property systems may fail to meet such goals. Thus, it is not the general system of property rights used for forest governance that is crucial in predicting whether forest conditions are sustainable. Rather, it is how a particular governance arrangement fits the local ecology, how the specific rules of a governance regime are developed and adapted over time, and whether users consider the system to be legitimate and equitable (for a more detailed overview of the IFRI research program, see Poteete, Janssen, and Ostrom 2010). Property rights are indeed important in affecting resource conditions, but the general names assigned to government, private, or community property regimes do not discriminate among the types of rules used in practice.

Diversity Rather than Uniformity of Rules in Property Rights Systems

Groups of individuals are considered to share common property rights when they have formed an organization that exercises at least the collective-choice rights of management and exclusion in relationship to a defined resource system and the resource units produced by that system. Communal groups most frequently establish some means of governing themselves in relationship to a resource. When communal groups are full owners, members of the group have the further right to sell their access, use, exclusion, and management rights to others, subject in many systems to approval by other members of the group.

Some communal ownership regimes are formally organized and recognized by legal authorities as having a corporate existence. Other communal proprietorships are less formally organized and may exercise de facto property rights that may or may not be supported by legal authorities if they are challenged by nonmembers

(Ghate 2000). Obviously, such groups hold less well-defined bundles of property rights than those that are secure in their de jure rights, even though the latter may not hold the complete set of property rights defined as full ownership. In other words, well-defined and secure property rights may not involve the right to alienation. Further, "communal" land tenure regimes in Africa and other developing countries are not as static and tradition bound as they are frequently portrayed in the literature (Cousins 2009). The specific attributes of land rights systems tend to evolve over time, but if government officials do not understand indigenous systems, the reforms they propose may be counterproductive.

Even though all common-pool resources are characterized by high costs of devising methods to achieve exclusion and determination of who owns the subtractable resource units, other attributes of these resources that affect the incentives of resource users and the likelihood of achieving outcomes that approach sustainability vary immensely. Further, whether it is difficult or costly to develop physical or institutional means to exclude nonbeneficiaries depends both on the availability and cost of technical and institutional solutions to the problem of exclusion and on the relationship of the cost of these solutions to the expected benefits of achieving exclusion from a particular resource.

Consider land as a resource system. Where population density is extremely low, and land is abundant and generates a rich diversity of plant and animal products without much husbandry, the expected costs of establishing and defending boundaries to a parcel of land of any size may be greater than the expected benefits of enclosure (Feeny 1993). Settlers moving into a new terrain characterized by high risk due to danger from others, from a harsh environment, or from lack of appropriate knowledge may decide to develop one large, common parcel before any divisions into smaller parcels (Ellickson 1993). Once land becomes scarce, conflict over who has the rights to invest in improvements and to reap the results of his or her efforts can lead individuals to want to enclose land through fencing or institutional means to protect their investments. Trade-offs in costs need to be considered. The more land included within one enclosure, the lower the costs of defending the boundaries, but the costs of regulating uses of the enclosed parcel may be higher than for small parcels.

The decision to enclose need not be taken in one step from an open-access terrain to a series of private plots owned exclusively by single families (Ellickson 1993; Field 1984; 1985; 1989). The benefits of enclosing land depend on the scale of productive activity involved. For some agricultural activities, considerable benefits may be associated with smaller parcels fully owned by a family enterprise. For other activities, the benefits of household plots may not be substantial. Moving all the way to private plots is efficient when the expected marginal returns from enclosing numerous plots exceed the expected marginal costs of defending a much more extended system of boundaries and the reduced transaction costs of making decisions about use patterns within boundaries (Nugent and Sanchez 1995).

In a classic study of the diversity of property rights systems used for many centuries by Swiss peasants, Robert Netting (1976; 1981) pointed out that the farmers fully divided their agricultural land into separate family-owned parcels. The grazing lands located on the Alpine hillsides, however, were organized into common property systems. For centuries, the same individuals used different property rights systems for different ecologies located side by side in these mountain valleys. Each local community had considerable autonomy to change local rules, so there was no problem of someone else imposing an inefficient set of rules on it. Netting argued that attributes of the resource affected which property rights systems were likely for diverse purposes. He identified five attributes that he considered most conducive to the development of common property rights systems:

1. Low value of production of resource units per unit of area.
2. High variance in the availability of resource units on any one potential parcel.
3. Low returns from intensification of investment.
4. Substantial economies of scale by utilizing a large area.
5. Substantial economies of scale in building infrastructures to utilize large areas.

Although the Swiss peasants were able to devote these harsh lands to productive activities at low cost, they had to invest time and effort in the development of rules that would reduce the incentives to overgraze and would ensure that investments in shared infrastructure were maintained over time. In many Swiss villages, "cow rights" to common pasturage were distributed according to the number of cows that could be carried over the winter by using hay supplies provided by the owner of the cows. Each village determined who would be allowed to use the Alpine meadow, the specific access and withdrawal rights to be used, how investment and maintenance costs were to be shared, and the formula used to share the annual returns from selling cheese made by the community from the cows milked in the Alpine meadows. All these systems included at least village proprietorship rights, but some Swiss villages developed full ownership rights by incorporating and authorizing the buying and selling of shares (usually with the approval of the village).

Netting's findings about the association of patchiness of a resource with common property arrangements are not unique. They are strongly supported by studies of mountain villages in Japan, where thousands of rural villages have held communal property rights to extensive forests and grazing areas located in the steep mountainous regions located above their private agricultural plots (McKean 1982; 1992). Similar systems have existed in Norway for centuries (Örebech 1993; Sandberg 1993; 2007), as well as in Ireland (Di Falco and van Rensburg 2008). The Masai herders of Kenya faced a patchy environment that they were able to develop before colonial rule by a set of rules allowing pastoral groups to move to regions within a large, jointly owned territory that had received the highest level of rainfall in recent times (Mwangi and Ostrom 2009). Patchy land environments in India are allocated in complex ways to farmers for part of the year and to roving pastoralists to graze their animals on the stubble and to fertilize fields during the other parts of the year (Agrawal 1999; Kaul 1996).

The importance of sharing risk is stressed in other theoretical and empirical studies of communal proprietorships (Antilla and Torp 1996; Bardhan and Dayton-Johnson 2002). Further, land rights that enable users to adapt to complex ecological conditions tend to be stronger than those that limit self-organized change (Lambin,

Geist, and Lepers 2003). Unpredictability and risk are increased in systems where resource units are mobile and where storage facilities, such as dams, do not exist (Schlager, Blomquist, and Tang 1994). Institutional facilities for sharing risk, such as formal insurance systems or institutionalized mechanisms for reciprocal obligations in times of plenty, also affect the kinds of property rights systems that individuals can devise. When no physical or institutional mechanisms exist for sharing risk, communal property arrangements may enable individuals to adopt productive activities not feasible under individual property rights. Empirical studies have shown that variance in the productivity of land over space, due largely to fluctuations in rainfall from year to year, is strongly associated with the size of communally held parcels allocated to grazing in the Sudan (Nugent and Sanchez 1995). Ellickson (1993) compares the types of environmental and personal security risks faced by new settlers in New England, in Bermuda, and in Utah to explain the variance in the speed of converting jointly held land to individually held land in each of these settlements.

A finding of many studies of common property systems is that these systems do not exist in isolation and are frequently used in conjunction with individual ownership. In most irrigation systems that are built and managed by farmers, such as those in Nepal discussed earlier, each farmer owns an agricultural plot (or plots) while participating as a joint proprietor or owner in a communally organized irrigation system (Coward 1980; Sengupta 1991; 1993; Tang 1992; Vincent 1995; Wade 1992). Water is allocated to individual participants under a variety of individually tailored rules, but those irrigation systems that have survived for long periods of time tend to allocate water and responsibilities for joint costs using a similar metric, frequently the amount of land owned by a farmer. In other words, benefits are roughly proportional to the costs of investing in and maintaining the system itself.

Further, formally recognized communal systems are usually nested in a series of governance units that complement the organizational skills and knowledge of those involved in making collective-choice decisions in smaller units. Since the Middle Ages, most of the Alpine systems in both Switzerland and Italy have been nested in a series of self-governing communities that respectively governed villages, valleys, and federations of valleys (Merlo 1989).

Factors Affecting the Performance of Common Property Regimes

The performance of common property systems varies substantially, as does the performance of all property rights systems. Some common property systems fail or limp along at the margin of effectiveness, just as private firms fail or barely hang onto profitability over long periods of time. In addition to the environmental variables discussed earlier that are conducive to the use of common property arrangements, the following variables related to the attributes of participants are conducive to their selection of norms, rules, and property rights that enhance the performance of communal property rights systems:

1. Accurate information about the condition of the resource and the expected flow of benefits and costs is available at low cost to participants. (Blomquist 1992; Gilles and Jamtgaard 1981; Steed 2010)
2. Participants share a common understanding about the potential benefits and risks associated with the continuance of the status quo as contrasted with changes in norms and rules that they could feasibly adopt.
3. Participants share generalized norms of reciprocity and trust that can be used as initial social capital. (Anderson, Locker, and Nugent 2003; Cordell and McKean 1992)
4. The group using the resource is relatively stable. (Berkes 2007; Seabright 1993)
5. Participants plan to live and work in the same area for a long time (and in some cases, expect their offspring to live there as well) and, thus, do not heavily discount the future. (Grima and Berkes 1989)
6. Participants use collective-choice rules that fall between the extremes of unanimity or control by a few (or even a bare majority) and, thus, avoid high transaction or high deprivation costs. (E. Ostrom 1990)
7. Participants can develop relatively accurate and low-cost monitoring and sanctioning arrangements. (Berkes 1992; Van Laerhoven 2010)

In turn, many of these variables are affected by the type of larger regime in which users are embedded. Larger regimes can increase the probability that a community will adopt more effective rules over time when they (these regimes) recognize the legitimacy of common property systems and facilitate local self-organization (McCay 2002). Some of the techniques used by facilitative governments include (1) providing accurate information about natural resource systems; (2) providing arenas in which participants can engage in discovery and conflict-resolution processes; and (3) providing mechanisms to back up local monitoring and sanctioning efforts.

Two additional variables, the small size of a group and its homogeneity, have been noted as conducive to the initial organization of communal resources and to the successful performance of organized users over time (Baland and Platteau 1996; Libecap 1989a; 1989b; E. Ostrom 2009). But neither of these variables is uniformly positive or negative. Changing the size of a group, for example, always involves changing some of the other variables likely to affect the performance of a system. Increasing the size of a group is likely to be associated with at least the following changes: (1) an increase in the transaction costs of reaching agreements; (2) a reduction of the burden borne by each participant for meeting joint costs, such as guarding a system and maintenance; and (3) an increase in the amount of assets held by the group that could be used in times of emergency. Libecap (1995) found that it was particularly hard to get agreements on oil unitization in groups larger than four. Blomquist (1992), on the other hand, documents processes conducted in the shadow of an equity court that involved up to 750 participants agreeing to common rules to allocate rights to withdraw water from groundwater basins in Southern California. The processes took a relatively long period of time, but the water systems have now survived with low administrative costs for half a century (Blomquist and Ostrom 2008). Agrawal (2000) has shown that communal forestry institutions in India that are moderate in size are more likely to reduce overharvesting than are smaller groups because they tend to invest in a higher level of monitoring by locally hired guards.

The basic causal processes and effects of group heterogeneity are also multifaceted (Agrawal and Gibson 2001; Bardhan and Dayton-Johnson 2002). Groups can differ along many dimensions, including assets, religion, information, valuation of final products, production technologies, landholdings, time horizons, exposure to risk (e.g., headenders versus tailenders on irrigation systems), and cultural belief systems (Keohane and Ostrom 1995; Ray and Bhattacharya 2010; Schlager and Blomquist 1998). Libecap's (1989b) research on inshore fisheries has shown that when fishers have distinctively different production technologies and skills, all potential rules for sharing withdrawal rights have substantial distributional consequences and are the source of conflict that may not easily be overcome.

Libecap and Wiggins's (1984) study of the rationing of crude oil production reveals an interesting relationship between the levels and type of information available to participants and the likelihood of agreement at various stages in a bargaining process. In the early stages of negotiation, all oil producers share a relatively equal level of ignorance about the relative claims that each might be able to make under private property arrangements. Oil-unitization agreements are most likely to be reached successfully at this time. If agreement is not reached early, each participant gains asymmetric information about his own claims as more and more investments are made in private information. Agreements are unlikely at this stage. If producers then aggressively pump from a common oil pool, all tend to be harmed by the overproduction and thus are willing to recognize their joint interests later, after the harm is obvious. Libecap (1995) also shows a strong negative impact of heterogeneity in his study of marketing agreements among orange growers.

The wealth of empirical information on real-existing property systems, only a fraction of which has been recounted here, belies naïve and simplistic theories of property rights that reduce all resource-conservation problems to either too little private-individual ownership or too little public ownership. Unfortunately, such naïve theories, which are usually premised on comparisons of flawed existing institutions with perfect but purely theoretical alternatives (Komesar 1997), continue to dominate the literature. It is high time to move from such simplistic and inaccurate models of property systems to theories that better account for the complexities and contingencies of actual resource governance regimes (rather than idealizations), based on comparative analyses of property institutions operating within larger social-ecological systems. It is hoped that the chapters presented in this volume will make a significant contribution to that effort.

REFERENCES

Agrawal, Arun. 1999. *Greener pastures: Politics, markets, and community among a migrant pastoral people.* Durham, NC: Duke University Press.
_____. 2000. Small is beautiful, but is larger better? Forest-management institutions in the Kumaon Himalaya, India. In *People and forests: Communities, institutions, and governance*, eds. Clark C. Gibson, Margaret A. McKean, and Elinor Ostrom, 57–86. Cambridge, MA: MIT Press.

Agrawal, Arun, Ashwini Chhatre, and Rebecca Hardin. 2008. Changing governance of the world's forests. *Science* 320(June 13):1460–1462.

Agrawal, Arun, and Clark C. Gibson, eds. 2001. *Communities and the environment: Ethnicity, gender, and the state in community-based conservation.* New Brunswick, NJ: Rutgers University Press.

Allen, P. M., and J. M. McGlade. 1987. Modelling complex human systems: A fisheries example. *European Journal of Operational Research* 30:147–167.

Alston, Lee J., Thráinn Eggertsson, and Douglass C. North, eds. 1996. *Empirical studies in institutional change.* New York: Cambridge University Press.

Anderson, C. Leigh, Laura A. Locker, and Rachel A. Nugent. 2003. A framework for analyzing the physical-, social-, and human capital effects of microcredit on common-pool resources. In *The commons in the new millennium: Challenges and adaptation,* eds. Nives Dolšak and Elinor Ostrom, 265–290. Cambridge, MA: MIT Press.

Anderson, C. Leigh, and Richard Zerbe. 2001. Culture and fairness in the development of institutions in the California gold fields. *Journal of Economic History* 61:114–143.

Antilla, Sten, and Aivind Torp. 1996. Environmental adjustment and private economic strategies in reindeer pastoralism: Combining game theory with participatory action theory. Working Paper. Östersund, Sweden: Mid-Sweden University.

Arnason, Ragnar. 1993. The Icelandic individual transferable quota system: A descriptive account. *Marine Resource Economics* 8(3):201–218.

Baland, Jean-Marie, and Jean-Philippe Platteau. 1996. *Halting degradation of natural resources: Is there a role for rural communities?* Oxford: Clarendon Press.

Banana, Abwoli Y., and William Gombya-Ssembajjwe. 2000. Successful forest management: The importance of security of tenure and rule enforcement in Ugandan forests. In *People and forests: Communities, institutions, and governance,* eds. Clark C. Gibson, Margaret A. McKean, and Elinor Ostrom, 87–98. Cambridge, MA: MIT Press.

Bardhan, Pranab, and Jeff Dayton-Johnson. 2002. Unequal irrigators: Heterogeneity and commons management in large-scale multivariate research. In *The drama of the commons,* eds. Elinor Ostrom, Thomas Dietz, Nives Dolšak, Paul C. Stern, Susan Stonich, and Elke U. Weber, 87–112. Washington, DC: National Academies Press.

Barzel, Yoram. 1989. *Economic analysis of property rights.* Cambridge, U.K. Cambridge University Press.

Becker, Lawrence C. 1977. *Property rights: Philosophic foundations.* Boston: Routledge and Kegan Paul.

Benjamin, Paul, Wai Fung Lam, Elinor Ostrom, and Ganesh Shivakoti. 1994. *Institutions, incentives, and irrigation in Nepal.* Decentralization: Finance and Management Project Report. Burlington, VT: Associates in Rural Development.

Berkes, Fikret. 1992. Success and failure in marine coastal fisheries of Turkey. In *Making the commons work: Theory, practice, and policy,* eds. Daniel W. Bromley, David Feeny, Margaret A. McKean, Pauline Peters, Jere L. Gilles, Ronald J. Oakerson, C. Ford Runge, James T. Thomson, 161–182. San Francisco: ICS Press.

———. 2007. Community-based conservation in a globalized world. *Proceedings of the National Academy of Sciences* 104(39):15188–15193.

Birks, Peter, and Grant McLeod, trans. 1987. *Justinian's Institutes.* Ithaca, NY: Cornell University Press.

Blackstone, William. 1979 [1766]. *Commentaries on the laws of England.* Vol. 2. Chicago: University of Chicago Press.

Blomquist, William. 1992. *Dividing the waters: Governing groundwater in Southern California.* San Francisco: Institute for Contemporary Studies Press.

Blomquist, William, and Elinor Ostrom. 2008. Deliberation, learning, and institutional change: The evolution of institutions in judicial settings. *Constitutional Political Economy* 19(3):180–202.

Bromley, Daniel W. 1989. *Economic interests and institutions: The conceptual foundations of public policy.* Oxford: Basil Blackwell.

———. 1991. *Environment and economy: Property rights and public policy.* Oxford: Basil Blackwell.

Busch, Jonah. 2008. Gains from configuration: The transboundary protected areas as a conservation tool. *Ecological Economics* 67(3):394–404.

Chhatre, Ashwini, and Arun Agrawal. 2008. Forest commons and local enforcement. *Proceedings of the National Academy of Sciences* 105 (36):13286–13291.

Christy, Francis T. 1973. Fisherman quotas: A tentative suggestion for domestic management. Working Paper. Kingston: University of Rhode Island, Law of the Sea Institute.

Ciriacy-Wantrup, Siegfried V., and Richard C. Bishop. 1975. "Common property" as a concept in natural resource policy. *Natural Resources Journal* 15(4):713–727.

Clark, Colin W. 1973a. The economics of overexploitation. *Science* 181:630–634.

———. 1973b. Profit maximization and the extinction of animal species. *Journal of Political Economy* 81:950–961.

———. 1980. Restricted access to common-property fishery resources: A game theoretic analysis. In *Dynamic optimization and mathematical economics*, ed. P. T. Lin, 117–132. New York: Plenum.

———. 2006. *The worldwide crisis in fisheries: Economic models and human behavior.* Cambridge, U.K.: Cambridge University Press.

Clay, Karen, and Gavin Wright. 2005. Order without law? Property rights during the California gold rush. *Explorations in Economic History* 42:155–183.

Coase, Ronald H. 1964. Discussion: The regulated industries. *American Economic Review* 54:194–197.

Cohen-Tanugi, Laurent. 1985. *Le droit sans l'état: Sur le démocratie en France et en Amérique.* Paris: Presses Universitaires de France.

Cole, Daniel H. 1998. *Instituting environmental protection: From red to green in Poland.* London: Macmillan; New York: St. Martin's Press.

———. 2002. *Pollution and property: Comparing ownership institutions for environmental protection.* Cambridge, U.K.: Cambridge University Press.

Cole, Daniel H., and Peter Z. Grossman. 2002. The meaning of property rights: Law vs. economics? *Land Economics* 78:317–330.

———. 2010. Institutions matter! Why the herder problem is not a prisoner's dilemma. *Theory and Decision* 69:219–231.

Coleman, Eric. 2009. Institutional factors affecting ecological outcomes in forest management. *Journal of Policy Analysis and Management* 28(1):122–146.

Coleman, Eric, and Brian Steed. 2009. Monitoring and sanctioning in the commons: An application to forestry. *Ecological Economics* 68(7):2106–2113.

Commons, John R. 1959. *The legal foundations of capitalism.* Madison: University of Wisconsin Press.

Copes, Parzival. 1986. A critical review of the individual quota as a device in fisheries management. *Land Economics* 62(3):278–291.

Cordell, John C., and Margaret A. McKean. 1992. Sea tenure in Bahia, Brazil. In *Making the commons work: Theory, practice, and policy*, eds. Daniel W. Bromley, David Feeny, Margaret A. McKean, Pauline Peters, Jere L. Gilles, Ronald J. Oakerson, C. Ford Runge, James T. Thomson, 183–205. San Francisco: ICS Press.

Cousins, Ben. 2009. Potential and pitfalls of "communal" land tenure reform: Experience in Africa and implications for South Africa. Paper for the World Bank conference "Land Governance in Support of the MDGs: Responding to New Challenges," Washington, DC (March 9–10).

Coward, E. Walter, Jr., ed. 1980. *Irrigation and agricultural development in Asia: Perspectives from the social sciences.* Ithaca, NY: Cornell University Press.

Deininger, Klaus, Daniel Ayalew Ali, and Takashi Yamano. 2008. Legal knowledge and economic development: The case of land rights in Uganda. *Land Economics* 84 (4):593–619.

Demsetz, Harold. 1967. Toward a theory of property rights. *American Economic Review* 57:347–359.

Di Falco, Salvatore, and Thomas M. van Rensburg. 2008. Making the commons work: Conservation and cooperation in Ireland. *Land Economics* 84(4):620–634.

Dowie, Mark. 2010. Conservation refugees. *Cultural Survival Quarterly* 34(1): 28–35.

Eggertsson, Thráinn. 1990. *Economic behavior and institutions.* Cambridge, U.K.: Cambridge University Press.

——. 2004. The subtle art of major institutional change: Introducing property rights in the Iceland fisheries. In *The role of institutions in rural policies and agricultural models*, eds. G. van Huyleborook, W. Verkeke, and L. Lauwers, 43–59. Amsterdam: Elsevier.

——. 2005. *Imperfect institutions: Possibilities and limits of reform*. Ann Arbor: University of Michigan Press.

Ellickson, Robert C. 1993. Property in land. *Yale Law Journal* 102:1315–1400.

Feder, Gershon, and David Feeny. 1991. Land tenure and property rights: Theory and implications for development policy. *World Bank Economic Review* 5(1):135–153.

Feder, G., T. Onchan, Y. Chalamwong, and C. Hangladoran. 1988. *Land policies and farm productivity in Thailand*. Baltimore, MD: Johns Hopkins University Press.

Feder, Gershon, and David Feeny. 1991. Land tenure and property rights: Theory and implications for development policy. *World Bank Economic Review* 5(1):135–153.

Feeny, David. 1993. The demand for and the supply of institutional arrangements. In *Rethinking institutional analysis and development*, eds. Vincent Ostrom, David Feeny, and Hartmut Picht, 159–209. San Francisco: ICS Press.

Fidzani, N. H. 2000. The Botswana tribal grazing land policy: A property rights study. In *Economic instruments for environmental management*, eds. Jennifer Rietbergen-McCracken and Hussein Abaza, 19–30. London: Earthscan for the United Nations Environment Programme.

Field, Barry C. 1984. The evolution of individual property rights in Massachusetts agriculture, 17th–19th centuries. *Northeastern Journal of Agricultural and Resource Economics* 14:97–109.

——. 1985. The optimal commons. *American Journal of Agricultural Economics* 67:364–367.

——. 1989. The evolution of property rights. *Kyklos* 42(3):319–345.

Freyfogle, Eric T. 2002. Property rights, the market, and environmental change in 20th century America. *Environmental Law Reporter* 32:10254–10266.

Frohlich, Norman, and Joe Oppenheimer. 1995. Alienable privatization policies: The choice between inefficiency and injustice. In *Water quantity/quality management and conflict resolution: Institutions, processes, and economic analyses*, eds. Ariel Dinar and Edna Loehman, 131–142. Westport, CT: Praeger.

Ghate, Rucha. 2000. The role of autonomy in self-organizing processes: A case study of local forest management in India. Working Paper. Bloomington: Indiana University, Workshop in Political Theory and Policy Analysis.

Ghate, Rucha, and Harini Nagendra. 2005. Role of monitoring in institutional performance: Forest management in Maharashtra, India. *Conservation and Society* 3(2):509–532.

Gibson, Clark C., Margaret A. McKean, and Elinor Ostrom, eds. 2000. *People and forests: Communities, institutions, and governance*. Cambridge, MA: MIT Press.

Gibson, Clark C., John T. Williams, and Elinor Ostrom. 2005. Local enforcement and better forests. *World Development* 33(2):273–284.

Gilles, Jere L., and Keith Jamtgaard. 1981. Overgrazing in pastoral areas: The commons reconsidered. *Sociologia Ruralis* 2:335–358.

Gordon, H. Scott. 1954. The economic theory of a common property resource: The fishery. *Journal of Political Economy* 62:122–142.

Grafton, R. Quentin. 2000. Governance of the commons: A role for the state. *Land Economics* 76(4):504–517.

Grapel, William, trans. 1994 [1855]. *The Institutes of Justinian, with the novel as to successions*. London: Wm. W. Gaunt and Sons.

Grima, A. P. Limo, and Fikret Berkes. 1989. Natural resources: Access, rights to use and management. In *Common property resources: Ecology and community-based sustainable development*, ed. Fikret Berkes, 33–54. London: Belhaven.

Hanna, Susan, and Mohan Munasinghe, eds. 1995. *Property rights in a social and ecological context: Case studies and design applications*. Stockholm and Washington, DC: Beijer International Institute of Ecological Economics and World Bank.

Hardin, Garrett. 1968. The tragedy of the commons. *Science* 162:1243–1248.

Hayes, Tanya. 2006. Parks, people, and forest protection: An institutional assessment of the effectiveness of protected areas. *World Development* 34(12):2064–2075.

Hohfeld, Wesley Newcomb. 1913. Some fundamental legal conceptions as applied in judicial reasoning. *Yale Law Journal* 23:16–59.

———. 1917. Fundamental legal conceptions as applied in judicial reasoning. *Yale Law Journal* 26:710–770.

Honoré, Toni. 1961. Ownership. In *Oxford Essays in Jurisprudence*, ed. Anthony Gordon Guest, 107–147. Oxford: Oxford University Press.

Hurst, James Willard. 1984. *Law and economic growth: The legal history of the lumber industry in Wisconsin, 1836–1915*. Madison: University of Wisconsin Press.

Joshi, Neeraj N., Elinor Ostrom, Ganesh P. Shivakoti, and Wai Fung Lam. 2000. Institutional opportunities and constraints in the performance of farmer-managed irrigation systems in Nepal. *Asia-Pacific Journal of Rural Development* 10(2):67–92.

Kaul, Minoti Chakravarty. 1996. *Common lands and customary law: Institutional change in North India over the past two centuries*. Oxford: Oxford University Press.

Keohane, Robert O., and Elinor Ostrom, eds. 1995. *Local commons and global interdependence: Heterogeneity and cooperation in two domains*. London: Sage.

Komesar, Neil. 1997. *Imperfect alternatives: Choosing institutions in law, economics, and public policy*. Chicago: University of Chicago Press.

Lam, Wai Fung. 1998. *Governing irrigation systems in Nepal: Institutions, infrastructure, and collective action*. Oakland, CA: Institute for Contemporary Studies Press.

Lam, Wai Fung, Myungsuk Lee, and Elinor Ostrom. 1997. The institutional analysis and development framework: Application to irrigation policy in Nepal. In *Policy studies and developing nations: An institutional and implementation focus*, ed. Derick W. Brikerhoff, 53–85. Greenwich, CT: JAI Press.

Lambin, Eric F., Helmut J. Geist, and Erika Lepers. 2003. Dynamics of land-use and land-cover change in tropical regions. *Annual Review of Environmental Resources* 28:205–241.

Larson, Bruce A., and Daniel W. Bromley. 1990. Property rights, externalities, and resource degradation: Locating the tragedy. *Journal of Development Economics* 33:235–262.

Lazarev, Nikolai. 2005. Hohfeld's analysis of rights: An essential approach to a conceptual and practical understanding of the nature of rights. *Murdoch University Electronic Journal of Law* 12. http://www.murdoch.edu.au/elaw/issues/v12n1_2/Lavarev12_2.html.

Libecap, Gary D. 1989a. *Contracting for property rights*. New York: Cambridge University Press.

———. 1989b. Distributional issues in contracting for property rights. *Journal of Institutional and Theoretical Economics* 145:6–24.

———. 1995. The conditions for successful collective action. In *Local commons and global interdependence: Heterogeneity and cooperation in two domains*, eds. Robert O. Keohane and Elinor Ostrom, 161–190. London: Sage.

Libecap, Gary D., and Steven N. Wiggins. 1984. Contractual responses to the common pool: Prorationing of crude oil production. *American Economic Review* 74:87–98.

Lovejoy, T. E. 2006. Protected areas: A prism for a changing world. *Trends in Ecology and Evolution* 21:329–333.

McCay, Bonnie J. 1992. Everyone's concern, whose responsibility? The problem of the commons. In *Understanding economic process*, eds. Sutti Ortiz and Susan Lees, 199–210. Lanham, MD: University Press of America.

———. 2002. Emergence of institutions for the commons: Contexts, situations, and events. In *The drama of the commons*, eds. Elinor Ostrom, Thomas Dietz, Nives Dolšak, Paul C. Stern, Susan Stonich, and Elke U. Weber, 361–403. Washington, DC: National Academies Press.

McCay, Bonnie J., Ian Wright, Richard Apostle, and Leigh Mazany. 1996. Fleet concentration in an ITQ fishery: A case study of the Southwest Nova Scotia Mobile Gear Fleet. Presented at the sixth annual conference of the International Association for the Study of Common Property, Berkeley, CA (June 5–8).

McDowell, Andrea. 2002. From commons to claims: Property rights in the California gold rush. *Yale Journal of Law and the Humanities* 14:1–72.

———. 2004. Real property, spontaneous order, and norms in the gold mines. *Law and Social Inquiry* 29:771–818.

McKean, Margaret A. 1982. The Japanese experience with scarcity: Management of traditional common lands. *Environmental Review* 6(2):63–88.

———. 1992. Management of traditional common lands (*iriaichi*) in Japan. In *Making the commons work: Theory, practice, and policy*, eds. Daniel W. Bromley, David Feeny, Margaret A. McKean, Pauline Peters, Jere L. Gilles, Ronald J. Oakerson, C. Ford Runge, and James T. Thomson, 63–98. San Francisco: ICS Press.

Merlo, M. 1989. The experience of the village communities in the north-eastern Italian Alps. In *Collective forest land tenure and rural development in Italy*, eds. M. Merlo, R. Morandini, A. Gabbrielli, and I. Novaco, 1–54. Rome: Food and Agriculture Organization of the United Nations.

Merrill, Thomas W. 1998. Property and the right to exclude. *Nebraska Law Review* 77:730–754.

Migot-Adholla, Shem E., Peter Hazell, Benoit Blarel, and Frank Place. 1991. Indigenous land rights systems in Sub-Saharan Africa: A constraint on productivity? *World Bank Economic Review* 5(1):155–175.

Mwangi, Esther, and Elinor Ostrom. 2009. Top-down solutions: Looking up from East Africa's rangelands. *Environment: Science and Policy for Sustainable Development* 51(1):34–44.

Netting, Robert McC. 1976. What Alpine peasants have in common: Observations on communal tenure in a Swiss village. *Human Ecology* 4:135–146.

———. 1981. *Balancing on an Alp: Ecological change and continuity in a Swiss mountain community*. New York: Cambridge University Press.

North, Douglass C. 1990. *Institutions, institutional change and economic performance*. New York: Cambridge University Press.

Nugent, Jeffrey B., and Nicolas Sanchez. 1995. The local variability of rainfall and tribal institutions: The case of Sudan. Presented to the Middle East Economic Association, Washington, DC (January 7).

Örebech, Peter. 1993. Common and public property rights regimes to non-private resources. Some legal issues on self-governing conservation systems. In *Common property regimes: Law and management of non-private resources; Proceedings of the conference*, ed. Erling Berge, 1:34–55. Ås: Agricultural University of Norway.

Ostrom, Elinor. 1990. *Governing the commons: The evolution of institutions for collective action*. New York: Cambridge University Press.

———. 2005. *Understanding institutional diversity*. Princeton, NJ: Princeton University Press.

———. 2009. A general framework for analyzing sustainability of social-ecological systems. *Science* 325(5939):419–422.

Ostrom, Elinor, Roy Gardner, and James Walker. 1994. *Rules, games, and common-pool resources*. Ann Arbor: University of Michigan Press.

Ostrom, Elinor, Marco A. Janssen, and John M. Anderies. 2007. Going beyond panaceas. *Proceedings of the National Academy of Sciences* 104 (39):15176–15178.

Ostrom, Elinor, Wai Fung Lam, Prachanda Pradhan, and Ganesh Shivakoti. 2011. *Improving irrigation in Asia: Sustainable performance of an innovative intervention in Nepal*. Cheltenham, U.K.: Edward Elgar.

Ostrom, Elinor, and Harini Nagendra. 2006. Insights on linking forests, trees, and people from the air, on the ground, and in the laboratory. *Proceedings of the National Academy of Sciences* 103(51):19224–19231.

Ostrom, Vincent, and Elinor Ostrom. 1972. Legal and political conditions of water resource development. *Land Economics* 48(1):1–14.

———. 1977. A theory for institutional analysis of common pool problems. In *Managing the commons*, eds. Garrett Hardin and John Baden, 157–172. San Francisco: W. H. Freeman.

Pinkerton, Evelyn. 1992. Conclusions: Where do we go from here? The future of traditional ecological knowledge and resource management in Canadian native communities. In *Traditional ecological knowledge and environmental assessment*, eds. P. Boothroyd and B. Sadler, chapter 12. Ottawa: Canadian Environmental Assessment Research Council.

———. 1994. Local fisheries co-management: A review of international experiences and their implications for salmon management in British Columbia. *Canadian Journal of Fisheries and Aquatic Sciences* 51(2):363–378.

Platt, Rutherford H. 2004. *Land use and society: Geography, law and public policy.* Washington, DC: Island Press.

Poteete, Amy R., Marco Janssen, and Elinor Ostrom. 2010. *Working together: Collective action, the commons, and multiple methods in practice.* Princeton, NJ: Princeton University Press.

Ray, Biswajit, and Rabindra N. Bhattacharya. 2010. Transaction costs, collective action and survival of heterogeneous co-management institutions: Case study of forest management organizations in West Bengal, India. *Journal of Development Studies* 46:1–21.

Robbins, Paul F., Anil K. Chhangani, Jennifer Rice, Erika Trigosa, and S. M. Mohnot. 2007. Enforcement authority and vegetation change at Kumbhalgarh Wildlife Sanctuary, Rajasthan, India. *Environmental Management* 40:365–376.

Rose, Carol M. 1998. Canon's of property talk; or, Blackstone's anxiety. *Yale Law Journal* 108:601–632.

———. 2003. Romans, roads, and romantic creators: Traditions of public property in the information age. *Law and Contemporary Problems* 66:89–110.

Sandberg, Audun. 1993. The analytical importance of property rights to northern resources. Colloquium presentation, Indiana University, Workshop in Political Theory and Policy Analysis, Bloomington (September 27).

———. 2007. "Property rights and ecosystem properties." *Land Use Policy* 24: 613–623.

Schlager, Edella, and William Blomquist. 2008. *Embracing watershed politics.* Boulder, CO: University Press of Colorado.

Schlager, Edella, William Blomquist, and Shui Yang Tang. 1994. Mobile flows, storage, and self-organized institutions for governing common-pool resources. *Land Economics* 70(3):294–317.

Schlager, Edella, and Elinor Ostrom. 1992. Property-rights regimes and natural resources: A conceptual analysis. *Land Economics* 68:249–269.

Scott, Anthony D. 1955. The fishery: The objectives of sole ownership. *Journal of Political Economy* 63:203–215.

Seabright, Paul. 1993. Managing local commons: Theoretical issues in incentive design. *Journal of Economic Perspectives* 7(4):113–134.

Sengupta, Nirmal. 1991. *Managing common property: Irrigation in India and the Philippines.* New Delhi: Sage.

———. 1993. *User-Friendly irrigation designs.* New Delhi, India: Sage.

———. 1996. The evolution of social norms in common property resource use. *American Economic Review* 86(4):766–788.

Sethi and Somanathan 1996.

Sheil, Douglas, Rajindra Puri, Meilinda Wan, Imam Basuki, Miriam van Heist, Nining Liswanti, Rukmiyati, Ike Rachmatika, and Ismayadi Samsoedin. 2006. Recognizing local people's priorities for tropical forest biodiversity. *Ambio* 35(1):17–24.

Shivakoti, Ganesh P., and Elinor Ostrom, eds. 2002. *Improving irrigation governance and management in Nepal.* Oakland, CA: ICS Press.

Shukla, Ashutosh K. 2002. Policies, processes, and performance of management: Turnover and agency-initiated interventions. In *Improving irrigation governance and management in Nepal,* eds. Ganesh Shivakoti and Elinor Ostrom, 71–102. Oakland, CA: ICS Press.

Singer, Joseph William. 2006. The ownership society and takings of property: Castles, investments, and just obligations. *Harvard Environmental Law Review* 30:309–338.

Sohm, Rudolf. 1994 [1907]. *The Institutes: A textbook of the history and system of Roman private law.* Trans. J. C. Ledlie. Oxford: Clarendon Press.

Steed, Brian C. 2010. "Natural Forces, Human Choices: An Over Time Study of Responses to Biophysical and Human Induced Disturbance in Los Angeles, California, Groundwater Governance." PhD diss., Indiana University.

Tang, Shui Yan. 1992. *Institutions and collective action: Self-governance in irrigation.* San Francisco: Institute for Contemporary Studies Press.

Terborgh, J. 1999. *Requiem for nature.* Washington, DC: Island Press.

Umbeck, John. 1981. *A theory of property rights, with application to the California gold rush.* Ames: Iowa State University Press.

Van Laerhoven, Frank. 2010. Governing community forests and the challenge of solving two-level collective action dilemmas—A large-N perspective. *Global Environmental Change* 20(3) (August): 539–546.

Vincent, Linden. 1995. *Hill irrigation: Water and development in mountain agriculture*. London: Overseas Development Institute.

Wade, Robert. 1992. Common-property resource management in South Indian villages. In *Making the commons work: Theory, practice, and policy*, eds. Daniel W. Bromley, David Feeny, Margaret A. McKean, Pauline Peters, Jere L. Gilles, Ronald J. Oakerson, C. Ford Runge, and James T. Thomson, 207–229. San Francisco: ICS Press.

Warming, Jens. 1911. Om "grundrente" af fiskegrunde. *Nationaløkonomisk Tidsskrift*, 495–506. Translated in P. Anderson. 1983. On rent of fishing grounds: A translation of Jens Warming's 1911 article, with an introduction. *History of Political Economy* 15:391–396.

Webb, Edward, and Ganesh P. Shivakoti, eds. 2008. *Decentralization, forests and rural communities: Policy outcomes in South and Southeast Asia*. New Delhi: Sage India.

Wilson, James A. 1990. Fishing for knowledge. *Land Economics* 66(1):12–29.

———. 1995. When are common property institutions efficient? Working Paper. Orono: University of Maine, Department of Agriculture and Resource Economics.

———. 2002. Scientific uncertainty, complex systems, and the design of common-pool institutions. In *The drama of the commons*, eds. Elinor Ostrom, Thomas Dietz, Nives Dolšak, Paul C. Stern, Susan Stonich, and Elke U. Weber, 327–359. Washington, DC: National Academies Press.

Wilson, James A., James Acheson, Peter Kleban, and Mark Metcalfe. 1994. Chaos, complexity, and community management of fisheries. *Marine Policy* 18(4): 291–305.

Wilson, James A., John French, Peter Kleban, Susan R. McKay, and Ralph Townsend. 1991. Chaotic dynamics in a multiple species fishery: A model of community predation. *Ecological Modelling* 58:303–322.

Wilson, James A., Liying Yan, and Carl Wilson. 2007. The precursors of governance in the Maine lobster fishery. *Proceedings of the National Academy of Sciences* 104(39):15212–15217.

Yandle, Tracy. 2001. Market-based natural resource management: An institutional analysis of individual tradable quotas in New Zealand's commercial fisheries. Ph.D. diss., Indiana University.

———. 2007. Understanding the consequences of property rights mismatches: A case study of New Zealand's marine resources. *Ecology and Society* 12(2):27.

Yandle, Tracy, and Christopher M. Dewees. 2003. Privatizing the commons . . . twelve years later. In *The commons in the new millennium: Challenges and adaptations*, eds. Nives Dolšak and Elinor Ostrom, 101–127. Cambridge, MA: MIT Press.

The California Gold Rush

Gold Rush Legacy

American Minerals and the Knowledge Economy

KAREN CLAY AND GAVIN WRIGHT

This chapter argues that the discovery of gold in California and a federal policy that gave all the rents in minerals on federal land to private parties led to two important and closely related outcomes. The first outcome was the development of a private-order property rights regime in the gold-mining region, key elements of which would later be adopted as federal law. This regime, often considered a canonical example of the emergence of private-order property rights, protected the rights of active users of gold-bearing land.[1] As Umbeck (1981) documented, the rights and responsibilities of miners in a particular area were memorialized in a mining-district code that defined who could hold rights, what the rights were, and procedures for transferring rights. These codes and associated norms were successful at controlling violence and so allowed miners to focus the bulk of their energies on mining.

Mining-district codes also included provisions for the reallocation of rights of inactive users through claim jumping. Clay and Wright (2005) argue that mining claims were not secure property rights as that concept is conventionally understood. This insecurity was in a sense built into the system, in that district codes gave considerable attention to the rights of claim jumpers, individuals who took over a claim deemed to be abandoned. Far from being a violation, claim jumping brought productive land into use and was the most common method of acquiring a claim.[2] Thus, codes both protected production on existing claims and regulated access to mining sites in a competitive race for high-value deposits.

The development of property rights in mineral land and the allocation of rents to private parties led to large-scale activity in mining. This scale fostered the second outcome, the development of a knowledge economy in minerals. U.S. mining during the nineteenth century displayed many of the features now associated with a knowledge economy, including synergies between higher education and industry, federal support for scientific research and infrastructure, diffusion of codified forms of useful knowledge, and economic progress based on extension of the knowledge

---

[1] See, for example, Umbeck's (1981) pioneering work, as well as Barzel (1997); Ellickson (1991); and Shavell (2004). Umbeck is also cited favorably in American economic history textbooks, for example, Walton and Rockoff (1998).

[2] The authors owe this insight to Andrea McDowell.

frontier. For nonrenewable resources like minerals, a prima facie analysis would suggest that open access would generate wasteful dissipation of rents through undue haste, excessive investment of labor and capital, and premature depletion as competitors race to extract dwindling resources ahead of their rivals. Some parts of the history conform to this scenario, but the larger picture is that of dynamic, innovative advances in resource discovery, extraction, and processing that together created the world's leading national mining sector.

Property Rights in the Gold Rush

The Rush

On 24 January 1848, James Marshall discovered gold at John Sutter's mill in Coloma in what would later be El Dorado County. Information about the discovery of gold took most of 1848 to spread, however. In March the *Californian*, a San Francisco newspaper, printed a story about the discovery of gold, but the streets of San Francisco did not immediately empty. In May Sam Brannan arrived in San Francisco and began to advertise the arrival of the gold rush. A store owner at Sutter's Fort and the publisher of the *California Star*, Brannan stood to gain from any increase in gold-mining activity. In June an estimated four thousand to five thousand miners were at work in the gold district, a very large share of the adult male population in California. By the end of July, two thousand copies of a special edition of the *California Star* had reached Missouri. In August the *New York Herald* printed a story on the discovery of gold. And in December President Polk confirmed the rumors in his address to Congress.

By late 1848 the whole American nation and many foreign countries knew about the California gold rush. Many headed for California in the spring of 1849, either overland or by ship. Estimates suggest that between five thousand and six thousand wagons left Missouri in the spring of 1849. Others took overland routes that began farther south or even in Mexico. For the period 1848 to 1850, lower-bound estimates of overland migration are more than 101,000.[3] Ships had also begun to leave New York and other cities on the Atlantic seaboard for California. The ships either took the long route around Cape Horn to California or left the passengers in Panama. In the latter case, the passengers then traveled across Panama and took a second ship from Panama to San Francisco. For the period 1849 to 1850, arrivals by sea are conservatively estimated at 75,462.

Clay and Jones (2008) show that by the end of 1850, 1.9 percent of native-born men aged 20 to 40 were already in California. Because of undercounting and the loss of census records for some counties, this number was probably closer to 3.1 percent. Only military-related migrations would induce a more rapid migration of young men in a comparably short period of time.

---

[3] Estimates of overland migration and passenger arrivals by sea are summarized in D. M. Wright (1940). A substantially higher figure for 1849 immigration is presented in the *State Register and Book of Facts* (1857). The fact that total arrivals were as much as 50 percent larger than the recorded 1852 non-Indian population of 223,856 suggests that many newcomers had already left.

Mining in a Legal Vacuum

Most national mining systems descend from the tradition that valuable minerals belong to the lord or ruler, who grants use rights as "concessions" in exchange for a share of the revenue. The U.S. government was by no means immune to the attractions of mineral revenues. Continuing colonial-era practice, the Land Ordinance of 1785 reserved for the federal government "one third part of all gold, silver, lead and copper mines, to be sold or otherwise disposed of, as Congress shall direct." Although minerals were not mentioned in the land laws of 1796, 1800, and 1804, Congress did act in 1807 to reserve lead mines in the Indiana Territory. Between 1824 and 1846, the government maintained a leasing system in the Galena District of Illinois, Iowa, and Wisconsin: miners were given exclusive permits to work certain areas and in return were required to bring their ore to one of the officially licensed smelters, who were required to pay a 10 percent royalty. The plan worked reasonably well in the 1820s, when production and federal revenue both grew. It fell apart in the 1830s, however, when nonpayment and noncompliance became widespread. Authorities in Washington lacked enforcement power, even over their own agents, who abetted evasion by smelters and fraudulently sold valuable mineral lands at minimum farmland prices, almost surely with side payments for personal profit.

The mining expansion of 1836 to 1840 generated no government revenues. British observer Frederick Maryatt commented: "How weak must that government be when it is compelled to submit to such a gross violation of all justice" (quoted in J. E. Wright 1966, 47). During the 1840s, the Ordnance Department attempted "reluctantly and halfheartedly" to reinstitute a leasing system for Michigan copper lands, but the results were no more successful, and the efforts were abandoned in 1846 (Mayer and Riley 1985; J. E. Wright 1966, 72).

By the eve of the California gold rush, the federal government had abolished all administrative apparatus and enforcement machinery pertaining to minerals in the public domain. Moreover, Mexican law was not in effect. On 12 February 1848, evidently still without knowledge of the gold strike, Colonel Richard B. Mason, commander of the American military forces, declared: "From and after this date, the Mexican laws and customs now prevailing in California, relative to the denouncement of mines, *are hereby abolished*" (quoted in Yale [1867], 17). Mason's intention was to protect private property in land from preemption for minerals under Mexican law. The effect, however, was to thwart any attempt to develop private mineral titles using Mexican rules. Having neither authorization nor capacity, Mason put no new system in place and declined to evict trespassers from the public domain. Thus, thousands of fortune seekers raced one another westward in the belief that gold was free for the taking, subject neither to government control nor to private land ownership.

Once the rush began in 1849, Congress considered many proposals to generate federal revenue from the gold fields, including mining licenses, auctions, leases, and sale of small mining tracts at farmland prices. The prospects for effective enforcement, however, were even more daunting at a distance of three thousand miles than they had been in the Midwest. After several early measures failed to gain support, both executive and legislative branches acquiesced in a policy of nonintervention.

Inaction was further supported by the arrival of political representatives from the new western states, who opposed any measures that might constrain the extension of the mining frontier and drain revenue from the region. As a result, no federal mining legislation was passed until 1866 (Ellison 1926).

Mining-District Codes

For some months, gold mining went forward under truly wide-open conditions, subject to no regulation of any kind.[4] This state of affairs could not last, however. Increased population in the mines, particularly after mid-1849, created a demand for some type of allocation system.

The first change was the emergence of the idea of a "claim." Legal historian Andrea McDowell shows that the concept of a claim as an area of land, as opposed to a hole in the ground, did not become standard until 1849, although there were scattered uses of the term earlier. Within a matter of months, however, some basic rules became widely accepted, which McDowell calls the "common law or customary law of the diggings" (McDowell 2002, 15). Perhaps the most fundamental of these rules was that tools left in a hole indicated that the miner was still actively mining, and so the hole and the immediately adjacent land should not be interfered with.[5]

Soon after the idea of a claim arose, miners began to meet to set down rules for a geographic area, the mining district. Writing in the tradition of Demsetz (1967), Umbeck theorized that "as land values rise and population increases, property rights will change from a communal sharing arrangement to private property in which each individual is assigned exclusive rights to a piece of land and all the income derived from it" (1981, 48). Umbeck refers to the mining codes as "contracts," Rousseauian agreements to foreswear violence for the sake of collective gain. But district rules were not contracts in any standard sense—agreements among a list of signers to respect and enforce one another's rights.[6] Mining-district codes were "laws of the land" for a specified area, rules and procedures binding on all miners in that district, founding members and newcomers alike. In the standard narrative, the mining districts were so effective and legitimate that they persisted long after the arrival of civil government, and their codes and customs ultimately became the basis for American mining law.

---

[4] As Mason wrote in his report of 17 August 1848: "Conflicting claims to particular spots of ground may cause collisions, but they will be rare, as the extent of the country is so great, and the gold so abundant, that for the present there is room and enough for all" (quoted in Paul [1966], 96).

[5] McDowell quotes from an account by miner Felix Paul Wierzbicki, written in September 1849: "A tool left in the hole in which a miner is working is a sign that it is not abandoned yet, and that nobody has a right to intrude there, and this regulation, which is adopted by silent consent of all, is generally complied with" (2002, 5).

[6] Libecap (1989, 11) extends this usage further, using the term "contracting" to refer not only to private bargaining but also to lobbying activity directed toward politicians and bureaucrats. Both authors mean to include all voluntary efforts to reduce the dissipation of rent. But their use of the term "contract" obscures the distinction between binding commitments by individuals and other forms of collective or political activity.

As one might expect in such a setting, miners drew on precedent and analogy in establishing these laws. Although the mining districts have long been celebrated as expressions of American frontier democracy (Shinn 1948 [1884]) early observers were well aware of the influence of Mexican mining law. Lawyer Henry Halleck wrote: "The miners of California have generally adopted as being best suited to their particular wants, the main principles of the mining laws of Spain and Mexico, by which the right of property in mines is made to depend upon *discovery* and *development*; that is, *discovery* is made the source of title, and *development*, or working, the condition of continuance of that title. These two principles constitute the basis of all our local laws and regulations respecting mining rights" (Halleck 1860, v).

In his 1867 treatise on mining law, Gregory Yale similarly argued that the role of American ingenuity in designing the codes had been exaggerated, in that most rules and customs were "easily recognized" from earlier mining traditions, primarily the Spanish-American system that had grown up under the ordinances of New Spain. The doctrine that claims must be worked or were subject to forfeiture, for example, was "precisely the principle of the *Ordenanzas de Mineria*" (Yale 1867, 58, 66). Mexicans were by no means dominant at the early miners' meetings, but their concepts may have had disproportionate influence because they had more experience in mining than most of the newcomers.[7]

It is not necessary, however, to view the mining codes as alien to American cultural values. As Zerbe and Anderson (2001) note, the first-come, first-served rule had strong salience as a fairness norm. Assigning ownership on the basis of "first possession" is a long-standing principle in Anglo-American common law (Lueck 1995; 1998). Nowhere was this dictum more vividly on display than in the settlement of American public lands in the nineteenth century. The Preemption Act of 1841 was the culmination of a long series of "special" preemption acts. It virtually institutionalized the practice of squatting and the principle that family-size plots would be provided to those who met settlement and improvement conditions. These analogies were frequently noted in gold rush discussions (Ellison 1926).[8] Elements of a typical mining-district code closely paralleled those of midwestern claim-clubs agreements pertaining to public land that had not yet been put up for sale: the size of claims; directions for marking, registering, and transferring claims; and procedures for settling disputes over contested claims (Bogue 1958).

Clay and Wright (2005) assembled a data set of surviving mining-district codes.[9] It included codes for 147 mining districts from the period 1849 to 1880, roughly 30 percent of all mining-district codes.[10] Because early mining districts were of

---

[7] Some of the Americans had participated in earlier gold rushes in the southern Appalachians, but their numbers could have been only a small part of the total, and there is no record of mining districts in these cases, most of which took place on privately owned land. See Williams (1993) and Young (1982).

[8] See also the discussion in Libecap (1989).

[9] Many of these codes were collected for the 1880 *Report on Precious Metals* (U.S. Bureau of the Census 1880). The rest of the set was assembled from county histories, newspapers, and surviving documents. A full list of codes and sources is available upon request.

[10] In his study of mining districts, Umbeck (1981) compiled a data set of 180 mining district codes. The difference between the two data sets is attributable to the incompleteness of Umbeck's citations and the fact that some references did not include the full text. These gaps prevented Clay and Wright from using 29 of his codes, but Clay and Wright's data set includes 10 codes that do not appear in Umbeck's data set.

TABLE 3.1

Summary Statistics for 52 Codes from 1850 Through 1852

Attribute	Number with Given Attribute
Claim size	52
Number of claims held by occupation	47
Work requirements	42
Existence of a recorder	42
Allowance for sale/transfer	36
Requirement that claim be recorded	33
Marking claim	30
Dispute resolution	24
Allowing claims by company	12
Bonus for discovery	10
Boundaries of mining district	9
Exceptions for working	8
Restrictions on foreign miners	8
Definition of claim abandonment	4
Property rights in water	3
Property rights in additional land	3
Rules for calling meetings	2
Rules for changing rules	1

SOURCE: Clay and Wright (2005, 165).

interest, the primary focus was on the 52 codes written between 1850 and 1852. Table 3.1 displays the attributes most frequently found in the early codes. Limits on claim size and number, as well as work requirements, were nearly universal. A majority of the codes specified procedures for marking and recording a claim, as well as for sale or transfer. For the most part, however, these early codes were sparse and incomplete, covering only a subset of what might be considered the basic elements of a mining-claim system. Clay and Wright's interpretation of this truncation is that the codes were understood as addenda, supplementary to the customs and usages that prevailed more generally. Indirect references to recording or work requirements suggest that such conventions often prevailed on matters that were not explicitly covered. When disputes were taken to court, judges typically referred to "customs and usages of miners," as well as to "regulations," as a basis for adjudication.

In one sense, the codes suggest that property rights were relatively secure, as Umbeck (1981) has argued, and that they were supported by norms of fairness, as Zerbe and Anderson (2001) have argued. Comparison across codes confirms Umbeck's (1981) view that mining codes were adapted to the circumstances of local mining districts. Some trends, such as greater attention to defining district boundaries, were common to both placer and quartz districts, perhaps reflecting greater uniformity statewide.[11] Others, such as exceptions to work requirements, allowance for sale or transfer, and rights to water, were much more prevalent in placer

---

[11] Yale stated that "these customs and usages have, in progress of time, become more general and uniform; and their leading features are now the same throughout the mining regions of the State" (1867, 62).

districts, presumably because of the difficulty of satisfying work rules in placer mining.

The Regulatory Function of Mining-District Codes

Previous interpretations have drawn on analogies to production-oriented activities, such as farming, and have neglected a basic feature of the gold rush context: miners were in a race to discover a limited number of high-yield, nonrenewable deposits. Typically a miner worked a claim only long enough to determine its potential. If he decided that it was a relatively low-value claim, as most were, he continued the search for one of the legendary bonanza sites. Because miners were continually looking for new and better sites even as they worked their present holding, mining-district rules were as much concerned with procedures for abandonment and re-possession of claims as they were with protection of the rights of holders of existing claims.

Although the analogy to farmland informed the design of the miners' codes, the effects in the two cases were quite different. Whereas squatters' rights and preemption rights were intermediate stages on the path to fully established ownership rights, such an evolution did not occur in the gold-mining districts. In understanding this divergence, one clue lies in a third widely accepted norm found in nearly all the early mining codes, the requirement that a claim must be worked to be maintained. Although work rules in gold mining were ostensibly only a logical extension of preemption-homestead principles, they compelled districts and later the courts to define "work." They also had to identify legitimate reasons for nonwork, such as illness or lack of water, which generated an endless stream of disputes and litigation. The system had some resemblance to the common-law doctrine of adverse possession, according to which property can be occupied and claimed if the original owner does not take active steps to evict trespassers (Lueck 1995). But on the spectrum from secure property rights to use-it-or-lose-it, the mining codes were at an extreme end in favor of the latter. Any slacking of effort on the miner's part exposed him to charges of having abandoned the claim. Prior occupation was not sufficient to re-possess a claim; the plaintiff also had to demonstrate that he had in fact complied with district work rules. Otherwise, the claim was liable to be "jumped," a standard procedure for entry into gold mining that was legitimated by the mining codes.

Clay and Wright (2005) argue that the main historical features of mining districts may best be understood by viewing them as institutions for managing access to mining sites in a high-turnover setting that approximated open access. As McDowell (2002; 2004) notes, participation in miners' meetings was not restricted to claim holders.[12] Typically, the codes begin with an announcement such as the

---

[12] There are some possible exceptions to this statement. The 1856 codes for both Little Humbug Creek and Maine Little Humbug state: "No person shall have voice or vote in a miners meeting or at arbitration that occurs in this mining District except he either holds a claim or is working in this mining district" (U.S. Bureau of the Census 1880, 291, 292). Clay and Wright interpret this as an exclusion of nonminers, but not a restriction to claim holders. The Empire Hill code was extended by one year "at a meeting held pursuant to a call by the claim holders" (U.S. Bureau of the Census 1880, 343); but the report of the next year's meeting uses the customary phrase, "a meeting of the miners." The only true documented case seems to be the Illinoistown quartz district code of March 1863, which barred persons who were not claim holders from future meetings (U.S. Bureau of the Census 1880).

following: "At a meeting of the miners of Union Quartz Mountain, held this 30th day of February 1851 ... the following Rules and Regulations were unanimously adopted" (U.S. Bureau of the Census 1880, 332). The internal politics of these early meetings cannot be recovered with any precision. If the group were divided between claim holders and latecomers without claims, it seems apparent that the only way to secure the votes of the latter was to assure them that the early arrivers would not be allowed to appropriate the entire district indefinitely. Both the provisions of the codes and their operation in practice suggest that a primary objective was not to strengthen the security of existing claims, but to place reasonable limits on those claims by setting explicit standards that an incumbent must meet to retain a claim against new arrivals.

McDowell (2002) advances a subtler argument. She suggests that whether they held claims or not at a point in time, miners operated behind a Rawlsian "veil of ignorance," visualizing themselves as claim jumpers as easily as claim protectors. This proposition is interpreted here as reflecting the pervasiveness of the "search" and "race" aspects of gold mining. The key difference between mining districts and claims clubs or cattlemen's associations was that gold mining was a race to find a small number of high-payoff claims. To be sure, search activity was inseparable from production, because only by the hard work of digging and sluicing could a miner-prospector learn whether a particular location was worth pursuing or not. Meanwhile, the "race" aspect was intensified by the keen awareness that high-yield gold sites were limited, gold was depletable, and many others were looking for the same limited number of deposits. If these features of the situation were paramount, it is perhaps understandable that mining-district codes made relatively little attempt to exclude new entrants and favor incumbents. In essence, they acquiesced in the high-turnover state of affairs and focused instead on prescribing rules for the orderly turnover of mining sites.

Even from a cursory reading, it is evident that the codes devoted as least as much attention to restrictions and requirements on claim holders as to protecting their rights. For example, the code for the Poverty Hill, Yorktown, and Chili Camp in Tuolumne County, adopted on 6 September 1851, contains nine articles. Two of these place size limits on claims; two restrict the number of claims that may be held; another sets down stringent marking procedures; and two others require that the miner be present and working the claim if water is available.[13] These rules hardly qualify as a pledge of mutual protection by property owners. But in the gold rush context, they can be understood as a codification of the rights of a larger group of would-be claimants.

To be sure, mining codes varied in the extent to which they favored claim holders over prospective jumpers. One of the oldest surviving codes, for the Gold Mountain Mining District in Nevada County (passed on 30 December 1850), might be considered proholder. It allowed claims to be held without tools being left or work being done until the first day of April 1851, and it provided stiff penalties for anyone who "takes away or uses tools of another without permission," or who "throws

---

[13] This code is recorded in the *Miners and Business Men's Directory* (1856). The remaining articles provide for exceptions when a person discovers a new lead, or when a claim is located on a ditch or ravine that has formerly been worked. In the latter case, ditch digging can qualify as labor sufficient to hold the claim.

dirt or rock upon the claim of another." Apparently influence had swung to the other side a year later, however, because the revised version required that claims be recorded by October 1851 "on pain of forfeiture" and severely tightened the rules for marking a claim.[14]

Subsequent Legal Developments

The endogenous development of a system of property rights that provided a reasonably stable framework within which search and production could occur shaped subsequent U.S. mining law decisively. Federal mining laws of 1866, 1870, and 1872 largely confirmed what by then was a well-established "free mining" precedent, dashing hopes that public-domain mining might be a major federal revenue source. In his exhaustive review of international mining laws, Theodore Van Wagenen (1918) concluded that prospecting was nowhere else as free as in the United States. In his study of comparative resource property rights, Anthony Scott (2008) concurs: "Essentially, for much of the nineteenth century, the American government acted as though it regarded mining law primarily as an instrument for bringing about an equitable and orderly disposal of the public lands" (2008, 286). These policy choices reflected not merely persistent mining-camp culture, but also political pressure in California and elsewhere in the West for rapid development of mineral resources. Although this perspective is often referred to as the "mining interest," it largely represented the interests of those who stood to gain from expanded mineral production, such as merchants, developers, and producers of mining equipment. The distinction is illustrated by the enactment of the foreign miners' tax by the California legislature in April 1850, imposing a $20 monthly license fee on all noncitizen miners in the state. After a chorus of opposition from merchants and editors, the tax was repealed in the following year and was reenacted at a more moderate rate in 1852. As mining activity spilled out from California into other western states and territories, and from placer gold to a range of hard-rock minerals, political priorities of both legislatures and courts favored rapid exploitation of mineral wealth (Bakken 1988; Libecap 1978).

The Federal Government as Mining Promoter

Rather than an extractor of rents, the U.S. federal government became a primary promoter of regional development through investment in the infrastructure of geological knowledge. In 1867 Clarence King, who had worked for the first state geological survey of California after graduating from the Sheffield Scientific School at Yale, approached the Corps of Engineers with a proposal that the War Department allocate funds for the geographic exploration of the fortieth parallel. The first publication from this project appeared in 1870, with contributions not just on the location of gold and silver deposits, but also on methods and equipment for digging and equipment for treating ores at the Comstock. The report was praised by the *American Journal of*

---

[14] "[E]very claim shall have a center stake driven upon it, which shall be three and a half inches in width by one in thickness of the length of two feet and which must be driven at least one half of its length into the ground" (U.S. Bureau of the Census 1885, 331).

Science as "the most valuable contribution yet made to the literature of the Mining Industry of the United States" (quoted in Manning [1967], 9).

When King exposed a fraudulent mining scheme in which an area had been secretly seeded with uncut diamonds, the *San Francisco Bulletin* lauded "the practical value, in the ordinary business of society, of scientific education and research . . . These public surveys 'pay' in more senses than one, and even those who care nothing for wider and fuller knowledge for its own sake, must hereafter admit that Government spends no money more wisely and usefully" (quoted in Manning [1967], 10–11). King was subsequently besieged by offers to examine property, and according to a friend, "He never charges less than $5000 to look at a mine" (Spence 1970, 113–114).

The United States Geological Survey, which emerged in 1879 under King's direction as the consolidation of several separate projects, became a leading center for topographic and metallurgical research in the post–Civil War era. The survey soon became known as a valuable employer for young men beginning a career in the industry, a "great graduate school of instruction," in the words of a mining journal (Spence 1970, 60). In 1882, under King's successor J. W. Powell, the survey was authorized to extend its operations east of the Mississippi and to begin preparation of a geological map of the entire country, not just the public domain. Thus it may fairly be said that the California gold rush enhanced and encouraged development of the entire national minerals sector, not just of the western region (David and Wright 1997).

Growth of the Minerals Sector

The result of this open and accommodating institutional setting was a vast expansion of activity in the minerals sector of the economy. The gold rush jump-started the western regional minerals enterprise. Figure 3.1 shows the evolution of the number of miners in the West over time (those in the East almost exclusively mined coal). The number of western miners fell between 1860 and 1870 and then began a steady rise in the 1870s. Opportunities in California declined as production shifted from surface mining of placer gold to more mechanized subsurface mining of quartz gold, but many miners migrated to other western states. Figure 3.2 shows that more than 20 percent of adult males were miners at some point in the history of six western states: California, Arizona, Colorado, Idaho, Nevada, and Montana. In every case except Arizona, miners were the largest share of the population in the first year of enumeration. For example, in 1860 they were 35 percent of the adult male population of Colorado and 56 percent in Nevada; in 1870, miners were 60 percent of adult males in Idaho and 49 percent in Montana.[15] Mining clearly drove settlement of these states. One can see this in maps of population distribution. The first map of this type was produced by the Census Bureau in 1870 and shows that the population in California, Colorado, Idaho, Nevada, and Montana was clustered in key mining districts.

---

[15] Percentages calculated from 1850–1910 public use samples of the census of population. Adult males are all aged 15 to 60.

FIGURE 3.1
Miners by Census Year

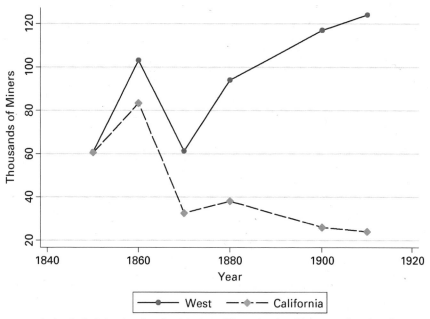

SOURCE: Authors' calculations based on the 1850–1910 public use samples of the census of population's occupation variable.

FIGURE 3.2
Miners as a Share of Adult Males, 1850–1910

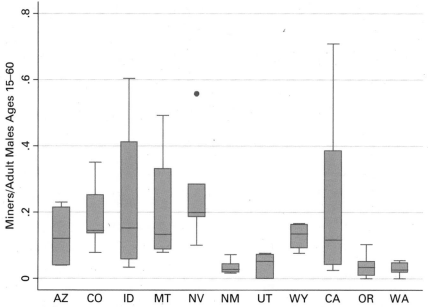

SOURCE: Authors' calculations based on 1850–1910 public use samples of the census of population. Adult males are all aged 15 to 60. The bars show the range of values for each state, while the boxes display the median, 25th and 75th percentiles, and adjacent values. The dot reflects an outlier year in which the percentage fell outside the upper adjacent value.

TABLE 3.2

Immigrants Reporting Occupation
as "Miner"

Years	Number
1820–1824	15
1825–1829	241
1830–1834	371
1835–1839	41
1840–1844	110
1845–1849	719
1850–1854	8,844
1855–1859	25,792
1860–1864	18,309
1865–1869	35,001
1870–1874	26,387
1875–1879	12,128
1880–1884	26,312
1885–1889	24,135
1890–1894	20,553

SOURCE: U.S. Department of the Treasury, Bureau of
Statistics (1903), 4406–4411.

Many of the western miners came from overseas. Table 3.2 shows the number of immigrants to the United States who gave their occupation as "miner" at the time of entry. The lasting impact of the gold rush is evident. Fewer than 2,000 miners entered the country before 1850, but more than 35,000 did so during the gold rush decade. Miner immigration actually increased during the 1860s and remained high for the rest of the century. Figure 3.3 shows that the share of foreign-born miners was high in most mining states in most years. Figure 3.4 shows the distribution of nationalities of all foreign-born miners from 1850 to 1910. The largest share was from the United Kingdom (England, Ireland, Scotland, and Wales). Chinese miners were the second-largest share, followed by Nordic, Mexican, Italian, German, Canadian, and other nationalities.

Although there is no way to measure their prior experience, many of these foreigners brought expertise that was highly valued in mining areas. In 1850s California, it was considered a great advantage to have a Cornishman or a Chilean in one's party. The shift to quartz mining further increased the prominence of skilled foreigners because of their experience at sinking and timbering shafts to reduce risks of rock falls or "caves" and their expertise in ore-reduction processes such as pulverizing rock. Cornishmen were held in particularly high esteem and were favored for positions both as miners and managers (James 1994; Paul 1947; Rowe 1974).

Figure 3.5 shows the course of gold production over time. The California series displays the classic pattern of a rush to discover a fixed number of rich ore deposits: Production peaked along with the number of miners in 1852 and drifted downward until 1865. But a focus on a single state is somewhat misleading because exploration spread to other western states, primarily Nevada and Colorado. Their rising gold production partially replaced California's declines. After 1885, total national

FIGURE 3.3

Foreign-Born Miners as Share of All Miners, 1850–1910

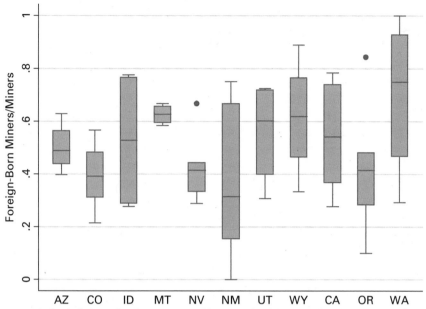

SOURCE: Authors' calculations based on 1850–1910 public use samples of the census of population. For an explanation of the diagram, see notes for Figure 3.2.

FIGURE 3.4

Nationalities of Foreign-Born Miners, 1850–1910

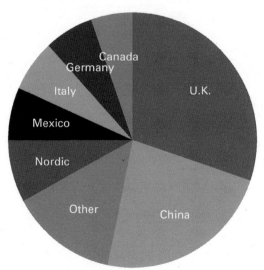

SOURCE: Authors' calculations based on 1850–1910 public use samples of the census of population.

FIGURE 3.5

Gold Production, California and U.S. Totals, 1835–1900 (in millions of dollars)

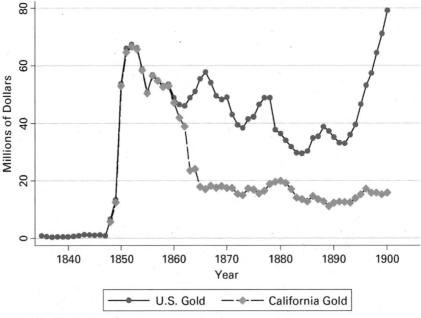

SOURCE: Berry (1984, 74, 76, 78).

gold production began to rise and by the 1890s had surpassed the peaks of the gold rush era.

But silver mining in the West was also a direct consequence of the California gold rush. The discoverers of the fabled Comstock Lode in what is now Nevada were gold prospectors who inadvertently stumbled on silver. Placer miners from California had worked a gulch called Gold Canyon for some years, unaware of the riches under their feet. Only in 1858, when more knowledgeable diggers detected bluish quartz mixed with the gold dust and had it assayed, was the area discovered to be rich in silver. A newspaper notice in July 1859 kicked off the Comstock rush, which in turn triggered searches for silver throughout the territories. Nevada became known as the Silver State, but its silver output was soon surpassed by that of Colorado, Montana, and Utah (Smith 1998 [1943]).

Figure 3.6 shows the dramatic growth of silver after 1860. If gold is combined with silver, the picture that emerges is not one of boom and bust, but of nearly steady growth throughout the century and beyond. From this perspective, the years of decline in California gold constituted a relatively minor setback in the larger story of expansion.

But the linkages did not stop with the transition from gold to silver. As the mining frontier progressed from west to east, prospecting became a specialized activity, conducted in small organized parties. These parties consisted of anywhere from five to fifty men, and experienced Californians were particularly prominent. Butte, Montana, became a gold placer camp in 1864 as the result of one such expedition. The camp became nearly deserted as the placers were exhausted, but interest in

FIGURE 3.6

U.S. Silver and Gold Production, 1835–1900

SOURCE: Berry (1984, 78).

Butte was revived in 1875 after some rich silver discoveries, by then a familiar object of mining attention. Butte silver was sufficiently promising to induce the Walker brothers of Salt Lake City to send their associate Marcus Daly, formerly a mine foreman on the Comstock Lode, to the area to examine and purchase claims. Early indications of plentiful copper deposits in the area were neglected at first, as they were elsewhere in the West. Rodman Paul observes, "Just when Daly came to realize that his silver mine was in fact one of the richest copper mines in the world, is not clear" (1963, 147–148). But by 1882 Daly induced a San Francisco group to finance a major investment in mining and smelting copper on a mass-production basis. By 1887 Anaconda was the largest copper mine in the country, propelling the United States into world leadership in copper production. Figure 3.7 shows that when copper is included, the path of post–gold rush mineral expansion in the West was almost continuously upward. Through similar path-dependent processes of discovery and learning, the value of base-metal production in the West (chiefly copper, lead, and zinc) came to exceed that of the precious metals by the 1890s.[16]

Inputs, Outputs, and Learning

To be sure, much of this expansion can be interpreted as the rise of inputs as much as of outputs, and from this perspective, one may question a linkage to common notions of a knowledge-based sector. But gold mining was technologically dynamic

---

[16] This paragraph draws on Richter (1927) and Trimble (1914).

FIGURE 3.7

U.S. Silver and Gold Production, plus Western Copper, 1835–1900

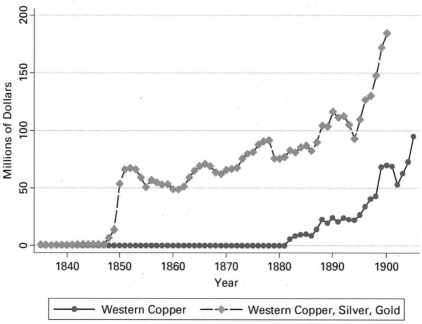

SOURCE: Data based on *The mineral industry: Its statistics, technology and trade.* Annual volumes, 1892–1905.

virtually from the beginning of the rush, so that the efficacy of mining labor improved over time despite ongoing depletion at particular deposit sites. Furthermore, the geographic expansion of the mining frontier was itself a learning process, deploying increasingly sophisticated forms of exploration and adaptation to new types of ore bodies and minerals. Perhaps most important, there was a positive complementarity between these two sources of progress: exploration brought new discoveries and technological challenges, while improvements in techniques of extraction, ore separation, and refining in turn facilitated the extension of mining into locations and ore qualities that would otherwise have been unprofitable, in effect creating new mineral resources from an economic standpoint.

The earliest placer miners extracted the metal from the gravel with a circular hand method performed by a single man with a pan. As early as 1848, miners began to make use of a larger machine called a "rocker" or "cradle," with which three or four men working together could produce a larger volume of "dirt" in a day. During the winter of 1849 to 1850, the "long tom" was first introduced in California. This instrument was a still-larger version of the cradle, with two 12-foot sections operated by three to six men, and required a continuous stream of water. Because the long tom allowed many of the finer gold particles to escape, a further improvement was implemented the following year in the form of the "sluice" or "sluice box," an open trough with riffle boxes perforated to allow gold particles to lodge. By the later part of 1849, all these techniques were enhanced by the use of quicksilver or mercury for more efficient separation of gold from the sand. Historian Rodman Paul argues that this package of innovations, together with investments in canals and ditches, constituted "a complete revolution in mining," and he notes that reductions in the unit cost of materials allowed miners to "extend their work into comparatively low-grade auriferous ground that had not previously been considered rich enough" for exploitation (1947, 65).

At that early stage, one could hardly have claimed that California mining technology was more advanced than elsewhere in the world. The use of mercury in gold mining was ancient, and the transition from panning to rockers to sluices did little more than recapitulate similar progressions in smaller previous rushes in Georgia and North Carolina. But even if one gives due allowance to all these considerations, one may still detect an emerging American pattern of progress in the minerals sector, in which higher-order forms of knowledge were deployed to address new technical challenges, and relationships between mining and other industries became increasingly complex.

Many of these linkages were functions of the scale of the mining sector. The rise of hydraulic mining in the late 1850s extended the range of accessible placer gold, albeit at high environmental cost, and dramatically increased the industry's demand for capital equipment (Isenberg 2005). Leather hoses for mining began to be made in San Francisco in 1857 and soon were exported to fire departments around the world. For quartz mining, San Francisco foundries and machine shops produced drills, belts, cables, explosives, pumps, and steam engines. The 1870 census recorded 42 steam engines in California mines and 604 in manufacturing firms. Manufacturing per capita in California was well ahead of that of midwestern states like Ohio and Illinois, and many industries that originated to serve the mines developed technologies with multiple additional uses, for example, in cable cars, shipbuilding, hydroelectric power, and sugarcane processing (St. Clair 1999).

Linkages from minerals to technology and science were accentuated with the shift from placer to quartz mining, and even more so with the rise of silver mining on the Comstock and elsewhere in the West. Barger and Schurr write that silver "ended the poor man's day in mining and ushered in the era of the financier and the engineer" (1944, 101). An important example of innovation endogenous to these new challenges was square-set timbering, in which rectangular sets of timbers replaced the ore as it was removed, increasing the strength of support and making possible the development of large underground ore bodies. The system was invented in 1860 by a German engineer who had been in California since 1851, and it soon became standard throughout the Comstock, an object of study and imitation by visiting experts from around the world (Paul 1963).

Of equal importance was a stream of innovations in methods of working ores that extended the intensive mining frontier for complex ores and low-grade deposits. An early breakthrough was the Washoe pan amalgamation process for separating silver and gold, developed in 1862 by the 49er Almarin Paul, who began by transferring stamp-mill technology from California quartz mining and then extended it to incorporate heavy iron mullers that would grind as well as mix the pulverized rock. Although standard historical narratives identify Paul and the Washoe process as the key breakthrough, he was only the most successful of the many gold rush veterans who were experimenting along related lines. Nor did the processes of innovation and adaptation stop there. For example, when the Washoe process was found not to work well for ores with arsenic or antimony sulfides, a variant known as the Reese River process (in which the ore was roasted with salt to convert silver sulfides into silver chlorides) was developed and used in a number of new silver-mining districts. In the 1860s and 1870s, the Comstock became known as a world center for hard-rock mining techniques, the "mining school of the world" (Barger and Schurr 1944, 102; Paul 1963).

Roughly simultaneous with the Comstock, but posing special geophysical challenges, was the gold- and silver-mining industry of Colorado. Although miners flocked to the area in large numbers between 1859 and 1865, output growth was inhibited by the extreme depths of the ores, and even more by the fact that Colorado gold ores were found in chemical combination with sulfides, known as "sulpherets" or "refractory ores" that resisted amalgamation. Initially, the main adaptation was a local variation of the California stamp mill that gave the ores a longer and finer crushing and a longer exposure to the action of mercury. These engineering methods were inherently limited in their ability to cope with what was in essence a scientific or metallurgical problem. As a mining newspaper wrote in 1870, "In Colorado we are having the privilege of solving some of the most difficult problems of metallurgy" (quoted in Paul [1963], 123). Numerous pseudoscientists, often self-titled professors, offered contraptions and processes to credulous mining companies. This led Rossiter Raymond, the U.S. commissioner of mining statistics, to declare that "desulphurization became the abracadabra of the new alchemists" (quoted in Fell [1979], 9).

Ultimately, Colorado investors reached out to real scientists for a solution, recruiting Nathaniel P. Hill from Brown University, an applied chemist who also maintained a vigorous consulting business. After visiting Colorado and gaining an appreciation of the technical challenge, Hill made trips to Britain and continental Europe to study techniques for smelting ores. In 1868 Hill built a smelter, largely copied from one in Wales. Its costs were prohibitively high, however, and the major breakthrough came only in 1871, when Hill allied himself with Richard Pearce, son of a Cornish miner who had studied both at the Royal School of Mines in London and in Freiberg. Their success provides a striking example of deployment of world-class scientific knowledge in the solution of a regional mining problem. Remarkably, Pearce's method was never patented but remained a company secret for the next 33 years.[17]

Hill's firm quickly drew the attention of the scientific community. James D. Hague visited the plant in 1868 as part of his geological study of the fortieth parallel and published data provided by Hill as part of Clarence King's study of the region. Pearce's technology was then discussed extensively in the first issue of the *Transactions of the American Institute of Mining Engineers* in 1871. In the *Transactions* for 1876, Thomas Egleston of the Columbia School of Mines published an article that discussed every aspect of the firm's technology except the secret process (Fell 1979).

---

[17] This paragraph draws on Fell (1979) and Paul (1960).

Successful development of Colorado smelting set the stage for the silver discovery at Leadville in 1877, a bonanza that was in many ways endogenous to the emerging regional technology. Leadville in turn became one of the first priorities of the United States Geological Survey (USGS), newly established in 1879. The USGS monograph on Leadville, prepared under the leadership of Samuel F. Emmons and published in 1882, was known for years as "the miners' bible." Paul writes: "More than any other event, the publication of this scientific study convinced skeptical mining operators that they could learn something of cash value from university men" (1960, 47). Emmons's thorough geological study of the entire district within a 10-mile radius generated a comprehensive view of the structural conditions affecting the distribution of ores. The survey's capacity to elucidate an area's complex system of faults led in turn to discoveries at Aspen and Rico, continuing the pattern of dynamic interaction among geological learning, processing technology, and new discoveries (Rickard 1932). Within a few years, other mining districts were petitioning the USGS for similar surveys.

The dynamic swung back to gold in the last decade of the nineteenth century with the invention and subsequent perfection of the cyanide process of gold extraction. A patent for a cyanide process was issued as early as 1867, and the pace of innovative effort accelerated in the 1880s. But the first demonstration of the commercial feasibility of cyanide was by the Scottish chemist John Stewart MacArthur, who obtained a British patent in 1887 and brought the process to Colorado in 1889. As with many metallurgical innovations, the process required extensive adaptation to local variations in ore quality. Between 1889 and 1905, 80 American patents were approved for various methods of extracting gold by cyanide, and the litigation was as intense as the experimentation. Ultimately, however, cyanide brought the required gold content of tailings down to as low as $1.80 per ton, leading to the "rediscovery" of many previously abandoned mines. The process also greatly increased the demand for technical skill and created a new niche for the metallurgical engineer, now clearly distinguished from assayers performing routine lab tests (Monroe 1905; Spude 1991).

The Rise of Western Copper

As previously mentioned, copper discoveries in Montana stemmed from the same exploratory process that spread gold and silver mining throughout the western states, which was traceable in turn to the California gold rush of the 1850s. Development of the region's potential in copper mining further extended the organizational and technological trends previously noted: greater capital intensity in mining operations, larger-scale enterprises, and complementary knowledge-intensive advances in ore processing and exploration. By 1884 the United States surpassed Chile as the world's leading copper-mining nation.

According to Richter (1927), the two most important innovations in American copper metallurgy during this period were the use of the Bessemer process for copper converting and the introduction of electrolysis for the final refining of copper. Converting brings copper matte forward to blister copper, a process that formerly required several melting or smelting operations plus roasting; the Bessemer pneu-matic converter reduced the process to a single operation in a few hours. Electrolysis allowed virtually complete recovery of the metal content of copper bullion, match-ing the naturally pure copper of the Lake Michigan district. In the early twentieth century, these metallurgical advances were further extended by the use of the oil-flotation process in concentrating the ore. Oil flotation called for and made possi-ble extremely fine grinding, which reduced milling costs sufficiently to allow the exploitation of low-grade porphyry copper ores on a commercial basis (Schmitz 1986).

Thus, advances in metallurgy effectively created new American mineral resources by fostering rediscoveries of deposits long known but considered submarginal. Indeed, there was an exponential link between the reduction in required yield and the expansion of ore reserves, a regularity known as Lasky's law, an inverse relation-ship between the grade of the ore and the size of the deposit (Lasky 1950; Schmitz 1986). Because the economies were in processing, commercial exploitation of this relationship encouraged large-scale, nonselective mining methods, using highly mechanized techniques to remove all materials from the mineralized area. This ap-proach was developed by Daniel Jackling, who graduated from the Missouri School of Mines in 1889 with a degree in metallurgy. In effect, Jackling's method was an application of mass-production, high-throughput technology and organization to mining. But this technology transfer between sectors was enabled by a prior revolu-tion in copper metallurgy.

From this perspective, reductions in average ore grades are a measure of techno-logical progress rather than depletion, especially in light of the downward trend in the real price of copper during this period. In her 2009 master's thesis, Kathryn Wood-ward assembled data on ore grades from the records of mining firms in Arizona, Michigan, and Montana between 1889 and 1909. Woodward's results are displayed in table 3.3. The inverse relationship between declining grades and expanding pro-duction in the western states is evident. By contrast, in copper-rich Chile, where

TABLE 3.3

Copper Production and Ore Grade, 1889–1909

		Copper Production (pounds)	Grade (%)
Arizona	1889	32,139,529	10.33
	1902	119,841,285	5.85
	1909	291,110,298	4.43
Michigan	1889	87,413,000	1.80
	1902	170,194,996	1.10
	1909	231,870,496	1.08
Montana	1889	104,189,353	8.56
	1902	266,500,000	4.33
	1909	314,858,291	3.03

SOURCE: Woodward (2009, 33). Production and grade for 1889 are from U.S. census data. Grades for 1902 and 1909 are averaged from firm data.

output was stagnant, yields averaged between 10 and 13 percent between 1880 and 1910 (Przeworski 1980; Woodward 2009).

Higher Mining Education

The expansion of mining and consequent encounters with new technical and scientific challenges gave rise to indigenous training institutions adapted to American conditions. The earliest efforts antedated the gold rush. For example, the Lawrence Scientific School at Harvard included mining and metallurgy as part of the founder's intended purpose in 1847. In practice, the Lawrence School concentrated on pure-science aspects of biology and chemistry. Before the late 1860s, Americans who wanted advanced training in mineral sciences were likely to enroll in one of the prestigious European mining colleges in Sweden, Freiberg, or Paris.[18] The first growth spurt for domestic mining schools came only in the 1860s (David and Wright 1997).

Although several of the eastern schools had strong links to in-state mining activity, the most successful of them all had no such connection, but was clearly producing mining engineers for a national market. When Columbia College in the City of New York opened what became the nation's first successful school of mines in 1864, twice as many students (29) appeared on the first day as had been expected. Within a year, that number had more than doubled. Visitors were impressed by the rigor of the Columbia curriculum; one of them wrote in 1867: "A graduate of the School of Mines will be well worthy of his degree" (quoted in Spence 1970, 38). The first-year curriculum included courses in drawing, stoichiometry, mathematics (analytic geometry and calculus), physics, electricity and magnetism, inorganic chemistry, quantitative analysis, mineralogy, and French and German. The second year added metallurgy, mechanics, geology, botany, and mining engineering (machines). The third year continued metallurgy and quantitative analysis and added the theory of veins, assaying, and "conservation of force." A well-informed 1871 survey declared Columbia "one of the best schools in the world—more scientific than Freiberg, more practical than Paris" (Church 1871, 79; Read 1941; Spence 1970).[19]

The Columbia School of Mines was dominant for the next quarter century. In 1893 Samuel B. Christy, a professor of mining and metallurgy at the University of California, noted that the United States had more mining students than any country in Europe except Germany, and nearly half of the national total as of that year had studied at Columbia (Christy 1893; figure 3.8). Notwithstanding the academic rigor of its program, the school also sought to expose its students to practical aspects of the mining industry. Professor Robert H. Richards developed the Mining Laboratory, where problems in ore dressing and metallurgy could be worked out by students. Professor Henry S. Monroe developed the Summer School of Practical Mining, which helped students become familiar with working conditions they would meet after graduation (Christy 1893).[20]

---

[18] Read (1941) presents a list of Americans enrolled.

[19] Read (1941) reports the opening-day enrollment at Columbia as 24 and enrollment in 1865–1866 as 97; Spence (1970) puts the opening-day figure at 29, followed by 79 in 1865–1866.

[20] Columbia College catalogs (1754–1894) are accessible through Google Books.

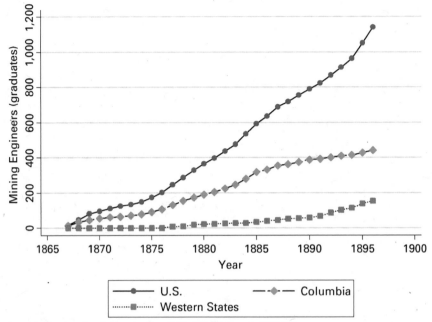

FIGURE 3.8

Cumulative Mining Engineering Graduates, Columbia and Western Mining Schools, 1867–1896

SOURCES: Data based on *Engineering News* (1892, 140); Wadsworth (1997, 731).

The majority of Columbia graduates stayed in the East, but many found work throughout the western states. They were sufficiently numerous in Colorado by 1884 for the School of Mines Alumni Association to establish a branch in Denver. The school journal reported Columbia clusters in Colorado, Utah, California, Arizona, Nevada, and Mexico, and many more traveled to the West on consulting trips. Clearly, Columbia was supplying mining expertise for a national market.[21]

Nonetheless, demands arose over time for mining schools in closer proximity to the mining districts. These efforts were an expression of state developmental impulses dating from the early nineteenth century, combined with the undeniable geographic specificity of much of the relevant knowledge about minerals. Inspired by the gold rush, many states initiated or revived geological surveys in the 1850s. When an 1867 proposal by a Nevada senator for a national school of mines was unsuccessful, the states quickly moved in. The Colorado School of Mines was the first to be set up as a separate institution; it was established by the territorial legislature in 1870 and began instruction in 1873. Mining education at the University of California began in the 1860s, although the first degree was not awarded until 1873. Mining schools were also established in Missouri, Michigan, South Dakota, Arizona, Nevada, and New Mexico. At Berkeley, registration at the mining college grew tenfold between

---

[21] Reports in the *School of Mines Quarterly*, summarized in Spence (1970).

1893 and 1903, supporting the school's claim to be "without doubt the largest mining college in the world" (Read 1941, 84; Spence 1970).[22]

Professionalization in American mining engineering was well ahead of its counterpart in Great Britain. Founded in 1871, the American Institute of Mining Engineers (AIME) was one of the earliest professional organizations, second in engineering only to the American Society of Civil Engineers. At the first meeting of the British Institution of Mining and Metallurgy in 1892, the organizers "found it more than a little irksome to have to acknowledge that in the U.S. some such organization had been operating successfully for nearly twenty years." The difference may have been mainly a matter of the scale of the national industry: whereas the AIME by that time had more than two thousand members, Britain "would be hard pressed to muster more than a couple of hundred" (Wilson 1992, 8–9).

Of course, advanced degrees and professional organizations do not necessarily imply that mining engineers and other scientifically trained personnel actually had a significant impact on mining technology and practice. But testimony is abundant that there was indeed a transition from reliance on the skills of apprenticeship-trained "mining captains," often foreign born, to deployment of college-trained engineers. The extension of the mining frontier to lower-quality ores was driven by scientific advances in geology and metallurgy and by a complementary technological shift toward nonselective mass-production methods, and both of these trends coincided broadly with the eclipse of traditional miners' skills in favor of those of professional engineers. The acceptance and legitimation of mining engineers is perhaps best indicated by their increasing presence in managerial and executive roles within large firms, an expected career path that came to be reflected in the curricula of mining schools.[23] But the high mobility and professional status of mining engineers gave them substantial independence, as confirmed by offers of extravagant salaries and bonuses to American engineers and metallurgists from such faraway locations as South America, Australia, Africa, Siberia, and China. A turning point in Australia's mining history came with the decision in 1886 to recruit high-paid engineers and metallurgists from the Rocky Mountain states, such as William H. Patton from the Comstock Lode and Herman Schlapp from the smelting towns of Colorado (Blainey 1969; Spence 1970).[24]

Property Rights and the Minerals Knowledge Economy

This chapter has argued that the American minerals sector of the late nineteenth century displayed many of the attributes associated with a knowledge economy: competitive research universities responsive to the private sector; entrepreneurial scientists and engineers who operated through active professional networks; government support for an infrastructure of public knowledge; and economic progress based on advances in the knowledge frontier. Most historical accounts date such

---

[22] Hendrickson (1961) lists state surveys.

[23] The association between the shift to nonselective mining methods and the rise of mining engineers is argued by Hovis and Mouat (1996). On the incorporation of administrative as well as technical skills at the Colorado School of Mines and elsewhere, see Ochs (1992).

[24] Harvey and Press (1989) note that large firms often opposed the trend toward mobility and independence on the part of engineers by imposing secrecy agreements in contracts.

developments only from the turn of the twentieth century, with the appearance of corporate laboratories and the emergence of research universities as a self-conscious group. This emergence is marked by the founding of the American Association of Universities (AAU) in 1900.[25] But the "modern" character of economic relationships in American minerals is impressive and suggests that many features of the twentieth-century "American innovation system" began much earlier in this sector.

What lessons does this analysis offer for assessing the relationship between property rights and natural resources? Most discussions of this matter deal mainly with efficiency in resource allocation in the presence of common-pool issues and other externalities. From this perspective, an open-access regime, such as that represented by U.S. mineral law, would lead to wasteful rent dissipation through excessive haste and costly, duplicative investments of labor and capital. The California gold rush displayed many of these symptoms (Clay and Jones 2008; Clay and Wright 2005). For the rest of the nineteenth century and beyond, the U.S. minerals sector was plagued by problems of high transaction costs, nuisance suits, overlapping claims, chronic litigation, and exorbitant legal fees, to say nothing of extensive environmental damage (Gerard 2001; Leshy 1987). Mining historian Clark Spence asserts: "No industry in any country was ever subject to as much or as complicated legal activity as mining in western America" (Spence 1970, 107).[26] But with all these shortcomings, the dynamism of the minerals knowledge economy generated the world's largest and most advanced national mining sector.

To some degree, intellectual property rights in mining technology could substitute for property rights in mineral-bearing lands. Indeed, figure 3.9 shows that the rate of patenting in mining accelerated at the time of the California gold rush and continued to rise thereafter. It is highly likely that the acceleration continued after 1870 as the training of mining engineers and metallurgists progressed, and mineral technology drew on increasingly advanced forms of knowledge. But intellectual property rights can hardly be a full resolution of the issue. As in modern times, patent claims were never fully secure because they were often objects of intense litigation and were vulnerable to technological obsolescence even if they were upheld. For these reasons, many new technologies were not patented but were protected instead by secrecy. Pearce's method for smelting refractory ores is but one example. Petra Moser's (2005; 2007) research on innovations displayed at nineteenth-century world's fairs suggests that less than half of them were patented, and mining had among the lowest industry patenting rates.

To be sure, American mining expanded within a larger society in which property rights and wealth accumulation were respected and protected. Under U.S. min-

---

[25] Goldin and Katz write that "something fundamental changed around the turn of the twentieth century," when "technological shocks" in scientific disciplines generated economically important findings that shocked the "knowledge industry" (1999, 38, 43, 51). A recent survey states that "the research university as we know it today did not emerge in the United States until around World War II" (Carlsson et al. 2009, 1197). On the founding of the AAU as a watershed, see Geiger (1986).

[26] Gerard (1998) shows that the rate of western mining claim disputes declined after 1900, suggesting that enforcement costs fell over time. There may be many reasons for this observation, but in any case, Gerard's evidence underscores the extremely high incidence of dispute during the period of U.S. ascendancy to world mining leadership.

FIGURE 3.9

Mining Patents by Five-Year Periods, 1835–1870

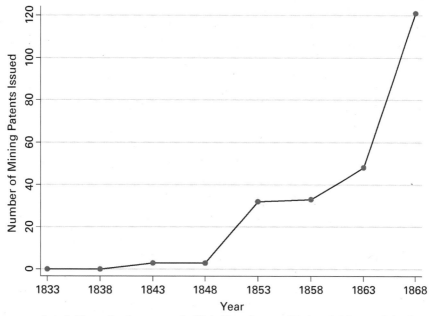

SOURCE: Compiled from a Google patent search of United States Patent and Trademark Office records for all patents using the terms "mine" or "mining" through 1870.

ing law, prospectors could acquire reasonably secure claims and legal title upon payment of modest fees. Claims could be sold and aggregated. Like patents on technology, mining claims were subject to nuisance suits and costly litigation. The promise of profit, however, was sufficient to attract large-scale capital into the sector from distant eastern and European investors. This was a thoroughly capitalist process from an early point. But it was a far cry from a standard account in which property owners invest willingly in improvements, secure in the knowledge that their asset values will capitalize the returns. Instead, the minerals knowledge economy was a complex institutional hybrid in which the prospect of large returns encouraged risky, long-distance private investments, with public and quasi-public support, assistance, and accommodation of various kinds. In short, it was much like a modern knowledge economy.

It would be imprudent to draw specific policy lessons from the U.S. experience for today's developing countries with mineral endowments. Engineering a gold rush to attract fortune seekers by the hundreds of thousands would be a challenge, and even if that were possible, one would hardly expect to kick-start a dynamic collective learning process as the result. The U.S. economy was already dynamic and innovative by the 1850s. The decentralized, endogenous, unregulated character of the episode reflected deep features of American society that are not readily transported across historical time and space. Perhaps the larger message is simply that property rights systems for natural resources should be appropriately adapted to specific cultural and historical contexts, rather than dictated by standardized formulas in isolation.

But one broad lesson does carry over from the American minerals experience, which is that minerals should not be understood as mere "endowments" given by nature, but as resources with potential for development. Realizing that potential requires investments of labor and capital, but above all, knowledge. And even in the modern globalized economy, in which the mineral sector draws on advanced frontiers of science-based technologies, useful forms of minerals knowledge still have strong geographically specific components. In general, the countries that have exploited their mineral potential successfully are those that have invested in indigenous, country-specific knowledge and human capital pertaining to exploration, extraction, processing, and sometimes usage of domestic resources. Because these learning processes have public-good properties, this sector deserves a legitimate place in the technology and engineering plans of developing countries with mineral potential.[27]

REFERENCES

Bakken, Gordon Morris. 1988. American mining law and the environment: The western experience. *Western Legal History* 1:211–236.

Barger, Harold, and Sam H. Schurr. 1944. *The mining industries, 1899–1939: A study of output, employment and productivity.* New York: NBER.

Barzel, Yoram. 1997. *Economic analysis of property rights.* 2nd ed. Cambridge, U.K.: Cambridge University Press.

Berry, Thomas Senior. 1984. *Early California: Gold, prices, trade.* Richmond, VA: Bostwick Press.

Blainey, Geoffrey. 1969. *The rush that never ended: A history of Australian mining.* 2nd ed. Melbourne: Melbourne University Press.

Bogue, Allan G. 1958. The Iowa claim clubs: Symbol and substance. *Mississippi Valley Historical Review* 45:231–253.

Carlsson, Bo, Zoltan J. Acs, David B. Audretsch, and Pontus Braunerhjelm. 2009. Knowledge creation, entrepreneurship, and economic growth: A historical review. *Industrial and Corporate Change* 18:1193–1229.

Christy, Samuel B. 1893. The rise of American mining schools and their relation to the mining industry. *Transactions of the American Institute of Mining Engineers* 23:444–465.

Church, John A. 1871. Mining schools in the United States. *North American Review* 112:62–81.

Clay, Karen. 2010. Natural resources and economic outcomes. In *Economic evolution and revolution in historical time*, eds. Paul Rhode, Joshua Rosenbloom, and David Weiman, 27–50. Stanford, CA: Stanford University Press.

Clay, Karen, and Randall Jones. 2008. Migrating to riches? Evidence from the California gold rush. *Journal of Economic History* 68:997–1027.

Clay, Karen, and Gavin Wright. 2005. Order without law? Property rights during the California gold rush. *Explorations in Economic History* 42:155–183.

David, Paul A., and Gavin Wright. 1997. Increasing returns and the genesis of American resource abundance. *Industrial and Corporate Change* 6:203–245.

Demsetz, Harold, 1967. Toward a theory of property rights. *American Economic Review* 57:347–359.

Ellickson, Robert C. 1991. *Order without law: How neighbors settle disputes.* Cambridge, MA: Harvard University Press.

Ellison, Joseph. 1926. The mineral land question in California, 1848–1866. *Southwestern Historical Quarterly* 30. Reprint. 1963. In *The public lands*, ed. Vernon Carstensen, 71–92. Madison: University of Wisconsin Press.

---

[27] These arguments are developed more fully in Clay (2010) and G. Wright and Czelusta (2006).

Engineering News. 1892. The engineering schools of the United States. XVII. The distribution of graduates. August 11: 139–140.

Fell, James E. 1979. *Ores to metals: The Rocky Mountain smelting industry*. Lincoln: University of Nebraska Press.

Geiger, Roger L. 1986. *To advance knowledge: The growth of American research universities, 1900–1940*. Oxford: Oxford University Press.

Gerard, David. 1998. The development of first-possession rules in U.S. mining, 1872–1920. *Resources Policy* 24:251–264.

———. 2001. Transaction costs and the value of mining claims. *Land Economics* 77:371–384.

Goldin, Claudia, and Lawrence F. Katz. 1999. The shaping of higher education: The formative years in the United States, 1890 to 1940. *Journal of Economic Perspectives* 13:37–62.

Halleck, Henry W. 1860. Introductory remarks by the translator. In *Fundamental Principles on the Law of Mines*, by J. H. N. de Fooz, i–cxlviii. San Francisco: J. B. Painter, printer.

Harvey, Charles, and Jon Press. 1989. Overseas investment and the professional advance of British metal mining engineers. *Economic History Review* 42:64–86.

Hendrickson, Walter B. 1961. Nineteenth-century state geological surveys: Early government support of science. *Isis* 52:357–371.

Hovis, Logan, and Jeremy Mouat. 1996. Miners, engineers, and the transformation of work in the western mining industry, 1880–1930. *Technology and Culture* 37:429–456.

Isenberg, Andrew C. 2005. *Mining California: An ecological history*. New York: Hill and Wang.

James, Ronald M. 1994. Defining the group: Nineteenth-century Cornish on the North American mining frontier. *Cornish Studies* 2:32–47.

Lasky, S. G. 1950. How tonnage and grade relations help predict ore reserves. *Engineering and Mining Journal* 151:81–85.

Leshy, John D. 1987. *The mining law: A study in perpetual motion*. Washington, DC: Resources for the Future.

Libecap, Gary D. 1978. *The evolution of private mineral rights: Nevada's Comstock Lode*. New York: Arno Press.

———. 1989. *Contracting for property rights*. Cambridge, U.K.: Cambridge University Press.

Lueck, Dean. 1995. The rule of first possession and the design of the law. *Journal of Law and Economics* 38:393–436.

———. 1998. First possession. In *The new Palgrave dictionary of economics and the law*. Volume 2, 132–144. New York: Stockton Press.

Manning, Thomas G. 1967. *Government in science: The U.S. Geological Survey, 1867–1894*. Lexington: University of Kentucky Press.

Mayer, Carl J., and George A. Riley. 1985. *Public domain, private dominion*. San Francisco: Sierra Club Books.

McDowell, Andrea. 2002. From commons to claims: Property rights in the California gold rush. *Yale Journal of Law and the Humanities* 14:1–72.

———. 2004. Real property, spontaneous order, and norms in the gold mines. *Law and Social Inquiry* 29:771–818.

The mineral industry: Its statistics, technology and trade. 1892–1905. New York: McGraw-Hill.

Miners and business men's directory. 1856. Tuolumne County, CA.

Monroe, Charles E. 1905. Precious metals recovered by cyanide processes. In *Special reports of the Census Office: Mines and quarries, 1902*, 591–645. Washington, DC: U.S. Government Printing Office.

Moser, Petra. 2005. How do patent laws influence innovation? Evidence from nineteenth-century world's fairs. *American Economic Review* 95:1214–1237.

———. 2007. Why don't inventors patent? National Bureau of Economic Research. Working Paper W13294.

Ochs, Kathleen. 1992. The rise of American mining engineers: A case study of the Colorado School of Mines. *Technology and Culture* 33:278–301.

Paul, Rodman. 1947. *California gold*. Cambridge, MA: Harvard University Press.

———. 1960. Colorado as a pioneer of science. *Mississippi Valley Historical Review* 47:34–50.

———. 1963. *Mining frontiers of the West, 1848–1880*. New York: Holt, Rinehart, and Winston.

———. 1966. *The California gold discovery*. Georgetown, CA: Talisman Press.

Pisani, Donald J. 1998/1999. "I am resolved not to interfere, but permit all to work freely": The gold rush and American resource law. *California History* 77:123–148.

Przeworski, Joanne Fox. 1980. *The decline of the copper industry in Chile and the entrance of North American capital, 1870–1916*. New York: Arno Press.

Read, Thomas Thornton. 1941. *The development of mineral industry education in the United States*. New York: American Institute of Mining and Metallurgical Engineers.

Richter, F. E. 1927. The copper-mining industry in the United States, 1845–1925. *Quarterly Journal of Economics* 41:236–291.

Rickard, T. A. 1932. *A history of American mining*. New York: McGraw-Hill.

Rowe, John. 1974. *The hard-rock men: Cornish immigrants and the North American mining frontier*. New York: Harper and Row.

Schmitz, Christopher. 1986. The rise of big business in the world copper industry, 1870–1930. *Economic History Review* 39:392–410.

Scott, Anthony. 2008. *The evolution of resource property rights*. Oxford: Oxford University Press.

Shavell, Steven. 2004. *Foundations of economic analysis of law*. Cambridge, MA: Belknap Press of Harvard University Press.

Shinn, Charles Howard. 1948 [1884]. *Mining camps: A study in frontier democracy*. New York: Alfred A. Knopf.

Smith, Grant H. 1998 [1943]. *The history of the Comstock Lode*. Reno: Nevada Bureau of Mines and Geology.

Spence, Clark C. 1970. *Mining engineers and the American West, 1849–1933*. New Haven, CT: Yale University Press.

Spude, Robert L. 1991. Cyanide and the flood of gold: Some Colorado beginnings of the cyanide process of gold extraction. *Essays and Monographs in Colorado History* 12:1–35.

State register and book of facts. 1857. San Francisco: Henry G. Langley and Samuel A. Mathews.

St. Clair, David. 1999. The gold rush and the beginnings of California industry. In *A golden state: Mining and economic development in gold rush California*, eds. James J. Rawls and Richard J. Orsi, 185–208. Berkeley: University of California Press.

Trimble, William J. 1914. *The mining advance into the inland empire*, 139–390. Madison: Bulletin of the University of Wisconsin.

Umbeck, John. 1981. *A theory of property rights, with application to the California gold rush*. Ames: Iowa State University Press.

U.S. Bureau of the Census. 1874. *Statistical atlas of the United States*. http://www.cartoko.com.

———. 1880. *Tenth census of the United States*. Vol. 14, *The United States Mining Laws and Regulations Thereunder, and State and Territorial Mining Laws, to which are appended Local Mining Rules and Regulations*. Washington DC: U.S. Government Printing Office.

U.S. Department of the Treasury. Bureau of Statistics. 1903. *Monthly summary of commerce and finance*. Washington DC: U.S. Government Printing Office.

Van Wagenen, Theodore. 1918. *International mining law*. New York: McGraw-Hill.

Wadsworth, M. E. 1997. Some Statistics of Engineering Education. *Transactions of the American Institute of Mining Engineers* 27:712–731.

Walton, Gary M., and Hugh Rockoff. 1998. *History of the American economy*. 8th ed. Fort Worth, TX: Dryden Press.

Williams, David. 1993. *The Georgia gold rush*. Columbia: University of South Carolina Press.

Wilson, Arthur J. 1992. *The professionals: The institution of mining and metallurgy, 1892–1992*. London: Institution of Mining and Metallurgy.

Woodward, Kathryn Morgan. 2009. Marvelous growth: Copper, technology and the firm, 1890–1913. M.S. thesis in economic and social history, Oxford University.

Wright, Doris M. 1940. The making of cosmopolitan California: An analysis of immigration, 1848–1870. *California Historical Society Quarterly* 19:323–343.

Wright, Gavin, and Jesse Czelusta. 2006. Resource-based growth past and present. In *Neither curse nor destiny: Natural resources and development,* eds. Daniel Lederman and William F. Maloney, 183–210. Stanford, CA: Stanford University Press and World Bank.

Wright, James E. 1966. *The Galena lead district: Federal policy and practice, 1824–1847.* Madison: State Historical Society of Wisconsin.

Yale, Gregory. 1867. *Legal titles to mining claims in California.* San Francisco: A. Roman.

Young, Otis E., Jr. 1982. The southern gold rush, 1828–36. *Journal of Southern History* 48:373–392.

Zerbe, Richard O., Jr., and Leigh Anderson. 2001. Culture and fairness in the development of institutions in the California gold fields. *Journal of Economic History* 61:114–143.

Commentary

PETER Z. GROSSMAN

Karen Clay and Gavin Wright argue that the U.S. mining industry underwent a transformation from the gold rush of 1849 through the end of the century that created economic progress based on the extension of the knowledge frontier. This thesis extends an argument made by one of the authors, Wright, who, along with Paul David in a 1997 article, argued that America's resource abundance was not a natural gift so much as a social construct that grew out of the "features that typify modern knowledge-based economies" (David and Wright 1997, 204). A difference in the two works is the impetus: In the article, David and Wright suggested that the gold rush was not as singular an event as is sometimes thought, but was only the most "spectacular" of the "'rushes' that occurred in almost every part of the country" (David and Wright 1997, 216). Here the argument is that the gold rush was in fact a catalyst that jump-started the process of technological innovation and generated various institutional and organizational changes that have come to characterize a knowledge economy. The chapter in a sense restores the place of the California gold rush as a central moment in U.S. economic history.

This chapter is divided into two parts. The first does a fine job of exploring the history of mineral property rights regimes and how they evolved during and after the gold rush. Of course, much has been written about the development of property rights in the California gold fields. Umbeck (1981) and McDowell (2002), as well as the authors of this chapter (Clay and Wright 2005), have provided substantial insights into how mining claims became conceptualized and codified as property in California. This chapter extends that work to delineate the way in which elements of California property institutions influenced U.S. mineral law for the rest of the century.

The second part traces the rise of the mining industry in the United States and the development of its knowledge components: higher education, government support, and technological advance. The authors make the point that the property regime was crucial in the development of the mining knowledge economy because the emphasis was on development of mining property, not just acquisition. They fit these parts together in some ways, but in the process, they raise a number of questions. For example, to what extent did the nature of mineral property institutions lead miners to focus so much on bonanza finds like silver in the Comstock Lode? Was it simply the fact that the government had no claim on appropriable rents, so the potential existed for enormous returns to the prospector-miner? It is not immediately obvious why a mine that produced steady, if unspectacular, returns would not have been a desirable goal of a miner. Also, did the particular American institutions of mineral rights create specific incentives to employ the latest technological advances? There is no doubt that colossal returns from Comstock-like finds provided incentives to innovate. But what role did institutions play in this process? Did the open-access character of prospecting or the opportunity to claim-jump abandoned or inactive properties give innovators particular advantages? Did so many skilled European miners come to the United States because of advantages in U.S. mining laws and enforcement over European laws, or did they cross the ocean just because here was where people were finding lots of gold and silver? What in particular about the rules of the game—if any—led to the identification of the mineral sector as a knowledge sector in the United States and not in other, and especially other common-law, countries?

Clay and Wright are able to show the synergies in the mining sector that developed similarly to those in a knowledge economy where there are productive ties between higher education, industry, and government. The chapter is particularly effective in explaining the rise in the United States of mining education and mining professionalism, and the impact this had in the field. Of course, it could be argued that far from blazing a particular new trail, mining was following general trends in the economy as a whole. In the period in question, sometimes referred to as the Second Industrial Revolution (especially by Chandler [1990]), there were transformative innovations in many industries that often led to innovations elsewhere. These, too, were often aided by institutional factors and by increasing specialization and professionalization of work and the creation of other specialized schools, such as Wharton's for business. Still, the chapter shows that mining, a major U.S. industry, was no bystander in this process but was a major part of the trends of the time.

Clay and Wright describe "the minerals knowledge economy" as "a complex institutional hybrid" that added up to something "like a modern knowledge economy." They make a compelling case on the whole, and no doubt they provide ideas for future research and analysis.

REFERENCES

Chandler, Alfred. 1990. *Scale and scope: The dynamics of industrial capitalism.* Cambridge, MA: Harvard University Press.

Clay, Karen, and Gavin Wright. 2005. Order without law? Property rights during the California gold rush. *Explorations in Economic History* 42:155–183.

David, Paul A., and Gavin Wright. 1997. Increasing returns and the genesis of American resource abundance. *Industrial and Corporate Change* 6:203–245.

McDowell, Andrea. 2002. From commons to claims: Property rights in the California gold rush. *Yale Journal of Law and the Humanities* 14:1–72.

Umbeck, John. 1981. *A theory of property rights, with application to the California gold rush.* Ames: Iowa State University Press.

Gold Rushes Are All the Same

4

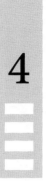

Labor Rules the Diggings

ANDREA G. MCDOWELL

In the popular imagination, the California 49er staked his mining claim, and woe betide the man who tried to jump it. The mining claim of myth is the very prototype of private property, combining the natural law principle of finders, keepers and a frontier right to shoot intruders if necessary. In reality, however, miners had very limited rights in their claims, and, by all accounts, miners were remarkably law abiding. From the beginning, claim holders and claim jumpers followed strict rules, and over time, those rules were codified at public meetings. The miners were impressed with their own law abidingness, and so has been almost everyone who has written about the California gold rush.

What were these rules? The earliest claims, those of 1848 and 1849, hardly qualified as property at all; they were barely more than use rights. A miner had about as much interest in his claim as a customer at Starbucks has in the armchair that he has been lucky enough to secure. As long as the customer is sitting in a seat, no one else can take it. He is entitled to get up from "his" chair briefly for a trip to the restroom or to get another cup of coffee if he leaves his coat on the seat and a coffee cup on the table to signal that he is coming back; but if he is gone too long and the place is crowded, someone else will move his coat aside and sit down. The more crowded it is, the sooner this will happen.

Similarly, a miner's right in his claim lasted only as long as he was actively mining. He was granted short absences to get provisions or to do a little prospecting, provided he left his tools on his claim; but if he was gone too long, his claim was deemed abandoned and could be jumped by anyone who did not already have a claim.

The rules in the richest diggings granted a miner little more than the space he and his tools occupied. In the spring and summer of 1848, there do not seem to have been any claims at all; men worked cheek by jowl in the richest diggings. "Every person takes the right to gather all they can, without regard to claims," reported the *Californian* on 3 May 1848. In October of that year, Walter Colton saw a miner strike gold in a hole he was digging for a tent pole. "As soon as it was known, some forty picks were flying into the earth all around the spot," Colton said. "You would have thought the ground had suddenly caved over some human being, who must be instantly disenhumed or die" (Colton 1850, 291). The discoverer in this case had no exclusive right to his treasure.

Claims emerged in some parts of the diggings before others, but there is no evidence of how or why they did. Perhaps when miners started to dig deeper and therefore stayed on one spot for several days, other miners automatically recognized their exclusive right to their investment. Edward Gould Buffum's observation that in November 1848, at Foster's Bar, "a claim [was] considered good when the claimant had cleared off the top soil from any portion of the bar" suggests that others could not take advantage of his labor (Buffum 1850, 53). In general, early claims took the form of miners' holes, and tools left on the site signified that they were still at work. The first codes standardized claim sizes at roughly the same size as the organic hole, that is, from 10 × 10 to 15 × 15 feet (McDowell 2002).

The formal rules, as opposed to the customary ones, also specified how long a miner could be away from his claim before he forfeited it; if he was inactive for three, or five, or more days, depending on the local code, his claim became "jumpable." The work requirement prevented a man from holding onto a claim that he was not using, for example, for purposes of speculation, while giving him time to run errands or do some prospecting without losing his claim (McDowell 2002).

The third feature of most mining codes was the notice requirement. For example, a miner could be required to "stake off" his claim and post a notice with his name and signature, the date of his claim, and its limits. Codes often required miners to register their claims with a local recorder, although this rule seems to have been largely ignored (McDowell 2002). A miner who did not give proper notice could come back from a trip to the merchant to find someone else on his claim.

Finally, many codes limited miners to one claim apiece. This seems to have been the majority rule in the early days and was probably the default rule. The humorous and very popular composition called *The Miner's Ten Commandments* states as the first commandment, "Thou shalt have no other claim than one" (Hutchings 1853).

A miner's limited use right in such a claim was different from any of the textbook forms of "property" in land. It belonged to the first comer, but it was not a speeded-up form of the traditional preemption right or adverse possession, both of which can eventually turn into ownership. The right to mine was also distinct from other rights in the same piece of land. A miner could locate a claim in another person's garden if the garden was on public land and the miner paid the occupant compensation for damages (Bancroft 1890; King 1885; McCurdy 1976; Parkinson 1921). One mining camp, Smith's Flat, had a specific rule allowing a family to hold a claim for gardening purposes, which suggests that bachelors were not allowed to garden on their claims (King 1885). The condition of continuous use and limits on the number of claims a man could hold, even by purchase, also differed in degree from the requirements for other sorts of preemption rights to such an extent that they amounted to a difference in kind. Instead, the mining claim was a codified variant of the mere occupancy that Blackstone imagined to have existed before property: "Thus the ground was in common, and no part of it was the permanent property of any man in particular; yet whoever was in the occupation of any determined spot of it, for rest, for shade, or the like, acquired for the time a sort of ownership from which it would have been unjust, and contrary to the law of nature, to have driven him by force: but the instant that he quitted the use or occupation of it, another might seize it, without injustice" (Blackstone 1827, Book 2, 2). In other words, before private property, all the world was a Starbucks.

Most of this chapter pertains to the simplest form of mining claim, the small, individual, surface claim. Generally, miners formed partnerships of three or four men to work their respective claims as a team. From the beginning, miners also joined together for large-scale undertakings, such as diverting a stream to get at the gold in the riverbed, working deep shafts, and tunneling into hillsides. Those group projects raised very different issues than individual mining claims. They lasted for longer periods, sometimes years, and required the cooperation of many miners, who organized themselves into joint-stock companies for the purpose. Moreover, whereas individual mining claims merely generated disputes between neighbors, river turning, that is, diverting the river from its bed, led to conflicts among companies upstream and downstream from one another, as well as among companies and individuals mining on the river banks. For these reasons, and because of the amount of money at stake, river turning in particular was not self-regulating like individual mining claims, but generated a great deal of litigation. I shall argue below that roughly similar systems of individual mining claims appear in gold rushes around the world, but there is more regional variation in the organization of large-scale projects.

The individual mining claims, however, are the ones that have fascinated the general public and scholars alike because they seem both simple and exotic. The first in-depth academic study of the claim system was by the economist John Umbeck (1981). Umbeck collected more than two hundred mining codes and compared their rules for individual claims, including claim size and work requirements. He concluded that the rules matched the outcome that would have resulted from fighting over claims. That is, he suggested that miners could spend their time mining or fighting for more land. The optimal claim size would be reached when the benefits of enlarging the claim were outweighed by the loss of time spent actually mining. Being rational actors, the miners agreed to skip the fighting and simply enacted rules reflecting the same result. The claim size in the code was what would have been reached by force of arms. The work requirement stemmed from the need to keep enough men in the diggings to protect one another's claims.

Zerbe and Anderson (2001) listed many problems with Umbeck's mechanical approach. Most important, it does not fit the evidence of what actually happened. There was almost no fighting among Americans over claims, although Americans did use force to expel other ethnic groups. Moreover, Umbeck had little to say about the miners' own accounts of the advantages of the claim system, namely, that it gave everyone an equal chance and prevented a relatively small number of "capitalists" from monopolizing the diggings. A further problem, not noted by Zerbe and Anderson, is that when guns are taken into account, the cost of fighting for more land is not measured in hours and therefore cannot be compared with the value of time spent mining. Without the fighting hypothesis, rational-choice accounts cannot predict what kind of property regime will emerge because many forms of property are equally viable.

Zerbe and Anderson (2001) rejected a purely functional explanation for the emergence of claims. They proposed instead that culture played an important and perhaps critical role in shaping the claims system because it provided focal points that helped the miners overcome the coordination problems inherent in creating a new property regime from scratch. First, common values supplied a basis for the rules. Zerbe and Anderson reasoned specifically that the claims system expressed both the Lockean labor theory of property and Jacksonian, small-labor ideology. Second, shared institutions, specifically, democratic meetings, enabled the miners to agree on specific laws. Finally, they argued, newcomers to the diggings accepted the codes as legitimate because they shared the basic notions of fairness underlying the codes and accepted the principle of majority rule. In support of their thesis, Zerbe and Anderson drew on the miners' own descriptions of the mining claims system with regard to equality, the rights of labor, and democratic self-government.

McDowell (2002) disagreed with Zerbe and Anderson's thesis and argued that American values alone were not enough to explain the mining-claim system. Fairness and equality are not sufficiently specific to determine a property regime. Eastern property norms were considered fair, although they did not include limits on buying and selling and allowed owners to do as they pleased with their property, including leaving it unused. But the miners chose a system radically different from the private property they had known back in the East. Moreover, in the gold rush, the Jacksonian idea that labor produces wealth and that capital is a mere passive partner in the process was a simple fact. Much of the Jacksonian rhetoric in California was an accurate description of the economics of mining and was not mainly ideological. McDowell suggested that mining claims developed spontaneously in 1848, before any meetings; and that the customary rules of that year acquired normative force and became the baseline for later codes. Later miners almost never gave reasons for the claims system. When they did, they talked about protecting the position that labor had enjoyed in the early gold rush.

Other Gold Rushes

In 2003, at a workshop in Halle, Germany, on mining frontiers, scholars who had studied contemporary gold rushes around the world described claims systems strikingly similar to those in California. The resemblances lie in the inability of individuals to control the mining area and the custom of temporary use rights. This suggests that the California system was not distinctively American.

A gold rush is, of course, a gold discovery that attracts crowds of people hoping to get gold. The geological requirement seems to be that the gold be near the surface and can be extracted with simple and affordable tools. The economic features of a rush are harder to characterize. It certainly is not true that all the miners will get rich. Even at the height of the California gold rush, most miners lost money. The Californians all hoped to get rich, but even that is not true of miners everywhere. In some rushes, like the current gold rush in Mongolia, the people hope merely for enough gold to feed their families that day; they are desperately poor and will endure anything, even police brutality, to scratch out a living from mining (Lim 2009). Elsewhere, in Africa and Brazil, for example, some diggings are more like seedy, adult summer camps than workplaces. The miners come to dig and be with other men and earn some money to spend on drinking, gambling, and prostitution. Indeed, in some parts of Africa, the gold is considered dangerous or evil and therefore is not to be used for family purposes such as buying land or paying dowries; it is only for frivolities. In short, an area does not have to be extraordinarily rich in gold to spark a gold rush (Werthmann 2008).

Mining claims are found in gold rushes around the world, present and past, from the most spectacular to the most humble, though it is unclear whether they appear in *all* gold rushes. In some cases, including the nineteenth-century gold rushes in Australia and Canada, the claim system was borrowed from California. Not only did the authorities in the British colonies say so explicitly, but many of the miners in Australia and Canada had previously worked in America (Goodman 1994). What is more striking is that variations on the theme of mining claims emerge in third world communities that know nothing about nineteenth-century western mining claims. The only thing that these places have in common is placer gold and, possibly, an irrational, risk-seeking population that is attracted to gold mining. It must therefore be the geological features that determine the property regime.

A number of modern gold rushes, perhaps most, share the following features with California in 1849: The discovery of surface gold, whether on private or public land, attracts hordes of gold seekers who cannot be stopped without 24-hour armed guards. The mining industry (capital), which may have discovered the gold, finds that it must accommodate the miners. A claims system emerges that is based on first possession and use. State laws and authorities are largely ignored; the miners themselves, or a committee of major claim holders or elders, decide disputes, which means that they determine the rules of mining. Finally, there is little violence except among miners of different tribes or ethnicities. The main differences between California and these other gold rushes are that the American miners passed codes, ran their own criminal justice system, and formed joint-stock companies to tackle bigger projects rather than working under a chief or boss. A brief description of gold booms in Africa, South America, and Southeast Asia will illustrate the similarities.

Of the three modern gold rush episodes described in this chapter, the Brazilian experience of the 1980s most closely resembles that in California. It is also particularly well documented by the anthropologist David Cleary (1990), who spent two years among the miners in the period from 1984 to 1986. The similarities to California are due mainly to types of mining that are possible in the Amazon, namely, placer mining with pan, cradle, and sluice box, on one hand, and a form of river mining, on the other hand. The Brazilian rush involved more miners and produced more gold than the California one (MacMillan 1995). Like California, too, Brazil had multiple boom-and-bust mining camps and thus developed an itinerant mining population with its own customs and routines (Cleary 1990). In Cleary's description of the population of the mining camps, there is a clearer division than in California between claim holders (or independent producers) and employees working for wages or on shares, presumably because of the greater use of mechanical pumps and crushers in mining.[1] He also notes, however that the two groups came from the same social class, that most claim holders began as employees, and that a significant number

---

[1] Gordon MacMillan (1995), another specialist on the Brazilian gold rush, found that almost all income in the diggings he studied was based on a share of the profits, so that mining was a gamble for all involved.

of claim holders failed and lost everything for which they had worked (Cleary 1990). This social mobility, upward and downward, was also characteristic of the California diggings.

In Brazil, as in California, gold either is embedded in quartz or has been brought down from the mountains by water and has come to rest on bedrock, in strata of earth, or even mixed with the topsoil. This last kind of deposit, known as alluvial or placer gold, is worked with the same tools used in California: mining pans, modified rockers called *cobra fumando* (Cleary 1990), and portable wooden sluices. Quartz gold, which gave the Californians great trouble, can now be worked by relatively simple motor-powered crushers and water pumps (Cleary 1990). Such crushers cost thousands of dollars and are difficult to transport because they have to be dismantled and loaded onto mules, but they are within the means of medium- and small-scale miners. Quartz mining and placer mining are carried out in many of the same diggings and together form the modern equivalent of California's dry diggings.

Riverbed mining in Brazil uses technology that was not available in 1849, but the stakes are still high and miners work on shares, as they did in California. The machinery is mounted on a raft. A motor pump attached to a wide, plastic hose is used to suck the alluvium up from the river bottom to the raft, from which it goes through pipes to a large version of the *cobra fumando* (Cleary 1990). The machinery requires a crew of three to operate it: one diver in full diving gear on the riverbed to work the hose, a second man on the raft to monitor the oxygen cylinders and to receive communications from the diver via pulls on a rope, and a third to work the *cobra*. A full team often has two crews to keep the process in continual operation, as well as a cook. The raft and machinery cost from $5,000 to $15,000, depending on quality. The running costs of the operation are also high, especially if fuel and supplies have to be sent in by airplane. Moreover, the work is dangerous, especially for the diver who works in the fast-moving stream with limited visibility; there is a risk that the sides of the hole he is excavating may collapse and bury him, or that logs floating downstream may cut his oxygen supply. This kind of mining can be very profitable, however, and individual miners are willing to take the risk for a share of the profits.

In short, the forms of mining in Brazil are roughly the same as in the California mines. The prospector, with his pan and cradle, pushes forward into the wilderness beyond the reach of roads and supply centers; the placer miners now work both as old-fashioned shovel-and-sluice-box partners and as teams using more advanced, motor-driven technology; and the crews are engaged in high-stakes, possibly highly rewarding, riverbed mining. It is interesting, therefore, to see the similarities to, and some differences from, the California mining-claim system in Brazilian diggings.

Mining conventions in the dry diggings of Brazil can best be described under three headings: establishing claims, disputes over claims, and the virtual impossibility of excluding miners from lucrative gold diggings, even when the diggings are on privately owned land. With respect to riverbed mining, the main point of interest is the internal organization of the crews.

As in California, Brazilian custom gives special privileges to the miner who discovers new diggings. If a prospector makes a rich strike, it attracts other miners, and if there are further strikes at the site, they set off a true gold rush. The first discoverer cannot grant himself an extra large claim or sell claims to newcomers, but he enjoys the status of *dono da fofoca* (owner of the rush). As *dono*, he marks out and allocates claims on request and in return receives a percentage of their earnings (Cleary 1990). The amount varies, but is usually about 10 percent. The earliest arrivals take claims near the *dono*'s own and honor their obligation to him, but as more and more miners arrive and take claims farther away, the *dono*'s authority becomes attenuated and eventually collapses. The latest newcomers refuse to pay a percentage, and soon everyone stops paying. The former *dono* becomes no more than an ordinary miner. After this, arrivals mark out claims for themselves in unoccupied spots (Cleary 1990).

Claims are small, about five meters by five meters for miners working without machinery and ten meters by ten meters for those with motor-driven pumps and crushers (Cleary 1990). Cleary does not say how such small claims came to be the norm, but he writes that the first discoverer "marks out a [claim], which can be no larger than the area he can realistically exploit, around ten meters by ten meters being the upper limit in most cases" (1990, 60). This is in line with maximum claim sizes in California in 1849. Cleary suggests that a claim holder is liable to forfeit his claim if he is not working it. Specifically, if a private landowner finds gold on his land, he becomes the *dono* and can also collect about 5 percent of earnings from the other miners. But if that landowner tries to reserve some land for himself without actually using it, the miners may simply move in and start mining. This suggests that there is a use requirement for claims, although possibly one that is not as formal as in California.

Once a miner has been assigned a claim by the *dono* or, later in the rush, has staked one off for himself, he has an exclusive right to the claim and may sell it or rent it to another (Cleary 1990). But, again, this is a use right: he may lose his claim if it is not worked.

Brazil does not appear to have a general custom of one claim per person, but at the spectacularly rich site at Serra Pelada in Brazil, Cleary reports that government geologists imposed such a rule with claims distributed by lot. Miners liked the arrangement because it was egalitarian, but it broke down because people found ways to buy and sell claims by letting the original owner retain 1 percent of his claim and keeping his name on the title (Clearly 1990). This was the same problem as in California.

The Brazilian diggings also resemble those in California in that there is very little fighting over claims. "Provided that a claim is in use," Cleary says, "it is very rare for it to be forcibly taken away from its owner, even by a rich and unscrupulous" opponent (1990, 63).[2] In fact, there are hardly any disputes about ownership of claims, violent or otherwise, although boundaries are often contested.

Cleary (1990) suggests two reasons for this, although neither can be verified. One is that someone who took another's claim by force not only would have to do serious

---

[2] Cleary (1990) does describe one case in which a group threw a miner off his claim, pistol-whipping him and threatening to kill him if he did not leave the diggings. The claim holder, a man of Japanese descent, had made himself unpopular by claiming a large area for himself on the basis of a faked document. Cleary does not say whether this was why he received no support from other miners.

damage to the claim holder and perhaps even kill him, but also would have to deal with the police and with the claim holder's friends and relatives. Second, his rights would not be recognized by others; laborers would not work for him, stores would not give him credit, and his neighbors would not lend him fuel or spare parts. Cleary further notes that new arrivals in the diggings would be particularly ill advised to try to force another off his claim. Newcomers are entering an area where there are already established relationships and personalities and are careful not to cause trouble when they are at their most vulnerable (Cleary 1990, 64). Both arguments could equally well apply to California and could help explain why disputes over claims were almost all between neighbors. More broadly, they are reminders that property is a relation among people and that possession of a claim does not create ownership unless the neighborhood acknowledges this relationship.

Boundary disputes are common in Brazil, however, as they were in California (Cleary 1990). Unfortunately, how they are resolved is unknown. According to Cleary, when the diggings are on private property, the miners recognize the landowner's authority to allocate claims and may ask him to arbitrate a dispute. An ordinary *dono* seldom enjoys this kind of prestige, and some diggings have no *dono* at all. It is not clear who arbitrates disputes in such cases.

Gold discoveries on private land are a Brazilian phenomenon that was unknown in California. Brazilian mining law allows miners to enter private land but requires them to pay 10 percent of their proceeds to the owner (Cleary 1990). A landowner can profit greatly from a gold rush on his property. He is the *dono* who assigns claims, many of which go to his relatives and employees and are effectively under his control. The other miners accept this arrangement, provided there is room for them, too, and the claims are seen to be worked. The landowner also sets up a store, with high markups. Finally, he can collect his 10 percent, although, interestingly, this is usually reduced to 5 percent to make the diggings more attractive to outside miners.

Some owners of land in remote areas where state control is weak, however, do try to run a private or "closed" diggings, and these are "the most violent and unstable" of all mining regions (Cleary 1990, 69). The owner must act quickly to seal the area and has to have enough gunmen to exclude independent miners. "If the attempt to restrict access is contested and the landowner loses, then he loses all legitimacy in the eyes of the [miners] and may even be killed by them" (Cleary 1990, 69). The owner controls his hired labor very tightly. The workers must sell their gold to the landowner and are searched when they leave the diggings to prevent them from smuggling. "Violence, or, more exactly, the threat of violence, becomes an integral part of the relations of production" (Cleary 1990, 71). Eventually, complaints against the landowner may lead the state to move in and take over the land. The Brazilian example suggests that it would have been impossible to privatize mineral land in California, as some members of Congress proposed in 1849.

Even more interestingly, Cleary explains that individual, small-scale mining is in many ways more efficient than industrial scale mining when it comes to placer mines in the Amazon: "It has very low overheads, it does not require more than minimal transport facilities, it is not reliant on a steady power supply, its basics are easily learned by newcomers to the [diggings] within a short time, it is an extremely effective form of gold prospecting, it has expanded both capacity and the range of deposits that it can work . . . over the last decade, and it is more efficient at extracting gold than it is generally given credit for" (Cleary 1990, 26). Moreover, it is difficult or impossible to transport large machinery to mining areas deep in the forest (Cleary 1990).

The same obstacles to capital investment would have applied in the Sierra Nevada. There, too, surface gold was often discovered deep in the wilderness and quickly worked out, and capital had no more effective equipment to offer than the sluice boxes and flumes that individual miners were already using. Walter Colton wrote of quartz mining, which would require capital investment, "Years must elapse before human enterprise can bridge a path to these mines, or render communication practicable in the rainy season; nor at any period can heavy machinery be transported here without an immense outlay of capital" (1850, 313–314). This is one reason why California capitalists were prepared to wait on the sidelines until the gold rush was over.

As for the limits of private property, landowners in Indonesia have also found it impossible to exclude independent miners. According to a 2001 article in the *Wall Street Journal*, there were 68,000 individuals working for themselves on land owned by mining companies at that time, taking out $250 million annually in gold and other minerals (Schuman 2001). On the island of Sulawesi, officials worried about the environmental impact of this activity, among other things, but were unwilling to act because "we don't want the people to demonstrate against us" (Schuman 2001, A8). Sixty-eight thousand people represent 68,000 votes.

In 1988 the Indonesian government did evict illegal miners from private land with military and police forces and then kept them out by staging "night raids on their camps and posting policemen in the mine full time" (Schuman 2001, A8). Years later, however, the trespassers were back, and the new, democratic government was no longer willing to crack down on them. In January 2001, one company, Aurora Gold, pulled out of Indonesia, taking a $42 million loss. At the time of the *Wall Street Journal*'s article, the miners ruled Aurora's former site and had a 20-man patrol guarding the area where they refined their gold. Again, private owners were no match for thousands of small-scale miners.

Since the early 1990s, West Africa has also experienced multiple gold rushes, which have sparked large labor migrations. Benin and Burkina Faso have been particularly closely studied; the following paragraphs are based on Tilo Grätz's work in Benin (Grätz 2002; see also Werthmann's work on Burkina Faso [2000]). Grätz studied mining near the village of Kwetana in northern Benin. When gold was discovered there in 1993, immigrants flooded in from Benin itself and from neighboring countries. As in California, mineral resources are owned by the state, and private mining is technically illegal. The government accordingly tried to force the miners from the field and confiscated their property, but this did not stop the miners. "At first a cohort of the *gendarmerie* deployed at the site were corrupted" (Grätz 2002, 3), permitting further mining in return for bribes. (Colonel Richard B. Mason in California also feared that his soldiers would desert and mine for themselves if they were stationed near the mines.) When the guards were withdrawn from the gold regions in Benin, many miners simply returned to work.

In 1999, having failed to expel the miners, the government changed its policy to partial legalization. It attempted to impose some rules, such as introducing mining licenses and requiring miners to sell gold to government agents rather than petty traders. The miners disregarded these measures.

The gold near Kwetana is reached by shafts. A shaft belongs to the person who first discovered the site and started exploiting it (called the chief or *patron*), but his rights last only as long as he is actually mining on the site. He has a use right, which lapses if the "chief" abandons his shaft, sells it, or rents it to others for a longer period. If the shaft later turns out to be rich, the original holder cannot reclaim it. Not surprisingly, there are many disputes about ownership rights.

Shafts must be worked in teams, and the hierarchy within these teams is one difference between Benin and California. The discoverer, as the owner, usually directs the work as the team leader and also supplies equipment, food, and medical care. Werthmann (2000) notes that in West African shaft mining, the workers may be paid wages, or the profits may be shared fifty-fifty between the pit owner and the crew. There is no class difference between owners and workers, however, because mining is so unpredictable that their positions can be quickly reversed. The owners may lose their investments and become laborers, while workers may make enough to buy shafts of their own.

Most disputes in the Benin mining camps are about claim boundaries or the rights of an owner who has apparently abandoned his shaft. These are almost always submitted to a gathering of other owners and team leaders. The miners very rarely take their cases to an outside court such as the village head or, even more rarely, government authorities. Moreover, they almost never appeal the arbitrator's decision, and if they do, it is to the village head, not to government agents (Grätz 2002). Grätz suggests that disputes are not pursued in part because miners have other options, such as moving to a new shaft, and because they do not want to waste their limited time on lawsuits.

This form of dispute resolution is reminiscent of that in California, but a difference appears in disputes between the discoverer of a claim who has abandoned it and moved on and a subsequent holder who strikes it rich. The arbitrators generally uphold the latter's rights, as in California, but they may ask him to pay some compensation to the first "explorer." Californians never split the difference between claimants.

Mining in Papua New Guinea is less well documented. In 1987 the mining company CRA Limited discovered fabulously rich placer gold at Mt. Kare on the island. News of the find leaked out in early 1988, and within five months, some eight thousand individuals were working at the site (Vail 1995). The gold was in a remote, uninhabited mountain area, and legal questions about the relative rights of the mining company and the two tribes that claimed use rights in the area created years of litigation; but in the short term, CRA had to write off hundreds of millions of dollars worth of surface gold (Ryan 1991).

Mt. Kare was even more chaotic than other gold rushes because it was so rich and so remote, and the miners had had little or no interaction with the market economy before the discovery of gold. CRA built a health clinic at the site, and there was a lot of helicopter traffic to and from the mountain, but those were the only signs of the twentieth century. There was no government presence, and the organization of the mines was left entirely up to the miners.

Evidently, the diggings were relatively orderly, but unfortunately, there is no good record of the rules or customs that the miners developed (Ryan 1991). It is known that the miners worked in holes six to ten feet square with crowbars, shovels, and pans. Some holes were much smaller; hardly wide enough for a man or boy to move in and three to four meters deep (Ryan 1991). Although the miners worked with only shovels and pans, not even cradles, they got out well over $100 million worth of gold (Ryan 1991). A number made a fortune, but most made just enough to support themselves, and others found no gold at all. Most of those who got rich squandered their money on sprees and luxury purchases. The cost of living in the mines was extraordinarily high, and transport to and from the mines used up much of the gold that was not spent on food.

Ethnic tensions at Mt. Kare were very like those in California. The two dominant ethnicities in the mines frequently came to blows, and there were two full-fledged battles with bows and arrows. Highlanders from farther away were tolerated as long as they worked holes that had been abandoned by local miners, but if they behaved badly or drew too much attention to themselves, they were moved on. Whites were not permitted to dig at all, although several tried to get a spot (Ryan 1991). A couple of miners tried using motorized pumps for sluicing. They might be compared with the Mexicans who brought their peons to the mines in California, and, like them, they were made to give up this unfair advantage and mine like everyone else (Ryan 1991).

These examples indicate that small, temporary, individual mining claims appear in gold rushes around the world. If the gold is found on private property, the owners find that it is difficult or impossible to stop the influx of miners. If, on the other hand, the strike is on public land, Cleary's research shows that in Brazil, custom grants the first discoverer some rights, but as more people pour into the locale, those rights are ignored. Meanwhile, capital cannot be used to advantage because it cannot control property; and also because heavy machinery is of little use when diggings are remote and no one knows how much gold there is until it is gone. It seems, therefore, that geological conditions, not culture, generate the mining-claim system.

It cannot be asserted that mining claims will emerge in all gold rushes in all circumstances. Very few of the hundreds of gold rushes in the past century have been studied, and the anthropologists who have worked on gold rushes have not focused particularly on property rights. A very different regime operated in ancient Egypt, where gold mining was a royal monopoly. One can also imagine that property rights would be different in a country that recognizes slavery, or in one that lies a in remote region where highly organized, well-armed gangs control the area, as the FARC does in parts of Colombia today (Romero 2011). That a California-like mining-claim system has appeared independently in vastly different societies around the world, however, and across time shows that it is not entirely a product of culture.

Back to California

In California, as in Brazil, the conventions of mining first evolved through interactions between miners and were not created at miners' meetings. By 1849 there was an almost universal expectation that claims would be small and that the rule was "use it or lose it." Where rich diggings were discovered, the crowds of miners arriving at the diggings picked their spots and got to work. The main difference between the American and Brazilian diggings from 1849 onward is that the Americans held meetings to formalize the new rules, whereas in Brazil, the rules remained unwritten. Although the miners said harsh things about capital, it was not the threat of a capitalist take over that roused them to create use rights. Miners and capitalists all agreed that capital was useless in the early stages of a gold rush, if only because wages were so high. Capital did finally step in when the gold rush was over; indeed, the time when individual mining was no longer profitable and expensive equipment was necessary marked the end of the rush.

Again, the subject of this chapter is the archetypical gold rush in which there is a lot of gold near the surface that individuals can reach with simple tools. Californians developed many other forms of mining to get at gold that was less accessible. As mentioned earlier, the 1850s mining operations included also river turning projects, deep-shaft mining, failed attempts at quartz mining, water companies, and enormous claims still worked by individual miners but now dependent on the water companies. The basic idea of the mining claim was carried forward through all these developments, but the spontaneous, self-enforcing, possibly even universal rules for whose existence this chapter argues are associated with very rich surface diggings.

The classic, individual claim had a relatively short history. Historians who have attempted to identify the end of the gold rush, that is, of the heyday of the independent miner, have put it in 1851 or 1852 (Clay and Wright 2005; Owens 2005; Paul 1947). Contemporaries began announcing its demise from 1850, as did the *Alta California* on 15 February 1851: "The man who lives upon his labor from day to day, must hereafter be employed by the man who has in his possession accumulated labor, or money, the representative of labor."

What makes it difficult to pinpoint the end of the gold rush is that miners continued to work individual claims for more than two decades. Amendments to local codes were still being enacted as late as 1878, long after any kind of rush (King 1885). After 1855 claims were huge; by 1857 some codes provided for claims as large as one hundred "yards square," or ten thousand square yards, and the cost of water was so high that many of those claims were not worth working (King 1885; Turrill 1876). At this point, mining was just a job, and not even a good job. These huge, almost worthless claims are not the subject of this chapter. For present purposes, 1852 is considered the last year of the rush, even though there were further mini-rushes in following years. As Clay and Wright (2005) note, a weakness of Umbeck's analysis as that two-thirds of the codes on which he based it were drafted after the gold rush proper.

The first appearance of claims is not documented. They did not appear everywhere at the same time, but were in use in some areas long before others. In 1848 there were only a few thousand men at work in the diggings, with almost no experience and only very primitive tools, and there were no general rules. Some miners were always on the move and probably did not think in terms of property. Miner William Jackson Barry, for instance, "mined" by "pulling up grass and shaking the earth from the roots into a pan, and then washing it off in the creek" (Barry 1879, 102). In some places, a miner did not have an exclusive right even to the spot where he was actively at work, that is, to the two or three yards occupied by his body and tools. Walter Colton observed this repeatedly, for instance, in the previously mentioned case of the miner who struck gold in the hole he was digging for a tent pole. Only a few days earlier, Colton saw or heard of a Mexican who had made a very rich find: "As soon as this was known, four of the New York volunteers struck in each side of the Sonorian, and dug him out" (1850, 287). (The Mexican at least had the satisfaction of seeing that they did not find any gold where he had been digging.) Many years after the gold rush, a former miner told the historian Charles Howard Shinn that when he began mining, there was not yet even a custom, "so that a man hardly objected to your digging close beside him so long as you gave him room to swing a pick" (1885, 166). In short, there were areas in the diggings with no property rights at all.

Elsewhere in the mines, however, someone who struck gold had at least a minimal right to his location. On their last day in the mines before leaving for Salt Lake City, Mormon Robert Petch and his partner Douglas "opened a hole" from which they got $398. They then sold the right to the hole for $150 (Owens 2005, 249). This hole must have been rather small, given that it was dug, worked, and sold in the course of one day. On 9 July 1848, about the same time that Robert Petch sold his hole, Charles Bolivar Sterling "bought a rich prospect from a Mormon," perhaps even the same one (Larkin 1960, 312). Bolivar Sterling and his partner got two to three ounces ($32 to $48) from their new "prospect" in part of an afternoon.

Meanwhile, during that same year, the custom emerged that a miner had a claim in his hole that would be respected as long as he left his tools in it to signal that he was still at work (McDowell 2002). Many miners referred to it in later years as a sort of default rule that held even in the wilderness where there was no community to enforce it. Bayard Taylor, for example, wrote that in 1849 "a man might dig a hole in the dry ravines, and so long as he left a shovel, pick, or crowbar to show that he still intended working it, he was safe from trespass" (Taylor 1850, 101). Taylor added that "his tools might remain there for months without being disturbed," but he may have been referring to the sanctity of the tools, not the claim (Taylor 1850, 101–102). There is no evidence about how long tools would hold a claim that was not being worked, but presumably it depended on how rich the diggings were and how many miners were eager to get claims there.

No source explains how this custom came about. That the claim was a hole suggests that it honored the miner's investment of labor. In some places, a hole would not pay until one got 12 feet down, and surely human nature, or even animal nature, would not accept a general rule that another party could jump in at that late point and take over.

Miners' meetings and rectangular, marked-out claims are first documented in 1849. The only description of an intermediate step between holes and square claims gives the impression that the transition was natural and unplanned: "As a general rule, it is a practice among the miners to leave each digger a sufficient space for a hole, upon which nobody has a right to encroach; from four to ten feet they allow among themselves to be sufficient for each, according as they may be more or less numerous and as digging may be more or less rich. A tool left in the hole in which a miner is working is a sign that it is not abandoned yet, and that nobody has a right to intrude there, and this regulation, which is adopted by silent consent of all, is generally complied with" (Wierzbicki 1933, 57). This passage suggests that all the essentials of a mining code were in place before actual miners' meetings and publications of miners' thoughts about the advantages of mining claims.

From the very beginning, the reversal of the usual power relationship between capital and labor was one of the wonders of the gold rush. William Thurston asserted that "labour has obtained the upper hand of capital, or rather, has become capital itself" (1849, 35); the *Californian* proclaimed on 14 August 1848 that the laboring class have now become the capitalists of the country. These two publications hoped to encourage emigration to California; their readers clearly believed that in the East, capital dominated labor, and that was a bad thing. But when they said that labor had the upper hand, they did not mean that labor made the rules to suit itself; they meant that as a matter of fact, only labor could generate wealth in the mines. Moreover, wages in the mines pulled up wages across the board. "The mechanic and artisan fixes his own price, and the capitalist is compelled from *necessity* to submit to that price, whatever it may be," James Collier, the newly arrived collector of customs, wrote on 13 November 1849 (1849, 30–31). As a result, equality simply happened. "We have no hired labourers—no servants; every man must black his own boots . . . This is a practical democracy—no theory—no talking about equality" (Thurston 1849, 40). Because the gold in California was distributed as it was, capital simply could not be used to advantage.

The capitalists, or those who thought like capitalists, realized from the very beginning that they could not get rich by using their money and other men's physical labor, at least not yet. "While gold can be found lying within a few inches of the earth's surface, and the only capital required to extract it consists in the capability to purchase a pick and a shovel, there is no need of combination; but when the hills are to be torn to their very bases . . . individuals must retire from the field, and make room for combined efforts" (Buffum 1850, 107). Similarly, Wierzbicki stated: "When this gold mania ceases to rage, individuals will abandon the mines; and then there will be a good opportunity for companies with heavy capital to step in" (1933, 34).[3]

That was exactly what happened. Thanks to technological innovations and cheap labor in the late 1850s, quartz mining and hydraulic mining became profitable. The few miners who were left were no longer able to support themselves on their own claims and had to hire themselves out to capital (Paul 1947). But by then, the men of the gold rush had taken their earnings or accepted their losses and moved on.

Calls for the sale of mineral lands came not from capitalists but from U.S. senators who understood nothing of all this. Presidents Polk (1845–1849) and Taylor (1849–1850) recommended dividing the gold-rich area into small parcels and leasing

---

[3] These words first appeared in *Alta California*, steamer edition, 31 August 1849, in a letter signed F. P. W. (Felix Paul Wierzbicki).

or selling them to miners (Ellison 1926; Yale 1867). A bill was duly debated in the U.S. Senate proposing the sale of mineral lands in California in lots not less than two acres each and at a minimum of $1.25 per acre (*Alta California*, 6 September 1849). Among the opponents to this ridiculous idea was Thomas Hart Benton, who argued that fee outright ownership of mineral land claims was unworkable. Because the gold was distributed irregularly, he argued, mining was more like hunting than like agriculture or any other steady industry. "For this purpose, it is not fee-simples in two acres that are wanted, but permits to hunt, and protection in the discovery when a deposit is found" (*Congressional Globe* 30th Congress, 2nd Session, 1849, 257).

A year later, the Senate debated another possible approach to the mineral lands in the form of a "bill for the temporary provision for the working and discovery of Gold Mines and Placers in California and for preserving order in the gold mine districts" (*Congressional Globe, Appendix* 31st Congress, 1st Session, 1850, 1362). The new proposal was to issue permits for mining at $1 per month, and to allow each miner to hold 30-feet square while he worked it in good faith. Selling the mining region was no longer an option; several senators stressed that they were against sale because if the land could be sold, "the poor will sell and the rich will buy; and by-and-by the necessary consequence will be, that the gold lands will be monopolized by a few persons" (*Congressional Globe, Appendix* 1850, 1371). At any rate, it looked that way from Washington.

The talk about selling mineral land alarmed some miners. Samuel McNeil, for instance, who was in the mines in 1849, said, "I shall blame Uncle Sam . . . if he is too hasty in selling the California gold lands in lots to speculators . . . that they may place it beyond the reach of our poorer classes, who, as true republicans, should have the full advantage of a republican government" (1957 [1850], 4). But the government never tried to introduce fee simple in mineral land, and even the idea of a $1 per month permit was never realized.

The California miners did not have to worry about big capital taking over the mines, and most of them did not worry about it. Fear of capital was not the reason for the claims system, which, in any case, evolved before the first miners' meetings took place. As in gold rushes around the world, capital had to wait for investment opportunities.

Variations on and Evasions of the Rules

It would be very difficult either to prove or to disprove that the mining-claim system was inevitable. One can, however, look at how much the rules varied from camp to camp and at attempts to evade or subvert the rules to see whether they ever resulted in a different form of property. It turns out that they did not.

First, none of the later diggings chose to adopt fee simple instead of claims. The codes enacted from 1849 to govern individual claims simply spelled out what custom had left hazy. Fifteen-by-fifteen-foot claims replaced holes; fixed work requirements replaced a vague good-faith standard; and stakes showing claim boundaries, or even registering the claim with a recorder, replaced tools left in a hole. The exact details varied from camp to camp, but the basic idea was the same.

Second, individuals or groups in California never managed to control a large area as a private domain. A few groups did attempt to dominate diggings by declaration or by assigning themselves very large claims, or by telling newcomers that all claims in the area were taken and they would have to move along (McDowell 2002; Shinn 1973 [1884]). In the early years, at least such attempts did not succeed for long.

There is one huge exception to the general rule that a group cannot control a particular diggings, namely, that one ethnic group frequently denies access to members of other ethnic groups, both in California and around the world. Not only did Americans collectively drive Indians, Spanish speakers, and Chinese from the mines, but individual American miners stole claims held by members of those ethnicities (Bancroft 1890; Hurtado 1988; Kanazawa 2005). Except for that aberration, however, the mines remained open to all.

There was one significant variation among codes where ideology could make a difference, namely that some codes restricted miners to only one claim at a time while others allowed them to purchase multiple claims on condition that they hire someone to meet the work requirements. The older and possibly default rule was one claim per person, as mentioned earlier, but many codes permitted a miner one claim by "location," that is, by staking off a regulation-sized bit of unclaimed land, and as many as he wanted by purchase (McDowell 2002, 34 n. 113). (To have let a miner hold multiple claims by location would have defeated the principle of limited claim size because the first miner on the scene of a new diggings could have "located" the whole area).

On the very few occasions on which miners who favored the one-claim rule explained their objection to the accumulation of claims, the reason was that it led to inequality. In 1852 the Miners and Settlers of Spring Valley urged the mining community "not to sanction the making of any new claims by men who already have enough," lest a mining aristocracy arise among them (Goodman 1994, 55–56). On a jocular note, Pringle Shaw wrote that he and his partner decided to jump a claim held by a man who "was well known to hold three or four claims in the same district." They were fairly confident that they would be able to keep the claim because "miners and mining laws are in most instances in radical opposition to all monopoly" (Shaw 1857, 132–133). In 1853 James H. Carson published a "Letter to the Miners of California" in the *Alta California*. He wrote that in the great majority of camps, the old rules of 1848, 1849, and 1850 had been replaced by regulations allowing miners to buy as many claims as they wanted. In those camps, Carson said, "New miners . . . find the ground all claimed, and they have no chance for a share" and "are forced to *hire out* for what they can get" (Carson 1853, 1). Even diggings with a one claim limit could be full, of course, but this was more likely to happen if existing miners could hold multiple claims.

Another problem with codes that let miners buy multiple claims, besides resentment against men who built up large holdings, was that a group of miners could use sham sales among themselves to circumvent the rule allowing only one claim by location. The Warren Hill code addressed this issue by stipulating that a purchaser had to "take a bill of sale, showing . . . the cost thereof attested by one or more witnesses," and that payment for the claim had to be "given in good faith and without collusion between the parties" (King 1885, 279–280).

It may have been abuses like this that led at least two diggings to change their rule to one claim per miner. In the summer of 1850, the miners at Murphy's Diggings voted "that from and after this date no person shall hold more than one claim" (Mining News, *Sonora Herald*, August 10, 1850, at 2). Presumably this meant that miners with several claims had to pick which one they wanted to keep, because the *Sonora Herald* advised miners who had claims at Murphy's to get back there if they did not want their claims to be jumped. Similarly, the first resolution of the 19 June 1850 code passed at Weaver Creek was that "[e]ach and every miner shall be entitled to hold one claim at a time and no more, either by purchase or otherwise from this time forth" (King 1885, 277).

Clearly, there was an ideological or principled difference between the one-claim rule and rules allowing multiple claims. In practice, however, the two regimes blurred into one another. Most importantly, the complexity of mining arrangements compromised the one-claim rule. In the worst case, a company of miners would take out extra claims in the names of fictitious "members." The codes allowed them to meet the work requirements for their individual claims by digging on one at a time, and if they were asked, they could always claim that the extra "members" were off running errands or whatever. The Warren Hill code also addressed this problem: "Whenever a company of miners take up or purchase claims and onely [*sic*] a part of said Company go before the Recorder. He may record the claim for the party present but shall refuse to record the claim of the absent party, unless the party present make affidavit of the existence of said partnership, which affidavit shall be taken by the recorder and made a matter of record" (King 1885, 280).

Then again, much of the rule bending was more benign and even necessary for miners who were short on cash and were happy to work for wages. In diggings where miners could buy multiple claims, an employer would offer work on one of his properties. If the local rules limited the employer to one claim, however, the same arrangement could be achieved by buying a second claim in the worker's name. One might think that the worker could take advantage and declare himself the owner (jump the claim he was working on), but according to Dame Shirley, that seldom, if ever, happened. "The person who is willing to be hired generally prefers to receive the six dollars per diem, of which he is *sure* in any case, to running the risk of a claim not proving valuable." And, in any case, "the holding of claims by proxy is considered rather as a carrying out of the spirit of the law than as an evasion of it" (Shirley 1922, 213).

Miners also got financial stakes in multiple claims through complicated buying and selling transactions. A claimholder selling to a buyer short on cash, for instance, might accept payment in installments from his earnings (Decker 1966). Alexander Barrington sold a rich claim at Shirt-Tale Hill for two-thirds of the future profits, a deal that would amount to rack-rent but for the fact that Barrington could probably have made a small fortune on a straight sale (McDowell 2002). Someone who made a number of such arrangements might in effect have shares in claims across the diggings without necessarily holding even one in his own name. The rules of Shirt-Tale Hill, which are not preserved, may have allowed such arrangements; but miners could very well have gotten away with them in one-claim diggings as well. In short, even when miners were officially limited to one claim each, some actually held interests in multiple claims.

At the same time, diggings that allowed miners to accumulate claims were not actually monopolized. No one had the money to buy up an entire mining district, and if he had, he would have lost it quickly because mining was a gamble. The difficulty of excluding other miners even from privately owned land in a modern state like Brazil suggests how powerful the claims system is.

In sum, the claim system not only reappeared in every new diggings, but also was largely resistant to cheating or manipulation. Although the bright-line rules of the codes were blurred in real life, only the one-claim rule was significantly eroded. That the system was so stable even though the rules were unofficial and there was no government suggests that there was no viable alternative to the claim system. American culture and values had little to do with it.

The argument of this chapter has been that the gold rush phenomenon is precultural or acultural: the same mining claim system has recurred around the world. In describing the California gold rush, Americans naturally used their own language, speaking in terms of the labor theory of value and a Jacksonian hostility to capitalists and speculators, but this was descriptive rather than normative.

There are both arcadian and nightmarish fairy tales of what the world would be like without private property. Gold rushes around the world have something of both. The California miners focused on the advantages of the mining claim system, where miners settle only in spots that are not already occupied, do not try to control more than they can use, and respect one another's claims during brief absences. Capitalists were more aware of the negative effects of individual, small scale mining: the wastefulness of working and reworking dirt, sometimes three times, over the course of the gold rush; the high wages that raised the cost of every enterprise; and the constantly changing population, consisting mainly of young men who had no intention of staying in the state. Both miners and capitalists realized, however, that temporary use rights would continue until the gold rush had run its course. When it was over, as Thomas Hart Benton said, "the sober industry will begin which enriches and ennobles a nation" (*Daily Alta California*, 6 September 1849, 2).

REFERENCES

Barry, William Jackson. 1879. *Up and down; or, Fifty years' colonial experiences in Australia, California, New Zealand, India, China, and the south Pacific*. London: S. Low, Marston, Searle, and Rivington.

Blackstone, William. 1827. *Commentary on the laws of England*. Vol. 1. New York: E. Duyckink, G. Long, Collins and Hannay, Collins and Co. and O. A. Roorbach.

Buffum, Edward Gould. 1850. *Six months in the gold mines*. Philadelphia: Lee and Blanchard.

Carson, James H. 1853. To the miners of California. *Daily Alta California*, March 19: 1.

Clay, Karen, and Gavin Wright. 2005. Order without law? Property rights during the California gold rush. *Explorations in Economic History* 42:155–183.

Cleary, David. 1990. *Anatomy of the Amazon gold rush*. Iowa City: University of Iowa Press.

Collier, James. 1849. *Letter to the Secretary of the Treasury W. M. Meredith, November 13, 1849*. 31st Cong., 1st sess., 1849–1850. H. Exdoc.17. Serial 573.

Colton, Walter. 1850. *Three years in California*. New York: A. S. Barnes and Co.

Congressional Globe. 1849. 30th Cong., 2nd sess.

Congressional Globe, Appendix. 1850. 31st Cong., 1st sess.

Decker, Peter. 1966. *The diaries of Peter Decker: Overland to California in 1849 and life in the mines, 1850–1851.* Georgetown, CA: Talisman Press.

Ellison, Joseph. 1926. *California and the nation, 1850–1869.* Berkeley: University of California Press.

Goodman, David. 1994. *Gold seeking: Victoria and California in the 1850s.* Stanford, CA: Stanford University Press.

Grätz, Tilo. 2002. Gold mining communities in northern Benin as semi-autonomous social fields. Working Paper No. 36. Halle/Saale: Max Planck Institute for Social Anthropology.

Halliday, J. S. 1999. *Rush for riches: Gold fever and the making of California.* Berkeley: University of California Press.

Hurtado, Albert L. 1988. *Indian survival on the California frontier.* New Haven, CT: Yale University Press.

Hutchings, J. M. [1853]. *The miner's ten commandments.* San Francisco: Sun Print.

Kanazawa, Mark. 2005. Immigration, exclusion, and taxation: Anti-Chinese legislation in gold rush California. *Journal of Economic History* 65:779–805.

King, Clarence. 1885. *The United States mining laws and regulations thereunder.* Washington, DC: U.S. Government Printing Office (compiled as part of the tenth census of the United States in 1880).

Larkin, Thomas Oliver. 1960. *The Larkin papers: Personal, business, and official correspondence of Thomas Oliver Larkin.* Vol. 7. Ed. George P. Hammond. Berkeley: University of California Press.

Lim, Louisa. 2009. Mongolians seek fortune in gold, but at a cost. NPR broadcast (September 7). http://www.npr.org/templates/story/story.php?storyId=112516360.

MacMillan, Gordon John. 1995. *At the end of the rainbow: Gold, land, and people in the Brazilian Amazon.* New York: Columbia University Press.

McCurdy, Charles W. 1976. Stephen J. Field and public land law development in California, 1850–1866. *Law and Society Review* 10:235–266.

McDowell, Andrea. 2002. From commons to claims: Property rights in the California gold rush. *Yale Journal of Law and the Humanities* 14:1–72.

McNeil, Samuel. 1957 [1850]. *McNeil's travels in 1849, to, through, and from the gold regions in California.* New Haven, CT: Yale University Press.

Owens, Kenneth N. 2005. *Gold rush saints.* Norman: University of Oklahoma Press.

Parkinson, John Barber. 1921. Memories of early Wisconsin and the gold mines. *Wisconsin Magazine of History* 5:119–141.

Paul, Rodman Wilson. 1947. *California gold: The beginning of mining in the Far West.* Cambridge, MA: Harvard University Press.

Romero, Simon. 2011. In Colombia, new gold rush fuels old conflict. *New York Times,* March 4: A1.

Ryan, Peter. 1991. *Black bonanza: A landslide of gold.* South Yarra: Hyland House Publishing.

Schuman, Michael. 2001. How big mining lost a fortune in Indonesia: The locals moved in. *Wall Street Journal,* May 16: 1, 8.

Shaw, Pringle. 1857. *Ramblings in California.* Toronto: J. Bain.

Shinn, Charles Howard. 1973 [1884]. *Land laws of mining districts.* Johns Hopkins University Studies in Historical and Political Science, 2nd Ser. No. XII. Baltimore: N. Murray, publication agent, Johns Hopkins University.

———. 1885. *Mining camps: A study in American frontier government.* New York: Charles Scribner's Sons.

Shirley, Dame [Louise Amelia Knapp Smith Clappe]. 1922. *The Shirley letters from California mines in 1851–1852.* San Francisco: T. C. Russell.

Taylor, Bayard. 1850. *Eldorado; or, Adventures in the path of empire.* 2nd ed. New York: G. P. Putnam.

Thurston, William. 1849. *Guide to the gold regions of upper California.* London: J. and D. A. Darling.

Turrill, Charles B. 1876. *California notes.* San Francisco: E. Bosqui and Co.

Umbeck, John R. 1981. *A theory of property rights, with application to the California gold rush.* Ames: Iowa State University Press.

Vail, John. 1995. All that glitters: The Mt. Kare gold rush and its aftermath. In *Papuan border-lands: Huli, Duna, and Ipili perspectives on the Papua New Guinea highlands*, ed. Aletta Bier-sack, 343–374. Ann Arbor: University of Michigan Press.

Werthmann, Katja. 2000. Gold rush in West Africa: The appropriation of "natural" resources; Non-industrial gold mining in south-western Burkina Faso. *Sociologus* 50(1):90–104.

———. 2008. "Frivolous squandering": Consumption and redistribution in mining camps. In *Dilemmas of development: Conflicts of interest and their resolutions in modernizing Africa*, eds. Jon Abbing and André van Dokkum, 60–76. Leiden: African Studies Center.

Wierzbicki, Felix Paul. 1933. *California as it is and as it may be*. San Francisco: Grabhorn Press.

Yale, Gregory. 1867. *Legal titles to mining claims and water rights in California*. San Francisco: A. Roman and Company.

Zerbe, Richard O., Jr., and C. Leigh Anderson. 2001. Culture and fairness in the development of institutions in the California gold fields. *Journal of Economic History* 61:114–143.

Commentary

MARK T. KANAZAWA

In this insightful chapter, Andrea McDowell has a number of things right about the California gold rush. This is not surprising, because she is a careful scholar who has done her homework. She is conversant with much of the relevant scholarly literature on gold rush mining rights, especially for California, and she has taken seriously the useful evidence contained in a number of contemporary accounts of the California gold rush, including the eyewitness accounts of miners who were there. This chapter asks interesting questions and reflects careful consideration and synthesis of a wide variety of evidence from both primary and secondary sources that do not always seem consistent. Coming up with a coherent story of the California gold rush is a challenging assignment, and McDowell has fulfilled it remarkably well. However, this work is unlikely to be the final word on the interpretation of mining rights in the California gold rush because it leaves certain important questions inadequately addressed. I offer three particularly important questions and provide some thoughts on each one.

When Did the California Gold Rush End?

Even though McDowell and every gold rush scholar offers an answer to this question, I believe that it cannot be answered with a specific cutoff year (in McDowell's case, 1852) without doing violence to what we mean by the gold rush. The problem is that regardless of the exact dating of the gold rush period, it was followed by a period of a more mature mining industry that no one wants to, or should, include as part of the gold rush. McDowell makes the distinction between small-scale, individual mining and large-scale mining and defines the former as the "gold rush." But there were all sorts of features of the period well before the end of 1852 that most people would consider "nonrushy," including townlike settlements exhibiting permanence in the gold fields as early as 1848, fairly large-scale river mining as early as 1849, capitalists hiring wage labor, and significant technological advances in placer mining. More generally, no matter what definition of "gold rush" one employs, it will not conform neatly to any particular period. This has created scholarly confusion in understanding the nature of gold rush mining rights, which were probably driven, as I will argue later, by a combination of generalized scarcity, economies of scale, and enforcement costs, all of which varied over time and from place to place within this early period. The punch line is that the precise combination that obtained at any particular time and place led to very specific and distinctive economic pressures driving the formation of mining rights.

How Much of Gold Rush Mining Rights Creation Was Driven by Economics?

The basic answer is, a lot, but this does not emerge clearly as an important determining factor in McDowell's account. For example, the vast majority of gold seekers from outside the state did not start arriving in California until the spring of 1849 at the very earliest. Given this fact, no scholar who ascribes to a scarcity theory of property rights formation should be surprised that 1848 witnessed very little explicit mining rights formation because there were relatively few miners chasing after the gold, and new discoveries were being made all the time. At the same time, the known isolated examples of anything like formal claims in 1848 only confirm that the growing scarcity of gold relative to demand contributed to the creation of something like formalized rights, because these claims were located right where, in all likelihood, gold first began to be significantly depleted: along the American and Yuba rivers, the first sites of major mining activity (McDowell 2002). Second, temporal changes in provisions in mining codes relating to claim size, the number of claims that could be held by individual miners, the ability of individual miners to associate to engage in mining cooperatively, and provisions governing water use are broadly consistent with the ongoing, rapid technological advances that are known to have been happening at the time, which resulted in growing economies of scale and a concurrent increase in the minimum efficient scale of a mining operation. Mining-code provisions, including those in the codes before 1853, cannot be fairly interpreted without taking this trend into consideration.

The only other economic factor I will mention here is that McDowell's entire story is a testament to the importance of enforcement costs, some of which McDowell makes obvious. However, it is not clear that enforcement costs will be equally controlling in different situations, which raises the question whether, for example, all placer rushes are indeed the same, a central claim of her chapter. Simple geography may, for example, make it easier for some governments to control mining regions within their borders (Allen 2007). In addition, politics may come into play in a complex fashion to create differential challenges to governments seeking to enforce their rights to their public lands (Kanazawa 1996), as the government tried to do in California.

How Do We Interpret the Emergence of Use Rights Rather than Property Rights?

McDowell considers this distinction quite important, arguing that mining rights were not really anything like full-fledged property rights, but rather were comparable to the tenuous rights of Starbucks patrons to the tables at which they have planted themselves. There is a question, however, whether this is in fact an actual distinction with real normative content. It could be argued, for example, that gold rush mining rights combined rights to exclude others with all sorts of restrictions imposed on the exercise of that right, an arrangement that serves the important function of economizing on the cost of measuring the complex attributes of a mining right (Smith 2002). If so, there is nothing particularly unusual or surprising about the way in which mining rights emerged.

REFERENCES

Allen, Douglas W. 2007. Information sharing during the Klondike gold rush. *Journal of Economic History* 67:4(December):944–967.

Kanazawa, Mark T. 1996. Possession is nine points of the law: The political economy of early public land disposal. *Explorations in Economic History* 33:2(April):227–249.

McDowell, Andrea G. 2002. From customs to claims: Property rights in the California gold rush. *Yale Journal of Law and the Humanities* 14:1–72.

Smith, Henry E. 2002. Exclusion versus governance: Two strategies for delineating property rights. *Journal of Legal Studies* 31:2(June):S453–S487.

Air

Property Creation by Regulation

Rights to Clean Air and Rights to Pollute

DANIEL H. COLE

overnment regulations impose on private property rights, as libertarian schol-
G ars remind us (Claeys 2003; DeAlessi 1980; Ely 1998; Epstein 1985). At the
same time, they also protect property rights by controlling negative externalities
created by neighbors (Karkkainen 1994). Indeed, in many cases, the same regulations that restrict property also protect it (much as common-law nuisance liability
protects and limits property at the same time).[1] Zoning laws (or subdivision regulations) may limit my right to develop my property as I see fit, for example, by pro-
hibiting gas stations from my neighborhood; but that same regulation also protects
my property by similarly restricting my neighbors. Less well understood and appreciated is the fact that government regulations can actually create property rights—
private, public, and/or common—in resources where property relations previously
did not exist or were underdetermined.[2]

This chapter, which elaborates on some ideas sketched in Cole (2002), examines
regulatory tools governments have used to convert the atmosphere from a nonproperty, open-access resource into public property and, to a more limited extent,
private property. The purpose is not to argue normatively that regulatory creation
of property is preferable to other methods by which property rights are established
(under either positive or natural-law theories),[3] but merely to establish that regulation

---

[1] Zoning may or may not be a particularly efficient means of limiting and/or protecting property rights. A size-
able literature exists on that issue (Ellickson 1973; Fischel 1978; 1980; 1987; Maser, Riker, and Rosett 1977), but it
is not relevant to the thesis of this chapter.

[2] Throughout this chapter, the phrase "property rights" is used as Cole and Ostrom define it in the introduction to
this volume. The term "right" is meant in its strict Hohfeldian sense as a correlative of "duty." To say that one person
or group possesses a "right" to some asset or resource, at least one other person must possess a corresponding duty to
avoid interfering with the right holder's lawful use of that asset or resource. The term "property" is a purely descriptive
appendage to "right" that distinguishes rights in things (including incorporeal things) from "personal rights," "human
rights," and so on. Other scholars define "property rights" differently, of course. Merrill and Smith (2001), for example,
define "property rights" in a way that requires the word "property" to do more work. They distinguish between property rights and contract rights, for example, because property rights are *in rem* (that is, in the thing itself) and supposedly apply against the entire world (a legal conceit if ever there was one), whereas contract rights apply only to the
parties to the contract. Merrill and Smith's definition reflects a venerable juridical view of property rights that arguably has grown obsolete as property rights have become increasingly malleable, thanks to instruments such as trusts,
and have been attenuated by various kinds of regulations, easements, servitudes, and other interests.

[3] This chapter also does not attempt to distinguish bad from good, or legitimate from illegitimate, regulatory
institutions, although this is admittedly an important concern, especially for developing countries. The focus is
on the experience of property creation by regulation in the United States and, to a lesser extent, the United Kingdom

both protects and sometimes creates property rights. The implications of this observation for property theory and jurisprudence, particularly in the realm of so-called regulatory takings law, are potentially significant.

The first part of the chapter compares two conceptions of regulation: (1) regulation as a governmental imposition on private property rights; and (2) regulation as a sometimes preferable alternative to the tort system for vindicating existing public and private property rights. The argument is made that the second conception, although not controversial among economists (at least since Coase 1960), is underappreciated by jurists and at least some justices on the U.S. Supreme Court. That part concludes with a call for property theorists to pay more attention to the role regulation serves in protecting and vindicating public, as well as private, property rights. The second part of the chapter argues, in the context of rights in airspace, that regulation not only vindicates and protects existing property rights, but creates property where none previously existed. In contrast to Roman law conceptions of the air as *res communes* and common law (or *faux* common law) conceptions of land boundaries extending up to the heavens, the historical record is clear that, prior to the last decades of the nineteenth century, the air was generally treated as *res nullius* or open-access, with only limited exceptions for cases where the pollution, over-hanging buildings, etc., interfered with the use and enjoyment of land-based activities. After the onset of the industrial revolution, which greatly increased the amount of pollution emitted into the air, the property status of the atmosphere began to change. Governments started to exercise sovereign authority over the airspace, initially in order to control aviation and later to regulate pollution. These sovereign acts implicitly, and sometimes explicitly, created and protected public property rights in clean air. More recently, governments have begun to privatize, albeit to a limited extent, property rights (notwithstanding government assertions that tradable permits are not property) to pollute the public's air. The chapter concludes by showing how the analysis might be expanded to marine resources, further strengthening its implications for property jurisprudence, particularly for the regulatory takings doctrine. Among those implications is the need for further development of theories of public property to complement existing theories of private and common property.

The Conventional Treatment of Regulation in Property Jurisprudence (and Its Problems)

Regulation is, generally speaking, a proactive alternative to the reactive tort system (Boyer and Porrini 2004; Glaeser and Shleifer 2003; Posner 1998; Shavell 1984: Wittman 1977).[4] Both systems share the ostensible purpose of preventing or internalizing the costs economic actors impose on neighbors, proximate or remote.[5] Some

---

and Europe, where property, market, and governmental institutions are generally well developed, functional, and adaptively efficient.

[4] Tort cases usually require proof of harm and therefore operate after the fact of harm. However, in rare cases involving so-called anticipatory or prospective nuisances, harm may be enjoined before the fact. Moreover, tort remedies generally have prospective incentive effects (Cole and Grossman 2005).

[5] Public choice theory has shed much light on the potential ulterior motives of regulators (Mueller 1989; Olson 1965) but has not focused nearly as much on the potential ulterior motives of judges (Beerman 1991).

jurists, however, tend to treat the two approaches to that goal as fundamentally different in kind. While tort suits for nuisance or trespass generally are presumed to vindicate personal and property rights violated by the actions (externalities) of neighbors (Cole and Grossman 2005; Posner 1998), regulations sometimes are portrayed too simply as government impositions on the property rights of regulated actors (Ogus 1994). Richard Epstein, for example, has claimed that "all regulations . . . are takings of private property *prima facie* compensable by the state" (1985, 95).[6]

Epstein's theory of property and takings has substantially influenced the U.S. Supreme Court's doctrine of "regulatory takings," which Justice Holmes invented (roughly speaking) in *Pennsylvania Coal Co. v. Mahon*, 260 U.S. 393 (1922).[7] Under that doctrine as expounded in subsequent cases, states must compensate regulated landowners for regulations that greatly diminish the value of their lands unless the externalities created by those regulated properties amount to common-law nuisances as in *Lucas v. South Carolina Coastal Council*, 505 U.S. 1003 (1992).

As regulatory takings doctrine has evolved, particularly in several cases where privately owned lands meet publicly owned waters,[8] the Court has shortchanged very real public property rights at issue by focusing exclusively on the complainant's private property rights.[9] This myopia has led to perverse arguments and, quite possibly, unjust outcomes. For example, in *Palazzolo v. State of Rhode Island*, 533 U.S. 606, 637 (2001), Justice Scalia, writing in concurrence, labeled the State of Rhode Island a "thief" for a claimed "regulatory taking" of tidal marshlands to which it in fact held legal title.[10]

Contrast the U.S. Supreme Court's relative disregard of public property rights under recent regulatory takings doctrine with the Wisconsin Supreme Court's famous ruling in *Just v. Marinette County*, 56 Wis. 2d 7 (1972). In that case, which involved regulation of dredging and filling of wetlands adjacent to navigable water bodies, the court ruled that even though the regulation limited the extent to which

[6] To be fair, Epstein (1985) recognizes that regulations also benefit property owners by protecting them. Thus, the presumption he creates in favor of compensation is rebuttable if the regulation at issue creates reciprocal benefits that offset its costs. That said, the presumption operates in the first instance as treating regulation as an imposition.

[7] Holmes hinted at the idea of compensable regulatory takings several years earlier, while he was a justice on the Supreme Judicial Court of Massachusetts, in *Rideout v. King*, 19 N.E. 390 (1889). However, the *Pennsylvania Coal* case constituted the first ruling by any court that an ostensible police power regulation could amount to a taking if it "went too far" in diminished the value of property rights. Holmes's diminution-in-value test has no basis in either the text or the original understanding of the Fifth Amendment's takings clause (Cole 2002). But, then, Holmes never claimed to be either a textualist or an originalist.

[8] Those cases included, in addition to *Lucas*, *Nolan v. California Coastal Commission*, 483 U.S. 825 (1987), *Dolan v. City of Tigard*, 512 U.S. 374 (1994); *Palazzolo v. Rhode Island*, 533 U.S. 606 (2001); *Tahoe-Sierra Preservation Council, Inc. v. Tahoe Regional Planning Agency*, 535 U.S. 302 (2002); and *Stop the Beach Renourishment v. Florida Department of Environmental Management*, 2010 U.S. Lexis 4971 (2010).

[9] Most recently, the Court paid more attention to preexisting public rights in *Stop the Beach Renourishment*. In that case, the Court unanimously upheld the State of Florida's assertion of property rights in artificially renourished (by avulsion as opposed to accretion) beaches above the mean high-tide line. It remains to be seen whether this ruling reflects a more general acknowledgment by members of the Court that public property rights deserve as much consideration as private property rights in takings claims where land meets water.

[10] The issue in *Palazzolo* was land use regulation that prevented the owner of oceanfront property from filling and building on coastal marshlands. Because those marshlands were subject to tidal flows, they were in fact owned by the state. State ownership became an issue, however, only after the case was remanded to the state courts. The main issue before the Supreme Court ruled was whether the petitioner could maintain a regulatory takings claim based on regulations that preceded his ownership. The Court was, however, briefed on the ownership issue, and had it decided the case on that basis in the first place, it would not have needed to reach the issue of compensation for a taking that occurred before the claimant's ownership.

the private landowner could develop his land, there was no compensable taking. Writing for a unanimous court, Chief Justice Hallows stated:

> [W]e think it is not an unreasonable exercise of [the police power] to prevent harm to *public rights* by limiting the use of private property to its natural uses . . . This is not a case of an isolated swamp unrelated to a navigable lake or stream, the change of which would cause no harm to *public rights*. Lands adjacent to or near navigable waters exist in a special relationship to the state. 56 Wisc. 2d at 17–18. (emphasis added)

The important point from *Just* is not that public property rights trumped private property rights; the outcome of the case is less important than the fact that the court properly treated it as a boundary dispute between privately owned lands and publicly owned waters.[11] I will return to this point later, when assessing the implications of a property theory that treats regulations seriously as a creator and protector of property.

To the extent that tort remedies and regulations share the goal of protecting some owners' property against unreasonable harm caused by other property owners' activities, such starkly differential judicial treatment of the two approaches seems inappropriate and even illogical. This is not to deny that regulations impose costs on the owners of regulated property, but so do common-law court rulings that hold landowners liable for nuisance or trespass. As Coase (1960) has noted, disputes over property are not about presumably innocent landowners seeking to vindicate harm/ costs externalized by neighboring wrongdoers. Rather, they are bilateral or multilateral (that is, social-cost) conflicts over entitlements to resources that amount potentially to zero-sum games between two or more landowners, each of whom may be using his land in a perfectly lawful way. Whichever party receives the entitlement, the outcome inevitably imposes costs on the other party (or parties).

Coase's observation is no less true of common-law tort decisions than of public law regulatory resolutions: both create or vindicate some owners' property rights while imposing costs on others. This observation is borne out in two classic property cases (among many others): *Amphitheaters, Inc. v. Portland Meadows,* 184 Or. 336 (1948), and *Miller v. Schoene,* 276 U.S. 272 (1928). In the first, the Oregon Supreme Court resolved a property conflict using common law; in the second, the supreme court upheld a state regulatory law that resolved the conflict. The institutional and organizational approaches differed, but the purpose was fundamentally the same.

In *Portland Meadows,* an auto racetrack operated next door to an outdoor movie theater. In order to maximize revenues, weekday races were held in the evenings (after work for most potential customers), which of course required the use of lights. Despite substantial efforts by the racetrack owner to reduce the flow of light from the track to the neighboring drive-in theater, the lights interfered with the theater's operations. Both of the neighboring land uses were fully lawful, but they were

---

[11] Legal scholars and other social scientists have yet to develop a workable normative theory for resolving such boundary disputes (in which cases should public property trump private property, and vice versa?). This problem is symptomatic of the absence of a more general theory of public property, a problem addressed later in this chapter.

incompatible. The theater owner sued, and the Oregon Supreme Court ruled in favor of the defendant, on the grounds that the drive-in theater's use of its property was abnormally light sensitive. The theater, thus, had to bear costs of either building a high enough fence to block out light from the racetrack or converting its use of the land to something less light sensitive.[12] This outcome of the judicial process was not necessarily less expensive for the theater owner than an alternative public regulation placing the burden of excluding light on outdoor movie theaters. Had the case gone the other way, the racetrack owner would have incurred costs roughly equivalent to those resulting from a public regulation requiring landowners to fence in light.[13]

In *Miller v. Schoene*, the State of Virginia enacted a regulatory law requiring the destruction of infected cedar trees to prevent the spread of cedar rust disease, a condition that is harmless for cedar trees but toxic for apple trees. The legislation's decision to entitle apple trees over cedar trees was purely commercial. Apples are an important cash crop in Virginia, while cedar trees are grown mainly for ornamental use. Cedar tree owners challenged the state law as a compensable taking under the Fifth Amendment (as applied to the states by the Fourteenth Amendment). The Supreme Court rejected that claim, holding that the regulation was a legitimate police power regulation. Planting either cedar or apple trees is a perfectly lawful activity in Virginia, but when cedar trees and apple orchards are planted in close proximity to one another, they are incompatible, just like the racetrack and the drive-in movie theater in the *Portland Meadows* case. The main difference in the treatment of the two disputes is that *Portland Meadows* was resolved in court pursuant to common-law rules, while *Miller v. Schoene* was settled by the state legislature (subject to subsequent judicial challenge). The cedar rust problem in Virginia placed the state in a position in which it really had no choice but to entitle one kind of tree over the other. Even if it had chosen to do nothing, that would have constituted an implicit grant of entitlement to cedar tree growers, at substantial cost to apple growers. By deciding, instead, to regulate infected cedar trees, the state decided that cedar tree growers, rather than apple growers, should bear the costs.[14] The state, not unreasonably, decided to regulate cedar trees because that resulted (in the state's estimation) in the lowest net costs (a Coasean solution). In other words, Virginia deemed cedar tree growers (rightly or wrongly) to be the lower-cost avoiders

---

[12] Whether the court achieved the most efficient solution in *Portland Meadows* is unclear. According to Coase (1960), the efficient ruling would put the onus on the least-cost avoider of the harm. The fact that the racetrack owner had already undertaken some efforts to avoid the harm suggests, but does not necessarily mean, that the theater owner had become the least-cost avoider. Instead of undertaking a real Coasean analysis, however, the court simply invoked the common-law doctrine of abnormally sensitive use to determine the outcome, perhaps because of its intuition that the theater owner was the lower-cost avoider of the harm. Indeed, the doctrine of abnormally sensitive use might be only one device (among others) courts employ to avoid imposing liability on defendants in cases where plaintiffs seem more likely to be lower-cost avoiders.

[13] This situation is analogous to the case of alternative rules requiring the fencing-in or fencing-out of cattle in agricultural areas (Ellickson 1991). Of course, as Ellickson points out, the official legal rules do not necessarily constitute the rules in use or determine the outcome of disputes.

[14] In the mythical world of the "Coase theorem," where all the assumptions of neoclassical economic theory hold and transacting is costless, state allocation of the entitlement would have been both unnecessary and irrelevant because cedar tree growers and apple tree growers would have costlessly contracted their way to the maximally efficient outcome. Unfortunately, despite the hopes and dreams of many property scholars, transaction costs are ubiquitous and often quite high in the real world. Coase himself understands this; many self-described Coaseans still do not.

of the harm.[15] Did the state's regulation impose costs on them in excess of a court ruling holding that infected cedar trees constituted a private or public nuisance? If a court held that infected cedar trees did not constitute a nuisance, would that ruling have imposed no costs on owners of apple orchards?

The purpose of pointing out similarities in the respective purposes of court decisions and regulations with regard to property is not to argue that the two mechanisms are necessarily equivalent in their effects, nor to argue that regulation is generally preferable to common-law judgments. The preferability of one approach to the other is likely to be circumstantial. For instance, common-law remedies might well be more efficient than regulation in small-numbers cases, such as *Portland Meadows*, and other cases in which transaction costs are likely to be fairly low. Regulation tends to be preferable where transaction costs are higher, for example, in larger-numbers cases such as *Miller v. Schoene*. As Coase observes in "The Problem of Social Cost":

> There is no reason why, on occasion . . . governmental administrative regulation should not lead to an improvement in economic efficiency. This would seem particularly likely when, as is normally the case with the smoke nuisance, a large number of people is involved and when therefore the costs of handling the problem through the market or the firm may be high. (1960, 18)

A year earlier, in his slightly less famous article "The Federal Communications Commission," Coase wrote in a similar vein:

> When the transfer of rights has to come about as a result of market transactions carried out between large numbers of people or organizations acting jointly, the process of negotiation may be so difficult and time-consuming as to make such transfers a practical impossibility. It may be costly to discover who it is that is causing the trouble. And, when it is not in the interest of any single person or organization to bring suit, the problems involved in arranging joint actions represent a further obstacle. As a practical matter, the market may become too costly to operate.
>
> In these circumstances it may be preferable impose special regulations (whether embodied in a statute or brought about as a result of the rulings of an administrative agency). Such regulations state what people must or must not do. When this is done, the law directly determines the location of economic activities, methods of production, and so on. (1959, 29)

Coase acknowledges the potential inefficiencies of such "special regulations," resulting, for example, from public choice pressures on the "political organization" (1959, 29). However,

> This merely means that, before turning to special regulations, one should tolerate a worse functioning market than would otherwise be the case. It does not mean that there should be no such regulation. Nor should it be thought that, because *some*

---

[15] *Miller v. Schoene* has been of great continuing interest to legal scholars and economists (Buchanan 1972; Buchanan and Samuels 1975; Fischel 2007; Griffin 1981; Mercuro and Ryan 1980; Samuels 1971; 1972).

rights are determined by regulation, there cannot be others which can be modified by contract. That zoning and other regulations apply to houses does not mean that there should not be private property in houses. Businessmen usually find themselves both subject to regulation and possessed of rights which may be transferred or modified by contracts with others. (Coase 1959, 29–30; emphasis added)

Other factors besides transaction costs, including deadweight costs, prospects of regulatory or judicial capture,[16] information asymmetries, and the potential for judgment-proof defendants, also can affect the choice between *ex ante* regulation and *ex post* liability (Boyer and Porrini 2004; Shavell 1984; White and Wittman 1983). And, of course, the two systems for vindicating or delineating property rights often are used in combination (Beckmann, Soregaroli, and Wesseler 2010).

Whatever reasons might exist for preferring one approach over the other in specific circumstances, it makes little sense for courts to treat regulations as something fundamentally different in kind from common-law remedies. Instead, property theory and jurisprudence should treat regulation with greater dignity as a legitimate means of vindicating or enforcing private, public, and common property rights.[17]

Creating Property out of Thin Air by Regulation and Other Acts of Sovereignty

Regulations and similar sovereign acts not only protect some property rights while imposing on others, but also can create property rights where they did not previously exist or were unclear. However controversial this assertion may seem at first blush, a simple uncontroversial example (unrelated to rights in the air) should mollify skeptics, at least to some extent.

The takings doctrine stems from language in the Fifth Amendment to the U.S. Constitution, which is a kind of meta- or superstatute (Howard 1968; Wood 1999).[18]

---

[16] Regulatory capture is a familiar category (Huntington 1952; Laffont and Tirole 1991). Judicial capture is less so, but only because too many legal scholars casually presume that at least in the United States, judges are independent and not subject to bias for or against parties appearing before them (Waldron notes that political scientists, "unlike law professors, . . . have the good grace to match a cynical model of legislating with an equally cynical model of appellate and Supreme Court adjudication" [1999b, 31]). The specter of judicial capture arose most recently in the wake of the British Petroleum Deepwater oil spill. After the spill, the Obama administration imposed a six-month moratorium on deepwater oil drilling. Various oil companies and associated service industries challenged that moratorium in federal court. Judge Martin L. C. Feldman of the U.S. District Court in New Orleans overturned the moratorium. Whether or not his decision was correct as a matter of law, many were troubled by Judge Feldman's substantial financial ties to the oil and gas industry, including investments in several firms that potentially benefited from his decision. Charlie Savage, "Drilling Ban Blocked; U.S. Will Issue New Order," *New York Times*, June 22, 2010, http://www.nytimes.com/2010/06/23/us/23drill.html. The Obama administration appealed Judge Feldman's ruling to the Fifth Circuit U.S. Court of Appeals. According to a report by the Alliance for Justice, "Judicial Gusher: The Fifth Circuit's Ties to Oil," fourteen of the twenty judges (including four senior judges) on that court, which covers Louisiana, Texas, and Mississippi, have significant financial ties to the oil and gas industry, with individual judges holding investments worth up to several million dollars. Before their appointments to the bench, eleven current Fifth Circuit judges represented oil and gas companies and/or worked at firms that specialized in oil and gas law; http://www.afj.org/about-afj/press/fifth_circuit_judges_report.pdf.

[17] This argument about taking regulation seriously as a means of vindicating existing private and public property is broadly consistent with the theory of legislation offered by Waldron (1999a).

[18] Eskridge and Ferejohn (2001) use the phrase "super-statute" to describe legislative enactments that are not constitutions but acquire some kind of constitutional force. That is not the meaning here.

The Fifth Amendment's takings clause created an enforceable right of landowners to prevent government expropriations that are either (1) not for public use[19] or (2) uncompensated.[20] No court created (or "discovered") those rights, along with the corresponding duties imposed on governments. Congress created them in 1789, and they were constitutionalized two years later upon ratification by three-fourths of the states. By literally regulating the government's exercise of eminent domain, the Fifth Amendment's takings clause created property rights and duties that had not previously existed anywhere in the world. This interpretation of the takings clause should not be controversial. It stands as a prime example of how regulation can create property.

This section explores two specific and interrelated contexts in which regulatory regimes have, either expressly or in effect, converted nonproperty air resources to private or public property (or public/private hybrids): (1) the implicit conversion of nonproperty atmosphere to public property through regulations and other acts of sovereignty; and (2) the subsequent conversion of some of that public property to private property in regulatory programs, such as the Clean Air Act's emissions-trading Acid Rain Program.

Air Rights at Common Law

A legal tradition dating back to Justinian's *Institutes* (Grapel 1994 [1855]) considers the air to be the common property of all, an open-access resource from which no person or state can exclude any other. Influenced by Roman law, the common law of England and Wales generally treated the atmosphere as an open-access commons, even where air pollution was involved. Polluters were limited only to the extent their emissions provably harmed people or property on the ground (Morag-Levine 2003).

By the later Middle Ages, however, a new legal conception of air as private property (*res privatae*) arose to compete with the Roman law conception of the atmosphere. Embodied in the maxim *cujus est solum, eius est usque ad caelum et ad inferos*, private property boundaries extended upward from the ground to the heavens and downward to the depths of the earth.[21] Although the maxim is sometimes misattributed to Roman law,[22] it was first articulated in the thirteenth century by the Italian lawyer Franciscus Accursius of Bologna (1225–1293), who lectured in

---

[19] The Supreme Court presently interprets the public use requirement of the takings clause to prohibit government exercises of eminent domain for purely private uses or purposes. See *Kelo v. City of New London*, 545 U.S. 469 (2005). The fact that the Court's interpretation is controversial should have no bearing on the fact that the takings clause itself creates rights in property by regulating (to whatever extent) government power.

[20] The Fifth Amendment also recognized, by necessary implication, the government's power of eminent domain, which can be thought of as, ostensibly at least, a public property right, albeit one that might exist regardless of a written constitution, as an inherent power of government (S. Reynolds 2010). Certainly, many jurists and judges have accepted it as such (Stoebuck 1972).

[21] Functionally similar phrases have been found in legal systems stretching from Portugal to Turkey (Banner 2008; Nijeholt 1910). However, in several European countries, including Switzerland and Germany, the extent of property rights above and below the ground was early on expressly restricted to areas that "may be of productive value" to the landowner (Banner 2008; Valentine 1910b, 96).

[22] According to Roman law, mines and treasures in what we now call the subsurface estate belonged to either the monarch or the finder, depending on the circumstances, rather than the landowner. Indeed, the landowner did not necessarily control any space above or below the surface of the earth (Banner 2008). More generally, the air was *res communes* (the common property of all) according to Roman law.

law at Oxford from 1275 to 1276 at the invitation of Edward I (*Bocardo SA v. Star Energy UK Onshore Ltd. and another,* [2009] EWCA Civ. 579).[23] In recent decades, some English jurists have mistakenly denied that it ever became part of the common law (*Bocardo*). Lord Wilberforce, writing for the Privy Council in the 1974 case *Commissioner for Railways v. Valuer General,* [1974] 1 A.C. 328 at 351H–352A, 3 All E.R. 268, [1973] 2 W.L.R. 1021, stated that "so sweeping, unscientific and unpractical a doctrine is unlikely to appeal to the common law mind." Lord Wilberforce's skepticism notwithstanding, there is no doubt that the maxim had a life in the common law of both England and the United States. The only real issue is whether it described actual legal rules in use or was a mere dictum.

The maxim's incorporation into the common law of England dates to Justice Coke, who quoted it approvingly in the late sixteenth century to resolve boundary disputes concerning overhanging buildings (Banner 2008). Coke also quoted the maxim in *Coke upon Littleton,* the first volume of his *Institutes of the Lawes of England* (1628–1644), but there he hedged a bit, noting that "the earth has, in law, a *great extent* upwards" (Coke 1832 [circa 1628], 4a; emphasis added). In fact, Coke, like later judges who cited the *cujus est solum* maxim, was practically concerned not with the maximal limits of property rights above and below the ground but with the immediately useful regions of airspace and subsurface. Beyond the relatively shallow areas above and below the ground that were actually in dispute in the cases Coke decided, his use of the maxim was hyperbole (Sprankling 2008). Perhaps most tellingly, Coke did not invoke the maxim when he decided *Aldred's Case,* [1611] 77 Eng. Rep. 816, the first common-law nuisance case to impose liability for air pollution.

After Coke, the *cujus est solum* maxim virtually disappeared from common-law jurisprudence until the end of the eighteenth century, when William Blackstone restated it with emphasis in his *Commentaries on the Laws of England*: "Land hath also, in its legal signification, an indefinite extent, upwards as well as downwards" (1979 [1766], 18). Blackstone inaccurately argued that the maxim was a bedrock principle of the common law of property, as exemplified in "every day's experience in mining countries." As Sprankling (2008) has noted, during Blackstone's own lifetime mines rarely reached a depth of even one thousand feet—hardly the center of the earth. With respect to airspace, Blackstone referred only to Justice Coke's cases of overhanging buildings, which rarely were more than a few stories high—hardly the heavens.

In the United Kingdom, Blackstone's resurrection of the *cujus est solum* maxim did not significantly affect the common law; the maxim was cited in only a handful of U.K. cases and treatises (Sprankling 2008). But Blackstone's outsized influence on the U.S. common law (Boorstin 1941) led to the widespread judicial quotation of the maxim in American case law (Banner 2008). As the Sixth Circuit U.S. Court of Appeals noted in *Swetland v. Curtiss Airports Corp.,* 55 F.2d 201, 202 (1932), "The popularity of the phrase with the courts of this country is attested by its repetition in the law reports of practically every state." Most courts quoted the phrase in the context of disputes over subsurface minerals; only rarely was it invoked in cases

---

[23] Others have asserted that the maxim was first articulated nearly one hundred years later by another Italian jurist, Gino da Pistoia (Banner 2008).

134 ■ Daniel H. Cole

involving property rights in the air. In virtually all cases, it was stated as a dictum rather than as a literal rule of law.

In cases involving alleged trespass on airspace, courts in both the United States and the United Kingdom early on limited property rights to the immediately usable atmosphere above the ground. This created a line-drawing problem: what part of the air was immediately usable? For the most part, however, the maxim was cited by judges "in connection with occurrences common to the era, such as overhanging branches or eaves" (*Swetland*, 55 F.2d at 203). However, as technological innovations, such as electrical wires, elevated railways, and skyscrapers, altered the extent to which airspace was usable, the line-drawing problems recurred (Banner 2008).

In drawing the lines, most courts refused to apply the *cujus est solum* maxim literally. The Georgia Supreme Court, in *Thrasher v. City of Atlanta*, 178 Ga. 514, 173, S.E. 817, 825 (1934), spoke for many courts in holding that the maxim was nothing more than a "generalization from old cases involving title to space within the range of actual occupation, and any statement as to title beyond was manifestly *mere dictum*" (emphasis added). On that account, *cujus est solum* never described the actual legal rule in use. Other courts accepted that the maxim might have once described the common-law rule, but they expressly overruled it. As one court put it, "If that maxim ever meant that the owner of land owned the space above the land to an indefinite height, it is no longer the law" (*Rochester Gas and Electric Corporation v. Dunlop*, 148 Misc. 849, 266 N.Y.S. 469, 471 [1933]).

Between 1930 and 1936, five courts addressed the issue of aerial trespass. None concluded that flights at high altitudes constituted trespasses (Banner 2008). In 1946 the U.S. Supreme Court once and for all eliminated *cujus est solum* from American law, at least insofar as airspace is concerned. In *United States v. Causby*, 328 U.S. 256, 261 (1946), the Court declared that the maxim "has no place in the modern world." The case arose from the extension of an airport runway used during World War II to accommodate bombers, transports, and fighters. The plaintiffs claimed that the runway extension amounted to a taking of their chicken farm because arriving and departing aircraft, flying low enough to blow leaves off the trees, literally scared their chickens to death.

The Court in *Causby* found a compensable taking—specifically, it held that the federal government had taken an easement over the plaintiffs' property—but it also took the opportunity to (1) repudiate the *cujus est solum* rule; and (2) redraw (if only vaguely) the boundaries between privately owned and publicly owned parts of the atmosphere. The Court found that "if the landowner is to have full enjoyment of the land, he must have exclusive control of the immediate reaches of the enveloping atmosphere. Otherwise buildings could not be erected, trees could not be planted, and even fences could not be run" (*Causby*, 328 U.S. at 264). Beyond those "immediate reaches," however,

> [t]he air is a *public* highway . . . Were that not true, every transcontinental flight would subject the operator to countless trespass suits. Common sense revolts at the idea. To recognize such private claims to the airspace would clog these highways, seriously interfere with their control and development in the public interest,

and transfer into private ownership that to which *only the public has a just claim*. (*Causby*, 328 U.S. at 261; emphasis added)

The Court's emphasis on public rights is crucial for understanding that the Court was not declaring the higher reaches of the atmosphere to be open access; rather, it was drawing boundaries, however vague, between private property in the usable airspace immediately above the ground and public property in the airspace beyond that area. The publicly owned airspace was not open access because the state asserted its sovereignty and limited access to it, for example, through civil aviation regulations. Interestingly, as Banner notes, not one of the five justices who ruled with the majority in *Causby* "expressed any support for recognizing private property rights in airspace" (2008, 249). But that was the outcome of their ruling.[24]

The *Causby* Court did not attempt to draw precise and rigid boundaries between the privately owned and publicly owned parts of the air, presumably because it understood that as a practical matter, the boundary would have be drawn at different altitudes in different locations. The immediately useful airspace above a given lot in midtown Manhattan is likely to be much higher than the immediately useful airspace above a farm in rural Iowa.[25] Indeed, in larger cities, private property rights in airspace have been legally recognized and bought and sold since before the twentieth century (Banner 2008).[26] Conceivably, a power company might seek to establish a wind farm in rural Iowa with generating towers and rotor blades reaching heights above four hundred feet. Doing so might constitute an act of occupation giving rise to private property rights in higher altitudes of airspace (implicitly converting some publicly owned airspace to private ownership). As always, the precise contours of the law are influenced by local circumstances, including commercial considerations.[27]

Beyond repudiation of the *cujus est solum* maxim, express recognition of public property rights in the higher atmosphere, and express recognition of private property rights at lower reaches of the atmosphere, the Court's opinion in *Causby* is important for several other reasons. It (1) illustrates how common-law property rules can and do change over time in response to changing circumstances, including technological changes; (2) takes seriously the importance of setting practicable boundaries between privately owned lands and publicly owned airspace; and (3) expressly

---

[24] Justice Black dissented from the Court's decision. In conference (but not in his written dissent), he argued that there could be no taking because the respondents could not have had private property rights in the air in the first place; the air "is supposed to belong to everyone" (Banner 2008, 248). Justice Reed, who for some reason did not dissent from the Court's ruling, went even farther in the conference, claiming that "air is public property" (Banner 2008, 248).

[25] Even at a single location, the boundaries might be changeable over time as changing circumstances dictate, in much the same way in which land boundaries move in response to accretion, avulsion, and erosion (Gletne 2008).

[26] In 2005 the value of "air rights"—essentially the right to develop upward to the limits set by local zoning rules—in Manhattan reached $430 per square foot (*San Diego Union Tribune*, November 30, 2005). Even in large cities, of course, ownership of higher reaches of the air is not absolute, but is subject to lawful public rights, including, for example, zoning restrictions and historic preservation rules (*Penn Central Transportation Co. v. New York City*, 438 U.S. 104 [1978]).

[27] That commercial considerations affect legal property relations has been clear at least since the 1707 case *Keeble v. Hickeringill*, 11 East 574, 103 Eng. Rep. 1127, which appears to be the first common-law ruling to define property relations functionally to distinguish lawful market competition from unlawful "malicious" interference with trade. Chief Justice Holt found a trespass to chattels (in this case, ducks) without any discussion of formal legal conceptions of possession, ownership, or boundaries.

recognizes the significance of transaction costs in setting those boundaries. Most important, the case shows that courts, like regulatory agencies, do not simply vindicate or enforce private property rights but allocate property rights in the first place. Explicit judicial recognition of public rights in the atmosphere allowed the government to organize and control access and use.

A legal formalist or old Roman lawyer might claim that the public rights recognized by the Court in *Causby* constituted *imperium* (sovereign authority) rather than *dominium* (property ownership). But arcane Roman law distinctions between *imperium* and *dominium* make little practical difference (Cole 2002). As Cambridge University's first professor of land economy, D. R. Denman, explained, property and sovereignty are both forms of power—"a sanction and authority for decision-making"—over resources (1978, 3).[28] In treating property and sovereignty as functionally similar concepts, Denman was participating in a legal tradition extending back to the early seventeenth century, when Grotius wrote of sovereignty as "a particular kind of proprietorship, such in fact that it absolutely excludes like possession by anyone else" (1916 [1609], 22). Three hundred years later, the Scottish legal scholar G. D. Valentine, writing specifically about use of the atmosphere, observed that "exclusive control" is "the most important element in sovereignty" (1910a, 19). He further argued that state sovereignty over the air amounts to *res publicae*: "The atmosphere, like a river, is public and cannot fall within the patrimony of any person" (Valentine 1910b, 87–88).[29] Valentine did not deny that private landowners possessed limited rights in the air based on use and enjoyment of underlying lands, but they could have "no direct right as owner[s] of the atmosphere" (1910b, 88).[30] More recently, Stuart Banner (2008) has noted how assignments of property and acts of sovereignty serve the same basic function. Richard Barnes concurs: "When sovereignty is exercised over things, say territory or natural resources, then sovereignty takes on the lineaments of property. Sovereignty in this sense is in effect a claim to an exclusive regulatory authority over a defined spatial extent or *res* . . . When . . . exercised over territory and the resources therein, it is clearly analogous to a regime of property" (2009, 223).[31] Each of these claims equating sovereignty and property, at least functionally, is consistent with a critical element of the argument that regardless of whether the state purports to act as sovereign or owner, the rights it asserts are in the nature of property (Cole 2002). This argument is, in turn, consistent with the definition of "property rights" provided earlier (see Chapter 2, note 2, above). Acts of sovereign authority over natural resources create legally enforceable rights over things, along with corresponding duties enforceable against others, including other states, private groups, and individuals.

---

[28] The legal philosopher Morris Cohen also sought to explode the distinction between *dominium* and *imperium*, but not by focusing on control of resources. Rather, Cohen claimed that "dominion over things is also *imperium* over our fellow human beings" (1927, 13).

[29] Interestingly for a legal scholar writing early in the twentieth century, Valentine expressly and pretty accurately defined air as a public good: "It can be enjoyed by many persons together and without their excluding each other" (1910b, 86).

[30] Somewhat confusingly, Valentine (1910b) later suggests that the right of free passage through airspace is basically an easement across what is otherwise private property in the air.

[31] Later, Barnes observes that "international law does not grant 'property rights' to States," but "defines the scope of their sovereignty." Nevertheless, he concludes, the phrase "sovereign rights," as used in international law, "amounts to much the same thing" as property (2009, 274).

As far as rights to pollute or rights to clean air are concerned, the *Causby* Court's eradication of the *cujus est solum* maxim was immaterial because courts had never even cited that maxim, let alone applied it as the legal rule, in cases involving air pollution. Long before *United States v. Causby*, courts in both the United States and the United Kingdom had treated air-pollution cases under nuisance law (which protects the rights to use and enjoy land) rather than trespass (which protects the right to exclude) (Morag-Levine 2003). The *cujus est solum* maxim concerns property boundaries, which gives it obvious relevance for trespass claims, but little utility in suits to vindicate use and enjoyment of the surface estate. As noted earlier, even Justice Coke, who first imported the maxim into the common law, did not so much as mention it in his famous air-pollution ruling (*Aldred's Case*), where liability was based not on trespass by smoke or odors (a cause of action the common law has never recognized) but on the "necessity" of "wholesome air" to the use and enjoyment of land (9 Co Rep 57b, 77 ER 816 [1610]). A comprehensive review of U.S. and U.K. case law turns up not a single instance in which a court relied on the *cujus est solum* maxim to resolve an air-pollution dispute.[32]

In the final analysis, the common law of property, both before and after *Causby*, was far more complex and nuanced than was implied either by the old Roman law assertion of pure common property or by the *cujus est solum* maxim's assertion of pure private property. Anglo-American property regimes governing the atmosphere are best viewed as admixtures of public, private, common, and nonproperty/open-access. Consider, for example, the modern common-law doctrine of nuisance. So long as air pollution does not unreasonably interfere with neighbors' use and enjoyment of land (and, of course, the neighbors must be able to prove the harm, the source, and causation), liability does not attach at all; the atmosphere itself remains, in effect, an open-access sink for "reasonable" levels of pollution. When air pollution causes "unreasonable" harm, the polluter is subject to damages or, much less frequently, injunctive relief. These nuisance remedies vindicate not only private property rights, but public property as well. As one English court explained, "[I]n cases of public nuisance the injury is to the property of mankind" (*Attorney General v. Sheffield Gas Consumers Co.*, 3 DeG.M. & G. 304, 320 [1853]). In sum, then, nuisance law provides limited protection for both private and public property, but leaves polluters at liberty to emit "reasonable" levels of pollution into the atmosphere.

Creating Property Rights in the Atmosphere by Acts of State Sovereignty and Regulation

Public property rights in air did not arise solely as a result of judicial rulings. They also came from express assertions of sovereign authority via treaties, legislation, and regulations.[33] Those assertions of sovereignty over the atmosphere arose both in Europe and in the United States at about the same time and in response to the same

---

[32] A Lexis search of all U.S. and U.K. case law using the search connectors "(cujus or cuius) w/seg ('air pollution' or smoke or odor)" turned up only a single mention of the maxim in an air-pollution case, *Gainey v. Folkman*, 114 F. Supp. 231 (D. Ariz. 1953), but the court expressly rejected it as a basis for decision.

[33] More generally, many property institutions usually considered to be solely creatures of the common law, including both nuisance and trespass, have deep roots in statutory law. Nuisance and trespass both originated in the twelfth century in an English statute known as the assize of novel disseisin (Loengard 1978; Woodbine 1925).

technological changes, especially the development of aviation, that created so much judicial consternation over the meaning and force of the *cujus est solum* maxim.

By the first decades of the twentieth century, lawyers and jurists were arguing for legal possession and control of the air as an incident of state sovereignty to facilitate and control aviation over states' territories (Banner 2008). H. Earle Richards, an Oxford professor of international law, wrote that "so long as the law of gravity prevails, a State must have unfettered control over air vessels passing above its territory in order to protect itself" (1912, 8). It was a matter of national security. Without the authority to restrict access to its airspace, as well as its land borders and sea ports, a state would be liable to attack from above (Richards 1912; Valentine 1910a). The irresistible logic of such claims, particularly given the specter of imminent war in Europe, led directly to state assertions of sovereignty over airspace. The British government was the first to act in 1913, introducing regulations that prohibited foreign aircraft from flying over British territory without advance permission. France and Germany quickly followed suit (Banner 2008). The onset of World War I, the first large-scale war in which aircraft routinely featured, a year later vindicated these decisions to exercise "complete sovereignty" over airspace (Banner 2008, 63).

The United States, which was not threatened by air attacks during World War I, did not enact a similar law regulating use of its airspace until the 1926 Air Commerce Act (69 P.L. 254, 44 Stat. 558), which provided that "the United States of America is . . . to possess and exercise complete and exclusive national sovereignty in the air space above the United States." This law, like earlier assertions of sovereign authority by European countries, hardly facilitated international civil aviation,[34] but the laws did, in effect, convert the atmosphere from open access to public property, at least as far as aviation was concerned. The phrase "to possess and exercise complete and exclusive . . . sovereignty," as used in the 1926 Air Commerce Act, is perfectly consistent with the property-law concept of "exclusive possession."

Early twentieth-century assertions of sovereignty in the atmosphere were not solely concerned with aviation. Increasing levels of air pollution also led to state actions that had consequences for property rights in the atmosphere. In *Georgia v. Tennessee Copper Co.*, 206 U.S. 230, 237–8 (1907), Justice Oliver Wendell Holmes, writing for a unanimous Court,[35] made clear that control over air pollution is a basic attribute of state sovereignty:

> The State owns very little of the territory alleged to be affected [by air pollution emissions from the respondent's copper mine], and the damage to it capable of estimate in money, possibly, at least, is small. This is a suit by a State for an injury to it in its capacity of quasi-sovereign. In that capacity the State has an interest independent of and behind the titles of its citizens, in all the earth and air within

---

[34] International treaties, including the Convention on International Civil Aviation, which took effect in 1947, subsequently facilitated international aviation without compromising state sovereignty.

[35] Justice Harlan authored a concurrence in which he disagreed with aspects of Justice Holmes's opinion not directly relevant to the section quoted here.

its domain. It has the last word as to whether its mountains shall be stripped of their forests and its inhabitants shall breathe pure air. . . .

It is a fair and reasonable demand on the part of a sovereign that the air over its territory should not be polluted on a great scale by sulphurous acid gas, that the forests on its mountains, be they better or worse, and whatever domestic destruction they have suffered, should not be further destroyed or threatened by the act of persons beyond its control.

States and municipalities had not been awaiting Justice Holmes's imprimatur to regulate air pollution. Long before the Supreme Court's decision in *Georgia v. Tennessee Copper Co.*, state and local governments had enacted numerous statutes, ordinances, and regulations to protect public health and property from air pollution. In 1867 St. Louis enacted what may have been the country's first air-pollution ordinance, which required all chimneys to rise at least 20 feet above surrounding buildings (Morag-Levine 2003).[36] Chicago followed in 1880 with a different approach to smoke regulation. Section 1650 of the Chicago ordinance summarily declared: "The emission of dense smoke from the smoke-stack of any boat or locomotive, or from any chimney, anywhere within the city, shall be deemed and is hereby declared to be a public nuisance." The provision did not define "dense smoke," and residential chimneys were exempted, but violators of the smoke ordinance were subject to a fine of "not less than five dollars nor more than fifty dollars" (§ 1651) (Cole 2002, 31).

Laitos (1975) has identified three specific types of air-pollution regulation in the late nineteenth century (not including the St. Louis tall-stacks approach). The first type, like Chicago's, declared air pollution a nuisance and imposed fines, rarely exceeding $100, for violations. A second type of regulation went further and required polluters to take affirmative steps to control or minimize their emissions, for instance, by building furnaces to consume more of the smoke they produced. A third type of regulation focused not on emissions, but on the fuel used, banning consumption of any coal containing more than 12 percent ash or 2 percent sulfur. This type of regulation actually had the longest pedigree of all. In 1306 the City of London for the first (but not the last) time attempted to deal with local air-pollution problems by banning, upon penalty of death, the importation and burning of "sea-coal," a heavily polluting bituminous coal shipped by sea from northeast England (Brimblecombe 1987, 9).[37] Parliament enacted the United Kingdom's first nationwide

---

[36] Tall-chimney requirements were a very popular form of air-pollution regulation into the late twentieth century. The legal and economic implications of such regulations are interesting. When emissions are emitted at a higher altitude, they typically drift farther away from the locality. This does not mean that they no longer constitute externalities, but only that they are externalized farther afield. The pollution may still harm public health and property when it falls to earth, but (1) that is not a problem so far as the local community, for example, the municipality of St. Louis, is concerned, and (2) nuisance suits are more difficult to sustain because plaintiffs located farther from the pollution source have a harder time identifying defendants and proving causation. From a property perspective, St. Louis's approach to local air-pollution problems implies that it was not concerned primarily with the use of the atmosphere as a pollution sink, but with the effects of the pollution on uses and users on the ground.

[37] The ban applied only to sea-coal ostensibly because it was less expensive, and therefore more widely used, than less-polluting anthracite coal, which was mined locally but in shorter supply. Public choice scholars have not yet examined the possibility that the City of London's ban on sea-coal was based (at least in part) on ulterior motives

smoke law in 1819, about half a century before American cities began enacting their first smoke ordinances (Morag-Levine 2003).[38]

Far from being a newfangled invention of the "nanny state" (Harsanyi 2007), public regulation of air pollution to protect public health and vindicate public property rights has a very long history. However, the air-pollution regulations that emerged during the twentieth century were different in several important respects: (1) they were greater in number; (2) they were more detailed and costly for polluters; (3) they were enacted at multiple levels of government—municipal, state, and eventually federal; and (4) their effectiveness was greatly enhanced by improving monitoring and enforcement technologies.

From the outset, some reviewing courts recognized that the various regulatory laws created and/or protected public property rights in the atmosphere. For example, when San Diego's Air Pollution Control District required gasoline stations to install vapor recovery devices on gas pumps, the California Court of Appeals, in *Mobil Oil Corp. v. Superior Court of San Diego City*, 59 Cal. App. 3d 293, 305 (1976), upheld the regulation as a valid measure designed to protect public property rights in clean air:

> Here it appears the Oil Companies are asking us to determine they have a fundamental vested right to release gasoline vapors while dispensing fuel to their customers. How are we to answer the public, on the other hand, who assert a fundamental vested right to breathe clean air? If either exists, it must be the latter.

The court expressly rejected the claim of a private entitlement to pollute and enforced public property rights in the atmosphere. But did those public property rights antedate the regulation, or were they created by it? The court's decision provides no guidance on this important question. Arguably, before state regulation, the atmosphere was de facto, and possibly de jure, open access for air pollution from gas pumps. The regulation itself converted the atmosphere from open access to public property subject to limited private access, not as of right, but as authorized by law.

Similarly, when a Michigan state appellate court upheld a judge's decision enforcing the state's 1965 Air Pollution Act (as amended) against a power plant, the court stated:

> [T]here exists no right to pollute. Since no such right exists, a polluter has not been deprived of any protected property or liberty interest when the state halts the pollution. (*Detroit Edison Co. v. Michigan Air Pollution Control Commission*, 167 Mich. App. 651, 661 [1988])

Moreover, the court agreed with the trial judge that "the Act read as a whole evince[s] a clear legislative intent to give the Commission broad authority to carry out its task of protecting the quality of Michigan's air" (*Detroit Edison Co.*, 167 Mich. App. at 659). The phrase "Michigan's air" is intriguing. Did the court mean to imply that

---

to support local mining interests. Certainly, such ulterior motives have affected U.S. regulation of air pollution under the Clean Air Act (Ackerman and Hassler 1981).

[38] On the history of smoke abatement in nineteenth-century Britain, see Flick (1980).

the 1965 Air Pollution Act constituted an assertion of state ownership, that is, public property, in the atmosphere above the state of Michigan? Such a claim would have been consistent with the court's assertion that "there exists no right to pollute." On the other hand, the court might have been making a simple jurisdictional or locational point in referring to "Michigan's air." But if that was the intended meaning, then how are we to understand the state's lawful exclusion of the utility's emissions within the conventional framework of property systems? Regulatory authority is generally said to emerge from the police power, which is an inherent element of state sovereignty (Dubber 2004; G. H. Reynolds and Kopel 2000). But if assertions of state sovereignty constitute implicit or explicit public property claims, as I claim, then the assertion of property rights is implicit rather than explicit. Either way, the 1965 Air Pollution Act asserts public property in "Michigan's air."

Some states have asserted public property rights explicitly. Consider the following provision from the Constitution of the State of Pennsylvania, entitled "Natural Resources and the Public Estate" (Article 1, Section 27):

> The people have a *right* to clean air, pure water, and to the preservation of the natural, scenic, historic and esthetic values of the environment. Pennsylvania's public natural resources are the *common property* of all the people, including generations yet to come. As *trustee* of those resources, the Commonwealth shall conserve and maintain them for the benefit of all the people. (emphasis added)[39]

If that is not an express assertion of public property (despite the somewhat misleading use of the phrase "common property"), then it is difficult to imagine what would be. It is unlikely for political reasons that state officials would ever seek to enforce to the fullest extent the state's property rights in the air, waters, and other natural amenities of Pennsylvania, that is, by excluding any and all private uses, but it would not be obviously unconstitutional. To avoid that politically untenable outcome, the state has interpreted Article 1, Section 27, with the Pennsylvania Supreme Court's approval, in a way that requires it to balance its role as trustee of publicly owned natural resources, including the air, against other state needs, including economic development (*Payne v. Kassab*, 468 Pa. 226, 246 [1976]).[40] In *Eagle Environmental II, L.P. v. Commonwealth of Pennsylvania*, 584 Pa. 494, 514 (2005), the Pennsylvania Supreme Court noted the need to balance the environmental protections constitutionally required under Article 1, Section 27, with the state's need to provide locations for solid waste disposal. Consequently, the state, as environmental trustee, is not always required to conserve the resources it owns in trust for the

---

[39] This constitutional provision was adopted in 1971.

[40] The court's conclusion that the protections of Article 1, Section 27, require balancing against other state obligations rests on a questionable foundation. The court merely notes that the state has other "duties," including, for example, the statutory duty to maintain an adequate public highway system (*Payne*, 469 Pa. 226 at 246). It is not at all clear, however, why or how a constitutional obligation to protect public resources requires balancing against duties created under ordinary statutes. Clearly, the court in *Payne* was looking for a hook to avoid interpreting Article 1, Section 27, in a way that would automatically disrupt all private or public development activities. However, it should have been able to find a better hook. The court left open the question whether the state could choose to apply Article 1, Section 27, to have that effect.

public. Thus, Article 1, Section 27 does not prohibit any and all development activities, but allows the state, by virtue of its legal ownership as trustee of state natural resources, to ensure "controlled development" (*Concerned Citizens for Orderly Progress v. Commonwealth of Pennsylvania, Dept. of Environmental Resources*, 36 Pa. Commw. 192, 199 [1977]).

But what if Pennsylvania chose to prevent all (or nearly all) development of privately owned lands to protect state resources, exercising to the utmost its constitutional authority under Article 1, Section 27? Such a choice would expose a latent constitutional conflict between Article 1, Section 27, and Article 10, which specifies, "[N]or shall private property be taken or applied to public use, without authority of law and without just compensation being first made or secured." Which constitutional provision would prevail over the other? The issue has not yet arisen in Pennsylvania,[41] but the California Supreme Court, in a closely analogous setting, has ruled that constitutional public property rights (under the so-called public trust doctrine) would prevail over private property in any taking suit.[42]

Federal Assertions of Public Rights in the Atmosphere to Control Air Pollution

Long after state governments began asserting sovereign authority and public ownership over the atmosphere, the federal government began to stake its own claims. The impetus for federal action came from increasing public concern over environmental issues that state and local pollution-control efforts did not appear to be resolving. During the 1950s and 1960s, air pollution from both stationary and motorized sources continued to increase despite state and local regulations (Menell and Stewart 1994). The federal government, however, did not simply jump into the fray with both feet. Federal environmental policy evolved slowly and cautiously, starting shortly after the end of World War II, at least partly because of uncertain constitutional authority for direct federal regulation of intrastate air pollution.

Before the mid-1960s, the federal government restricted its role in air-pollution control, generally speaking, to funding research and providing aid to state programs. Initial federal forays into direct regulation began in 1965 with the Motor Vehicle Air Pollution Control Act (Pub. L. 89-272, 79 Stat. 992), which authorized the secretary of health, education, and welfare (HEW) to set national standards for motor vehicle emissions, and continued in 1967 with the Air Quality Act (Pub. L. 90-148, 81 Stat. 485), which authorized the HEW secretary to designate air-quality-control regions around the country, including interstate regions, for which states would be required to promulgate air-quality standards and plans for achieving

[41] It seems clear, however, that the State of Pennsylvania could be required to compensate for a taking under the U.S. Constitution, given current Supreme Court doctrine, if its "controlled development" policies greatly diminished the value of affected privately owned lands. The Fifth Amendment's takings clause, applicable to the states via the Fourteenth Amendment, sets a federal constitutional limit that no state can avoid through contrary state constitutional provisions (Cole 2006). The federal limit is only a floor; states are allowed to provide greater (but not lesser) protections.

[42] See *National Audubon Society v. Superior Court of Alpine County*, 658 P.2d 709 (1983) (holding that private interests in water are limited to nonvested use rights, which remain perpetually subject to the state's superior title under the public trust doctrine, embodied in Article 10 of the state's constitution). Of course, California Supreme Court decisions carry no necessary influence in Pennsylvania.

those standards. These limited federal intrusions into the state-dominated field of air-pollution control turned out to be merely precursors to a major federal incursion, which occurred three years later in the 1970 Clean Air Act Amendments.[43]

The 1970 Clean Air Act (42 U.S.C. §§ 7401–7671q) marked a major, but incomplete, shift of power over environmental protection from the states to the federal government, symbolized by the creation of an entirely new federal agency, the Environmental Protection Agency (EPA), to implement and enforce the new law.[44] The act subsumed and greatly expanded on precursor laws, including the 1965 Motor Vehicle Pollution Control Act and the 1967 Air Quality Act, and it set the standard for other federal environmental statutes that followed, including the Clean Water Act of 1972, the Coastal Zone Management Act of 1972, the Endangered Species Act of 1973, the Safe Drinking Water Act of 1974, the Toxic Substances Control Act of 1976, and the Resource Conservation and Recovery Act of 1976.

The federal government's large-scale takeover of environmental regulation was facilitated by the Supreme Court's adoption of a more expansive interpretation of the commerce clause in the wake of the New Deal and continued use of this interpretation by the Warren Court. By the time the Court upheld the constitutionality of the Civil Rights Act of 1964 (*Heart of Atlanta Motel Inc. v. United States*, 379 U.S. 241 [1964]; *Katzenbach v. McClung*, 379 U.S. 294 [1964]), it was clear that the federal government had all the constitutional authority, if not necessarily the economic justification, it needed to regulate even local sources of air pollution (Futrell 1993).[45]

The 1970 Clean Air Act does not expressly assert federal, state, or other public ownership of the atmosphere; nor does it make explicit reference to any public "right"

---

[43] Technically, they were amendments to the 1955 Clean Air Act (as amended in 1963), which was not a regulatory statute. In reality, the 1970 Clean Air Act started a whole new ballgame. For that reason, the statute is referred to as the "Clean Air Act," rather than "the Clean Air Act Amendments," in the remainder of this chapter.

[44] The Clean Air Act is premised (in conception more than in reality) on a notion of cooperative federalism, according to which state and federal governments each supposedly play important and complementary roles in the regulatory regime. In the 1970 act, the federal government was to establish uniform, national air-quality standards, and the states were left with primary responsibility to control emissions from existing stationary sources of air pollution within their respective boundaries to meet those standards. However, new and substantially modified stationary sources, as well as mobile sources, had to meet federal, rather than state-set, emissions standards. Each time Congress has amended the act since 1970 (especially in 1977 and 1990), federal authority has been expanded at the expense of state authority. Today, state governments are relegated, more or less and for better or worse, to serving as functionaries of the federal EPA. Perhaps the only reason that the states do not rebel and resign their commissions is fear that the EPA might impose draconian measures if required to promulgate federal implementation plans, which are provided for in 42 U.S.C. § 7410(c), for air-quality-control regions in states that decline to prepare state implementation plans.

[45] The chief economic justification for federal intervention in environmental regulation was the problem of interstate pollution, which individual states were unlikely to resolve alone. For example, the State of Illinois would not likely take action against a Chicago-based pollution source whose emissions caused damage only in neighboring Indiana. Even some scholars who believe that the federal government has seized too much regulatory authority over pollution control, relative to the states, accept this argument (Butler and Macey 1996). Another, more controversial, justification for federal intervention was the belief that state competition for economic development would precipitate a "race to the bottom" in environmental standards (Stewart 1985, 919). Whether such a race to the bottom actually occurred or was ever likely to occur has been a source of still-unresolved disagreement among academics (Engel 1997; Engel and Saleska 1998; Revesz 1992; 2001). Another, sometimes overlooked, but very important factor in the federalization of environmental law was concern among interstate industries about the proliferation of varying environmental standards in dozens of states. As Lazarus (2004) notes, in 1967 alone, state governments enacted 112 pollution-control laws, which were neither well coordinated nor necessarily consistent. In these circumstances, "the possibility of a uniform, federal preemptive standard became increasingly attractive to those in the regulated community" (Lazarus 2004, 45; also see Smith [2000]). This public choice explanation of federalization is, to some extent at least, at odds with the race-to-the-bottom hypothesis.

to clean air.[46] In what way, then, does it create public, common, or private property rights (and corresponding duties) with respect to the atmosphere? It does so simply through the sovereign act (under the police power) of regulating access to and use of the atmosphere by polluters. More specifically, it imposes enforceable duties on polluters to not pollute beyond certain levels along with corresponding public rights, which can be exercised by federal or state government agencies, citizens' groups, or private individuals. Like most federal environmental statutes, the Clean Air Act contains a "citizen suit" provision in § 304 (42 U.S.C. § 7604), which provides that "any person may commence a civil action on his own behalf . . . against any other person . . . who is alleged to have violated . . . an emission standard or limitation" under the act. All persons are potential enforcers of the rights to clean(er) air created by the Clean Air Act. That the rights created in the Clean Air Act are contingent and changeable by statutory amendment hardly distinguishes them from other kinds of property, which can be sliced and diced (and resliced and rediced) in all kinds of ways under common-law rules. Those rules expressly recognize, for example, conditional and contingent fee interests (e.g., fee simple determinable, fee simple subject to a condition subsequent, and determinable life estate), not to mention legal rules governing trusts and simple contracts, which are almost completely malleable.[47] More generally, common-law court rulings governing property relations can alter both the quantum and distribution of property rights after the initial assignment (Cribbet 1986).

A simple thought experiment illustrates the property-like effect of the Clean Air Act's regulatory regime. Suppose, counterfactually, that before the Clean Air Act was enacted, there was no pollution regulation of any kind, including common-law restrictions, at any level of government. In that circumstance, the atmosphere would be a nonproperty/open-access resource. Everyone would, in Hohfeld's (1913; 1917) terminology, have a "privilege" or "immunity" (but no "right") to pollute; and no one would possess a "right" to any quantum of clean air. The atmosphere would truly be a pollution sink "open to all" (Hardin 1968, 1244). Suppose that this situation prevailed just before the federal government enacted the Clean Air Act, which restricts access to and use of the atmosphere (for pollution purposes). In Hardin's (1968) schema, the regulation would amount to a regulatory or socialist solution to the "tragedy of the commons," as opposed to the capitalist, privatization solution. The argument here is that the distinction between Hardin's two solutions is not a difference in kind because both solutions create property rights and duties (or something functionally identical to property rights and duties) in the atmosphere. Where previously no one had any duty not to pollute, and no one had the right to prevent anyone else from polluting, after the regulation, polluters have a duty not to pollute the public atmosphere beyond legal limits (set by the government), and government officials and private citizens both have rights to enforce those duties

---

[46] By contrast, the 1972 Clean Water Act expressly declares as its "objective" the restoration and maintenance of the "chemical, physical, and biological integrity of the *Nation's waters*" (33 U.S.C. § 1251[a]) (emphasis added) and declares unlawful the "discharge of any pollutant by any person" except in accordance with federal permits granted by the EPA (33 U.S.C. §§ 1311[a], 1342).

[47] On defeasible fees and other contingent property interests, see Dukeminier et al. (2006). On the malleability of legal instruments assigning property interests, see Grey (1980). But Merrill and Smith (2001) argue that property rights, properly conceived, are not nearly as malleable as most contemporary scholars suppose.

against polluters. In other words, the Clean Air Act by necessary implication has created rights to a minimal level of clean air, as specified in the act and subsidiary regulations.

Relaxing the assumptions of this thought experiment complicates, but does not fundamentally alter, the picture. In reality, the common law, as well as earlier state and local government regulations, constrained access to and use of the atmosphere as a pollution sink (at least to some extent) before the federal Clean Air Act. Nevertheless, the Clean Air Act allocated (or reallocated) rights and duties with respect to the atmosphere that meet the strict Hohfeldian definition provided by Cole and Ostrom (chapter 2 in this volume).

Partial Privatization of the Atmosphere for Use as a Pollution Sink

The federal government, having asserted a public ownership interest in the atmosphere for purposes of limiting pollution, initially left polluters at liberty to emit pollutants within (changeable) legal limits. There was as yet no "right" to pollute;[48] at most, polluters possessed "privileges" to emit or limited "immunities" from liability for lawful levels of pollution.[49] Such entitlements are not different in kind from the privilege to emit under common-law nuisance doctrine, which enforces only property rights to be free of "unreasonable" pollution.

In the 1990 Clean Air Act Amendments, the federal government made another important institutional move that again altered property relations between air polluters and others with respect to the atmosphere. In a new effort to control sulfur dioxide emissions from power plants in order to reduce the incidence of acid rain,[50] Congress enacted an emissions-trading program that in effect, despite express congressional claims to the contrary, established limited private rights to pollute. Because earlier regulations had converted the open-access atmosphere to some ill-defined form of public property, the Acid Rain Program converted a small amount of that public property to private ownership.

Here is how it worked. The government (1) set an overall pollution-control goal, expressed in terms of overall ambient concentration levels of sulfur dioxide in the atmosphere; (2) determined how much existing emissions had to be reduced to

---

[48] It would be inaccurate to claim that polluters had even a limited "right" to emit within lawful limits because (1) those limits were changeable and therefore were not enforceable against the government, and (2) even pollution emissions that were lawful under the Clean Air Act might still be unlawful under private or public nuisance law. Compliance with air-pollution regulations is not, generally speaking, a defense against common-law claims (*Orchard View Farms, Inc. v. Martin Marietta Aluminum, Inc.*, 500 F. Supp. 984 [D.Or. 1980]; *Borland v. Sanders Lead Co.*, 369 So. 2d 523 [Ala. 1979]; *Galaxy Carpet Mills, Inc. v. Massengill*, 338 S.E. 2d 428 [Ga. 1986]; *Maryland Heights Leasing, Inc. v. Mallinckrodt, Inc.*, 706 S.W. 2d 218 [Mo. Ct. App. 1986]).

[49] Even this immunity was imperfect, however, because the federal regulatory regime did not preempt common-law actions, which could be used to impose stricter limits on emissions if they were necessary to vindicate the property rights of injured neighbors (Rogers 1994). Also, the Clean Air Act specifies that states may impose stricter limits on emissions than the minimal federal standards (42 U.S.C. § 7416). No state has yet done so, perhaps because the federal floor is already set very high, pursuant to the statutory mandate requiring that national ambient air-quality standards be set to protect the health of the most sensitive subgroups within the population with "an adequate margin of safety" (42 U.S.C. § 7409[b][1]).

[50] Acid precipitation occurs when sulfur molecules recombine in the atmosphere with oxygen molecules and then fall to earth, where the acid has various deleterious effects, including eroding structures, corroding cars and other metallic objects, burning forests, and acidifying water bodies (Likens and Bormann 1974).

meet that goal; (3) subtracted necessary emissions reductions from current emissions to determine an overall quota limit; and (4) unitized and allocated quota limits for each regulated facility, based on the historic emissions rates of each facility (42 U.S.C. § 7651c[e]).[51] The sum of all plants' quota limits was supposed to match the maximum emissions level that would meet the government's overall air-quality goal. If the government's calculations were correct, the pollution-control goal would be achieved if each regulated facility complied with its quota, regardless of emissions trading.

At this point, all the government had done was to create a traditional form of environmental regulation known as a "performance standard" (Cole and Grossman 2005, 332). What made the Acid Rain Program novel, and not just another performance-based regulatory regime, was Congress's express authorization for regulated facilities to buy and sell units of emissions, known as "allowances" (with each allowance equaling one ton of sulfur dioxide emissions), on the open market.[52] The primary purpose of allowance trading was not to achieve the government's emission-reduction goal—that was already more or less guaranteed by the aggregate quota—but to minimize the compliance costs for regulated facilities. According to the theory of emissions trading first analyzed by J. H. Dales (1968), emissions trading improves the economic efficiency of a regulatory regime because it (1) implicitly recognizes that different firms have different compliance cost structures; and (2) uses the market to reallocate the emission-reduction burden to those regulated facilities that can reduce emissions at the least cost.

> Firms with low pollution control costs may find it worthwhile to reduce their emissions below mandated levels, leaving them with excess rights to sell to firms with higher pollution control costs. In theory, exchanges of pollution rights should occur at any price below the marginal pollution reduction costs of some firms and above the marginal pollution control costs of others. As a result of these exchanges, firms with the lowest costs of control should end up taking on the biggest emissions reduction burden, thereby minimizing the overall compliance/abatement costs of attaining the government's pollution control goal. (Cole 2002, 47)

Firms with higher costs of control will not be forced to reduce their emissions as much, but they will have to pay for the privilege of emitting above their initial quotas.[53]

---

[51] Various other distributional criteria were available. Instead of allocating allowances based on historical emissions from each source, the government might have chosen to split the overall quota evenly among all 110 of the originally regulated power plants, or it might have allocated more credits to those plants that had taken earlier steps to reduce emissions (as a reward). Such distribution choices can potentially affect the overall cost savings associated with an emissions-trading regime.

[52] It was not entirely novel. Congress, the EPA, and the states had previously experimented with various forms of emissions (or pollution-content) trading. However, the Acid Rain Program was an experiment in emissions trading on a much larger scale (Cole 2002).

[53] It is sometimes inaccurately presumed, including by J. H. Dales, the economist who first developed the idea of emissions trading, that emissions trading minimizes the "total costs to society" of a pollution-control regime (Dales 1968, 107). As Cole and Grossman (1999; 2002) have explained, the total costs of environmental protection equal the sum of compliance/abatement costs, administrative costs (including monitoring and enforcement), and residual pollution costs. Emissions trading results in total cost savings only if the other costs of pollution control are lower than or the same as those of other regulatory regimes. It is sometimes the case, however, that emissions-trading regimes entail higher administrative costs than traditional forms of regulation, such as technology-based standards (Cole and Grossman 1999). If and when those higher administrative costs offset, or more than offset, the lower compliance costs associated with emissions trading, emissions trading cannot be said to minimize total costs.

The Acid Rain Program was, by all accounts, highly successful, leading to emissions reductions that were greater than expected at costs that were not only lower than expected but much lower than under a traditional regulatory system using design or performance standards (Burtraw et al. 1997; Ellerman et al. 2005; Percival, Miller, and Schroder 1996).[54] For current purposes, however, the most important aspect of the Acid Rain Program is its effect on property rights and duties in the atmosphere.

In effect, the Acid Rain Program converted some of the public's property in the atmosphere (which had been converted from open access to public property pursuant to earlier regulations) into limited private rights to pollute, with corresponding duties on others not to interfere with those permitted pollution emissions. Put differently, the Acid Rain Program took what had previously been only a privilege to pollute (or immunity from liability for pollution) and converted it into a bona fide right. And it did so despite Congress's express disclaimer that an emissions allowance is only a "limited authorization" that does "not constitute a property right" (42 U.S.C. § 7651b[f]). The statutory assertion that emissions allowances are not property rights is simply incorrect, or at least overbroad.[55] But how can the law itself be wrong about the legal status of emissions allowances?

Congress made a simple conceptual error—or what the philosopher Gilbert Ryle would have labeled a "category mistake" (1949, 16)—in presuming that it had to declare emissions allowances nonproperty in order to insulate the EPA against takings claims for future regulatory decisions that might reduce the number of allowances in circulation (e.g., to ensure attainment of national environmental goals). Perusal of the legislative history makes clear that all Congress really meant to say is that emissions allowances are not property enforceable against the government (Dennis 1992–1993); no evidence exists that Congress intended emissions allowances to be unenforceable against anyone else. As Cole has explained, Congress's assertion that emissions allowances are not property is "premised on a typical confusion between property rights in something and the thing itself. An emissions allowance is not a property right, but there certainly are property rights in emissions allowances. A utility that holds an allowance to emit SO_2 cannot prevent the government from confiscating it but certainly can exclude all others from interfering with it. The rights to possess and exclude certainly are property rights in allowances" (2002, 54).

That possessory rights in emissions allowances are enforceable as property is clear from actual litigation over disputed possession. In *Ormet Primary Aluminum Corporation v. Ohio Power Co*, 207 F.3d 687 (4th Cir. 2000), the plaintiff claimed an 89 percent proportionate share of emissions allowances allocated under the Acid Rain Program to the defendant's power plant, based on a long-term contractual

---

[54] The success of the Acid Rain Program is not attributable to emissions trading alone, but to the combination of emissions trading with strict, government-imposed monitoring requirements, specifically, the installation of continuous emissions monitors, reporting in real time to EPA headquarters, at each regulated power plant (42 U.S.C. § 7651k). In the absence of accurate, reliable, and cost-effective monitoring technologies, the program would never have gotten off the ground because emissions sources could not have been held accountable for actual emissions (Cole and Grossman 2005).

[55] Rose tacitly agrees, referring to transferable emissions allowances as "regulatory property," but without a substantial discussion of their status as property (2002, 233).

relationship with the owner of the power plant, of which it is the primary customer (under 42 U.S.C. § 7651g[i], which provides for distribution of allowances among coowners of regulated facilities). The court rejected the claim, finding that the plaintiff's contracts with the defendant did not establish the plaintiff as a joint owner of the regulated power plants pursuant to the requirements of the act. Although the court was careful not to discuss disputed possession of emissions allowances in terms of property ownership, the case was nevertheless about possessory rights in emissions allowances. In other words, it was about the allocation of property between rival claimants.[56] Once again, however Congress might define "emission allowances," they still function as property.

The fact that not every single right is included in a particular owner's bundle of rights—in the case of emissions allowances, the right against uncompensated government expropriation is missing—hardly means that the owner has no property rights at all.[57] If that were the case, the only legally recognized property rights would amount to fee simple absolute.[58] But the law has for many centuries recognized lesser (that is, incomplete) ownership interests in land and other things. Land held in joint tenancy is not freely heritable. Life tenants do not have the right to use land in such a way as to destroy its value to remaindermen (those who take after the life estate ends), under the doctrine of waste. Owners of land that is fee simple determinable can lose their title if they put the land to a use that violates a condition on the fee. All of these are cases of incomplete ownership, in which some typical ownership right is missing or only weakly present, but they are all well-recognized forms of property ownership, even if they are economically less valuable than fee simple absolute.

That emissions allowances under the Clean Air Act may be devalued or even expropriated by the government without compensation hardly means that they do not amount to property (regardless of what Congress says). By creating and allocating emissions allowances, Congress has, in effect, partially privatized the atmosphere, creating very real rights for power plants to pollute that cannot be defeated by the competing claims of a right to clean air. In fact, those competing claimants have a legally enforceable duty not to interfere with emissions of regulated power plants in compliance with their emissions quotas. No one other than the government can stop the power plants from emitting within (changeable) quota limits. Just like the Supreme Court in *Causby*, the U.S. Congress in the 1990 Clean Air Amendments created a mixed property system in the atmosphere, recognizing a combination of private and public property rights. If anything, the boundaries between the publicly owned and privately owned parts of the atmosphere are better

---

[56] For a similar case, see *City of Owensboro v. Kentucky Utils. Co.*, 2008 U.S. Dist. LEXIS 68587 (W.D. Ky. 2008).

[57] Were freedom from uncompensated government expropriation the sine qua non of property, no such thing as property would exist, technically speaking, in the United Kingdom, where no constitutional right to compensation for government takings exists, although Parliament regularly offers compensation as a matter of statutory law and "convention" (Cole 2007, 154–155).

[58] "Fee simple absolute" is the law's technical phrase for ownership of a complete bundle of property rights, including right to exclusive possession, use and enjoyment, alienation, and so on, without any conditions or contingencies other than common-law nuisance restrictions, zoning and other valid police power restrictions, the possibility of adverse possession, or compensable taking by the government. As these exceptions indicate, fee simple absolute ownership turns out to be far from absolute.

defined in the Clean Air Act than in the case of liability for airplane overflights under *Causby*.

Unresolved Normative Issues

This chapter's thesis of property creation by regulation applies not only to the atmosphere, but also to other natural resources, including marine fisheries, where property rights have been created by similar acts of sovereignty. The regulatory establishment of individual transferable quotas (ITQs) in fisheries is closely analogous to the creation of emissions allowances in air pollution.[59] They amount to private property rights in otherwise public fisheries. The fisheries are public, rather than open-access, resources in the first place because governments long ago claimed public property rights by assertions of sovereignty, including the declaration of exclusive economic zones extending two hundred miles from shore.[60] As Barnes explains, "Exclusive competence over a geographically determinate zone is the crucial prerequisite to the establishment of property rights in marine natural resources" (2009, 311). The assertion of sovereignty is critical because marine resources are plagued by a "problem of physical excludability," which can only be "overcome through the use of positive law to assert legal excludability" (Barnes 2009, 252). Once sovereign rights, that is, public property rights, were in place, governments could allocate limited private property rights to improve efficient, partly market-based resource management.[61]

If, as has been argued, regulatory regimes and other acts of sovereignty sometimes create and vindicate public and private property rights, as well as restrict them, the next step is to address the significance of that observation. Two related implications of this argument highlight its importance.

As noted earlier, regulatory takings doctrine is premised on theories of property according to which regulations are essentially impositions on private property rights, rather than assertions or attempts to vindicate existing public or private property rights. Consequently, even in several takings cases where privately owned lands have abutted publicly owned waters, the Supreme Court has (at least until very recently) focused exclusively on the private rights at issue to the detriment of real, existing public rights (Cole 2002: ch. 8). The arguments in this chapter raise important questions about the meaning, scope, and doctrine of regulatory takings, including its theoretical underpinnings.

Among the most important of those questions is whether private property rights should trump conflicting public property rights (or vice versa) in regulatory takings

---

[59] On the history of property rights in fisheries, from open access to ITQs, see Scott (2008). Macinko and Bromley (2004) deny that ITQs constitute property rights because one fisherman cannot enforce a quota limit against another. They seem to confuse the ITQ holder's private right to take fish, which is clearly a property right enforceable against those who might interfere with the ITQ holder's efforts to take fish within the quota limit, with the ITQ holder's duty not to take fish beyond the quota limit, which is enforceable not by other private individuals, but by the state. The fact that the ITQ holder's duty is enforceable only by a government agency merely confirms that the property right that corresponds to that duty is a public property right rather than a private property right.

[60] Historically, these assertions of sovereignty were not intended primarily to facilitate fisheries conservation, but to control exploration for valuable offshore mineral deposits (Barnes 2009).

[61] Heller (1999) observes that regulations establishing ITQs create, rather than destroy, private property.

disputes. Before that question can reasonably be answered, more work needs to be done on the development of a theory (or multiple theories) of public property that goes beyond existing, almost equally naïve, public interest and public choice models. These theories are needed to complement the numerous, well-developed theories and studies of private property that already exist. Even common property, thanks to the work of Ostrom (1990) and others, has been more rigorously studied in recent years than has public property. Therefore, this chapter ends with a general call for more legal and social scientific research on the theory and empirics of *res publicae*, particularly as it interrelates with other property systems.

Acknowledgments

For many helpful comments, criticisms, and suggestions, the author is grateful to Richard Epstein; Peter Grossman; Yu-Hung Hong; Gerard Magliocca; Mike McGinnis; Wallace Oates; Elinor Ostrom; Jouni Paavola; Mike Pitts; colloquium participants in the Workshop in Political Theory and Policy Analysis; participants in a presentation at the Michael Maurer School of Law at Indiana University, Bloomington; and participants in the Lincoln Institute of Land Policy conference entitled "Evolution of Property Rights Related to Land and Natural Resources."

REFERENCES

Ackerman, Bruce A., and William T. Hassler. 1981. *Clean coal, dirty air; or, How the Clean Air Act became a multibillion-dollar bail-out for high-sulfur coal producers.* New Haven, CT: Yale University Press.

Bagli, Charles V. 2005. Sky-high cost of Manhattan air may leave you gasping. *San Diego Union Tribune.* Nov. 30.

Banner, Stuart. 2008. *Who owns the sky? The struggle to control airspace from the Wright brothers on.* Cambridge, MA: Harvard University Press.

Barnes, Richard. 2009. *Property rights in natural resources.* Oxford: Hart Publishing.

Beckmann, Volker, Claudio Soregaroli, and Justus Wesseler. 2010. Ex-ante regulation and ex-post liability under uncertainty and irreversibility: Governing the coexistence of GM crops. *Economics* 4:1–32.

Beerman, Jack M. 1991. Interest group politics and judicial behavior: Macey's public choice. *Notre Dame Law Review* 67:183–229.

Blackstone, William. 1979 [1766]. *Commentaries on the laws of England.* Vol. 2. Chicago: University of Chicago Press.

Boorstin, Daniel J. 1941. *The mysterious science of the law.* Boston: Beacon Press.

Boyer, Marcel, and Donatella Porrini. 2004. Modeling the choice between regulation and liability in terms of social welfare. *Canadian Journal of Economics* 37:590–612.

Brimblecombe, John. 1987. *The big smoke: A history of air pollution in London since medieval times.* London: Methuen.

Buchanan, James M. 1972. Politics, property, and the law: An alternative interpretation of *Miller et al. v. Schoene. Journal of Law and Economics* 15:439–452.

Buchanan, James M., and Warren J. Samuels. 1975. On some fundamental issues in political economy: An exchange of correspondence. *Journal of Economic Issues* 9:15–38.

Burtraw, Dallas, Alan J. Krupnick, Erin Mansur, David Austin, and Deirdre Farrell. 1997. The costs and benefits of reducing acid rain. Discussion Paper 97-31-REV. Washington, DC: Resources for the Future.

Butler, Henry N., and Jonathan R. Macey. 1996. Externalities and the matching principle: The case for reallocating environmental regulatory authority. *Yale Law and Policy Review* 14:23–66.

Claeys, Eric R. 2003. Takings, regulations, and natural property rights. *Cornell Law Review* 88:1549–1671.

Coase, Ronald H. 1959. The Federal Communications Commission. *Journal of Law and Economics* 2:1–40.

———. 1960. The problem of social cost. *Journal of Law and Economics* 3:1–44.

Cohen, Morris R. 1927. Property and sovereignty. *Cornell Law Quarterly* 13:8–30.

Coke, Edward. 1832 [circa 1628]. *The first part of the institutes of the laws of England; or, A commentary upon Littleton.* London: James and Luke G. Hansard and Sons.

Cole, Daniel H. 2002. *Pollution and property: Comparing ownership institutions for environmental protection.* Cambridge, U.K.: Cambridge University Press.

———. 2006. Why *Kelo* is not good news for local planners and developers. *Georgia State University Law Review* 22:803–856.

———. 2007. Political institutions, judicial review, and private property: A comparative institutional analysis. *Supreme Court Economic Review* 15:141–182.

Cole, Daniel H., and Peter Z. Grossman. 1999. When is command-and-control efficient? Institutions, technology, and the comparative efficiency of alternative regulatory regimes for environmental protection. *Wisconsin Law Review* 1999:887–938.

———. 2002. Toward a total-cost approach to environmental instrument choice. In *An introduction to the law and economics of environmental policy: Issues in institutional design*, ed. T. Swanson, 223–241. *Research in Law and Economics*, 20. New York: Elsevier Science.

———. 2005. *Principles of law and economics.* Upper Saddle River, NJ: Prentice-Hall.

Cribbet, John Edward. 1986. Concepts in transition: The search for a new definition of property. *University of Illinois Law Review* 1986:1–42.

Dales, J. H. 1968. *Pollution, property, and prices: An essay in policy-making and economics.* Toronto: University of Toronto Press.

DeAlessi, Louis. 1980. The economics of property rights: A review of the evidence. *Research in Law and Economics* 2:1–47.

Denman, D. R. 1978. *The place of property: A new recognition of the function and form of property rights in land.* Berkmansted, U.K.: Geographical Publications.

Dennis, Jeanne M. 1992–1993. Smoke for sale: Paradoxes and problems of the emissions trading program of the Clean Air Act Amendments of 1990. *UCLA Law Review* 40:1101–1144.

Dubber, Markus Dirk. 2004. "The power to govern men and things": Patriarchal origins of the police power in American law. *Buffalo Law Review* 52:1277–1345.

Dukeminier, Jesse, James E. Krier, Gregory S. Alexander, and Michael H. Schill. 2006. *Property.* 6th ed. New York: Aspen.

Ellerman, A. Denny, Paul L. Joskow, Richard Schmalensee, Juan-Pablo Montero, and Elizabeth M. Bailey. 2005. *Markets for clean air: The U.S. Acid Rain Program.* Cambridge, U.K.: Cambridge University Press.

Ellickson, Robert C. 1973. Alternatives to zoning: Covenants, nuisance rules, and fines as land use controls. *University of Chicago Law Review* 40:681–781.

———. 1991. *Order without law: How neighbors settle disputes.* Cambridge, MA: Harvard University Press.

Ely, James. 1998. *The guardian of every other right: A constitutional history of property rights.* Oxford: Oxford University Press.

Engel, Kirsten H. 1997 State environmental standard-setting: Is there a "race" and is it "to the bottom"? *Hastings Law Journal* 48:271–376.

Engel, Kirsten H., and Scott R. Saleska. 1998. "Facts are stubborn things": An empirical reality check in the theoretical debate over the race-to-the-bottom in state environmental standard-setting. *Cornell Journal of Law and Public Policy* 8:55–88.

Epstein, Richard A. 1985. *Takings: Private property and the power of eminent domain.* Cambridge, MA: Harvard University Press.

Eskridge, William N., and John Ferejohn. 2001. Super-statutes. *Duke Law Journal* 50:1215–1276.

Fischel, William A. 1978. A property rights approach to municipal zoning. *Land Economics* 54:64–81.

———. 1980. Externalities and zoning. *Public Choice* 35:37–43.

———. 1987. *The economics of zoning laws: A property rights approach to American land use controls*. Baltimore: John Hopkins University Press.

———. 2007. The law and economics of cedar-apple rust: State action and just compensation in *Miller v. Schoene*. *Review of Law and Economics* 3:133–195.

Flick, Carlos. 1980. The movement for smoke abatement in 19th-century Britain. *Technology and Culture* 21:29–50.

Futrell, William. 1993. A history of environmental law. In *Environmental law: From resource to recovery*, § 1.2(H)(2), eds. Celia Campbell-Mohn, Barry Breen, and J. William Futrell. Minneapolis: West.

Glaeser, Edward L., and Andrei Shleifer. 2003. The rise of the regulatory state. *Journal of Economic Literature* 41:401–425.

Gletne, John. 2008. Changes in riparian boundary location due to accretion, avulsion, and erosion. *Surveying and Land Information Science* 68:47–52.

Grapel, William, trans. 1994 [1855]. *The Institutes of Justinian, with the novel as to successions*. London: Wm. W. Gaunt and Sons.

Grey, Thomas C. 1980. The disintegration of property. In *Property*, eds. J. Roland Pennock and John W. Chapman, 69–85. Nomos 22. New York: New York University Press.

Griffin, Ronald C. 1981. Property rights and welfare economics: *Miller et al. v. Schoene* revisited; Comment. *Land Economics* 57:645–651.

Grotius, Hugo. 1916 [1609]. *The freedom of the seas; or, The right which belongs to the Dutch to take part in the East Indian trade*. Oxford: Oxford University Press.

Hardin, Garrett. 1968. The tragedy of the commons. *Science* 162:1243–1248.

Harsanyi, David. 2007. *The nanny state: How food fascists, teetotaling do-gooders, priggish moralists, and other boneheaded bureaucrats are turning America into a nation of children*. Louisville: Broadway Press.

Heller, Michael A. 1999. The boundaries of private property. *Yale Law Journal* 108:1163–1223.

Hohfeld, Wesley Newcomb. 1913. Some fundamental legal conceptions as applied in judicial reasoning. *Yale Law Journal* 23:16–59.

———. 1917. Fundamental legal conceptions as applied in audicial reasoning. *Yale Law Journal* 26:710–770.

Howard, A. E. Dick. 1968. *The road from Runnymeade: Magna Carta and constitutionalism in America*. Charlottesville: University of Virginia Press.

Huntington, Samuel P. 1952. The marasmus of the ICC: The commission, the railroads, and the public interest. *Yale Law Journal* 61:467–509.

Karkkainen, Bradley C. 1994. Zoning: A reply to the critics. *Journal of Law Use and Environmental Law* 10:45–89.

Laffont, Jean-Jacque, and Jean Tirole. 1991. The politics of government decision-making: A theory of regulatory capture. *Quarterly Journal of Economics* 106:1089–1127.

Laitos, Jan. 1975. Legal institutions and pollution: Some intersections between law and history. *Natural Resources Journal* 15:423–451.

Lazarus, Richard J. 2004. *The making of environmental law*. Chicago: University of Chicago Press.

Likens, Gene E., and F. Herbert Bormann. 1974. Acid rain: A serious regional environmental problem. *Science* 184:1176–1179.

Loengard, Janet. 1978. The assize of nuisance: Origins of an action at common law. *Cambridge Law Journal* 37:144–166.

Macinko, Seth, and Daniel W. Bromley. 2004. Property and fisheries in the twenty-first century: Seeking coherence from legal and economic doctrine. *Vermont Law Review* 28:623–661.

Maser, Steven M., William H. Riker, and Richard N. Rosett. 1977. The effects of zoning and externalities on the price of land: An empirical analysis of Monroe County, New York. *Journal of Law and Economics* 20:111–132.

Menell, Peter S. and Richard B. Stewart. 1994. *Environmental law and policy.* New York: Aspen.

Mercuro, Nicholas, and Timothy P. Ryan. 1980. Property rights and welfare economics: *Miller et al. v. Schoene* revisited. *Land Economics* 56:203–212.

Merrill, Thomas W., and Henry E. Smith. 2001. The property/contract interface. *Columbia Law Review* 101:773–852.

Morag-Levine, Noga. 2003. *Chasing the wind: Regulating air pollution in the common law state.* Princeton, NJ: Princeton University Press.

Mueller, Dennis C. 1989. *Public choice II: A revised edition of Public choice.* Cambridge, U.K.: Cambridge University Press.

Nijeholt, J. F. Lycklama à. 1910. *Air sovereignty.* The Hague: Martinus Nijhoff.

Ogus, Anthony. 1994. *Regulation: Legal form and economic theory.* Oxford: Clarendon Press.

Olson, Mancur. 1965. *The logic of collective action.* New York: Shocken Books.

Ostrom, Elinor. 1990. *Governing the commons: The evolution of institutions for collective action.* Cambridge, U.K.: Cambridge University Press.

Percival, Robert, Alan S. Miller, and Christopher H. Schroder. 1996. *Environmental regulation: Law, science, and policy.* Boston: Little, Brown.

Posner, Richard A. 1998. *Economic analysis of law.* 5th ed. New York: Aspen Law and Business.

Revesz, Richard L. 1992. Rehabilitating interstate competition: Rethinking the "race-to-the-bottom" rationale for federal environmental regulation. *New York University Law Review* 67:1210–1254.

———. 2001. Federalism and environmental regulation: A public choice analysis. *Harvard Law Review* 115:553–641.

Reynolds, Glenn H., and David B. Kopel. 2000. The evolving police power: Some observations for a new century. *Hastings Constitutional Law Quarterly* 27:511–537.

Reynolds, Susan. 2010. *Before eminent domain: Toward a history of expropriation of land for the common good.* Chapel Hill: University of North Carolina Press.

Richards, H. Earle. 1912. *Sovereignty over the air.* Oxford: Clarendon Press.

Rogers, William H., Jr. 1994. *Environmental law.* 2nd ed. St. Paul, MN: West Publishing Co.

Rose, Carol M. 2002. Common property, regulatory property, and environmental protection: Comparing community-based management to tradable environmental allowances. In *The drama of the commons*, eds. Elinor Ostrom, Thomas Dietz, Nives Dolšak, Paul C. Stern, Susan Stonich, and Elke U. Weber, 233–257. Washington, DC: National Research Council.

Ryle, Gilbert. 1949. *The concept of mind.* New York: Barnes and Noble Books.

Samuels, Warren J. 1971. Interrelations between legal and economic processes. *Journal of Law and Economics* 14:435–450.

———. 1972. In defense of a positive approach to government as an economic variable. *Journal of Law and Economics* 15:453–459.

Scott, Anthony. 2008. *The evolution of resource property rights.* Oxford: Oxford University Press.

Shavell, Steven. 1984. Liability for harm versus regulation for safety. *Journal of Legal Studies* 13:357–374.

Smith, John K. 2000. Turning silk purses into sows' ears: Environmental history and the chemical industry. *Enterprise and Society* 1:785–812.

Sprankling, John G. 2008. Owning to the center of the earth. *UCLA Law Review* 55:979–1040.

Stewart, Richard B. 1985. Allocating responsibility between the federal and state courts: Article; Federalism and rights. *Georgia Law Review* 19:917–980.

Stoebuck, William B. 1972. A general theory of eminent domain. *Washington Law Review* 47:553–608.

Valentine, G. D. 1910a. The air—A realm of law. I. *Juridical Review* 22:16–27.

———. 1910b. The air—A realm of law. II. *Juridical Review* 22:85–104.

Waldron, Jeremy. 1999a. *The dignity of legislation.* Cambridge, U.K.: Cambridge University Press.

———. 1999b. *Law and disagreement.* Oxford: Oxford University Press.

White, Michelle J., and Donald Wittman. 1983. A comparison of taxes, regulation, and liability rules under imperfect information. *Journal of Legal Studies* 12:413–424.

Wittman, Donald. 1977. Prior regulation versus post liability: The choice between input and output monitoring. *Journal of Legal Studies* 6:193–212.

Wood, Gordon S. 1999. Oliver Wendell Holmes Devise Lecture: The origins of judicial review revisited; or, How the Marshall Court made more out of less. *Washington and Lee Law Review* 56:787–809.

Woodbine, George E. 1925. The origins of the action of trespass. *Yale Law Journal* 34:343–370.

Commentary

WALLACE E. OATES

Daniel Cole provides a fascinating and insightful examination of the nature of regulation as it relates to the complex issues surrounding the definitions and enforcement of both private and public property rights. The basic thesis is that regulation should not be seen solely as an encroachment on private property rights; regulatory measures, in fact, often create, modify, and protect property rights. The chapter develops this argument through an intriguing historical examination and interpretation of the evolution of air-quality management.

Cole's thesis seems quite correct. The recent history of the regulation of air pollution in the United States encompasses a variety of measures that not only define and protect certain existing rights, but also (at least in a practical sense) create new property rights. As a public finance and environmental economist, I want to explore Cole's argument from an economic perspective and develop the implications of the economic view for the role of property rights in regulatory design.

The central concern of the discipline of economics is the efficient and equitable use of scarce resources. Basic analysis suggests that competitive markets will generally do a good job of allocating these scarce resources to their most valued use in the case of wholly private goods. However, problems arise where varying sorts of publicness arise, where the use of resources by one party encroaches on the well-being of others outside the market. In the case of common property resources, for example, use of the resource by one individual typically has adverse effects on others. The use of the atmosphere as a dumping ground for polluting waste emissions by one person or firm can have negative effects (negative externalities) on others who depend on clean air. The equilibrium level of use of such open-access resources typically involves excessive use, an outcome often described as the "tragedy of the commons." In the economic literature, this is an instance of so-called market failure.

Economists have proposed a number of different regulatory approaches for correcting the distortions associated with such an open-access equilibrium. The oldest (and traditional) approach is the use of a tax that serves to internalize the external costs associated with the use of the resource. Such a Pigouvian tax effectively serves as a surrogate price for the scarce resource; in this way, it serves to ration the use of the resource efficiently. Economists refer to this regulatory device as a price instrument. From this perspective, one can think of a Pigouvian tax as providing the missing price needed for the efficient allocation of the open-access resource. From Cole's perspective, this amounts to viewing the resource (e.g., clean air) as a form of public property whose use the regulator rations through the pricing mechanism.

An alternative economic approach is the use of a quantity instrument. Instead of putting a price on the use of the resource, the regulator can limit its use to the efficient level by controlling this level directly through the issuance of an appropriate number of licenses or permits. As Cole discusses, this is the approach that the U.S. government adopted in the Clean Air Act Amendments of 1990 to address the problem of acid rain. In this case, the regulator directly limited the level of sulfur emissions into the atmosphere through the distribution of the requisite number of permits to the major sources of emissions, power plants. These permits were tradable, and a reasonably well-functioning market developed fairly quickly. Subsequent studies (cited by Cole) suggest that this cap-and-trade system was quite effective in limiting emissions to their target level and did so at relatively low cost. In contrast to the price instrument, a system of tradable emission permits (a quantity instrument) involves what for most practical purposes can be regarded as the creation of private property rights in the use of the atmosphere.

It is interesting in this regard that (as economic analysis shows) price and quantity instruments can produce fully equivalent outcomes when the permits are distributed through an auction. If they are simply given away, the distributive properties of the two outcomes will differ, but they both produce the same efficient result: the optimal use of the scarce resource at the minimum level of aggregate abatement (pollution-control) costs. When permits are auctioned, it is straightforward to show that the outcomes are identical: there is effectively a one-to-one mapping from the workings of the price instrument (Pigouvian tax) to that of the quantity instrument (cap-and-trade system).

However, the implications of the two approaches from the legal perspective on property rights seem to be quite different. For the case of Pigouvian taxes, it would appear that the regulator is claiming, in effect, that the resource is public property and is allocating its use through an appropriate price. In contrast, under a cap-and-trade system, the regulator is effectively creating private property in the resource, the ownership of which can be transferred through a market. As Cole points out, however, there are some important and subtle issues here. In the 1990 Clean Air Act Amendments, for example, he notes that although an emissions allowance is not a property right, there certainly are property rights in emission allowances, such as the rights to possess and to exclude. Should the government (regulator) decide that further reductions in emissions are required, it would not necessarily have to expropriate existing allowances; the regulator could simply go into the market and buy back the requisite quantity, an approach that would effectively recognize the standing of these allowances (or permits) as privately owned property. There are many complicated issues here from the perspective of property theory.

Finally, price and quantity instruments by no means exhaust the list of regulatory alternatives. As Cole discusses, legal liability is another avenue for regulating externalities. Pushing even further, as we have learned from Coase's theorem, so long as property rights are clearly defined and certain other important conditions are satisfied, voluntary transactions will correct any distortions resulting from externalities. For such public goods as air quality, however, these other conditions

effectively rule out voluntary approaches. In any practical sense, Coase's mechanism requires a small group of participants who can sit down together and strike
the requisite bargains. In the case of urban air quality, it would be virtually impossible for the thousands of victims of air pollution and the many sources of the polluting emissions to reach voluntary agreements on how to control air quality. The
Coase mechanism clearly has very limited relevance to such issues.

Rights to Pollute

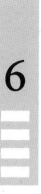

Assessment of Tradable Permits for Air Pollution

NIVES DOLŠAK

Scholars often attribute deterioration of natural resources to ill-defined property rights and suggest privatization and tradable-permit markets as a solution to environmental problems. Environmental resources differ in physical characteristics and use patterns, and policies regulating their use must be tailored to these differences as well as to resource user characteristics. This chapter draws on Dolšak (2007) to examine factors that contribute to well-performing tradable-permit markets for reducing air pollution. Comparative analysis of market performance suggests that tradable permits are not successful in all cases. Much analytic work has identified individual sources of transaction costs that have led to market failures. However, a holistic framework that looks at key sources of costs enables one to find cases of successful use of tradable permits where partial analytic frameworks would have predicted failure. For example, nonuniform pollution cases (cases where emission of one unit, e.g, a ton of pollutant, causes different pollution outcomes across space) should have high exchange costs and a low level of trading, but appropriate design of a tradable-permit system can reduce these challenges.

The problem of air pollution dates to at least the nineteenth century. Indeed, from the 1860s to the 1880s, many cities passed ordinances to regulate smoke and odor (see chapter 5 by Daniel Cole in this volume). At the federal level, the key statutes were not enacted until the 1970s. The Clean Air Act Amendments (CAAA) of 1970 mandated that the newly established Environmental Protection Agency (EPA) list substances causing local air deterioration and set maximum allowable concentration levels for these pollutants to avoid health hazards and destruction of property.[1] Consequently, the EPA established the National Ambient Air Quality Standards (NAAQS) for six major criteria pollutants: ozone, carbon monoxide (CO), nitrogen oxides (NO_x), sulfur dioxide (SO_2), particulate matter (PM), and lead. The EPA requires states to develop and implement policies to meet NAAQS guidelines. If the ambient quality in an area is worse than the standard set by the EPA, the area is designated as "nonattainment." States with nonattainment areas must submit a state implementation plan (SIP) to the EPA indicating how they will meet the

---

[1] For a detailed discussion of the legislative and judicial processes involved in the Clean Air Act and its amendments, see chapter 5 by Daniel Cole.

standards in the future. The sanction for noncompliance is economic: nonattainment areas can be denied permits to construct new facilities unless they come into compliance with the NAAQS. Additionally, in some cases, the EPA may not accept the SIPs and may decide to administer the clean air policy itself (Crotty 1987; Lester 1986).

Despite four decades of federal air-quality regulation, some areas continue to suffer from serious air pollution. In April 2011 a large number of counties in southern California failed to meet the NAAQS for several criteria pollutants, and areas in Nevada, Montana, Arizona, midwestern states, and the northeast states failed to meet NAAQS for one or two pollutants. (For detailed county level information, see the EPA Green Book information at http://epa.gov/airquality/greenbk/mapnpoll. html.) Although lead is no longer a significant pollutant in the United States, many states continue to find it impossible to meet standards for ozone and PM, and several still exceed standards for SO_2.

The EPA's Air Quality Index (AQI) measures health hazards of air pollution above certain levels. AQI values above 100 indicate levels of air pollution that pose risk to sensitive populations with respiratory and coronary problems. AQI values above 150 indicate pollution levels that are unhealthy for anyone undertaking extensive outdoor activities. In 2008, the most recent year for which data are available for the entire United States, air quality in a large number of counties was at a level that was unhealthy for sensitive populations. As depicted in figure 6.1, most of southern California, central and southern Arizona, and many areas in the Midwest, Florida, the Atlantic coast, and the Northeast experienced AQIs above 100 for more than 10 days a year.

A comparison of data for 1998 and 2008 gives a sense of changes over time. The data for 1998 suggest that air quality was significantly worse 10 years earlier in the eastern United States, the Midwest, the southern states, and states along the Atlantic coast (figure 6.2). Although air quality has significantly improved in the eastern United States since 1998, several western states have not seen such improvement.

In 2008, 52.4 million people lived in areas where the 90th percentile value of annual AQI exceeded 100, and 31.9 million lived in areas where the 90th percentile value of annual AQI exceeded 150, the value at which air becomes unhealthy for outdoor activities for anyone. Although these numbers are high, notable improvement had occurred since 1998. In that year, 111.1 million people lived in areas where the 90th percentile value of annual AQI exceeded 100, and 21.4 million lived in areas where the 90th percentile value of annual AQI exceeded 150.[2] The key point here is that the increase in the number of people living in the most polluted areas is the result of population growth (Riverside–San Bernardino and the Los Angeles Metropolitan Statistical Area) rather than pollution increases.

What is local often becomes global. Winds transport pollutants across countries and continents. Recent data suggest that some toxic pollutants cross oceans and travel around the globe. Similarly, the use of certain chemicals, such as ozone-depleting

---

[2] These estimates are based on data on air quality and population for metropolitan statistical areas, available at the EPA (http://www.epa.gov/air/data/monaqi.html?us~USA~United%20States) and the U.S. Census Bureau (http://www.census.gov/prod/3/98pubs/98statab/saappii.pdf and http://www.census.gov/population/www/metroareas/metroarea.html).

FIGURE 6.1

Air Quality in U.S. Counties in 2008

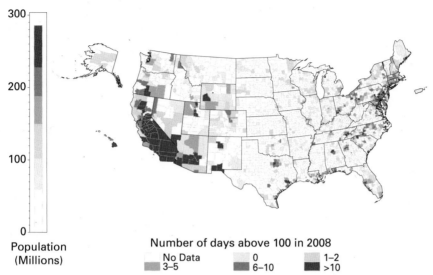

Number of days above 100 in 2008

No Data 0 1–2
3–5 6–10 >10

Population (Millions)

SOURCE: Environmental Protection Agency, http://www.epa.gov/air/data/msummary.html?us~usa~United%20States.

FIGURE 6.2

Air Quality in U.S. Counties in 1998

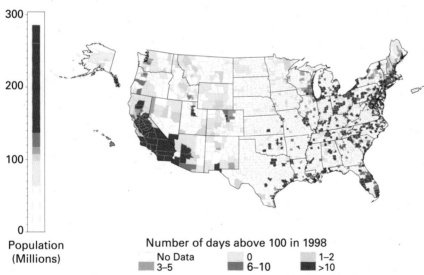

Number of days above 100 in 1998

No Data 0 1–2
3–5 6–10 >10

Population (Millions)

SOURCE: Environmental Protection Agency, http://epa.gov/airquality/greenbk/mapnpoll.html.

substances, has led to deterioration of the atmospheric shield that protects the earth's surface from harmful radiation. Since the late 1970s, scientists have measured a hole in the ozone layer over Antarctica where up to 66 percent of the ozone is depleted. The Vienna Convention for the Protection of the Ozone Layer and its subsequent protocols since 1989 devised a phaseout schedule for ozone-depleting substances.

This regime has been fairly successful. The United Nations Environment Programme (UNEP) estimates that the total consumption of a key group of ozone-depleting substances, chlorofluorocarbons (CFCs), dropped from 1.1 million tons in 1986 to 35,000 tons in 2006.[3] Global problems require international cooperation in developing, monitoring, and enforcing institutions for pollution reduction. As it would be extremely difficult to exclude anybody from benefitting from reduction in global pollution, incentives for free-riding are significant. Although the institutional challenges of devising and enforcing effective international regimes for air pollution are beyond the scope of this chapter, the use of tradable permits in the regime protecting stratospheric ozone is reviewed here and is compared with national and regional tradable-permit systems.

Governments have historically developed policies to reduce air pollution. First, governments have regulated the use of the atmosphere as a pollution sink by prescribing technologies polluters must employ, such as catalytic converters for vehicles and scrubbers to clean up exhausts of power plants, or by setting minimum requirements for the use of renewable sources of energy in electricity generation (the so-called Renewable Portfolio Standards). Second, governments have enacted policies requiring firms to provide information to consumers about the environmental impact of their products and production processes. For example, many U.S. states require electric utilities to provide information on the portfolio of energy sources used in electricity generation. The idea is that informed consumers will vote with their dollars to reward firms that minimize environmental harm (Dietz, Ostrom, and Stern 2003). Finally, governments have created market incentives, such as taxes, fees, and tradable quotas, to alter the benefits and costs of air pollution for individual actors. This approach has drawn much attention, especially in the context of the ongoing global climate change debate.

If ill-defined property rights are an important cause of the overuse of environmental resources and of negative externalities (Coase 1960; Cornes and Sandler 1996), defining property rights better may solve the externality problem. Dales suggested that "it is high time that we began to devise some new forms of property rights, not to air and water, but to the *use* of air and water" (1968, 76). Because "a property right is enforceable authority to undertake particular actions related to a specific domain" (Commons 1968, cited in Ostrom and Schlager 1996, 130), one expects that property owners will design institutions to prevent resource overuse and deterioration.

Privatization proponents suggest that when property rights are well defined and easily enforced, markets efficiently determine what and how much should be produced (by means of market prices), how it should be produced (through the relationships between marginal productivities of inputs and their prices), how it should be distributed (depending on individuals' income and preferences), and how consumption should be allocated over time (through differences in individuals' discount rates).[4] In addition, tradable permits have dynamic advantages over command-and-control instruments, the alternative to privatization. Various studies suggest that

[3] UNEP, http://ozone.unep.org/Events/ozone_day_2008/press_backgrounder.pdf.
[4] Although this chapter focuses on the effectiveness of tradable permits for reduction of air pollution, fairness in access to the resource may be more important than effectiveness and/or economic efficiency. The right-allocation

market-based systems create greater incentives for technological innovation and diffusion than command-and-control instruments (Jaffe and Stavins 1995; Montero 2002).[5]

However, empirical analyses of individual cases suggest that this broad endorsement of privatization is too optimistic. Tradable-permit markets have been found to be thin and to have high transaction costs (Gangadharan 2000; Hahn and Hester 1989a; 1989b). Data problems have impeded monitoring and enforcement of trading rules (Coy et al. 2001; EPA 2002; Wilkinson and Thompson 2006). Scholars question whether tradable-permit systems stimulate innovation (Driesen 2003; Montero 2005) and have the ability to respond to sudden and substantial changes in the market (Coy et al. 2001; EPA 2002). About 40 years after the implementation of the first tradable-permit market in the United States, researchers are somewhat careful about endorsing tradable-permit markets as a universal approach to solve the pollution problem: "All of our analysis suggests one final observation: Experience with and lessons learned from the Acid Rain Program must be applied with care to other environmental objectives" (Ellerman et al. 2000, 321).

Privatization is a complex undertaking. Scientifically uncertain and politically sensitive issues must be resolved before there is any allocation of individual rights among individual users. For example, what total level of resource use can prevent deterioration of future resource stocks? How many fish can be harvested without jeopardizing future stocks (Gordon 1954)? How many tons of SO_2 can be emitted without causing significant damage to physical and biological environments in areas downwind from the pollution? The ability of science to provide answers to such questions significantly diminishes as the complexity of the environmental resource or pollution problem grows.

Scientific estimates become the basis for a government's decisions on what the limits on resource use should be. These decisions, however, are influenced not only by scientific information, but also by political factors. Some environmental resource users may be able to influence the decision on the overall level of the use of a resource, how it should be allocated among current users, and how future users should obtain permits to access and use the resource. Title IV of the CAAA followed more than a decade of political struggle over how SO_2 emissions could be reduced (E. M. Bailey 1998; Burtraw and Palmer 2004; Ellerman et al. 2000).

Arguably, monitoring and enforcement rules might be easier to design for tradable-permit systems for environmental resources that extend across a smaller geographic area and involve a smaller number of resource users (Rose 2001; Tietenberg 2001). On the other hand, a larger area and, therefore, a larger number of resource users may create incentives for specialized brokers to enter the market, thereby reducing transaction costs and increasing trading activity in the market for tradable permits.

---

process takes place in the political arena and may have redistributional consequences (McCay 2001). It therefore deserves special attention.

[5] Although emissions trading might create more incentives for innovation than technological standards for the regulated industries, technological standards can encourage innovation in pollution-control industries. Hence, which policy approach can encourage innovation across industry types remains an open question. For an empirical analysis of the impacts of the 1971 New Source Performance Standards on patent activity, performance, and costs of emission-control technologies in emission-control industries following the introduction of tradable permits in 1990, see Taylor, Rubin, and Hounshell (2003).

Thus, there is no definitive answer regarding the optimal market size or user base for the functioning of any environmental resource tradable-permit system.

Resolving these issues requires the development of an analytic framework that enables a comparison of different tradable-permit regimes and their effectiveness, controlling for factors that are external to the regime's design, such as characteristics of the resource, patterns of its use, and characteristics of resource users. The following section outlines an analytic framework to compare effectiveness of tradable-permit regimes. This framework is then employed to compare the tradable-permit performance of four U.S. tradable-permit regimes.

The Analytic Framework

A growing body of literature on tradable-permit markets identifies several factors that affect their performance. Although empirical studies since the 1970s have analyzed the performance of tradable permits and other transferable quotas, these analyses have mostly focused on a single environmental resource, with a few notable exceptions, such as Sorrell and Skea (1999) and Tietenberg (2006).[6] Little systematic effort has been invested in developing comprehensive frameworks that would "identify the universal elements that any theory relevant to the same kind of phenomena would need to include" (Ostrom 1999, 40).

Two approaches to comparative work are noteworthy. The first is often used when an existing tradable-permit design is used as a template for designing a system for another pollutant (e.g., the Acid Rain Program for a carbon dioxide allowance market). This approach focuses on similarities and differences between these environmental resources and/or pollution issues (P. Bailey and Jackson 1999; Ellerman et al. 2000; Farrell and Morgan 2003; Schmalensee 1998). There is no clear guidance, however, about what characteristics of the environmental resource and its users have to be included in such an analysis and how they will interact. An alternative approach provides a list of factors that affect the performance of tradable-permit systems, including characteristics of the tradable permit (timescales, banking, and allocation), spatial characteristics of the resource (local versus global impact of resource use), enforcement and monitoring, and size and knowledge of regulatees. This approach, however, does not specifically address how these variables are interlinked (Sorrell and Skea 1999).

The problem with these frameworks is not merely analytic, but also practical. Recommendations from such partial frameworks can lead policy makers to devise a tradable-permit system that addresses the impact of a subgroup of factors, not recognizing that they may be sacrificing critical aspects of the tradable-permit design and, thereby, performance. For example, when a greenhouse gas tradable-permit design follows a frequent recommendation that regulatees be large, point-source emitters, it focuses on fossil-fuel-burning electricity generators. Although focusing on large stationary sources that are easy to monitor may be a plausible start for many developed economies, thereby signaling the willingness of the major emitters to

---

[6] For an excellent example of a study of the Acid Rain Program, see Ellerman at al. (2000).

curtail their emissions, this approach misses the fact that in some areas, the largest sources of greenhouse gas emissions are not electricity generation, but deforestation, waste management, and/or transportation. It is important, then, that a framework be developed that incorporates all major factors affecting market performance so that the limitations of tradable-permit designs can be recognized and supplemented with other regulatory approaches.

The analytic framework used in this chapter seeks to overcome the limitations of partial frameworks. It is based on the comparative literature on common-pool resources (Dietz, Ostrom, and Stern 2003; Ostrom 1990). It also builds on the literature on transaction costs and the factors affecting market performance. Performance of a tradable-permit system depends on the ability of permit holders to trade permits at low cost and of system administrators to monitor and enforce rules (Cason and Gangadharan 2003; Ellerman at al. 2000; Gangadharan 2000; Hahn and Hester 1989a; 1989b; Tietenberg 2006). Therefore, the analytic framework applied here augments the institutional analysis and development (IAD) framework developed by Elinor Ostrom in her influential book *Governing the Commons* (1990) by incorporating elements of the transaction-costs literature. The IAD framework is used because it focuses on how resource characteristics and resource use patterns affect institutional design and therefore performance.

The following groups of factors are identified as affecting market performance (figure 6.3):

FIGURE 6.3

Factors Affecting Performance of Tradable Permits

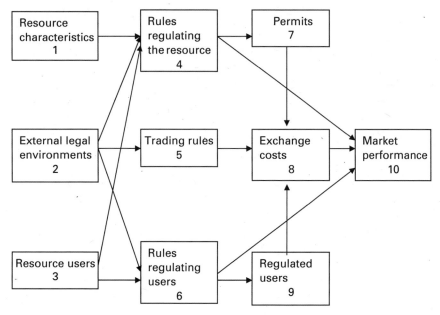

1. External factors, such as resource characteristics, external legal and regulatory environments, and characteristics of resource users (boxes 1, 2, and 3).
2. Rules regulating resource use and users (boxes 4 and 6).
3. Characteristics of the tradable-permit markets, including trading rules, permits, and exchange costs (boxes 5, 7, and 8) and their participants (box 9).

Resource Characteristics

Resource characteristics (box 1 in figure 6.3) include predictability of the resource stocks (i.e., air quality), availability of reliable indicators of resource flows (emissions), spatial extent of the resource, and effects of use of the resource on resource stocks (uniform versus nonuniform effects). If predictability of the impact of emissions on air quality is low, the rules need to be easily adaptable as new information becomes available. However, frequent changes in the rules make property rights embedded in tradable permits insecure and thereby reduce the incentive for right holders to curb their resource use with the objective of generating a surplus to be traded.

Further, if there are no reliable indicators of resource flows (e.g., emissions of air pollutants from vehicles), monitoring and enforcement become more difficult. However, this obstacle can be addressed by relying on measurements of the use of related resources. For example, if continuous measurements of emissions are not easily obtainable or reliable, one could measure the amount of combusted fossil fuels and thereby estimate pollution using emission coefficients. Consequently, one could devise permits for the levels of inputs into the resource-using activity (e.g., sulfur or carbon content of fuels) or the outputs from the process (e.g., kilowatt hours of electricity generated or barrels of gasoline produced in a refinery).

The spatial extent of the resources is crucially important. If the resource expands over large areas (e.g., the atmosphere or the oceans), monitoring becomes difficult and expensive. It is difficult to relate changes in the stocks of large, dispersed resources to different resource use patterns and to estimate the appropriate level of emissions. For example, when air pollution travels across large areas, computations of the impact of local versus regional or global emissions on air quality require extensive air-pollution modeling and data monitoring. In estimating the impact of the resource use rules on resource stocks, one has to separate so-called background pollution (pollution from upwind sources) from pollution by local sources. When the Houston area in Texas was not meeting the NAAQS in the early 2000s, arguably because of the transport of air pollution from Mexico, the EPA granted it an extension of two years to meet the standards. Such adjustments can decrease the pollution-reduction efforts and affect the environmental outcome and trading activity.

Another problem arises if the effects of resource use by different users are not uniform, and, therefore, the property rights cannot be traded on a unit-to-unit basis (Baumol and Oates 1975). For example, if the effect of a ton of emitted pollutant in the coastal area near Los Angeles is not the same as the effect of a ton of emitted pollutant in the mountains, permits for these pollutants cannot be traded one-to-one. Rules have to be created that reflect varying environmental effects of pollution from different locations and enable their comparability. Alternatively, trading can be allowed only in subareas with uniform impact. Consequently, air-pollution measurability is highest where a unit of pollution has the same impact on air quality no matter where it is emitted, for pollution that spans small areas (local rather than regional or global air pollution), and where emissions of each polluter can easily be measured or reliably estimated.

Resource Users

Resource users (box 3 in figure 6.3) can be few or many. If a small number of resource users appropriate a large proportion of the resource, the institutional arrangements regulating resource use are more likely to be developed and well functioning. A small number of users may find it easier to solve the collective-choice dilemma and craft institutional arrangements to manage the resource. However, even if the institutional arrangement is imposed by an authorized agency, it is easier to monitor a smaller group because transparency of the resource use is higher, and thus, the need for complicated monitoring is reduced. For example, in the case of the CFC production-quota trading system, the number of companies capable of manufacturing CFCs was small. On the other hand, if the number of users is small, the potential for reducing costs through trade decreases.

The number of resource users may be directly related to the spatial extent of the resource. A global resource, such as the atmosphere, would be expected to have a large number of widely dispersed resource users all over the world. This is indeed true of many forms of global pollution, such as ocean pollution or emissions of greenhouse gases. There are, however, also cases where the use of the common pool resource (CPR) requires special technology that is available to a relatively small number of users. Thus, the two variables are not perfectly correlated.

Rules Regulating the Resource

Three types of rules regulating the resource use (box 4 in figure 6.3) are of particular importance: rules determining the severity of resource use limitation, rules requiring adjustments in the severity levels in response to external shocks or newly available information about the resource, and rules regulating how the resource is transformed into a private good (permit). These rules affect the actual environmental effectiveness of the permit system, as well as the level of trading (the value the permits hold and the security of the permits).

As outlined in figure 6.3, resource characteristics influence resource rules. Low measurability of resource stocks or flows requires that the rules be flexible to allow for adjustments in light of new information, and this flexibility potentially reduces the security of the permit for the holder.

Rules on the severity of the resource use limitation prescribe how much resource use must be reduced. The severity of the resource-management targets can significantly affect the success of the institutional arrangement, both in environmental effectiveness and in trading incentives (EPA 2002; Hall and Walton 1996), but in which direction is unclear. Theoretical literature and empirical results for the Regional Clean Air Incentives Market (RECLAIM) in southern California (SCAQMD 2007) suggest that if the targets are not restraining, they have a small environmental effect and also lead to low permit prices and a low level of investment in pollution-reduction technologies. However, empirical work presented elsewhere indicates that severity alone is not sufficient to spur high trading (Dolšak 2007).

Two broad types of rules regulating how the environmental resource is transformed into a private good have been implemented: case-by-case systems, and standardized systems depending on an emission baseline used in their definition and the actors who can participate in the market-based exchange. The case-by-case or emission-reduction credit (ERC) system is based on individual emission standards. Each polluter is required to adhere to a given emission standard, defined as emissions by unit of input or unit of output. The ERC regime does not control the aggregate emissions; it focuses on standards for emissions per unit. The total emissions depend not only on the emission coefficient but also on the level of input (output). Because input is controlled by the polluters, the regulators cannot determine the aggregate level of emissions. Therefore, this system is less environmentally effective than the emission allowance system. In this system, the right to an emission-reduction credit is issued only when the emissions are recognized by the authorized agency. Everyone with a capacity to reduce resource use can participate in this market.

The emission allowance system entitles the user to pollute the air up to the maximum level allowed by the permit. This system requires that an authorized agency determine the total level of pollution for a given period and then allocate the aggregate among the polluters included in the permit system. This system (e.g., the SO_2 allowance system authorized by the CAAA of 1990) is based on setting the maximum resource use rights (total emission allowances) for a particular period, dividing that amount among polluters, and enforcing that an individual polluter does not emit more in that period than the allowed amount. An individual polluter can purchase additional allowances for that period from other polluters whose emissions are lower than the initially allocated allowances. Thus, although every polluter holds a permit to emit an allocated amount of the pollutant, if the allocated amount is not used in the period, it can be sold to other regulated polluters or kept for future use.[7] The level of pollution from the regulated polluters is limited by the maximum amount of allowances.

Each system has advantages and disadvantages. The emission allowance system sets the maximum level of pollution and reduces transaction costs because the traded permit is standardized (a given emission allowance) and issued beforehand. However, a major disadvantage of this closed-market system is that it requires that regulators have knowledge about the pollution problem, especially the sources and acceptable levels of pollution. Also, there must be political consensus about the initial quota allocation. This system also creates barriers for new entrants. (These barriers are one way to secure the political support of existing polluters.)

The ERC system, on the other hand, allows everyone to participate in market exchange once emission reductions are certified. However, a key finding from the initial EPA emissions-trading programs has been that the quantification and cer-

---

[7] Not all tradable-permit systems, however, allow banking for future use. RECLAIM permits, for example, expire at the end of the compliance year for which they were issued.

tification of the ERCs can require much time and effort, increase exchange costs, and impede trading.

Rules Regulating Users

The most important rules pertaining to resource users (box 6 in figure 6.3) are those that determine who is regulated and how the nonregulated resource users can opt in or become regulated at a later time. If the proportion of resource users that are not regulated is large, these markets may not be environmentally effective. Rules determining which resource users are regulated must be crafted carefully because they may result in significant leakage, that is, a shift of CPR use from regulated to nonregulated users. The Clean Development Mechanisms defined in the Kyoto Protocol are particularly prone to this problem (Richards and Andersson 2001). A developing country without a national emission-reduction target does not have a mechanism to measure whether the pollution reduced at a particular site has leaked to a different project. Therefore, it is necessary to identify the largest resource users and examine how their activities might shift. In some cases, rules can be created to prevent this shift; in others, this may not be possible at low cost and in a short period of time. This shift can be regulated by specific rules stipulating the requirements that nonregulated users must meet. These characteristics must also be closely monitored.

The second challenge is the decision to allow some resource users to opt in for regulation. This decision again must be carefully considered, and the permits must be allocated so that the process does not lead to adverse selection. This clearly was the problem in the SO_2 market, where opt-in units were allocated allowances to undertake emission reductions that they would have undertaken even in the absence of opting in (Ellerman et al. 2000). Permit programs also require that once a polluting facility opts in, it can no longer elect to leave the permit program.

Trading Rules

One of the most important sets of trading rules (box 5 in figure 6.3) determines who can participate in trading. Rules that allow brokers to enter the markets can reduce exchange costs and thereby improve market performance. Brokers do much more than just match potential counterparts. In less standardized traded goods, brokers can provide standardization services (additional measurements that better define property rights) and even insurance services. Once brokers entered the EPA's lead phasedown program and the SO_2 allowance market, trading activity in both markets substantially increased.

Permit Exchangeability and Security

Polluters' incentives to invest in pollution permits depend on the permits' exchangeability and security (box 7 in figure 6.3). Exchangeability has two dimensions: space and time. The more restricted exchangeability is, the lower are the incentives for investing in permits. If resource use is not uniform (its effect on resource stocks varies depending on its location), complex exchangeability rules have to be created.

One unit of resource use at one location cannot be traded for one resource unit at another location because these uses affect stocks in different ways. Policy makers propose several ways to handle this issue (Klaassen 1996). One option is to establish trading rules based not on the flows, but on the effect the flows have on stocks. For example, permits might be allocated to biological oxygen demand, the outcome of pollution, rather than a flow of a pollutant into a water body. A second option is to divide the resource's use rights between two subunits and allow trading only within the two units, but not between them. This option will create two smaller markets, and some economically beneficial trades might not occur because of location restrictions. A third option is to allow resource users to trade between the two subunits but with restrictions on either the stock status or the total flows of resource use. Alternatively, trading can be allowed as long as the total flow of the resource in the subunits is below a threshold level. This creates incentives to use or trade resource permits early and not to bank them because it limits trading over time. All these options have higher transaction costs than single-zone trading, which has been successfully implemented for SO_2 and lead permit trading (Klaassen 1996).

Constraints on exchangeability over time might also reduce the incentives to invest in pollution permits. If permits are issued for a particular compliance year, incentives for polluters to invest in them will be higher at the beginning of the period and will decline toward the end of the period. Arguably, the desired length of the exchangeability period should reflect the level of investment in the pollution-reduction technology and the time required to obtain the permit and install the technology.

Security of permits also increases the incentives for polluters to invest in pollution-reduction technologies with the purpose of generating excess permits, selling them, or banking them for future use. Resource users are most certain that permits will continue in the future if they themselves regulate their use. The external legal and regulatory environments (box 2 in figure 6.3) can grant this authority to them or authorize a regulatory agency to regulate resource use. In many cases, the issue is whether state or federal regulators affect the security of permits. For example, if a state fails to meet the NAAQS, the federal EPA may step in and override the existing permit system. Because permits are not treated as private property, they are rarely protected by the takings laws. Therefore, the security of permits is not certain and can only be estimated by permit holders from the information they have on the past policies of the regulators.

Exchange Costs

High exchange costs (box 8 in figure 6.3) decrease the number of trades and the total trading volume and thereby diminish the potential cost savings of tradable-permit systems. Exchange costs are a function of permit characteristics: the number of issued permits, their denomination, their exchangeability (Hall and Walton 1996), the availability of information, and the existence of past trading among permit holders. Past trades among resource users can reduce current exchange costs if trades produce positive informational externalities.

High exchange costs, however, may not completely prevent trading. Resource users search for options that reduce these costs. These options include trading within firms (if firms consist of smaller units that were allocated permits; intrafirm trade) rather than between firms (interfirm trade), and trading a cluster of pollutants rather than trading each pollutant individually (Foster and Hahn 1995).

Market Performance

Market performance (box 10 in figure 6.3) can be assessed by two indicators: environmental effectiveness and market liquidity. Environmental effectiveness reflects whether and to what extent tradable-permit systems reduce air pollution. Ideally, this indicator would measure the resource stocks before and after the implementation of a tradable-permit system. For example, if a tradable permit has been designed to reduce acidification of surface waters due to SO_2 emissions, the indicator of environmental performance would measure a reduction in acidity levels in surface waters subsequent to the introduction of the permit system.

However, in many cases, data on resource stocks (either before or after the introduction of the permit system) are not available. Therefore, environmental effectiveness is frequently measured in terms of flows from or to an environmental resource. The flows from or to the resource resulting from the regulated resource users are compared with the flows in the absence of the tradable-permit system (Burtraw and Palmer 2004). The difference is then attributed to the tradable-permit system. This measurement is problematic when other policy instruments are implemented concurrently for the same environmental problem.

Although flow measures attempt to isolate program effectiveness, they miss an important aspect of market performance. When a tradable-permit system is adopted to protect an environmental resource, to keep transaction costs low, it must focus on a particular subset of resource users whose flows from or into the resource can easily be measured and monitored and on whom restrictions can be enforced. At the extreme, one could visualize a tradable-permit design that would exclude some resource users if they negatively affected the effectiveness of the market. For example, when prices for NO_x allowances in the RECLAIM market increased by a factor of four beyond what was anticipated in 2000, electric utilities were excluded from RECLAIM. This exclusion of specific market participants significantly reduced the demand for allowances and thereby stabilized the price of allowances, but the pollution merely shifted to resource users outside the tradable-permit system. Although prices stabilized (indicating higher efficiency of the market) and NO_x emissions of market participants were reduced (indicating higher environmental effectiveness of the market), the indicator focusing solely on pollution by the market participants would be an incorrect measure of environmental performance of this tradable-permit market.

In this chapter, environmental effectiveness is operationalized in terms of resource flows (emissions) after the tradable-permit market has been implemented as compared with the resource flows (emissions) before its implementation. In using this measure, all of the caveats discussed earlier should be kept in mind. The value of this variable is coded as low when emissions were reduced by less than 30 percent (RE-CLAIM [EPA 2002]; early EPA emissions trading); moderate when emissions were reduced by between 30 and 60 percent; and high when CPR use was reduced by more than 60 percent (lead phasedown program [EPA 1995]; ozone-depleting substances production-quota trading [UNEP 1999]).

Market liquidity is the second general indicator of market performance.[8] Market liquidity or trading activity is measured by comparing quantities of the resource flows exchanged in the markets among economically nonrelated entities (quantity of permits traded) with the entire quantity of the resource flow allocated to market participants (quantity of permits issued).[9] The values of this variable are coded as low when fewer than 10 percent of the tradable permits are exchanged in a market (early EPA emissions trading [Hahn and Hester 1989a; 1989b]); moderate when this share was between 10 percent and 20 percent (RECLAIM); and high when this share exceeded 20 percent (lead phasedown program [Nussbaum 1992]; ozone-depleting substances production-quota trading [Lee 1996; UNEP 1999]). Although the coding cutoff points are arbitrary, there is a clear difference between markets with high trading activity and those with low trading activity. Surprisingly, a majority of the analyzed markets have comparable trading activity, with measures of trading varying from 20 percent to about 30 percent.

Tradable-Permit Systems for Reducing Air Pollution

This section examines the factors that affect the performance of four U.S. tradable-permit systems to reduce air pollution. These systems range from local (lead emissions) and regional (NO_x) to global air pollution (ozone-depleting substances). The data used in this analysis come from published empirical case studies on these markets and from regulators, such as the EPA, California's South Coast Air Quality Management District (SCAQMD), and the Department of Energy (DOE).

The Lead Phasedown Program

The lead phasedown program sought to reduce the use of the atmosphere as a sink for lead pollution from gasoline-burning vehicles. By focusing on gasoline producers, the program drastically reduced emissions of lead into the atmosphere. Between 1988 and 1997, the maximum quarterly average lead concentrations decreased by 67 percent. At the end of the program, all gasoline refineries met the standards and required no extensions. Section 218 of the CAAA of 1990 eliminated the last remnants of leaded gasoline in 1996. Today, no area in the United States violates the NAAQS for lead.

---

[8] Market liquidity is an important precondition for economic efficiency. However, there are exceptions. First, trading may be low if actors choose to bank rather than sell their quotas (Fraas and Richardson 2010). The incentives for banking may be enhanced when there is an expectation that emission-control stringency will increase in the future.

[9] Although some have argued that a larger number of allowances exchanged does not necessarily mean a better-functioning market (Ellerman et al. 2000), others have argued that a low volume of trading indicates barriers to trading and a poorly performing market. Those barriers then have to be identified and removed (E. M. Bailey 1998; Gangadharan 2000; Hahn and Hester 1989a; 1989b; Kerr and Mare, 1997; Lile, Bohi, and Burtraw 1996; Newell and Rogers 2004; Schmalensee 1998).

Lead concentrations closely follow lead emissions. Because of the short residence time of lead, changes in emission levels are followed within a year by changes in concentrations (Brown, Kasperson, and Raymond 1993). This makes it easier to devise the necessary reductions in resource use to accomplish the required effects on resource stocks. Because lead content does not differ across gallons of gasoline produced in the same refinery at any given time, it was measured in samples, and the values were averaged over a three-month production period (the compliance period).

The extent to which air pollution travels depends on the physical state of the pollutant (gaseous, vapor, or particulate), the height of the emission source, and wind speed. Lead does not travel very far. In the past, concentrations were highest in the vicinity of highways. They decrease drastically as the distance from highways increases. Therefore, lead concentration monitoring must occur not only at road sites, but also at a neighborhood level.

Gasoline combustion accounted for nearly 86 percent of lead emissions in 1970, whereas the next-largest contributors, such as primary lead smelting, coal burning, and waste oil combustion, each accounted for about 2 percent of the total emissions (EPA 1984). The lead phasedown program, therefore, focused on gasoline refineries. Three hundred to four hundred oil refineries were included in the lead phasedown program. Gasoline production was fairly concentrated: 25 percent of the refineries accounted for 70 percent of production, while the remaining 75 percent of the refineries accounted for about 30 percent of production (Nussbaum 1992). Modern refineries (mainly located on the west coast) were capable of producing gasoline with 0.7 grams of lead per gallon. Some opting in was allowed, but gasoline blenders played a minor role in the market.

At the peak in the 1970s, the average content of lead in a gallon of gasoline was about 2 grams per liquid gallon (gplg), but the content could be as high as 4 gplg. In 1982 the standard of 1.1 gram of lead per gallon of gasoline was introduced for refineries. The use of lead as a gasoline additive was to be phased out by 1987. During the initial period, from 1983 to the end of 1985, the resource use regulations were not stringent. The actual lead content was significantly below the standard. The standard was tightened on 1 July 1985 (0.5 gplg) and again on 1 January 1986 (0.1 gplg).

Refineries were allocated rights to use lead as a gasoline additive for each quarter of a year on the basis of their quarterly production of gasoline, multiplied by the currently valid lead content standard. With banking (exchangeability of rights across time periods), trading became more active and new actors entered the market. Gasoline suppliers could blend gasoline with alcohol, thereby reducing lead content per gallon and obtaining lead-use permits. At the end of 1984, there were about one hundred blenders. By late 1985, the number grew to nine hundred. Many of them, unfortunately, did not know how to report lead usage, and many trades included rights that could not be claimed legitimately (Nussbaum 1992). Brokers also entered the market, but they merely acted as intermediaries.

Allocated rights were fully tradable within the commitment period. No prior EPA approval was required for transferring the permits. In 1985 banking (exchangeability of rights across time periods) was allowed; refineries could bank unused rights for the last two years of the program (1986 and 1987), when the leaded gasoline would be phased out As a result, trading became more active, and new actors entered the market.

Trading of lead permits did not cause high exchange costs for refineries, which were used to trading with one another. In addition to trading gasoline, they would add the lead rights. For them, trading lead rights resulted in "little more paper work costs than the addition of a contractual paragraph and, perhaps, the price of a stamp" (Nussbaum 1992, 32). Although brokers were allowed to enter the market, they faced the same information problems as the traders. Large traders did not rely on brokers because of high costs; it was mostly small traders who used their services.

The program exhibited active trading and banking, even though no price information was publicly available, and brokers played only a limited role (predominantly for small traders). With the enactment of tighter standards in 1985 and 1986, refineries had to use the banked rights to comply with the standards. From the beginning of the program in 1983 to its end in 1987, between one-fifth and one-third of the facilities purchased lead rights (Nussbaum 1992). Intrafirm trading was also important. Kerr and Mare (1997) report that about 67 percent of trades in their sample, covering the second half of 1983 and 1984, were internal.

The value of lead rights rose with the introduction of banking. Initial prices were about 3.5 cents per gram and subsequently increased to slightly more than 4 cents per gram. Price information was not collected and reported by any entity in the market. The only way to learn the price was to negotiate it with potential trading partners (Kerr and Mare 1997).

Emissions of lead from on-road vehicles declined from about 172,000 short tons of lead in 1970 to about 62,000 short tons in 1980 and to only 1,387 in 1995 (EPA 1995). At the same time, total lead emissions were reduced from about 220,000 short tons in 1970 to about 5,000 short tons in 1995 (EPA 1995). The average lead content in gasoline fell from about 2 gplg in 1973 0.7 gplg in the first quarter of 1985. At that time, the standard was 1.1 gplg. In the third quarter of 1985, the average lead content fell to 0.4 gplg. In the same year, the standard was tightened to 0.5 gplg (Nussbaum 1992). In 1987, at the end of the lead phasedown program, no refinery asked for additional time to comply with the 0.1 gplg standard (Nussbaum 1992).

Early EPA Trading and RECLAIM

This section reviews two tradable-permit systems implemented in southern California: a federal early EPA trading program implemented in the 1970s and the subsequent local tradable-permit system, the Regional Clean Air Incentives Market (RECLAIM), implemented in the 1993 by the SCAQMD.[10]

The following discussion offers lessons about the impact of institutions on environmental effectiveness and market liquidity.[11] First, predefined, standardized emission allowances do not necessarily outperform case-by-case-defined emission-

---

[10] The SCAQMD was established in 1977 to address the persistent air-pollution problems in Southern California.

[11] Generalization of the SCAQMD trading data to other air-quality-control regions, however, is limited. The SCAQMD exhibited a more active market than other areas, most likely because of high demand caused by rapid development in the area and more stringent classification requirements for major emission sources.

reduction credits in environmental effectiveness when predictability of resource stocks is low and resource use is not severely constrained. Market liquidity, however, improves. The number of trades increases, traded rights represent a larger proportion of resource use, and specialized agents enter the market. However, market liquidity improvements do not occur instantaneously with the shift to standardized allowances, because right holders must take time to learn the new property institutions.

Measurability of resource stocks and flows is moderate in southern California. More than 30 locations throughout the SCAQMD measure air pollution. However, attributing the pollution data directly to any policy is problematic because 60 to 80 percent of variability in daily maximum ozone concentrations depends on weather.

The reliability of measurements of resource flows, that is, air emissions, varies. Stationary sources, such as power plants, have been installing devices for continuous measurements of emissions of SO_x and NO_x since the 1990s to meet the RECLAIM requirements (about two-thirds of the RECLAIM units are required to do so). However, such devices were not in place before the 1990s, and measurability was limited in the early EPA trading systems. Mobile sources' emission rates are measured annually during emissions tests.

SO_x and NO_x pollution in this area has a clear nonuniform effect; a ton of criteria pollutant emitted in the coastal area affects air quality not only in this area but also in the inland area because of the direction of prevailing winds. The reverse, however, does not hold.

The main polluters are transportation, electric utilities, and industry. Transportation accounts for more than half the emissions of five important pollutants. Ozone's two major precursor gases, NO_x and volatile organic compounds (VOCs), come predominantly from transportation and industrial facilities. Two major emission sources of NO_x are transportation and stationary fuel-combustion sources (electric utilities and industrial boilers). Industrial and commercial sectors are the second-largest polluters. Major sources of ambient SO_2 are coal and oil combustion, steel mills, refineries, pulp and paper mills, and nonferrous smelters (EPA, 2010).

The severity of restrictions on resource use depends on three factors: (1) the level of resource stocks—the most stringent regulation of resource users is in the nonattainment areas, for example, SCAQMD; (2) the history of resource use by a given resource user (its presence in the resource area and its past compliance); and (3) planned future resource use (major or minor user).[12]

Rules for defining tradable permits differed between the early EPA trading and RECLAIM. The early EPA trading system defined permits through a case-by-case review of emission levels. This review was fraught with uncertainty regarding the amount of ERCs to be given. Because neither the baseline (until 1986) nor the estimation method was defined, neither the seller nor the buyer knew how many ERCs were actually involved in the trade (National Academy of Public Administration 1994).

In RECLAIM, each existing facility was allocated RECLAIM Trading Credits (RTCs) for equipment or processes that emitted NO_x and SO_x, starting in 1994. The

---

[12] Chapter 5 by Daniel Cole addresses the issues of access to resources in greater detail.

allocation was based on past peak emissions and was very generous. However, NO_x allowances were scheduled to decline annually by 7.1 percent until 2000 and by 8.1 percent from 2000 to 2003. SO_x emissions were scheduled to decline 4.1 percent annually until 2000 and by 8.1 percent until 2003 (Gangadharan 2000). New facilities have to purchase emission rights (as in the EPA policy in the 1970s). To obtain a permit, they have to demonstrate that best available control technology will be applied. Permit review is more stringent for "major" than for "minor" emitters.

The early EPA trading program and RECLAIM regulate different resource users. The former was focused on new sources that had to obtain ERCs to offset their emissions. RECLAIM, on the other hand, focuses on existing sources and also regulates new sources. As of 1992, about 30,000 firms had obtained permits in the Los Angeles Basin, but only facilities emitting more than four tons or more from permitted equipment per year are included in RECLAIM. There are approximately 390 facilities in the NO_x market, which account for about 65 percent of the emissions from all permitted stationary sources in the basin, and about 41 facilities in the SO_x market, which account for about 85 percent of reported emissions from all permitted stationary sources. Stationary sources, however, account for only 40 percent of the air pollution in the area, whereas mobile sources account for 60 percent (SCAQMD 1997). Electric utilities (until 2000), industrial boilers, manufacturers, and refineries are included in RECLAIM. Transportation projects are allowed to opt in. RECLAIM resource users have two different compliance cycles, the calendar year and the fiscal year, to avoid fluctuations in the market.

Nonregulated resource users can employ three programs to enter RECLAIM: ERCs resulting from scrapping of old vehicles (ERCs are converted to RTCs at a 1.2 discount factor); area source credits (ASCs) resulting from changes in applied technologies (ASCs are converted to RTCs at a ratio of 10 to 9); and Air Quality Investment Program credits, obtained from an investment fund operated by the SCAQMD.

State regulatory agencies served as brokers in the early EPA trading, bringing "the two partners to the negotiation table 'kicking and screaming'" (Liroff 1980, 18). RECLAIM, on the other hand, has several active broker companies. Data from the 1990s suggest that brokers played an important role in reducing transaction costs. By 1996 about 70 percent of the trades were conducted by brokers. RTC exchanges in which brokers were involved were traded at prices about 43 percent higher than those in which the polluters were trading directly (Gangadharan 2000). These price differences were eliminated by 2010.

The early EPA trading allowed four types of transfers of ERCs: bubbles, netting (used for existing sources), offsets (used by new sources), and banking. Bubbles (after 1979) provided flexibility to a facility to achieve emission reductions across its many processes rather than implementing a prescribed technology for each one. Netting (after 1974) allowed an existing facility to use ERCs in planning for a technology modification. The key advantage of using netting was that it allowed modifications and sources to qualify as "minor" rather than "major" and thereby avoid more stringent regulations. Offsets were devised in 1976 to be purchased by new major emitters from existing emitters. ERCs were discounted at each trade, and the extent of discounting was not known beforehand (National Academy of Public Administration 1994). Banking (beginning in 1979) allowed firms to hold unused ERCs for either future use or future sale. As of 1986, only five states had their banking regulations approved by the EPA.

The EPA's 1975 exchange rules used discounting to adjust for the nonuniform effect of pollution and restricted areas in which ERCs could be traded. Offsets for SO_x, for example, had to originate from sources in the immediate vicinity of the polluter. Similarly, the farther apart the seller and the buyer were, the more discounted the offsets were.[13] The discounting factors and sophisticated air-pollution modeling, required for such trades, impeded trading. Banking involved additional uncertainty; there was no assurance that the ERCs would not be discounted or even confiscated if the NAAQS were not met.

RECLAIM simplified the exchange rules with respect to nonuniformity of the pollutant. The SCAQMD area was divided into two homogeneous areas: coastal and inland. Trading was allowed within areas. Trading between areas, however, was restricted; facilities in the coastal areas could purchase only RTCs originating in the coastal area. This resulted in higher prices of RTCs from coastal areas. RECLAIM does not allow exchange of RTCs across time periods. Although facilities with different compliance periods can trade RTCs, RTCs can be used only in the year for which they are issued. This rule does not stimulate early achievement of environmental targets, but it does prevent occurrence of temporal hot spots.

The early EPA trading program had low trading volumes. Furthermore, trading activity varied across the four ERC transfer options because of different exchange rules and severities of resource use regulation. Netting was the most widely used (Hahn and Hester 1989a; 1989b; Liroff 1980). It brings significant savings because it allows that a source be classified as a minor source. Thereby, the firm avoids more stringent emission limits, modeling, and monitoring, which can all be costly (Hahn and Hester 1989a). Unfortunately, detailed data are available only for 1984. In this year only, nine hundred sources applied for netting in the entire United States.

Offsets were the second most used form of trading. Between 1977 and 1980, approximately 1,500 sources used offsets, and between 1981 and 1986, 500 sources used offsets. Traded offsets represented a small proportion of total emissions. For example, in 1985 there were five NO_x external offsets in the SCAQMD, with a total volume of 575 tons per year traded, accounting for less than 0.5 percent of total emissions. There were only two external SO_x offsets, with 310 tons per year traded at an average price of $3,000, accounting for less than 0.5 percent of total emissions.

Initial trading in RECLAIM was also modest, but then increased substantially over the years. In the first year of the policy, only about 9,000 tons of NO_x RTCs were traded. In subsequent years, the volume of NO_x RTCs increased to about 40,000 per year until 2000. The SCAQMD removed electric utilities from RECLAIM in 2000. Trading volumes after 2000 declined to about 15,000 tons annually. Traded volumes of SO_x RTCs were similarly high in the years before 2000. The volume of trade varied between a low of 10,000 tons in 1998 and a high of 22,000 in 1999. The crisis of 2000 reduced the traded volume to about 5,000 tons of SO_x. Since then, annual traded volume has varied from fewer than 1,000 tons to 13,000 tons.

---

[13] If the sources were relatively close, predetermined ratios were used. If the distance exceeded 30 miles, air-pollution modeling was required.

RTC prices also varied over the years. Average NO_x RTC prices were about $800 per ton in 1995, but more than $31,000 in 2001. After 2001 the prices decreased substantially, ranging from $3,147 in 2004 to $9,400 in 2006 (Coy and Luong, 2007). Prices for SO_x RTCs similarly started low at $600 per ton in 1995 and were at their highest in 2002, $7,850 per ton. After two years of high prices in 2002 and 2003, prices dropped to $2,000 in 2004 and $3,500 in 2005.

As previously noted, there are approximately 390 facilities in the NO_x market and about 41 facilities in the SO_x market. In 1995 only about 95 facilities (about 24 percent) actually traded in the NO_x market. The number of companies trading in the market increased over the years. In the third quarter of 2010 alone, almost 60 nonbroker companies traded in both markets.

If the environmental effectiveness of RECLAIM is judged by the actual emissions of the units included in the program, it was a success. Emission targets for SO_x were met in all years. Emission targets for NO_x were met in all years but 2000 and 2001, when electricity shortages required that old, polluting units be used again for electricity generation, resulting in increased pollution.

A review of resource stocks similarly suggests that pollution is decreasing in this area, although it still exceeds the NAAQS. For example, in the late 1970s, this area exceeded the permissible concentrations of ozone standards for almost two hundred days. In the late 1980s, the number of days when ozone concentrations exceeded standards were around one hundred and fifty. In 1993, the year in which RECLAIM was implemented, the number dropped below 120. In addition to the decline in the number of days in violation, there has also been a reduction in maximum concentrations of pollutants. In 1976 the highest eight-hour concentration of ozone was 0.268 parts per million (ppm); in 2008 the highest eight-hour concentration of ozone was 0.131ppm (the standard in 2008 was 0.075 ppm). As noted earlier, the major causes of ground ozone are NO_x (addressed by RECLAIM) and VOCs (SCAQMD, 2011).

Ozone-Depleting Substances

The ozone (O_3) layer is found in the earth's atmosphere between about six and thirty-one miles above the ground. In the early 1970s, scientists discovered human interference with stratospheric ozone. The substances causing the damage were CFCs emitted on the earth's surface but reaching the stratosphere because of their chemical stability. The reason for concern about ozone depletion and increased ultraviolet-B (UV-B) radiation is that the latter is associated with skin cancers and cataracts. The U.S. EPA estimated that continued depletion of the ozone layer could result in an additional 800,000 cancer deaths in the United States over the next century (McKinney and Schoch 1998). Further, increased UV-B radiation can adversely affect photosynthesis, metabolism, and growth of a number of plants. Phytoplankton, which form the basis of many food chains, are also susceptible to increased UV-B radiation. The international community limited the use of ozone-depleting substances (ODSs) in the Montreal Protocol to the Vienna Convention in 1987 that was then subsequently revised seven times. Countries accepted limitations on their production and consumption of ODSs. The analysis in this chapter focuses on the U.S. tradable-permit system only.

Although resource stocks were fairly well understood in the 1990s, the impact of resource flows, that is, emissions of ODSs, on the ozone hole was estimated only with high uncertainty (Hollandsworth and Binder 1998). Emissions of ODSs are measured by using production data. By multiplying production data for these substances by their ozone-depleting potential (ODP), one can estimate the total quantity of ODSs. The damage caused by emissions of ODSs varies across the globe. Maximum ozone depletion occurs in high latitudes, where trends are close to a 6 and an 8 percent reduction per decade in the Southern and Northern hemispheres, respectively. There is less depletion in the tropics, and there are even positive trends at the equator (Hollandsworth and Binder 1998). However, ODSs have uniform effects in that it does not matter where a ton of ODSs is emitted.

ODSs are used in a variety of products and processes, and resource users vary from households to the car industry. CFCs are widely used in plastic foams (32 percent), solvents (21 percent), car air conditioning (20 percent), other refrigeration (17 percent), medical sterilants (6.5 percent), and aerosols (3.5 percent) (Cook 1996).

Production and consumption of ODSs were regulated in the United States by imposing production and consumption limits, as well as by imposing taxes on these substances. The 1990 CAAA also banned nonessential products containing CFCs or hydrochlorofluorocarbons (HCFCs), such as flexible and packaging foams, most aerosols, and pressurized dispensers, and required labeling of products that contained or were manufactured with ODSs. To implement the CAAA, the EPA issued deadlines for phasing out the production and consumption of Class I substances (CFCs, carbon tetrachloride, methyl chloroform, and halons) in 1992. End users were also regulated. Standards were set for servicing equipment using CFCs, and car air-conditioning substitutes were established (62 Fed. Reg. 68,026; EPA, 2010).

Permits to produce ODSs were allocated to five CFC producers, three halon producers, fourteen CFC importers, and six halon importers (Lee 1996). This is the smallest group of regulated users of all markets examined in this chapter. Because this group is also very homogeneous and has a history of intragroup trading, identifying potential partners was not too difficult or costly.

Users of CFCs and halons (or products containing these substances) were allocated consumption permits. The EPA estimated that in the 1980s there were more than 10,000 CFC and halon user sectors (Lee 1996). Their emissions were regulated by standards. For example, the 1990 CAAA enacted standards for CFC-recycling equipment for air conditioners and refrigerators. Users, however, also adjusted their use patterns to the new market situation. This shift in demand (for example, the solvent industry stopped using CFC-113, recycled used substances, and started substituting) made CFC-113 allowances available for trading. They were traded and used as allowances for substances that were still in demand, such as CFC-12.

As the United States banned some uses of CFCs and scheduled other ODSs for a phaseout by 1996, the severity of resource use limits in the case of CFCs is comparable to that of the lead phasedown program. However, some of these substances and products containing them were taxed, and their prices increased; in some cases (CFC-11 and CFC-12), they doubled. By 1995 the taxed price was nearly triple the untaxed price.

The right to use the atmosphere as a sink for ODSs was expressed as the right to produce a given amount of these substances. However, because manufacturers produced substances with various ODPs, the issue of assigning rights arose. Should the permits be allocated for each substance, or should they be allocated as an ODP-weighted aggregate? Under the first system, each user is allocated permits for each ODS. Under the second system, the user is issued ODP-weighted allowances.

The CFC and halon trading systems were initially based on weighted averages. The 1990 CAAA enacted substance permits. If a user wanted to trade allowances of one substance for allowances of another substance, the EPA based the calculation of the trading ratio on the ODP. In this way, the EPA could track who had allowances of which substance. At the time of reducing allowances or completely phasing out a substance, information was then available on whose allowances were being reduced. If allowances are based on ODP-weighted averages, information about which substances are the base of the allocated permits is lost. The EPA does not know how much to issue to which user the next time the permits are issued.

Exchangeability of permits is based on the ODPs of the substances and the origin of the substance (manufactured or recycled). Difficulties in distinguishing between manufactured and recycled substances in the absence of a carefully documented recycling process result in illegal trades of these substances. Each manufacturer must have a sufficient amount of permits to cover the production of the substances. Each consumer must have a sufficient amount of consumption permits to cover the purchased substances. Each transfer of substances must be accompanied by a transfer of permits. If substances are imported from countries that do not have limits on CFC production (Article 5 countries), no transfer of permits is possible. Transfers of substances from these countries are therefore limited to recycled substances. Close examination of the flow of recycled substances, their origin, and the recycling capabilities of the industry in those countries indicates that large amounts of CFCs and halons are illegally exported to the United States and the European Union, predominantly from China, India, and Russia. The economic motivation is clear. The excise tax and the domestic production reduction and phase-out increased the price of these substances in non–Article 5 countries, such as the United States. The price of domestically reclaimed halon 1301 is about $26 per kilogram, whereas the price of supposedly recycled halon from China is $7.5 per kilogram (EIA, 1998).

The market for ODSs in the United States was a small club with a total of 28 producers and importers who were initially allocated permits. All these facilities were listed in a *Federal Register* notice. The Alliance for Responsible Atmospheric Policy, an industrial organization, brought together potential traders. Trades had to be preapproved by the EPA, which promised to process requests within three days. Two EPA offices were involved in the program: the Office of Atmospheric Programs tracked allowances, and the Office of Enforcement monitored compliance. Because the definitions of traded goods and quantities did not depend on a case-by-case review, but on issued allowances, approval required only that the two offices cross-check their data. All these aspects suggest that exchange costs were low.

Targets for reductions in production and consumption of CFCs and halons were not only met, but exceeded. The 1989 target for CFC production was about 342,000 ODP tons, but actual production was about 320,000 tons. The target for 1994 was about 109,000 tons, but actual production was about 78,000 tons. By 1996 the United States produced only 676 tons of CFCs. The CFC consumption-reduction targets were also exceeded. The target for 1989 was about 337,000 tons, but actual consumption was about 318,000 tons. The 1994 target was about 107,000 tons, with actual consumption of about 73,000 tons, and the 1996 target was about 46,000 tons, with actual consumption of about 2,000 tons. Similarly, the 1992 target for halon production was about 65,000 tons, but actual production was about 26,000 tons, and the 1992 target for halon consumption was about 64,000 tons, but actual consumption was about 24,000 tons. The 1994 production and consumption targets were each about 6,000 tons, but the United States had completely phased out halon production and consumption by then (UNEP, 1999).

However, the question is to what extent these reductions can be attributed to tradable permits and to what extent they were caused by the excise taxes, introduced in 1990. Allowances were already assigned in 1989, but production had not fallen drastically, whereas in 1990, the first year when the tax was paid, production decreased substantially.

Lee (1996) claims that permit trading helped American companies exceed the Montreal Protocol targets. He argues that the drop in anticipated costs of reducing CFC production from $3.55 per kilogram of CFC to $2.45 was a result of the marketable system, which lowered administrative costs and offered the flexibility needed to meet the reduction goals. There is no question that allowance trading offers flexibility.

However, the trading data for 1989 and 1990 suggest modest trading levels. Each year, allowances for not more than 1 million kilograms of ODSs were traded between companies. In 1991 the trading increased to 80 million kilograms of ODSs (45 trades). The amount of traded ODSs then remained fairly stable until 1995, when it dropped to 60 million kilograms. Therefore, the major overcompliance that Lee (1996) identifies in 1990 cannot plausibly be attributed to trading. Further, in 1990, when U.S. actual production was 6 percent below the allowed limit, the productions of France, Germany, and the United Kingdom were 29, 23, and 33 percent, respectively, below their allowed production.

The market saw little activity in trades until 1992 (5, 15, and 45 trades in 1989, 1990, and 1991, respectively). In 1992 the number of trades increased to 217 and then declined to 95 in 1995. Although production and consumption were reduced beyond the targets, it is not likely that these results were accomplished solely because of the tradable-permit system. Without additional data, it is impossible to conclude how much of the effectiveness was due to the excise tax and how much to the tradable-permit system.

Findings

This chapter has examined the effectiveness of four tradable-permit systems for emissions of pollutants: emissions of lead (lead phasedown program); emissions of nitrogen oxides (early EPA emissions trading and RECLAIM); and emissions of ODSs (CFC and halon production and consumption quota trading). Table 6.1 presents an overview of the characteristics of these tradable-permit systems.

The examined air-pollution cases vary from small and local (for example, using the atmosphere as a sink for pollutants that have local effects, such as lead) to those with a global extent (emission of ODSs). They include cases with a very small number of users (CFCs) and with large numbers (RECLAIM). The security and the exchangeability of permits vary from very limited in some markets (early EPA emissions trading) to high for others (lead phasedown program in the second stage).

Two markets exhibited high environmental performance and high trading activity: the lead phasedown program and ODS production-quota trading. High environmental performance is associated with severe limits on resource use in all markets. Although theory would predict that nonuniform impacts of emissions would have reduced trading, the institutional design appropriately addressed it. Instead of assigning permits to the users who cause pollution (cars), the permits were assigned to those who produced polluting fuel (refineries). So-called hot spots could have occurred if gasoline from the lead-permit buyers (high lead-content gasoline) were concentrated in one market. However, because gasoline from overcomplying refineries was mixed in the pipeline system with gasoline from refineries that used higher amounts of lead, the hot spots did not occur. Nonetheless, the accomplished reductions in resource use cannot be attributed solely to the tradable permits; other policy instruments (excise taxes) and external factors (technological changes that provided substitutes for polluting substances) were also involved. Therefore, we must be cautious about attributing environmental effectiveness to tradable permits.

In sum, comparative case analysis suggests that two factors commonly perceived to affect market effectiveness negatively—large spatial extent of the environmental resource and nonuniform effect of resource flows on resource stocks—do not necessarily reduce the effectiveness of tradable permits. Transaction costs, identified as significantly hindering trading activities in earlier markets, have successfully been reduced over time. These findings suggest that tradable permits can be applied to a larger number of environmental problems than the critics of this approach would admit.

In contrast, the other two tradable-permit markets exhibited low environmental performance. This result can be linked to low severity of limits on resource use and to lack of information available for monitoring and enforcement (RECLAIM). Therefore, future research will need to focus on political factors that affect the design of tradable permits, especially the severity of resource use limits and rules regulating opting in.

Several lessons emerge from this study. First, the environmental effectiveness of tradable-permit regimes is influenced by the severity of restrictions imposed on resource users. Of course, severity leads to the erosion of political support among existing polluters. Thus, tradable-permit regimes need to find a balance between political imperatives and institutional requirements. Second, policy makers should

TABLE 6.1

Tradable-Permits Systems for Air Pollution

| Permit System | Independent Variables | | | | | Outcome | |
	Resource	Users	Regulated Users	Permits	Exchange Costs	Environmental Effectiveness	Trading Activity
Lead phasedown program	High predictability; local once emitted; nonuniform	Moderate number	Homogeneous group; trading experience; little opting in; samples monitored	Clearly defined; no property right; severe limits; exchangeable in space, but not in time	Low	High	High
RECLAIM	Moderate predictability; local extent; nonuniform	Large number	Not very homogeneous; opting in; partially continuous monitoring	Clearly defined; exchange ratios (space); exchangeable in time; modest severity	Moderate	Low	Moderate
ODS production-quota trading	Moderate predictability; global extent; uniform effect	Small number	Very small number; homogeneous group; no opting in; phased self-reporting	Clearly defined; substance-specific; exchange ratios; high value; severe limits on resource use	Low	High	High
Early EPA emissions trading	Moderate predictability; local extent; nonuniform	Large number	Large number; not very homogeneous; opting in	Case-by-case definition; exchange ratios; high severity	High	Low	Low

introduce tradable permits at appropriate points of the resource use cycle and devise and enforce credible rules for reducing resource use over time. Because the findings presented in this chapter are based on limited data, the causal inferences have high uncertainty. To reduce this uncertainty, future efforts should target compilation of a set of measures that are comparable across tradable-permit markets. In particular, researchers need to identify better data to measure cost savings of tradable-permit systems and to develop comparable measures of environmental performance. They also need to control for the share of the resource that is not regulated by the tradable-permit system, for potential leakage of resource use to non-participants in the market, and for the policy effect of related policy instruments implemented concurrently with tradable permits.

Resource users participate in a variety of markets, including the market for the tradable permits. Two kinds of markets are especially important: the market for products requiring the use of the regulated resource (increased electricity demand will likely increase demand for tradable permits for air pollution; increased timber and cash-crop demand will likely lead to increased deforestation); and markets that enable resource users to decouple their income from resource use (for example, markets for technologies that reduce the use of the atmosphere as a sink for pollution). These markets can either increase or alleviate pressure on environmental resources and thereby influence the efficacy of tradable-permit regimes. In the future, it will be important to examine the impact of these markets on the effectiveness of tradable-permit markets. Globalization and access to markets with high demand for resource conservation may actually help reduce the exploitation of natural resources in countries with lower ability to postpone current resource use with the goal of protection. It is obvious, then, that it is not possible to discuss only one way in which private rights allocation and privatization affect natural resources and air pollution. Rather, it is necessary to study factors affecting market outcomes and perhaps suggest how privatization can be used to protect environmental resources.

Acknowledgments

The research for this chapter was partially supported by the Workshop in Political Theory and Policy Analysis, Indiana University, and by the Center for the Study of Institutions, Population, and Environmental Change, Indiana University. The author thanks Elinor Ostrom, Daniel H. Cole, Shi-Ling Hsu, and Aseem Prakash for their comments on earlier versions of this chapter.

REFERENCES

Bailey, E. M. 1998. Allowance trading activity and state regulatory rulings: Evidence from the U.S. Acid Rain Program. Working Paper Wp-98005. Cambridge, MA: Massachusetts Institute of Technology.

Bailey, P., and T. Jackson. 1999. Joint implementation for controlling sulphur in Europe and possible lessons for carbon dioxide. In *Pollution for sale: Emissions trading and joint implementation*, eds. S. Sorrell and J. Skea, 255–271. Northampton, MA: Edward Elgar.

Baumol, W. J., and W. E. Oates. 1975. *The theory of environmental policy.* Englewood Cliffs, NJ: Prentice Hall.

Brown, Halina Szejnwald, Roger E. Kasperson, and Susan Raymond. 1993. Trace pollutants. In *The Earth as transformed by human action: Global and regional changes in the biosphere over the past 300 years,* eds. B. L. Turner II, et al., 437–454. Cambridge, U.K.: Cambridge University Press.

Burtraw, D., and K. Palmer. 2004. SO_2 cap-and-trade program in the United States: A "living legend" of market effectiveness. In *Choosing environmental policy: Comparing instruments and outcomes in the United States and Europe,* eds. W. Harrington, R. D. Morgenstern, and T. Sterner, 41–66. Washington, DC: Resources for the Future.

Cason, T. N., and L. Gangadharan. 2003. Transactions costs in tradable permit markets: An experimental study of pollution market designs. *Journal of Regulatory Economics* 23(3):145–165.

Coase, R. H. 1960. The problem of social cost. *Journal of Law and Economics* 3:1–44.

Cook, Elizabeth, ed., 1996. *Ozone protection in the United States: Elements of success.* Washington: World Resources Institute.

Cornes, R., and T. Sandler. 1996. *The theory of externalities, public goods, and club goods.* Cambridge, U.K.: Cambridge University Press.

Coy, C., et al. 2001. *White paper on stabilization of NO_x RTC prices.* South Coast Air Quality Management District. http://www.aqmd.gov/hb/2001/010123a.html.

Coy, Carol, and Danny Luong. 2007. RECLAIM: Key lessons learned. South Coast Air Quality District. http://www.aqmd.gov/reclaim/docs/Policy_Paper_Part2.pdf.

Crotty, Patricia McGee. 1987. The new federalism game: Primacy implementation of environmental policy. *Publius* 17 (Spring): 53–67.

Dales, J. 1968. *Pollution, property, and prices: An essay in policy-making and economics.* Toronto: University of Toronto Press.

Dietz, T., E. Ostrom, and P. C. Stern. 2003. The struggle to govern the commons. *Science* 302(5652):1907–1912.

Dolšak, N. 2007. An assessment of tradable permits for common-pool resources. *Review of Policy Research* 24(6):541–565.

Driesen, D. M. 2003. *The economic dynamics of environmental law.* Cambridge, MA: MIT Press.

Ellerman, D. A., et al. 2000. *Markets for clean air: The U.S. Acid Rain Program.* Cambridge, U.K.: Cambridge University Press.

EIA (Environmental Investigation Agency). 1998. *A crime against nature: The Halon trade.* http://www.eia-international.org/old-reports/Ozone/Reports/CrimeAgainst/halon_trade03.html.

EPA (U.S. Environmental Protection Agency). 1984. *National air quality and emissions trends report, 1984.* http://www.epa.gov/nscep/index.html.

———. 1995. *National emission standards.* http://www.opa.gov:80/airprogram/oar/emtrnd95/natemtr.pdf.

———. 2002. *An evaluation of the South Coast Air Quality Management District's regional clean air incentives market—Lessons in environmental markets and innovation.* http://www.epa.gov/region9/air/reclaim/reclaim-report.pdf.

———. 2010. *The accelerated phaseout of Class I ozone-depleting substances.* http://www.epa.gov/ozone/title6/phaseout/accfact.html.

Farrell, A. E., and M. G. Morgan. 2003. Multilateral emission trading: Heterogeneity in domestic and international common-pool resource management. In *The commons in the new millennium: Challenges and adaptations,* eds. N. Dolšak and E. Ostrom, 169–218. Cambridge, MA: MIT Press.

Foster, V., and R. W. Hahn. 1995. Designing more efficient markets: Lessons from Los Angeles smog control. *Journal of Law and Economics* 38(1):19–48.

Fraas, Arthur G., and Nathan Richardson. 2010. Banking on allowances. RRF Discussion Paper 10–42. Washington, DC: Resources for the Future.

Gangadharan, L. 2000. Transaction costs in pollution markets: An empirical study. *Land Economics* 76:601–614.

Gordon, H. S. 1954. The economic theory of a common property resource: The fishery. *Journal of Political Economy* 62:124–142.

Hahn, R. W., and G. L. Hester. 1989a. Marketable permits: Lessons from theory and practice. *Ecological Law Quarterly* 16:361–406.

———. 1989b. Where did all the markets go? An analysis of EPA's emissions trading program. *Yale Journal on Regulation* 6:109–153.

Hall, J. V., and A. L. Walton. 1996. A case study in pollution markets: Dismal science vs. dismal reality (California's Regional Clean Air Incentives Market). *Contemporary Economic Policy* 14(2):67–78.

Hollandsworth, S. M., and M. D. Binder. 1998. Stratospheric ozone, an electronic textbook. Goddard Space Flight, Center Atmospheric Chemistry and Dynamic Branch of NASA.

Jaffe, A. B., and R. N. Stavins. 1995. Dynamic incentives of environmental regulations: The effects of alternative policy instruments on technology diffusion. *Journal of Environmental Economics and Management* 29 (3rd Suppl. pt. 2):S43–S63.

Kerr, S., and D. Mare. 1997. Transaction costs and tradable permit markets: The United States lead phasedown. Manuscript. College Park: University of Maryland.

Klaassen, G. 1996. *Acid rain and environmental degradation: The economics of emission trading.* Cheltenham, U. K.: Edward Elgar.

Lee, D. 1996. Trading pollution. In *Ozone protection in the United States: Elements of success*, ed. E. Cook, 31–38. Washington, DC: World Resources Institute.

Lester, James P. 1986. New federalism and environmental policy. *Publius* 16 (Winter):149–165.

Lile, R. D., D. R. Bohi, and D. Burtraw. 1996. An assessment of the EPA's SO_2 emission allowance tracking system. Discussion Paper 97-21. Washington, DC: Resources for the Future.

Liroff, Richard A. 1980. Air pollution offsets: Trading, selling, and banking. Washington, DC: Conservation Foundation.

McCay, B. J. 2001. Emergence of institutions for the commons: Contexts, situations, and events. In *The drama of the commons*, eds. E. Ostrom et al., 361–402. Washington, DC: National Academy Press.

McKinney, Michael L., and Robert M. Schoch. 1998. Environmental science: Systems and solutions. Sudbury, MA: Jones and Bartlett Publishers.

Montero, J. P. 2002. Permits, standards, and technology innovation. *Journal of Environmental Economics and Management* 4:23–44.

———. 2005. Pollution markets with imperfectly observed emissions. *RAND Journal of Economics* 36(3):645–660.

National Academy of Public Administration. 1994.

Newel, R. G., and K. Rogers. 2004. Leaded gasoline in the United States: The breakthrough of permit trading. In *Choosing environmental policy: Comparing instruments and outcomes in the United States and Europe*, eds. W. Harrington, R. D. Morgenstern, and T. Sterner, 175–191. Washington, DC: Resources for the Future.

Nussbaum, B. 1992. Phasing down lead in gasoline in the U.S.: Mandates, incentives, trading, and banking. In *Climate change: Designing a tradeable permit system*, 21–34. Paris: OECD.

Ostrom, E. 1990. *Governing the commons: The evolution of institutions for collective action.* Cambridge U.K.: Cambridge University Press.

———. 1999. Institutional rational choice: An assessment of the institutional analysis and development framework. In *Theories of the policy process*, ed. P. A. Sabatier, 35–72. Boulder, CO: Westview Press.

Ostrom, E., and E. Schlager. 1996. The formation of property rights. In *Rights to nature: Ecological, economic, cultural, and political principles of institutions for the environment*, eds. S. Hanna, C. Folke, and K. G. Maeler, 127–156. Washington, DC: Island Press.

Richards, K., and K. Andersson. 2001. The leaky sink: Persistent obstacles to a forest carbon sequestration program based on individual projects. *Climate Policy* 1:41–54.

Rose, C. M. 2001. Common property, regulatory property, and environmental protection: Comparing community-based management to tradable environmental allowances. In *The drama of the commons*, eds. E. Ostrom et al., 233–258. Washington, DC: National Academy Press.

SCAQMD (South Coast Air Quality Management District). 1997. *1997 Air quality management plan.* http://www.aqmd.gov/aqmp/97aqmp/.

———. 2007. Over a dozen years of RECLAIM implementation: Key lessons learned in California's first air pollution cap-and-trade program. http://www.aqmd.gov/reclaim/docs/Policy_Paper_Part1.pdf.

———. 2011. Historic ozone air quality trends. http://www.aqmd.gov/smog/o3trend.html.

Schmalensee, R. 1998. Tradable emissions rights and joint implementation of greenhouse gas abatement: A look under the hood. In *The impact of climate change policy on consumers: Can tradable permits reduce the cost?* eds. C. E. Walker, M. A. Bloomfield, and M. Thorning, 39–55. Washington, DC: American Council for Capital Formation.

Schmalensee, R., et al. 1998. An interim evaluation of sulfur dioxide emissions trading. *Journal of Economic Perspectives* 12(3):53–68.

Sorrell, S., and J. Skea. 1999. Introduction. In *Pollution for sale: Emissions trading and joint implementation,* eds. S. Sorrell and J. Skea, 1–26. Northampton, MA: Edward Elgar.

Taylor, Margaret, Edward Rubin, and David Hounshell. 2003. Effect of government actions on technological innovations for SO2 control. *Environmental Science and Technology* 27(2):4527–4534.

Tietenberg, T. H. 2001. The tradable permits approach to protecting the commons: What have we learned? In *The drama of the commons,* eds. E. Ostrom et al., 197–232. Washington, DC: National Academy Press.

———. 2006. Emissions Trading: Principles and Practice. 2nd ed. Washington, DC: Resources for the Future Press.

UNEP (United Nations Environment Programme). 1999. *Production and consumption of ozone depleting substances, 1986–1998.* United Nations Environment Programme, Ozone Secretariat. http://www.unep.ch/ozone/DataReport99.shtml.

Wilkinson, J., and J. Thompson. 2006. *2005 status report on compensatory mitigation in the United States.* Environmental Law Institute. http://www.elistore.org/reports_detail.asp?ID=11137.

Commentary

SHI-LING HSU

N ives Dolšak's chapter is a very useful review of several different air-pollution trading programs, analyzed together for the purpose of assessing the value of trading programs as instruments to reduce air-pollution. The stated goal of the chapter is to "examine factors that contribute to well-performing tradable-permit markets for reducing air pollution." This chapter has largely achieved this objective. It does a thorough job of identifying the main factors that go into the success of air-pollution trading programs and, importantly, moves the discussion past the simplistic prescription of reducing transaction costs as a salve to make markets work more efficiently. The variety of objectives of air-pollution trading, as Dolšak notes, is more complicated, and therefore, the ability of trading programs to meet those manifold objectives is also more complicated. This chapter makes an important advance in this discussion.

In the spirit of building on this contribution, the bulk of this commentary will focus on new directions and extensions for this important discussion. My comments fall into four categories: (1) the choice of trading programs; (2) the extent to which conclusions can be drawn from this type of analysis; (3) whether institutional analysis is an appropriate lens through which to view air-pollution trading programs; and (4) if institutional analysis is appropriate, how it might proceed.

Choice of Trading Programs

The data set for this analysis consisted of four programs: (1) the EPA's lead phase-down program to reduce the lead content of gasoline, (2) Southern California's Regional Clean Air Incentives Market (RECLAIM), (3) trading in ozone-depleting substances after the 1987 Montreal Protocol, and (4) what Dolšak calls "early EPA emissions trading," which included some early EPA initiatives to introduce some flexibility in emissions regulations. At the outset, it is worth noting that more recent examples of trading programs might be worth attention. The SO_2 trading program under the 1990 Clean Air Act Amendments, for example, surely contains many lessons for future program design. Other more recent programs may be even more relevant for policy analysis, given the current attention to climate change: NO_x trading in the United States, the European Union Emissions Trading System for greenhouse gases, and the Regional Greenhouse Gas Initiative. The most important product of this chapter might be insights that can be used for better design of incipient and still-developing greenhouse gas trading programs, such as that under the Western Climate Initiative.

The analysis in this chapter also prompts us to revisit what we might mean by "emissions trading" or "tradable permits." In particular, one of the analyzed programs, early EPA emissions trading, does not really seem to be trading at all, but a series of one-off policies and regulatory bargains with individual emitters or groups of emitters that EPA struck in its earliest years. "Emissions trading" might better be viewed as a concept in which trades are decentralized, are not made with the EPA, and do not require some adjudication by the EPA or any other government agency in order to be consummated. Emissions trading must be decentralized; there can be no structural information asymmetry, as there would be when individual emitters come to the EPA peddling an emissions-reduction bargain. In light of this, the lessons from early EPA emissions trading would seem to be of somewhat limited value in the design of future emissions-trading programs.

Robustness of Conclusions

This chapter's identification of the important factors that go into what can plausibly be considered "success" or "failure" is valuable, but some care is needed in concluding whether programs actually achieve success. A fundamental problem with drawing conclusions from this type of analysis is that the baseline counterfactual against which the outcomes of the trading program can be measured is difficult to draw. To say that a trading program is "successful," either environmentally or economically, requires some construction of what would have occurred without the program. Establishing this baseline counterfactual requires a great deal of data analysis and economic ingenuity, but it has been done. One of the best pieces of economic analysis of trading is that of Carlson et al. (2000), which measures the gains from SO_2 emissions trading. These gains derive not only from the trades themselves, but from the flexibility offered by emissions trading. Just by making other compliance options possible, emissions trading created new opportunities to lower compliance costs. For example, scrubbing costs were lowered redesigning scrubbers so that they no longer carried a spare scrubbing module (which was, in essence, a designed redundancy) to provide for scrubbing during maintenance and repair periods. During maintenance and repair periods, emissions could simply be vented, and permits could be bought to cover that relatively small blip in emissions. These types of compliance strategies are also described in Ellerman et al. (2000) and accounted for a large part of the compliance cost savings under the SO_2 program.

The Appropriateness of Institutional Analysis

The importance of institutional analysis in environmental and natural resource problems can hardly be overstated. Dolšak's approach is institutional, but the most important lessons from this chapter, which concern the factors contributing to the success of trading programs, are not fundamentally institutional. Many important lessons seem to concern market design, for which an institutional approach has some limitations. For example, we know that price breadth is important to maximize the coverage of subindustries in which innovation might take place and lead to unexpected compliance cost savings. We know that price breadth is also important to ensure that leakage into nontrading sectors does not cancel out the hard-won emissions reductions in the trading sectors. We know that price volatility deters development of alternative energies that reduce emissions. And we know that if trading markets allow offsets that are worth hundreds of thousands of dollars more than the underlying product behind the pollution, then pollution may increase because of the enormous incentive to manufacture a false counterfactual that exaggerates the impact of the offset project. This increases overall pollution because the offsets permit pollution that might otherwise not be allowed. The now-familiar horror story of how Chinese hydrochlorofluorcarbon plants have been constructed for the sole purpose of securing offsets is the sort of lesson that is of crucial importance. The mix of institutional and market-design questions therefore calls for a broad approach that is less explicitly institutional in nature. At the very least, institutional choices have to be investigated against the backdrop of an array of market-design principles. For example, a descriptive account of how the Clean Development Mechanism (CDM) program of the Kyoto Protocol developed and of the institutional factors that went into its design offers only a partial lesson. A truly useful lesson in how to make emissions-trading markets work effectively would also include a normative analysis that would guide future trading program development to avoid some of the problems stemming from the CDM program. In that kind of analysis, institutional analysis may provide a cautionary note on institutional pitfalls rather than normative guidance on program and institutional design.

Whither Institutional Analysis?

Despite the limitations of a pure institutional approach, it is worth noting that emissions-trading programs might be the subject of some very interesting institutional analysis research. For example, what accounts for the many decisions that were made in developing the RECLAIM program? What exactly was the mandate of the South Coast Air Quality Management District in developing RECLAIM? Did monitoring and enforcement capabilities dictate how RECLAIM was structured? The evolution of the EPA over time must be one of the most interesting institutional analysis projects that could be imagined. How, in institutional terms, does an agency move from early emissions trading, such as bubbling and netting and offsetting, to the hard SO_2 cap-and-trade program and even defy political interests in pushing forward with NO_x trading? And the current climate, in which the EPA is pushing forward (under court mandate) in regulating the emissions of greenhouse gases under the Clean Air Act, begs for an institutional analysis. Analyzing changes in staffing of the EPA, with its external political influences, would seem to be one of the great institutional analysis projects that could be undertaken.

In summary, Dolšak's chapter moves discussion forward. This commentary is intended to highlight new directions suggested by Dolšak's contribution. The paths not taken, and their relative attractiveness, are never apparent until at least one path is taken.

REFERENCES

Carlson, Curtis, Dallas Burtraw, Maureen Cropper, and Karen L. Palmer. 2000. Sulfur dioxide control by electric utilities: What are the gains from trading? *Journal of Political Economy* 108:1292–1326.

Ellerman, A. Denny, Paul L. Joskow, Richard Schmalensee, Juan-Pablo Montero, and Elizabeth M. Bailey. 2000. *Markets for Clean Air.* Cambridge, U.K.: Cambridge University Press.

Wildlife

7

Who Owns Endangered Species?

JASON F. SHOGREN AND GREGORY M. PARKHURST

The United Nations declared 2010 the International Year of Biodiversity, a commemoration of the biological capital that makes human life possible. This declaration came 14 years after the publication of *Global Biodiversity Assessment*, the UN's analysis of the state of knowledge about risks to threatened and endangered species (Heywood 1996), and nearly 40 years after the United States Congress passed the Endangered Species Act (ESA) of 1973 (see the review edited by Goble, Scott, and Davis [2006]). The Year of Biodiversity, *Global Biodiversity Assessment*, and the ESA all capture the idea that some form of classic market failure exists such that a decentralized private property approach fails to protect biodiversity and endangered species for the social good. The market fails to price accurately the social benefits of species because ownership of species is typically not exclusive to any one person.

So who owns these endangered species? The brief answer is that we all do. But a full answer is more complicated because private landowners frequently pay the cost to shelter species that provide these nonrival and nonexcludable benefits to the general public. The bioeconomic property right challenge is the same it has always been: the benefits of species protection are widespread public goods, whereas the costs can be private when species live on private lands. In the United States, by one estimate nearly 90 percent of endangered species are sheltered on private lands (Brown and Shogren 1998).

Property and the ESA

The tension between private property and protection of endangered species has a long history. In the United States since 1973, the ESA has codified the idea that species have "ecological, educational, historical, recreational and scientific value" unaccounted for in the course of "economic growth and development" (ESA, sec. 2). The ESA has broadened the scope of species protection, making every species, subspecies, and discrete population, restricted to plants and animals, eligible for protection by being listed as either endangered or threatened. The original language of the act also implies that all species will be protected regardless of cost, a reversal of the preceding doctrine that species protection would be "practicable and consistent with primary purposes" of land use on both public and private property. The ESA prohibits landowners, public and private, from taking any threatened or endangered species on their private property; here a "taking" means any action that injures or kills a member of an endangered species or degrades its habitat. The U.S. Supreme Court has upheld this interpretation. Once an endangered species is found on property, a landowner works with a federal agency whose basic goal is to protect species by putting explicit restrictions on how the land can be used.

But private property owners do not see themselves as going against social norms with their land use decisions. Secure private property rights have long been promoted by Western countries as the key for sustained and prosperous economic growth; landowners are more likely to see themselves as stewards of the land who provide public goods than as corporate producers who create negative wedges between private and social objectives. A historical perception of entitlement and endowment arises with ownership of private property, irrespective of owners' actual rights and responsibilities as defined by current legal standards. People appreciate that neither land restrictions nor calls for conservation on private land are new. For centuries in Europe and in Euro-America, common-law restrictions have limited what people could do to or with their property (North and Thomas 1973).

But the ESA has produced a backlash because private property has held special status in the history of many nations, including the United States. Laws impose inequitable burdens every day (e.g., horse riders pay taxes for interstate highways). Many Americans, however, view laws that restrict private landowner autonomy to protect obscure species a threat to both the economic system and the broader social order (Epstein 1985; 1995; Norton 2002). They view land as capital, albeit natural capital, and they believe that capital is the key ingredient that allows people the ability to create, store, and share the wealth necessary for national prosperity.

Following the utilitarian view of nature promoted by John Stuart Mill and Gifford Pinchot, the resource conservation ethic is "the greatest good to the greatest number for the longest time" (Pinchot 1947, 382). Utilitarian landowners believe that their land ethic is valid, and they would like their ongoing stewardship to be appreciated. This classical liberal viewpoint takes a Hamiltonian perspective: the government should abdicate to market forces that create wealth by allowing resources to move freely from low-valued to high-valued uses. Classical liberals agree with James Madison's argument in the *Federalist Papers* that "the wide diffusion of independent property rights . . . was the essential foundation for stable republican government" (McEvoy 1998, 101). Rightly or wrongly, they fear that restricting private land for species protection without just compensation is another step down the slope toward collectivism.

In contrast, the romantic conservation ethic promoted in the United States by Ralph Waldo Emerson, Henry David Thoreau, and John Muir takes a different perspective on private property and endangered species. The preservationists believed that land had other uses than just for human financial gain. Landowners would be free to pursue private profits provided they also behaved as responsible social citizens, because by definition, land was already in public service. All land uses should be viewed as harm preventing rather than as public good providing. "The conviction that the freedom to wring the last speculative penny from one's land is of a piece with one's most fundamental civil, political, and personal liberties seems to be grounded less on argument than on assumption" (Sagoff 1997, 845).

A more pragmatic mind-set toward property and endangered species that emerged in the 1940s, in part from frustration with the other two views, is Leopold's evolutionary-ecological land ethic. Leopold (1949) based his ethic on the scientific notion that nature is not a collection of separate parts but an integrated system of actions, reactions, and feedbacks. This science-based mind-set focuses on defining the natural system within the context of human interaction and well-being. By integrating natural science and social science, one can promote more understanding by defining evaluative criteria that reflect the range of ethical views. For the private lands challenge, these criteria can address perceived biological needs, regulatory concerns, and landowner interests, such as compensation for land use restrictions.

But enforcement of the ESA typically has not risen to the level of a Fifth Amendment "taking"—private property shall not be taken for a public use without just compensation. Supreme Court decisions, for example, *Lucas v. South Carolina Coastal Council*, 506 U.S. 1003 (1992) and *Dolan v. City of Tigard*, 512 U.S. 374 (1994), have established rules that say that a regulation related to the public purpose will require compensation only if it singles out a vulnerable minority, deprives a landowner of all viable uses of his property, or physically invades or occupies the property (Sagoff 1997).

Although the courts have ruled that the government does not always need to compensate landowners, they have not answered the question whether the government should compensate private landowners who shelter endangered species (Innes, Polasky, and Tschirhart 1998). Bean believes that "without positive incentives, the Act's goals are unlikely to be achieved" (1998, 28 ELR 10707). Approaches exist that offer compensation to landowners for the costs of protecting species on their land. These approaches rely on incentives and financial rewards for better practices rather than prosecution for violating ESA's prohibition on harming listed species or their habitat. Policy makers have addressed the compensation question by offering voluntary programs to landowners to increase their incentives for private species protection and biodiversity conservation. The idea is to transform an environmental liability into a marketable asset.

The U.S. Fish and Wildlife Service and more than a thousand nonprofit land trusts promote habitat conservation by using voluntary incentive mechanisms to elicit the cooperation of private landowners. Mechanisms include conservation easements, leases, habitat banking, habitat-conservation planning, safe harbors, candidate conservation agreements, and the "no-surprises" policy (Bean 1999). A survey of state incentive programs found that at least 400 incentive programs enrolling some 70 million private acres existed in the 50 states by 2001, 50 percent of which had originated between 1990 and 2001. State departments of fish and game or wildlife administered 80 percent of these incentive programs (Defenders of Wildlife 2002). The typical state offered about four to six conservation incentives, usually in some form of direct payment and easement with tax relief. About 28 percent of the states made direct payments, 22 percent provided education and technical support,

20 percent gave tax relief, and 13 percent used property right tolls like easements and deed restrictions. Market institutions for species protection were used in about 3 percent of the programs.

The compensation question, however, has split both sides of the ESA debate. Some landowners want compensation; some want nothing to do with it. Some conservation groups want to pay compensation; others do not. Some ranchers and farmers say that they will retire acres for habitat or will put up with large predators (e.g., grizzly bears or wolves) provided they are compensated. Those landowners willing to consider compensation demand a fine level of detail about the program, need to see a local precedent, and need some basic reassurances to overcome an instinctual distrust of the regulatory aspects of the government (Korfmacher and Elsom 1998). Examples exist in which private landowners have voluntarily become partners in positive and proactive plans to protect and enhance natural resources on their land. Turner and Rylander (1998), for instance, describe several examples in which incentives have worked to protect species like the Louisiana black bear and the red-cockaded woodpecker.

Many ESA defenders agree that compensation is needed. They see compensation as a pragmatic way to bring private land into the fold of species protection. Compensation would reduce a landowner's incentive to wipe out the potential environmental value of land, thereby avoiding any potential ESA restrictions. Defenders of Wildlife, for example, has paid out more than $64,000 for nearly one hundred grizzly depredations since 1997 and more than $200,000 to about 180 ranchers for livestock losses to wolves since 1987.

But other landowners do not want to be paid to protect species. They say that they want nothing to do with a compensation policy because they fear further public erosion of autonomy and private control. They also fear the risk of unenforceability of contracts between private and federal ESA protection (Melions and Thorton 1999). They see compensation as a set of golden handcuffs through which more and more will be required of them and taken from them. Their view is that sometimes compensation is not enough; landowners want their privacy respected, their prior stewardship efforts acknowledged, and their ability to protect their investments flexible. As one rancher puts it, "It sounds to me like you're basically selling the state or federal government the right to control, not necessarily your land, but down the road it seems to me that the government then has control of private lands" (Korfmacher and Elsom 1998, 7).

Conservationists also think that compensation is a bad idea, both on moral grounds and because of pragmatic fears. They do not want compensation as part of the ESA because they view payments as a tool to paralyze the ESA through continual congressional underfunding of budget sources. They fear that mandatory compensation that is not coupled with the necessary federal funding would effectively gut the ESA.

The compensation question has helped stall ESA reauthorization for more than a decade. No one sees a quick end to the ESA controversy. Society is faced with difficult economic choices affected by biological needs and political realities. Working through this tangle requires more explicit attention to how economic incentives might affect private landowners, ESA supporters, and policy makers. People can point to voluntary programs that have worked to encourage some landowners to protect endangered species on their private property. These programs offer a regulatory safeguard to promote cooperation; some use explicit economic incentives, such as payments for easements. A variety of such flexible compensation schemes are possible: direct compensation from the government to owners of land; conservation banking and tradable rights in habitat, under which those who wish to develop land would buy permits from those who would then not be able to develop; insurance programs under which landowners are compensated if endangered species impose costs on them, like the fund created by Defenders of Wildlife; estate tax relief to allow large chunks of land to be preserved, rather than broken up to pay federal estate taxes; and tax deductions for conservation expenses. Private companies also are now playing a role. The goal of the developers Greenvest, for example, is to develop land to balance profit maximization with new green residential communities and commercial developments.

Creative suggestions on how to generate and use public monies more effectively are also welcome, even those with low odds of short-term political success. Easterbrook (1998) has proposed that Congress should codify a "build-and-save" plan: for each and every acre developed, another acre of habitat must be purchased and conserved for species protection. The idea is to align developers' and conservationists' interests such that if the economy grows, so do national parks and forests and grasslands. Over the last few decades, new development of about 1.5 million acres has occurred each year; therefore, a development fee of $1,000 per acre would generate a conservation fund of about $1.5 billion per year.

Other approaches try to add creative uses of compensation to existing programs in the government. The difficulties of implementing new programs suggest that one could fund conservation through existing programs such as the Wetlands Reserve Program (WRP) run by the Natural Resource Conservation Services of the U.S. Department of Agriculture (USDA). The WRP is a voluntary nationwide program that offers payment based on agricultural value for wetlands that have been drained and converted to agriculture uses. Another USDA incentive is the Wildlife Habitat Incentive Program, which provides cost sharing to assist landowners who use their habitat to protect wildlife and threatened and endangered species. In addition, Title II of the Farm Security and Rural Investment Act of 2002 budgeted about $17 billion for incentives for conservation on agricultural lands, including the newly created Conservation Security Program (CSP). The CSP pays producers who adopt and maintain conservation practices on private lands. Contracts run for periods of five to ten years, and annual payments range from $20,000 to $45,000. The CSP uses an initial "secretary's" bonus to encourage people to sign up.

Another imaginative bonus scheme that could be incorporated into these existing incentive options is an agglomeration bonus. Suppose that the dual goal is to maximize species protection cost-effectively and to minimize private landowner resentment. The agglomeration bonus mechanism pays an extra bonus for every acre a landowner retires that borders on any other retired acre (Parkhurst et al. 2002). The mechanism provides an incentive for landowners to voluntarily create a contiguous reserve across their common border that provides a single large habitat usually desired for effective conservation. A government agency's role is to target the critical habitat, to integrate the agglomeration bonus into the compensation package, and to provide landowners the unconditional freedom to choose which acres to retire.

Oregon's Conservation Reserve Enhancement Program (CREP) illustrates the idea of an allied land retirement bonus scheme. The CREP pays an extra bonus to enrollees along a stream if at least 50 percent of the stream bank within a five-mile stream segment is enrolled in the USDA's Conservation Reserve Program (CRP). Additional increases in the CREP payment are made when in-stream water leases are made available on enrolled lands (OWEB 2011).

Spatial Configurations of Private Property

Protecting threatened and endangered species requires the creation of landscape-scale contiguous reserves and corridors to support viable species populations and ecological processes (Cincotta, Wisnewski, and Engelman 2000). Creating contiguous protected areas cannot be accomplished without the voluntary cooperation of private landholders. Their cooperation is more likely if they are compensated for financial losses, for example, through the CRP (Ferraro and Kiss 2002). Aldo Leopold stressed nearly half a century ago that the key to conservation was to compensate landowners for their efforts to protect nature on private lands. He argued that conservation "ultimately boil[s] down to reward the private landowner who conserves the public interest" (Leopold 1934, 136–137; see Innes, Polasky, and Tschirhart [1998]; R. B. W. Smith and Shogren [2002]). Compensation can be used to create an incentive to encourage landowners to maintain their land in an undeveloped state or to mitigate the environmental impact of development by helping the landowner meet costs of maintenance and restoration of environmentally sensitive areas. Compensation aligns a landowner's private incentives with the social desire to create nature reserves that shelter species at risk. In the United States compensation also reduces the odds that a landowner might claim a Fifth Amendment "taking" (private property taken for a public use) without just reimbursement. Landowners with a financial stake in conservation should provide more environmental stewardship if they are reimbursed for their efforts.

The U.S. Fish and Wildlife Service and many state agencies have started to design compensation programs to reduce the risk of defensive habitat destruction by providing landowners with regulatory relief in the event that restrictions are levied against their land (e.g., Safe Harbor Plans and Habitat Conservation Plans in the ESA of 1973; Bean 1998). Compensation takes the form of grants, loans, cash payments, and tax allowances offered by federal or state agencies or nonprofit organizations (Parkhurst and Shogren 2005). These programs are funded from numerous sources, including tax revenue, lottery funds, and special permits. A good example is Idaho Fish and Game's (IFG) Habitat Improvement Program (HIP). HIP is a cost-share program that allocates funds for improvements on both private and public lands. Recognizing the role landowners play in providing habitat for upland game and wild birds, the primary objective of HIP is to encourage private landowners to invest in habitat restoration and enhancement projects that increase the populations of wild birds. The agreements and compensation under HIP have evolved over time; compensation currently depends on the type of project and the duration of the project commitment. As much as 100 percent of costs can be reimbursed, and payments can be as large as $10,000 (IFG 2011).

But landowner compensation by itself does not guarantee the creation of habitats most suitable for species protection. Landowners still have no incentive to coordinate their land retirement decisions to create, say, one contiguous reserve that falls across property lines or to create optimal habitat configurations within their own property lines. Fragmented retirement decisions will affect species that prosper within a large habitat (e.g., the northern spotted owl, the red-cockaded woodpecker, or the grizzly bear). Most voluntary compensation programs are not designed to address directly biologists' concern that landowners may not coordinate conservation efforts across property lines or create habitat within their own property (Brown and Shogren 1998). Conservation biologists argue that many species face extinction because of fragmented habitats on both public and private lands. Habitat fragments are either too small to provide species with the physical and biological landscape characteristics necessary for survival and breeding or are too isolated from other fragments and cause species "bottlenecks," which are reduced chromosome types in the DNA of a species that emerge from inbreeding and increase susceptibility to changes in the environment of that species (Saunders, Hobbs, and Margules 1991). But biologists also point out that how one reconfigures fragmented habitat matters because different species thrive under different spatial habitat designs (Noss 1993).

The more private property fragments landscape, the more conservation and management of the habitats that shelter endangered species matter. Fragmentation results in a reduction of biodiversity and a loss of critical habitat. Regulators charged with the oversight and provision of natural resources have several incentive mechanisms at their disposal to combat the negative impacts on the environment and on ecosystems resulting from human consumptive uses. Two of the primary concerns of the regulator in implementing incentive mechanisms for conserving habitat are inducing voluntary participation by private landowners and coordinating conservation efforts in a desired spatial configuration.

Incentives that fail to compensate landowners for the cost of conserving their land potentially result in a decrease of available land and an increase in the cost of conservation. Alternatively, incentive mechanisms that compensate landowners for the foregone private use of their land are more effective at inducing landowners to assign their land to habitat protection. Increasing the available land for conservation objectives provides more options with the likelihood of lower costs.

In addition, many species require spatial habitat configurations to enhance the benefits they provide to society. Recently, spatially explicit models have been designed to capture the trade-offs between spatial allocation of conservation within the landscape and conservation costs (Ando et al. 1998; Grout 2009; Hamaide and Sheerin 2010; Hartig and Drechsler 2009). These research projects focus on low-cost landscape configuration in the absence of individual and group landowner decisions. However, these authors do not propose a method for transferring funds from the conservation coffers of governments and nongovernmental organizations to landowners (Chomitz et al. 2006). Given the current shortfalls in agency budgets, choosing an allocating mechanism is not a trivial matter. The assumption that compensation subsidies minimally equivalent to foregone productive use will induce landowners to voluntarily conserve the desired configuration ignores the strategic actions of landowners as they optimize the various land use rents and minimize the risk associated with coordinating conservation decisions within the landscape (Parkhurst and Shogren 2005). Furthermore, landowners possess private information concerning the productive value of their land and can use their private information to exact information rents from regulators (Ferraro 2008). A one-dimensional subsidy will be insufficient to meet a voluntary spatially dependent conservation agenda.

Meeting multiple objectives requires the use of multiple incentive mechanisms—potentially one for each objective. If the regulators' objective is to conserve a targeted spatial configuration voluntarily on private land, the incentive mechanism will need one component to induce voluntary participation and a second component to create the desired spatial configuration. Parkhurst et al. (2002) propose a mechanism, the agglomeration bonus, that is multidimensional and, as such, can be implemented to protect habitat critical for endangered species. The following section explores this mechanism in more detail.

Agglomeration Bonus

The agglomeration bonus, also referred to as a smart subsidy, is an incentive for landowners to conserve land voluntarily in a predetermined desired spatial configuration. This bonus is a set of subsidies that can be positive or negative and that attach to specific landscape characteristics. A flat subsidy induces voluntary participation, while a shared-border subsidy coordinates conservation within the landscape. Positive subsidies create an explicit network externality between adjacent land parcels and neighboring landowners by paying an additional agglomeration bonus when they retire land adjacent to other conserved parcels, both their own and their neighbors' (Parkhurst et al. 2002). Negative subsidies work to discourage land retirement decisions along the fence of a neighbor; rather, they encourage each landowner to create his or her own contiguous parcel that is separate and distinct from his neighbors' retired lands. Combining positive and negative subsidies makes smart subsidies flexible because they can create many different spatially conserved landscape configurations.

Parkhurst and Shogren (2007; 2008) examined the effectiveness of smart subsidies at conserving four different spatial configurations in the experimental lab. In a context-free experiment with four participants, each possessing 25 cells (parcels), a smart subsidy containing a menu of agglomeration bonuses was effective at conserving a coordinated landscape of long corridors, large contiguous regions, corridors with a midcorridor nesting area (resembling a cross), and isolated patches.

Their experimental results were promising and showed that subjects were able to identify the underlying incentives and meet the spatial objective. Further research showed that the agglomeration bonus was better than a simple per unit subsidy or coerced conservation at meeting spatial conservation objectives.

Experimental Test

Landscape and Landowners

Parkhurst and Shogren represented the landscape with a 10×10 land grid divided into four private 5×5 landholdings. They used this grid design to extend and test the robustness of conservation incentives that used a classic normal-form 8×8 payoff matrix game in which the spatial element is implicit and embedded in the payoffs. As far as is known, this land grid is the first spatially explicit design in the experimental economics literature. Each cell in the land grid was assigned an economic value ranging from $20 to $50 per cell, which was the land's opportunity cost if it was retired for conservation. Land values differed across landholdings. Each landowner knew his own land values and those of the three other owners.

Policy Treatments and Subsidy Design

Parkhurst and Shogren compared three land retirement policy tools: compelled land retirement without a subsidy (figure 7.1), a simple $93 flat-fee subsidy per retired parcel (figure 7.2), and the subsidy with agglomeration bonus (figure 7.3). The subsidy divides a landowner's payment into four distinct parts: (1) a $20 flat fee per cell retired; (2) a $50 own-border bonus for each common border shared between two of his own retired cells; (3) a $24 row-border bonus for each shared border with his row neighbor; and (4) a $22 column-border bonus for each shared border with his column-neighbor (to the east). The amount of each bonus payment depends on the productive values and desired configuration and location of the habitat and can be positive, negative, or zero. Parkhurst and Shogren kept the absolute values of the simple and smart subsidies the same by equating the $93 simple fixed-fee subsidy with the average per cell payoff generated in the smart subsidy treatment. They conducted two 20-round sessions for each policy option. Eight subjects participated in each session.

Parkhurst and Shogren followed standard economic experimental procedures. All experiments were run on computers. Subjects were not told the objective of the experiment, and all wording in the instructions and on the computer screens was context free. Following standard protocol, subjects were recruited campuswide and were told to report to a computer lab at a given time. Experimental instructions were provided to each of the participants, and the monitor read them out loud while the subjects followed along. The experimental instructions are available upon request. Subjects had an opportunity to ask questions concerning the experimental procedures, which were answered by the monitor. The monitor also walked the subjects through two practice rounds to familiarize the subjects with the experimental design. The monitor handed out the agglomeration bonus specification page, which

FIGURE 7.1

Compelled-Retirement Results

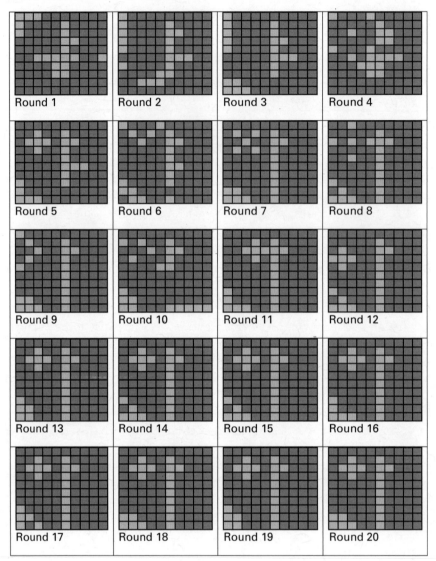

the subjects were allowed to review. The subjects then entered their name and student identification numbers into the computer, and the computer randomly assigned the subjects to groups of four.

Game Strategies

In the compulsion session, each subject was required to retire 5 cells (the white cells in the figures); the remaining 20 cells were left in production (the black cells in the figures) and earned the specified value for the cell. In the simple and smart subsidies, each subject could retire up to 5 cells {0, 1, 2, 3, 4, or 5} to receive the policy

FIGURE 7.2

Simple-Subsidy Results

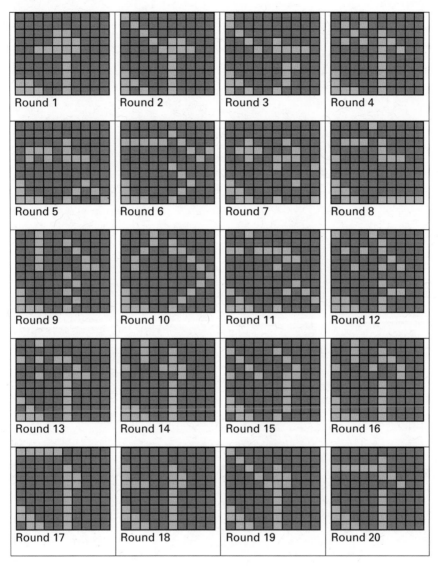

subsidy; the remaining cells were left in production. Note the large set of potential strategy permutations. Subjects presented with the land grid and allowed voluntary participation had 68,406 strategies to choose from. (N was an element of the set {0, 1, 2, 3, 4, 5}, and the number of cells to choose from was 25. The equation is $[25!/5!20!] + [25!/4!21!] + [25!/3!22!] + [25!/2!23!] + [25!/1!24!] + [25!/0!25!] = 68,406$.) With four subjects in each group, the possible group outcomes for the corridor treatment are $(68,406)^4$.

For the compulsion and simple-subsidy policies, each subject has one clear dominant strategy: retire his five lowest-valued cells. A dominant strategy is any strategy

FIGURE 7.3
Subsidy with Agglomeration Bonus Results

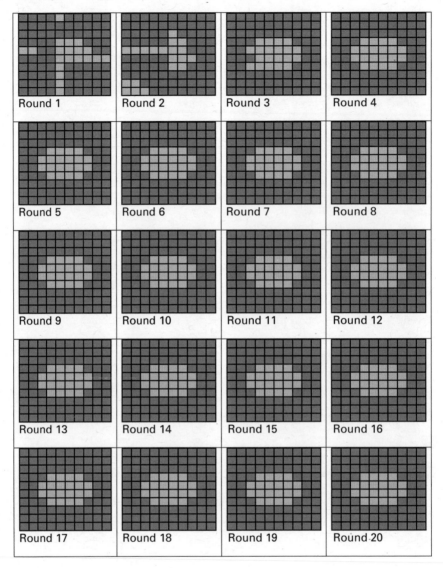

that maximizes a player's payoffs irrespective of the strategy choices of the other players. In the smart-subsidy policy, however, each player has at least two non-dominated strategies. The players in the northwest, northeast, and southeast sections of the land grid have two dominant strategies: both strategies retire land at the borderline with the three neighbors, although only one of these strategies creates exactly one-quarter of the targeted habitat. The southwest player has five dominant strategies, four at the borderline and one in the far corner with lowest land values.

Calculator and Communication

Each subject had a 10×10 grid calculator on the computer screen for assistance in calculating profits. The subject could experiment with different retirement strategies for himself and for the other three landowners before having to make a binding decision. The subject's potential profits based on the configuration of retired cells on the calculator were calculated and displayed. Subjects could send one message per round to the group. Communication was nonbinding and unstructured, with no restrictions on timing or content, and a common language was implemented by allowing subjects to send messages in their natural language. Subjects had two minutes to send messages, use the calculator, and send their choices.

Information and History

After all four subjects' retirement choices were submitted, the resulting land grid was shown to the group. The subjects' 5×5 grid of values, the maximum allowed number of retired cells, a message box, and the grid calculator came up on the computer screen, and players chose the cells to retire. Subjects had common knowledge regarding payoffs and strategies. Each subject's individual payoffs and accumulated payoffs were private information. The entire 10×10 grid showing the configuration of retired cells and the payoffs for each subject within the group then appeared in the history box. Subjects had record sheets and the history box to help them keep track of their own and the other group members' choices of strategies and associated payoffs in previous rounds.

Results

Three illustrative examples are presented of groups' land retirement decisions and the resulting habitat configurations given each policy treatment. For the compulsion treatment, figure 7.1 shows that a noncontiguous pattern of habitat retirement emerges. Once all subjects learned to play their dominant strategies (by round 6), they retired their cheapest cells and created fragmented habitat. Figure 7.2 illustrates a similar noncontiguous pattern for the simple-subsidy treatment. Here subjects played their dominant strategy in every round and again created a fragmented reserve. In contrast, figure 7.3 shows that the smart subsidy induced the desired contiguous spatial pattern. Once all subjects realized the dominant strategy created by connectivity incentives of the agglomeration bonus (rounds 4–20), they voluntarily created a contiguous reserve. The smart subsidy provided the proper incentives for subjects to minimize the fragmentation of the conservation efforts.

Now consider all data from two perspectives of efficiency, economic and biological. Economic efficiency (EE) measures the frequencies with which groups make land retirement choices that maximize personal wealth. EE ([group earnings − minimum earnings]/[maximum earnings − minimum earnings]) is the percentage of available program rents captured by the group, and an EE of 100 percent means that all rents are captured. Biological efficiency (BE) measures the connectivity of the group's habitat. Formally, BE is the percentage of the shared borders between conserved parcels achieved by the group relative to the maximum number of shared borders. A BE of 100 percent implies that the targeted contiguous habitat was created.

For the agglomeration bonus treatment, in which the incentive mechanism is positively correlated with the conservation objective, if a group coordinates to achieve the desired habitat, all efficiency measures equal unity (EE = BE = 100 percent). For the simple-subsidy and compulsion treatments, no correlation, positive or negative, exists between economic and biological efficiency. For expediency, the three efficiency measures are average group outcomes for 5-round intervals {1–5, 6–10, 11–15, and 15–20}. The group outcome is the most precise measure of effectiveness because all four players must select the dominant payoff strategy for the outcome to be considered first best.

All three policies induced approximately the same range of economic efficiency, between 80 and 99 percent. The groups captured most of the rents. In contrast, biological efficiency differed substantially by policy option. For compulsion, BE starts at 50 percent and drops to about 40 percent in rounds 6–20; for the simple subsidy, BE starts at about 60 percent and drops to about 52 percent in rounds 6–20. For the smart subsidy, however, BE increases with rounds, starting at 91 percent and increasing to about 99 percent. In summary, the smart subsidy, which links earnings and the conservation objective, is more biologically efficient at creating contiguous conservation reserves than the current status quo policies of compulsion and a simple flat-fee subsidy.

Applications

A need exists for coordinated landowner conservation efforts when natural ecosystem services benefit many landowners within the landscape (Zhang et al. 2007). When conservation efforts benefit the common good, landowners underinvest in conservation efforts. Understanding the dynamics of ecosystem services provides the opportunity to pool conservation dollars across landowners and reduce the collective costs by coordinating conservation efforts spatially. A mechanism such as the agglomeration bonus is proposed as an alternative to the incentives currently offered at the individual landowner level.

The agglomeration bonus also appears to be an important approach for conserving spatial habitat when regulatory budgets are small (Drechsler et al. 2007). Using an ecological-economic model for protecting an endangered butterfly species in Landau, Germany, Drechsler et al. (2007) show that when budgets are small, the need to coordinate conservation efforts across the landscape increases. They conclude that under some conditions, heterogeneous payments may be dominated by the agglomeration bonus. Kurttila et al. (2008) discuss agglomeration bonuses in Finnish forests, and Stoneham et al. (2005) study agglomeration and auctions in marine management.

Researchers have examined how to implement voluntary incentive mechanisms to induce private landowner conservation in the Brazilian Atlantic Forest in southern Bahia (Chomitz et al. 2006). Their research suggests that individual contracts targeting larger contiguous parcels of land for conservation will be more effective at creating continuity within the landscape. They suggest payment schemes that include an agglomeration bonus to increase connectivity.

Challenges

Competing Objectives

Conservation efforts within an organization or across organizations may have competing objectives in a common target area for conservation. Spatially targeted conservation efforts that increase the benefits for one objective may decrease the benefits for a secondary objective. The overall impact of conservation may be less than expected because of the competing spatial conservation demands for the various objectives. Nelson et al. (2008) explore this scenario in examining the spatial conservation needs for meeting different objectives such as species habitat, carbon sequestration, and riparian protection. Further, anthropogenic conservation programs are typically myopic in their focus on measurable human benefits and do not account for all the dynamic characteristics and needs of ecosystems, such as natural fires and floods. Models should identify the trade-offs between anthropogenic and biological objectives (Chan et al. 2006).

Administration of Conservation Contracts

Ferraro (2008) evaluates the differing approaches to allocating contracts for conserving biological amenities. Information rents exist in all scenarios because of landowners' private information. A common approach to allocating conservation contracts is to have landowners submit bids indicating the payment they require to conserve their land. The regulator can then compare the environmental benefits per dollar derived from each contract and choose those contracts that provide the largest benefit per dollar. Adjusting this process to satisfy an agglomeration bonus when each contract represents a contiguous land mass and several landowners may not be simple. The number of contracts offered decreases, potentially creating market power for landowners that could increase information rents (Ferraro 2008). Further, educating landowners and facilitating their understanding of the agglomeration bonus and coordinated bids could impose additional costs on landowners and regulatory agencies (Parkhurst et al. 2002). Evidence on combinatorial auctions suggests that when the items being auctioned are complements, as is the case with spatially configured habitats, combinatorial auctions outperform simultaneous auctions (Tanaka 2007).

Budgetary Constraints

The agglomeration bonus provides landowners an extra payment to coordinate their conservation in the desired landscape configuration. The extra payment offsets transaction costs associated with coordinating landscapes and the risk associated with reliance on others' initial and continual conservation actions. If contract payments are contingent on landowners maintaining conserved land for endangered species protection, payments are contingent on the actions of all landowners. The larger the custodial costs, the larger the number of coordinating landowners, and the longer the contract horizon, the greater the risk that must be incorporated into a landowner's land use decision. Consequently, the agglomeration bonus will need to be sufficient to compensate for the risk. With limited conservation dollars, the open question is under what conditions agglomeration bonuses are preferable to other payment mechanisms, such as heterogeneous landowner subsidies (Drechsler et al. 2007; 2010).

Further, landowners earning a disproportionate share of the subsidy are incentivized to coordinate group conservation efforts to ensure their earnings. The agglomeration bonus can be designed to provide for landowners to earn excessive rents which could facilitate members of the group to incur the costs of collaboration. Heterogeneous payments serve to compensate landowners for lost productivity. They do not create network externalities that will promote collaborative conservation efforts (Raymond 2006).

Uniqueness of the Nash Equilibrium

The agglomeration bonus creates a coordination game in which landowners coordinate their conservation within the landscape. Many equilibrium points may exist within the framework of the incentive mechanism design and the landscape costs and benefits in which it is implemented. The design of the agglomeration bonus makes the desired landscape configuration the payoff dominant Nash equilibrium (the equilibrium with the largest payoff). In practice, however, achieving this payoff dominant Nash equilibrium is a challenge (Parkhurst and Shogren 2007). M. D. Smith, Sanchirico, and Wilen (2009) find that the agglomeration bonus is a promising policy instrument for allocating effort across patches in fisheries.

Who owns endangered species? We all do. But it makes economic sense to compensate private landowners who shelter species for their stewardship. Economic incentives can help align their land use decisions with social goals of species protection. The challenge is to provide a compensation mechanism that both is voluntary and can create spatially contiguous habitats across holdings of several private landowners. The agglomeration bonus is one potential incentive mechanism that could help meet this challenge. By making participation voluntary, the agglomeration bonus creates a setting that aligns landowners' incentives and species protection goals into contiguous habitat preserves. Although the laboratory test discussed in this chapter was conducted under stylized conditions, its results suggest that an agglomeration bonus subsidy could work. The scheme was more effective than current policy options of compulsion and a simple fixed-fee subsidy at inducing people to coordinate their conservation decisions voluntarily By formally creating a link between the payment and the conservation objective, the agglomeration bonus achieves both economic and biological goals without resorting to compulsion or land-specific compensation schemes. The landowners in the experiment chose to retire the targeted land willingly, whereas with compulsion and fixed fees, people still secured the economic rents but did not create the desired habitat.

But can the agglomeration bonus subsidy be implemented in the natural environment with real private property? The answer will depend on specific local bioeconomic and political conditions of a given site. For example, will landowners accept the idea that their compensation is linked to the actions of a neighbor?

Will there be holdouts and holdups as land values increase once neighbors agree to retire land? The results presented in this chapter cannot answer these questions directly, but they do suggest that policy makers might consider adding the agglomeration bonus to their list of potential policy options for cost-effectively conserving habitat across private or public-private landholdings to protect endangered species.

REFERENCES

Ando, Amy, Jeffrey Camm, Stephen Polasky, and Andrew Solow. 1998. Species distributions, land values, and efficient conservation. *Science* 279:2126–2178.

Bean, Michael. 1998. The Endangered Species Act and private land: Four lessons learned from the past quarter century. *Environmental Law Reporter News & Analysis*, 10701–10710. http://www.edf.org/documents/826_elr.pdf.

———. 1999. Endangered species? Endangered act? *Environment* 41:12–38.

Brown, Gardner, and Jason Shogren. 1998. Economics of the Endangered Species Act. *Journal of Economic Perspectives* 12:3–18.

Chan, Kai, Rebecca Shaw, David Cameron, Emma Underwood, and Gretchen Daily. 2006. Conservation planning for ecosystem services. *PLOS Biology* 4(11):2138–2152.

Chomitz, Kenneth, Gustava da Fonseca, Keith Alger, David Stoms, Miroslav Honzak, Elena Landau, Timothy Thomas, Wayt Thomas, and Frank Davis. 2006. Viable reserve networks arise from voluntary landowner response to conservation incentives. *Ecology and Society* 11(2):40.

Cincotta, Richard, Jennifer Wisnewski, and Robert Engelman. 2000. Human population in the biodiversity hotspots. *Nature* 404:990–992.

Defenders of Wildlife. 2002. Conservation in America: State government incentives for habitat conservation. http://www.defenders.org/programs_and_policy/.

Drechsler, Martin, Frank Watzold, Karin Johst, Holger Bergmann, and Josef Settele. 2007. A model-based approach for designing cost-effective compensation payments for conservation of endangered species in real landscapes. *Biological Conservation* 140(1–2):174–186.

Drechsler, Martin, Frank Watzold, Karin Johst, and Jason F. Shogren. 2010. An agglomeration in payment for cost-effective biodiversity conservation in spatially structured landscapes. *Resource and Energy Economics* 32:261–275.

Easterbrook, Gregg. 1998. Getting around the takings problem. *PERC Reports* 16(2):3–5. [Originally published in the *New Republic*, 2 March 1998.]

Epstein, Richard. 1985. *Takings: Private property and power of eminent domain.* Cambridge, MA: Harvard University Press.

———. 1995. *Simple rules for a complex world.* Cambridge, MA: Harvard University Press.

Ferraro, Paul. 2008. Asymmetric information and contract design for payments for environmental services. *Ecological Economics* 65:810–821.

Ferraro, Paul, and Agnes Kiss. 2002. Direct payments to conserve biodiversity. *Science* 298:1718–1719.

Goble, Dale, J., Michael Scott, and Frank Davis. 2006. *The Endangered Species Act at thirty.* 2 vols. Washington, DC: Island Press.

Grout, Cyrus. 2009. Incentives for spatially coordinated land conservation: A conditional agglomeration bonus. *Western Economics Forum* 8(2):21–29.

Hamaide, Bertrand, and Jack Sheerin. 2010. Species protection from current reserves: Economic and biological considerations, spatial issues and policy evaluation. *Ecological Economics* 70(1):667–675.

Hartig, Florian, and Martin Drechsler. 2009. Smart spatial incentives for market-based conservation. *Biological Conservation* 142:779–788.

Heywood, V., ed. 1996. *Global biodiversity assessment.* Cambridge, U.K.: Cambridge University Press.

IFG (Idaho Fish and Game). 2011. *The Idaho Habitat Improvement Program.* http://fishandgame .idaho.gov/cms/wildlife/hip/.

Innes, Robert, Stephen Polasky, and John Tschirhart. 1998. Takings, compensation, and endangered species protection on private lands. *Journal of Economic Perspectives* 12(3):35–52.

Korfmacher, Katrina, and Emily Elsom. 1998. Voluntary incentive for farmland preservation in central Ohio: What do farmers think? Working Paper 98–4. DeKalb, IL: Center For Agriculture in the Environment.

Kurttila, Mikko, Pekka Leskinen, Jouni Pykäläinen, and Tiina Ruuskanen. 2008. Forest owners' decision support in voluntary biodiversity-protection projects. *Silva Fennica* 42(4):643–658.

Leopold, Aldo. 1934. Some thoughts on recreational planning. *Parks and Recreation* 18(4):136–137.

———. 1949. *A Sand County almanac, and sketches here and there.* New York: Oxford University Press.

McEvoy, Arthur. 1998. Markets and ethics in U.S. property law. In *Who owns America? Social conflict over property rights,* ed. H. Jacobs, 94–113. Madison: University of Wisconsin Press.

Melions, Jean, and Robert Thorton. 1999. Contractional ecosystem management under the Endangered Species Act: Can federal agencies make enforceable commitments? *Ecology Law Quarterly* 26:489–524.

Nelson, Erik, Stephen Polasky, David Lewis, Andrew Plantinga, Eric Lonsdorf, Denis White, David Bael, and Joshua Lawler. 2008. Efficiency of incentives to jointly increase carbon sequestration and species conservation on a landscape. *Proceeding of the National Academy of Sciences* 105(28):9471–9476.

North, Douglass, and Robert Thomas. 1973. *The rise of the Western world: A new economic history.* Cambridge, U.K.: Cambridge University Press.

Norton, Gale. 2002. Helping citizens conserve their own land—and America's. *New York Times,* April 20. http://phoenix.liu.edu/~uroy/externalities/NORTON.html.

Noss, Reed. 1993. The Wildlands Project: Land Conservation Strategy. *Wild Earth. Special Issue* (1)10–25. http://www.connix.com/~harry/nosswild.txt.

OWEB (Oregon Watershed Enhancement Board). 2011. Oregon Conservation Reserve Enhancement Program. http://www.oregon.gov/OWEB/CREP.shtml.

Parkhurst, Gregory, and Jason Shogren. 2005. An economic review of incentive mechanisms to protect species on private land. In *Species at risk: Economic incentives to protect endangered species on private property,* ed. Jason Shogren, 65–127. Austin: University of Texas Press.

———. 2007. Spatial incentives to coordinate contiguous habitat. *Ecological Economics* 64:344–355.

———. 2008. Smart subsidies for conservation. *American Journal of Agricultural Economics* 90:1192–1200.

Parkhurst, Gregory, Jason Shogren, Chris Bastian, Paul Kivi, Jennifer Donner, and Rodney W. Smith. 2002. Agglomeration bonus: An incentive mechanism to reunite fragmented habitat for biodiversity conservation. *Ecological Economics* 41:305–328.

Pinchot, Gifford. 1947. *Breaking new ground.* New York: Harcourt, Brace.

Raymond, Leigh. 2006. Cooperation without trust: Overcoming collective action barriers to endangered species protection. *Policies Study Journal* 34(1):38–57.

Sagoff, Mark. 1997. Muddle or muddle through: Takings jurisprudence meets the Endangered Species Act. *William and Mary Law Review* 38:825–993.

Saunders, Denis A., Richard J. Hobbs, and Chris R. Margules. 1991. Biological consequences of ecosystem fragmentation: A review. *Conservation Biology* 5:18–32.

Smith, Martin D., James Sanchirico, and James Wilen. 2009. The economics of spatially-dynamic processes: Applications to renewable resources. *Journal of Environmental Economics and Management* 57(1):104–121.

Smith, Rodney B. W., and Jason F. Shogren. 2002. Voluntary incentive design for endangered species protection. *Journal of Environmental Economics and Management* 43:169–187.

Stoneham, Gary, Nicola Lansdell, Anne Cole, and Loris Strappazzon. 2005. Reforming resource rent policy: An information economics perspective. *Marine Policy* 29:331–338.

Tanaka, Tomomi. 2007. Resource allocation with spatial externalities: Experiments on land consolidation. *B. E. Journal of Economic Analysis and Policy* 7(1):7.

Turner, John, and Jason Rylander. 1998. The private lands challenge: Integrating biodiversity conservation and private property. In *Private property and the Endangered Species Act: Saving habitat, protecting homes*, ed. Jason Shogren, 138–144. Austin: University of Texas Press.

Zhang, Wei, Taylor Ricketts, Claire Kremen, Karen Carney, and Scott Swinton. 2007. Ecosystem services and dis-services to agriculture. *Ecological Economics* 64(2):253–260.

Commentary

JAMES WILSON

This chapter suggests what appears to be a sensible approach to the compensation of landowners who set aside land necessary for the conservation of endangered or threatened species. In particular, the chapter is concerned with compensation in circumstances in which the land supporting the species to be conserved crosses private property lines, for example, migration corridors and large contiguous parcels.

The first section of the chapter presents a useful overview of the wide range of public and private (e.g., land trusts) policies that offer landholders compensation for setting aside land inhabited by endangered or threatened species. To this reader, who is more familiar with conservation problems in the ocean, the description is informative and helpful.

The second part of the chapter presents the interesting idea of an agglomeration bonus. The authors argue that this kind of bonus is a new policy tool designed to apply to situations in which the spatial extent of a public resource, in this instance, the land required to support an endangered or threatened species, is not contained within an individual private holding. The wider problem they address, of course, is that there is no mechanism built into the system of private landholding that is able to coordinate the broader public interest in the spatial continuity of certain lands supporting wildlife. The idea of the agglomeration bonus is to make the amount of compensation contingent on neighbors voluntarily coordinating their land retirement decisions so that the resulting preserves better match the biological needs for corridors or large wildlife areas. The intent is to find an alternative to ill-informed, arbitrary bureaucratic decisions.

To illustrate their approach, the authors describe an experimental test of three kinds of bonus schemes:

1. A compulsory scheme in which landowners are required to withdraw a given amount of land from production but are compensated. Landowners can choose the land they retire without regard to its biological value. (The authors do not state whether any private or state agency actually permits this kind of choice mechanism.)
2. A scheme in which bonus compensation is given when an individual landowner creates contiguous parcels of biologically valuable land within the boundaries of his own holdings; the landowner has the option of retiring up to five parcels and is able to pick the parcels to be retired. The value of the compensation the owner receives is tied to the overall biological value of the retired land.

3. A third scheme that includes the features of the second and adds another bonus that rewards landowners if they retire biologically valuable land adjacent to similar land retired by their neighbor.

The authors "test" their idea with a "spatially explicit" experiment. Four landowners (students) are each given a gridded 5 × 5 piece of property, 25 parcels. Each student has one of four such properties that occupy a 10 × 10 grid. Each of the four landowners know the market value of each of their own and the other landowners' 25 parcels. The biological value of each parcel is determined independently by the compensating authority. In the second bonus scheme, the compensation for any retired parcel depends upon the retirement decisions made by adjacent landowners. Communications between adjacent landowners are the source of coordinated activity.

The experiment follows the usual procedures of experimental economics. Students' land is represented on a grid on a computer screen and they are given the rules for each bonus scheme. In each case they are asked to retire up to five of their 25 parcels. The bonuses for each scheme are calculated so that the total payoff for the student is the same in each case. Each experiment consists of 20 rounds; in each round students are asked to indicate which parcels they intend to retire. After each round students learn the results of their own actions and their neighbors'. Over the course of the rounds of the experiment they are able explore various retirement patterns and, consequently, to discover retirement patterns that best suit their self-interest, i.e., patterns that maximize the sum of the compensation they receive and the value of their continuing use of unretired land.

Not too surprisingly, the first scheme leads to the quick discovery that the least valuable or productive land, without regard to biological worth, should be retired. The implication, of course, is that this kind of scheme is not likely to accomplish much of biological or public value.

In the second scheme, the landowners quickly learn that they can achieve greater private value by aggregating their retired land into contiguous biologically valuable parcels. The extent to which this might occur is clearly a function of the compensation offered compared with the value of the land if it is left in production. A low bonus presumably would lead to no retired land. At higher bonus levels the large number of combinations of land holding and biological patterns and of market factors determining the expected value of land left in production could be expected to lead to an equally large number of outcomes, many of which might be surprising. In spite of this possibility the authors' main point is clear: if the spatial pattern of compensation offered to individual landowners by private and public agencies matches the agglomeration patterns of biological value, the outcome is likely to be more conservation.

In the third scheme, the landowners also learn, a little less quickly, that their private interest is best served by retiring biologically valuable land adjacent to similar land retired by their neighbors. Here also it can be expected that the particulars of local situations will produce a variety of sometimes surprising outcomes; nevertheless, the authors' point is clear: if the spatial pattern of individual compensation is consistent with the biological value of agglomerated land or corridors, the outcome is likely to be more conservation.

In this third experiment, the spatial design places all landowners immediately adjacent to one another; this minimizes the potential communication problem among landowners and leads to an optimistic overstatement of the coordination potential of the bonus scheme. Because each agent is in contact with all the others, there are no problems of distance, such as those that might occur in long corridors or large areas, for example. When distance is part of the problem and agents are able to respond only to the actions of their immediate neighbors, there is no guarantee that the actions of all agents will be consistent. As agents in one part of the space adjust their behavior toward locally efficient solutions, their actions can cascade through the system, disturbing the locally efficient decisions of other groups of agents. In other words, both landowners and compensating agencies might find that their expectations about the outcome of the compensation process are defeated by circumstances elsewhere that are out of their control. The most obvious example is a monopolist landowner holding a corridor proposal hostage. Neither landowners nor compensating agencies are likely to consider a local contract desirable if the outcome of distant negotiations might undo the investment of the local parties. Consequently, the ability of the scheme to assemble large areas or corridors in these instances can be fatally impaired.

The authors avoid this substantive problem by not subjecting their experiment to an analysis which would seek to determine the sensitivity of conservation outcomes to the different amounts of compensation offered and the possible spatial combinations of landholding, land productivity (in private production), and biological value. The number of combinatorial possibilities that could arise even in a simple model like the one illustrated in the chapter is huge and presents an intractable analytic problem. Even if the analysis were done in an experimental setting, it would be very costly and time consuming. (It is understandable that the authors did not pursue such an analysis.) Further, as the spatial scale of the problem and the number of interacting agents are extended to address questions like corridors, the problem is compounded. Put simply, the large number of particular situations that arise because of the spatial complexity of the problem rules out neat, generalizable conclusions.

The authors appear to recognize this. Their response is to suggest that the bonus scheme simply be added to the toolbox of land compensation methods and used where possible. But are compensating agencies not doing this already? It is hard to imagine that an agency interested in the establishment of a large area or of a corridor would not take into consideration the advantages of compensating in a way that contributes to contiguity of preserved land, explore alternative routes that might reduce the chances that, for example, a single holdout might hold a corridor hostage, or do any one of a number of things that are tailored to the particular spatial circumstances of their proposal.

The interesting problem here lies in exactly the direction the authors chose not to go when they avoided a costly sensitivity analysis. Valuable learning might occur in an exploration of the spatial patterns that could arise in this complex problem space. For example, it would be very interesting to know whether there are regular landholding patterns that arise at various scales and under various biological circumstances, and if there are, what the relationship of those patterns to successful collective action is. For example, a bonus scheme such as the one the authors suggest might work if the nature of the biological problem, that is, the corridor and contiguity requirements, were unspecialized and allowed for a range of alternative spatial solutions. Under these conditions, it might be possible for a spatially acceptable biological outcome to be assembled incrementally, from the bottom up. Other spatial arrangements might require top-down design or other explicit coordination methods. And, of course, it is highly probable that any large scheme would require a combination of both.

The interesting analytic question is the circumstances in which (assisted) self-organization, such as the authors' bonus scheme, and designed coordination are more likely to work. In a heterogeneous environment these instances are likely to be a function of very particular local circumstances; those circumstances are not likely to be easy to identify or analyze using a methodology whose power is dependent upon relatively simple environments with a small number of homogeneous elements.

Enclosing the Fishery Commons

From Individuals to Communities

BONNIE J. MCCAY

The oceans and their fish and shellfish are classic instances of "open access" (places and goods with essentially no protection at all), "common property" governance arrangements (places and goods subject to legal and customary protections of shared use rights), and "common-pool" resources (resources that are hard to draw defensible boundaries around and are subject to overexploitation). Depending on the extent of effective regulatory constraint, demand for resource flows, and conditions of the resource systems, marine fisheries are so vulnerable to "tragedies of the unmanaged commons" (Hardin 1994) that one scholar argues that the tragedy of the commons can be thought of as "the fisherman's problem" (A. F. McEvoy 1986).

The long history and widely distributed occurrence of small or large and modest or grandiose efforts to create exclusive places and rights at sea constitute a historical geography of marine environments and resources that are subject to various forms of enclosure, rather than open access. The great diversity of tenurial systems in the world's fisheries, past and present, lends credence to the notion that, at least on local and smaller scales and under certain conditions (Ostrom 1990), people who fish are capable of coordinating and restraining their activities to avert tragedies of the commons (Cordell 1989; Dyer and McGoodwin 1994; McCay and Acheson 1987; McGoodwin 1990; Pinkerton 1989; 1994; Pinkerton and Weinstein 1995; Ruddle 1989). But exploration, colonization, modernizing technologies, and institutions contributed to the marginalization or disappearance of such community-oriented, common-property-based systems of marine resource management throughout the world (Johannes 1978; McCay 1987), even though important dimensions of community affiliation persist and newly emerge even in the most technologically sophisticated fisheries (St. Martin 2006).

Consequently, marine geographies can be characterized very simply in most regions of the world's oceans. In oceans outside territorial waters, there are open-access fisheries that are beyond national limits of jurisdiction and are limited by international institutions of very modest effectiveness. Within national limits, there are broadly defined public rights of access subject to national and local regulatory institutions with similarly modest effectiveness. The thesis that open access creates conditions for overexploitation and economic loss was developed by resource economists and is a well-known justification for enclosing the fisheries commons (H. S.

Gordon 1954; Scott 1955). Open access has been construed as the fundamental component of the incentive structure for overexploiting a shared resource. Open access makes it difficult to formulate collective agreements on management; for instance, there is nothing to prevent newcomers from reaping the benefits of the efforts or sacrifices of present users. Free-rider problems are rampant.

The resultant "tragedy of the commons" scenarios contribute to disappointing performance of fisheries worldwide. The latest global statistics show a leveling off of wild fish catches and increased dependence on farmed production (FAO 2009). Data are even more dismal for many coastal fisheries, as well as some open-sea fisheries; from the perspective of biodiversity, the situation is grave indeed (Worm et al. 2006; but see Branch 2008). The lack of alternatives to fishing in many poorer regions, the difficulties of controlling fisheries beyond national zones of extended jurisdiction because of the weaknesses of international institutions, and the underdevelopment of knowledge about fish and fisheries are major barriers to restoration and sustainable exploitation of fish stocks. However, it is also widely agreed that combinations of closed areas, gear modification, and catch restrictions can and do make a difference, depending on local context (Worm et al. 2009), and that key conditions include restricting access and reducing effort. Controlling access, especially by granting exclusive property rights to individuals or other social units, reduces free-rider and overcapitalization incentives and is also said to improve incentives for stewardship by giving resource users a clear-cut and defensible stake in the resource, present and future, and hence, the motivation to follow the rules and also to participate in developing them.

Spatial Enclosure of the Fisheries Commons

A major step toward enclosure that reshaped fisheries policy and, to some extent, fisheries science was taken in the mid-1970s during a series of United Nations Law of the Sea conferences, when nations agreed to claim two hundred miles of extended jurisdiction over seas and fish stocks that formerly had been treated as part of the international "freedom of the seas" regime. This agreement encouraged the development of new domestic and international institutions for fisheries research and management while restricting access to rich coastal fishing grounds. However, the trend within many nations was to encourage fuller domestic exploitation of fish stocks in adjacent waters, which resulted in expansion of domestic fisheries. In the United States and Canada, many coastal fish stocks had been overfished before implementation of the two-hundred-mile limit; the pattern was for domestic fisheries to continue what foreign fishing had begun (Hennessey and Healey 2000; Ludwig, Hilborn, and Walters 1993). Tragedies of the fisheries commons continued, but within, rather than outside, national boundaries.

In this context and in response to multiple signals of trouble at sea, other forms of enclosure began to take shape in policy planning. A major one is the use of marine protected areas (MPAs), spatially bounded places that are managed to protect marine organisms and habitats from human activities. Establishing MPAs may involve closing areas during spawning seasons or making some fish habitats out of bounds in general or for specific types of fishing gear, but they may also be set aside as "no-take" zones. MPAs have been heavily promoted by environmental groups (Agardy 2000) and are part of national marine resource policies throughout the developed world and in poorer countries as well. They are advocated as measures to complement other management tools and particularly as precautionary measures where scientific knowledge is scarce and highly uncertain (Clark 1996). Also, when resources are not harvested, they have tourist and other values. From a fisheries perspective, MPAs may be thought of as "exclosures," and much research effort has been devoted to exploring the complex parks and people issues involved (Brechin et al. 2003; Christie et al. 2003). MPAs are increasingly subsumed into the topic of marine spatial planning, which is an important thrust of the most recent U.S. ocean policy and central to policy in Canada, the European Union, and other developed countries (Crowder et al. 2006).

Spatial enclosures are also used to provide privileges and assign some management responsibilities to fishing groups. They may be set aside, for example, for those who use certain types of fishing gear, but not others. Of particular interest are territorial use-rights fisheries (TURFs), which grant community groups exclusive fishing rights to certain fishing grounds, or certain species within those grounds. For example, in Chile and Mexico, local fishing syndicates or cooperatives have exclusive concessions for mollusks and crustaceans in marked territories that are usually adjacent to the coastal communities involved (Castilla and Defeo 2001; Ponce-Díaz et al. 1998; Ponce-Díaz, Weisman, and McCay 2009). The TURF model affords an important alternative to individual and marketable fishing rights, which will be discussed later.

Enclosure of the Marine Commons: Commodifying the Right to Fish

A major trend since the 1980s has been to treat fishing rights as commodities that can be parceled out and are subject to negotiation and exchange. Not long after nations claimed two-hundred-mile limits, the view of fishing rights began to change in many countries from the notion of the freedom of citizens to fish, with or without permits and rules, to that of more exclusive and individualized rights (Huppert 2005). The ultimate step, in the eyes of economists and other advocates, is individual transferable quotas (ITQs).

The ITQ management system, also known as individual vessel quota (IVQ) or individual fishery quota (IFQ), has become a popular, but controversial, innovation in fisheries management. The ITQ system for the Atlantic surf clam (*Spisula solidissima*), combined with one for ocean quahogs, another species in the fishery, closely followed examples created earlier in Canada, Iceland, The Netherlands, and New Zealand (National Research Council 1999b). Its design reflected some experiences from work of Lee Anderson, a university professor who had advised the New Zealand fisheries agency on ITQs before working with the Mid-Atlantic Fishery Management Council (Anderson 1989a; 1989b; 2000). Portions of an overall allowable catch are granted to participants in a fishery, who use them as marketable commodities and can buy, lease, and sell them. In the surf-clam fishery, each ITQ owner or lessee receives a percentage of the annual quota and is given tags for the steel cages for clams after dredging. The ITQ system is analogous to cap-and-trade programs for the control of air pollutants in that the government retains the critical rights and responsibilities of setting and enforcing the caps and other rules of the game. Within those constraints, enterprises can make many other critical decisions. The goal is a win-win outcome where private entities are profitable while the goal of environmental protection or resource conservation is achieved.

The process of changing property rights is often incremental and historically specific although general in outcome (North 1990). Measures to address management issues can lead to new or intensified problems that call for new measures, some of which, like ITQs, result in privatizing the right to harvest fish or shellfish, that is, make them exclusive to the holder and potentially divisible and tradeable. This is evident in the case of the Atlantic surf-clam fishery of the eastern seaboard of the United States, the first in U.S. federal waters to become managed by ITQs. Surf clams are large mollusks found in sandy and muddy bottoms on the continental shelf. They are harvested by hydraulic dredges and are used in processed products, such as frozen or canned clam meats that are sold to consumers as breaded clam strips, spaghetti with clam sauce, or clam chowder (Jacobson and Weinberg 2006). In the 1970s clear signs of stock decline and increased effort led to a diagnosis of a tragedy of the commons, but until the United States created its fisheries act, the Magnuson-Stevens Act, in 1976, little could be done to address the issue of open access in federal waters, outside the states' three-mile limits. The Magnuson-Stevens Act provided for a two-hundred-mile limit of extended federal jurisdiction, as well as regional fishery management councils with the power of enacting fishery regulations. In 1978 the Atlantic surf-clam fishery outside the three-mile limit of state jurisdiction became the first fishery in the United States to be managed by limited entry. The Mid-Atlantic Fishery Management Council imposed a moratorium on new vessels in the fishery, as well as a minimum size limit, a closed area to protect juvenile clams, and an overall catch quota. About 120 vessels were allowed to continue fishing for surf clams.

Programs that cap the number of permitted users create smaller groups of commons users, but they can also replicate the commons dilemma on a smaller scale as users continue to compete freely for limited resources, and management continues to depend heavily on efforts to restrict how people harvest (effort controls) or how much they harvest (output controls). In the surf-clam case, catches were controlled through an overall competitive quota that replicated open-access incentives to invest in better technology to race for the resource before the quota was reached and the fishery would have to close. Managers countered the race somewhat by restrictions on vessel and dredge size but also by restrictions on the amount of fishing time allowed per week. The latter were imposed to help spread out production over the year to fit the capacity of clam processing plants.

Such systems create their own inefficiencies, congestion problems, and enforcement challenges, which can lead to demands for further management innovations. In the Atlantic surf-clam case, as clam abundance increased through the growth of two successful year-classes, that is, unusually large populations of clams born in 1977 and 1978 and controls on harvests, it became easier to catch huge amounts of clams in a short period of time. The overall quota remained the same because of management concern given evidence that there were no more large year-classses to follow those of 1977 and 1978, and the consequence was a reduction in allowable fishing time. By 1984 the surf-clam vessels were allowed to work the clam beds no more than six hours per week. Because participation in the fishery required using a vessel that had been in it before limited entry was imposed, the trip limits were attached to specific vessels, and people with multiple vessels were not allowed to combine their trip-limits on one vessel, a clear-cut case of overcapitalization emerged. Management meetings focused on the question of allowing vessel owners to combine the allowable times of two or more vessels into that of one vessel in order to economize. That proposal was a major step toward privatization because access rights (allowable fishing time) came to be thought of as units that could be moved around independently of the boats.

Meanwhile, unknown to many of the actors in this scenario, the key unit being restricted through management began to shift from fishing time to amounts of clams that could be caught. The Atlantic surf-clam fishery was on the verge of becoming a program that "stinted" the limited access rights by attaching some quantified allocation to these rights, the "stinting" practice of the archetypal village commons (Christy 1973; Moloney and Pearse 1979). Talk of combining allowable fishing days or hours into one vessel, which was resisted by those who owned only one vessel because they feared the competitive advantage of large fleet owners, was transformed over time into talk of assigning portions of the overall quota to individual vessels. Economists had long seen the prospect of privatization for this fishery; as early as 1979, some form of stock certificates for this fishery had been discussed, and in the mid-1980s the overcapitalization caused by management through limited entry offered an opportunity for economists to insert the notion of tradable vessel quotas into management debates. Assigning shares of a quota to individual vessels made little sense in this case without the ability to consolidate them into fewer vessels because each of the 120 original vessels would have far too low a share to make economic sense. Hence, the discussion quickly moved past the notion of attaching shares to vessels and cast them as separate from the boats, making them far more fungible commodities.

Marketable shares provide incentives and mechanisms to adjust investments to resources in theory and practice (Grafton et al. 2006; Hannesson 2004). Despite much opposition, particularly from the smaller-scale fishers who felt that their initial allocations would be too small to allow them to continue profitably, the regional fishery management council agreed in 1988 to allow the Atlantic surf-clam fishery to be managed with ITQs (McCay and Creed 1988). The new system began in 1990 and resulted in a very rapid decline in the number of vessels and the amount of vessel capacity (McCay and Brandt 2001a). Today there are fewer than 35 vessels. Thus, in little more than a decade, that fishery shifted from open access to limited entry with complex, costly, and inefficient controls on effort and then to a privatized system of marketable extraction rights embedded within a government-run management system.

Economics and ITQs

The economic performance of ITQs is well known and amply depicted in the literature (Grafton, Squires, and Fox 2000). The intent and theory of an ITQ program are that it will cause a reduction in the overcapitalization and regulated inefficiencies that occur in many common-pool resource systems by downsizing the fishery as the more efficient and/or better-capitalized firms buy out the others. A case study review reports, "Improving transferability of quota is likely to be the only feasible solution to reduce overcapacity and generating resource rents in the fishery . . . The incentives inherent in a tradable [ITQ] scheme provide Adam Smith's 'invisible hand' to direct the fishery in the right direction" (Asche et al. 2008, 926–927). Those who remain in the fishery as quota holders tend to make more money than they did before, countering the tendency in open-access fisheries for the resource rent from nature to be dissipated through competition and overharvesting.

ITQ programs often replace fisheries that were organized with competitive quotas that led to "derby fishing," or races to catch fish before the quota was reached. As in the Atlantic surf-clam case, they may also replace fisheries management regimes that developed extraordinarily complex and costly regulatory measures. ITQs guarantee to their owners that they will be able to catch a certain amount of fish during the year. Because fishing can take place at different paces, the dangers and other costs of races to fish are reduced, and fishers can time their work according to markets, weather, and personal life choices. ITQs can also transform markets, as shown for halibut in the Pacific Northwest, where the gluts created by competitive quotas had necessitated a frozen-fish product. The implementation of ITQs allowed fishermen to time their harvests according to markets, no longer fearing an early closure, and they were able to sell the fish for higher prices on fresh fish markets (Casey et al. 1995; Pinkerton and Edwards 2009).

Conservation and ITQs

Recently, much attention has been devoted to the conservation outcomes of ITQs, following the notion central to bioeconomic theory that privatized ownership—expressed also as owning a secure asset—may provide stronger incentives for ecological stewardship than are found in conventional fisheries management (Costello, Gaines, and Lynham 2008). This notion is controversial; many scientists and social scientists argue for it, but others deny or cast doubt on the argument (Beddington, Agnew, and Clark 2007; Copes 1986; Grafton et al. 2006; Hilborn, Orensanz, and Parma 2005; Macinko and Bromley 2002; McCay 1995b).

Empirical research on the question is now possible because ITQ programs have a three-decade history, are numerous in developed nations, and can be studied within the framework of large databases on fisheries and fish stocks that enable large comparative studies. Costello, Gaines, and Lynham (2008) revived the question and used a database of more than 11,000 commercial fisheries plus a database that had been used to assess trends in fisheries collapse, defined as less than 10 percent of the maximum recorded harvest. They claimed that ITQ-managed fisheries were much less likely to show signs of biological collapse and, when ITQs were implemented, they did much to avert or reverse collapse.

Other scholars found less convincing results that underscore the fact that ITQs are only parts of complex fisheries institutions. They are usually accompanied by more restrictive and/or better-enforced fishing rules, a factor not included in Costello, Gaines, and Lynham's study. Two studies found that whether stock biomass continued to decline after the introduction of ITQs had less to do with ITQs per se than with other changes in management, such as more effective total allowable catch levels and better enforcement and monitoring (Branch 2009; Chu 2009). In addition, Branch found that "ITQs have largely positive effects on target species but mixed or unknown effects on nontarget fisheries and the overall ecosystem" (2009, 39). This result highlights the challenge of melding market-based and ecosystem-based approaches to marine resource management.

Essington (2010) used more refined measures of behavior and ecological outcomes, as well as efforts at controlled comparison. He found that ITQ-managed fisheries differed from non-ITQ fisheries in his study only by markedly reduced variability in year-to-year levels of indicators such as exploitation rate and landings. Essington speculated on the causes and implications of this finding. The end of a race to fish, improved catch reporting (necessitated when individual catches must be monitored), and changes in incentives when individuals must stay within their own quotas and can trade within a fishing season all make it possible both to catch the entire quota and not to exceed the quota. The next result is that resource managers can be more certain about whether a given strategy for management will have a desired outcome in an ITQ fishery. However, the use of ITQs to distribute access to a resource is still dependent on the overall quota and other measures to protect the resource.

The findings about the importance of other management measures in the success of ITQ fisheries are further supported by the biomathematician Colin Clark. In 1973 he raised a warning to those who cast the problem of the commons as defined by the lack of private property. He presented a formal mathematical argument that a private owner could be motivated to harvest a resource to extinction if the growth or replenishment rate was low and the discount rate was high; whaling was the compelling example (Clark 1973). This observation has been treated as either wrong or merely a theoretical possibility in several analyses of the economics of marine fisheries examining the benefits of privatized fishing rights such as ITQs (e.g., Grafton et al. 2006). In response, Clark and colleagues revisited, extended, and broadened the 1973 analysis and concluded that the result "cannot be safely dismissed as being no more than a theoretical possibility. There is a nontrivial number of resources that cannot be safely entrusted to complete private control and management. There are indeed limits to private resource ownership" (Clark, Munro, and Sumaila 2010, 216).

Social and Power Relations and ITQs

There are other reasons that a society cannot and should not rely on privatized property rights alone in managing a public trust and common-pool resource (Bromley 2003; 2009; Macinko and Bromley 2002; Rose 1994; 2002). These reasons support the need to look not only at improving government management of common-pool resources, but also at the roles of user-based institutions, such as communities, in resource management.

In the initial phases of a privatized resource system, processes of downsizing and consolidation tend to result in fewer owners, more leaseholders, and fewer crew members. The leaseholders and crew members, who in some fisheries, as shares decline, become more transient and less skilled than before, may believe that they have little stake or at least little power in the fishery (Pinkerton and Edwards 2009). This perception can work against the dynamic of ownership and stewardship. Lessees and crew are less likely to be in a position to share knowledge about and interest in the fate of the resource with owners and managers. More generally, they have little incentive to follow sustainable fishing practices (Olson 2011). ITQ holders do have strong incentives for engagement in management decision making, and these incentives increase the odds of effective collaboration and even comanagement. However, ITQ holders also may be powerful enough to influence the management agencies and raise the "foxes in the henhouse" problem (McCay 1995a). Such industry control over management decision making can reduce the capacity for adaptation to environmental, institutional, or climate change. Essington's (2010) finding of greater stability in ITQ fisheries was mentioned earlier; rights-holding businesses may be inclined to emphasize maintaining stability not only in performance, but also in the conditions of management affecting the value of their capitalized rights. This emphasis on stability can result in disincentives to adapt to environmental or other changes that might otherwise call for adjustments of the annual quota, as noted in a study of United Kingdom fisheries (Christensen et al. 2009).

More generally, ITQs have been criticized for their socially inequitable outcomes. In an extensive review of the literature on ITQs and similar catch-share programs involving privatized fishing rights, Julia Olson (2011) identifies evidence of significant negative effects of ITQs on crew employment, small-scale boat owners, fishing practices, households and communities, and culture. For instance and quite obviously, the downsizing of the fishing fleet that usually occurs results in fewer boats and fewer people working in them and has direct social consequences for fishery-dependent communities. Equally significant is the fact that trades in quota shares can result in major redistribution of access to fishing and fish-processing opportunities, favoring some enterprises and communities and hurting others (Copes and Charles 2004; McCay 2004; McCay et al. 1995). An important and widely discussed social issue is the difference between the first generation of rights holders, who in all historic cases received a windfall allocation (rather than one that was purchased), and future generations who eventually must pay for access to the fishing rights, taking on major debts and obligations (Copes 1986). Taxation policies often intensify barriers to entry; for example, capital gains taxes lead many initial rights holders to resist selling out in favor of leasing, creating a class of "sea lords," or people who no longer fish but continue to gain wealth from the sea, contrary to deeply embedded notions about rightful relationships with the sea and work.

The social equity implications of privatization were immediately evident in the Atlantic surf-clam fishery (Apostle, McCay, and Mikalsen 2003; Brandt 2005a; 2005b;

Creed and McCay 1996; GAO 2004; Hicks, Kirkley, and Strand 2004; McCay and Brandt 2001b; McCay and Creed 1987; 1990; 1994; D. McEvoy et al. 2009). They were of even greater consequence in other parts of North America, where communities were more heavily dependent on fisheries (McCay 1995b; McCay et al. 1995). In the United States the concerns led to a nationwide moratorium on the use of ITQs in fishing between 1995 and 2006. One of the troubled outcomes that led to such measures was the creation of a generation of people who lost access to fishing as a livelihood, as reported for small Alaskan native communities left behind as a result of ITQ trading (Langdon 2008; Lowe and Carothers 2008). In New Zealand the claims of the indigenous Maori population led to a costly reorganization and settlement (Boyd and Dewees 1992; Crothers 1988). In Iceland there have been several major legal cases on the matter, and today efforts are under way to dismantle the country's ITQ system (Copes and Pálsson 2000). As Huppert observes, privatizing fishing rights can initiate radical changes in how fisheries are organized, "ultimately changing who fishes, where and when they fish, the products sold, the balance of power among industry sectors, incentives to support conservation, the size of incomes from fishing, and the location of shore-side economic activity. Changes of this sort are bound to provoke controversy" (2005, 201). These social dimensions of ITQs have sparked resistance and calls for reform, including calls for greater involvement of communities in management.

Reclaiming "Rights" for Communities

In fisheries policy, the language of "rights" or "property rights" has become shorthand or a euphemism for privatized property rights; the phrase "rights-based management" almost always means systems that use individualized assignments of rights to fishing quotas or related measures (Neher, Arnason, and Mollett 1989). Resistance to ITQs has led to efforts to represent the needs and claims of poorer groups and resource-dependent communities as driven by "rights" as well, as in this report on a workshop in Brazil in 2006: "The tendency to privatize fish resources [goes] . . . against the rights of fishing communities and represents a direct consequence of the neoliberal model aiming to transfer to the private bank the property of fish resources that in most countries are considered as national goods for public use. By this means those who control the fishing capital become the owners of the fishing wealth of nations" (Avendaño 2006, 7). From the perspective of small-scale fisheries and the communities that depend on them, the absence of rights over fisheries resources is a problem quite different from what Hardin (1968) meant in his analysis of the conditions for tragedies of the commons. One recent and thoughtful review of the situation in the developing world concludes that a major impediment to resilient small-scale fisheries "is the inability of fishers to secure and exercise rights and responsibilities over fisheries resources" (Andrew et al. 2007, 228). Rights regimes are contested or are inappropriately assigned, given the scales at which power is exercised versus the scales over which social and ecological systems function.

The refusal to equate "rights" with "private property rights" raises the idea that fishing rights are human rights, as in a statement from a 2008 workshop in

Zanzibar:[1] "The fishing rights should not be treated as a tradable commodity and they should be seen as an integral part of human rights. A rights-based approach to fisheries should not lead to the privatization of fisheries resources"(Kumar 2008). This statement goes on to define a "rights-based" approach to fisheries as one that recognizes "the customary rights, local knowledge, traditional systems and practices, and the rights to access marine and inland resources of small-scale, artisanal and indigenous fishing communities, as well as the right to land for homestead, fishery-related, and other livelihood-related activities. Furthermore, such an approach should enhance collective, community-based access and management regimes" (Kumar 2008). The workshop statement, signed by 45 participants from eastern and southern African nations, also called for gender equality: "All the rights and freedoms that are agreed to as relevant for rights-based approach to fisheries, should apply equally to all men and women of fishing communities" (Kumar 2008). This complicated claim incorporates both a notion of universal and hence "human" rights to access the wherewithal for a livelihood and more specific and somewhat contradictory notions of rights linked to specific cultures, communities, and experiences. Both notions gain rhetorical strength, however, from their opposition to what is viewed as a neoliberal instrument (Mansfield 2004a; 2004b) that threatens the welfare of poor and fishery-dependent communities.

For many resource-dependent coastal communities, a big question now is how such a rights-based approach can be created, given a history of privatized access rights and a context of economic difficulties worldwide, government downsizing, and pressures to reduce participation in the fisheries altogether. How can residents of coastal communities in rural areas or even the fishing communities of urbanized coasts maintain access to the livelihoods, infrastructure, and culture they need to participate viably in the fisheries of the future and, perhaps, to be stewards of the resources of the sea? Is there some way they can benefit from a fisheries management system that depends on control of how many fish are taken and allocates that amount to participants in the fishery? Are there alternatives to criteria such as historical participation and vessel ownership, the most common bases for assignment of ITQ rights? Is there an argument for communities or community-related organizations as "rightful" entities that should participate in such an allocation? Although these questions seem most pertinent to poor communities in the developing world, they are highly relevant to fishery-dependent communities in the developed world as well. The remainder of this chapter addresses these questions through the lens of recent shifts in fisheries policy and practice in the United States, Canada, and western Europe, with a focus on catch shares.

[1] The workshop in Zanzibar, Tanzania, was titled "Asserting Rights, Defining Responsibilities: Perspectives from Small-Scale Fishing Communities on Coastal and Fisheries Management." It was organized by the International Collective for Support of Fishworkers (ICSF), headquartered in Chennai, Tamil Nadu, India, together with the World Forum of Fisheries Peoples, the Western Indian Ocean Marine Science Association, and the Masifundise Development Trust (an independent, nongovernmental organization working with small-scale and traditional fishing and coastal communities in the west and south coasts of the Western Cape, South Africa). The ICSF has been active over the past two decades in defining such positions.

Catch Shares and the Commons

On 4 November 2010, the U.S. agency responsible for the nation's fisheries beyond state jurisdiction, the National Oceanic and Atmospheric Administration (NOAA), published a policy statement on "catch shares" (NOAA Office of Sustainable Fisheries 2010). Earlier, while the policy was still in draft form, the agency provided funding to facilitate the adoption of catch shares in commercial fisheries on both the west and the east coasts of the United States. The term "catch share" follows on other terms—including "limited access privileges" and "individual fishery quotas" (IFQs)—used in the United States to indicate the privatization approach to fisheries management, assigning exclusive extraction rights to individuals or groups. The difference in terms also seems to indicate a progressive semantic widening. IFQ was a synonym for ITQ, the market-based tool for allocating fishing rights long promoted by resource economists. Controversy over the use of ITQs led to a congressional moratorium on their use in 1995, a major national study of ITQs (National Research Council 1999b), and a broadening of the concept in the nation's fisheries law under the term "limited access privilege" (LAP). The language of LAPs asserted and supported the national policy that allocating exclusive fishing rights from a public resource was better construed as granting revocable privileges rather than enduring property rights. It also avoided controversy about giving away public resources, a salient issue in the context of the U.S. public trust doctrine (McCay 1993; Turnipseed et al. 2009).

The broadened notion of LAPs also opened up the possibility of allocation of shares of a quota to units other than individuals. The most recent catch-share policy is more explicit about the range of units that can be involved in the allocation of exclusive fishing privileges or property rights:

> "Catch share" is a general term for several fishery management strategies that allocate a specific portion of the total allowable fishery catch to individuals, cooperatives, communities, or other entities. Each recipient of a catch share is directly accountable to stop fishing when its specific quota is reached. The term includes specific programs defined in law such as "limited access privilege" (LAP) and "individual fishing quota" (IFQ) programs, and other exclusive allocative measures such as Territorial Use Rights Fisheries (TURFs) that grant an exclusive privilege to fish in a geographically designated fishing ground. (NOAA 2010, i)

Changing the vocabulary and broadening the scope of the catch-share policy have not done away with controversy because the policy is about enclosing the fisheries commons, restricting access to formerly open or publicly available places and resources. Catch shares have been subject to vigorous debate and public protest just as their predecessors, particularly IFQs, have been, largely because most of the programs understood to be covered by this rubric are, to date, mainly based on the allocation of exclusive and usually tradable fishing rights to individuals or individual firms. Implementation also coincides with a tightening of fishery limits, which intensifies criticism of the policy. But the new catch-share policy does create opportunities for fisheries management programs that better reflect and support the needs of a wider range of fisheries and fishing communities.

Defining Community

One difficult question is that of defining "community" in the context of fisheries management. U.S. fisheries law and popular culture view communities as defined by place, but anthropological theory and social science research in fisheries point to more fluid notions of community that are marked less by physical or political boundaries than by broadly conceived interactions on multiple scales (Clay and Olson 2007; 2008). Geographic towns, ports, and municipalities serve as place-based fishing communities because of their significant dependence on and/or heritage of fish harvesting or processing. Examples are Dutch Harbor, Alaska, and Gloucester, Massachusetts. There are also enclaves and occupational subcultures within urban areas, such as the commercial fishermen of San Francisco. However, given the mobility of fish and fishermen, significant social interactions can take place away from land locations and can create virtual communities of people who pursue the same prey with similar technologies and in similar places, such as the long-liner fishermen who specialize in large pelagic species, for example, swordfish and tuna, and might be working the Grand Banks off Newfoundland one year and the deep waters off the Hawaiian Islands another.

Each of these cases has dimensions of community, as expressed by the capacity to act collectively on the basis of some degree of shared history, values, and interests and some chance of interaction in the future. One can also find instances of enduring social ties in management arenas as something approximating either an "epistemic community" of expertise and shared concerns and values (Haas 1992) or, in science-policy discourse, extended peer communities (Funtowicz and Ravetz 1993). These types of communities are significant for the development of post-normal science, based on both lay and professional expertise, which is very important in fisheries (St. Martin et al. 2007). However, the discussion that follows refers mainly to place-based fishery-dependent communities and to more or less discrete and localized groups of people with similar fishing technologies or interests, the kinds of communities that have been the focus of studies of small-scale fisheries and irrigation, forest, and other commons management.

Roles of Communities in Fisheries Management

Apart from social impact assessments, there has been little explicit acknowledgment of the fishing rights of communities in the United States and Canada. However, in Japan, Mexico, and some other nations, community-based management has a strong foothold and is particularly connected with fisheries cooperatives and their exclusive concessions. Fishing communities are engaged in fisheries management through political processes (the power of the vote; advisory, consultative, and other participatory institutions), as well as public and private acts of compliance, resistance, and subterfuge. Moreover, community interests are recognized in the U.S. federal law for marine fisheries, the Magnuson-Stevens Act (MSA),[2] which as of 1996 included a provision that fisheries management plans should promote the

---

[2] Magnuson-Stevens Fishery Conservation and Management Act (16 U.S.C. §§ 1801 et seq.).

sustained participation of fishery-dependent communities and minimize economic hardships for such communities. Community-related provisions occur throughout the MSA. For example, in a section in the part of the MSA that requires the rebuilding of overfished stocks, the needs of fishing communities are mentioned, as is the requirement that both restrictions and recovery benefits be allocated fairly and equitably among sectors of the fishery (Clay and Olson 2008). However, it is understood from court cases that requirements for biological conservation and recovery trump the concerns of fishing communities when fishery management choices must be made (Heinz Center 2002).

The topic of community-based management intersects with the movement toward decentralized and industry-based management or "comanagement," with implications for communities. In the northeastern United States, for instance, decentralized, industry-based management has long been practiced in both formal and informal institutions for the region's highly territorial lobster fisheries, and today both the federal waters lobster fishery management regime and a zonal system developed in the state of Maine bear testimony to the capacity for delegating much management authority to industry groups (Acheson 2003). Marketing and dock cooperatives have long existed in the area (Pollnac and Poggie 1988). To a limited extent, they have been involved in managing local fisheries mainly for market purposes (McCay 1987), taking advantage of a Depression-era law that protects cooperatives from antitrust allegations (Sullivan 2000).

Strong industry involvement in management occurs in some of the region's small, specialized fisheries, particularly for tilefish, red crabs, and, as noted earlier, surf clams and ocean quahogs (Kitts, Pinto da Silva, and Rountree 2007; McCay and Brandt 2001a; Pinto da Silva and Kitts 2006). In those cases, fisheries industry associations or small networks of industry leaders play key roles together with management councils to craft regulations that suit industry and community needs and provide considerable flexibility to members. Some have also been particularly active in cooperative research to supplement government scientific research (Johnson 2007).

The notion of providing exclusive quota shares to communities or other groups that are associated with communities is more radical and innovative than previous efforts to reflect the needs and values of communities in fisheries management. Some such programs have evolved parallel with, as reforms of, or in reaction to ITQ management. A recent trend toward sector management offers the potential for greater community engagement in fisheries management.

Community Quotas in Alaska

In the United States the first major instance of assigning quota shares to communities came about through the creation of community development quotas (CDQs) in western Alaska in 1992. The goal was to give remote and mostly native communities bordering the Bering Sea a financial stake in fisheries that were heavily industrialized and often distant (Tryon 1993). Percentages of the overall quota for commercially valuable species, particularly groundfish like pollock, halibut, and, more recently, crabs, have been granted to six corporations. These corporations were created to represent the interests of 65 local communities for the purpose of community development. In most cases, the corporations lease their shares of the quota to commercial fishing businesses rather than operate their own vessels, but the system is characterized by great diversity and dynamism (National Research Council 1999a). CDQs may be exchanged among the six corporations, but they do not have the right to sell their CDQs or accumulate more by purchase from other groups, and they do not have a seat at the table for fisheries management, although they are active politically. Their performance as vehicles for community development has been criticized and is highly variable (Langdon 2008).

More recently, in Alaska the individual fishery quota (IFQ) program for halibut, sablefish, and other species was modified to help redress the movement of quotas away from many small communities because of transfers among quota holders. In 2004 the North Pacific Fishery Management Council enacted a provision allowing 42 small, isolated, and fishery-dependent communities in the Gulf of Alaska to organize as nonprofit community quota entities (CQEs) with the right to purchase quotas on behalf of community members.[3] Each year the CQE then leases its quota to one or more persons deemed to be permanent members of the community. This provision was in response to an unexpected consequence of another provision of the IFQ program intended to promote community values: quota ownership is supposed to be restricted to bona fide fishers, that is, individuals with experience in fishing. Moreover, to preserve the owner-operator nature of the fishery, the owner of the quota being used for a fishing trip should be on board the boat (there are numerous grandfathered exceptions). Both provisions made it difficult for larger businesses to purchase quotas, the intent of the program, but they also made it impossible for entities like communities or cooperatives to do so. However, the CQE program was very narrowly designed, with neither an allocation of quotas to CQEs nor a program to support financing purchase of IFQs on the open market. As of 2010, only one community has been able to get financing to purchase a quota, and it purchased the quota from one of its own retiring members (Ed Backus, personal communication, 1 June 2010).

The nonprofit group Ecotrust has created the North Pacific Fisheries Trust as a potential financing mechanism to help the CQE program realize its goals.[4] Trusts are emerging as important vehicles for development of community-related fisheries in the context of privatized rights, reflecting their use more generally for environmental, housing, and other purposes. Another trust, the Cape Cod Fisheries Trust, was formed in 2009 and is playing a major role in community-based management in New England.

Community Management Boards in Atlantic Canada

A less well-known innovation in North America is the community management board program created in the 1990s for small-scale fisheries in the Scotian Shelf region of Atlantic Canada (Kearney 2005; Kearney et al. 1998). In 1990 ITQs were

[3] Community Quota Program Final Rule, 69 Fed. Reg. 23,861, 30 April 2004; effective 1 June 2004. NOAA Fisheries: Restricted Access Management: Community Quota Program, http://www.fakr.noaa.gov/ram/cqp.htm.
[4] Ecotrust: North Pacific Fisheries Trust, http://www.ecotrust.org/npft/.

put in place for the mobile-gear (otter-trawl or dragger) groundfish fishery in the region (Apostle, McKay, and Mikalsen 2003; McCay, Apostle, and Creed 1998). Very strong and even violent opposition to the expansion of ITQs to other fleets or the possibility that owners of vessels with ITQs could buy up quotas held by smaller-scale fishers contributed to efforts by fishery leaders, community workers, and others to find a more community-oriented alternative. These efforts were focused on the small-scale fixed-gear fleet (mostly hand-line and gill-net fishers) (Kearney et al. 1998). The Canadian government's Department of Fisheries and Oceans (DFO) was supportive, apparently seeing the community program as a way to reduce the allocational conflict that occurred every season among the numerous small associations that had emerged over the years to represent the interests of hand-liners and other small-scale fishers and their communities (Peacock and Annand 2008). A pilot program began in 1995, and by 1997 DFO had worked with community development representatives and local fishing associations to create eight community management boards (CMBs) that covered all the small-scale fixed-gear fisheries of the region.

"Community" was defined in terms of both geography and "like-minded" fisheries, that is, "groups of fisheries who have common management objectives" (Peacock and Annand 2008, 102), but in all but one case, geography sufficed for like-mindedness. In that one exception, the geographic community was divided into two boards, one mindful of the benefits of ITQ-like ways of allocating the catch share among board members, the other preferring a competitive fishery modified by trip limits. The CMBs received portions of the overall quotas for cod, haddock, and other species that were based on historic landings of individuals in the areas (as well as records from processors, given the difficulty of getting documentation for all individual landings). All registered fishers in an area within the vessel categories involved become members of the CMBs, although they have the right to opt out and fish in a competitive fishery (the size and limitations of which have discouraged most fishers) (Peacock and Annand 2008). Each CMB must put together a "conservation harvesting plan" that has to be approved by the DFO and becomes the contractual agreement with the agency.

This example shows the importance of using community-based programs to reduce conflict, enable diversity and experimentation in management, and improve compliance. Government participants have emphasized the last factor. The CMB has the obligation to ensure that the rules are obeyed, in accordance with standards developed over time between government and industry. It uses a dockside monitoring program that evolved with ITQs in the region. The CMBs are said to have been effective in using peer pressure to enforce compliance. In some communities, they have instituted more draconian penalties than would be issued by courts, typically reductions in quotas and/or time that can be spent at sea (Peacock and Annand 2008).

The communities, on the other hand, have been behind efforts to limit transferability, in sharp contrast with the local ITQ fishery management regime. The CMBs have been able to trade quotas with other communities (but not with the ITQ fleet, with one exception), and fishers are able to move between communities, but these movements require agreement from both communities (Peacock and Annand 2008).

The CMB system is a genuine comanagement system. The government plays a significant role in enhancing the capacity of the CMBs and in quality control. The DFO has responsibility for licensing, through which many conditions of the fishery are established and enforced (e.g., vessel and gear features and fishing areas). It also has the function of auditing to ensure that the sharing works as planned and that conservation approaches are adopted. It further helps the CMBs manage the limits they have imposed, as well as those dictated by the DFO for conservation purposes, by providing data on individual vessel landings (Peacock and Annand 2008). The CMBs have the responsibility to determine how the assigned allocations are to be harvested. The options range from competitive fishing by gear type (hand-liners have one competitive quota; gill-net fishers have another competitive quota), trip limits, or time limits at sea to an industry-developed ITQ system. The CMBs can be divided into smaller groups with different approaches to the fishery. In the Shelburne area, the largest, there are two CMBs. One of the Shelburne CMBs has five different associations, each with its own harvesting plan; the other has three.

A major benefit of the CMB system has been reduced conflict among the small-scale fishing communities. Examples of enhanced cooperation include some trading of quotas and the creation of the Bay of Fundy Council, made up of two CMBs and other groups, which seeks to develop an ecosystem-management approach (Kearney et al. 1998; Peacock and Annand 2008). This council was a significant institutional shift toward more explicit industry-based stewardship over ecologically defined areas, but reports suggest that standard fisheries conservation benefits have been mixed. There has been a marked improvement in the science-advisory process, and the fishers are more meaningfully involved in participatory research (Peacock and Annand 2008; Wiber et al. 2008). On the other hand, fish stocks in the region, particularly cod, have been in poor shape. One assessment notes the continued problem of discarding and high grading, that is, given strict quota limits, bringing in only the fish that are more valuable and throwing away much else that is actually caught, dead or alive (Peacock and Annand 2008).

Assessment of conservation and economic outcomes is complicated by the fact that community-based management in the Scotian Shelf region has taken place in a context of severe and continuing resource decline. Participation in these fisheries has dropped dramatically in the area as people have left fishing altogether or have focused more on lobsters.[5] It is remarkable that community-based management evolved as it did, given the high transaction costs, observer fees, and other costs of this form of fisheries management (Peacock and Annand 2008), but those costs may have contributed to movement out of the groundfish fisheries.

Greg Peacock and Chris Annand, who were both deeply involved in the government side of the program, believe that the CMBs enabled a "more business-like" way of managing fisheries and facilitated the readjustment of efforts to be more in line with the resource; that is, they helped downsize the fishery (2008, 107). However, they also point out that the CMBs are strongly divided about the use of "business-like" methods, particularly the assignment of individual quotas to members of the CMBs.

---

[5] The number of active vessels in all communities fishing in the region decreased from 1,274 in 1996 to 384 in 2005 (Peacock and Annand 2008).

Consequently, there are no formal or official ITQ programs in this fishery even though some groups have informal means of assigning and managing quotas that are functionally equivalent to ITQs. For example, they may allow some degree of "license stacking," where one boat uses two license-attached quotas (Peacock and Annand 2008, 108).[6] Nonetheless, all groups resisted "self-rationalization" schemes allowing the buyout of members by others, and the fishery was still in economic trouble, with incentives that worked against conservation, including incentives to discard less valuable fishes (Peacock and Annand 2008, 109).

The system was run without legally binding arrangements between the DFO and the fishing groups; such arrangements were not allowed for in Canada's Fisheries Act. The DFO agreed to the measure informally, without specific legislative basis, and the boards used contracts for their internal organization (Kearney 2005; Kearney et al. 1998). Several of the CMBs persist as institutions to represent local interests vis-à-vis the government, but the fisheries have changed greatly, with further problems in groundfish populations and economics, such that the traditional handline fishery is virtually gone. One longtime proponent and participant in the system from the community development side, Arthur Bull, believes that the major limitation was that the CMBs were not granted exclusive rights to fishing areas (TURFs) and instead had to share fish stocks with the larger-scale, industrialized fishing fleets. Representing what were always seen as marginal fishers, the CMBs were ill equipped to compete for sizable shares of overall quotas and had little incentive to cooperate for tighter management (Arthur Bull, personal communication, 2 June 2010).

Sector Allocations in The Netherlands and the United Kingdom

The Producer Organisation (PO) quota management programs in the United Kingdom and the Biesheuvel groups in The Netherlands involve the allocation of shares of overall quotas to organized groups of fishers (Christensen et al. 2009). The Biesheuvel system began as an ITQ-based fishery, but it evolved into a system whereby smaller, geographically distinct groups of fishers in the large-scale cutter fleet belong to organizations that have responsibility for managing a share of the overall quota, within which ITQs are used (Dubbink and van Vliet 1996).[7] The PO system in the United Kingdom is similar but has developed within a policy framework that is generally opposed to ITQs, allowing individual vessel allocations but no trading of quotas independent of transfers of the vessels. POs are artifacts of the European Community that were intended originally for marketing purposes, but in the 1980s they became vehicles for allocating shares of overall quotas to groups of fishermen within which decisions about more detailed allocations are made. The POs have responsibilities to the larger fishery management system for ensuring that the quotas are not exceeded and that other conservation measures are met, and they are involved in purchasing or leasing quotas from other groups.

---

[6] Peacock and Annand refer to the license permits as "quasi-property rights" and note that there has been controversy in the larger fishing industry about them because the more informal ITQ fishers pay much lower fees than do those involved in formal ITQ fisheries (2008, 108).

[7] The Dutch Biesheuvel system is named after a minister of food and fisheries of the 1960s who not only promoted methods for improving fish quality but also presided over a group which was mandated to find ways to make the fisheries sector take more responsibility for its activities.

Some of the POs operate like ITQs, allowing some accumulation of purchased or leased quotas on individual boats. Others remain wholly or in part committed to a more egalitarian mode of allocating quotas among boats (Christensen et al. 2009; Goodlad 2005; Philippson 1999). The POs can trade quotas with one another and obtain quotas from other sources. They provide many of the advantages of both ITQs and comanagement. By allowing fishers to make many crucial decisions about allocation through the democratic processes of the POs, they give them a sense of ownership, as well as responsibility.

From a management perspective, it appears that the value of such community-oriented management that matters most to the larger system is the use of group responsibility and peer pressure to ensure better compliance with a management regime, as well as getting government out of the sticky business of deciding how to distribute allocations. In contrast with the Canadian case, in the Dutch and U.K. systems, there may be little relationship to specific fishing communities or to larger objectives of community development, including maintaining opportunities for fishing as a livelihood. Indeed, the U.K. system has evolved into a full-fledged quota-trading system, despite an anti-ITQ policy. Nonetheless, the system is a strong comanagement one, where the POs and fishers function as interacting social beings who play important roles in the management of quotas. Government manages the POs, but POs manage the fishers (Goodlad 2005).

Within this setting, one true community-owned fish quota has been instituted, in the Shetland Islands (Goodlad 2005). In the United Kingdom it has been possible since 1993 to purchase fish quotas through fleet-decommissioning schemes, where vessel owners sell their quota entitlements (which come from the records of their fishing performance) to their PO, relinquish their licenses, and thereby separate entitlements from the vessels. By entitlement is meant that share of the quota assigned by a given vessel. The Shetlands PO purchased such quota entitlements with the intent of retaining them as a whole to secure future fishing opportunities for members. Through that and another quota investment scheme, the Shetlands community held two pools of demersal (groundfish) fish quotas, more than the quotas owned privately by the individuals and companies within the Shetland fleet (Goodlad 2005). The part held by the PO was never to be sold and was to be used only to augment the quota allocations of member vessels. The other part, held by an islands development fund, was used to help new entrants get started in the industry, to counter the problem common in remote regions where people surrounded by fish and dependent on the fish industry see access to marine resources and livelihoods being eroded through quota trading.

Sector Management in New England

On 1 May 2010, the groundfish fisheries of New England under the auspices of the New England Fishery Management Council came under a management system very similar to what is found in the systems in Canada, The Netherlands, and the United Kingdom described earlier. The system is called "sector management" and can be viewed as an example of a more collective form of a catch-share policy. The groundfish fleet from Maine to New Jersey is organized into cooperative-like sectors, each of which is allocated a portion of the overall catch for each stock of fish in the management unit on the basis of the historic performance of members of the sectors from certain years, as in the PO system in the United Kingdom. In this system, too, it is up to the organization that receives the allocation to decide how the sector's share is to be allocated among members of the sector. Fishers who are not able or willing to join a sector remain in a common-pool fishery subject to strict controls on days at sea and other measures (*Federal Register* 2010). Fishers are apparently free to move from one sector to another from year to year, taking their historic catch records with them.

The current system of sector management owes much to the example set by a group of fishers and others based in Cape Cod, Massachusetts, which had an explicit community orientation. As controls on fishing effort in the demersal fisheries tightened through limited days at sea, and cod were reduced to a bycatch for most fishers, the Cape Cod Commercial Hook Fishermen's Association (CCCHFA) came up with a proposal for a special allocation to a "sector" of the fishing industry that would be awarded a share of an allowable catch quota for cod. In 2004 an amendment to the multispecies groundfish plan included a provision for the Georges Bank Cod Hook Sector, and in 2006 a second sector was authorized by a framework of the plan, the Georges Bank Fixed Gear Sector. Both sectors were based largely on vessels from two Cape Cod ports, Harwich and Chatham. As sectors, they were responsible for keeping catches under a certain limit, but they also were exempt from some of the rules that the small-scale hook-and-line and gill-net fishers felt would end their participation in fishing. Each sector decided to distribute its allocations in the form of monthly quotas fished competitively by members (K. Gordon 2010).

These programs have been described by their designers, participants, and others as exemplars of community-based fisheries management. They have received a great deal of media attention, as well as foundation and public support. Their Web site (http://www.ccchfa.org) reads: "The sector system, pioneered by the Hook Association, allows fishermen to work collectively to harvest a combined quota of fish. These fishing cooperatives work for our community by increasing flexibility and profit for fishing businesses, encouraging sustainable fishing methods, and making it easier for fishermen to stay within annual limits."

The amendments to the fishery management plan that resulted in the Georges Bank Cod Hook and Fixed Gear sectors were written generically, enabling other sectors to form, but it was not until 2009 that the New England Fishery Management Council agreed on a full-fledged sector program, to begin in May 2010. This program was strongly supported by the Environmental Defense Fund (EDF), a representative of which was appointed to the New England Fishery Management Council, along with an employee of the CCCHFA. The EDF was among several environmental groups that promoted catch-share management in New England and nationally (Environmental Defense Fund 2009). The context was a long period of continuous decline in allowable fishing days, attrition in fisheries participation, and deep economic and social distress for individuals, enterprises, families, and communities that threatened to worsen because of a management shift from indirect controls on fishing mortality, such as days at sea and closed areas, to strict caps or quotas (NOAA Northeast Fisheries Science Center 2010). The effect on fishing communities was mitigated somewhat by the fact that some shifted to other fisheries, particularly lobsters, scallops, and monkfish, but many people left fishing altogether, and the infrastructure of the fisheries in some areas was in peril. The direness of the situation was compounded by a new provision in the 2006 revision by the U.S. Congress of the Magnuson-Stevens Act that required precautionary lowering of allowable catches where there was significant scientific and/or implementation uncertainty, even for fish stocks thought to be in fairly good shape, no longer overfished, or on their way to restoration.

Anticipating even further cuts in allowable fishing time, the New England Fishery Management Council combined its mandate to impose caps on catches with sector management in 2009, to start in May 2010. Extremely hard choices are required, and these are being delegated to industry groups, which have to decide how limited fish quotas are to be parceled out among their members, as well as what the criteria for membership should be. By January 2010, the deadline for sector organization, the Northeast Seafood Coalition, an industry group, had established 12 of its eventual 13 sectors, representing more than 500 fishing vessels, and the coalition expected allocations of about two-thirds of all the fish authorized to be caught under the new program for the new fishing year, to begin in May 2010 (Gaines 2010). Another industry trade association, Associated Fisheries of Maine, organized a large sector, the Sustainable Harvest Sector, which then had 93 permitted vessels enrolled and expected a few more. This group represented the larger, mobile trawlers of Maine and nearby states and had a large portion of the haddock quota for the region (Gaines 2010). The common pool varied greatly in size and share of fish-stock quotas as owners of fishing vessels vacillated between sectors and the common pool, but ultimately it had very low allocation and, as expected, was on the verge of being closed within a month of the opening of the fishery, exemplifying the "derby" dynamic that sectors were intended to help people avoid.

Although the official language of the national catch-share policy emphasizes that catch shares can be allocated to communities, as well as individuals, and the sectors are good examples, leaders of the New England Fishery Management Council publicly stated their intent that sector management would usher in ITQs (personal observation, Gulf of Maine meeting, October 2009). The size of a sector's allocation is a function of the historic performance of its members, the same condition that applies to the U.K. POs. Some of the U.K. POs have long awarded their members equal fishing rights despite what they bring to the PO from their historic records as entitlements attached to their vessels, and other allocations have been devised. It appears that the New England sectors are not moving into such terrains. By and large, they are choosing instead to share the sector allocations according to what each member brings in and to allow trades among members, coming close to ITQ systems despite a long history of resistance to ITQs. Therefore, the sectors may prove to have little "community" significance beyond their roles in comanagement. This is recognized in the fervor of opposition to the system, exemplified by a recent movement called Who Fishes Matters, led by a small advocacy group, the Northwest

Atlantic Marine Alliance (http://www.namanet.org), although most opposition has focused on the size of the catch limits.

Sector management does provide a structure that could enhance community interests, as might have been expected, given the strong community orientation of the Georges Bank Cod Hook and Fixed Gear sectors. There was a semblance of like-minded community in the early composition of many of the sectors, but by and large, the larger ones emerged as business enterprises that had little identity linked to place or even technology and gave early indications, as mentioned earlier, of moving toward ITQs. However, several very small sectors also signed up by May 2010 with the intention of protecting and enhancing opportunities for fishing communities. These were the Georges Bank Cod Fixed Gear Sector, the Port Clyde Community Groundfish Sector, and the Northeast Coastal Communities Sector, each of which is organized around themes of social equity and community survival.

Sectors and Communities

Community-oriented sector management in New England has emerged mainly within the three very small sectors and in conjunction with other innovations designed to help keep small-boat, local, and family-based fishing businesses alive at a time of severe cutbacks in fishing opportunities. Financial trusts and a system known as permit banking have been introduced to help local groups obtain financing to acquire increasingly scarce and costly permits. The Cape Cod group combined its former sectors into one, the Georges Bank Fixed Gear Sector, and as of January 2010 was set up to receive a large portion, 28 percent, of the Georges Bank cod allocation (Gaines 2010). Furthermore, in order to realize the group's commitment to the goal of helping keep fishing as a livelihood in Chatham and other Cape Cod communities, the CCCHFA obtained help from environmental groups and foundations to fund the Cape Cod Fisheries Trust through which it can purchase limited licenses in other fisheries, particularly scallops, to enable its members to participate in more diversified fisheries.

Similar innovations are taking place in the two other small sectors. Although its membership went beyond the Port Clyde fleet, the Port Clyde Community Groundfish Sector is based on a local fishing cooperative that had already begun community-based initiatives, including its Community Supported Fishery program (http://www.portclydefreshcatch.com), the first in the United States, with the goal of enabling fishermen to make adequate incomes from smaller catches. A similar strong commitment to local fisheries and community development was demonstrated by the organization that became the Northeast Coastal Communities Sector, led by the Penobscot East Resource Center of Stonington, Maine, but combined with a small group of fishers from Martha's Vineyard, Massachusetts. Together they were able to muster 19 permit holders as members for the 2010 fishing year (Schreiber 2010b). Their allocations were very small. It was a challenge to find people with groundfish permits from Maine because many had given up groundfishing for lobstering. That difficulty played a role in Penobscot East's decision to work with Martha's Vineyard, even though the two places are in separate states and many miles apart.

The mission of the Northeast Coastal Communities Sector is explicitly community oriented: "To rebuild a sustainable groundfishery and ensure access for traditional fishing communities" that have come to have very limited access to groundfish (Garrett-Reed 2010). The sector system reopens possibilities for participation in the cod and other groundfish fisheries as the fish populations recover. A Maine fisherman from Swans Island explained: "In my case, coming from a small-boat community that traditionally fished groundfish seasonally, this is my only opportunity to fish" (Jason Joyce, quoted in Schreiber [2010b]). His father had lost his groundfish permit many years ago, and he had purchased one about 15 years ago, keeping up the paperwork but never able to use it for want of allocated days at sea. Now, as a member of the sector, he is able to participate according to how many groundfish the sector is allocated, given the combined landings history of the members. The situation on Martha's Vineyard is similar. Its fishing community sees the sector program as a way to revive and preserve its fishing heritage for coming generations. Only five groundfish permit holders are left; they fish for other species during the summer and fall and hope that access to groundfish allocations will enable them to revive a winter cod season.

However, allocations have been very small for the Port Clyde and Northeast Communities sectors, and survival in fishing for the fishermen and communities involved is increasingly dependent on trusts and permit banking. In 2009 the Penobscot East Resource Center partnered with The Nature Conservancy to purchase groundfish permits, up to now from local fishermen, which are being banked for future use or leased at relatively low cost to local fishers who can use the days at sea or annual catch shares involved, as well as being made available to local fishermen for research into more sustainable fisheries (Cartwright 2009). Similarly, the Port Clyde sector has access to quotas from a permit bank created by The Nature Conservancy and the Island Institute. The Penobscot East sector is using the groundfish permits to establish a "sentinel fishery" research program. Days at sea, which are attached to permits, are leased from the bank so that a vessel can participate in cooperative research projects. "This is a really important project for the future of the groundfish fishery here," said the Penobscot East Resource Center's director, Robin Alden. "Even this small start has taken getting past almost insurmountable obstacles. Without the permit bank, the sentinel fishery would not be possible. Without the sentinel fishery research, we couldn't find out what's happened to the fish. On top of that, we are restarting the shoreside infrastructure—ice, offloading, and marketing. The door is no longer closed on groundfishing in eastern Maine" (Schreiber 2010a).

In the winter of 2009–2010, the NOAA announced an expansion of permit banking as part of an appropriation to help with the transition to catch shares and sector-based management. About $5 million was announced for funding permit banks in the New England states of Maine, New Hampshire, Massachusetts, and Rhode Island. The State of Maine had received $1 million as seed funding in 2009 and will receive $2 million more. Notable is the existence of regulations that "indicate a new commitment in Washington to community-based fisheries" (Hayden and Conkling 2010). Recognizing that limited-access programs and the consolidation that follows them tend to squeeze out small boats and hence hurt fishery-dependent coastal communities, the new permit-banking program restricts participation in the permit banks to fishermen whose vessels are 45 feet or less in length and who either reside in or operate from communities with 30,000 or fewer residents. For organized sectors to obtain permits from the bank, at least 65 percent of the member fishermen must meet those requirements (Hayden and Conkling 2010).

The Northeast Coastal Communities sector exemplifies one of the potential contributions of sector management that makes it close to the Shetlands example. The sector uses collective access to a share of a resource as the basis for reaching agreements on conservation and allocation measures beyond the catch limits established by the regional fisheries management council, that is, to create locally devised resource management. Thus, Northeast Coastal Communities sector management not only seeks to restore traditional fishing patterns, as in the case of the Swans Island fisherman quoted earlier, but also sets constraints on technology to encourage methods that are deemed to be more selective and protective even though they are more labor intensive. At least for the first year, the vessels in the sector are allowed to use only longline, tub-trawl, or pots/traps gear. A Martha's Vineyard small otter trawler is the only exception (Schreiber 2010b).

Permit banking and sector management are closely intertwined, and both depend on a far more decentralized and potentially community-oriented system of fisheries management than before in this region. They require the existence of legitimate organizations representing subgroups in the fisheries and the capacity of people in those organizations to devise and work out viable systems for allocating and using scarce resources, as well as support from the outside, in this case from political representatives and administration officials who have included line items in federal budgets. But most of all, permit banking has emerged as a tool for sector management to enable communities to ensure future and viable participation in the fisheries.

If decision making and monitoring are devolved to smaller units of fishers, the sector management system of New England, which has many similarities to cases described from Canada and the United Kingdom, may become more participatory, which should increase the legitimacy of practices and rules that evolve and strengthen the sense of ownership that seems critical to stewardship in the longer term. At the same time, participants in the fishery are rewarded according to their past performance (catch histories determining catch shares) and are granted the option of trading or purchasing shares, at least within their sectors, to counterbalance constraints created by the initial allocations. Following the logic of exclusive fisheries based on tradable rights, this incentive structure could allow for the exercise of individual choice, investment, and skill and increase efficiencies of production within a system, the sector, that provides some security for future participation (the catch shares) within a more or less collective framework.

The extent to which the sector institution of New England will become a transition to full-fledged ITQs or remain an instrument for comanagement is uncertain. Whether and where sectors will be managed on behalf of small-scale fishers and fishery-dependent communities is also an open question. At this point, the use of sectors for fishery-dependent communities is happening on very small scales and is heavily dependent on subsidies from interested foundations and nongovernment organizations, as well as leadership from strongly motivated and highly principled individuals. More generally, fisheries management in the northeastern United States is moving toward the ITQ end of the spectrum, while enclosure itself, in its many forms, is fully under way through the events and processes of "creeping enclosure" that have affected individual fisheries, fishery by fishery and region by region (Murray et al. 2010). But these small-scale experiments keep alive the possibility and practice of community in fisheries, as do current laws and policy statements (St. Martin 2001; 2005).

Communities, Places, and the Future of Fisheries

There are many ways in which communities and their needs are involved in marine fisheries management. Even in many ITQ programs, there are provisions to protect community-oriented values, such as owner-operated fishing enterprises (McCay 2004). However, if community participation in catch-share-managed fisheries is to be taken seriously, communities must be included in the initial allocations of catch-share programs. A major barrier for many communities is financing, particularly when catch-share programs take place during downturns in the fisheries. Permit banking and fishery trusts are significant innovations, but they are heavily dependent on government subsidies and grants from private charities, neither of which is reliable or even desirable on a permanent basis. Efforts are currently under way, through the NOAA, the Pacific Fisheries Management Council, and groups such as Ecotrust, to adapt enabling legislation on "fishing communities" and "regional fishery associations" to establish the administrative framework for allocations to community-based organizations or "community fishing associations."

Whether communities will have a genuine role as recipients of catch shares will depend on the politics of specific fisheries management efforts, as well as regional and national organizing by advocacy groups. In the United States, when a catch-share program is implemented, granting initial windfall allocations to community-based groups is highly unlikely in most circumstances, given political pressures to recognize the claims and interests of individual vessel owners and fishery companies. It is more likely, as in Alaska's CQE program and the New England sectors, that community groups will have to struggle to obtain financing in order to purchase catch-share allocations after they have been granted. Consequently, effort is being directed toward finding capital from public and private sources or creative mixtures, as in the development of innovative financing mechanisms through trusts or the fisheries equivalent of community development corporations, for example, Coastal Enterprises of Maine (http://www.ceimaine.org).

In this context, it is also worthwhile to consider the development of TURFs, which provide exclusive access or governance rights to coastal communities over the resources found in adjacent waters, a version of the marine protected area rather than the catch-share system of management. In TURF systems, local communities or user groups claim or are granted exclusive fishing rights to certain fishing grounds or certain species within those grounds. The best-known examples are in Japan (Barrett and Okudaira 1995; Lim, Matsuda, and Shigemi 1995; Makino and Matsuda

2005; Ruddle 1989; Takahashi, McCay, and Baba 2006; Weinstein 2000), Chile (Castilla and Defeo 2001; 2005; Defeo and Castilla 2005), and Mexico (Ponce-Díaz et al. 1998; Ponce-Díaz, Weisman, and McCay 2009), where local fishing syndicates or cooperatives have exclusive concessions for benthic resources in marked territories usually adjacent to the coastal communities involved.

In some regions, such as the Gulf of California, Mexico, such exclusive claims may be associated with marine protected areas, where the local fishers forbid harvesting in an area and claim the exclusive right to harvest once it has recovered (Cudney-Bueno et al. 2009). Research in Mexico and the Philippines shows that where communities are able and willing to defend their territories and to develop high levels of compliance, local, community-oriented management through exclusive fishing territories can be successful in achieving economic, social, and conservation goals. However, defense of territories requires getting recognition and some enforcement support from the larger government, which is often difficult (Cudney-Bueno et al. 2009). Furthermore, enforcing compliance is a complex matter involving process legitimacy, well-defined boundaries, and other factors (Pollnac et al. 2010).

Considerable effort has been directed toward understanding these systems, including recent research on a federation of fishing cooperatives on the Pacific coast of Baja California, Mexico (Ponce-Díaz, Weisman, and McCay 2009). The concession system used for lobsters, abalones, turban snails, and a few other benthic and sedentary species has an impressive history of community-based sustainable fishing, especially for lobsters, whose system received ecocertification from the Marine Stewardship Council in 2004. The ability of fishing cooperatives to fish sustainably is closely tied to the property-rights incentives afforded by the exclusive concessions (Costello and Kaffine 2008). It is also due to conditions well known in the common property literature, including well-defined social and geographic boundaries, high dependence of the local community on the fisheries at stake, high value of the concession species, good comanagement and cooperative research relationships with government agencies, and wide involvement of resource users in monitoring, research, and policy through their cooperatives (McCay et al. 2008).

The TURF model affords a noteworthy alternative to individual and marketable fishing rights. In the best-known cases, the resources at stake are benthic and relatively sedentary, mainly shellfish and crustaceans, or are found mainly on discrete coral reef or lagoon structures. Territorial solutions may be easier to create and enforce for these kinds of resources than for mobile and migratory finfish, a fact that has contributed to much stronger policy and academic interest in enclosure through privatization of access rights and a long delay in addressing whether and how privatized rights might be used in ways that protect and benefit coastal communities. However, in the future, fisheries management may see increased interest in more spatially discrete and place-based management controls even for finfish.

During the past decade, more place-based management of finfish has been a topic of discussion in marine fisheries management, particularly for the Gulf of Maine region. Academic scientists, industry leaders, community development specialists, and The Nature Conservancy have discussed ways to develop more place-based appreciations of both human behavior and fish-stock biology in the Gulf of Maine. For example, they have recognized the earlier history of discrete inshore spawning events and likely subpopulations and have posed the notion of complex metapopulations (Ames 2004). The metaphor of "roving bandits" has been used to depict the incentive-driven and predatory behavior of fishers in New England, as elsewhere, which poses challenges to effective management (Berkes et al. 2006). Discussions have taken place about ways to change institutions in order to provide the incentives and wherewithal for improved knowledge and harvest management in highly uncertain, complex, and multiscaled natural systems (Wilson 2007). One outcome of these discussions was a set of efforts by the Island Institute, a regional nonprofit organization, and The Nature Conservancy to create permit banking with the explicit intent of increasing fishers' participation in improving the knowledge base for fisheries management in local areas and protecting the future of small-scale fisheries, which are dependent on local fishing grounds.

Whether exclusive use rights and other property rights will be claimed and defended over local fishing territories in the United States is doubtful, given public trust and constitutional legal constraints. But the history of lobster territoriality in the region suggests that it is premature to ignore TURFs as possible outcomes, particularly where maintaining local control can be a prerequisite for year-round community survival, as in the case of some of the more remote fishing communities (Acheson 1988; 2003; Princen 2005). The larger point of this overview of trends in fisheries enclosure is that greater attention should be given to alternative property rights systems, including community-oriented ones. The current catch-share policy has room for a broader construction. Giving support to communities and small-scale fisheries through permit banking and other measures may help slow trends toward consolidated control and ownership of the right to fish and provide opportunities to experiment with socially and ecologically sensitive, as well as economical, ways to manage fisheries.

REFERENCES

Acheson, James M. 1988. *The lobster gangs of Maine.* Hanover, NH: University Press of New England.
———. 2003. *Capturing the commons: Devising institutions to manage the Maine lobster industry.* Hanover, NH: University Press of New England.
Agardy, Tundi. 2000. Information needs for marine protected areas: Scientific and societal. *Bulletin of Marine Science* 66:875–888.
Agrawal, Arun. 2002. Common resources and institutional sustainability. In *The drama of the commons,* eds. Elinor Ostrom, Thomas Dietz, Nives Dolšak, Paul C. Stern, Susan Stonich, and Elke U. Weber, 41–85. Washington, DC: National Academy Press.
Ames, Edward P., 2004. Atlantic cod stock structure in the Gulf of Maine. *Fisheries* 29:10–28.
Anderson, Lee G. 1989a. Conceptual constructs for practical ITQ management policies. In *Rights based fishing,* eds. Philip A. Neher, Ragnar Arnason, and Nina Mollett, 191–209. Dordrecht: Kluwer Academic Publishing.
———. 1989b. Property rights in fisheries: Lessons from the New Zealand experience. Working Paper 89-22. Bozeman, MT: Political Economy Research Center.

———. 2000. The effects of ITQ implementation: A dynamic approach. *Natural Resource Modeling* 13:435–470.

Andrew, Neil L., Christophe Béné, Stephen J. Hall, Edward H. Allison, Simon Heck, and Blake D. Ratner. 2007. Diagnosis and management of small-scale fisheries in developing countries. *Fish and Fisheries* 8:227–240.

Apostle, Richard, Bonnie McCay, and Knut Mikalsen. 2003. *Enclosing the commons: Individual transferable quotas in a Nova Scotia fishery.* St. John's, Newfoundland: Memorial University of Newfoundland, Institute of Social and Economic Research.

Asche, Frank, Håkan Eggert, Eyjulfur Gudmundsson, Ayoe Hoff, and Sean Pascoe. 2008. Fisher's behaviour with individual vessel quotas—Over-capacity and potential rent; Five case studies. *Marine Policy* 32:920–927.

Avendaño, Pedro. 2006. *Proceedings of Workshop on Land, Territory and Dignity Forum and Artisanal Fisheries, Porto Alegre, Brazil (6–10 March).* World Forum of Fish Harvesters and Workers. http://www.foodsovereignty.org/new/documenti/pescaforoen.pdf.

Barrett, Gene, and Tadahi Okudaira. 1995. The limits of fishery cooperatives? Community development and rural depopulation in Hokkaido, Japan. *Economic and Industrial Democracy* 16:201–232.

Beddington, J. R., D. J. Agnew, and C. W. Clark. 2007. Current problems in the management of marine fisheries. *Science* 316:1713–1716.

Berkes, F., T. P. Hughes, R. S. Steneck, J. A. Wilson, D. R. Bellwood, B. Crona, C. Folke, L. H. Gunderson, H. M. Leslie, J. Norberg, M. Nyström, P. Olsson, H. Österblom, M. Scheffer, and B. Worm. 2006. Globalization, roving bandits, and marine resources. *Science* 311: 1557–1558.

Boyd, Rick O., and Christopher M. Dewees. 1992. Putting theory into practice: Individual transferable quotas in New Zealand's fisheries. *Society and Natural Resources* 5:179–198.

Branch, Trevor A. 2008. Not all fisheries will be collapsed in 2048. *Marine Policy* 32:38–39.

———. 2009. How do individual transferable quotas affect marine ecosystems? *Fish and Fisheries* 10:39–57.

Brandt, Sylvia. 2005a. The equity debate: Distributional impacts of individual transferable quotas. *Ocean and Coastal Management* 48:15–30.

———. 2005b. A tale of two clams: Policy anticipation and industry productivity. *Regulation* 28:18–21.

Brechin, Steven R., Peter R. Wilshusen, Crystal L. Fortwangler, and Patrick C. West. 2003. *Contested nature: Promoting international biodiversity with social justice in the twenty-first century.* Albany: State University of New York Press.

Bromley, Daniel W. 2003. Rights-based fishing: The wrong concept and the wrong solution for the wrong problem. In *Managing marine fisheries in the United States: Pew Oceans Commission Workshop on Marine Fishery Management,* 35–39. http://www.pewoceans.org/reports/pew-managing-fisheries.pdf.

———. 2009. Abdicating responsibility: The deceits of fisheries policy. *Fisheries* 34:280–290.

Cartwright, Steve. 2009. Permit banking could help save fishery. *Working Waterfront,* August. http://www.workingwaterfront.org.

Casey, Keith E., Christopher M. Dewees, Bruce R. Turris, and James E. Wilen. 1995. The effects of individual vessel quotas in the British Columbia halibut fishery. *Marine Resource Economics* 10:211–230.

Castilla, Juan Carlos, and Omar Defeo. 2001. Latin American benthic shellfisheries: Emphasis on co-management and experimental practices. *Reviews in Fish Biology and Fisheries* 11:1–30.

———. 2005. Paradigm shifts needed for world fisheries. [Letter to the editor]. *Science* 309:1324–1325.

Christensen, Anne-Sophie, Martin Aranda, Bonnie McCay, H. Anne McLay, Carl Rova, Andrea Leme da Silva, and Franziska Wolff. 2009. Understanding social robustness in selected European fisheries management systems. In *Comparative evaluations of innovative fisheries management,* eds. K. H. Hauge and Douglas C. Wilson, 163–189. Dordrecht: Springer.

Christie, Patrick, Bonnie J. McCay, Marc L. Miller, Celia Lowe, Alan T. White, Richard Stoffle, David L. Fluharty, Liana Talaue McManus, Ratana Chuenpagdee, Caroline Pomeroy, Daniel O. Suman, Ben G. Blount, Daniel Huppert, Rose-Liza Villahermosa Eisma, Enrique Oracion, Kem Lowry, and Richard B. Pollnac. 2003. Toward developing a complete understanding: A social science research agenda for marine protected areas. *Fisheries* 28:22–26.

Christy, Frances T., Jr. 1973. Fishermen's quotas: A tentative suggestion for domestic management. In *Occasional Papers 19*. Kingston, RI: Law of the Sea Institute, University of Rhode Island.

Chu, Cindy. 2009. Thirty years later: The global growth of ITQs and their influence on stock status in marine fisheries. *Fish and Fisheries* 10:217–230.

Clark, Colin W. 1973. The economics of over-exploitation. *Science* 181:630–634.

———. 1996. Marine reserves and the precautionary management of fisheries. *Ecological Applications* 6:369–370.

Clark, Colin W., Gordon R. Munro, and U. Rashid Sumaila. 2010. Limits to the privatization of fishery resources. *Land Economics* 86:209–218.

Clay, Patricia M., and Julia Olson. 2007. Defining fishing communities: Issues in theory and practice. *NAPA (National Association of Practicing Anthropologists) Bulletin* 28:27–42.

———. 2008. Defining "fishing communities": Vulnerability and the Magnuson-Stevens Fishery Conservation and Management Act. *Human Ecology Review* 15:143–160.

Copes, Parcival. 1986. A critical review of the individual quota as a device in fisheries management. *Land Economics* 62:278–291.

Copes, Parcival, and Anthony T. Charles. 2004. Socioeconomics of individual transferable quotas and community-based fishery management. *Agricultural and Resource Economics Review* 33:171–181.

Copes, Parcival, and Gísli Pálsson. 2000. Challenging ITQs: Legal and political action in Iceland, Canada and Latin America; A preliminary overview. *IIFET Proceedings 2000*, 1–6.

Cordell, John, ed. 1989. *A sea of small boats*. Cambridge, MA: Cultural Survival.

Costello, Christopher J., Steven D. Gaines, and John Lynham. 2008. Can catch shares prevent fisheries collapse? *Science* 321:1678–1681.

Costello, Christopher J., and Daniel Kaffine. 2008. Natural resource use with limited-tenure property rights. *Journal of Environmental Economics and Management* 55:20–36.

Creed, Carolyn F., and Bonnie J. McCay. 1996. Property rights, conservation, and institutional authority: Policy implications of the Magnuson Act reauthorization for the mid-Atlantic region. *Tulane Environmental Law Journal* 9:245–256.

Crothers, Stan. 1988. Individual transferable quotas: The New Zealand experience. *Fisheries* 13:10–12.

Crowder, L B., G. Osherenko, O. R. Young, S. Airame, E. A. Norse, N. Baron, J. C. Day, F. Douvere, C. N. Ehler, B. S. Halpern, S. J. Langdon, K. L. McLeod, J. C. Ogden, R. E. Peach, A. A. Rosenberg, and J. A. Wilson. 2006. Resolving mismatches in U.S. ocean governance. *Science* 313:617–618.

Cudney-Bueno, Richard, Luis Bourillon, Andrea Saenz-Arroyo, J. Torre-Cosi, P. Turk-Boyer, and W. W. Shaw. 2009. Governance and effects of marine reserves in the Gulf of California, Mexico. *Ocean and Coastal Management* 52:207–218.

Defeo, Omar, and Juan Carlos Castilla. 2005. More than one bag for the world fishery crisis and keys for co-management successes in selected artisanal Latin American shellfisheries. *Reviews in Fish Biology and Fisheries* 15:265–283.

Dubbink, Wim, and Martijn van Vliet. 1996. Market regulation versus co-management: Two perspectives on regulating fisheries compared. *Marine Policy* 20:499–516.

Dyer, Christopher, and James McGoodwin. 1994. *Folk management in the world's fisheries: Lessons for modern fisheries management*. Boulder: University Press of Colorado.

Environmental Defense Fund. 2009. Catch shares design manual: A guide for fishermen and managers. Draft. http://www.environmentaldefensefund.org/documents/10400_catch_shares _design_manual_09.09.09.pdf.

Essington, Timothy E. 2010. Ecological indicators display reduced variation in North American catch share fisheries. *Proceedings of the National Academies of Science* 107:754–759.

FAO (Food and Agriculture Organization). 2009. *FAO yearbook: Fisheries and aquaculture statistics, 2007*. Rome, Italy: Food and Agriculture Organization of the United Nations. ftp://ftp .fao.org/docrep/fao/012/i1013t/i1013t.pdf.

Federal Register. 2010. 50 CFR Part 648. Fisheries of the Northeastern United States; Northeast Multispecies Fishery; Framework Adjustment 44; Final Rule. Page 18356. http://edocket .access.gpo.gov/2010/2010-7235.htm.

Funtowicz, Silvio O., and Jerome R. Ravetz. 1993. Science for the post-normal age. *Futures* 25:739–755.

Gaines, Richard. 2010. NMFS extends sector deadline. *Gloucester Times*, January 4. http://www .gloucestertimes.com/local/x546183983/NMFS-extends-sector-deadline.

GAO (U.S. General Accounting Office). 2004. Individual fishing quotas: Methods for community protection and new entry require periodic evaluation. Report to congressional requesters. GAO-04-277. Washington, DC: U.S. General Accounting Office.

Goodlad, John. 2005. Co-management and community-based fisheries management initiatives in Shetland. In *Successful fisheries management: Issues, case studies and perspectives*, eds. Stephen Cunningham and T. Bostock, 91–110. Delft: Eburon.

Gordon, H. Scott. 1954. The economic theory of a common property resource: The fishery. *Journal of Political Economy* 62:124–142.

Gordon, Kimberly. 2010. Catch share management in New England: Groundfish sectors. Master's thesis. Duke University.

Grafton, R. Quentin, Ragnar Arnason, T. Bjørndal, D. Campbell, H. F. Campbell, Colin W. Clark, Robin Connor, Diane P. Dupont, Rågnvaldur Hannesson, Ray Hilborn, James E. Kirkley, Tom Kompas, Daniel E. Lane, Gordon R. Munro, Sean Pascoe, Dale Squires, Stein I. Steinshamm, Bruce Turris, and Quinn Weninger. 2006. Incentive-based approaches to sustainable fisheries. *Canadian Journal of Fisheries and Aquatic Sciences* 63:699–710.

Grafton, R. Quentin, Dale Squires, and K. J. Fox. 2000. Private property and economic efficiency: A study of a common-pool resource. *Journal of Law and Economics* 43:679–713.

Haas, Peter M. 1992. Epistemic communities and international policy coordination: Introduction. *International Organization* 46:1–35.

Hannesson, Rågnvaldur. 2004. *The privatization of the oceans*. Cambridge, MA: MIT Press.

Hardin, Garrett. 1968. The tragedy of the commons. *Science* 162:1243–1248.

———. 1994. The tragedy of the unmanaged commons. *Trends in Ecology and Evolution* 9:199.

Heinz Center. 2002. *Managing summer flounder: A Heinz Center dialogue on marine fisheries initiative*. Washington, DC: H. John Heinz III Center for Science, Economics, and the Environment.

Hennessey, Timothy M., and M. C. Healey. 2000. Ludwig's ratchet and the collapse of New England groundfish stocks. *Coastal Management* 28:187–213.

Hicks, Robert L., James E. Kirkley, and Ivar E. Strand, Jr. 2004. Short-run welfare losses from Essential Fish Habitat designations for the surf clam and ocean quahog fisheries. *Marine Resource Economics* 19:113–129.

Hilborn, Ray, J. M. Orensanz, and Ana Parma. 2005. Institutions, incentives and the future of fisheries. *Philosophical Transactions of the Royal Society* B 360:47–57.

Huppert, Daniel D. 2005. An overview of fishing rights. *Reviews in Fish Biology and Fisheries* 15:201–215.

Jacobson, Larry, and James Weinberg. 2006. Atlantic surfclam (*Spisula solidissima*). In *Status of Fishery Resources of the Northeastern US, 2006*. NOAA/NEFSC, Resource Evaluation and Assessment Division. Revised December 2006. http://www.nefsc.noaa.gov/sos/spsyn/iv/ surfclam/index.html.

Johannes, Robert E. 1978. Traditional marine conservation methods in Oceania and their demise. *Annual Review of Ecology and Systematics* 9:349–364.

Johnson, Teresa. 2007. Integrating fishermen and their knowledge in the science policy process: Case studies of cooperative research in the northeastern U.S. Ph.D. diss., Rutgers University.

Kearney, John. 2005. Communities-based fisheries management in the Bay of Fundy: Sustaining communities through resistance and hope. In *Natural resources as community assets*, eds.

M. W. Lyman and B. Child, 83–100. Washington, DC: Aspen Institute and Sand County Foundation.

Kearney, John, Arthur Bull, Maria Recchia, Mary Desroches, L. Langille, and G. Cunningham. 1998. Resistance to privatisation: Community-based fisheries management in an industrialised nation. Paper presented to International Workshop on Community-Based Natural Resource Management, the World Bank, May 10–14. Washington, DC.

Kitts, Andrew, Patricia Pinto da Silva, and Barbara Rountree. 2007. The evolution of collaborative management in the Northeast USA tilefish fishery. *Marine Policy* 31:192–200.

Kumar, K. G. 2008. Workshop on perspectives from small-scale fishing communities on coastal and fisheries management in eastern and southern Africa, Zanzibar, Tanzania, 24–27 June 2008. Chennai, India: International Collective in Support of Fishworkers. http://www.icsf .net/icsf2006/uploads/publications/proceeding/pdf/english/issue_100/ALL.pdf

Langdon, Steve J. 2008. The community quota program in the Gulf of Alaska: A vehicle for Alaska native village sustainability? In *Enclosing the fisheries: People, places, and power,* eds. Marie E. Lowe and Courtney Carothers, 155–194. Bethesda, MD: American Fisheries Society.

Lim, Christina P., Yoshiaki Matsuda, and Yukio Shigemi. 1995. Co-management in marine fisheries: The Japanese experience. *Coastal Management* 23:195–221.

Lowe, Marie, and Courtney Carothers, eds. 2008. *Enclosing the fisheries: People, places, and power.* AFS Symposium 68. Bethesda, MD: American Fisheries Society.

Ludwig, Donald, Ray Hilborn, and Carl Walters. 1993. Uncertainty, resource exploitation, and conservation: Lessons from history. *Science* 260:17–18.

Macinko, Seth, and Daniel W. Bromley. 2002. *Who owns America's fisheries?* Covelo, CA: Center for Resource Economics and Island Press.

Makino, Mitsutaka, and Kiroyuki Matsuda. 2005. Co-management in Japanese coastal fisheries: Institutional features and transaction costs. *Marine Policy* 29:441–450.

Mansfield, Becky. 2004a. Neoliberalism in the oceans: "Rationalization," property rights, and the commons question. *Geoforum* 35:313–326.

———. 2004b. Rules of privatization: Contradictions in neoliberal regulation of North Pacific fisheries. *Annals of the Association of American Geographers* 94:565–584.

McCay, Bonnie J. 1987. The culture of the commoners: Historical observations on Old World and East Coast U.S. fisheries. In *The question of the commons: The culture and ecology of communal resources,* eds. Bonnie J. McCay and James M. Acheson, 195–216. Tucson: University of Arizona Press.

———. 1993. The making of an environmental doctrine: Public trust and American shellfishermen. In *Environmentalism: The view from anthropology,* ed. Kay Milton, 85–96. London: Routledge.

———. 1995a. Foxes and others in the henhouse? Environmentalists and the fishing industry in the U.S. regional council system. In *Fisheries resource utilization and policy: Proceedings of the World Fisheries Congress, Theme 2,* eds. R. M. Meyer, Chang Zhang, Malcolm L. Windsor, Bonnie McCay, Leroy Hushak, and Robert Muth, 380–390. New Delhi: Oxford and IBH Publishing Co.

———. 1995b. Social and ecological implications of ITQs: An overview. *Ocean and Coastal Management* 28:3–22.

———. 2004. ITQs and community: An essay on environmental governance. *Review of Agricultural and Resource Economics* 33:162–170.

McCay, Bonnie J., and James M. Acheson, eds. 1987. *The question of the commons: The culture and ecology of communal resources.* Tucson: University of Arizona Press.

McCay, Bonnie, Richard Apostle, and Carolyn Creed. 1998. ITQs, comanagement, and community: Reflections from Nova Scotia. *Fisheries* 23:20–23.

McCay, Bonnie J., Richard Apostle, Carolyn Creed, Alan C. Finlayson, and Knut Mikalsen. 1995. Individual transferable quotas (ITQs) in Canadian and U.S. fisheries. *Ocean and Coastal Management* 28:85–116.

McCay, Bonnie J., and Sylvia Brandt. 2001a. Changes in fleet capacity and ownership of harvesting rights in the United States surf clam and ocean quahog fishery. In *Case studies on the effects of transferable fishing rights on fleet capacity and concentration of quota ownership*, ed. Ross Shotton, 44–60. Rome: Food and Agriculture Organization of the United Nations.

———. 2001b. *Initial allocation in the Mid-Atlantic surf clam and ocean quahog individual transferable quota fisheries: Report*. Rome: Food and Agricultural Organization of the United Nations.

McCay, Bonnie J., and Carolyn F. Creed. 1987. *Crews and labor in the surf clam and ocean quahog fleet of the mid-Atlantic region*. Dover, DE: Mid-Atlantic Fisheries Management Council.

———. 1988. Dividing up the commons: Management of the U.S. surf clam fishery. In *Marine resource utilization: A conference on social science issues*. Mobile: University of South Alabama.

———. 1990. Social structure and debates on fisheries management in the mid-Atlantic surf clam fishery. *Ocean and Shoreline Management* 13:199–229.

———. 1994. *Social impacts of ITQs in the sea clam fishery: Final report to the New Jersey Sea Grant College Program*. Fort Hancock, NJ: New Jersey Marine Sciences Consortium.

McCay, Bonnie J., Wendy Weisman, German Ponce-Díaz, Geoff Shester, and Saudiel Ramírez-Sánchez. 2008. Conditions that enable self-governance in managing common-pool resources: A view from the Pacific Coast of central Baja California. Unpublished paper, revised 10 October.

McEvoy, Arthur F. 1986. *The fisherman's problem: Ecology and law in the California fisheries, 1850–1980*. Cambridge, U.K.: Cambridge University Press.

McEvoy, David, Sylvia Brandt, Nathalie Lavoie and Sven Anders. 2009. Effects of ITQ management on fishermen's welfare in the presence of an imperfectly competitive processing sector. *Land Economics* 85:470–484.

McGoodwin, James R. 1990. *Crisis in the world's fisheries: People, problems, and policies*. Stanford, CA: Stanford University Press.

McKean, Margaret. 1996. Common-property regimes as a solution to problems of scale and linkage. In *Rights to nature: Ecological, economic, cultural, and political principles of institutions for the environment*, eds. Susan S. Hanna, Carl Folke, and Karl-Göran Mäler, 223–243. Washington, DC: Island Press.

Moloney, David G., and Peter H. Pearse. 1979. Quantitative rights as an instrument for regulating commercial fisheries. *Journal of the Fisheries Research Board of Canada* 36:859–866.

Murray, Grant, Teresa Johnson, Bonnie J. McCay, Satsuki Takahashi, and Kevin St. Martin. 2010. Cumulative effects, creeping enclosure, and the marine commons of New Jersey. *International Journal of the Commons* 4:367–389.

National Research Council. 1999a. *The Community Development Quota Program in Alaska*. Washington, DC: National Academy Press.

———. 1999b. *Sharing the fish: Toward a national policy on individual fishing quotas*. Washington, DC: National Academy Press.

Neher, Philip A., Ragnar Arnason, and Nina Mollett. 1989. *Rights-based fishing*. Dordrecht: Kluwer Academic Publishing.

NOAA (National Oceanic and Atmospheric Administration) Northeast Fisheries Science Center. 2010. NOAA announces new northeast groundfish management measures. March 31. http://www.nefsc.noaa.gov/press_release/2010/News/NR1008/index.html.

NOAA (National Oceanic and Atmospheric Administration) Office of Sustainable Fisheries. 2010. Catch share policy. November 4. http://www.nmfs.noaa.gov/sfa/domes_fish/catch-share/docs/noaa_cs_policy.pdf.

North, Douglas C. 1990. *Institutions, institutional change, and economic performance*. Cambridge, U.K.: Cambridge University Press.

Olson, Julia. 2011. Understanding and contextualizing social impacts from the privatization of fisheries: An overview. Ocean and Coastal Management 54:353–363.

Ostrom, Elinor. 1990. *Governing the commons: The evolution of institutions for collective action*. Cambridge, U.K.: Cambridge University Press.

Peacock, F. G., and Christina Annand. 2008. Community management in the inshore groundfish fishery on the Canadian Scotian Shelf. In *Case studies on fisheries self-governance*, eds. Ralph E. Townsend, Ross Shotton, and H. Uchida, 101–110. FAO Fisheries Technical Paper 504. Rome: Food and Agriculture Organization.

Philippson, Jeremy. 1999. The fish producers' organisations in the U.K.—A strategic analysis. In *Alternative management systems for fisheries*, ed. D. Symes, 79–92. Oxford: Blackwell Science.

Pinkerton, Evelyn W. 1989. *Cooperative management of local fisheries*. Vancouver: University of British Columbia Press.

——. 1994. Local fisheries co-management: A review of international experiences and their implications for salmon management in British Columbia. *Canadian Journal of Fisheries and Aquatic Sciences* 51:1–17.

Pinkerton, Evelyn, and D. N. Edwards. 2009. The elephant in the room: The hidden costs of leasing individual transferable fishing quotas. *Marine Policy* 33:707–713.

Pinkerton, Evelyn, and M. Weinstein. 1995. *Fisheries that work: Sustainability through community-based management*. Vancouver, BC: David Suzuki Foundation.

Pinto da Silva, Patricia, and Andrew Kitts. 2006. Collaborative fisheries management in the Northeast U.S.: Emerging initiatives and future directions. *Marine Policy* 30:832–841.

Pollnac, Richard B., Patrick Christie, Joshua E. Cinner, Tracey Dalton, Tim M. Daw, Graham E. Forrester, Nicholas A. Graham, and Timothy R. McClanahan. 2010. Marine reserves as linked social-ecological systems. *Proceedings of the National Academy of Sciences* 107(43):18282–18265.

Pollnac, Richard B., and John J. J. Poggie. 1988. The structure of job satisfaction among New England fishermen and its application to fisheries management policy. *American Anthropologist* 90:888–901.

Ponce-Díaz, German, A. Vega-Velázquez, Mario Ramade-Villaneuva, G. León-Carballo, and R. Franco-Santiago. 1998. Socioeconomic characteristics of the abalone fishery along the west coast of the Baja California peninsula, Mexico. *Journal of Shellfish Research* 17:853–857.

Ponce-Díaz, German, Wendy Weisman, and Bonnie J. McCay. 2009. Co-responsabilidad y participación en el manejo de pesquerías en México: Lecciones de Baja California Sur. *Pesca y Conservación* 1:1–9.

Princen, Thomas. 2005. *The logic of sufficiency*. Cambridge, MA: MIT Press.

Rose, Carol M. 1994. The comedy of the commons: Custom, commerce, and inherently public property. In *Property and persuasion: Essays on the history, theory, and rhetoric of ownership*, ed. Carol M. Rose, 105–162. Boulder, CO: Westview Press.

——. 2002. Common property, regulatory property, and environmental protection: Comparing community-based management to tradable environmental allowances. In *The drama of the commons*, eds. Elinor Ostrom, Thomas Dietz, Nives Dolšak, Paul C. Stern, Susan Stonich, and Elke U. Weber, 233–257. Washington, DC: National Academy Press.

Ruddle, Kenneth. 1989. Solving the common-property dilemma: Village fisheries rights in Japanese coastal waters. In *Common property resources*, ed. Fikret Berkes, 168–198. London: Belhaven Press.

Schreiber, Laurie. 2010a. Shrinking the fleet, A16, banks and buyouts. *Fishermen's Voice: News and Comment for and by the Fishermen of Maine 15*. http://www.fishermensvoice.com/0510Shrink ingTheFleet.html 15.

——. 2010b. Swans Island fisherman inaugurates sector fishing. *Bar Harbor Times*, May 22. http://mdi.villagesoup.com/news/story/swans-island-fisherman-inaugurates-sector-fishing/327117.

Scott, Anthony. 1955. The fishery: The objectives of sole ownership. *Journal of Political Economy* 63:116–124.

St. Martin, Kevin. 2001. Making space for community resource management in fisheries. *Annals of the Association of American Geographers* 91:122–142.

——. 2005. Disrupting enclosure in New England fisheries. *Capitalism Nature Socialism* 16:63–80.

——. 2006. The impact of "community" on fisheries management in the U.S. Northeast. *Geoforum* 37:169–184.

St. Martin, Kevin, Bonnie J. McCay, Grant Murray, Teresa Johnson, and Bryan Oles. 2007. Communities, knowledge, and fisheries of the future. *International Journal of Global Environmental Issues* 7:221–239.

Sullivan, Joe. 2000. Harvesting cooperatives and antitrust law—Recent developments and implications. Paper presented at the annual meeting of the International Institute of Fisheries Economics and Trade, Corvallis, Oregon, July 10–15. http://oregonstate.edu/dept/IIFET/2000/papers/sullivan.pdf.

Takahashi, Satsuki, Bonnie J. McCay, and Osamu Baba. 2006. The good, the bad, or the ugly? Advantages and challenges of Japanese coastal fisheries management. *Bulletin of Marine Science* 78:575–591.

Tryon, Luanne E. 1993. An overview of the CDQ fishery program for western Alaskan native communities. *Coastal Management* 21:315–325.

Turnipseed, Mary, Larry B. Crowder, Rafael D. Sagarin, and Stephen E. Roady. 2009. Legal bedrock for rebuilding America's ocean ecosystems. *Science* 324:183–184.

Weinstein, Martin S. 2000. Pieces of the puzzle: Solutions for community-based fisheries management from native Canadians, Japanese cooperatives, and common property researchers. *Georgetown International Environmental Law Review* 12:375–412.

Wiber, Melanie, Anthony T. Charles, John Kearney, and Fikret Berkes. 2008. Enhancing community empowerment through participatory fisheries research. *Marine Policy* 33:172–179.

Wilson, James. 2007. Scale and costs of fishery conservation. *International Journal of the Commons* 1:29–41.

Worm, Boris, Edward B. Barbier, Nicola Beaumont, J. Emmett Duffy, Carl Folke, Benjamin S. Halpern, Jeremy B. C. Jackson, Heike K. Lotze, Fiorenza Micheli, Stephen R. Palumbi, Enric Sala, Kimberley A. Selkoe, John J. Stachowicz, and Reg Watson. 2006. Impacts of biodiversity loss on ocean ecosystem services. *Science* 314:787–790.

Worm, Boris, Ray Hilborn, Julia K. Baum, Trevor A. Branch, Jeremy S. Collie, Christopher Costello, Michael Fogarty, Elizabeth A. Fulton, Jeffrey A. Hutchings, Simon Jennings, Olaf P. Jensen, Heike I. Lotze, Pamela M. Mace, Tim R. McClanahan, Colin Minto, Stephen R. Palumbi, Ana M. Parma, Daniel Ricard, Andrew A. Rosenberg, Reg Watson, and Dirk Zeller. 2009. Rebuilding global fisheries. *Science* 325:578–585.

Commentary

ANTHONY SCOTT

A few decades ago, it seems, most conference papers on the general subject of fishery management were about regulation. Most authors favored individual transferable quotas (ITQs). Although their early reckless advocacy was soon toned down, the fisheries-economics literature has remained pro-ITQ. Today's writers on the newer subject of "communities" are less unanimous. Communities have many dimensions, and these suggest many alternative versions (Scott 2008). In any case, because actual communities are relatively few in number, many economists have yet to inspect one, and Bonnie McCay's descriptions are most welcome. She also brings law, history, anthropology, and political science to bear. I have chosen only a few topics from the resulting wealth of theory and observation.

McCay gives a brief account of the progress of ocean fishery management. First, governmental rules began to regulate the time, gear, vessels, and size and species selection in particular ocean harvesting areas. In the century that followed, these were made less absolute and more quantitative. The past forty years saw them being transformed into individual quotas, and the past twenty saw these quotas become tradable. Today, as McCay explains, fisher associations or "communities" are emerging and taking over much of the government's regulatory function. McCay's three key words for this progression are that the common-property ocean fishery became, in effect, "enclosed" by regulation; enclosed fisheries became "privatized" by license limitation and the distribution of individual quotas; and "communities" are now being assembled out of quota holders.

Having briefly described the enclosed-fishery phase, she draws attention to the problems encountered in privatizing it. They arise because whatever procedure is followed in allotting quotas to fishermen is bound to permit some of them to land larger catches than before. Thus, the relative distribution of income within the group receiving quotas will be changed. It is not surprising, therefore, that the suggestion that a regulated fishery become an individual-quota fishery will kindle enthusiasm from the "high-liner" fishermen who expect to better their status, but will provoke distrust and opposition from the rest.

For example, consider a group of fishermen to whom the government decides to distribute equal quotas that are nontransferable. This means that the fishers who previously landed the largest catches will be reduced to landing no more than the others. These people will likely be well known, and their bitter opposition to the equal-quota system may well be influential in persuading the government to abandon the idea of equal quotas.

In its place, the authorities may offer one of a variety of "grandfather" endowment systems, designed precisely to preserve the former distribution of catches and family incomes, and so to prevent the quota-distribution procedure from rocking the distributional boat. Naturally, these systems will excite the hostility of those who receive small quotas and will seem fated never to be allowed to take large catches.

Alternatively, the quotas can be bought and sold. In one version, they are allotted equally to all at the outset. However, because of their marketability, they are quickly redistributed. In the long run, they become concentrated in the hands of only a few holders, perhaps newcomers, whose quotas cover a busier, but smaller, number of vessels.

It is this compression of previously large groups of ocean fishers that leads to the opposition to which McCay alludes. Whole families may now have no economic connection with their fishing community. The author, following Olson (2011), describes the scattering effects as "distorting," "imperiling," "hurting," and "devastating." Families, and indeed whole communities, are fated to receive less income. Middle-aged and older men have taken advantage of the new transferability of rights and have sold out. The new system typically results in a longer fishing season and perhaps a redirection of the catch to different docks or ports, different final markets along different channels, and different storage, processing, or marketing firms or cooperatives, where it involves different people from those who would have handled it under the previous system.

Fishermen, fishing as skillfully as they ever did, see that they have become victims of government's arbitrary addition of transferability to quota characteristics, much as a whole manufacturing district can become the victim of a government's decision to cancel its protective tariff. McCay thinks of this as an offense against social equity, conveying the opposition and outrage of those in the community and, evidently, her own opposition and sympathy.

But one wonders whether economic redistribution should be given as much prominence as it gets here. Any innovation that results in the downsizing of the fishing fleet, be it more powerful trawlers, more effective gear, or more privatized rights, results in fewer boats and fewer people working in them. Such results are typical of laborsaving innovations. In the fisheries, not only past technical changes in fish packing and transportation, but also changes responding to new final consumer tastes have resulted in social changes in jobs, incomes, and locations. Furthermore, the present state of the groundfish fishery shows that disastrous natural fluctuations in fish stocks can destroy fishers' community welfare more thoroughly than the mere introduction of new systems of rights.

One must recognize that throughout the economy, many of today's hardships arise from official attempts to correct old policies. This is certainly so in the fisheries. For a long time, governments, first passively, then actively, protected open access to coastal and ocean fisheries. When open access led to the hardship of declining harvests, they "enclosed" some fisheries by regulation and closure. Then, carefully and politically, they imposed boundaries around territories where the new restrictions were to apply. These changes imposed hardship on those who had already adopted larger vessels and more effective gear. This hardship forced governments to modify their previous closures and gear regulations. Some did this by introducing individual catch quotas or days-at-sea permits. For example, there have been instances of coastal fishing-port communities founded in remote locations so that vessels based there could dash in when nearby fishing grounds were briefly opened. When individual quotas were introduced, these fishing grounds could be, and are today, open most of the time. Now crews and families could move back from the remote communities to city ports with schools and shopping. The simple privatizing of rights had caused the exodus, perhaps comparable to that suffered in Labrador. The point is that all changes in fishery policy have hurt some fishermen and their families. The hardship attributed to the privatization of quotas is just the latest example.

It must also be recognized that politics is involved. McCay's case studies describe fragmentations of fishing regimes that may reflect local politicians' attempts to please voters if they have a constituency with a special interest in only one aspect of the coast's fishing enterprises (such as a particular species, a particular fishing ground, a specific type of gear, or schools and employment for crews' families). Often, perhaps usually, there has been a welfare or relief element in the forming and shaping of various boards and sectors, much as bridges and highways have often been obtained by politicians to favor their own districts. For desperate politicians, populations of hard-up fishermen and companies in remote areas may serve well as policy targets. Certain groups of fishers need only be given quotas (amounting to no less than quantities that are already being landed) and formed into harmless communities or boards with decision-making powers.

Politics may also be the reason that the illustrative community-oriented systems, seem sometimes not to have corrected fishery mismanagement. McCay observes that studies of certain fisheries with ITQs, or with communities, or both, show little or no improvement in the biological dimensions. She does not note that such reports may be distorted by the inclusion of fisheries where political support, not stock improvement, has been the main purpose.

McCay's account of the various mixtures of government rules, individual quotas, and collective communities is a great source of information about the strengths and defects of fishing institutions in Alaska, Atlantic Canada, Britain, The Netherlands, and New England. She begins with places where local fishery "communities" already exist. Instead of becoming stewards of the resources of the sea and participants in building fisheries for the future (Clark and Munro 1975), some of them often reinforce their members' resistance to unpopular official decisions. For example, if ITQs are being introduced, existing communities may focus on protecting members' shares. Or they may seek to expel nonmembers from certain fishing grounds.

At the end, McCay essentially abandons recent U.S. policies. Instead, she opts for direct initial acquisition and holding of fishery use rights, not by fisherman-members but by the communities. Thus, she would go further than the Shetlands program, where the community (or at least its Producer Organization), never freely endowed with quotas, used its own resources to buy entitlements. She also commends other locally based forms of collective property, claiming that ownership by the community will "enhance the sense of ownership and stewardship without risking their being traded away."

The real test is in relations with communities with which she is not concerned: that majority of the world's fishers who work in waters in which several or many commercial species live, or through which they migrate. Such waters are not used only for commercial fishing; they are exploited for sports/recreation, shipping, local transportation, and waste disposal. Employers and owners will be in conflict with fishers in different specializations and markets or in different territories, with sports fishermen, and/or with users who are dumping wastes, docking freighters, running ferries, and engaging in other activities. In some parts of the world, individual fishers, endowed with quotas, can implicitly contract with one another so that the community's members regulate and share with one another. But when the waters have multiple users and purposes, and when the fish are of many species and migratory, the fishermen must be represented collectively as against other kinds of users. Their community may speak for them all in bargaining, litigation, and contracting. (On a visit to Japanese inshore fishermen, I gathered that the village's fishing community was working things out contractually with a giant marine construction firm whose project threatened to ruin its fishing grounds [Hersoug, Jentoft, and Degnbol 2004].)

McCay says little about such coordination. The fishers need more powers than a village community can put together. When the threats come from outside, they need the capacity of alliance with other fishing communities to negotiate overall ocean uses. Such bargaining and contracting are complex and daunting responsibilities. At one extreme, a community could go through a bargaining process with adjoining fishery communities so that they might bargain collectively with representatives of other types of ocean users. As an alternative, communities might make conditions so as to concede their bargaining and contracting powers permanently to the members of a higher level—a board or council. (Note the similarities to the choices to be made by the water-supply organizations discussed by Gary Libecap in chapter 13.) The fisherman's community must be the basic unit of any quota system, regardless of whether it is established by a government, a high-level alliance, or more local contracting. By portraying a range of such units, McCay has shown many of the strengths and weaknesses of fishermen's right-holding communities.

REFERENCES

Clark, C. W., and G. R. Munro. 1975. The economics of fishing and modern capital theory: A simplified approach. *Journal of Environmental Economics and Management* 2:92–106.
Hersoug, B., S. Jentoft, and P. Degnbol. 2004. *Fisheries development: The institutional challenge.* Delft: Eburon Publishers.
Olson, Julia. 2011. Understanding and contextualizing social impacts from the privatization of fisheries: An overview. *Ocean and Coastal Management* 54:353–363.
Scott, Anthony. 1955. *Natural resources: The economics of conservation.* Toronto: University of Toronto Press.
———. 2008. *The evolution of resource property rights.* Oxford: Oxford University Press.

Land and Water

The Evolution of Zoning Since the 1980s

The Persistence of Localism

WILLIAM A. FISCHEL

The word "evolution" in the title of this chapter pulls together three themes. One is an assessment of where the practice of zoning has gone since the publication of *The Economics of Zoning Laws* (Fischel 1985). The major pressures for zoning to change have come from above: the courts and the federal and state governments. There has not been a grassroots movement. Most of the changes have made zoning more restrictive than it otherwise would have been. Zoning has remained resolutely local despite (or perhaps because of) political and legal movements seeking to change it. The second theme is how my views about the American practice of land use regulation have changed over the past 25 years. This has less to do with changes in zoning itself and more with my subsequent scholarship, almost all of which has concerned the economic role of local government in the United States. I have come to see zoning as a critical part of the process of local government and local government as an essential part of a federal system.

The third theme is a gingerly advanced proposition about local government in general, although the focus is land use regulation. Zoning's historical development should be regarded as comparable to that of the common law and thus should be taken more seriously by scholars than it normally is. An example is the development of zoning in Los Angeles that led to the puzzling U.S. Supreme Court decision *Hadacheck v. Los Angeles*, 239 U.S. 394 (1915), which permitted the city to expel a previously established brickyard from a subsequently developed residential area without compensation. The fulcrum issue is why most zoning allows nonconforming uses to continue despite that decision.

This chapter is both postscript and prologue. It is in part an assessment of what has happened to zoning and a prospectus for a revision of *The Economics of Zoning Laws* that I hope to undertake in the next few years. It falls under the rubric of "public rights in private land." Zoning fills that category in a particular way. "Zoning" may be designated as almost all local land use regulation, including subdivision regulations, historic preservation, and public master planning for location of infrastructure. Although different political actors make these decisions, all of them respond to the same underlying local political forces.

Zoning is one land use regulation that affects almost all Americans, and if revealed political preference is any guide, it is the local government function they are least inclined to give up. Municipalities have incorporated just to control their zoning (Fischel 2001; Miller 1981). National regulations concerning wilderness, endangered species, and water pollution certainly affect land use, but they are usually of only episodic concern to most people. Indeed, one of the puzzles to be explained here is why American land use regulation has remained so steadfastly local despite the many political movements that would seem to undermine its parochial governance.

"Rationality" in *The Economics of Zoning Laws*

The Economics of Zoning Laws (Fischel 1985) was subtitled *A Property Rights Approach to American Land Use Controls*. The "property right" is municipal zoning. Zoning extends to local voters (or to those who are decisive in local politics) the right to control other people's property within a jurisdiction. This was not a new idea. Robert Nelson (1977) had come up with it earlier. Both Nelson and I were quick to disclaim the idea that zoning is formally a property right. That is, courts of law do not recognize zoning as a property right in the same sense in which fee-simple ownership or its varieties, such as covenants and easements, are recognized as one's property. No individual has an enforceable right to a particular zoning category.

The term "property right" is applied to zoning in a sense that is less precise but broader in scope. Zoning is a collectively held entitlement that redounds to the benefit of the politically dominant faction in the community. Lest this definition be thought too adventurous, Jeremy Bentham called property "a basis for expectation" (Michelman 1967, 212), and that is what most zoning offers to community residents. They have some reasonable basis for expecting that zoning categories will persist over time, in large part because they and their neighbors have a lot to say about any changes. This basis is firm enough to encourage property owners to make long-term investments and to assure buyers of property that such uses will not be summarily altered, so that the benefits and burdens of zoning can be capitalized in the price of land that is subject to it. Henneberry and Barrows (1990) present an empirical study supporting this.

The hypothesis that underlies this chapter is that the local electorate exercises its land use authority in ways that look economically rational. Such rationality does not require exact calculation or necessarily result in admirable outcomes. The zoning process can be messy and error prone, as are collective decisions in all areas of life. But the assumption of rationality rules out outcomes that do not generally advance the economic interests (broadly conceived) of those in charge of the local political process. More specifically, it rules out the two models of zoning that economists usually adopted in the rare pre-1980 instances in which they thought about zoning at all, one of which was highly optimistic and the other of which was unthinkingly cynical.

The first theory might be called the goody-two-shoes theory: zoning authorities adopted regulations that would internalize externalities so as to correct market failures in the real estate market. The source of their authority was not investigated. Local authorities were regarded in this mix of normative and positive modeling as folks who sought to maximize social welfare. This view stems largely from the tradition of Arthur Pigou (1920), commonly regarded as the founder of welfare economics, but his most severe critic, Ronald Coase (1960), actually offered an offhanded endorsement of zoning in the presence of high transaction costs. Coase may have subsequently changed his mind about zoning as a result of the work of Bernard Siegan (1972), whose investigation of Houston, Texas, the only large American city without zoning, was encouraged by Coase. In any case, it was not hard to persuade economists that this model did not yield useful behavioral insights. Neither the motivation of authorities nor the outcome of the process seemed to jibe with reality.

More resistant to intellectual reform was the other model of zoning adopted by economists, which sees it as a cantankerous constraint on real estate development (Mills 1979). This view persists because it captures two true features of zoning: it is a constraint on development, limiting both the gross ratio of capital to land and the type of activities permitted, and it seems contentious in the sense that it is difficult to modify the initial constraint on development even when there seem to be substantial mutual gains to be had.

The problem with the cynical view is that it takes existing zoning laws as somehow exogenous rather than as the product of rational calculation. As a result, resistance to change is seen by theorists as irrationally stubborn. It certainly is stubborn. A good deal of economic research finds that zoning-constrained development results in lower metropolitan density (of capital and people) than would seem optimal. Why would rational economic agents, the kind who control zoning changes, forgo the potential gains from trade that could be had by allowing higher capital-to-land ratios that have the potential to make almost everyone better off? In law and economics terms, why does Coase's theorem seem not to work very well?

The answer proposed in *The Economics of Zoning Laws* was transaction costs. Zoning is a collective property right, and modifying it requires navigating an obstacle course of hearings and procedures whose rules of decision are not always evident to the outside observer. The establishment of this obstacle course is not an accident. It exists because real property is durable, not very movable, and subject to many neighborhood effects. The majority of local property owners in most American jurisdictions own their own homes and not much else, and they are decisive in the zoning process. The theory was expanded in a later book, *The Homevoter Hypothesis* (Fischel 2001): home ownership places most people's major asset in a single local basket, and they cannot obtain insurance against its devaluation from adverse municipal events. The high transaction costs that impede zoning changes are an alternative to an insurance policy against local devaluations of existing homes (Breton 1973).

The success of my 1985 book can be judged by citations and by the current scarcity of the foregoing economic models (goody-two-shoes and cantankerous) against which it railed. Not as many studies assume from the outset that zoning is a welfare-maximizing institution, and at least a few ask what the economic motivation for a zoning regime might be (Bogart 1993; Hilber and Robert-Nicould 2009; Rolleston 1987; Rothwell 2009). Probably more important to the success of *The Economics of Zoning Laws* is that local zoning has proven so durable despite the many criticisms of its shortcomings and the development of political movements that threatened to displace it.

Resistance of Local Zoning to Change

The most striking quality of zoning is that it is still local. Its durability threatens to bury the idea of evolution, but the localness of zoning is itself an evolutionary puzzle. After all, many formerly local activities, such as road building, public health, care for the poor, school finance, prosecution of corruption, and water-quality regulation (even drinking-water regulation), have been largely preempted by federal and state governments. In their book about large central-city governments, Frug and Barron (2008) address the many ways in which local government authority has been circumscribed by the state government, but zoning (with the exception of Boston) is the power that in their description remains almost entirely in the local sphere.

The biggest threat to local zoning was the federalization of environmental law in the 1970s. Informed observers forecast that state and national laws would take over zoning (Mills 1979), and a federal study headed by Laurence Rockefeller (Reilly 1973) encouraged a larger and implicitly preemptive state and federal role. Planners eagerly anticipated that their professional status and incomes would be enhanced as national land use planning took over most of the functions of local zoning (Popper 1988).

It was not to be. Localism has had to make only slight adjustments to accommodate the federalization of environmental law in the 1970s. Indeed, it is arguable that new environmental law supplemented rather than supplanted local zoning, at least where the community was inclined to reduce the rate of development. Opponents to local development could invoke nonlocal hurdles, such as the requirement of an environmental impact statement and legal challenges to those statements that were provided. Prodevelopment communities did have to find their way around new hurdles, especially where wetlands were at issue, but wholesale displacement of local decision making along the lines of the Federal Communications Commission, the Interstate Commerce Commission, or the Federal Aviation Administration has not happened. Federal land use policy is confined to specific activities (soil conservation) and geographic areas that lack local government (and population), chiefly land to which the federal government still holds title. These holdings are vast in area, but small in their contribution to the economy.

The accommodation of federal environmentalism by local zoning was well established by the time *The Economics of Zoning Law* was published in 1985. The federal role was not so much beaten back as it was absorbed by local governments. Wetlands overlays, for instance, are a routine part of most zoning laws (where wetlands are present) and have seldom altered other aspects of zoning regulation. More vigorous federal intrusions were dealt with more directly. A brief attempt by the federal courts to apply antitrust law to municipal zoning (among other local enterprises) was beaten back by congressional legislation in 1982 and a change of heart by the Supreme Court in 1990 (Kinkade 1992). State preemption of local zoning had been identified as "the quiet revolution" by the authors of a book with that title (Bosselman and Callies 1971), but within a few years, even its enthusiasts had conceded that the revolution had gotten so quiet as to be inaudible (Plotkin 1987). Where state regulations have persisted, they continue to be of the double-veto variety: a state agency can veto a lower government's approval of a project, but a higher government can in only rare circumstances make a local government accept a development that it does not want.

The double veto appears to hold even for most of the more elaborate statewide programs for "smart growth" that have appeared since 1990. The Lincoln Institute of Land Policy embarked on an elaborate and well-conceived evaluation of smart growth by comparing the results from four states (New Jersey, Florida, Oregon, and Maryland) that had at least a decade's experience with it with four that lacked conscious statewide programs (Colorado, Indiana, Texas, and Virginia) (Ingram et al. 2009). Somewhat surprisingly, the objective measures that the researchers could obtain indicated very little difference between the two groups of states. One cannot conclude from the study that statewide policies failed, but the effect of adopting a conscious statewide program of smart growth, as opposed to local initiatives, is difficult to detect.

For purposes of this chapter, I examined the Lincoln Institute volume to see whether any of the smart growth states (or those in the control group) had adopted and enforced regulations that would force localities to rezone for higher densities or for uses that they did not wish to have. Two of the states, New Jersey and Oregon, had long-standing programs (adopted before the smart growth movement became self-conscious) to override local zoning. Most of the smart growth programs identified by Ingram et al. had mild incentives (access to state funds for infrastructure) or requirements to accommodate higher-density housing as a goal for local plans, but none had any serious enforcement along the lines of New Jersey, Massachusetts (not examined in the Lincoln Institute study), or Oregon, all of which had preexisting laws. Smart growth advocates are aware of the double-veto problem, but they have not been able to deal with it effectively, at least in the states the Lincoln Institute's study examined.

The rise of "urban growth boundaries" is a specific aspect of smart growth that also has the potential to compromise local zoning. (As the Lincoln Institute's study notes, some of the states that had not adopted statewide smart growth policies nonetheless had cities that had embraced growth boundaries.) The rationale for growth boundaries is not so much affordable housing as urban form. The general idea is to draw a line somewhere near the existing suburban and rural transition zone and add a little room for expansion (Phillips and Goodstein 2000). Outside the line, development is severely restricted (limited, say, to agricultural structures), but inside the line, infill development is encouraged or even required. In principle, this should not adversely affect housing supply, because the development that is forbidden outside the line should be offset by additional development inside the line. (Standard urban economic theory would predict that more centrally located housing should be more costly per unit because of higher land costs, but it is not clear what the effect would be on average household expenditures on housing.) The higher density, it is thought, would allow more efficient use or development of alternative transit systems, promote walkable neighborhoods, and keep the cost of public infrastructure and services down.

Two problems seem to beset these goals. One is that in most metropolitan areas, numerous governments must be brought on board to agree with the goals. If only one or two adopt growth boundaries, development that is excluded from the municipality in the rural zone simply jumps to another municipality. This appears to be what happened in Boulder, Colorado, which has an effective urban growth boundary out to its city limits, but no control over nearby municipalities, which have grown inordinately as a result (Pollock 1998).

The other problem is that even when a metropolitan federation can be formed, it is necessary for the close-in, partially developed suburbs to be inclined to rezone their available land for higher densities. The area that seems to have achieved this result is Portland, Oregon. (It is actually part of a statewide program [Knaap and Nelson 1992], but almost all of Oregon's urban population is in the Portland area.) The key to making this program work politically was to have a metropolitan council that was elected from districts whose boundaries did not correspond to local governments, so that local resistance to the infill obligations would not fall on local officials. The Seattle area has a similar program, but its more generously sized boundaries and weaker obligations on local governments to develop make it a less obvious test (Fischel 2001). The success of such programs may require a kind of regional solidarity among communities (which in Oregon could be characterized as "we aren't California") that is rare in other states.

The most notable overrides of local zoning since the 1980s have come from specific federal directives. Most notorious and controversial is the Religious Land Use and Institutionalized Persons Act (RLUIPA), which gives religious organizations a federal boost in local zoning controversies and makes it more difficult for local governments to stop projects that are sponsored by churches and similar institutions. The controversy is due more to high-level constitutional debate about congressional deployment of the Fourteenth Amendment than to actual evidence of discrimination against religious institutions (Clowney 2007). Somewhat less controversial are amendments to the Fair Housing Act that give special status to group homes for persons covered by the Americans with Disabilities Act. Thus, group homes for the aged, the developmentally disabled, and recovering narcotics addicts must be accommodated amid ordinary residential uses (Salkin and Armentano 1993). Another federal intervention concerns the location of communications towers for cell phones, which must be granted reasonable accommodation (Eagle 2005). These exceptions are episodically problematic for local governments, but taken as a whole, they seem to have had modest effects on local zoning.

Housing Price Inflation Pressured Zoning (and Vice Versa)

A second threat to local zoning has been renewed attention to its effects on the price of housing. The housing affordability issue has taken two forms. The older has to do with zoning's retardation of the construction of low-income housing in high-income communities. Economists have given an explanation and a related rationalization for this exclusionary zoning. The explanation is widely understood: low-income housing is a fiscal drain on high-income communities because the property taxes they generate do not cover the additional public service expenditures, chiefly for public schools, required by the new housing.

The economic rationalization for this brake on local redistribution of wealth is grounded in the model of Tiebout (1956). From this perspective, the exclusive community is but one of many municipalities or school districts from which foot-loose households can choose (Hamilton 1975). If one cannot afford a home in Richdale and attend its fine schools, a more modest dwelling is available in lower-wealth but high-tax-and-spending Strivertown. Households with low demand for public schools would choose a low-tax, low-spending district. (The reason that the two-thirds of all households who do not have children at home do not all choose such communi-ties is their appreciation of the local social capital that public schools create [Fischel 2009].) With enough municipal and school-district variety, people end up getting the housing and public services (schools and police departments) that they are will-ing to pay for, and local property taxes are no more than a fee for services. Zoning is seen as a mechanism to ensure that developers do not cheat the system and build homes that do not pay their own way.

A brief comment on the empirical relation of zoning to property taxation (Fischel 1992) and subsequent work have pushed me into the somewhat unexpected role of the leading academic proponent of the benefit view of the property tax (Nechyba 2001). It turns out that almost all economists agree that if zoning operates as a nu-anced and effective fiscal gatekeeper for municipal development, property taxes, the mainstay of local finance, are not really taxes at all (Zodrow 2007). They serve simply as a price for local public services and have none of the inefficiency qualities of most taxes.

The main issue for the benefit view is the extent to which local zoning can actually fulfill its gatekeeper function. Zoning does this about as well as corporate finance fulfills its role in the business world (Fischel 2006). This is not an exalted standard. Critics of corporate governance point out the many ways in which business manag-ers overlook the interests of stockholders. Local government's "stockholders," who are resident property owners, are actually more attentive to local governance than are the stockholders of business corporations. Homeowners' lack of diversification of their major asset makes them watchful of local decisions that affect its value. This watchfulness is offset in part by local governments' much greater insulation from bankruptcy and outside takeovers and, as a consequence, closer oversight by the state government of their activities. But this greater supervision has not done much to undo the local hold on zoning. It remains a challenge to determine the extent to which zoning turns local property taxes into fees for services. School finance reform has reduced the connection between taxation and education services, but the connec-tion is still evident in many empirical studies (Hilber and Mayer 2009).

Two movements have attacked the apparent fiscal segregation that zoning creates. One is the "open-suburbs" campaign. Its two most famous successes have been the *South Burlington County NAACP v. Township of Mount Laurel*, 92 N.J. 158 (1983) judicial decisions in New Jersey and the legislatively adopted "antisnob zoning" laws of Massachusetts (Hughes and Van Doren 1990). New Jersey's courts viewed local exclusion as a constitutional infirmity, and they eventually adopted a highly contro-versial remedy. Builders who could demonstrate that their proposals would add to the stock of low-income housing in communities deemed by the court to be inade-quate on this account could get a "builders' remedy." The derelict community would be ordered by the court to rezone the land in question to accommodate both the builder's request for market-rate housing and a quota of low-income housing. The extra market-rate housing permits (and extra density of development) were in effect a subsidy to make it possible to build low-income housing that was otherwise uneconomical. A similar program was developed in Massachusetts. Towns and cities whose affordable housing was below 10 percent of the total stock are liable for a "40–B" development, named for the statute that authorized the requirement. As in New Jersey, builders can obtain an entitlement to build more housing than is locally allowed if they earmark a significant fraction of it for low-income residents. This often involves protracted negotiations and litigation, but builders do get permits under the law (Fisher 2007).

The success of these programs is best measured by their durability. Both are more than 30 years old. It is not clear that they have produced more low-income housing than would have been available otherwise. Aside from simply crowding out some market-rate housing that would have filtered down from older stock (Sinai and Waldfogel 2005), the problem with both programs is that they rely on percentages for success. A town that finally meets its *Mount Laurel* or 40-B goals will be unmolested by the court (in New Jersey) or the state (in Massachusetts) as long as its ratio of low-income units to total units does not decline. This acts as an incentive for towns to restrict further growth altogether (Schmidt and Paulsen 2009; see also *In the Matter of the Adoption of N.J.A.C. 5:96 and 5:97*, 2010 N.J. Super. Lexis 20 [2010]). The disincentives to grow may account for the immense popularity of open-space preservation in both Massachusetts and New Jersey. From 1998 to 2003, these two states led the nation in voter initiatives to purchase farmland-development rights (Kotchen and Powers 2006). More than 40 percent of all open-space initiatives in the United States between 1997 and 2004 took place in New Jersey and Massachusetts (Banzhaf et al. 2006). It might be understandable that these two urban, eastern states value farmland preservation more than, say, Nebraska or Texas, but it is unclear why they lead other urban and eastern states by such a wide margin. The inclination for growth avoidance has been made much stronger by the effectiveness of the *Mount Laurel* and 40-B programs.

The important point, however, is that New Jersey and Massachusetts are exceptional. Courts and legislatures in other states have made bows in their direction, but no others have adopted their intrusive remedies. "Inclusionary zoning" schemes are popular in some cities and counties, especially in California (Rosa 2010), but their practical impact appears to be modest. Robert Ellickson (1981) first speculated that they are a cover for the more exclusionary regulations that apply to most of the rest of the community. It should be kept in mind that inclusionary zoning operates essentially as a tax on new development, not on current residents. (Tax revenues would have an opportunity cost for the community at large if the money could be used for projects other than housing, a possibility that may be foreclosed by judicial insistence—for example, in *Nollan v. California*, 483 U.S. 825 [1987]—that spending have an identifiable relationship to the purpose of the regulation.) The "tax" is the in-kind obligation imposed on developers to subsidize the below-market-rate housing. Such a tax is much more easily collected where all housing has been made artificially scarce by restrictive regulations. This may explain why inclusionary zoning is more prevalent in cities with highly restrictive zoning (Bento et al. 2009).

The other housing price issue has been the overall affordability of housing. This issue has been taken up by prodevelopment interests and has been around at least since the 1970s. Presidential commissions addressing the affordable housing problem have been convened since 1968 (President's Committee on Urban Housing 1969). They have appeared so frequently that the U.S. Department of Housing and Urban Development (HUD) seems to have institutionalized them. Its Regulatory Barriers Clearinghouse disseminates information on the mostly local hurdles to developing new housing, including a how-to-overcome-them feature on its Web site titled, without apparent irony, "Strategy of the Month." (One wonders why, if HUD had an effective strategy, it would need to come up with a new one every month.)

What has been new in the past two decades has been the amount and quality of the evidence that links land use regulation with high and rising housing prices. A topic that used to be a back-office activity for graduate students without great prospects has now engaged some of the best minds in the economics profession. Edward Glaeser at Harvard is one of the leading scholars to have discovered the link between zoning regulations (especially those that constrain overall density) and general housing affordability (Glaeser, Gyourko, and Saiz 2008; Glaeser, Gyourko, and Saks 2006; Glaeser and Ward 2009). Much of this research has been advanced by economists at the University of Pennsylvania, who have accumulated their own data on local zoning and have lent it to many other researchers (Gyourko, Saiz, and Summers 2008). Among their more robust and puzzling findings is that zoning constraints appear to matter most in metropolitan areas on the Atlantic and Pacific coasts. Cities in the Midwest and South do have zoning, but it appears not to constrain development nearly as much as it does in the Northeast and the West Coast. (Much of the West Coast inflation followed the California Supreme Court's many rulings that were hostile to development in the early 1970s [diMento et al. 1980; Fischel 1995], but why the court took this particular tack is not clear.) Explaining this disparity is an ongoing effort that is related to the more profound issue of why cities in these areas have generally become more attractive to employers and residents in the past three decades.

Regulatory Takings Came and Went

The rise in scholarly interest in zoning's macroeconomic effects (in the sense of affecting large areas) has been paralleled by the property rights movement, whose most notable scholarly work was *Takings* (Epstein 1985). Although Epstein has drawn few formal connections between just compensation and housing prices, I made that connection in my 1985 book, as well as in later works. The problem was that local governments (and the voters who elected them) were making decisions about the use of other people's property without having to face the economic consequences of doing so (Ellickson 1977; Fischel 1985). When local voters do not have to face any budgetary outlay (or an immediate opportunity cost) to expand the scope of regulation, they are inclined to substitute zoning excessively for other public outlays to enhance the value of their property. It is sometimes efficient to substitute regulation for spending, as Gilbert White (1986) pointed out in the context of flood control. The economic problem arises when one input to local public welfare, zoning, is under-priced relative to other inputs, such as purchases of land for parks.

The traditional legal method of protecting property rights from the excesses of popular legislation was pursued under the due process clauses of the U.S. Constitution and most state constitutions. The remedy for government misbehavior was injunctive relief, which simply ordered the government to do the right thing. The problems with this approach were its dubious constitutional legitimacy and its clunky and intrusive remedial tools, which presumed that judges know more about local conditions than most would admit they did (Ellickson 1977).

The alternative was to invoke the takings clause, which has more constitutional legitimacy (at least property is mentioned in the Fifth and Fourteenth Amendments and parallel state bills of rights), and which in principle does not require that judges know what the right zoning should be. A locality that rezoned a prime and vacant section of land from a quarter-acre minimum lot size (a former suburban standard) to a five-acre minimum would be allowed to do so if it was willing to pay the landowner the difference in the value of his parcel (Fischel 1995). If it was not, it would have to revert to the previous (presumably constitutional) zoning category. This gave the government a choice. If its citizens valued the more restrictive standard more than the money required to compensate for the downzoning (payable through higher local taxes), it could do so. Localities do purchase development rights for open space. The damages remedy also gave the complaining landowner a better bargaining position. Even if he had won his case under the old due process standards, the response by the government might be to rezone his property to something only slightly less burdensome, giving him little more than a ticket to sue again. With a takings claim, which would include profits lost by undue delay, the municipality has a stronger reason to pay attention to his complaint.

The federal courts, for federalism reasons that have not been well articulated, have been reluctant to embrace this remedy. The Supreme Court breathed life into the takings clause in a series of decisions in 1987 (Fischel 1988). The clause's high-water mark was *Lucas v. South Carolina Coastal Council*, 505 U.S. 1003 (1992), in which the Court announced a sweeping per se rule. A land use regulation that destroys all "economic use" should in most situations be compensable. Although this left open the question whether a regulation that destroyed 99 percent of economic use should be allowed to stand, *Lucas* led much of the legal and planning community to predict that the Court was about to cut a wide swath through land use regulations (Callies 1994).

However, the Supreme Court imposed burdensome and perplexing procedural barriers to access to the federal courts. A concerted effort to get the Court to impose another *Lucas*-like rule for delaying development was a failure (*Tahoe-Sierra Preservation Council, Inc. v. Tahoe Regional Planning Agency*, 535 U.S. 302 [2002]). The Court further pared the regulatory takings issue in a Hawaii case by knocking out a previous rule that had given some hope (but not much relief) to development-minded plaintiffs (*Lingle v. Chevron U.S.A. Inc.*, 544 U.S. 528 [2005]).

The Supreme Court seemed to be pushing the takings litigation down to the state courts, which have been unwilling to grasp that nettle. Indeed, several of the Supreme

Court's rulings can be thought of as attempts to keep the state courts from abandoning the damages remedy for regulatory takings altogether (Fischel 1995). State legislatures have actually appeared to be slightly more receptive to property owners' complaints than their courts. A spate of state legislation that required compensation for regulatory takings appeared in the 1990s, but it has not had an appreciable effect on zoning. Florida adopted a carefully crafted regulatory takings bill in 1995 (Powell, Rhodes, and Stengle 1995). It seems to have had sufficiently little effect that it was not even mentioned in the Lincoln Institute's study of that state's growth-management program (Ingram et al. 2009). The more robust schemes that libertarian and prodevelopment groups have proposed in state plebiscites since about 1990s have largely failed. The exception was Oregon's Measure 37, which in 2004 required compensation for devaluations caused by many land use regulations, and which was subsequently amended by an initiative in 2007 (Measure 49) that pulled out almost all of its remedial teeth (Berger 2009).

One of the reasons for the failure of regulatory takings to do much to rein in local zoning was the inability to agree on a normative baseline for compensation (Fischel 2004b). What minimum lot size would pass muster? Is the income tax system a taking? How about jury service? Deregulation of electric utility markets proposed by Sidak and Spulber (1996)? Without a consensus, the enterprising power of American attorneys would open a flood of cases that would make asbestos litigation look tame and uncomplicated.

An experience that aroused caution was teaching a law and economics course for more than ten years in which I had students closely examine regulatory takings cases of their choosing and talk with participants to find out what had happened before and after the decision. The revealing aspect of their reports was how few students sided with the plaintiff landowners. Often I was convinced by their more searching examination that just compensation was not warranted. But almost as often, students simply thought that the public benefits of the regulation in question were sufficiently important, and the private losses sufficiently minor, that compensation would not have met the fairness and efficiency criteria of Michelman (1967), which they had been taught along with Coase's (1960) theorem and Epstein's (1985) more property-protective theory. If the students had any systematic biases, I would have expected them to fall toward the development-minded landowner whose plans were frustrated. It was like one of those psychological experiments where everyone else turns the wrong way in the elevator, and you start to think that the wrong way is the right way.

My gradual retreat from the regulatory takings doctrine led me to wonder what process might take its place. One possibility is the old-fashioned due process doctrine of the Pennsylvania Supreme Court. This court routinely issues orders to communities to adopt "curative amendments" for zoning rules that it deems outside the pale of proper regulation. Although there is much complaining about abuse of curative amendments (Rowan 2007), at least one economic study found that they had more benign effects on housing-market diversity in Pennsylvania than neighboring New Jersey's self-consciously redistributive zoning reforms (Mitchell 2004).

The problem with the Pennsylvania approach is that it is almost universally disdained by planning lawyers. Urban economists likewise have some difficulties with its guiding principle, which is that every community should have land zoned for every use. The municipal specialization that lies at the heart of the Tiebout (1956) model would seem not to be allowed in Pennsylvania. A study of diversity within communities by Pack and Pack (1977) found that the state's municipalities indeed displayed an internal heterogeneity that seems inconsistent with the predictions of the Tiebout model. Nonetheless, the long-standing ability of the Pennsylvania courts to make localities pay attention to land uses and densities that local residents would be reluctant to accept without a judicial prod is intriguing.

Contract Zoning Versus Environmental Justice

One of the explanations for the difficulty in changing zoning to accommodate new development that was offered in *The Economics of Zoning Laws* was the legal trans-action costs of purchasing development rights (Fischel 1985). "Zoning for sale" was a put-down of many proposals by developers to ease their way through the zoning obstacle course. Courts abetted this hostility with doctrines that undercut what was called "contract zoning."

Hostility to contract zoning seems to have abated considerably in the past quar-ter century. Communities seem so willing to put dollar amounts on rezonings that Lee Anne Fennell (2009) has used contract zoning as a lead to reformulate basic ideas about home ownership. Courts have increasingly tolerated obvious end runs around the supposed ban on contract zoning (Serkin 2007). At least some of the greater tolerance for cash exchanges has been the rise of tradable emissions per-mits. Buying and selling "the right to pollute" was once disdained by environmen-talists. Now it is eagerly embraced by many such organizations. The fungibility of public environmental entitlements seems to have trickled down to everyday zoning controversies. "Zoning for sale" is no longer a trump card for people opposed to neigh-borhood change.

One argument in Fischel (1985) was that hostility to cash settlements was a major transaction cost that retarded the transfer of development rights from the commu-nity to development-minded landowners. But relaxation of that apparent cost does not seem to have resulted in a great deal of infill development in suburban commu-nities. Housing costs have continued to soar, and land use regulations have regularly and accurately been blamed for at least part of the inflation. I also (Fischel 1985) blamed what economists somewhat nebulously call "the endowment effect" for continuing excess restrictiveness (Knetsch 1989). Because zoning gives entrenched suburban homeowners a generous entitlement to keep nearby densities low, it is more difficult to persuade voters to give up something that they would be unwilling to purchase even if they were endowed with an equivalent amount of money. (This has sometimes been called the wealth effect, but because most suburban residents pur-chase their homes after zoning has put been in place, they have to pay more for their piece of the community's endowment, and their wealth is correspondingly reduced.)

The endowment effect is not well supported empirically. Most of the evidence for it comes from psychological experiments that lack the rich contextual world in which exchange normally takes place. People regularly sell their homes and move elsewhere, despite indubitable affections for their neighborhood. A more coherent explanation for reluctance to trade is homeowner risk aversion (Fischel 2001). The concentration of their wealth in their homes and the inability of most homeowners to insure against neighborhood decline seem to offer a better explanation of the fact that American suburban voters are wary of value-enhancing transactions that would promote the higher-density development desired by both profit-minded developers and public-spirited promoters of smart growth.

The lesser constraints on contract zoning would seem to make local land use outcomes more prodevelopment. A parallel movement promoting "environmental justice" seems to push in the opposite direction. Prodevelopment decisions by local governments are second-guessed by both judicial and legislative reviews for their impact on the poor. Some of the acceptance of second-guessing is promoted by economists who view political competition for industry as a destructive "race to the bottom" or, at best, a zero-sum game in which the gains to one community are offset by losses to another (Esty 1997). Even if there were no geographic advantages of one location over another, variation in preferences among residents of communities would justify the competitive process (Fischel 1975). Residents see a trade-off between the loss of environmental amenities and the rewards of nearby industry, chiefly a lower tax price for local public goods, but sometimes more convenient access to jobs and shopping.

Because of ordinary income effects, low-income communities would be more likely to give more weight to the gains from obtaining an industrial development than to the loss of local environmental amenities that it caused. Higher-income communities demand better local environmental amenities (Kahn and Matsusaka 1997). As long as people are less mobile than industry, an efficient outcome will result in more (but not all) noxious industries being located in lower-income communities. Most evidence indicates that higher-income communities are indeed more leery of commercial and industrial development (Fox 1981). Lower-income communities either developed around preexisting industry or were more inclined to allow it to come into their communities (Been and Gupta 1997). Environmental justice advocates may take less resistance to industrial development to be a sign of political ineptitude or corruption by local officials, but there seems to be little systematic evidence of this.

A more controversial issue is whether land use policies have systematically discriminated against African Americans. Because African American communities tend to have lower incomes, the evidence for this is complicated by an identification problem. Also, disfranchisement of blacks in the first part of the twentieth century certainly made them more vulnerable to dumping of noxious land uses in their neighborhoods (Hinds and Ordway 1986). But since voting rights have been restored, the argument seems to have lost its punch, and evidence that African American communities suffer more environmental injuries than otherwise similar nonminority neighborhoods is almost nonexistent. Nonetheless, there continue to be special reviews by the Environmental Protection Agency of industrial location on this account, and such reviews should count as an additional (perhaps desirable) transaction cost for locating problematic land uses.

School Finance and Property Taxation

Another change in the past three decades that should have undermined, or at least changed, local zoning is the school-finance-equalization movement (Hanushek and Lindseth 2009). As described in a previous section, much of zoning's suburban appeal was that it made it possible to exclude housing development that did not "pay its own way" for community services. Zoning kept developers from building modest dwellings that would pay little in property taxes but would generate large expenses for education. Communities that spent more than average on schools used zoning to make sure that their school funding would not be undermined by low-cost development. This is such a common motive that there are standard manuals on how to compute the impact of new housing on local fiscal conditions, including local school taxes (Burchell, Listokin, and Dolphin 1993). These manuals need to be recalibrated in light of the continuing decline in childbearing among native-born Americans, but school costs are a continuing concern in all zoning decisions.

The considerable success of the school-finance-equalization movement should have changed these calculations. Among the earliest equalizations were those that came about as a result of the *Serrano* decisions in California in the 1970s. After Proposition 13 dealt the coup de grâce to local financing for schools (Fischel 1989), fiscal opposition to low-cost housing in the formerly high-spending school districts should have melted away. If the new units housed low-income families with schoolchildren, there was no reason for local property taxes to rise or school spending to fall. Taxes were in effect frozen by Proposition 13, and school spending was determined by a statewide formula that was not affected by the local property tax base.

This radical change in local public finance did not seem to make suburban zoning any less exclusionary, although it did affect some location decisions. Some high-income families seem to have moved to cities whose schools they otherwise would have disdained because suburban schools now hold less of an advantage for them (Aaronson 1999). But most of these high-income families either had no children in school or sent their children to the burgeoning private schools in the urban districts. By far the most distinctive changes in California schools have been the high average class size (by national standards) and diminished participation in the public school system by high-income families (Brunner and Sonstelie 2006). But there is no evidence that California communities have been any more welcoming to low-income housing (or any other controversial developments). The chief trend appears to be requiring new development to pay its own way by land use exactions and to pay for facilities by Mello-Roos bonds, which require homebuyers to pay more of school costs, neither of which appear to be more welcoming of development (Dresch and Sheffrin 1997). The notion that local property taxation for education is the basis for exclusionary zoning is not supported by California's experience or by that of any other state.

This is not to say that school-finance-equalization programs have not changed location decisions. Aside from the back-to-the-city movement mentioned in the preceding paragraph one interesting result emerged from Texas's "top 10 percent" plan (Cortes and Friedson 2010). In response to court decisions that undid affirmative action in Texas state universities, the legislature adopted a facially neutral plan. Students in the top 10 percent of their class in any public high school would gain automatic admission. Thus, the best students in the worst high schools had a much improved opportunity to attend state universities, and students in the best high schools faced a reduced chance of admission. This resulted in some redistribution of population. Families with children started moving into poorer high-school districts, apparently in the hope that their children would have a better chance to get into college. This movement in turn raised housing values in those districts, although it did not appear to reduce home values in the better districts. A similar capitalization effect occurred in Minnesota as a result of its cross-district enrollment programs (Reback 2005). Homes in poorer districts began to appreciate faster than those in richer districts because families could to a large extent ignore the district line, purchase cheaper homes, and still send their children to better schools outside the district. Whether any of the better school districts in Minnesota and Texas became more welcoming to low-income housing is a subject yet to be addressed in the zoning literature.

Google Earth, Crime, and Covenants

Another change in the past three decades has been in the capacity to get information about land use. The development of geographic information systems has enhanced the ability of both practicing planners and scholars to learn about patterns of development. Real estate values and U.S. census information are now easily obtainable. Details of local zoning ordinances and controversies are easily searchable and accessible to scholars far away from the communities in question. Estimating the effects of various kinds of borders—municipal, school district, and zoning—on home values is now an undergraduate exercise, and my own students have confirmed or sometimes altered my views about the effects of zoning.

As a result of such information, it is now more difficult to base justifications of restrictive zoning policies on geographic fables. A federal study in the early 1980s seriously advanced the idea that urban development was proceeding at such a rapid rate that the United States was in danger of running out of farmland (National Agricultural Land Study 1981). Many communities seized on this idea as a rationale for adopting extremely large minimum lot sizes in their rural areas. (In fact, the movement for agricultural land preservation had started in the 1970s.) It was also a justification for some proposed statewide plans to preserve rural farmland both by purchase and by regulation. Fischel (1982) contested the running-out-of-farmland data, and the U.S. Department of Agriculture eventually disavowed the original alarmist data (Heimlich, Vesterby, and Krupa 1991). But Google Earth and similar satellite photography can now demonstrate even to a casual observer that urban development is such a small fraction of the total land area that it is difficult to sustain the original alarmist view about running out of farmland. Remote sensing methods have also been used to get accurate data on the amount of urbanization in North America and in the rest of the world. All these studies show a steadily urbanizing and suburbanizing world that is nonetheless a tiny fraction of the world's stock of arable land (Angel, Sheppard, and Civco 2005; Burchfield et al. 2006).

A more recent trend that potentially affects zoning is the remarkable decline in American crime rates. Anxiety about crime was an important explanation for suburbanization and exclusionary zoning (Fischel 1985). Crime rates rose considerably during the 1960s and 1970s, and at least some opposition to further suburban development was predicated on the possibility that low-income housing development made local crime more likely. Like equalization of school financing, the decline in urban crime seems to have been a discernible factor in reducing the flow of middle-class residents to suburbs (Ellen and O'Regan 2010). It is too early to tell whether this trend will make suburban residents more inclined to accept low-income housing or otherwise loosen zoning constraints. A further complication is the possibility that lower crime and not-so-bad schools in central cities may make poorer people less inclined to move to the suburbs.

The last trend that has become more prominent since 1985 is the development of residential private governments (RPGs). RPGs are associations of homeowners that are governed by legal covenants and are almost always designed by a developer of multiunit housing projects. They are universal in apartment condominiums, but they are also widespread in single-family developments. The most obvious physical manifestation of RPGs is gated communities, but this understates their influence. Almost a third of new residential construction in the United States between 1970 and 2000 was governed by such private arrangements (Nelson 2003). Like municipalities, RPGs come in a wide variety of flavors, from progressive political experiments to conservative religious retreats, although most appear to be supplements to ordinary zoning regulations.

Whatever else the rise of privately regulated communities signifies, it affirms that American homebuyers are not fed up with regulation. The regulations in RPGs are considerably more detailed and intrusive than even the most aggressive zoning laws. Voluntary entrance into private agreements, in contrast to zoning's police power origins, is a distinction without a difference for most home buyers. The real difference is that zoning can be applied to a set of landowners who do not agree to its terms, and so there is a greater hazard that zoning will result in excessive substitution of regulation for public expenditures. But for buyers of already-built homes (or platted lots), zoning and RPGs are essentially the same. Neither is likely to be changed in ways that adversely affect most homeowners' specific investment.

The growth of RPGs has paralleled the development of private substitutes for governments, such as business improvement districts (Nelson, McKenzie, and Norcross 2009). This trend has led some observers to hope (and others to worry) that the private institutions will displace the public institutions. Under this scenario, zoning would be displaced by consensual regulations as residents found that private governance offered them more control over their environs. This has not yet happened. If anything, RPGs have strengthened zoning laws. In many cases, community associations have monitored zoning changes, and many participate (through representatives) in zoning hearing decisions. If zoning is to wither away, it seems unlikely to do so because of RPGs.

A separate trend in private land use regulation is the growth of conservation easements (Pidot 2005). Federal and state tax laws make it attractive for owners of large (and some smaller) undeveloped parcels to donate them to conservation organizations. This would hardly be of much public concern except that the tax subsidies appear to be very generous (largely because of uncontested appraisals), so that the opportunity cost of private large-lot zoning would seem almost as low as it is for municipalities. The other potentially distorting aspect of conservation easements is that federal tax rules require that donated land remain undeveloped indefinitely. This requirement was instituted primarily to prevent owners from simply avoiding taxes on speculative land investments, but its effect in growing areas is to remove large patches of developable land from the available stock, potentially making suburban infill development more costly.

Overstatement of Zoning Board Misrule

After I had completed my 1985 book, I got some practical experience on zoning by serving on my local zoning board. Zoning boards are not the agencies that formulate or administer the laws. Zoning laws and, more important, the many changes in the laws are passed only by elected officials or, in an increasing number of jurisdictions, the voters themselves in formal plebiscites (Nguyen 2007). Zoning boards are adjuncts of the regulatory process designed to hear appeals from administrative rulings and to grant exceptions, usually minor, to the literal application of zoning laws. Being on a board is a good way to see zoning's application.

An observation about zoning boards that might be useful to scholars is that visiting the site in question is essential. Site visits can change the views of the case enormously. An applicant may show charming pictures of his antique-car hobby and seek a variance only to park some storage trailers. A visit might reveal that he actually harbors a private junkyard. Local knowledge is important because there is a literature on zoning boards, most often by attorneys, that finds fault with their decisions. One early and well-known critique is the article by Dukeminier and Stapleton (1962). A more recent study was conducted by an attorney who statistically examined variance decisions in five New Hampshire towns, one of which was Hanover, during the years 1987–1992, when I was on the zoning board. His chief finding was that variances are disproportionately granted if abutters do not object (Kent 1993; Ellickson and Been 2000). To which most board members would say, "Who knows better whether the variance will have an adverse effect?" The practice of granting variances if abutters do not object illustrates the recurrence of an early, grassroots approach to land use regulation, which required nonconforming uses to obtain permission of local property owners. It was struck down as unlawful delegation of the police power in several early cases, such as *Eubank v. City of Richmond*, 226 U.S. 137 (1912), but most local zoning boards informally operate as if it were still in effect.

Kent (1993) neglected to point out that four of the five towns in his sample have administrative officers who could discourage applicants with weak cases (Hanover's certainly did), but none of the other "misrule-by-variance" studies worry much about selection bias either. Kent also accurately reported that during the period he examined, the New Hampshire Supreme Court overturned the decisions of all ten towns whose opponents appealed their granting of variances. This seems to support his conclusion that local boards were prodigal in this regard. However, the decision in *Simplex v. Newington*, 145 N.H. 727 (2001), changed the court's previous zoning variance criteria, on which Kent had relied as the source of proper variances, to a less exacting standard that more closely reflected actual practice.

Legal error is not practical error, much less economic harm. Although the articles critical of boards mention the possibility that variances will degrade the neighborhood, even anecdotal evidence in support of that contention is scarce. Without visiting the site in question, it is often extremely difficult to tell whether the variance was warranted by legal, practical, or economic criteria. An underappreciated study by David Bryden (1977) established this more systematically. Bryden examined scores of Minnesota lakeshore building and septic variances (which he had no part in granting) and concluded that what looked like a travesty from the legal record in almost all cases made perfectly good sense to local board members who were acquainted with the details of the sites in question. For example, building setback variances, which by themselves seemed to have been issued with little regard to the state's standard criteria, were granted most often to allow septic systems to be even farther from the lake than the state required. The local officials knew the sites and made what Bryden inferred were appropriate trade-offs between the serious risk of septic-tank pollution of water bodies and the less consequential aesthetic concerns of building setbacks.

This is not to say that zoning boards are faultless. Some members can be inclined to promote a political agenda. Favoritism and score settling can influence some members' votes. But even the least sophisticated zoning boards have an asset that is almost never available to appellate judges or to statistical analysts: they know at least the neighborhood and usually the specific site from personal experience. This makes a big difference that critics of boards need to take into account.

The Development of Zoning and Treatment of Nonconforming Uses

The second new perspective I have acquired since 1985 is historical, as is implied by the term "evolution" in the title of this chapter. *The Economics of Zoning Laws* had almost no historical analysis. Zoning just appeared in the 1920s as a result of state legislation (following model acts developed by the U.S. Commerce Department) and Supreme Court rulings that upheld zoning against legal attack. Just why zoning appeared only in the early twentieth century, spread rapidly to both cities and suburbs, and took the form of residential (as opposed to business) protection was not addressed. I attempted to remedy my oversight in an article addressing the economic history of zoning (Fischel 2004a). The main point in that article was that technological change in the form of automobiles, motor trucks, and passenger buses created a demand for more formal and durable land use regulation.

When people walked to work and urban factories were anchored by railroad junctions, river wharves, and seaports, separation of businesses and residences was not practical. The development of intraurban rail transport allowed residents to live farther from their jobs, and this resulted in more demand for exclusive districts. But most of this demand could be handled by protective covenants and informal agreements, as well as by the simple expedient of locating one's home far enough from the railroad. Once cars, trucks, and buses were introduced, covenants and informal methods were overwhelmed by footloose businesses seeking cheaper land (Moses and Williamson 1967) and apartment developers seeking more pleasant neighborhoods for their clients (Fogelson 2005). Only then did home developers embrace public regulation in order to assure their risk-averse buyers that their investments would not be devalued by subsequent developments (Weiss 1987).

My explanation for zoning emphasized the "bottom-up" demand for zoning (Fischel 2004a). Prospective homeowners were not eager to buy homes where neighborhoods could change in undesirable ways. In Marc Weiss's (1987) account, this demand was transmitted to the first large-scale home developers in the Los Angeles area. They lobbied for regulations at municipal and state levels and eventually persuaded their fellow Californian Herbert Hoover, then secretary of commerce in the Coolidge administration, to promulgate the wildly successful Standard State Zoning Enabling Act (SSZEA) in 1928 (Knack and Meck 1996).

The success of the SSZEA gave rise to the view that zoning was a top-down arrangement. The planning profession promoted the view that zoning arrived as a tidy package in New York City in 1916 with the protection of Fifth Avenue carriage-trade stores from the inroads of low-class manufacturing (Toll 1969). In this popular story, residential protections played a minor role. The story is reinforced by the common account of how the U.S. Supreme Court came to its decision to uphold early zoning ordinances in *Euclid v. Ambler*, 272 U.S. 365 (1926). The Court in its first hearing seemed inclined to overturn zoning until Cincinnati planner Alfred Bettmann filed an amicus brief that carried the day for zoning after a rehearing.

The apparent simultaneity of supply of zoning laws by planners and demand for zoning by homeowners and developers presents an identification problem: which was the primary mover, the planning establishment or the homeowners and developers? One way of identifying the more important factor is to consider an element of zoning that the planners wanted and initially obtained but that the public subsequently rejected. If the demanders (the public) trump the suppliers (the planners), the hand goes to the demand side.

The element is important and current. The planners who promulgated zoning regarded zoning districts as seriously flawed if any nonconforming uses were allowed to persist (Veiller 1916). They consistently proposed that nonconforming commercial and industrial uses be expelled from residential neighborhoods. Expulsion was required regardless of how long the nonconforming use had been there or whether it had arrived long before the residences. A brief grace period to facilitate relocation of the activity might be allowed, but no compensation was to be paid. The idea of terminating nonconforming uses has never faded away. Harland Bartholomew (1939) succinctly stated his thesis in the title of his article, "Nonconforming Uses Destroy the Neighborhood." A *Stanford Law Review* student note (1955) strenuously advocated termination. A modern expression of the same idea, though more nuanced in its application, has been advanced by Christopher Serkin (2009).

American courts bought into this idea without much trouble. The illustrative case—Frank Michelman called it (and thus helped make it) "the undying classic" (1967, 1237)—was *Hadacheck v. Los Angeles*, 239 U.S. 394 (1915). John C. Hadacheck had built a brick-making facility in a rural part of Los Angeles County seven years before the city of Los Angeles annexed territory containing his property. (See an excellent dissertation by Kathy Kolnick [2008], whose title, "Order Before Zoning," honors Ellickson's 1991 book *Order Without Law*.) Hadacheck had moved to his initially rural site specifically to avoid conflicts with his residential neighbors. His business had been expelled from a previous site nearer downtown by a 1902 ordinance aimed at brickyards in general and the objections to his operations by his residential neighbors, who included the owner of the *Los Angeles Times*. Hadacheck moved his operations about a mile west to an eight-acre site at the corner of what is now Pico and Crenshaw. The site was at the time outside the boundaries of the city of Los Angeles. However, Hadacheck's new neighborhood also became largely residential soon after he built his facility. After the new residents petitioned that the area be annexed to the city, the city's "districting" laws—the precursor to its comprehensive zoning law—designated the area as exclusively residential.

The city demanded that Hadacheck (and another nearby brickyard) discontinue operations. Hadacheck demurred, noting the large investment he had made and the considerable drop in value of his property if only residential use was allowed. Expensive and difficult-to-move machinery had been installed on the site, and deep pits from which the clay for bricks had been mined rendered the site problematic for alternative uses. Kolnick (2008) found that sometime afterward, Hadacheck's land was actually developed as mixed residential. However, she does not say what Hadacheck was paid for the land or what remediation was necessary in order to build on it. In any case, both the California and U.S. supreme courts upheld this ruling without a dissent, the U.S. Supreme Court blandly declaring that "there must be progress" (239 U.S. at 410).

Hadacheck is intriguing for two reasons. It seemed to involve a zoning controversy in Los Angeles that arose several years before New York's supposedly first-in-the-nation zoning ordinance of 1916. Los Angeles was not yet a huge city—in 1910 its population was only a little more than 300,000, while New York's was nearly 5 million at the same time—but it was growing rapidly because of migration, especially from the Midwest. Indeed, the major industry in Los Angeles at the time was residential development. Why had Los Angeles not been regarded as the mother of American zoning?

Kolnick's answer is that the zoning to which Hadacheck was subject was not comprehensive or citywide. Indeed, the word "zoning" was not used. Neighborhoods would petition the city to be placed in an exclusive residential district either because business had invaded the area or because residences were now invading areas where industries had come first (as in Hadacheck's case). The city government became especially responsive to these requests after its first experience with a voter initiative on land-use issues, which was a novelty at the time. But the process was actually done piecemeal. What is now called zoning was merely called "districting," and the entire city was not covered with districts. Indeed, the city itself was rapidly growing in land area (by annexation), as well as population, so comprehensive zoning would have been especially difficult to undertake. New York's title for first in the nation in 1916 was based on the comprehensiveness of its zoning map, which designated the entire city for some zone or another. Los Angeles did not get around to that until the 1920s.

The more pressing question is why the *Hadacheck* precedent had not led to a general rule that allowed nonconforming uses to be expelled without compensation. One reason that *Hadacheck* is not a clear guide is that it looked like a nuisance case. If that was all it was, then the fact that his brickyard had to move despite its precedence would not be especially unusual. First in time does not establish an entitlement to continue a nuisance. As Richard Epstein (1985) succinctly analyzed, Hadacheck had been granted an implied but temporary easement by neighboring landowners to conduct a nuisance that did no damage as long as the land nearby was vacant. Once neighboring landowners developed their property for residential use, the brickyard was obliged to leave.

There are two problems with the nuisance theory of *Hadacheck*. One is that both the California Supreme Court and the U.S. Supreme Court did not treat it as a simple nuisance case. *Hadacheck* was a test of the police power, not of the common law of nuisance. (Contemporary defenders of zoning, such as Pollard [1931], specifically emphasized this distinction.) The difference is that under the police power, the city of Los Angeles could have designated Hadacheck's neighborhood an industrial zone, and Hadacheck would have been protected from the wrath of his neighbors. In fact, the city did have to deal with this issue. The other problem is that *Hadacheck* was preceded by two cases that also tested the city's districting regulations, but did not involve uses that would have been considered nuisances.

Ex parte Quong Wo, 161 Cal. 220 (1911), involved the creation by local petition of a residence district near downtown Los Angeles, on Flower near Seventh Street. Quong's was one of more than a dozen Chinese hand laundries (no power machinery was employed) that were affected by the 1911 ordinance. They had long been interspersed with homes and other commercial buildings, as indicated on the map constructed by Kolnick (2008). Quong Wo had operated in the area for more than 14 years but was ordered to close his business. He declined, was arrested (as Hadacheck was in his later case), and appealed his conviction to the California Supreme Court, which upheld the ordinance and the conviction. Chinese laundries would not have met almost any traditional definition of nuisances, and several of Quong Wo's neighbors testified that his laundry was inoffensive (Kolnick 2008). Prejudice against Chinese, which surely informed earlier cases, was declining in Los Angeles as the city's population grew as a result of non-Chinese immigrants from other states. The California court in this instance seems to have treated this simply as a test of the breadth of municipal discretion in the police power and did not mention nuisance issues at all.

The second case was *Ex parte Montgomery*, 163 Cal. 457 (1912). It involved a lumberyard located at North Avenue 61 and North Figueroa Street. It was also required to discontinue operations as a result of a newly adopted residential district. It was possible that some nuisancelike activities occurred in lumberyards at the time, but they surely could have been abated without requiring that the use be entirely removed. The more remarkable aspect of *Montgomery*'s specific circumstance was that the lumberyard was adjacent to a railroad (the Santa Fe), across from which was a commercial neighborhood. The California Supreme Court specifically noted that a lumberyard was not a per se nuisance but then added that it might be considered a hazard to residential property because it harbored flammable materials.

Politics and People Overruled *Hadacheck*

One would think that the court losses by Hadacheck and the other two defendants would be the end of it. The planners had their way, and the highest courts of the state and the nation gave uncompensated removal of nonconforming uses their unqualified support. Indeed, Illinois courts in the 1920s briefly declared that "grandfathering" was illegal (Schwieterman, Caspall, and Heron 2006). But anyone familiar with zoning law knows that this was not the end of the story. In fact, Hadacheck would nowadays likely prevail, although his brick making might be scaled back by environmental laws. Nonconforming uses are now handled with kid gloves. Some states regard their status as constitutionally protected (Serkin 2009). Others have statutes that support them. Some of the more nuisancelike nonconformers were given a term of years to operate under so-called amortization statutes, reflecting the public unease with simply terminating them.

But *Hadacheck* is still good law (diMento et al. 1980). The explanation for its de facto reversal is twofold. One was popular revulsion at the law. According to Weiss (1987), as well as Kolnick (2008), Hadacheck's case and the other two were causes célèbres. It just did not seem fair that a long-established business could be eliminated by the stroke of a pen. The same popular feeling emerges in modern "right-to-farm" laws, which protect preexisting farming operations against nuisance suits (and sometimes zoning changes) that arise when residential neighborhoods are built around farms. The new neighbors find that the smells and sounds of agriculture are not to their liking, but the right-to-farm laws stay their hands (Adelaja and Friedman 1999) despite common-law principles that disfavor the "moving-to-the-nuisance" defense that right-to-farm laws support, and despite the writings of economists, who disparage the "first-in-time" principle as a general rule. This principle creates incentives for landowners to opportunistically establish what they know will be problematic uses in advance of the regulations or to lazily ignore neighborhood changes that they should anticipate (Wittman 1980).

Aside from popular perceptions of fairness, the city of Los Angeles faced a practical problem. Although the biggest business in Los Angeles in the early twentieth century was residential development, both the city council and voters were aware that some industrial and commercial developments were essential both for the residences and for longer-term employment. The immigrants who flocked to Southern California's pleasurable climate were not all retirees or rentiers. But development was happening so rapidly that *Hadacheck*'s problem cropped up time and again.

The impetus for the industrial districts was the fear that the city would be unable to attract industry. As Kolnick observed, "Though the California state and federal courts had declared it constitutional to require what were considered as nuisance businesses to be removed from residence districts, an anti-industry reputation was one the city council and civic organizations were at pains to avoid" (2008, 254).

City council members were aware that nearby cities were attracting industry with promises of exclusive districts. El Segundo brought in a refinery and established worker housing nearby, apparently able to persuade the refiner that it would not be chased out as Hadacheck had been.

The answer for that problem was the industrial zone. Within such zones, businesses could be more secure. They were not exempt from nuisance litigation, but that was not what caused the problem. What was problematic was residential development and the subsequent demand for an exclusive residential district. People who moved to an industrial zone, on the other hand, could be told that they did not have the right to demand removal of offending businesses.

At first, Los Angeles struggled to determine the location of its industrial zones. Centered on the Los Angeles River (east of downtown), the initial district was fitfully expanded to accommodate industry and was divided into degrees of noxiousness, with the worst being placed farthest from the residential areas. The city council had no stomach for actively removing residents from the industrial zone, but it appears that they left of their own accord over time, and at least those who owned property profited from the sales.

Kolnick's more remarkable finding, however, was that most of the firms that had been officially banished from residential zones actually did not leave. Hadacheck departed, but most of the Chinese laundries remained for many years, probably as long as the ordinary lifespan of an urban business. Other banned businesses often were in place years after the exclusive residential area had been established. Kolnick, an assiduous researcher, found no official record of their being granted exceptions, but after a while, controversies over expulsions simply died out.

Although zoning's national advocates continued to decry the persistence of nonconforming uses, most seemed to accept that it was politically difficult to dislodge them. Some attempted to justify their acceptance of nonconformers by claiming that the California courts were extreme in their deference to the police power. But the bland and unanimous acceptance of California's practice by the U.S. Supreme Court in *Hadacheck* suggests that however extreme California may have looked initially, there would be no opposition from the federal courts. This is not to say that the federal courts always deferred to state courts in these matters. In *Buchanan v. Warley*, 245 U.S. 60 (1917), the U.S. Supreme Court unanimously overturned an attempt by Louisville to establish separate residential zones for blacks and whites. (The city's defense invoked *Hadacheck*.) Louisville's apartheid scheme had been spreading throughout much of the South and the border states in response to the increase in migration of blacks in search of industrial jobs in the World War I era.

Most state courts, as well as many commentators, continue to regard grandfathering previous uses as strictly a matter of noblesse oblige or political necessity on the part of local jurisdictions. Many have accepted the concept of an "amortization period" during which nonconforming uses are granted a reprieve from discontinuance. But even amortization periods have gone out of fashion (Serkin 2009). This seems to be a case in which the leaders of zoning called for a practice that the public was unwilling to accept, even though the courts either endorsed the practice or tolerated it. For this reason, the continuing practice of grandfathering nonconforming uses supports the demand-side or bottom-up theory of zoning's development. The argument is not that courts have no effect on local government behavior. *Buchanan v. Warley* was indeed important in that it undermined the ability of local governments to perpetuate racial segregation (Fischel 1998). That a less-than-perfect substitute for racial zoning, the private racial covenant, continued to be available may have helped southern cities accept *Buchanan*.

The principle that nonconforming uses need not adapt to current zoning is hardly absolute. Unlike conforming uses, a discontinuation of a nonconforming use for a period of months (usually set by statute) may cause its owner to lose its legally protected status. Even accidental destruction of a nonconforming building may require that it be rebuilt subject to current zoning regulations. And a nonconforming use that threatens health and safety (as opposed to the more nebulous "general welfare") is more likely to be shut down, although the same can be said for conforming uses. The special status of nonconforming uses is largely contrary to the supply side view of zoning and to zoning theory generally. It has been integrated into zoning practice for such a long time that most planners now regard it as entirely natural, but that natural feel is actually illustrative of the power of the demand side of zoning.

Zoning has remained the premier function of local governments everywhere in the United States. The political and technical trends that at first blush seemed destined to undermine it have either strengthened it (although in the direction of more restrictiveness) or been absorbed by the indigenous regulatory culture. This is a reflection of the grassroots appeal of local land use regulation. This appeal is not new. As suggested earlier, bottom-up forces substantially modified the force of zoning on previously existing, nonconforming uses.

Although most professional advocates for zoning urged (and continue to urge) the discontinuance of nonconforming uses, and court decisions have seldom stood in their way, public sentiment has generally favored their continuance. This sentiment has gradually solidified into what appears to be a popular legal entitlement. Although there are serious arguments against recognizing such entitlements, their development might be taken by scholars as an indicator of the ongoing evolution of property rights.

Acknowledgments

I thank without implicating Peter Buchsbaum, Daniel Cole, Robert Ellickson, Elinor Ostrom, and other participants at the conference "Evolution of Property Rights Related to Land and Natural Resources" for helpful comments and observations.

REFERENCES

Aaronson, Daniel. 1999. The effect of school finance reform on population heterogeneity. *National Tax Journal* 52:5–29.

Adelaja, Adesoji O., and Keith Friedman. 1999. Political economy of right to farm. *Journal of Agricultural and Applied Economics* 31:565–579.

Angel, Solly, Stephen Sheppard, and Daniel Civco. 2005. *The dynamics of global urban expansion.* Washington, DC: Transport and Urban Development Department, World Bank.

Banzhaf, Spence, Wallace Oates, James N. Sanchirico, David Simpson, and Randall Walsh. 2006. Voting for conservation: What is the American electorate revealing? *Resources* 160:7–12.

Bartholomew, Harland. 1939. Nonconforming uses destroy the neighborhood. *Land Economics* 15:96–97.

Been, Vicki, and Francis Gupta. 1997. Coming to the nuisance or going to the barrios? A longitudinal analysis of environmental justice claims. *Ecology Law Quarterly* 24:1–56.

Bento, Antonia, Scott Lowe, Gerrit Knaap, and Arnab Chakraborty. 2009. Housing market effects of inclusionary zoning. *Cityscape: A Journal of Policy Development and Research* 11:7–11.

Berger, Bethany R. 2009. What owners want and governments do: Evidence from the Oregon experiment. *Fordham Law Review* 78:1281–1330.

Bogart, William T. 1993. "What big teeth you have!": Identifying the motivations for exclusionary zoning. *Urban Studies* 30:1669–1681.

Bosselman, Fred P., and David Callies. 1971. *The quiet revolution in land use control.* Washington, DC: Council on Environmental Quality.

Breton, Albert. 1973. Neighborhood selection and zoning. In *Issues in urban public economics*, ed. Harold Hochman, 718–750. Saarbrücken: Institute Internationale de Finance Publique.

Brunner, Eric J., and Jon Sonstelie. 2006. California's school finance reform: An experiment in fiscal federalism. In *The Tiebout model at fifty*, ed. William A. Fischel, 55–93. Cambridge, MA: Lincoln Institute of Land Policy.

Bryden, David P. 1977. The impact of variances: A study of statewide zoning. *Minnesota Law Review* 61:769–840.

Burchell, Robert W., David Listokin, and William R. Dolphin. 1993. *The development impact assessment handbook and model.* Washington, DC: Urban Land Institute.

Burchfield, Marcy, Henry G. Overman, Diego Puga, and Matthew A Turner. 2006. Causes of sprawl: A portrait from space. *Quarterly Journal of Economics* 121:351–397.

Callies, David L. 1994. *Preserving paradise: Why regulation won't work.* Honolulu: University of Hawaii Press.

Clowney, Stephen. 2007. Comment: An empirical look at churches in the zoning process. *Yale Law Journal* 116:859–868.

Coase, Ronald H. 1960. The problem of social cost. *Journal of Law and Economics* 3:1–44.

Cortes, Kalena E., and Andrew Friedson. 2010. Ranking up by moving out: The effect of the Texas top 10% plan on property values. IZA Discussion Paper No. 5026. Bonn, Germany: Institute for the Study of Labor. http://ssrn.com/abstract=1634493.

DiMento, Joseph F., Michael D. Dozier, Steven L. Emmons, Donald G. Hagman, Christopher Kim, Karen Greenfield-Sanders, Paul F. Waldau, and Jay A. Woollacott. 1980. Land development and environmental control in the California Supreme Court: The deferential, the preservationist, and the preservationist-erratic eras. *UCLA Law Review* 27:859–1066.

Dresch, Marla, and Steven M. Sheffrin. 1997. *Who pays for development fees and exactions?* San Francisco: Public Policy Institute of California.

Dukeminier, Jesse, Jr., and Clyde L. Stapleton. 1962. The zoning board of adjustment: A case study in misrule. *Kentucky Law Journal* 50:273–350.

Eagle, Steven. 2005. Wireless telecommunications, infrastructure security, and the NIMBY problem. *Catholic University Law Review* 54:445–496.

Ellen, Ingrid G., and Katherine M. O'Regan. 2010. Crime and urban flight revisited: The effect of the 1990s drop in crime on cities. *Journal of Urban Economics* 68:215–290.

Ellickson, Robert C. 1977. Suburban growth controls: An economic and legal analysis. *Yale Law Journal* 86:385–511.

———. 1981. The irony of "inclusionary" zoning. *Southern California Law Review* 54:1167–1216.

———. 1991. *Order without law.* Cambridge, MA: Harvard University Press.

Ellickson, Robert C., and Vicki L. Been. 2000. *Land use controls: Cases and materials.* Gaithersburg, MD: Aspen.

Epstein, Richard A. 1985. *Takings: Private property and the power of eminent domain.* Cambridge, MA: Harvard University Press.

Esty, Daniel C. 1997. Revitalizing environmental federalism. *Michigan Law Review* 95:570–653.

Fennell, Lee Anne. 2009. *The unbounded home: Property values beyond property lines*. New Haven, CT: Yale University Press.

Fischel, William A. 1975. Fiscal and environmental considerations in the location of firms in suburban communities. In *Fiscal zoning and land use controls*, eds. Edwin S. Mills and Wallace E. Oates, 119–174. Lexington, MA: Lexington Books.

———. 1982. The urbanization of agricultural land: A review of the National Agricultural Land Study. *Land Economics* 58:236–259.

———. 1985. *The economics of zoning laws: A property rights approach to American land use controls*. Baltimore: Johns Hopkins University Press.

———. 1988. Introduction: Utilitarian balancing and formalism in takings. *Columbia Law Review* 88:1581–1599.

———. 1989. Did *Serrano* cause Proposition 13? *National Tax Journal* 42:465–474.

———. 1992. Property taxation and the Tiebout model: Evidence for the benefit view from zoning and voting. *Journal of Economic Literature* 30:171–177.

———. 1995. *Regulatory takings: Law, economics, and politics*. Cambridge, MA: Harvard University Press.

———. 1998. Why judicial reversal of apartheid made a difference. *Vanderbilt Law Review* (Colloquium issue: Rethinking *Buchanan v. Warley*) 51:975–991.

———. 2001. *The homevoter hypothesis*. Cambridge, MA: Harvard University Press.

———. 2004a. An economic history of zoning and a cure for its exclusionary effects. *Urban Studies* 41:317–340.

———. 2004b. Why are judges so wary of regulatory takings? In *Private property in the twenty-first century*, ed. Harvey M. Jacobs, 50–74. Northampton, MA: Edward Elgar.

———. 2006. A theory of municipal corporate governance with an application to land use regulation. In *A companion to urban economics*, eds. Richard Arnott and Daniel McMillen, 372–388. Malden, MA: Blackwell.

———. 2009. *Making the grade: The economic evolution of American school districts*. Chicago: University of Chicago Press.

Fisher, Lynn. 2007. *Chapter 40B permitting and litigation: A report by the housing affordability initiative*. Cambridge, MA: MIT Center for Real Estate.

Fogelson, Robert M. 2005. *Bourgeois nightmares: Suburbia, 1870–1930*. New Haven, CT: Yale University Press.

Fox, William F. 1981. Fiscal differentials and industrial location: Some empirical evidence. *Urban Studies* 18:105–111.

Frug, Gerald E., and David J. Barron. 2008. *City bound: How states stifle urban innovation*. Ithaca, NY: Cornell University Press.

Glaeser, Edward L., Joseph Gyourko, and Albert Saiz. 2008. Housing supply and housing bubbles. *Journal of Urban Economics* 64:198–217.

Glaeser, Edward L., Joseph Gyourko, and Raven Saks. 2006. Urban growth and housing supply. *Journal of Economic Geography* 6:71–89.

Glaeser, Edward L., and Bryce A. Ward. 2009. The causes and consequences of land use regulation: Evidence from Greater Boston. *Journal of Urban Economics* 65:265–278.

Gyourko, Joseph, Alberto Saiz, and Anita Summers. 2008. A new measure of the local regulatory environment for housing markets: The Wharton residential land use regulatory index. *Urban Studies* 45:693–729.

Hamilton, Bruce W. 1975. Zoning and property taxation in a system of local governments. *Urban Studies* 12:205–211.

Hanushek, Eric A., and Alfred A. Lindseth. 2009. *Schoolhouses, courthouses, and statehouses: Solving the funding-achievement puzzle in America's public schools*. Princeton, NJ: Princeton University Press.

Heimlich, Ralph E., Marlow Vesterby, and Kenneth S. Krupa. 1991. *Urbanizing farmland: Dynamics of land use change in fast growth counties*. Washington, DC: U.S. Department of Agriculture, Agricultural Information Booklet 629.

Henneberry, David, and Richard Barrows. 1990. Capitalization of exclusive agricultural zoning into farmland prices. *Land Economics* 66:249–258.

Hilber, Christian A. L., and Christopher Mayer. 2009. Why do households without children support local public schools? Linking house price capitalization to school spending. *Journal of Urban Economics* 65:74–90.

Hilber, Christian A. L., and Frederic Robert-Nicoud. 2009. On the origins of land use regulations: Theory and evidence from U.S. metro areas. CEPR Discussion Paper No. DP7604. London: Centre for Economic Policy Research.

Hinds, Dudley S., and Nicholas Ordway. 1986. The influence of race on rezoning decisions: Equality of treatment in black and white census tracts, 1955–1980. *Review of Black Political Economy* 14:51–63.

Hughes, Mark Alan, and Peter M. Van Doren. 1990. Social policy through land reform: New Jersey's *Mount Laurel* controversy. *Political Science Quarterly* 105:97–111.

Ingram, Gregory K., Armando Carbonell, Yu-Hung Hong, and Anthony Flint. 2009. *Smart growth policies: An evaluation of programs and outcomes*. Cambridge, MA: Lincoln Institute of Land Policy.

Kahn, Matthew E., and John G. Matsusaka. 1997. Demand for environmental goods: Evidence from voting patterns on California initiatives. *Journal of Law and Economics* 40:137–173.

Kent, David L. 1993. The presumption in favor of granting zoning variances. *New Hampshire Bar Journal* 34:29–34.

Kinkade, Brent S. 1992. Municipal antitrust immunity after *City of Columbia v. Omni Outdoor Advertising*. *Washington Law Review* 67:479–500.

Knaap, Gerrit, and Arthur C. Nelson. 1992. *The regulated landscape: Lessons on state land use planning from Oregon*. Cambridge, MA: Lincoln Institute of Land Policy.

Knack, Ruth, and Stuart Meck. 1996. The real story behind the standard planning and zoning acts of 1920s. *Land Use Law and Zoning Digest* 48:3–9.

Knetsch, Jack L. 1989. The endowment effect and evidence of nonreversable indifference curves. *American Economic Review* 79:1277–1284.

Kolnick, Kathy A. 2008. Order before zoning: Land use regulation in Los Angeles, 1880–1915. Ph.D. diss., University of Southern California.

Kotchen, Matthew J., and Shawn M. Powers. 2006. Explaining the appearance and success of voter referenda for open-space conservation. *Journal of Environmental Economics and Management* 52:373–390.

Michelman, Frank I. 1967. Property, utility, and fairness: Comments on the ethical foundations of "just compensation" law. *Harvard Law Review* 80:1165–1258.

Miller, Gary J. 1981. *Cities by contract: The politics of municipal incorporation*. Cambridge, MA: MIT Press.

Mills, Edwin S. 1979. Economic analysis of urban land-use controls. In *Current issues in urban economics*, eds. Peter Mieszkowski and Mahlon Straszheim, 511–541. Baltimore: Johns Hopkins University Press.

Mitchell, James L. 2004. Will empowering developers to challenge exclusionary zoning increase suburban housing choice? *Journal of Policy Analysis and Management* 23:119–134.

Moses, Leon, and Harold F. Williamson, Jr. 1967. The location of economic activity in cities. *American Economic Review* 57:211–222.

National Agricultural Land Study. 1981. *Final report*. Washington, DC: U.S. Government Printing Office.

Nechyba, Thomas. J. 2001. The benefit view and the new view: Where do we stand, twenty-five years into the debate? In *Property taxation and local government finance*, ed. Wallace E. Oates, 113–121. Cambridge, MA: Lincoln Institute of Land Policy.

Nelson, Robert H. 1977. *Zoning and property rights*. Cambridge, MA: MIT Press.

———. 2003. The rise of private neighborhood associations: A constitutional revolution in local government. In *The property tax, land use, and land use regulation*, ed. Dick Netzer, 209–272. Cambridge, MA: Lincoln Institute of Land Policy.

Nelson, Robert H., Kyle R. McKenzie, and Eileen Norcross. 2009. *Lessons from business improvement districts: Building on past successes.* Arlington, VA: Mercatus Center at George Mason University.

Nguyen, Mai Thi. 2007. Local growth control at the ballot box: Real effects or symbolic politics? *Journal of Urban Affairs* 29:129–147.

Pack, Howard, and Janet R. Pack. 1977. Metropolitan fragmentation and suburban homogeneity. *Urban Studies* 14:191–201.

Phillips, Justin, and Eban Goodstein. 2000. Growth management and housing prices: The case of Portland, Oregon. *Contemporary Economic Policy* 18:334–344.

Pidot, Jeff. 2005. *Reinventing conservation easements.* Cambridge, MA: Lincoln Institute of Land Policy.

Pigou, Arthur C. 1920. *The economics of welfare.* London: Macmillan.

Plotkin, Sidney. 1987. *Keep out: The struggle for land use control.* Berkeley: University of California Press.

Pollard, W. L., ed. 1931. Zoning in the United States (symposium). *The Annals of the American Academy of Arts and Sciences* 155:1–227.

Pollock, Peter. 1998. Controlling sprawl in Boulder: Benefits and pitfalls. *Land Lines* 10:1–3.

Popper, Frank. 1988. Understanding American land use regulation since 1970. *Journal of the American Planning Association* 54:291–301.

Powell, David L., Robert M. Rhodes, and Dan R. Stengle. 1995. A measured step to protect private property rights. *Florida State University Law Review* 23:255–314.

President's Committee on Urban Housing. 1969. *A decent home: The report of the President's Committee on Urban Housing.* Washington, DC: U.S. Government Printing Office.

Reback, Randall. 2005. House prices and the provision of local public services: Capitalization under school choice programs. *Journal of Urban Economics* 57:275–301.

Reilly, William K., ed. 1973. *The use of land: A citizen's policy guide to urban growth.* New York: Thomas Crowell.

Rolleston, Barbara S. 1987. Determinants of restrictive suburban zoning: An empirical analysis. *Journal of Urban Economics* 21:1–21.

Rosa, Josh. 2010. Inclusionary housing in Sacramento County: Costs, benefits, and politics. http://ssrn.com/abstract=1638624.

Rothwell, Jonathan T. 2009. The origins of zoning: Rural settlements vs. urbanization. http://ssrn.com/abstract=1422737.

Rowan, Katrin C. 2007. Anti-exclusionary zoning in Pennsylvania: A weapon for developers, a loss for low-income Pennsylvanians. *Temple Law Review* 80:1271–1304.

Salkin, Patricia E., and John M. Armentano. 1993. The Fair Housing Act, zoning, and affordable housing. *Urban Lawyer* 25:893–904.

Schmidt, Stephan, and Kurt Paulsen. 2009. Is open-space preservation a form of exclusionary zoning? The evolution of municipal open-space policies in New Jersey. *Urban Affairs Review* 45:92–118.

Schwieterman, Joseph P., Dana M. Caspall, and Jane Heron. 2006. *The politics of place: A history of zoning in Chicago.* Chicago: Lake Claremont Press.

Serkin, Christopher. 2007. Local property law: Adjusting the scale of property protection. *Columbia Law Review* 107:883–948.

———. 2009. Existing uses and the limits of land use regulation. *New York University Law Review* 84:1222–1291.

Sidak, J. Gregory, and Daniel F. Spulber. 1996. Deregulatory takings and breach of the regulatory contract. *New York University Law Review* 71:851–999.

Siegan, Bernard H. 1972. *Land use without zoning.* Lexington, MA: Lexington Books.

Sinai, Todd, and Joel Waldfogel. 2005. Do low-income housing subsidies increase the occupied housing stock? *Journal of Public Economics* 89:2137–2164.

Stanford Law Review. 1955. Note: The elimination of nonconforming uses. *Stanford Law Review* 7:415–421.

Tiebout, Charles M. 1956. A pure theory of local expenditures. *Journal of Political Economy* 64:416–424.

Toll, Seymour. 1969. *Zoned American*. New York: Grossman.

Veiller, Lawrence. 1916. Districting by municipal regulation. In *Proceedings of the Eighth National Conference on City Planning, Cleveland*, 147–178. New York: National Conference on City Planning.

Weiss, Marc A. 1987. *The rise of the community builders: The American real estate industry and urban land planning*. New York: Columbia University Press.

White, Gilbert F. 1986. Human adjustment to floods. In *Geography, resources, and environment: Selected writings of Gilbert F. White*, vol. 1, eds. Robert W. Kates and Ian Burton, 10–25. Chicago: University of Chicago Press.

Wittman, Donald. 1980. First come, first served: An economic analysis of "coming to the nuisance." *Journal of Legal Studies* 9:557–568.

Zodrow, George R. 2007. The property tax incidence debate and the mix of state and local finance of local public expenditures. *CESifo Economic Studies* 53:495–521.

Commentary

ROBERT C. ELLICKSON

William Fischel occupies a premier niche in the pantheon of American scholars of land use policy. Over the course of his distinguished career, he has exhibited an exceptional knack for bringing theory to reality and reality to theory. His chapter exhibits many of his characteristic strengths—a command of a wide range of literatures, a holistic and sophisticated view of local government, and an engaging and down-to-earth writing style.

Fischel's conception of local politics has bested the competition. In essence, Fischel sees homeowners, the dominant political faction in most suburbs, as seeking to enhance the value of their houses. Local officials serve, more or less faithfully, as these homevoters' agents. Fischel's model is far more realistic, in particular, than what he calls the "goody-two-shoes theory," which envisions local officials as acting to compel developers to internalize externalities. For example, where the demand for housing is somewhat inelastic, homevoters are likely to favor restricting the supply of new housing in order to raise their value of their own houses to monopoly levels. Instead of eliminating market imperfections, local politics thus can foster zoning practices that affirmatively misallocate resources.

Although Fischel's stimulating chapter addresses other subjects as well, I restrict my comments to the topic identified in his title, that is, the evolution of zoning since the 1980s. For the most part, I agree with his description of recent trends. His core assertion, reflected in his subtitle, is the persistence of localism in land use regulation. In 1971, Bosselman and Callies famously detected a "quiet revolution" under whose banner state planning agencies increasingly were either preempting local zoning or obtaining authority to veto locally approved projects or plans. Fischel observes, as previous commentators have, that by the 1980s this quiet revolution had stalled. Most legal scholars would also endorse another of his basic conclusions, namely, that the threat of landowners' takings claims—the constitutional centerpiece of the property rights movement—in practice rarely constrains local zoning officials.

Two of Fischel's other central assertions, however, warrant closer scrutiny. He maintains that local zoning generally became more restrictive after the 1980s, and that the states and the federal government have been largely responsible for this trend. At the close of this comment, I will conclude that the recent history of land use controls in Massachusetts indeed supports these two central claims. Nonetheless, I have reservations about both Fischel's methods of supporting these assertions and the generality of his articulation of them.

Although Google Earth and local government Internet sites have greatly eased the study of zoning practices, it remains difficult to have a sense of what the 20,000 or so zoning governments in the United States are up to. A few intrepid researchers have investigated practices in a sample of either localities (Gyourko, Saiz, and Summers 2008; Pendall, Puentes, and Martin 2006) or states (Ingram et al. 2009). These investigators, however, have generally been more interested in describing contemporaneous differences in these jurisdictions' policies than in examining how these policies have changed over time. In addition, empirical measurement of actual zoning practices is exasperatingly difficult because many localities, when offered sufficiently generous concessions by developers, are happy to alter the ordinances on their books. For example, as Justice Hall's famous opinion in *Southern Burlington County NAACP v. Township of Mount Laurel*, 336 A.2d 713 (N.J. 1975), describes, the Township of Mount Laurel, New Jersey, frequently waived its nominal zoning restrictions to permit far denser planned-unit developments.

In light of the dearth of good survey sources about zoning trends, Fischel offers some general impressions. Because his knowledge of the pertinent secondary literature is unsurpassed, these warrant respect. He might have made use, however, of another source of evidence, namely, changes over time in the relative prices of housing in different states and localities. Except in markets where housing demand is perfectly elastic, the tightening of regulations on housing supply can be expected to raise house prices. The meaning of a relative price change should be interpreted with caution, however, because it may also manifest, in whole or part, a shift in either the demand for housing or the relative quality of a jurisdiction's housing stock. Table C9.1, calculated from gross data gathered by the Census Bureau, nonetheless suggests that trends in a state's relative home values can serve as a rough proxy for changes in the strictness of the development regulations within that state. The figures in the table confirm, for example, that constraints on housing supply became much tighter in California from 1960 to 1980, a fact previously well documented by Fischel (1995). From 1980 to 2000, by contrast, the figures in the table suggest that housing developers in Massachusetts witnessed a greater incremental regulatory tightening than did their counterparts in either California or Texas. The winds of zoning politics do not blow nationally, it appears, but differently from state to state.

Is there evidence to support Fischel's second broad assertion that since the 1980s, the federal and state governments have been pressuring localities to zone more restrictively? Fischel recognizes that the pertinent legal history is mixed, especially at

TABLE C9.1

Median Existing Home Value, by State, as a Percentage of U.S. Median Home Value

	1960	1980	2000
California	127	179	177
Massachusetts	116	103	155
Texas	74	83	69

SOURCE: U.S. Census Bureau (2010).

the federal level. He mentions several pro-development federal actions in recent decades, for example, ones that selectively override local zoning constraints on religious land uses, towers for cell-phone communications, and group homes for the disabled.

The history of changes in state land use policies since the 1980s is similarly mixed. Two of the most ballyhooed state initiatives of the 1990s, the Maryland Smart Growth statutes (Knaap and Frece 2007) and the Washington Growth Management Act (McGee 2007), intrude far less on local autonomy than did, for example, the Oregon and Florida statutes that highlighted the quiet revolution of the 1970s. Both Oregon and Florida eventually required each local government to prepare a comprehensive plan and to submit it to a state agency for determination of its consistency with state-articulated goals. In both states, there have been noisy, if not always successful, counterrevolutionary efforts to vitiate these planning mandates. Opponents of Oregon's planning scheme have repeatedly attacked it with ballot initiatives, two of which have won voter approval (Berger 2009), if only to be subsequently defanged by statute or court ruling. In 2011 lawmakers in Florida, over the intense opposition of environmentalists, greatly eased the state's planning mandates on local governments (Alvarez 2011). New Jersey, home of the famous *Mount Laurel* decisions, has similarly witnessed counterrevolutionary stirrings. The New Jersey Fair Housing Act of 1985 is widely regarded as a retreat from *Mount Laurel*'s affordable housing mandates (Haar 1996). And Charles Christie, on assuming the New Jersey governorship in 2010, made clear his desire to lighten further the municipal burdens generated in the aftermath of *Mount Laurel* (Carroll 2010).

What causes the tides of land use regulation to rise and fall? Fischel, like other urban economists (Glaeser & Gyourko 2002), is fully aware that development controls tend to be much stricter in the blue states that tilt Democratic than in the red states that tilt Republican. Although economists strive as hard as scholars in other disciplines to shape ideas, they nonetheless seem, with rare exception (e.g., Kahn [2011]), to harbor an antipathy to the notion that ideological beliefs importantly influence political outcomes. For example, when Fischel (2004) and Glaeser, Gyourko, and Saks (2005) sought to explain why local governments had tightened their zoning restrictions in the 1970s, they gave little weight to the flowering of environmentalist sentiment at that time.

By contrast, I attribute the noisy counterrevolutionary stirrings since the 1980s in significant part to shifts in national and subnational political zeitgeists. In the mid-twentieth century, many Americans envied the economic trajectory apparently achieved by the planned economy of the Soviet Union and also supported Robert Moses–style urban renewal. Today, confidence in the wisdom of the ambitious planning of either economies or cities has ebbed. In the 1980s promarket neoliberal ideas were ascendant around the globe and remain a central, if contested, paradigm. Friedrich Hayek's book *The Road to Serfdom* (1944), a classic attack on the assumptions underlying centralized planning, has reappeared on a few best-seller lists (Schuessler 2010). Although the environmental movement certainly has remained vibrant, the property rights movement, energized in part by Richard Epstein's *Takings* (1985), has emerged as a partially offsetting political force in many venues. A sign of the times is the outpouring of outrage that followed the Supreme Court's decision in *Kelo v. City of New London*, 545 U.S. 469 (2005). *Kelo* upheld the constitutionality of what would have been a ho-hum event during the heyday of urban renewal: a city's use, for the purpose of economic development, of the power of eminent domain to acquire a modest home. That the Obama administration has been keeping "smart growth" initiatives on the back burner is another clue that federal measures of this stripe are not thought to enjoy widespread popular support.

Contemporary legal scholars and judges also seem to be less enthusiastic than their forebears were about the merits of comprehensive planning. For example, a central issue in zoning law is whether local officials should be required to make piecemeal zoning decisions "in accordance with a comprehensive plan," or are instead free to muddle through case-by-case. In 1955 Charles Haar famously advanced the view that the formal local plan should control. By the 1980s, however, Carol Rose (1983) and other highly regarded legal scholars had begun to challenge Haar's pro-planning stance. A trend against the exaltation of formal planning is also evident in the pattern of decisions of various state supreme courts. Compare, for example, *Fasano v. Board of County Commissioners*, 507 P.2d 23 (Or. 1973), a decision that explicitly endorses Haar's view, with *Campion v. Board of Aldermen*, 899 A.2d 542 (Conn. 2006), which stresses the need for flexibility in modern zoning practices.

In sum, the political zeitgeist of the 1970s generally helped nurture support for robust state planning mandates. The zeitgeist of the 2010s is everywhere more muddled and, in some states, on balance hostile to ambitious planning efforts. But any national generalization about political and ideological trends invariably is too sweeping. The data presented in table C9.1 strongly imply, for example, that since the 1980s development restrictions have tightened, at the margin, more in Massachusetts than in either Texas or California. Studies focused on Massachusetts confirm the burgeoning use during the past few decades of at least three specific legal devices that crimp housing production. First, more and more Massachusetts towns have been compelling developers to help finance the provision of affordable (i.e., reduced-price) housing. Schuetz, Meltzer, and Been (2011) have found that this policy functions as a tax on housing supply and actually inflates Massachusetts housing prices across the board. Second, towns in Massachusetts increasingly acquire tracts for use as open space, obviating their use for housing development (Hollis and Fulton 2002). Fischel, inspired by Schmidt and Paulsen (2009), insightfully attributes this phenomenon partly to the Massachusetts Anti-Snob Zoning Act, which immunizes a suburb's exclusionary zoning policies from state override when more than 10 percent of the suburb's housing stock has been deemed affordable. He notes that this formula encourages homevoters to oppose all proposed housing subdivisions, including ones exclusively marketed to the well-to-do. Third, Bray (2010) has shown that after 1980 voluntary landowner donations of conservation easements became much more common in Massachusetts. These donations, largely motivated to obtain tax write-offs, inevitably constrain housing supply, although by how much is largely unknown.

Each of these three examples of a burgeoning grassroots practice supports Fischel's general thesis that inducements from higher-level governments have fostered the tightening of constraints on development. The Massachusetts Anti-Snob Zoning Act has spurred municipalities both to acquire open space and compel developers to provide inclusionary housing, and federal tax policies have helped foster gifts of conservation easements.

Land use laws have made housing unduly expensive in many jurisdictions, disproportionately ones in the Northeast and along the west coast. In these areas especially, beleaguered housing consumers would benefit from legal reforms at every level of government.

REFERENCES

Alvarez, Lizette. 2011. Florida legislature votes to ease rules on development. *New York Times*, May 11: A16.

Berger, Bethany R. 2009. What owners want and governments do: Evidence from the Oregon experiment. *Fordham Law Review* 78:1281–1330.

Bosselman, Fred P., and David Callies. 1971. *The quiet revolution in land use control*. Washington, DC: Council on Environmental Quality.

Bray, Zachary. 2010. Reconciling development and natural beauty: The promise and dilemma of conservation easements. *Harvard Environmental Law Review* 34:119–177.

Carroll, Thomas F. III. 2010. Court enjoins portion of Governor Christie's executive order imposing moratorium on COAH proceedings. http://nj-landuselaw.com/web-content/pdf/coah021110rev2.pdf.

Epstein, Richard A. 1985. *Takings: Private property and the power of eminent domain*. Cambridge, MA: Harvard University Press.

Fischel, William A. 1995. *Regulatory takings: Law, economics, and politics*. Cambridge, MA: Harvard University Press.

———. 2004. An economic history of zoning and a cure for its exclusionary effects. *Urban Studies* 41:317–340.

Glaeser, Edward, and Joseph Gyourko. 2002. Zoning's steep price, *Regulation* 25(3):24–30.

Glaeser, Edward L., Joseph Gyourko, and Raven Saks. 2005. Why have housing prices gone up? *American Economic Review* 95:329–333.

Gyourko, Joseph, Alberto Saiz, and Anita Summers. 2008. A new measure of the local regulatory environment for housing markets: The Wharton Residential Land Use Regulatory Index. *Urban Studies* 45:693–729.

Haar, Charles M. 1955. "In accordance with a comprehensive plan." *Harvard Law Review* 68:1154–1175.

———. 1996. *Suburbs under siege: Race, space, and audacious judges*. Princeton, NJ: Princeton University Press.

Hayek, Friedrich. 1944. *The road to serfdom*. Chicago: University of Chicago Press.

Hollis, Linda E., and William Fulton. 2002. *Open space protection: Conservation meets growth management*. Washington, DC: Brookings Institution Center on Urban and Metropolitan Policy.

Ingram, Gregory K., Armando Carbonell, Yu-Hung Hong, and Anthony Flint. 2009. *Smart growth policies: An evaluation of programs and outcomes*. Cambridge, MA: Lincoln Institute of Land Policy.

Kahn, Matthew E. 2011. Do liberal cities limit new housing development? Evidence from California. *Journal of Urban Economics* 69:223–228.

Knaap, Gerrit-Jan, and John W. Frece. 2007. Smart growth in Maryland. *Idaho Law Review* 43:445–473.

McGee, Henry W., Jr. 2007. Washington's way. *Seattle University Law Review* 31:1–34.

Pendall, Rolf, Robert Puentes, and Jonathan Martin. 2006. *From traditional to reformed: A review of the land use regulations in the nation's 50 largest metropolitan areas*. Washington, DC: Brookings Institution Metropolitan Policy Program.

Rose, Carol M. 1983. Planning and dealing: Piecemeal land controls as a problem of local legitimacy. *California Law Review* 71:839–912.

Schmidt, Stephan, and Kurt Paulsen. 2009. Is open-space preservation a form of exclusionary zoning? The evolution of municipal open-space policies in New Jersey. *Urban Affairs Review* 45:92–118.

Schuessler, Jennifer. 2010. Hayek: The back story. *New York Times Book Review*, July 11: 27.

Schuetz, Jenny, Rachel Meltzer, and Vicki Been. 2011. Silver bullet or Trojan horse? The effects of inclusionary zoning on local housing markets in the United States. *Urban Studies* 48:297–329.

U.S. Census Bureau. 2010. Historical census of housing; tables; home values. http://www.census.gov/hhes/www/housing/census/historic/values.html.

Psychological Entitlement, Reference Levels, and Valuation Disparities

The Case of Native American Land Ownership

C. LEIGH ANDERSON AND RICHARD O. ZERBE

Ownership, in the economics literature, is primarily established by property rights. As a general concept, however, ownership can be defined by both a legal and moral or personal facet, such as "legal or just claim" and "the relation of an owner to the thing possessed."[1] We posit that a relevant concept of ownership, as it affects willingness to pay (WTP) and willingness to accept (WTA) for the right to property, derives from psychological entitlement, which is informed not only by legal rights, but also by cultural and historical norms and expectations that give rise to moral claims.

Valuation disparities between WTP and WTA are important because they can influence individual and market behavior and can hinder exchange involving real property, such as land. Valuation disparities are measured in relation to a reference level—that set of perceived rights from which one measures gains and losses—and are associated with an endowment effect posited to arise with ownership.[2] A fairly recent series of articles has challenged the existence of valuation disparities, suggesting they arise from experimental design, rather than as a function of preferences, and has prompted an equally vigorous response (Knetsch and Wong 2009; Plott and Zeiler 2005). This debate hinges in part on what is meant by ownership; that is, it is largely a debate over semantics.

Legal land disputes, particularly between indigenous and nonindigenous groups, commonly involve moral claim and sentimental value (Fishel 2006/2007; Rolfe and Windle 2003; Snyder, Williams and Peterson 2003). Indeed, in the landmark 1823 *Johnson v. M'Intosh* decision, Chief Justice Marshall "declared the Indian nations 'to be the rightful occupants of the soil, with a legal as well as just claim to retain possession of it, and to use it according to their own discretion'" (Watson 2011, citing *Johnson v. McIntosh*, 21 U.S. [8 Wheat] 543, 574 [1823]). When ownership is not simply legal, the reference point from which gains and losses are perceived will

---

[1] The Collaborative International Dictionary of English v.0.48, *Webster's Revised Unabridged Dictionary* (1913), WordNet 2.0.

[2] Valuation disparities that give rise to differences between WTA and WTP are also attributed within the confines of standard neoclassical utility theory to income and substitution effects, signaling, transaction costs, regard for others, and other factors (Knetsch and Wong 2009). The endowment effect and loss aversion (under uncertainty) favor prospect theory.

differ from the legal one, and psychological entitlement can explain valuation disparities not covered by income or substitution effects.[3] Psychological entitlement can
also explain valuation disparities across individuals with different moral claims over
a property, who might otherwise value it identically. The sentimental value attached
to a good can likewise produce valuation disparities by increasing the good's subjective value and heightening losses relative to gains. In the absence of loss aversion,
however, sentimental value reduces to a substitution effect. Either way, sentimental
value will not change the reference level, whereas a change in moral claim derived
from views of fairness or sovereignty will change the reference level by altering
expectations of ownership.

Valuation disparities and the reference level will vary depending on the subset of
rights held and the property regime. Hence, a more complete treatment of ownership
must consider subsets of property rights and the property regime under which those
rights are held. Ownership is distinguished by a set of operational and collective-
choice rights, where de jure or de facto ownership may include all or only a subset of
these rights (Schlager and Ostrom 1992). Who possesses which rights, and whether
ownership resides with a group or a single residual claimant, have implications for
property valuation and moral claim. The source of these rights and the property regime depends in part on the physical characteristics of the property, and in part on
the cultural characteristics of the community to which the owners/occupants belong.
Which rights are legitimate bases of land ownership (for example, use, occupancy,
and discovery) have long been debated (Watson 2011).

This chapter develops a theory of ownership that argues that a moral claim underlies psychological entitlement, which affects reference levels and can create valuation
disparities. Hypotheses are developed about psychological entitlement that are, in
principle, testable. The basis for testing these hypotheses is the relevance of initial allotments to moral claim. The relevance of initial position challenges the Coase theorem and the claim that the rate of exchange is invariant to whether property is being
acquired or is given up (Tversky and Kahneman 1991).[4] Empirical testing is left to
future experiments or applications with more recent data on real property values;
instead, a survey of the available historical evidence on Native American valuation of
land is presented.[5] The historical record brings into question arguments for valuing
Native American land that do not consider the effect of psychological entitlement.
This work is specifically important because of the complexities of and conflict over
valuing indigenous property and generally important for assessing the integrity and
validity of contingent valuation methods (Altman 2004; Sjaastad and Bromley 1997).

A Theory of Psychological Entitlement

In welfare economics, gains are measured by the WTP for the gain, and losses by
the WTA for the loss (Zerbe and Dively 1994). Gains and losses are measured from

---

[3] Tversky and Kahneman noted that "in accord with a psychological analysis of value, reference levels play a
large role in determining preferences" (1991, 1039). See Zerbe (2001) on psychological reference points.

[4] Attributed to Ronald Coase, the theorem states that in the absence of transaction costs, bargaining will lead to
the socially efficient allocation of resources regardless of which party holds property rights.

[5] We use the terms "Native American," "Indian," and "tribe" as closely as possible to the original source and
apologize for any offense that is taken at a particular or historical usage.

a reference level that defines the status quo. A rich literature examines economic and psychological theories on both the factors that influence the level of WTP or WTA and the regularly observed disparity between the two. Economic models predict that for normal goods, those for which demand increases as income rises, the amount one will pay for ownership is less than the amount one would accept to give it up. That is, WTA is greater than WTP because of income and substitution effects. This gap has also been attributed to uncertainty, signaling, transaction costs, public goods, imprecise preferences, and experimental design (Dubourg, Jones-Lee, and Loomes 1994; Graves 2003; Plott and Zeiler 2005). From the psychological perspective, the disparity has been attributed to an endowment effect (Kahneman, Knetsch, and Thaler 1990; 1991; Tversky and Kahneman 1991), moral responsibility (Boyce et al. 1992), punitiveness (Rachlinski, Croson, and Johnston 2005), and moral outrage (Kahneman and Ritov 1994). For environmental goods, for example, economic models assume that WTP is a proxy for acquisition or monetary value of the resource. Psychological models, however, focus on motives to address social problems or on whether the source of the environmental loss is natural or human induced (Kahneman and Ritov 1994; Ryan and Spash 2010).

Recent debates about economic and psychological hypotheses center on the endowment effect, a reported causal result in which ownership qua ownership influences valuation. Plott and Zeiler (2005) suggest that valuation disparities can be attributed to experimental controls rather than preference effects. Knetsch and Wong (2009) have countered by showing that rather than changing the endowment effect, experimental controls affect the reference level from which valuations are made. In particular, they posit that ownership is not a prerequisite to the endowment effect, but that attachment value may be. That is, the degree to which individuals are attached to an object or property, regardless of their de jure ownership, affects the reference level.

There are at least two issues that challenge conventional economic models in the debate over reference levels and valuation disparities and favor using a value function rather than traditional indifference curves to represent individual choice behavior. The first is loss aversion, where losses matter more than commensurate gains (a value function is steeper in the negative than in the positive domain), and the second is calibrating value to initial endowments, where value is assigned to gains and losses from a reference level rather than just to final assets. A considerable literature exists on the gap between WTP and WTA, but as Knetsch and Wong (2009) point out, less work has been done on the determinants of reference levels (the inflection point where the concavity of the value function changes).

Valuation disparities can arise from a change either in the slope of the value function or in its inflection point that represents a reference level. Therefore, one must distinguish between purely sentimental value and moral claim. Sentimental value increases the value of the good and, hence, the slope of the value function over gains and losses. For example, one may attach sentimental value to a good, increasing its intrinsic value to the individual and the potential sense of loss. Sentimental value can be attached to private or public goods, can grow over time, or can be discovered (for instance, when one learns that a piece of jewelry was owned by one's grandmother, or that an ancestor's grave lies within a piece of land that otherwise had little value). This type of sentiment is not presumed to give a moral claim and is therefore unlikely to affect the reference level from which WTA and WTP are measured. Sentiment can, however, affect valuation disparities through loss aversion or a simple substitution effect and be relevant in property disputes. Goods with limited substitutes in consumption, which can include goods that have sentimental value arising from unique histories or associations, can have WTA-WTP disparities even with modest income effects (Hanemann 1991).

Moral claim underlies psychological entitlement and can affect valuation disparities by changing the reference level from which WTP and WTA are measured. "Although the reference state usually corresponds to the decision maker's current position, it can also be influenced by aspirations, expectations, norms and social comparisons" (Tversky and Kahneman 1991, 1046). Religious, traditional, or otherwise-derived moral claims affect realizations or expectations of property ownership; that is, they affect the reference level from which gains and losses are measured. The psychological reference level may differ from the legal one because of perceived moral claim based on fairness or sovereignty. Fairness and a sense of what is right will affect the expected probability of ownership. If ownership is already presumed, for example, the WTP for a good that one believes is rightly his to begin with may be lower as a result of indignation that one is asked to pay for what ought to be free (Seip and Strand 1992).

Sovereignty presumes ownership over the constitutional and collective-choice rights that allow for self-determination. But the unconventional sovereignty of Native Americans' "domestic dependent nations" status raises competing interpretations of the collection of rights that constitute land ownership. Unlike a traditional economic view where the right to alienate is prime, many Native American tribes have recognized and been granted only exclusion and management rights (Watson 2011). Hence, a discussion of ownership requires investigating the subset of ownership rights at issue.

Subsets of Property Rights

Ownership consists of a bundle of different rights, which are authorized and enforced actions derived from rules (Ostrom 1976). For common-pool resources, Schlager and Ostrom (1992) distinguish between operational-level rights that allow for access and withdrawal of a resource and collective-choice rights that allow for participation in management, exclusion, and alienation decisions. Management is the right to "regulate internal use patterns and transform the resource," exclusion the right to determine who has access and how that right is transferred, and alienation the right to sell or to lease management or exclusion rights over the property (Schlager and Ostrom 1992, 251).[6]

The particular bundle of rights owned can be expected to affect reference levels for gains and losses over a resource differentially. Management, exclusivity, and alienation rights—participating in collective-choice decisions—confer both economic

---

[6] Existence and option value are often considered in tandem with use value for environmental goods (Rachlinski, Croson, and Johnston 2005). Existence value is a moral sentiment that is expected to affect reference points and loss aversion, and hence, valuation disparities.

value through the incentives to make current and long-term resource investments and psychological entitlement through assumed or expected ownership. Changes to collective-choice rights, therefore, can affect valuation disparities through loss aversion and reference levels through moral claim. Conversely, operational-level use rights (withdrawal and access) contribute primarily to economic value through supporting livelihoods and can affect valuation disparities through loss aversion.

Although collective-choice rights are primal in conferring moral claim, the specific rights within that set may vary and may be the underlying source of WTA discrepancies in land disputes. First, there can be disagreement between indigenous and nonindigenous parties over the basic legitimacy of alienation rights over land. Second, legal decisions have conferred differing "limited ownership" and "limited possessor" conceptions of land rights, although both conceptions limit alienation rights (Watson 2011). If alienation rights are not acknowledged, for example, then management and exclusivity rights may be sufficient to confer psychological entitlement. Indeed, some scholars view use and exclusion rights as generally held together.[7] Further, in cases where collective-choice rights have not been established, repeated use can also create ownership expectations.

Private Versus Common Property Regimes

Property rights may be held individually or in common. Private property generally refers to a single individual holding a property right, while common property regimes refer to situations in which multiple individuals share ownership over some set of rights. All rights may be held by the same entity, generally referred to as the owner. The term "proprietor" is used to indicate that all but alienation rights are held, "claimant" when all but alienation and exclusion rights are held, and "authorized user" when only operational-level rights are held (Schlager and Ostrom 1992, 252).

Although cultural predispositions for common or private property are often assumed, at any one time, a single community may hold a multiplicity of regime types, often depending on the property type. C. L. Anderson and Swimmer (1997) document how different tribes simultaneously held multiple access regimes across different kinds of property, depending on the costs of defining, maintaining, and enforcing rights over the property. Tools, weapons, regular food (plants and berries), and shelter, for example, were often private property, while joint food (animals) and undeveloped land had fewer access restrictions. Others have argued that the value of risk spreading in variable environments may outweigh the benefits of specialization and the incentives that come with private property (Allen and Lueck 1998; Rose 1999, citing Ellickson [1993]).

Whether property evolves to be held privately or in common also has an economic basis. Demsetz (1967) argued that private property rights emerge when the benefits, because of changing relative prices, outweigh the costs of establishing and enforcing private property. This argument implicitly assumes common property as a starting point from which a regime switch occurs when the externalities from

---

[7] See Penner (1997) and Merrill and Smith (2007), citing Penner. The authors thank Robert Ellickson for noting this viewpoint.

common property grow to exceed those from private property. Demsetz examined the origin of private rights among the Montagne Indians of the Labrador Peninsula in response to a developing fur trade and the increasing price of furs. This switch from common to private property occurs when the burden of common property resulting from overuse is greater than the transaction costs of maintaining a private property system along with its external effects on tracts of private property.[8] For any society, the point at which this regime change occurs is hypothesized to depend on population growth of the resource users or new markets, changes in the physical condition and availability of the resource, or changes in the technology of production or consumption.

Rights, particularly those held in common, may originate with resource users or community elders and may be de facto rather than de jure (although legal rights may ultimately be based on social mores). Rights are considered de facto if they are not recognized by governmental authorities (Schlager and Ostrom 1992), although they represent another set of cultural constraints that affect behavior (Usher, Tough, and Galois 1992). As Johnsen notes, "While legal constraints consist of coercive sanctions imposed by the state on socially undesirable behavior, ideological constraints consist, at least in part, of social mores backed by social disapproval and ingrained patterns of guilt or shame imposed by the group when behavior is contrary to the prevailing ideology" (1986, 43).

The source of these rights is intimately tied to how they are secured. The integrity of the source stems from an understanding of the benefits of cooperation or the costs of competition and noncompliance. A single leader, a governing body, or a community of users may sanction rights via recognized formal or informal law and may punish defections by force, removal from the group, fines or other economic penalties, or social ridicule.

De facto property systems, especially those that have evolved over time and across users, can be attendant on local physical resource and social conditions and can internalize the costs of monitoring and exclusion among the locals who benefit from the regimes (Schlager and Ostrom 1992). These observations underlie the argument that the endogenous structure of indigenous property rights is efficient, that is, that the governing institutions minimize transaction costs (Johnsen 1986). In the evolution of the common law, for example, justices attempted to adopt existing de facto norms as de jure and thus to avoid creating inefficiencies (Zerbe 2006). There is no consensus, however, that existing property rights systems are necessarily efficient, at least with regard to social welfare, nor is there a clear distinction between de jure and de facto rights. Schlager and Ostrom note that "within a single common-pool resource situation a conglomeration of de jure and de facto property rights may exist which overlap, complement, or even conflict with one another" (1992, 254). Nonetheless, there is support for a Darwinian argument that to survive over time, evolved regimes must move toward efficiency. Certainly, one might expect more complementarities within internally evolved regimes than from an external regime overlaid on an existing one. Hence, replacing one de jure regime with another,

---

[8] Ault and Rutman (1979) well illustrate this pattern.

or a de facto regime with an externally imposed de jure regime, is likely to have economic (and social) consequences.

In addition to the economic argument behind common property and de facto rights, the methods to preserve these regimes can create moral claims. Common property is often intentionally regulated to reduce external effects through complex social norms or rules. "Complex entitlement structures encourage continuity in a common property regime's membership, because outsiders cannot easily buy in and insiders cannot easily sell out . . . This structure provides a background condition of 'repeat play' among group members, often said to be an important factor in solving collective action problems; repeat play helps participants to build up cooperation and trust, and hence it impedes breakdown from internal shirking and cheating" (Rose 1999, 65). To promote cooperative behavior, land may become rooted in spiritual or religious tradition, in which case the value of the land in common can exceed its commercial value; that is, the whole is greater than the sum of the parts.

Hence, replacing rights, either in principle or in practice, with the de jure rights of another authority and altering the balance of private and common ownership has at least three consequences. First, if common ownership is more efficient when all costs and benefits are measured, a forced move to private property, rather than one that evolves naturally, represents a loss in economic value. An externally imposed change from common to private property can be expected to contribute to valuation disparities by imposing an untimely and possibly inefficient economic solution. Second, the complex entitlement structures and religious or social norms that promote cooperative behavior within the commons and support de facto rights intentionally foster moral claim. Historically held common property, therefore, may carry a higher moral entitlement than private property. Finally, a change in any collective-choice right that represents a change in the authority to construct operational-level rules is a change in moral claim and can be expected to affect reference levels.

The Hypotheses of Psychological Entitlement and Evidence from Historical Valuations of Real Property Among Native Americans

A useful definition of ownership must allow for psychological entitlement. Strictly legal definitions of ownership and simple commercial valuations of property are often operationally valid. For example, stock traders, realtors, and multiple daily transactions for standardized items, such as gas and prepackaged foods, do not appear to be hampered by valuation disparities that limit exchange. But for more complex property and infrequently traded property for which repeat market values do not exist, ignoring psychological entitlement that affects reference points and valuation disparities is likely to bias contingent valuation estimates.

Both sentimental value and moral claim can increase the divergence between WTA and WTP, sentimental value from an increase in intrinsic value (with or without loss aversion) and moral claim by affecting reference levels. Testing for reference-level effects involves demonstrating a change in one's baseline sense of ownership, holding constant changes in how the good is valued. In the simple mug example used in Plott and Zeiler (2005) and Knetsch and Wong (2009), testing would entail measuring WTA in cases that varied by expectations of ownership; for example, where moral entitlement had been created (e.g., by indicating that "ownership" meant that the individual had a right to determine who had access to the mug and how those rights could be transferred) relative to cases where the individual was told that he had only a temporary right to use the mug for consumption purposes.

The effect of moral claim on reference levels can be examined in the long-standing debate on the valuation of Native American lands. Although the historical record limits rigorous empirical testing, there are three compelling features of these lands. First, Native American land ownership contained a unique cultural or intrinsic value. Second, lands that were commonly owned by the tribe were split among tribal members through the operation of external laws, and not through self-reorganization by the tribe. Third, the role of alienation rights in land ownership was indeterminate, stemming from both internal and external sources: common tribal disregard of these rights as legitimate or meaningful and a diminishment of these rights accorded to tribes beginning with the 1823 *Johnson v. McIntosh* decision and to individual "owners" of lands held in trust by the U.S. government (Watson 2011).

Our goal is to use the available historical records on collective-choice rights and spiritually significant common property to illustrate that psychological entitlement affects reference levels. The focus is on the sequence of U.S. government actions that changed Native American collective-choice rights and property regimes, the moral claim of tribes, and the relevance of initial allotments as a factor affecting psychological entitlement. Evidence is sought that changes in these rights (1) were exogenously imposed and not evolutionary or in accordance with Native American constitutional choice actions; (2) altered collective-choice rights, not just operational-level rights; and (3) caused an economic and psychological loss through the move from common to private property.

> *Hypothesis 1: Exogenously imposed changes in collective-choice-level rights will affect valuation disparities and reference points, regardless of the property regime or type.*

Changes in property rights for a community that do not originate or accord with indigenous constitutional choice actions and that change collective-choice rights management, exclusivity, and/or alienation will affect psychological entitlement and, hence, reference levels.

Early tribal collective-choice rights appear to have been based on management and exclusion, or the "work-use-ownership" principle. "If you did the work to acquire a thing and used it productively, it belonged to you" (Isakson and Sproles 2008, 66, citing T. L. Anderson and LaCombe [1999]; Zerbe and Anderson 2001). Aboriginal rights in Canada, for example, "included: use by the group itself, and the right to include or exclude others (by determining the composition of the social group); and the right to permit others to utilize lands and resources. Rights to alienate or sell land to outsiders, to destroy or diminish land or resources, or to appropriate lands or resources for private gain without regard to reciprocal obligations, were all excluded" (Usher, Tough, and Galois 1992, 112).

Cronon (1983) suggests that northeastern Indians held usufruct rights, but not alienation rights, and that changes in ecological value drove land use and the trading of rights. He offers additional support for the work-use-ownership principal:

"Beginning with personal goods, ownership rights were clear; people owned what they made with their own hands" (Cronon 1983, 61). Objects recognized as individually owned were usually utilitarian. Resources collected from the land could be individually owned, and tribal boundaries were generally recognized, with a middle ground used for trading. "Insofar as a village 'owned' the land it inhabited, its property was expressed in the sovereignty of the sachem . . . When Roger Williams wrote that 'the Natives are very exact and punctuall in the bounds of their Lands, belonging to this or that Prince or People,' he was refuting those who sought to deny that legitimate Indian property rights existed. But the rights of which he spoke were not ones of individual ownership; rather, they were sovereign rights that defined a village's political and ecological territory" (Cronon 1983, 60).

In a broader study of 40 tribes, C. L. Anderson and Swimmer (1997) found distinct and varied collective-choice rights across tribes. Records indicate, for example, that access restrictions to hunting territories were quite varied across tribes, including four tribes with access restricted to the nuclear family, three tribes with access restricted to the extended family, and thirteen tribes with unrestricted access. This variation may be explained by different degrees of abundance of food or other goods relative to user demands and by the technologies available to the tribes. The value of the potlatch—an exchange system among the Southern Kwakiutl of the Pacific coast, described in detail by Johnsen (1986)—rests on rights of exclusion and alienation. Many of these collective-choice rights were the basis of common property regimes, preserved wealth in important natural assets, and provided a risk-diversifying strategy for livelihoods subject to the variability of nature.

T. L. Anderson and LaCombe (1999) note that the introduction of the horse reduced the need for cooperative hunting behavior. One hypothesized result was a dramatic increase in conflict as each tribe attempted to protect and expand its traditional territories (Isakson and Sproles 2008). T. L. Anderson and LaCombe (1999) observe that externalities associated with common property, were expanding before the treaty era but were not yet sufficient to overcome the difficulties or costs of creating mutually agreeable private land rights, so that common property remained the norm (T. L. Anderson and LaCombe 1999). In the ordinary course of events, there might have been a "natural" evolution toward private property. But with the arrival of Europeans in the late fifteenth century, the evolutionary process from common to private property regimes was abruptly interrupted (Schlager and Ostrom [1992] in general; Demsetz [1967] and Johnsen [1986] for Native American communities in particular).

The evolving relationships between Native Americans and European Americans changed the pace and pattern of rights evolving at the discretion of the resource users. Conflicts between Native Americans and European settlers were initially generally resolved through treaties. At least 322 treaties between the United States and Native American tribes were recorded between 1778 and 1886 (Kappler 1904). "These nation-to-nation agreements with the United States are the source of their [the Native Americans'] legal leverage, and the fount of their moral authority" (Dupris, Hill, and Rodgers 2006, xxi).

The historical record suggests that across the country, at least some of these negotiations were unwelcome, were born of limited choices, and led to a solution that would not have evolved indigenously. R. T. Anderson et al. report on several cases, including an 1824 correspondence from the chiefs of the Creek Nation responding to a request from earlier attempts by federal treaty commissions to persuade the southeastern tribes to exchange their lands for lands west of the Mississippi:

> Brothers, we have among us aged and infirm men and women, and helpless children, who cannot bear the fatigues of even a single day's journey. Shall we, can we, leave them behind us? Shall we desert, in their old age, the parents that fostered us? The answer is in your own hearts. No! Again: we feel an affection of the land in which we were born; we wish our bones to rest by the side of our fathers. Considering, then, our now circumscribed limits, the attachments we have to our native soil, and the assurance which we have that our homes will never be forced from us, so long as the government of the United States shall exist, we must positively decline the proposal of a removal beyond the Mississippi or the sale of any more of our territory. (2010, 50)

Forty years later, in discussions with multiple tribes from the plains, Comanche leader Ten Bears responded to the reservation policy at the 1867 Medicine Lodge treaty negotiations:

> There are things which you have said to me which I do not like. They were not sweet like sugar, but bitter like gourds. You said that you wanted to put us upon a reservation, to build our houses and make us medicine lodges. I do not want them. I was born upon the prairie where the wind blew free and there was nothing to break the light of the sun.
>
> I was born where there were no enclosures and where everything drew a free breath. I want to die there and not within walls. I know every stream and every wood between the Rio Grande and the Arkansas, I have hunted and lived over that country. I lived like my fathers before me, and like them, I lived happily. (R. T. Anderson et al. 2010, 85)

Referring to the three treaties that established 18 reservations in the Northwest, the commissioner of Indian affairs opined that "their sole purpose . . . was to extinguish Indian title to large tracts of land" (Porter 1990, 114). "Treaties are supposed to be the law of the land, but we owned all the land before this" (Larry Campbell, a historian for the Swinomish tribe, in the August 22, 2010 *Seattle Times*). A recent article acknowledged the bitterness about the 1855 signing of the Point Elliot Treaty with a headline: "155 Years Later, Descendants of Treaty Signers Gather to Apologize, Reconcile" (Liu 2010).

Reconciliation, however, may be the exception rather than the norm. The 1863 Treaty of Ruby Valley with the Western Shoshone Indians allowed American settlers operational use rights, but there was no cession of property or waiver of alienation and management rights by the Shoshone, who did not acknowledge the notion of "owning" the land and, therefore, the right to alienation. Today, the United States claims the majority of Western Shoshone property as public or federal lands. A trust established in the Shoshone name as payment for the sale of alienation rights is currently worth $26 million, but the Shoshone continuously refuse to accept this monetary compensation. Says Shoshone Carrie Dann of the $26 million trust: "I have said this a thousand times, I am not taking money for this land. This land has no value, there is no price for it. In Western Shoshone culture, the earth is our mother. We cannot sell it. Taking our land is a not [sic] only a cultural genocide, it is also a spiritual genocide" (Dann 2004).

The argument here is that regardless of whether the treaties were fair or reasonable, they were an abrupt change in course discordant with the path of at least some tribes. Further, treaties represented a change in collective-choice rights and hence altered psychological entitlement. Treaties generally created reservation land that was "owned" by the tribe in common and held in trust by the U.S. government; that is, it was nonalienable by tribes.

Withholding alienation rights has likely weakened the economic development prospects of tribes and tribal land. But the impact on psychological entitlement comes from losing previously held collective-choice rights, which may or may not have included alienation rights. Whether these rights were de jure or de facto, organized, rule-bound trade and exchange mechanisms among tribes make it clear that collective-choice rights existed, were recognized, and were an important part of managing the risks of livelihoods based on the variability of nature and subsistence living (Johnsen 1986). Indians could and did sell operational rights to European settlers, but they retained ownership of certain activities and management or exclusion rights, although Europeans probably misunderstood, whether unintentionally or intentionally, what the treaties entitled them to (Cronon 1983). "While it is a convenient aside that the tribe's land provides the raw materials for their material welfare, it is not central to their ownership and only constitutes a part of it. Often, indigenous people are not concerned about exclusive occupancy, despite being fiercely jealous of having the land recognized as their property. There is something beyond occupation and use rights that constitutes a core value in indigenous ownership. This means that the alienation of rights pertaining to land cannot be fully evaluated using material/commercial equivalencies" (Small and Sheehan 2008, 110).

Treaties, which focused on operational-level rights and economic valuation, were working from a reference point that failed to recognize the psychological entitlement many Native Americans held over these lands and the way "ownership and sovereignty among Indian peoples could shade into each other in a way Europeans had trouble understanding" (Cronon 1983, 58–59). This is a primary way in which culture affects moral sentiments. Citing Myers and Shah (2004), Small and Sheehan note the following methodological problem with valuing indigenous land: "The interpretation of indigenous interests in land as a set of use rights misses the fundamental issue in the indigenous understanding of ownership" (2008, 116). The same holds for a narrow economic interpretation of collective-choice rights as dependent only on exercising alienation rights.

Before the treaties, tribes held moral claims and exercised collective-choice rights over land, with or without alienation rights. There is sufficient support for psychological entitlement in cases of indigenous valuation of real property to render untenable presumptions that the allocation of rights and initial allotments are irrelevant to exchange.

Hypothesis 2: Exogenously imposed changes from common property to private property regimes will affect valuation disparities and reference points.

Common property with spiritual value and historically subject to complex entitlement structures, regardless of the underlying economic rationale, will have a greater whole value than the economic sum of its parts. Moral claim is present because of shared ownership of rights, regardless of whether changes are to operational-level or collective-choice-level rights.

The common view is that before contact with Europeans, tribes treated land as a common resource (Isakson and Sproles 2008). From around 1778, when records and written treaties became more common, through the period of the Indian Removal Act of 1830,[9] "Native Americans held, at best, a collective ownership concept of land, if they held any concept of land ownership at all" (Isakson and Sproles 2008, 69).

The General Allotment Act of 1887 (commonly referred to as the Dawes Act) altered the balance of commonly versus privately held land by assigning allotments of reservation land to individual tribal members (e.g., 160 acres to each family head, 80 acres to a single person under 18). "Allotment was a radical departure from the Indian's concept of land tenure. Land was not something which could be alienated or exchanged for something else. Although there were various concepts of land tenure and land use, to the Indian the land was a whole and individually-owned parcels were unknown" (Porter 1990, 116, citing Sutton [1975]).

The Dawes Act led to the much-criticized fractional estates by inheritance rules and restrictions on the rights of alienation, because allotment land was held in trust (Shoemaker 2003). "Because the land was held in trust by the U.S. Government, the heirs could not simply sell the land, not even to their tribe, and divide up the proceeds. As the heirs died, additional fractionalization of the ownership rights occurred"; further, "The fractionalization of allotment lands makes it extremely difficult for Native Americans to pool together their individual interest to the benefit of the tribe or others who might be interested in developing the land" (Isakson and Sproles 2008, 70).

In addition to the imposed inefficiencies of the Dawes Act's alienation rules, economic loss stems from unrecognized sentimental value and the relative efficiency of Indian de jure and de facto common property rights. Citing Myers and Shah (2004), Small and Sheehan note: "The valuation of indigenous interests on the basis of use rights ignores the fundamental and categorically distinct cultural value of land to indigenous peoples and is impossible to render equivalence in commercial terms" (2008, 116). The efficiency of common property regimes, argued by Schlager and Ostrom (1992) and illustrated for tribes in the Northwest by Johnsen (1986) and in the Northeast by Demsetz (1967), supports the contention that switching to a nonevolutionary property rights regime could result in a less optimal economic arrangement.

---

[9] The Indian Removal Act empowered the president to negotiate for land exchanges with Native Americans and make payments for improvements on the land; it ended up enabling the forced removal of some tribes (Isakson and Sproles 2008).

Psychological entitlement arose through the complex entitlement structures, often rooted in spiritual and religious traditions, of common property to support cooperative behavior on these common lands. Norms included status systems, which are argued to have supported social sanctions that restricted individual accumulation (Cronon 1983). "Indigenous people do not view land as individual property per se but rather as a part of an ethical/spiritual/legal matrix of rights, obligations, and community relationships" (Small and Sheehan 2008, 106).

Historians suggest that among many pre–Columbian Native American, cooperation was a necessary condition for survival (T. L. Anderson and LaCombe 1999).

> The aboriginal management system, operated through consensus by the local harvesting group, rested on communal property arrangements. Management and production were not separate functions, although leadership and authority within the group were based on knowledge, experience, and their effective use. Spiritual values and ceremonial activities also helped define appropriate and necessary modes of behavior in harvesting resources. Although these practices did not operate in the paradigm or manner of western "scientific" management, they served to regulate access to resources. It was these cultural constraints on behavior, rather than "natural" predator-prey relationships, that normally guarded against resource depletion. (Usher, Tough, and Galois 1992, 112)

> American Indian beliefs often assert the full integration of the spiritual with the physical, and the sacredness and interrelatedness of all creation. Thus, while some American Indian tribes or individuals are quite comfortable with putting dollar values on land and water resources, many other tribes or individuals find this highly offensive. (Hammer 2002, 3)

> While usage of indigenous land may have a discernible rental value, it may not necessarily capitalize into a fair market price for alienation. This is because indigenous people see their relationship to the land as more than a commercial interest, even if they traditionally rely on their land for material support. In this respect, indigenous land is more like a body part than a conventional external discretionary possession. Part of a body part's value may be expressed in terms of material utility, such as a pianist's fingers, but few would deny that one's fingers are not worth more to a person than their potential contribution to paid work. This means that there also exists a separate, metaphysically distinct, category of value for which a fair market value cannot be established. (Small and Sheehan 2008, 114)

The goal of these structures was to promote cooperative behavior. Hence, the intentional result was the creation of shared moral entitlement and a value of the land as a whole that was greater than the economic sum of its parts.

Incomplete consideration of psychological entitlement is illustrated in a detailed account of the 1997 Grass Mountain/Huckleberry Divide Trail Land exchange between the U.S. Forest Service and Weyerhaeuser. The exchange involved selling land to the logging company that had spiritual and economic value to the Muckleshoot tribe. "In addition to the physical sustenance provided by these extra-reservation places that originally comprised their traditional territory, the Muckleshoot's use of their traditional homelands remained part of 'an integrated system . . . all within a spiritual whole'" (Hanson and Panagia 2002, 177). Moreover, "The Muckleshoot Tribe was omitted from the original conveyance of the land, although their presence had long been part of the area, and non-Indian anthropological, historical, and settler accounts had long documented this presence" (Hanson and Panagia 2002, 171). Hanson and Panagia refer to the case as a "legalistic" dismissal of the psychological entitlement of the Muckleshoot to historically important sections of the mountain and trail, a "bureaucratic dispossession" that prompted more than 20 years of effort by the tribe to preserve the trail, now with much greater spiritual than economic value, from further damage (2002, 170).

The 1934 Indian Reorganization Act ended the allotment process and restored tribal ownership in common of the remaining surplus lands. The 1983 Indian Land Consolidation Act makes it possible for tribes to consolidate fractional interests by purchasing them, but the lands must be held in trust by the U.S. government or be owned collectively by the tribe. These acts may prevent further erosion of economic value, but the effect on psychological entitlement is perhaps more interesting. Like the Western Shoshone, eight Sioux tribes hold over $900 million in federal trusts but refuse to accept monetary compensation for land that a 1980 court case determined to be illegally acquired by the United States. Sovereignty requires land in common. Hence, incentives to continue social and other tribal norms supporting land in common are necessary to maintain sovereignty, which is itself necessary to gain or reestablish treaty rights.

For Native Americans, the right to land has been in large part a fight for sovereignty, necessary for cultural survival and the gains from treaties. As Sarah Krakoff notes, "To put it bluntly, without sovereign American Indian tribes, there would be no American Indians" (2006, 804).[10] The relationship among sovereignty, land, and treaty rights may explain some of the Native American attitude and response toward land treaty rights.[11] This suggests a subsidiary hypothesis that the holding of rights in common was necessary for sovereignty, although the collective-choice rights normally associated with sovereignty remain in debate.

Debates over the source of valuation disparities are, in some cases, debates over the meaning of ownership. We have theorized that for property or circumstances that create moral claim and change expectations of ownership, psychological entitlement will differ from legal ownership and change the points from which gains and losses are measured. Treaties represented an exogenously imposed change in collective-choice rights, and this represented a loss of psychological entitlement, as

---

[10] See also Riley (2005); *Lyng v. Northwest Indian Cemetery Protective Association*, 485 U.S. 439, 108 S. Ct 1319 (1988).

[11] Rights to fisheries show a pattern of sentiment similar to those for common land. In the case of fisheries, the Muckleshoot said that money could never compensate for the loss of the fisheries, and when they were forced to accept it, they interpreted the payments as representing temporary intrusions on their fishing properties, not permanent repeal (Dupris, Hill, and Rodgers 2006). "Through it all . . . the Tribes have never surrendered the conviction that they had solved the problem of salmon management" (Dupris, Hill, and Rodgers 2006, xxii). To what extent these claims represent expediency is not easily determined, if at all. But whatever their source, there can be no doubt of their psychological validity.

well as an economic loss, for American Indians. Additionally, the untimely transitions from common to private property eroded psychological and possibly economic value through changes in the complexity of the structures that promote cooperative behavior.

Comparing valuation disparities that arise between coerced and evolutionary changes in collective choice level rights for additional cases of indigenous peoples with moral claim to property would be helpful for testing our hypotheses. Likewise, comparing buying and selling prices for commonly and privately held land exchanged among tribal members, and between Native and non-Native Americans, could test for valuation disparities according to the historical moral claim over the land exchanged, independent of its current commercial value. Even absent this empirical evidence, however, the historical record on Native American land valuation suggests that psychological entitlement is credible.

Acknowledgments

We would like to thank Catherine Kilbane Gockel, Nevena Lalic, Tyler Scott, Kiana Scott, and Katie Stahley for valuable research help, and Robert Anderson for useful guidance and comments.

Appendix

In cases where legal rights are uncertain, the welfare economics of efficient allocation would assign the right to that party which valued it most. Where the value is simply the commercial value, WTP and WTA for any one party would be the same at a given level of information and expertise. Commercial value is the value of a right where no emotional or reference point is attached (e.g., a retail seller would regard his goods without attachment). The values would differ among parties only due to differences in their discount rates and expertise. The policy solution for property of purely commercial value then is to auction the right as its efficient allocation is governed solely by the WTP.

Where there is a divergence between the WTP and the WTA, the matter is different. For simplicity, suppose that there are two parties, A and B. Each party has a sense of psychological ownership with respect to some property. This would represent an incompletely defined reference point. Let P_a and P_b represent the subjective sense (probability or extent to which ownership is felt) of psychological ownership by A and B. When expectations of ownership are less than 100 percent, both WTP and WTA enter into the evaluation. On welfare economic grounds, the right goes to A when

$$\text{WTP}_a(1-P_a)+\text{WTA}_a(P_a) > \text{WTP}_b(1-P_b)+\text{WTA}_b(P_b), \tag{1}$$

that is, when the value to A is greater than the value to B, weighing WTP and WTA, respectively, by the probabilities of no psychological ownership and ownership. Equation (1) can be manipulated to give

$$\text{WTP}_a+P_a(\text{WTA}_a-\text{WTP}_a) > \text{WTP}_b+P_b(\text{WTA}_b-\text{WTP}_b). \tag{2}$$

In equation (2), the size of the difference between WTA and WTP (the quantities in parentheses) arise, in part, from the strength of the moral divergence between what one would pay for the right and one's psychological claim to it. The difference represents a "willingness to fight" for one's reasonable expectations.

Suppose that for land of purely commercial value for B, A has some sense of psychological ownership, but B has none. A's divergence, however, results from income, substitution, loss-aversion, and endowment effects associated with sense of ownership. In this case, there is no difference between B's WTP and WTA. The requirement for A's ownership is then

$$WTP_a(1 - P_a) + WTA_a(P_a) > WTP_b. \tag{3}$$

If A and B have an equal WTP, then A's value will be higher than B's because $WTA_a > WTP_b$, so the left-hand side of equation (2) will be greater than the right-hand side.

Of course, in many cases of interest, the party with the higher WTA may have the lower WTP. For example, an environmental group may be able to pay little to buy the environmental preservation of trees but would be unwilling to sell it if it owned it. A commercial timber company, however, would attach a purely commercial value to the trees. For an actual example of such a situation, see the Head Waters Grove case in Zerbe (2001).

The social gain is not invariant under who is initially given the right when both parties have loss aversion with respect to psychological ownership. This is a nontraditional exception to Coase's theorem. It is generally held from Coase's theorem that if transaction costs are zero, economic efficiency is invariant under the initial assignment of rights, income effects aside. The owner will sell his right to anyone to whom it is worth more. The concept runs into difficulty when it is applied to goods with a meaningful difference between WTA and WTP. Consider two parties A and B and property that is a normal good and is held by the government, which will distribute it, but otherwise does not value it. Parties A and B both wish to obtain the right. The transaction costs of a sale are represented by T. When $T > 0$, efficiency considerations clearly suggest giving the good to A because this either saves transaction costs or prevents the good from remaining with B, who has the lower valuation. Where $T = 0$, the right will also end up with A as long as $WTP_a > WTA_b$, which indicates also that $WTA_a > WTP_b$, so that there is no sale if A is given the right.

When the good has only commercial value for B, so that $WTA_b = WTP_b$, there is no efficiency loss when the good is given to B. The social gain is $WTP_a - (WTA_b - WTP_b)$. This is less than the gain of WTP_a when A is given the initial right.

However, the social gain can be greater if the right is given to A rather than B when B has psychological expectations that create a divergence between WTA_b and WTP_b. B's gain from the initial right is WTP_b. A will buy it if $WTP_a > WTA_b$. Because B loses more from the sale than he initially gained, there is a social loss. Then, the social value is just WTP_a. This results in a social loss of WTA_b.

One might argue that B would always regard himself as an intermediary in a Coasean world in which zero transaction costs imply perfect information. In the real world, however, it serves to increase the argument for giving the good to A initially.

For the purposes of this chapter, the important effect occurs when A has a greater WTA but a lower WTP than B. In this case, social value is greater when the new right is initially given to A. Native Americans' sense of psychological ownership of land based both on first-claimant grounds and on a sense of moral right would suggest they should have been given the initial right, had they had standing.

REFERENCES

Allen, Douglas W., and Dean Lueck. 1998. The nature of the farm. *Journal of Law and Economics* 41(2):343–386.

Altman, Jon C. 2004. Economic development and indigenous Australia: Contestations over property, institutions and ideology. *Australian Journal of Agricultural and Resource Economics* 48(3):513–534.

Anderson, C. Leigh, and Eugene Swimmer. 1997. Some empirical evidence on property rights of first peoples. *Journal of Economic Behavior and Organization* 33(1):1–22.

Anderson, Robert T., Bethany Berger, Philip P. Frickey, and Sarah Krakoff. 2010. *American Indian law: Cases and commentary*. St. Paul, MN: Thomson Reuters/West.

Anderson, Terry L., and Steven LaCombe. 1999. Institutional change in the Indian horse culture. In *The other side of the frontier: Economic explorations into Native American history*, ed. Linda Barrington, 103. Boulder, CO: Westview Press.

Ault, David E., and Gilbert L. Rutman. 1979. The development of individual rights to property in tribal Africa. *Journal of Law and Economics* 22(1):163–182.

Boyce, Rebecca R., Thomas C. Brown, Gary H. McClelland, George L. Peterson, and William D. Schulze. 1992. An experimental examination of intrinsic values as a source of the WTA-WTP disparity. *American Economic Review* 82(5):1366–1373.

Cronon, William. 1983. *Changes in the land: Indians, colonists, and the ecology of New England*. New York: Hill and Wang.

Dann, Carrie. 2004. Statement on George W. Bush signing House Resolution 884, July 7, 2004. Western Shoshone Defense Project. http://www.h-o-m-e.org/Shoshone/Shoshone%20Docs/Distribution.Dann.htm.

Demsetz, Harold. 1967. Toward a theory of property rights. *American Economic Review* 57:347–359.

Dubourg, W. R., Michael W. Jones-Lee, and Graham Loomes. 1994. Imprecise preferences and the WTP-WTA disparity. *Journal of Risk and Uncertainty* 9(2):115–133.

Dupris, Joseph C., Kathleen S. Hill, and William H. Rodgers. 2006. *The Si'lailo way: Indians, salmon, and law on the Columbia River*. Durham, NC: Carolina Academic Press.

Ellickson, Robert C. 1993. Property in land. *Yale Law Journal* 102:1315–1400.

Fishel, Julie Ann. 2006/2007. United States called to task on indigenous rights: The Western Shoshone struggle and success at the international level. Symposium: Lands, Liberties, and Legacies: Indigenous Peoples and International Law. *American Indian Law Review* 31(2):619–650.

Graves, Philip E. 2003. The simple analytics of the WTA-WTP disparity for public goods. Working Paper. Boulder: University of Colorado. http://spot.colorado.edu/%7Egravesp/WTA-WTPDisparity.PDF.

Hammer, Miriam Z. 2002. *Valuation of American Indian land and water resources: A guidebook*. U.S. Bureau of Reclamation. http://www.usbr.gov/pmts/economics/reports/Valuation%20of%20Indian%20Resources%20Land%20and%20Water%20Resources.pdf.

Hanemann, William M. 1991. Willingness to pay and willingness to accept: How much can they differ? *American Economic Review* 81(3):635–647.

Hanson, Randel, and Giancarlo Panagia. 2002. Acts of bureaucratic dispossession: The Huckleberry land exchange, the Muckleshoot Indian tribe, and rational(ized) forms of contemporary appropriation. *Great Plains Natural Resources Journal* 7(1):169–203.

Isakson, Hans R., and Shauntreis Sproles. 2008. A brief history of Native American land ownership. *Indigenous Peoples and Real Estate Valuation* 10(1–13):63–76.

Johnsen, D. Bruce. 1986. The formation and protection of property rights among the Southern Kwakiutl Indians. *Journal of Legal Studies* 15(1):41–67.

Kahneman, Daniel, Jack L. Knetsch, and Richard H. Thaler. 1990. Experimental tests of the endowment effect and the Coase theorem. *Journal of Political Economy* 98(6):1325–1348.

———. 1991. Anomalies: The endowment effect, loss aversion, and status quo bias. *Journal of Economic Perspectives* 5(1):193–206.

Kahneman, Daniel, and Ilana Ritov. 1994. Determinants of stated willingness to pay for public goods: A study in the headline method. *Journal of Risk and Uncertainty* 9(1):5–37.

Kappler, Charles J. 1904. *Indian affairs: Laws and treaties*. Washington, DC: U.S. Government Printing Office.

Knetsch, Jack L., and Wei-Kang Wong. 2009. The endowment effect and the reference state: Evidence and manipulations. *Journal of Economic Behavior and Organization* 71(2):407–413.

Krakoff, Sarah. 2006. The virtues and vices of sovereignty. *Connecticut Law Review* 38:797–812.

Liu, Marian. 2010. 155 years later, descendants of treaty signers gather to apologize, reconcile. *Seattle Times*, August 22.

Mary and Carrie Dann v. United States, Case 11.140, Report No. 75/02, Inter-Am. C.H.R., Doc. 5 rev. 1 at 860 2002. University of Minnesota Human Rights Library. http://www1.umn.edu/humanrts/cases/75-02a.html.

Merrill, Thomas W., and Henry E. Smith. 2007. The morality of property. *William and Mary Law Review* 48:1849. http://scholarship.law.wm.edu/wmlr/vol48/iss5/15.

Myers, Matthew S., and Krishn Shah. 2004. Why native lands are worth less than freehold. Paper presented at the Pacific Rim Real Estate Society International Conference, Bangkok.

Ostrom, Vincent. 1976. John R. Commons's foundations for policy analysis. *Journal of Economic Issues* 10(4):839–857.

Penner, James E. 1997. *The idea of property in law*. Oxford: Clarendon Press.

Plott, Charles R., and Katherine Zeiler. 2005. The willingness to pay–willingness to accept gap, the endowment effect, subject misconceptions, and experimental procedures for eliciting valuations. *American Economic Review* 95(3):530–545.

Porter, Frank W. 1990. In search of recognition: Federal Indian policy and the landless tribes of western Washington. *American Indian Quarterly* 14(2):113–132.

Rachlinski, Jeffery, Rachel Croson, and Jason Johnston. 2005. Punitiveness as an explanation of the WTA-WTP discrepancy in contingent valuation: Theory and evidence. Working Paper. Philadelphia: University of Pennsylvania. http://cbees.utdallas.edu/papers/07-17.pdf.

Riley, Angela R. 2005. Straight stealing: Towards an indigenous system of cultural property protection. *Washington Law Review* 80:69–164.

Rolfe, John, and Jill Windle. 2003. Valuing the protection of aboriginal cultural heritage sites. *Economic Record* 79(June):s85–s95.

Rose, Carol M. 1999. Expanding the choices for the global commons: Comparing newfangled tradable allowance schemes to old-fashioned common property regimes. *Duke Environmental Law and Policy Forum* 10(51):45–65.

Ryan, Anthony M., and Clive L. Spash. 2010. Testing Kahneman's attitudinal WTP hypothesis. http://mpra.ub.uni-muenchen.de/22468/.

Schlager, Edella, and Elinor Ostrom. 1992. Property-rights regimes and natural resources: A conceptual analysis. *Land Economics* 68(3):249–262.

Seip, Kalle, and Jon Strand. 1992. Willingness to pay for environmental goods in Norway: A contingent valuation study with real payment. *Environmental and Resource Economics* 2(1):91–106.

Shoemaker, Jessica A. 2003. Like snow in the spring time: Allotment, fractionation, and the Indian land tenure problem. *Wisconsin Law Review* 5:729–788.

Simons, Robert A., Rachel Malmgren, and Garrick Small. 2008. *Indigenous peoples and real estate valuation*. New York: Springer.

Sjaastad, Espen, and Daniel W. Bromley. 1997. Indigenous land rights in sub-Saharan Africa: Appropriation, security and investment demand. *World Development* 25(4):549–562.

Small, Garrick, and John Sheehan. 2008. The metaphysics of indigenous ownership: Why indigenous ownership is incomparable to Western conceptions of property value. *Indigenous Peoples and Real Estate Valuation* 10(1–13):103–120.

Snyder, Robert, Daniel Williams, and George Peterson. 2003. Culture loss and sense of place in resource valuation: Economics, anthropology, and indigenous cultures. In *Indigenous people: Resource management and global rights*, eds. S. Jentoft, H. Mindle, and R. Nilson, 107–123. Delft, Netherlands: Eburon Publishers.

Sutton, Imre. 1975. *Indian land tenure: Bibliographical essay and guide to the literature.* New York: Clearwater.

Tversky, Amos, and Daniel Kahneman. 1991. Loss aversion in riskless choice: A reference-dependent model. *Quarterly Journal of Economics* 106(4):1039–1061.

Usher, Peter J., Frank J. Tough, and Robert M. Galois. 1992. Reclaiming the land: Aboriginal title, treaty rights and land claims in Canada. *Applied Geography* 12:109–132.

Watson, Blake A. 2011. The impact of the American doctrine of discovery on native land rights in Australia, Canada, and New Zealand. *Seattle University Law Review* 34:507–551.

Zerbe, Richard O. 2001. *Economic efficiency in law and economics.* Northampton, MA: Edward Elgar.

———. 2006. Justice and the evolution of the common law. *Journal of Law, Economics and Policy* 3(1):81–122.

Zerbe, Richard O., and C. Leigh Anderson. 2001. Culture and fairness in the development of institutions in the California gold fields. *Journal of Economic History* 61(1):114–143.

Zerbe, Richard O., and Dwight Dively. 1994. *Benefit-cost analysis in theory and practice.* New York: HarperCollins College Publishers.

Commentary

JOHN A. BADEN

Anderson and Zerbe's chapter deals substantially with the "endowment effect" arising from a sense of ownership. This effect is a reported causal result in which ownership qua ownership influences valuation; the reference level is that set of perceived rights from which one measures gains and losses. They also observe that the degree to which individuals are attached to an object or property, regardless of their de jure ownership, affects the reference level. They then note that the sense of ownership is a function of culture, physical characteristics, and use patterns.

They conclude their chapter with a discussion of the alienation of tribal lands in the Pacific Northwest as a result of treaties signed in the mid-1800s. They argue that these treaties marked an abrupt change in course discordant with the path of at least some tribes. Further, the treaties represented a change in collective-choice rights and hence altered psychological entitlement. A key variable is whether the change is exogenously imposed. When it is imposed from the outside, it represents a loss of psychological entitlement, as well as an economic loss, regardless of the property type or regime.

I believe that Anderson and Zerbe's perspective can alert us to consequences of changes in rights, especially those that are imposed by higher authority. When rights to land or valuable resources that flow from it are unclear and changing, conflict naturally follows.

A sense of ownership can come from traditional uses that engender psychological entitlement. Anderson and Zerbe apply this sense of ownership in reference to lands taken from various American tribes. Their framework offers insights regarding two self-identified tribes in the states surrounding Yellowstone Park: Montana, Wyoming, and Idaho. These are the Greens and the "cowboys." These two groups are contending for management of and traditional rights in the greater Yellowstone area, some 20 million acres.

From the Civil War until Earth Day, the states surrounding Yellowstone had a coherent culture, politics, and economy. The glue holding this culture together was the use of natural resources. Water was to be dammed for mines and irrigation, trees were to be cut for lumber, and grass was to be grazed by livestock. Big game existed to be enjoyed and hunted. Many hunters and the outfitting industry organized their lives around fall hunting.

Roughly half of this land is in federal and state ownership. The public lands not in parks were traditionally available for livestock grazing and big-game hunting. For every person holding grazing permits on these public lands, there were thousands holding a big-game license. Together, the ranching and hunting interests made a powerful and vocal constituency.

The U. S. Biological Survey killed the last wolf in Yellowstone Park in 1927. A few years after Earth Day in 1970, a few individuals began studying the reintroduction of wolves to Yellowstone Park; others began advocating it. In 1994 the environmental impact statement (EIS) on wolf reintroduction generated more than 150,000 comments. The Wyoming Farm Bureau protested with a lawsuit, and the Idaho state government opposed wolves' return.

In a move that demonstrated a shift in control, in 1995, 66 Canadian wolves were released in Yellowstone Park. The population has since expanded by a factor of 15 to 25, and the wolves' range has grown far beyond the park's boundaries. In Yellowstone Park, elk constitue up to nine-tenths of the winter diet of wolves, some 22 ungulates per wolf annually, twice the level predicted by the EIS.

During the 2004 hunting season, the number of elk permits issued by Montana Fish Wildlife and Parks for the hunting districts contiguous to Yellowstone Park dropped by 50 percent. The next year it went down to 100, less than one-twentieth the number issued in 1995. Some big-game outfitters claim that their business, often marginal at best, has been devastated by wolves.

Wolves also kill some livestock. One family just north of Dillon, Montana, lost 121 sheep one night. However, death is not the only cost of wolf predation. There is a loss of grazing because cows avoid areas frequented by wolves. Successful pregnancy rates are reputed to be lower, and stress leads to weight loss. There is also a huge psychological and monitoring cost accompanying predation.

Although wolves account for only a low percentage of total livestock losses, the cultural effect is huge, a bright marker of the transfer of control from the cowboys to the Greens. In terms of population, wolf reintroduction has been a great success. It represents a shift of control from one "tribe" to another.

Anderson and Zerbe's chapter concludes with the observation that for property or circumstances that create moral claim and change expectations of ownership, psychological entitlement will differ from legal ownership and will change reference levels. Exogenously imposed changes can result in a loss of psychological entitlement, as well as an economic loss. The conflict so evident in impassioned letters to the editor regarding wolf reintroduction in the greater Yellowstone area supports these insights.

Playing by Different Rules?

Property Rights in Land and Water

RICHARD A. EPSTEIN

Property Regimes for Land and Water

One of the ancient philosophical conceits about the nature of the universe was that it was divided into three separate elements: air, water, and land. As an explanation of elementary particles, this antique tripartite division is an arid intellectual curiosity. But, ironically, in dealing with the organization of property rights systems, this early classification system is right on the mark. The focus of this chapter is not primarily air rights of all kinds and descriptions, although the topic does come up.[1] Instead, it deals systematically with the differences and similarities that arise in forming property rights systems in both land and water.

One point common to the two types of systems is that each works in two dimensions. One dimension asks about the assignment of property rights to two or more private parties. The second dimension deals with the relationship of all private right holders, either individually or in groups, to the state. Viewed globally, these cases are concerned with the taking or regulation of land, including land use, which the government may do only if it provides an owner with just compensation for any property interest that is eliminated or reduced. The usual prism through which this topic is raised in the United States is the takings clause, "[N]or shall private property be taken for public use, without just compensation" (U.S. Constitution, Fifth Amendment), and the allied doctrines that develop under analogous state constitutional provisions.

On the first issue, dealing with private disputes, the uniform rule with respect to both land and water starts with an assumption of parity of entitlements among all participants in the original position. Although the remedial side of the question will not be stressed here, the implicit assumption is that both damages and injunctions are available to provide redress for past grievances and protection against future ones, all in an effort to steer the realignment of property rights through voluntary transactions. In contrast, that assumption (to some extent) cannot be fully realized in any takings context because, by definition, the government exercises a set of unique powers in relationship to all private parties. In these situations, once the public use

---

[1] For a discussion of these issues in connection with the Clean Air Act, see Epstein (2010).

requirement is satisfied, as it typically is, injunctive relief is off the table so long as the government is prepared to pay just compensation. These second-order questions are again put to one side.

This chapter addresses the key challenge of outlining the main features of a private and public system of law with respect to both land and water. The feel, texture, and characteristics of these two resources differ in ways that tend to create large differences in the legal regimes that govern them. The dividing line between land and water has huge staying power in this area, but it is by no means the sole relevant categorical division. As Daniel Cole and Elinor Ostrom (2010) have stressed (see chapter 2 of this volume), differences in property rights within each of these broad categories are at least as important as the similarities. A sensible conception of the much-criticized notion of natural law helps inform analysis of the many doctrines of private and public law that are discussed in this chapter.

The Utilitarian Origins of Natural Law

In dealing with the broad set of issues raised in this chapter, it is important to note something about the much-vexed relationship between natural law and the consequentialist approach.[2] Many writers think that the use of natural law arguments is a form of mumbo jumbo that is best excluded from political analysis. Itai Sened, for example, offers an explanation of how property rights evolve within a set of political institutions by consciously dismissing the role of natural law in the analysis: "The essence of any social contract should no longer be understood as a delegation of authority by private individuals to a central entity so that this entity becomes the guardian of their 'natural' rights. On the contrary, the foundation of any social contract is based on the willingness of government officials to grant individual rights to their constituents in return for political and economic support" (Sened 1997, 7). Without a doubt, there is some grim truth to this proposition. A system of rent control, for example, arises from the combined efforts of tenants to force price controls on landlords for their own short-term benefits. This system exactly fits this definition of "individual rights" because it gives full sway to the political pressures that generate this system of wealth transfer from tenants to landlords. All sorts of tax subsidies can be explained in exactly the same fashion. But the purpose here is not to explain how legislation can ruin a perfectly good system of common-law property rights, but to offer some normative justification of the particular types of property rights that serve human interests well.

In dealing with this question, one can fault the natural laws of classical times for their inability to offer the best functional explanations for the rules that they championed, but they cannot accurately be accused of taking a naïve view of property rights that assumed that nature itself offered an account of property rights. Nor did they make any assumption that any set of property rights established by the political system through interest-group politics was entitled to normative respect. Rather, their general orientation was to try to figure out what set of rules was conducive to

---

[2] For development of these themes, see Epstein (1989; 2000).

bringing out the best in human nature by avoiding the inconveniences that were routinely found in a state of nature. Although they did not have a strong theory on how this was to be measured, natural law placed great confidence in those customary institutions that grew up through long use, many of which were employed as building blocks by wise sovereigns who wanted to retain the loyalty of their subjects by protecting these ancient rights.

Indeed, writers like Sened miss the key elements of the classical tradition by treating David Hume, for example, as though he disregarded the natural rights tradition by insisting that individual property "rights are not deriv'd from nature but from *artifice*," or that property rights were human "conventions" that "acquire force by . . . our repeated experience of the inconveniences of transgressing it" (Hume 1739–1740, 489, 490). The sole force of this passage was to show that people learn the utility of property rights by seeing what happens when the traditional rules are disregarded. That account differs in key respects from the positivist notions that the proper content of property rights should be determined solely by reference to the political struggles that generate this or that configuration of property rights. For Hume, the major task was to justify the traditional rules of property by linking these artifices and conventions to human well-being. His effort was to give a strong account of justice, not to follow out the grisly consequences of interest-group politics: "Our property is nothing but those goods, whose constant possession is establish'd by the laws of society; that is, by the laws of justice . . . A man's property is some object related to him. This relation is not natural, but moral, and founded on justice" (Hume 1739–1740, 491).

Hume's basic point is that no one can run a good society if the property of one is subject to constant expropriation by others. The wisdom of this rule is confirmed by long experience. He may use the terms "artifice" and "convention" in opposition to that of "natural law," but his own theory is no paean to public choice theory; it is at every point heavily dependent for its normative foundations on Roman law. Indeed, as a Scotsman trained in Roman law, he extensively discusses the standard rules by which property is acquired, dealing in success with "Occupation, Prescription, Accession, and Succession," praising at one point the "remarkable subtilty of the *Roman* law," and quoting thereafter from Justinian's *Institutes* on that topic (Hume 1787, 514, 512 n.2 [beginning on 509]). His major intellectual effort is to prove the importance of the "stability of possession" a phrase that he uses on multiple occasions (e.g., Hume [1787], 490, 503, 514, 515, 567), and one that comes directly from the Roman tradition on this problem. It is all too easy to be misled by his use of the terms "artifice" and "convention." These terms are not meant to repudiate the property conceptions of the Roman lawyers working in the natural law tradition. They are meant only to establish a firmer foundation for these rules by showing how they can be justified by their consequences—a position that no natural lawyer of the time would have categorically rejected. This is evidenced by Blackstone's justification of property, written some years later, which also relies on a mix of natural law and consequentialist arguments, where again the central challenge is to explain why a person who took property at one moment is entitled to retain possession even when he relinquishes immediate physical possession:

Thus the ground was in common, and no part of it was the permanent property of any man in particular; yet whoever was in the occupation of any determinate spot of it, for rest, for shade, or the like, acquired for the time a sort of ownership, from which it would have been unjust, and contrary to the law of nature, to have driven him by force; but the instant that he quitted the use or occupation of it, another might seize it without injustice . . . But when mankind increased in number, craft, and ambition, it became necessary to entertain conceptions of more permanent dominion; and to appropriate to individuals not the immediate *use* only, but the very *substance* of the thing to be used. Otherwise innumerable tumults must have arisen. (Blackstone 1765–1769, 2:3–4)

Jeremy Bentham relied on just this type of example to buttress his ostensible critique of natural law. But his differences with his archenemy Blackstone are at root terminological. On matters of substance, he adopts Blackstone's position root and branch. His most famous aphorism reads, misleadingly, like a tribute to positivist accounts of property rights: "Property and law are born together, and die together. Before laws were made there was no property; take away laws and property ceases" (Bentham 1882 [1802], 113). This view apparently rejects any notion that customary practices prior to state decree can have the force of law unless and until they are endorsed by the state. It also gives no direction whatsoever about why the rules should be as they are. In context, Bentham's remark comes after a longish passage that derides, as did Blackstone, the limitations of possession in the state of nature, which lasts only as long as one is able to grasp a particular object.[3] But this hardly establishes the naked positivism for which it is cited. A fuller account shows that the shift in the rights of possession creates a Pareto improvement (whereby everyone is either as well off or better off than under the previous legal regimes that is clearly justified on efficiency grounds).[4] Quite simply, any regime that fosters the stability of possession allows those who already have some things to acquire others without having to worry about keeping others away. More precisely, it means that the state will make good on these claims in any dispute by refusing to treat the relaxation of physical control as the abandonment of possession. The key point here is that the normative improvement drives the example. But to the determined nominalist, it would be a matter of total indifference if the arrival of the state was used to reinforce the notion that the person who walks out of his house or leaves his catch untended has abandoned it to the next taker.

It is critical to note that all these examples are drawn from the law of land and personal chattels. There is no doubt that the philosophical writings on the subject of property rights in water are far thinner. Writers like Blackstone are content to

---

[3] "There have been from the beginning, and there always will be, circumstances in which a man may secure himself, by his own means, in the enjoyment of certain things. But the catalogue of these cases is very limited. The savage who has killed a deer may hope to keep it for himself, so long as his cave is undiscovered; so long as he watches to defend it, and is stronger than his rivals; but that is all. How miserable and precarious is such a possession! If we suppose the least agreement among savages to respect the acquisitions of each other, we see the introduction of a principle to which no name can be given but that of law. A feeble and momentary expectation may result from time to time from circumstances purely physical; but a strong and permanent expectation can result only from law. That which, in the nature state, was an almost invisible thread, in the social state becomes a cable" (Bentham 1882 [1802], 112–113).

[4] For further elaboration of this point, see Epstein (2007).

state that the interest of any person in water is (using the Roman term out of context) "usufructuary" (Blackstone 1765–1769, 1:339). That is, of course, an insufficient account of the system, and for perfectly clear reasons. The difficulties in the context of water are greater than they are with land because of the far greater diversity of circumstances that any comprehensive system of property rights has to address. Some of these problems relate to the highly varied settings in which water rights have to be organized. That physical diversity in turn increases the need to balance competing uses, so that much of the major litigation on the question deals with whether this system governs in the first place.[5] For these purposes, however, it is evident that the rules that work for a small English river will not do well to harness waters that barrel down a gorge etched out by the Colorado River. That river is governed by a prior-appropriation system that, roughly speaking, gives strict priority to order of acquisitive use. Strong preferences for out-of river consumptive uses make good sense in physical settings where riparian uses are of minimal value. Taking cows to the edge of the river produces rather different consequences in the two different riparian settings. In addition, natural variations in water environments alter the rate of topological change with respect to water, and to the land that abuts it, far more than with land. This level of natural variation necessitates rules that determine ownership as water levels rise and fall or as rivers are redirected. These concerns gave rise to the doctrines of alluvium and avulsion, which have their origins in Roman law (Gaius 1932, 2.70–72).[6] Although Joshua Getzler (2006) does not discuss this particular body of law, he rightly notes in his exhaustive treatise that many Roman law doctrines have had a heavy influence on the common-law development of water rights.[7]

On balance, the key insight is that the levels of topological differences, which are easy to underestimate with respect to land, have, if anything, far greater salience with water. At the same time, the rules that govern the state regulation of water rights are largely insensitive to these variations and, in general, tend to reduce the set of circumstances in which compensation is provided, appealing chiefly to the new and distinctive property rights that are applicable.

This discussion leads to the following conclusions: On one hand, the system of private rights and duties, while far from perfect, often ends up with the right divisions between private and common property, and with more or less the right rules for each of these subdivisions. On the other hand, the constitutional doctrines of takings are far too underprotective in both contexts because they make two grave doctrinal errors, each of which serves as a mirror image of the other.

With respect to land, the mistake is to fragment the bundle of rights so that strong protection is given to the right to exclude but weak protection is given to every

---

[5] See, e.g., *Coffin v. Left Hand Ditch Co.*, 6 Colo. 443 (1882).

[6] The footnote was added by the translator, Scott, to reflect the point that these rules were incorporated in their entirety into the English Law. See, e.g., Bracton v. 2 at 44 (1969) for his version of the distinction between alluvion and avulsion, which uses the first term but not the second.

[7] "The new water doctrines were built from Roman law and Roman-derived civil-law concepts of common goods and the natural rights of ownership, together with the English sources of Bracton and Blackstone, part-civilians themselves. Water law is one of the most Romanesque parts of English law, demonstrating the extent to which common and civilian law have comingled. Water law stands as a refutation of the still-common belief that English and European law parted ways irreversibly in the twelfth century" (Getzler 2006, 1–2).

other element within the bundle of rights.[8] Essentially, the government knows that if it tries to take property outright, full compensation is owed. But if it engages in partial takings, its actions will often be demoted, so it is said that they create a "mere" diminution of value (in the millions of dollars, of course) for which no compensation is required.[9] The excessive fragmentation of private interests thus leads to an insufficient protection of private rights, with consequent resource losses, and the government is spurred on to take private assets for public use without having to make an explicit comparison of the private values that are lost with the public values that are gained. What is ideally, in effect, a system of Kaldor-Hicks efficiency, where the winners could in principle compensate the losers and still come out ahead, breaks down in practice, for reasons that will shortly become apparent.

With water, the courts make the opposite mistake. They treat it as a single unitary thing for public law purposes, even though as a matter of private law, water rights are highly fragmented to reflect the underlying set of multiple inconsistent uses. Any accurate assessment of an individual claim has to deal with trade-offs at the margin, which are often made explicitly in cases involving water rights.[10] Everything that is traded off at the margin goes exactly the opposite way in takings disputes, where the uniform judicial recognition of the so-called navigation easement has long been regarded to dominate every private interest in the water. Total state takeover therefore generates virtually no compensation for either in-stream or riparian private rights. The bottom line is that the same strong, progovernment bias in the takings area manifests itself in different ways, precisely because of the conscious effort to distance all rules in the law of takings from their private law analogies. The path toward reform is not to deny the complexity of property rights, a well-rehearsed theme. Instead, it is to strengthen the relationship of the laws that govern private disputes with those that govern public disputes.

Equal Rights in Property Law

Private Parties

In cases involving private parties, the uniform assumption is that some position of equal rights between the parties is the appropriate point of departure for the analysis. One reason for this particular allocation is that it provides an indispensable focal point in ordinary two-party disputes. That focal point, in turn, avoids the need to ask which party to any future dispute should occupy a preferred position. Any other path is a sure road to danger. Choosing to bestow a preference on one party necessarily gives rise to a second question of even greater complexity: if there is any built-in preference, just how large is it, and by what particular reasons can it be justified?

---

[8] For a conventional account of the incidents of ownership, see Honoré (1961). For a discussion of whether fragmentation of rights either strengthens or weakens the constitutional protection of property rights, see Claeys (2006); for a response, see Epstein (2006).

[9] For the key doctrinal statement, see *Penn Central Transportation Co. v. New York City*, 438 U.S. 104 (1978).

[10] For an account of the marginalist nature of these trade-offs, see Epstein (1994).

Herein lies the difficulty. Improving the lot of one party relative to another produces both gains and losses, which means that the only social measure of efficiency that can be used to deal with the situation is the Kaldor-Hicks measure that will bestow its benediction of an efficient government action only if the gains to the winner are larger than the losses to the loser. All these actions assume, of course, that the transaction occurs in a world in which no transfer of payment, either in cash or in kind, is made (or needs to be made) to the other side. Finding a transaction that satisfies this constraint requires more delving into the particulars of any given case than does the more stringent Pareto formula, which requires that both sides be at least as well-off in the new state of the world as in the previous one, without committing itself to any distribution of the net gains between them.

Formal parity in position between the two parties tends to generate gains for one side only if it generates gains for the other. Given that the judgment of parity in positions is made largely behind a veil of ignorance, there is, moreover, no particular reason to assume that the two parties enjoy some differential level of gains. The much more plausible assumption is that the two sides gain in roughly equal proportion. The position of parity of rights, therefore, is more likely to produce a system of property that generates more overall gains than the less restrictive Kaldor-Hicks test. It is for just this reason that the postulate of equality of persons in the state of nature is used not only in setting out property relations, but in assigning the equal or like liberties of human beings within the general Lockean framework.[11] The parity principle thus creates a focal-point equilibrium that any two people, wholly without regard to their previous connections, can sustain.

The second great advantage of the like-liberty or equal property rights position is that it is scalable in ways that preserve the desired focal point. The same rule that works for two people can easily be generalized to n people, at least so long as noninterference with the like rights of other individuals remains the norm.[12] This ability is absolutely critical in property settings, because even if the issue is not property rights that are good against the world, as with land, but those that are binding against a substantial number of people, as with riparian rights, any asymmetry in the definition of rights introduces a new round of complexity from which there is no avenue of easy escape.

The explanation, as usual, rests on a transaction-costs view of the world. Any effort to create preferences in a dispute among n individuals has to be at the very least well ordered, so that a system in which A has priority over B, who in turn has priority over C, has unalterable transitive features. In addition, the magnitude of the preferences again has to be assayed without knowing the alternative conceptual solution or the types of evidence that could lend it empirical credibility. Equal liberty against force and fraud, for example, avoids this problem because everyone can follow a rule that requires him to keep his hands (or feet) to himself against a stranger. At this point, the noninterference rules set a background situation where any two people can form a cooperative venture without the approval of the rest of the world, so long as they do not by any voluntary cooperation or combination infringe on the

---

[11] See generally Locke (1980 [1690]).
[12] These considerations are also tied closely to rule-of-law concerns; see Epstein (2011a).

rights of third parties. By similar reasoning, they are protected against a diminution of rights to third parties, which would otherwise be an implicit tax against voluntary transactions that improved the position of both parties to the transaction. The stabilization of the overall system thus goes a long way to resolve various suits between parties.

The actual way in which this parity constraint operates depends in part on the rules in question. The physical rules of noninterference just mentioned are particularly amenable to this type of approach because it simultaneously creates a perimeter of rights around all persons in which they are free to do as they please. Positive entitlements to external resources, however, are less easily crafted. Thus, all the rules dealing with the occupation of land, the capture of animals, or the taking of various natural resources gravitate to a system of first possession, whereby the first to bring the thing into possession is its presumptive owner.[13] The key feature that makes this system work is the focal-point equilibrium (whereby everyone recognizes instantly who is the preferred party) if the party in possession is, and is widely known to be, entitled to ward off all others. It is the possession that singles out the owner from the rest of the world, which any system of exclusive rights must do, and it does so long before there are state actions designed to coordinate individual behavior.

Indeed, this first-possession rule is susceptible only to cautious generalization, because in some property settings (e.g., the capture of whales), a single party often cannot land the whale by himself. At this point, the initial logic becomes a bit more complicated, but the basic contours of the first-possession rule bend without breaking. The huge portion of humanity that has had nothing to do with landing whales continues to have no claims against the whale. However, the individuals whose efforts contribute to its successful capture must work out some accommodation that reflects their respective contributions to the catch. The system will break down if all contributors to the catch do not receive a return that equals or exceeds their contribution to the overall venture. In this sense, the strict sequential role of the various players means that any defection at any point in the process results in the loss of the catch for all. All players, therefore, have to be incentivized simultaneously. That set of mutually consistent rewards, moreover, must be created by custom, because there is no direct communication between them at the time they act. Just these conditions, for example, are satisfied in the rule that requires the ship that brought down a fin whale to pay a finder's fee to the person on the beach who gave it information about where it landed.[14] The fee exceeds the cost of the notice, but it does not deny the fishermen the needed return on their investment. (This analysis neglects all the common-pool difficulties that arise from overfishing, which require major adaptations.)

In the area of water rights, moreover, the interlocking nature of claims to running bodies of water make it more difficult to follow the parity position, especially as the level of use intensifies with the introduction of mills and dams, which generate

---

[13] For the Roman origins, again, see Gaius (1932, 2.66); see also Justinian (2009), 2:1:12.
[14] See *Ghen v. Rich*, 8 F. 159 (D. Mass. 1881).

much conflict.[15] It cannot be said, therefore, that following a parity principle solves all problems, for two simple reasons. First, rivers flow downhill, and oceans are often influenced by the tides. By the same token, though, the effort to observe those natural conditions does help eliminate certain legal configurations that are less stable than their rivals. But in the absence of any system of boundaries, it is not credible to think that common-law rules can bring the legal system to its fruition without legislative intervention, which occurred with great regularity in both the English and American systems (Getzler 2006). In sum, all that can be said about the parity restraint is that it is a safeguard against the worst abuses but is not in and of itself a sure guide to the optimal system of property rights in water, even if there is some confidence about what the optimum is.

Public Versus Private

Resolution of disputes between the state and individuals cannot, as a general matter, be completely guided by the general principle of parity. The very talk of eminent domain power suggests that there lie in the state some rights that are superior to those held by ordinary citizens. Unlike ordinary private disputes, there is no real difficulty in figuring out who should get the extra rights and no formidable obstacle to applying the applicable rules to large numbers of disputes simultaneously; whether the government takes from one party or from many, it always occupies the distinctive role of the government. The problems of coordinating the behaviors of multiple actors that arise in private disputes do not arise when the state claims pride of place.

The principle of parity does not work as well with systems of direct government. In order to begin that inquiry, it is necessary to concede, without question, that the state can rise above ordinary citizens in using compulsion against individuals, whether on land or water. But just how far above those citizens can it rise? In particular, the most difficult question is often whether the state can act under its police powers so that the regulations it imposes are not offset by any duty to compensate private individuals who are, at least in some instances, cast in the role of wrongdoers, as in the case of pollution. However, not all state initiatives are directed toward private parties as wrongdoers. In some instances, the state demands sacrifices from individuals who have done no wrong in order to advance the common good. The common requirement that just compensation be supplied in those cases is an effort to convert a set of government initiatives that might provide a Kaldor-Hicks improvement into one that provides a Pareto improvement: the purpose of compensation is to ensure that no one is left worse off by the state's use of coercion.

But putting the point in this way introduces the need to determine which cases fall on which side of the line. As a brute historical fact, the systematic errors in dealing with eminent domain are not those that make the state too feeble to meet the challenges that it faces; in fact, they create the opposite risk. The duty to compensate is systematically separated from the conceptions of right and wrong that govern

---

[15] For a historical account, see Rose (1990). For an extensive critique of this position as oversimplifying the differences between English and American law on the rise of the reasonable-user doctrine, see Getzler (2006).

disputes between neighbors, specifically under the law of nuisance. That gap opens up enormous opportunity for political arbitrage between the private law and the public administrative process. Within the land use context, if it is not possible for a group of neighbors to purchase the right to a view over someone else's land via a restrictive covenant, they may turn to the zoning board, where the restrictive covenant is theirs for the asking if they can prevail by majority vote, particularly given the nearly unbroken history of judicial cases giving deference to zoning authorities since the initial Supreme Court decision in *Village of Euclid v. Ambler Realty Co.*, 272 U.S. 365 (1926).

The space for this kind of behavior is very large. First, the gains from obtaining a desired view are not trivial: the value of land with a protected view can easily increase by as much as 50 percent in the right coastal settings. Second, gains that large can become the focal point of political action because once the restrictions are imposed, future enforcement of the political deal is usually not a major obstacle to its initial realization. The durability of the purchase increases the willingness to make it. Third, the losses on the other side are almost always larger, which is why there seldom are voluntary transactions that implement the restrictions imposed by zoning ordinances. In virtually all cases, the party who is prohibited from building has the same view as the party who gets the zoning order. Those values are lost, and that owner will therefore fight. However, in a political arena, votes count for more than the dollars of economic gains or losses, so that the side with the larger coalition can win even if its result is inefficient. In the end, therefore, there is only one structure with a good view instead of two structures, one of whose view is better than the other's. Fourth, an even greater problem is that the ability to work through political means does not lead to compromise solutions in which, for a fee, the coastal owner will agree to some concessions on the size, type, or location of the new construction for the benefit of the party one level removed from the beach.

There is only one way to avoid the political arbitrage that leads to these zoning battles, and that is to use the same set of liability and boundary rules for the resolution of both public disputes and private disputes. But which set? On this point, the ultimate choice is easy. The private law rules between like parties are all honed with the efficiency of the whole in mind. The guiding principle is that the greater the parity in position, the higher the level of expected efficiency. But there is no similar veil-of-ignorance-type protection with public rules, which no amount of ingenuity could render serviceable in dealing with private law disputes. At this point, then, the private law rules supply a baseline for dealing with the key problem of demarcation, which asks how to distinguish between those government actions that generate some obligation to compensate and those that do not. It is instructive to see how these insights play out with regard to land and to water.

Private and Public Disputes over Land Use

Private Disputes

The implicit private law strategy for resolving disputes between two parties proceeds in two stages. At stage one, the law adopts the position of implicit parity between the parties so as to rule out favoritism, for reasons stated earlier. At stage two, the legal system, when it works correctly, adopts rules that maximize the value for each of the participants. Given the way in which the project is organized, the second task is made easier in most cases by the adoption of the parity rule. To the extent that all the parties to the system are in a lockstep position, the only way in which one party could seek to improve its own position is to adopt a rule that improves the position of all other persons. Stated otherwise, when the first condition is satisfied, the second task becomes far more tractable than would otherwise be the case. Any effort by one party to maximize its own position will result in parallel improvements for all other parties.

EXCLUSIVITY

It is just this procedure that leads to the traditional bundle of rights for the ownership of land—rights that are found in both civil law and common-law systems. Thus, the first question on exclusivity initially receives an easy answer: unless each person can exclude all others, investments in real property can be made by no one. The initial argument in favor of exclusivity of private land is powerful enough that it goes a long way to shape the inquiry into the proper understanding of private property, which is one reason that exclusion has always been included in the general bundle of rights.

The process in this case, however, is iterative and incremental.[16] The best way to look at exclusivity is as an improvement of the state of nature—that is, the situation where no party has any rights of any sort in land. That test requires no detailed empirical inquiry to conclude that exclusivity marks an improvement over a brawl and a free-for-all. But the question then arises whether there are further improvements to be had, and if so, how they should be made. It is well established in every legal system, for example, that the right of exclusion is trumped by a narrowly conceived exception permitting one to enter the land of another in times of necessity in order to escape death, serious injury, or major property loss from forces of nature or third persons. That privilege lasts only as long as the necessity lasts, after which the status quo ante is restored. In most cases, moreover, that right to enter is usually accompanied by a duty to make compensation for property losses inflicted, or even for lost rental value of the property in question. The large empirical hunch is that salvation counts for more than exclusion, so much so that if the owner tries to exclude under conditions of necessity, he can be rebuffed, at least if the issue is whether the outsider can moor his boat at a dock. In general, however, there is no universal duty to rescue (a principle that has problems of its own), and the situation becomes murky if the outsider in cases of necessity wishes to claim access by right to the interior of one's home. The more complicated the accommodations, the less clear the general gain.

In addition to the necessity cases, an exception to the norm of exclusive property arises in connection with common property, which operates as a network link. For those properties that are long, thin, and suitable for transportation, the initial property regime can easily be one that operates in common, as with waters, beaches, and

---

[16] For a discussion of moral incrementalism, see Epstein (2003).

often customary trails. At this point, the dominant regime assures that each property owner who abuts the common element has access to the transportation (or, today, communication) grid, given the obvious gains in question. There are evident limits to what a purely private system of law can do, but for now, the analysis can proceed at least this far.

USE RIGHTS

The same type of argument that applies to rights of use with respect to water applies to rights of use with respect to land: does the allowance of some use rights work an overall social improvement? In a system in which no one is allowed to build anything, the legal definition of property rights would consign all individuals to states of permanent deprivation. So use rights in property are necessarily allowed, given the manifest Pareto improvements they create. But again, the incrementalist approach dominates because the right to use does not cover all uses, for these are in every jurisdiction hemmed in by some law of nuisance dealing with filth, pollution, odors, and the like on the generalized assumption that all parties are, as a first approximation, better off with these restrictions than without them.[17] But the heterogeneity of nuisances gives rise to a needed notion of caution, so that this first approximation is modified both ways, but always under a principle of reciprocity that applies to all parties in all cases. Thus, for instance, negative reciprocal easements impose duties on landowners to refrain from digging up their soil in ways that cause their neighbors' land to collapse.[18] On the opposite side, the live-and-let-live rule carves out from the general nuisance law those reciprocal low-level interferences with respect to all parties—the rule easily generalizes to n persons, where all persons are better off if none is allowed to sue.[19] Similar logic applies to such matters as the broadcast of radio waves or the overflight of airplanes, for which no relief at all is allowed.

This argument, moreover, applies not only to land use, but also to land development, where, again, the gains are so large that the contrary position is not sustainable as a general rule, given the mutual gains that follow if all parties in the state of nature are allowed to develop their land, instead of a situation where none are allowed to do so. How far these rights can generally go is always a question, and on this matter, the question of lateral support, whereby the land of one neighbor supports all others, often requires individuals to set back their buildings from boundary lines. More controversially, height restrictions, intended to preserve air and light, could also be imposed if they worked well on a reciprocal basis, but the case for imposing those restrictions as a matter of law also tends to be weak. In rural settings, large plot sizes tend to make these height restrictions unnecessary. In urban settings, the close density of property tends to make these blocking rights prohibitively expensive, so that they are usually denied.[20] It was for that reason that Justice Holmes, in his usual blunt fashion, wrote: "At common law, a man has a right to build

---

[17] For discussion, see Epstein (1979).
[18] *Birmingham Corp. v. Allen*, [1877] 6 Ch. D. 284 at 288–289 (discussing the rights of owners of mines to extract coal, preventing the extraction of coal from neighboring mines).
[19] *Bamford v. Turnley*, [1862] 122 Eng. Rep. 27 at 32–33 (Ex.) (Bramwell, B., concurring).
[20] See, e.g., *Fontainebleau Hotel Corp. v. Forty-Five Twenty-Five, Inc.*, 114 So. 2d 357 (Fla. Dist. Ct. App. 1959).

a fence on his own land as high as he pleases, however much it may obstruct his neighbor's light and air" (*Rideout v. Knox*, 19 N.E. 390, 391 [Mass. 1889]). In dealing with these issues, moreover, it is always critical to remember that any assessment of rights should be made as of the moment that property has been acquired in its natural state. The judgments become completely skewed when the unilateral actions of one side introduce a key asymmetry in dealing with rights. Thus, if A builds on his land, he has a strong case to argue that the law of nuisance should now prevent B from blocking his view by building on her land. The correct analytical framework denies A the opportunity to gain an advantage over his neighbor by taking the unilateral step of building first. His earlier action gives him the benefit of an unobstructed view until she decides to build. It does not create a prescriptive right whereby, through the passage of time, she forfeits her right of construction.

There are, of course, situations where the parity principle cannot be observed, not because of what the law says, but because nature does not allow the parties to interact on what is instructively called "a level playing field." The most obvious case concerns conflicts that arise between uphill and downhill owners. This situation, which is the norm in dealing with water rights, makes it impossible to devise any rule that exhibits perfect parity, so the question is what compromises will be available. The rule that says that no physical invasion is possible will favor the downhill owner but will kill all development from above. What developed, then, was a tripartite solution that had a fair bit of wit to it. Any discharge from the higher land to the lower land, such as dumping filth from an upper-story window onto a neighbor's land, was treated as tortious.[21] On the other hand, a decision to remove coal from the upper land, such that water could come through, was not tortious. Let the lower fellow fend for himself under the "common enemy" or purchase some protection from the defendant.[22] The sense here is that forcing the uphill landowner to supply the protection puts all the cost on one side and leaves all the benefit on the other. In addition, it creates an added cost of coordination between two parties that does not arise when the same person has to keep coal in place, knowing what will happen if he does not.

That leaves the intermediate case, where the upper party wants to engage in ordinary husbandry, from which some level of runoff is inevitable. Here any decision that the uphill landowner had to avoid all interference meant that the lower landowner had a huge strategic advantage that was the reverse of the one nature created. The legal impulse, therefore, was to avoid either of the two end points involved in the other cases, which in turn led to the adoption of a reasonableness rule of the sort that quickly developed in connection with water rights. In the famous case *Middlesex Co. v. McCue*, 21 N.E. 230 (Mass. 1889), Justice Holmes refused to enjoin the defendant from filling up the plaintiff's mill pond with the inevitable runoff generated when the defendant gardened on his plot. His eye for the middle position

---

[21] See, e.g., *Baird v. Williamson*, [1863] 143 Eng. Rep. 831 at 831 (C.B.). The great case *Rylands v. Fletcher*, 3 H.L 330 (H.L.E. 1868) (affirming *Fletcher v. Rylands*, 159 Eng. Rep. 737 [Ex. 1865]) is best understood as a variation on the discharge theme that applied to cases in which a defendant brings, keeps, collects, or accumulates water on his land that is likely to do mischief if it escapes. Both cases were judged by a strict liability rule in which the negligence of the defendant was immaterial.

[22] See, e.g., *Smith v. Kenrick*, 137 Eng. Rep. 205 (C.P. 1849).

was expressed thusly: "[A] man has a right to cultivate his land in the usual and reasonable way, as well up a hill as in the plain, and that damage to the lower proprietor of the kind complained of is something that he must protect himself against as best he may. The plaintiff says that a wall would stop the trouble. If so, it can build one upon its own land" (*McCue*, 21 N.E. 230 at 231).

Note that protection is not supplied against actions that count as unusual and unreasonable cultivation, which means, as Holmes loved to say in many other contexts, that the protection of the law was a matter of degree, which in some cases it is.[23] But a simple physical test indicates which cases can be governed by categorical rules and which ones cannot. For those cases in which the field is level, hard boundary lines work because the risk of downward flow is not present. It was for that reason in *Rideout v. Knox* that Holmes gave the categorical rule that denied the easement of light and air. But in cases that involve land on a slope, a reasonableness accommodation is needed to avoid the complete domination of the one by another. It will become clear which category water is in.

DISPOSITION

The third key element in the ownership bundle is the right of disposition. Rights of exclusion, use, and development make no allowance for gains from trade, either between neighbors or with strangers. These rules must be included in the ownership bundles for the system to function. Between strangers, the nuisance rules are first approximations that are subject to limited correction by legal rule. It is also useful to allow parties to make additional adjustments through contracts that bind both themselves and their successors in title. The law that deals with *ius in re aliena* (rights in the property of others) handles that problem by allowing for the consensual creation of servitudes, which can either permit individuals to enter the land of their neighbors without committing a trespass or to restrict the neighbors' use of their own property without it being an impermissible form of domination.[24] These consensual easements may well be reciprocal, as is commonly the case when they are included in a planned unit development, which contains an elaborate crisscross of covenants and easements among the various participants. But these covenants and easements need not be created by a common grant; they can be done in one direction only, upon payment of compensation. No matter how these interests are created, they follow two strict rules for the conservation of property rights. The first is that the parties to the transaction cannot expand their legal rights as against the rest of the world, which is thereby protected against their machinations. The second is that the parties to the transaction are not thereby forced to sacrifice rights to the rest of the world as a condition of finishing the deal. In essence, the rights of A, separately, and B, separately, against the rest of the world are carried over to any admixture of A+ and B− or, indeed, any more complex situation of A++ and B++, where the pluses and minuses represent the paired deviation from the initial set of rights.

---

[23] See *Rideout v. Knox*, 19 N.E. 390, 391 (Mass. 1889).

[24] For the current rules, see French (1994).

These rights of disposition, moreover, are not limited to adjustments among neighbors. Several points are in order. First, these rights also apply where the owner of a single plot of land chooses to create multiple interests in the same plot. Here again, no matter how many parties are involved, and no matter how complex the arrangements are, the same conservation of rights necessarily applies. The question that then arises is what kinds of division of property interests can follow. The list is long and impressive, but the key feature is that two or more deviations from the initial position may always be combined so long as the same constraints are met. Thus, mature institutions have been developed that have divided ownership of property over time, with the creation of life estates (both present and future), contingent remainders, and executory interests, both of which vest only on the occurrence of some future event. In effect, the owner of a piece of land is entitled to give a road map for the disposition of the property that will move from party to party at death, marriage, or some other event. There are some nontrivial limitations on this freedom of disposition, most notably, the rule against perpetuities, which invalidates some contingent remainders and executory interest because they take too long to vest.[25] But none of these have any material effect on the ability to divide the actual control.

Second, it is possible to create commercial interests in the form of leases (and subleases), which may ordinarily be assigned to third persons. Again, the accounting among the parties gets complex as the number of these interests increases, but the key point is that no matter how many different ways the fee simple (as the land is called when the title is indefinite) is sliced, the sum of the parts is always equal to the whole in regard to strangers.

Third, it is possible to create mortgages over the fee simple or any part of it, and to do so not once, but repeatedly with second and third mortgages whose respective claims can be organized by precise priority rules.

Fourth, it is possible to divide management from the control of any interest through the use of the trust mechanism, which is not very common today for land, but which is the dominant form for the holding of financial assets. But again, the same tactic works. The parties govern the relationships among themselves by contract. As against the rest of the world, they have the same arm's-length arrangement. The one adaptive response is that often the defensive function of property management and control is vested in the hands of a single person (usually the life tenant or the trustee) for reasons of administrative convenience. At one time, the proliferation of interests made it hard for outsiders to keep track of ownership and thus reduced the ability for further alienations of given pieces of the whole. Modern systems of recording have largely mitigated that problem. A bulletin board, now often available and searchable online, records all interests so that any outsider can determine the state of the title if he wishes either to purchase the property or to lend on the strength of it as security. The proliferation of interests produces gains from trade. The system of deeds and recording reduces the transaction costs that stand in the way of further fragmentation of the interests.

---

[25] For an explanation of the technicalities of the rule, see Bergin and Haskell (1984).

Public Taking of Private Property

The key insight for a proper approach to eminent domain is that the government cannot short-circuit the division of rights in question. The state of the title as a matter of private law binds the sovereign. It may decide to take or not to take land or some interest in it. So long as the taking is for a public use, there is no way for any landowner to resist that takeover. The distinctive feature of the takings clause is that it allows the state to force exchanges on even terms (by payment of just compensation) to prevent the holdout problems that could otherwise prevent the coherent assembly of land that is needed for some kinds of collective ventures.

The success of this operation depends socially on the judgment that the value of the property, when it is placed in the hands of the government, is greater than it is in the hands of private parties, when all spillover effects on third persons are taken into account. Without that constraint, the entire process will be consumed by various forms of public policy intrigue. Unfortunately, however, just that situation results because the current law of "property" as it is conceived under the law of eminent domain does not correspond to the law of private property with its strong system-wide efficiency effects. Here are some of the reasons that this situation flounders badly.

PARTIAL TAKINGS

One key mistake is that the law draws an artificial distinction between the taking of property as a whole and the partial taking limited to an interest in property. A sound system of private property encourages unlimited division of interests until all gains from trade are exhausted. The constitutional version of property law assumes that the only interest that is fully protected is the right to exclude, which is violated when the government enters property, at which point there is a nearly per se, or automatic, rule for compensation of the interest taken (*Loretto v. Teleprompter Manhattan CATV Corp.*, 458 U.S. 419 [1982]). But even in these cases, the compensation is commonly stated to be only for the "property taken," which excludes from the mix all the dislocations that occur when the owner is deprived, for example, of property for use in his trade or business.[26] But these consequential damages are routinely allowed (to the extent measurable) against private defendants, and the failure to include them in the social calculus leads to excessive takings relative to the proper standard of social welfare.

Starting from its misconceived view of private property, the current takings law offers only scant protection for fractional interests in property, which has the unfortunate effect of discouraging owners from entering into transactions that make business sense. One illustration of this position involves the famous case *Penn Central Transportation Co. v. New York City*, 438 U.S. 104 (1978), where the private owners of the ground sold the air rights to a separate buyer. There was no question that air rights were just one form of sensible property division under New York law, which allowed them to be sold, divided, inherited, traded, bequeathed, leased, and mortgaged. In essence, they were folded into the standard system of property

---

[26] See *Monongahela Navigation. Co. v. United States*, 148 U.S. 312 (1893).

rights. In *Penn Central*, New York's Landmark Commission denied the owner of those air rights the right to exploit them. No private party could have used its muscle to do so, but if New York City chose to preserve the view down Park Avenue (which was already blocked by what was then the Pan Am Building), its scenic endeavors counted as a public use, so long as just compensation was paid, as measured by the market value of these air rights in a voluntary transaction. But Justice Brennan deviated from the private law rule that protected divided interests. Instead he held that the air rights had to be considered as part of the "parcel as a whole" (*Penn Central*, 438 U.S. 104 at 131). At the very least, that maneuver is incorrect, for putting the land back together implicitly denied the holder of the air rights the gains from the separation. But in fact, Brennan's agenda was more aggressive. In his view, the development rights received a zero valuation so long as the current operations of the Penn Central terminal allowed the company to cover its costs and make a normal profit. Again, this rule is surely wrong by analogy to the private system, where the taking or destruction of any interest in land has its value lost, not its original cost to the owner, as its proper measure. Brennan's argument was that diminution in value should be treated as though it were a loss from competition, which again deviates from the cardinal principle of private law that even competitive losses are noncompensable, while the removal of any stick from the bundle of property rights is compensable. Otherwise, the risk is too great that the government will achieve its goals by a succession of small takings of partial interests.

This initial error creates a serious question about how to value development rights on land that is at present undeveloped and thus cannot cover its costs. On that issue, the current rules are still incoherent because they have deviated from the only rules that make sense: those that govern the taking or destruction of private property by other private parties. This effort to create a set of preferred property rights in government invites the form of political arbitrage identified earlier. Needless to say, virtually every exercise of the zoning power has the same consequence when it is not tightly tethered to private law conceptions of private ownership.

EXACTIONS

Next, the entire doctrine of exactions is another abuse that follows from the deviation from private law. The standard definitions of coercion involve the threat or use of force against another person or his property. That definition works in a straightforward sense when the two parties stand as strangers to each other. But the account of coercion must be flexible enough to cover other cases. There is a clear case of coercion if I have both your money and your ring and offer you a choice between them when you are entitled to both (Epstein 1993). Unfortunately, that is what is usually done with the law of exactions. An individual should have the right to build his house and to keep his access to the beach. The government announces that it will allow the construction of a new building (which is in no sense a nuisance) only if the owner of the property consents to having a lateral easement across the front of his land. Here there is a choice between two entitlements, and the Supreme Court was right to hold that this choice was not permissible (*Nollan v. California Coastal Commission*, 483 U.S. 825 [1987]). But that decision rested on the notion that an easement (but not a restrictive covenant, even though both are servitudes) was a possessory interest in land that was subject to the per se compensation rule in *Loretto*. The danger of this illicit choice is everywhere. Thus, the government will only allow the construction of a new apartment complex (which, again, is no nuisance) if the owner agrees to fund a new park, school, or train station that is available to all members of the community. Here the game is that the burdens are borne exclusively by some even though the benefits are shared by others who do not contribute to the cost. There is an implicit wealth transfer through regulation, which courts have refused to guard against outside the context of easements. Once again, the distortions are palpable.

In sum, it should be noted that these key decisions exhibit the same general feature. The deviations from the (efficient) rules used to resolve private disputes all favor the government, almost always on the ground that government officials have an expertise and high-mindedness that no private landowner could hope to match. That naïveté leads to substantial social losses.

Water Law

Private Law

THE RISE OF CORRELATIVE RIGHTS
The private law of water is organized on a principle that is the polar opposite of the law of land. No longer is exclusivity the dominant term of analysis. Rather, in these systems, the rights of all parties are shared, such that the dominant language (as in the case of disputes concerning hillsides) is that of reasonableness, in which no one party is entitled to dominate over any other. The position of any claimant to water is often described as "usufructuary,"[27] which means that the person is entitled to some of the use and fruits of the water, but not to the entire stock of water, whose "going concern" value would be diminished if a running river were diverted into a private barrel or reservoir.[28] This effort to borrow a term from Roman law leads to a distortion of its primary meaning, which, in connection with land, referred to the right of an individual, the usufructuary, to take the use and the fruits of the land, while the title to that land remained in the hands of the bare proprietor. The exact division of assets in the land context covers a wide variety of issues, from cutting trees to opening mines to remodeling houses. But those conflicts are strictly between the two parties in question and are subject to modification by explicit agreement. There is, however, no one person who stands in the position of a bare proprietor with respect to water. Instead, there are multiple classes of claimants, such as riparians, owners of boats, mill owners, recreational users, and fishermen, each with its own distinctive class of uses that may or may not be valuable in connection with certain rivers. In these cases, topography matters so greatly that the delineation of rights that work in one context need not work in another.

To understand how the system works with respect to rivers, it is useful to set out the deviations that are needed from the law of land in order to develop a system of sensible water rights, which in fact begins with a simple form of riparianism. Once

---

[27] See, e.g., Blackstone (1765–1769, 4:14).
[28] For further development of this theme, see Epstein (1985).

that is done, one can ask, as with land, the extent to which it is possible to devise modifications of that body of rules when the potential valuable uses of water are expanded either by technology or changes in the natural topography of water.

On this question, it is instructive to begin with a short passage from John Locke that roughly assumes parity between the rules of acquisition of land and of water. As is well known, Locke thought that the proper way in which any individual separated his property from the common was to mix it with his labor: "Whatsoever, then, he removes out of the state that Nature hath provided and left it in, he hath mixed his labour with it, and joined to it something that is his own, and thereby makes it his property" (Locke 1980 [1690], par. 26).

Locke's "mixing" image is somewhat overdrawn because it is quite clear that a minimal amount of labor can then separate something from the common; for example, "the acorns he picked up under an oak" would do the job (Locke 1980 [1690], par. 27). Locke is not so foolish as to think that extraordinary levels of effort should be required where simple labor will do. The real issue here is that of the focal point: the simplest way to have one person own property is for him to take it and for others to recognize that claim of ownership and stand aside. From this perspective, it appears to follow that taking water out of the common should be governed by the same rules, given the need to establish a unique owner. Locke, for example, appeared to endorse the parity of position between land and water when he wrote as follows: "Nobody could think himself injured by the drinking of another man, though he took a good draught, who had a whole river of the same water left him to quench his thirst. And the case of land and water, where there is enough of both, is perfectly the same" (Locke 1980 [1690], par. 32).

This approach is, of course, a particular application of the more general Lockean proviso, "Nor was this appropriation of any parcel of land, by improving it, any prejudice to any other man, since there was still enough and as good left, and more than the yet unprovided could use" (Locke 1980 [1690], par. 32). But it also shares the same defect. In both cases, Locke tries to make the case easy for himself by insisting that there is no injury at all, when some injury to the common pool is a physical necessity under the conditions of scarcity. The difference between a draught of water and the wholesale diversion of a river is just a matter of degree. The same point was raised by the plaintiffs' lawyers in *Embry v. Owen*, when they attacked the claim that the defendant had caused no injury at all: "if this defendant were allowed to take an inappreciable quantity of water for the purpose of irrigation, fifty other persons might do the same" (155 Eng. Rep. 579, 582–583 [Ex. 1851]). Just as the longest journey starts with a single step, so too does the destruction of the largest river start with a single drop.

The great strength of this response is that it reveals a logical objection to a practical position. The difficulty in both these cases is that Locke and his followers are not asking the right question when they focus exclusively on the inappreciable diminution of the river as if it caused no harm at all. That all-or-nothing response is much too categorical. What is needed is a marginalist approach. The correct way to put the issue is to ask what happens to overall welfare if each person takes some portion out of the common for private use. In the case of land, the interdependence between separate parcels is generally small, so that the gains that come from privatization are likely to exceed the losses that accrue to others who now have limited access to the common. Indeed, these persons could easily be made better off because the privatization of land generates improved productivity, which in turn increases the opportunities of third persons to gain through trade. In most cases, there is no disruption of any common-pool asset, which is what distinguishes the situation with land from that with water. At this point, the first approximation of letting no one take anything from a river will surely do better than the opposite first approximation of allowing the first possessor to take whatever he wants from the common, which is the case for land. Nonetheless, it is impossible to improve on that first approximation by allowing a system of limited, pro rata, access as the common law did. In light of these adjustments, it should be evident, therefore, that Locke's purported equivalence of land and water is misguided.

FROM NATURAL FLOW TO REASONABLE USER

English Cases. The difficulty in finding the optimal system of water rights is reflected in the early English and American common law cases.[29] The first approximation is thus that riparians, as a matter of natural right, have access to the natural flow of water. This posture is explicitly defensive because the first objective is to protect each riparian landowner against the unilateral actions of any person who threatens to abstract all the water from the river for himself, as is permissible under an unrestricted first-possession rule. As Lord Wensleydale wrote, the riparian has "the right to have [a natural stream of water] come to him in its natural state, in flow, quantity and quality, and to go from him without obstruction; upon the same principle that he is entitled to the support of his neighbour's soil for his own in its natural state. His right in no way depends upon prescription, or the presumed grant of his neighbour" (*Chasemore v. Richards*, 11 Eng. Rep. 140, 153 [1859]).

It is worth exploring how this formulation both follows land law and deviates from it. To do so, it is necessary to consider the differences between the law of prescription and the law of original occupation. On this issue, the brief allusion to the right of lateral support is most instructive. Recall that as a first approximation, all boundary lines in land are rigid: no one can invade the property of another, but one is nevertheless allowed to do as he will with his own property. The lateral-support easement is a deviation from that rule in that it meets the strict test of reciprocity because each person owes the identical duty to a neighbor. That reciprocal duty is justified as a Pareto improvement, precisely because the values of all affected parcels of land are increased by its uniform application. It is critical, therefore, to make it clear that this right of lateral support is not acquired by prescription or its close cousin, the theory of the lost grant.[30] The doctrine of prescription is triggered only by open and notorious use over a long period of time. The conceptual difficulty with the doctrine of prescription is the same as that for the kindred doctrine of adverse possession in land: why does a continuous trespass at some point become the source

---

[29] For a comprehensive account of the developments in English law, which were heavily influenced by early nineteenth-century writings on the subject, see Getzler (2006).

[30] For a discussion of prescription and the lost grant, see Getzler (2006).

of a valid title?[31] The answer to that question depends less on the dispute between the parties than on the need to assign title on a systematic basis so that ordinary development and trade of real property can take place without fear of the dead hand of the past.[32] To achieve that objective, a firm line dominates a wavy principle, and its arbitrariness is in large part mitigated by its clear publication so that all parties know the rules of the game.

These rules, however, are utterly unsuitable for creating a universal set of correlative rights and duties to govern all individuals from the outset, without any waiting period at all. There are no acts of prescription and no conceivable grants. The social objective is to install the most efficient system of property rights from the beginning, which is what the natural law approach does. This is not to say that doctrines of prescription have no place in dealing with water rights, for clearly they do. But the doctrine of prescription is applied only to those cases in which one person deviates from the natural rights position of common-law parity by open and notorious moves that claim greater rights than the natural flow system allows (Getzler 2006). For the upstream party, that requires blocking water or removing excessive quantities of it for the appropriate limitations period, say, 20 years. For the downstream party, it requires constructing a dam, which backs up water beyond the natural level to the prejudice of the upstream holder. In both these cases, prescription serves its proper function by acknowledging changes in the original rights structure brought about by long use without also altering the general system, which remains intact for all other users.

The second issue raised by the brief passage in *Chasemore* goes to the content of those natural rights. It is at this point that the clear intellectual distance between the rules governing the acquisition of rights in water and those governing the acquisition of rights in land becomes apparent. Recall the two-step analytical framework: first, establish parity; next, pick that set of parallel rules that maximizes overall utility. The parity on the river is preserved among all riparians because each has a right to have the water run past his land, but by the same token, he must allow it to run past the land of others. That initial parity, unfortunately, fares quite poorly under the second test of value maximization for riparians as a group, because there are surely social gains if some amount of water may be removed from the river. Put otherwise, the first drop of water in the river in private hands is worth more than the last drop of water that remains in the river.

The challenge, therefore, that the Lockean proviso's rigid formulation misconceives is to see how to introduce marginalist analysis to deal with water on the river. At this point, the gaps between land and water regimes grow larger. With land, the unilateral action of one person establishes priority over all others under the first-possession rule. But that rule cannot possibly function well (notwithstanding Locke's superficial acceptance of it) in connection with any river, particularly in light of its

---

[31] For one prominent early formulation of the question, see Ballantine (1918). For the analogous Roman rules on *usucapio* (taking ownership by use), see Nicholas (1962) and Getzler (2006).

[32] "The statute [of limitations] has not for its object to reward the diligent trespasser for his wrong nor yet to penalize the negligent and dormant owner for sleeping upon his rights; the great purpose is automatically to quiet all titles which are openly and consistently asserted, to provide proof of meritorious titles, and correct errors in conveyancing" (Ballantine 1918, 135).

large class of actors, each of whom may have acquired a parcel of land at different times. The first-possession rule gives too much power to the first taker (aside from the difficulty of determining who that person is in the absence of any system of deeds to record when riparian lands were first occupied or water rights were first used). So the property rule switches over to one that allows all persons the right to remove some small quantity of water from the river, regardless of when they acquired their interest in the land. It is better, on the whole, if all riparians are allowed to take a good draught out of the river, so long as its overall level does not shrink too much. That is likely when the amount of water removed by these low-level uses is less than the natural variation in the level of the river attributable to rainfall, evaporation, and other natural phenomena.

In lockstep progression, therefore, all riparians can, under established doctrine, make use of water for their modest domestic purposes. After water is removed from the river, the first-possession rule transfers ownership to the water, just as Locke thought.[33] The key question, however, is not how that person acquires ownership of the water he takes. Instead, it is how to determine the amount of water that can be taken in the first place, for which Locke's labor theory of value does not supply the slightest help. At this point, the hard question is how much more water can be removed from the river. In principle, the same marginalist test that applied to the easier cases should also apply to these harder cases. It is never a question of whether "as much again and as good" is left over; by definition, this is never the case. Rather, the correct question compares the sum of instream and consumptive rights when all riparians are allowed to increase their withdrawals from the stream. And the question whether overall levels increase or decrease with uniform consumption levels admits to a uniform a priori response that is independent of the volume of water in the river and the value of the private riparian uses to which it is put. The challenge is to ask just how much the pro rata removals can be increased until the reduction of instream uses becomes larger than the consumptive uses.

This issue intensified, and ultimately came to a head, with the transformation of the relatively passive system of riparian rights to the more muscular system of reasonable use. The issue was fought out in both England and the United States over key questions arising from irrigation and mills. With irrigation, the question in England was whether a riparian could take water out of the river for irrigation purposes so long as the return flow after irrigation did not reduce the levels of water for the downstream riparian to any appreciable extent. The argument against allowing this right was that its repeated application could easily put such pressure on the notion of appreciable loss that the entire system of negative rights (those that kept the river intact) could in practice be undermined by the recognition of this greater right. The argument on the other side is that the appreciable-loss test could be applied separately by each individual riparian, thereby obviating the risk that a succession of such deviations could undermine the whole system. If, therefore, the right in ques-

---

[33] "Though the water running in the fountain be every one's, yet who can doubt but that in the pitcher is his only who drew it out? His labour hath taken it out of the hands of Nature where it was common, and belonged equally to all her children, and hath thereby appropriated it to himself" (Locke 1980 [1690], par. 29).

tion could be restricted, the overall value of the water in the river would be increased by the very large gains that came from this additional use. Indeed, that condition could hold even if there were an appreciable decline in water levels, so long as that decline did not prejudice disproportionately the position of downstream users.

The English battle over this question came to a head in a series of cases toward the mid-nineteenth century, which Getzler (2006) describes in complete and accurate detail. The key case is *Embrey v. Owen*, 155 Eng. Rep. 579 (Ex.) (1851), where it is not quite coincidence that the lawyer for the victorious defendant was none other than George Bramwell, who, as Baron Bramwell, announced eleven years later in *Bamford v. Turnley*, 122 Eng. Rep. 27 (Ex.) (1862), the live-and-let-live principle that gave a principled, Pareto improvement account of why rigid boundaries should not govern disputes in low-level nuisance cases between neighboring landowners. In modern terminology, his view was that the detriments from these diversions, even if universally applied, were trivial compared with their gains. He noted that the diversions tended to take place in the wet seasons, when the harm to downstream users would be negligible. Further, much of the water that was used for irrigation returned to the river, thereby moderating any harm to downstream riparians. He concluded by insisting that the gains from the effective utilization of the land worked for the benefit of all. That argument was sufficient to persuade the trial court to adopt instructions that expanded the use of water from an earlier list of limited classes. Thus, Bramwell noted that it had always been accepted that water could at all times be used for "all natural and normal purposes, domestic and agricultural, provided [the riparian user] does not interfere with the rights of other riparian proprietors. For instance, he may, either by himself, his family, or his cattle, drink the water; he may bathe in it, use it in his habitation, and for watering his garden" (*Embrey*, 155 Eng. Rep. at 582). The only difference was that irrigation was a more intensive use than the others listed. But so long as the overall level of diminution was kept low, that point counted in favor of allowing the use, not cutting it back. As stated, the law is universalizable so that all participate in it, and all can enforce the limitation. Indeed, there was evidence at the time that many cooperative ventures between adjacent riparians allowed for more intensive use of water for their mutual benefit.[34] By way of analogy in land cases, the locality rule allows for higher levels of pollution in certain industrial districts because the greater reciprocal intensity of use continues to produce gains for all affected landowners.[35] In sum, this initial deviation from the older regime of riparian rights led to overall increases in utility without any clear shift in wealth among riparians.

The situation was quite different with the mills that sprang up in great profusion in England's Midlands during the seventeenth and eighteenth centuries (Getzler 2006). These mills were a source of power for the various factories that sprang up

---

[34] "According to the law so enunciated . . . it would be competent for a [riparian] to erect a mill . . . and take the water from the stream to work it, provided he neither penned back the water upon his neighbour above, nor injuriously affected the volume and flow of the water of the stream to his neighbour below. And the law favours the exercise of such a right: it is at once beneficial to the owner and to the commonwealth" (*Nuttal v. Bracewell*, 2 Ex. 1 [1866], quoted in Getzler [2006, 320–321]).

[35] For the adoption of this rule in England at this time, see *St. Helen's Smelting Co. v. Tipping*, 11 Eng. Rep. 1483 (H.L.) (1865), and the discussions of this case in Brenner (1974) and Simpson (1995).

along the rivers. There is little question that the introduction of some mills could increase the overall value of the river for its consumption and in-stream uses. Unlike the irrigation cases, these mills did not normally create the risk that water would be lost to the downstream users. Also, the use of these mills could generate strong distributive consequences for the riparians along the river. The power of a mill depends on the height of the falling water that is used to turn the wheel. That distance can be increased by building dams behind the mill, which could easily raise the river or even flood the uplands of upstream neighbors. Conversely, the size of that head could be reduced if the downstream owner built his own dam, which in turn would raise the height of the water at the foot of the upstream mill. Clearly, the total value of all mills, and the particular value of any given mill, depended on the number, size, and location of the mills along the river. Given the negative impact that each mill could have on the creation of other mills, the issues of number and spacing along the river became acute. It could be a matter of simple physics and geography that some riparians could construct no mills at all on their land, while the construction of some mills could easily foreclose the construction of others that might have proved equally valuable.

American Cases. The question, therefore, is how to design a regime that can deal with these situations. The closest parallels in the land use context are the disputes between farmers located at the top and the bottom of a hill, which in *Middlesex v. McCue*, 21 N.E. 230 (1889), generated a compromise that allowed ordinary farming at the top, even if it generated runoff that hurt the farmer at the bottom, who otherwise would have had the dominant hand in the matter. Just that solution was adopted in the reasonable-use cases, which reached the same uneasy conclusion about mills. For instance, in *Dumont v. Kellogg*, 29 Mich. 420 (1874), which involved simple but instructive facts, the plaintiff (the downstream owner) constructed a mill that was powered by water from above. The defendant (the upstream owner) subsequently constructed a dam that materially diminished the flow to the downstream mill. The question of "prejudice," as that term is used in irrigation cases, has to be resolved conclusively for the plaintiff. But in this instance, the decision came out clearly for the defendant. Justice Cooley put the proposition as follows:

> [A]s between different proprietors on the same stream, the right of each qualifies that of the other, and the question always is, not merely whether the lower proprietor suffers damage by the use of the water above him, nor whether the quantity flowing on is diminished by the use, but whether under all the circumstances of the case the use of the water by one is reasonable and consistent with a correspondent enjoyment of right by the other. (*Dumont*, 29 Mich. at 423–424)

Elsewhere, the point is put as follows:

> The person owning an upper mill on the same stream has a lawful right to use the water, and may apply it in order to work his mills to the best advantage, subject, however, to this limitation; that if, in the exercise of this right, and in consequence of it, the mills lower down the stream are rendered useless and unproductive, the law, in that case, will interpose, and limit this common right, so that the

owners of the lower mills shall enjoy a fair participation. . . . —Woodworth, J., in *Merritt v. Brinkerhoff*, 17 Johns., 320, 321 [N.Y., 1829]

It is fair participation and a reasonable use by each that the law seeks to protect. (*Dumont*, 29 Mich. at 420)

At this point, the system comes apart at the seams. There is no way to preserve parity between upstream and downstream users in ways that give both of them fair participation and reasonable use. It is easy to think of situations in which parity results in a situation where neither riparian can maintain a successful mill, so that one mill must remain useless if the other is to be viable. The carrying capacity of the river over the relevant interval supports only one but not two mills. The system of social welfare, even if it is carried to the maximum, can no longer meet a Pareto standard, at least in the absence of side payments, which, as far as I know, were never used. The best that can be done is to create a system in which it is hoped that the gains to the upstream riparian exceed the losses to those of a downstream riparian, as judged by the sense of the community, however determined. In essence, there is no clear hierarchy among the correlative uses of instream users. The only clear rules in this context are those that involve a diversion of the water from the river for nonriparian uses, which will always be forbidden if there is any diminution in flow; the same is true of any diversion by a stranger.[36] In effect, both of these activities are no different from the strict rules on exclusion of others that govern the use of land. Whatever the complications among coowners, the hard boundary lines reassert themselves in two contexts: those situations where a stranger takes from the group as a whole, or those cases in which an insider converts what is common property into sole property.

Even if the common-law rules work well in those two contexts, they surely fall short with respect to conflicts among in-stream users, for there is no obvious reason that unilateral moves by various riparians will be able to maximize the value along the river. If the legal rules fall short when there are only two parties to the dispute, they cannot work well with more. At this point, it seems as though some administrative solution is required to deal not only with the question of mill size and separation, but also with compensation for those persons whose lands are flooded. Schemes of this sort were developed during the nineteenth century and managed to survive constitutional challenges on the ground that the takings were not for public use.[37] A more accurate set of procedures would follow the unitization rules for oil and gas, where the common practice was to limit the number of wells that could be drilled in the field and to provide compensation for those surface owners who were denied rights to drill on their own land. Stated otherwise, there is no way to avoid reasonableness solutions so long as water flows downhill, but there are ways to supply compensation to the losers in the all-or-nothing choices for construction.

---

[36] "No person has a right to cause such a diversion, and it is wholly a wrongful act, for which an action will lie without proof of special damage. It differs, also, from the case of an interference by a stranger, who, by any means, or for any cause, diminishes the flow of the waters; for this also is wholly wrongful, and no question of the reasonableness of his action in causing the diminution can possibly arise" (*Dumont*, 29 Mich. at 422). For the same result, see also *Stratton v. Mt. Hermon Boys' School*, 103 N.E. 87 (Mass. 1913).

[37] See *Head v. Amoskeog Mfg. Co.*, 113 U.S. 9 (1885). For discussion, see Epstein (1997).

ALLUVION AND AVULSION

The last of the distinctive features of water law involves the long-established doctrines of alluvion and avulsion, which arise when the watercourse itself changes direction. In dealing with rivers, there is a good deal of sense in the Roman solution referred to earlier. The gradual changes in the course of the river essentially lead to automatic changes in the ownership of the land. If the river moves away from X, his holdings expand; if it moves toward him, they contract. *Ex ante*, there is no particular reason to believe that the river will move in one direction or the other, and certainly no reason to think that any action subject to human control can alter its course. The great advantage of this rule is that it keeps all riparians riparians, thereby eliminating the loss in value that would arise if a former riparian could no longer access the river. It also eliminates the task of having to decide who owns any new sliver of land that emerges between the river and the former riparian's land. By the same token, a sharp change in the course of a river from one channel to another cannot be handled by this means. Other landowners could easily own land between the new and the old courses, and their holdings would be wiped out if the alluvion doctrine applied. Hence the new stream has new riparian owners who are subject to the same rules.

The situation with respect to littoral property, which borders either lakes or oceans, is different. If the waters move in, the land is lost; if they move out, the additional land accretes to the landowner. These additions and diminutions are not trivial. Along Lake Michigan, the lake has moved out well over 100 feet in the last 15 years. The new and substantial dunes accrete to the owners of the beachfront property. Any losses, of course, would affect the same parties. The issue has great importance because the expansion of lands should not be allowed to destroy the key components of value in any lakefront or oceanfront property. The difficulty of applying these rules depends on the rapidity with which these shores change direction. Although the topic is beyond the scope of this chapter, Florida water law is especially complicated because the issue of moving is coupled with the issues of flooding and drainage, which give rise to difficult questions about who owns the beds of lakes that have been drained (the answer appears to be the state, which owned them when they were covered with water).[38] In essence, the introduction of yet another element of complexity puts additional strains on the system of property rights as among the parties. The question that now remains is how this complexity plays itself out in a constitutional setting.

Constitutional Protection of Water Rights

THE NAVIGATION SERVITUDE

The final piece of this inquiry seeks to integrate the discussion of water rights into the general principles of American constitutional law. This issue arises most saliently with regard to a question that has not yet been discussed, namely, the rights of navigation along rivers. Given the obvious government interest in transportation within and across state lines, this question has loomed large in the constitutional

---

[38] See, e.g., *Martin v. Busch*, 112 So. 274 (Fla. 1927), discussed in *Stop the Beach Renourishment, Inc. v. Florida Department of Environmental Protection*, 130 S. Ct. 2592, 2611 (2010). For my views, see Epstein (2011b).

decisions devoted to this topic. The Roman law on this subject was not fully developed, and it contained some internal complexities. One was that not all rivers were necessarily public, particularly if their entire course lay within the boundaries of a single owner. But many rivers obviously were public, and for those, the matter of correlative rights and duties quickly became paramount: what was the relationship between the public's rights of navigation and the rights of riparians? The answer was that the navigation rights could not be impaired by the use of riparian rights, by which it was meant that the natural course could not be blocked by improvements from the land, nor could the waters in question be drained from the channel in a way that impeded passage (MacGrady 1975). It was in this sense only that it can be said, as Getzler does, that "in the Digest, navigation and irrigation are given absolute priority over other consumptive uses" (2006, 13–14). There are no references in the Roman materials that deal with the converse question whether public improvements to a river could be allowed to entrench on the riparian rights of landowners.

English law in many respects follows from the Roman principles. The original common-law rules in England held that rivers were navigable only to the extent that their levels varied with the tides. That rule made sense for most small English rivers, but clearly not for the longish rivers in the United States, which were then governed by a rule of navigability "in fact," wholly without regard to the tides.[39] To the extent that a river is navigable in fact, its use is open to all, not just to the riparians who border it. That rule makes perfectly good sense because otherwise the river would have a large unused carrying capacity. But so long as the general public cannot make any consumptive use of the water, the net gains from increased utilization of these waters seem positive.

The phrase "open to all," however, is a natural law phrase that does not take into account the power of sovereign governments to limit access to the navigable waters of the state (or, indeed, any other property). The Roman law texts of Gaius and Justinian never address this issue but assume that these relationships are governed by the *ius gentium*, or the law of nations, which are general principles that are thought to be applicable to common situations whenever and wherever they occur. There is a deep tension between natural law and political power because natural law principles are not tied in any way to the power that a sovereign exercises of its own territory.[40] Quite the opposite, the broad outlines of natural law were thought to bind all sovereigns to general principles, leaving to particular states questions of implementation, which might determine, for example, which individuals enjoy the status of riparian owners. The peculiar role of the sovereign never rose to the fore in the English context with its unitary system of laws administered by one central government. But the potential collision between natural law and sovereign power arises with special urgency in the United States because of its federal system of divided state and national power. One consequence of making property rights part of the law of nations is that all persons in the world, regardless of citizenship, have equal access to the various forms of common property. Indeed, the phrase "law of

[39] For discussion, see *United States v. Cress*, 243 U.S. 316, 320–322 (1917).
[40] For a recent explication of the natural law theme in relationship to sovereign power, see Hamburger (2008). For comments on the matter, see Epstein (2011c).

nations" is no stranger to the U.S. Constitution, which at times also takes the natural law approach to these matters. Thus, it provides explicitly that Congress shall have the power "[t]o define and punish Piracies and Felonies committed on the high Seas, and Offences against the Law of Nations" (U.S. Constitution, Article I, § 8, cl. 10).[41]

In any real-world context, however, sovereign states and nations enforce the particular mandates of natural law. Side by side, therefore, with the earlier tradition lies the view that all property rights are the creature of the sovereign that has created them, whose power is essentially unlimited. Thus, Justinian not only speaks of the law of nations, but also expresses the famous phrase of royal power, "Quod principi placuit legis habet vigorem," or "That which is pleasing unto the prince has the force of law" (Justinian, quote in Thatcher 1907, 1.2.6).[42] Within the context of American federalism, the question of sovereignty gives rise to a further complication: which sovereign, state or federal, takes this responsibility? That question has special relevance in connection with the takings clause, which, in its original construction, offered protection only against the federal government (*Barron v. Baltimore*, 32 U.S. 243 [1833]). But historically, all water rights long antedated the creation of the federal government, so that the common and correct conclusion on this matter has always been that the delineation of the property rights to which the takings clause attaches is determined by state law.[43] Where else could they come from, given the limited powers of the federal government? The question of navigable easements pertains to all rivers, not just those that lie in two or more states. But as *Gibbons v. Ogden* makes unmistakably clear, from the time of the founding of the United States until the early twentieth century at the earliest, the commerce clause did not extend to any navigation that took place entirely within the confines of a single state.[44]

---

[41] Note the implicit tension between the law of nations, which is generally customary and thus discoverable by inspection, and the ability to "define" the offenses that are subject to punishment, which can, it appears, be done only in some bounded way.

[42] A second translation of this critical passage differs in instructive ways. In the Moyle version, the same passage is rendered, "Again, what the Emperor determines has the force of a statute" (Translated into English by J. B. Moyle, D.C.L. of Lincoln's Inn, Barrister-at-Law, Fellow and Late Tutor of New College, Oxford Fifth Edition (1913), http://www.gutenberg.org/files/5983/5983-h/5983-h.htm#2H_4_0003), which likewise misses the level of arbitrariness found in the word "placuit"). On these matters not one ounce of literalism beats a pound of creativity.

[43] See, e.g., *United States v. Cress*, 243 U.S. 316, 319–320 (1917) (the same view is taken in connection with the modern due process cases); see also *Board of Regents v. Roth*, 408 U.S. 564, 577–578 (1972) ("Property interests, of course, are not created by the Constitution. Rather, they are created and their dimensions are defined by existing rules or understandings that stem from an independent source such as state law—rules or understandings that secure certain benefits and that support claims of entitlement to those benefits"). *Roth* involved claims of procedural due process for property rights that arose from contracts with the United States, for which there is no natural law origin, as in the case of water rights.

[44] "Comprehensive as the word 'among' is, it may very properly be restricted to that commerce which concerns more States than one. The phrase is not one which would probably have been selected to indicate the completely interior traffic of a State, because it is not an apt phrase for that purpose; and the enumeration of the particular classes of commerce, to which the power was to be extended, would not have been made, had the intention been to extend the power to every description. The enumeration presupposes something not enumerated; and that something, if we regard the language or the subject of the sentence, must be the exclusively internal commerce of a State" (*Gibbons v. Ogden*, 22 U.S. 1, 194–195 (1824). This passage is quoted in full here because it has been twisted in subsequent decisions to make it appear that the commerce clause covers all productive activities. See, e.g., *United States v. Wrightwood Dairy Co.*, 315 U.S. 110 (1942) (holding valid an act regulating prices of milk that has traveled through interstate channels or that affects the marketing of such milk). In it, *Gibbons* was redacted to read in a manner at war with its original meaning: "The power of Congress over interstate commerce is plenary and complete in itself, may be exercised to its utmost extent, and acknowledges no limitations other than are prescribed in the Constitution (*Gibbons*, 22 U.S. at 196). It follows that no form of state activity can constitutionally

CRESS AND THE LIMITED SERVITUDE

At this point, one can address the central question: to what extent can the federal government alter the distribution of rights to protect and advance the interests of the public at large? This issue arises with protection of the uplands, access to the river, and the variety of in-stream uses insofar as they relate to the navigation servitude of uncertain scope. The correct approach to this question was taken in *United States v. Cress*, 243 U.S. 316 (1917). The two separate plaintiffs in *Cress* complained of the destruction by the increase of a variety of interests: the frequent inundation of fast land next to the river caused the destruction of a ford over the river, and a mill on the river was rendered inoperable by increases in the water level. In both cases, the government activities took place on navigable rivers. In one case, it was likely, and in the other, certain, that the harm took place on nonnavigable rivers.

The conclusion that these acts were for public use is, in the context of a navigable river, too obvious to contest. Accordingly, on this view, the only issue left for decision is the compensation, if any, that the government should be paid for undertaking its particular action. In line with decisions like that in *Dumont*, the government's ability to flood uplands was governed by ordinary eminent domain principles. Flooding for public use could not be enjoined, but full compensation was owed. To reach that conclusion, Justice Pitney applied the simple agency test developed earlier, namely, that actions that are wrongful when done by private parties are compensable when done by the state. At that point, he examined the scope of the navigation servitude in terms that relied heavily on the natural law origins of water rights. The key passage is worth quoting in full, if only because it has in many instances been disregarded:

> In Kentucky, and in other States that have rejected the common-law test of tidal flow and adopted the test of navigability in fact, while recognizing private ownership of the beds of navigable streams, numerous cases have arisen where it has been necessary to draw the line between public and private right in waters alleged to be navigable; and by an unbroken current of authorities it has become well established that the test of navigability in fact is to be applied to the stream in its natural condition, not as artificially raised by dams or similar structures; that the public right is to be measured by the capacity of the stream for valuable public use in its natural condition; that riparian owners have a right to the enjoyment of the natural flow without burden or hindrance imposed by artificial means, and no public easement beyond the natural one can arise without grant or dedication save by condemnation with appropriate compensation for the private right. (*Cress*, 243 U.S. at 321)

Thereafter, he describes the relationship of the federal power under the commerce clause: "Congress shall have the power . . . to regulate commerce with foreign Nations,

---

thwart the regulatory power granted by the commerce clause to Congress. Hence the reach of that power *extends* to those intrastate activities which in a substantial way interfere with or obstruct the exercise of the granted power" (*Wrightwood*, 315 U.S. at 119; emphasis added). Constitutional law becomes all too easy if "restricts" and "extends" have the same meaning.

and among the several States, and with the Indian tribes" (U.S. Constitution, Article I, § 8, cl. 3).

> The States have authority to establish for themselves such rules of property as they may deem expedient with respect to the streams of water within their borders both navigable and non-navigable, and the ownership of the lands forming their beds and banks subject, however, in the case of navigable streams, to the paramount authority of Congress to control the navigation so far as may be necessary for the regulation of commerce among the States and with foreign nations; the exercise of this authority being subject, in its turn, to the inhibition of the Fifth Amendment against the taking of private property for public use without just compensation. (*Cress*, 243 U.S. at 319–20 [citations omitted])

And further:

> The authority to make such improvements is only a branch of the power to regulate interstate and foreign commerce, and, as already stated, this power, like others, must be exercised, when private property is taken, in subordination to the Fifth Amendment. (*Cress*, 243 U.S. at 326)

Justice Pitney's excellent opinion in *Cress* is quite explicit in insisting that the "natural condition" of waterways sets the baseline from which the takings analysis should proceed. He correctly identifies the relationship between the public use and just-compensation requirements. The riparian interests that are good against other riparians are also good against the United States. In this regard, there is little question that the United States can, without compensation, take necessary steps in order to ensure that navigation is not blocked along the original channel by silting or other human actions, including those by riparians or others lawfully on the river. It is a closer question, in principle, whether the United States can counter natural changes in the course or depth of a navigable river. In addition, Pitney says (but only once) that the interest of the United States in the navigation servitude is "paramount," but only in this restrictive sense: it lets the United States expand the scope of the navigation servitude so long as it pays just compensation when it exercises the privilege. In this regard, he follows the applicable law for easements in land, where it is well established that no private party is allowed to "surcharge" an easement by making more extensive or intensive use of it than is allowed by the terms of the original grant, for example, by using an easement meant to allow the holder of the dominant interest to enter the land of a servient tenement also to encroach on the interests of third parties.[45] If the easement is acquired by prescription, the scope of the original use also determines its proper limits. Thus, an easement to walk over someone's land cannot be used to drive cattle over it. A new and broader easement is required. Private parties thus face an injunction if they do not purchase the broader easement. In like fashion, the government can take that wider navigation easement, but it must pay for its expansion. Pitney sees the point and refuses to allow the government to rise above the natural easement as determined by sensible private law principles.

---

[45] *Penn Bowling Recreation Center, Inc. v. Hot Shoppes, Inc.*, 179 F.2d 64, 66 (D.C. 1949); see also Restatement of Property § 478 & cmt. e (1944).

In dealing with this particular problem, such a solution is the only way to avoid the problem of political arbitrage noted earlier. The politics of water rights is always intense, given the multiple interests in any given body of water. The want of a just-compensation requirement thus incentivizes dominant political factions to seek extensions of the navigation easement through political action, well knowing that they need not pay for the change or ask the taxpayers to come up with the needed funds. The only way to control the abuse of government powers is to insist that all takings for public use require payment of just compensation in the absence of any common-law nuisance. The nuisance issue, of course, always lingers in the background. In *Cress*, the issue was not explicitly raised, probably because the matter had been put to rest in earlier cases, which limited the power of the state to redefine nuisances at will in ways that negated its duty of compensation. Thus, in *Yates v. Milwaukee*, the Supreme Court said: "It is a doctrine not to be tolerated in this country, that a municipal corporation, without any general laws either of the city or of the State, within which a given structure can be shown to be a nuisance, can, by its mere declaration that it is one, subject it to removal by any person supposed to be aggrieved, or even by the city itself" (77 U.S. 497, 505 [1871]).

The statement in *Yates* arose in the context of efforts by the private landowner to build a pier that reached the navigable waters of the local river. The precise decision in the case held that the state could not block that effort by calling the wharf a nuisance in the absence of a showing of any interference with navigation along the river. The government here was called out for an overaggressive defense of its navigation servitude, not for its effort to expand the servitude where it had not previously run, as in *Cress*. If a state seeks to expand its sphere of influence for the navigation servitude, the nuisance issue is dead on arrival, which is why it never surfaced in *Cress*. Instead, everything turns on the compensation question and its relationship to the various types of interests that the government's construction project hurt. If there are any damages to the fast lands by the river, the compensation issue is easy because of the per se rule in private law that protects these upland interests from any action by any user of the river. The government is bound by that rule. Damage in the river proper, including the loss of power of the mill, is a more difficult issue because the correlative nature of all private rights and duties means that to prevail, the private parties must show actual damages and the unreasonableness of the government's action. That inquiry could, in some cases, give rise to delicate questions of fact, which could turn on the natural scope of the navigation easement. But in *Cress*, the artificial expansion was in and of itself enough to establish that result. At that point, the takings finding followed. The navigation easement is one of a group of correlative interests in waters. It cannot by this logic become the dominant one.

SCRANTON AND THE PARAMOUNT NAVIGATION SERVITUDE

Cress is virtually the only twentieth-century Supreme Court case that gets the correct sequence from top to bottom. In all other situations, it is said that the navigation easement of the United States is paramount over all interests in the river. The delicate balance is thus put to one side. The cases that take this position are legion. In *Scranton v. Wheeler*, 179 U.S. 141 (1900), the question was whether the government owed compensation when its canal construction project cut off the access of a private riparian to a navigable river. Justice John Marshall Harlan rejected the claim by reading the term "paramount" to cover not only the public use issue, but also the just-compensation question. "All the cases concur in holding that the power of Congress to regulate commerce, and therefore navigation, is paramount, and is unrestricted except by the limitations upon its authority by the Constitution" (*Scranton*, 179 U.S. at 162). He went on: "It was not intended, by that provision in the Constitution, that the paramount authority of Congress to improve the navigation of the public waters of the United States should be crippled by compelling the Government to make compensation for an injury to a riparian owner's right of access to navigability that might incidentally result from an improvement ordered by Congress" (*Scranton*, 179 U.S. at 164–165).

The two key assertions of this passage are wholly erroneous, relating first to the nature of the navigation easement and second to the role of the commerce power. Harlan's reading of "paramount" is utterly inconsistent with the usual understanding of water rights as mixed and correlative. An instructive parallel to this claim for the paramount easement is Blackstone's overwrought (and widely criticized) definition of the ownership of real property as "[t]hat sole and despotic dominion which one man claims and exercises over the external things of the world, in total exclusion of the right of any other individual in the universe" (Blackstone 1765–1769, 2:2). But ironically, Blackstone is closer to the truth because exclusive rights are the initial starting point for delineating property rights in land, while correlative rights and duties are surely the best way to think about this subject for water. This imperial definition of "paramount" is surely inferior to Pitney's more measured use of the term in *Cress*.

Nor does Harlan offer any compelling reason for this extravagant argument. His use of the word "crippled" makes it appear that the riparian could block the project, but all that can be done is to demand compensation for the property loss attendant to the improvement. That requirement does not "cripple" the land acquisition of the government, but instead puts an accurate price on the social costs of its adventures. The same conclusion applies here. Nor are matters made better by the use of the weasel word "incidental," which makes it appear as though only intentional takings done solely to hurt the private property owner are covered by the takings clause. But that term is neither here nor there. The government knows full well that most dams will back up water, and if it does not, its ignorance is hardly an excuse to allow it to keep the benefit for the public at large by inflicting harm on some of its members. The private law governing the rights of riparians among themselves in no way turns on whether or not any riparian who dams or diverts a river intends to harm the riparians above or below him on the river. A strict liability norm takes hold that is equally useful in this context.

Harlan's second error is to read the commerce clause as though it were on steroids. In particular, his entire argument rests on a deep confusion between federal sovereign power, on one hand, and the federal ownership of specific assets, on the other hand. In the initial Supreme Court foray into the scope of the commerce clause, Chief Justice Marshall, in *Gibbons*, opined correctly and at great length that the commerce power of the United States covered navigation, including navigation that extended into the interior of a state (22 U.S. 1 [1824]). That power surely gives the federal government the power to regulate existing sources of navigation and to expand or enlarge them. But there is no reason to convert this grant of federal power into an overarching claim of property rights that ignore other elements of the Constitution.

THE *WILLOW RIVER* SYNTHESIS

The same confusion manifested itself in the important case *United States v. Chandler-Dunbar Water Power Co.*, 229 U.S. 53 (1913) (where Justice Pitney was oddly silent), which split the difference by allowing recovery for any flooding of uplands but denied compensation for the loss of power of the company's mills attendant to the expansion of the river in question. The most notable decision in the sequence, however, is that of Justice Robert Jackson in *United States v. Willow River Power Co.*, 324 U.S. 499 (1945), where the question was whether the actions of the government that raised the water level of the St. Croix, a navigable river, created a compensable loss to the owner of a power plant on the Willow River, an upstream nonnavigable river, whose power was diminished when the height of the St. Croix River was raised. On its facts, the case is indistinguishable from *Cress*, which exhibited the same interaction between navigable and nonnavigable rivers. The cases, however, were duly "distinguished," leaving *Cress*, as it were, dead in the water, which is its current status in the law.[46] Key to the argument in *Willow River* was the asserted dominance of the navigation servitude. Use of the natural law baseline makes this an easy case, which is why the surge for positivism dominated Jackson's opinion: "[T]he claimant in this case cannot stand in the Cress shoes unless it can establish the same right to have the navigable St. Croix flow tail waters away at natural levels that Cress had to have the non-navigable stream run off his tail waters at natural levels" (*Willow River*, 324 U.S. at 506–507). The agency theory of government rights is then brushed aside on the ground that the correlative duties between riparians of equal stature before the law do not bind the government with its superior rights:

> Rights, property or otherwise, which are absolute against all the world are certainly rare, and water rights are not among them. Whatever rights may be as between equals such as riparian owners, they are not the measure of riparian rights on a navigable stream relative to the function of the Government in improving navigation. Where these interests conflict they are not to be reconciled as between equals, but the private interest must give way to a superior right, or perhaps it would be more accurate to say that as against the Government such private interest is not a right at all. (*Willow River*, 324 U.S. at 510)

There is a delicious irony in a decision that deprecates the recognition of "absolute" rights while elevating the navigation servitude to that lofty state. But the rejection of one position, without argument, requires the creation of an alterna-

---

[46] See, e.g., *United States v. Grand River Dam Authority*, 363 U.S. 229 (1960); *United States v. 531.13 Acres of Land*, 366 F.2d 915, 922 (4th Cir. 1966). These cases relied on *Willow River* for a broad construction of the navigation easement that allowed the federal government to trump all state interests in power sources and other uses of nonnavigable rivers.

tive. Rather than face this question head on, Jackson offers a variety of function-
alist considerations by insisting:

> [N]ot all economic interests are "property rights"; only those economic advantages
> are "rights" which have the law back of them, and only when they are so recog-
> nized may courts compel others to forbear from interfering with them or to
> compensate for their invasion. The law long has recognized that the right of own-
> ership in land may carry with it a legal right to enjoy some benefits from adjacent
> waters. But that a closed catalogue of abstract and absolute "property rights" in
> water hovers over a given piece of shore land, good against all the world, is not in
> this day a permissible assumption. We cannot start the process of decision by call-
> ing such a claim as we have here a "property right"; whether it is a property right
> is really the question to be answered. Such economic uses are rights only when
> they are legally protected interests. Whether they are such interests may depend
> on the claimant's rights in the land to which he claims the water rights to be ap-
> purtenant or incidental; on the navigable or non-navigable nature of the waters
> from which he advantages; on the substance of the enjoyment thereof for which
> he claims legal protection; on the legal relations of the adversary claimed to be
> under a duty to observe or compensate his interests; and on whether the conflict
> is with another private riparian interest or with a public interest in navigation.
> The claimant's assertion that its interest in a power head amounts to a "property
> right" is made under circumstances not present in any case before considered by
> this Court. (*Willow River*, 324 U.S. at 502–503)

Jackson's passage is a fog of words that explains the challenge to be faced without
answering it. Further, it does not address any of the functional explanations for the
stabilization of property rights that the natural law system so powerfully and freely
supplies. It is true enough to say that property rights exist only when the law is behind them. However, it is critical to explain why the law should not back the plaintiff in this case. Jackson treats the situation as though it is one of *damnum absque
iniuria*, which, literally translated from the Latin, means harm without legal injury.
The modern, equally unilluminating term is "pecuniary externality," which refers
to losses from changes in prices and quantities in the operation of the competitive
economy. But these losses do not arise because people prefer to patronize power that
is now derived from cheaper sources. It comes from wiping out the mill by actions
that would not be tolerated under the standard of reasonableness in riparian use
developed in *Dumont*. The effort to demote them thus anticipates the same misguided
move in *Penn Central*, when Justice Brennan relies explicitly on the muddled argument in *Willow River* to equate the loss of a property interest to a competitive loss.
Brennan thus points to

> the decisions in which this Court has dismissed "taking" challenges on the ground
> that, while the challenged government action caused economic harm, it did not
> interfere with interests that were sufficiently bound up with the reasonable expec-
> tations of the claimant to constitute "property" for Fifth Amendment purposes.
> See, e. g., *Willow River* (interest in high-water level of river for runoff for tailwaters

to maintain power head is not property); *Chandler-Dunbar* (no property interest can exist in navigable waters). (*Penn Central*, 438 U.S. at 124–125)

That error follows hard on the heels of Justice Brennan's original mistake in belittling the possibility of articulating any clear rules by insisting wrongly that everything depends on "ad hoc" inquiries that balance various factors (*Penn Central*, 438 U.S. at 124), which denatures the internal structure of any system of property rights.

Willow River thus marks a regrettable decline in how modern cases approach the question of property rights relative to earlier authorities, like *Yates* and *Cress*, which followed the natural law principles even if they were not always clear about why they had such explanatory power. In most instances the strength of the natural law lies in the soundness of its implicit utilitarian foundations (Epstein 1989).

AVULSION AND *STOP THE BEACH RENOURISHMENT*

For most standard waterways, the takings law developed in the sequence of cases from *Scranton* through *Willow River* has set the path for further developments. The most novel development in this area comes with the question of how to apply takings principles to government actions that take place in the shifting Florida waters. In *Stop the Beach Renourishment, Inc. v. Florida Department of Environmental Protection*, 130 S. Ct. 2592 (2010), the issue was a strong antierosion program introduced by the State of Florida that was designed to stabilize conditions on lakefront properties. The key to this situation was a decision to build walls and other supports that would prevent the erosion of the beach. The statutory scheme fixed a new boundary line between the public and the private lands at the place where this erosion line was established. That line replaced the usual mean high-water-mark line that could vary widely with circumstances. It was clear that this system could, with the expansion of the littoral lands, demote the original littoral owner by allowing the government to claim title to the new lands that emerged from the water.

In light of what has been said here, that interposition constitutes a rejiggering of the fundamental private relationships, counting as a taking of the property for which compensation is owed. It is easy to see the strength of the state's claim in this situation, for why would it invest its resources in beach renourishment at public expense if all the benefit inured to the private landowners? However, this objection can be met within the framework of traditional eminent domain law once the full arrangement is examined (Epstein 2009). The key point in favor of the current arrangement is that all the benefits of the renourishment did not fall to the state. As the statutory scheme was constructed, the landowners not only received the benefits of a stabilized water line, but also had their access and view rights explicitly preserved. This troika of rights is surely impressive and may well have left the landowners better off with the new scheme than they were before, at which point no cash compensation is appropriate. The record on this point, however, was not developed, so that one possibility was to remand the case for a determination of relative values, with the understanding that the most the state would owe would be the net diminution in value, once all pluses and minuses were taken into account, including the prospect that the general public could make use of the land seaward to the antierosion line.

The sensible framework gives protection to the state interest, but this entire line of argument was lost on Justice Scalia. Far from concentrating on the details of the particular scheme, he instead relied on the view that the private law in this area did not establish any background expectations. Relying on his earlier decision in *Lucas v. South Carolina Coastal Council*, 505 U.S. 1003 (1992), he concluded that "a regulation that deprives a property owner of all economically beneficial use of his property is not a taking if the restriction 'inhere[s] in the title itself, in the restrictions that background principles of the State's law of property and nuisance already place upon land ownership'" (*Stop the Beach*, 130 S. Ct. at 2609).[47] His application of this test in *Stop the Beach* was quite useless because he relied on *Martin v. Busch*, 112 So. 274 (Fla. 1927), to support the proposition that no such expectation had been formed. That was odd because the distinctive feature of the Florida statute was that it preserved both the former littoral owner's right of access to the beach and his right of view over it as part of the grand settlement. The correct approach, therefore, was to raise a factual issue on which the government could well prevail, namely, whether the stabilization of the shoreline (which prevented retreat or "reliction," which would have resulted in the loss of the lake front land to which ownership rights attached), coupled with the easements of access and view, made the parcel worth more than before.

Moreover, it is instructive why Scalia went so far astray. In dealing with the Florida law, he cited several early treatises that dealt with the subject for the rules that had developed.[48] But at no point did he pay any attention to the natural law framework that dominated their discussions.[49] Because of his utter lack of mooring in the traditional literature, Scalia adopted a framework that was devoid of insight when he should have followed the analysis in *Cress*. Once again, the utter separation of the public and private law, coupled with the total disregard of the natural law tradition, led the Supreme Court astray.

This chapter has traced two sets of interconnections that are of vital concern in understanding the law and economics of natural resources. The first task is to figure out, within the context of private law, the overlap and differences between the rules that govern land and those that govern water. It should not be supposed that there is no connection between them because the natural law tradition in which these relationships are all involved featured two considerations. First, private rights were acquired through a decentralized customary system that did not depend for its inception on the use of public power. The first-possession rule was operative in

---

[47] There are two great weaknesses of this approach. First, it implies that there are two regimes for takings, one that deals with total wipeouts (loss of all economically beneficial uses) and one that does not. Second, it never specifies the explicit police power issues that surround the law of nuisance. Interestingly enough, Justice Pitney never made that mistake in *Cress*. There he noted first that permanent flooding of land created a compensable taking whether or not the government formally took title to the property. See *Pumpelly v. Green Bay Co.*, 80 U.S. 166 (1872). *Cress* did not involve permanent flooding. "It is true that in the *Pumpelly Case* there was an almost complete destruction . . . of the value of the lands, while in the present case the value is impaired to the extent of only one-half. But it is the character of the invasion, not the amount of damage resulting from it, so long as the damage is substantial, that determines the question whether it is a taking" (*Cress*, 243 U.S. at 328).

[48] Farnham (1904); Lewis (1909); Maloney, Plager, and Baldwin (1968), cited with approval in *Stop the Beach*, 130 Sup. Ct. at 2598.

[49] See, e.g., Farnham (1904).

both contexts, albeit in very different ways. For land, the dominant trope was always that of exclusive rights to possession, use, and disposition, not as the ultimate assignment of rights, but as the best first approximation to preface a more comprehensive solution. For water, the notion of riparianism denoted a class of individuals who had complex rights among themselves, much like joint tenants or tenants in common for land, but who, as a group, did have a set of exclusive rights (for consumptive uses) that they did not have to share with the rest of the world. Starting from these simple components, a larger system of property rights that was in some rough sense efficient could develop in both areas.

A successful public law—one that can distinguish between takings and legitimate regulations requiring no compensation—is possible only in a legal environment that builds on the full set of private water rights. The distinctive power of the government is not to redefine the common law of nuisance in ways that work to its short-term advantage. It is that it may initiate for public use changes in private rights without consent of the riparian owners only if it pays the appropriate compensation for the rights so taken. In dealing with this question, the property rules in government cases follow those developed in private law contexts. For real estate, this means that fractional interests must receive as much protection as the larger fee interest of which they are a part. For water, it means the exact opposite, such that the government's effort to expand its navigation servitude has to respect (or pay compensation for) the many correlative interests in water.

The course of takings law in the United States has not followed that path. Instead, for both sets of resources, the traditional conceptions of property rights developed in private law contexts are either belittled or ignored. This disregard has opened a vast public space for political intrigue, which often leads to political conflict and wasteful allocation systems that a more definite and coherent approach to property rights would avoid. Time after time, the new learning is said to reflect an intellectual sophistication that the intuitive natural law jurists were said to ignore. And time after time, the modernists are wrong, precisely because they have lost all sight of the key fundamentals.

Acknowledgments

I thank Daniel Cole, Joshua Getzler, and Yu-Hung Hong for their very helpful comments on an earlier draft of this chapter, and Isaac Gruber of the University of Chicago Law School and Brett Davenport of New York University School of Law for their usual excellent research assistance.

REFERENCES

American Law Institute. 1944. *Restatement of property*. Philadelphia.
Ballantine, Henry W. 1918. Title by adverse possession. *Harvard Law Review* 32:135.
Bentham, Jeremy. 1882 [1802]. *Theory of legislation*. 4th ed. Trans. R. Hildredth. London: Trübner and Co.
Bergin, Thomas F., and Paul G. Haskell. 1984. *Preface to estates in land and future interests*. New York: Foundation Press.

Blackstone, William. 1765–1769. *Commentaries on the law of England*. Vols. 1–4. Oxford.

Bracton, Henry. 1969. *Laws and customs of England*. Bracton Online, Harvard Law School Library. http://hlsl5.law.harvard.edu/bracton/Common/SearchPage.htm (Samuel Thorne translation 1969).

Brenner, Joel Franklin. 1974. Nuisance law and the Industrial Revolution. *Journal of Legal Studies* 3:403.

Claeys, Eric R. 2006. Takings: An appreciative retrospective. *William and Mary Bill of Rights Journal* 15:439.

Cole, Daniel H., and Elinor Ostrom. 2010. The variety of property systems and rights in natural resources: An introduction. Paper delivered at the conference "Evolution of Property Rights Related to Land and Natural Resources," Lincoln Institute of Land Policy, Cambridge, MA (September 20). http://ssrn.com/abstract=1656418.

Epstein, Richard A. 1979. Corrective justice and its utilitarian constraints. *Journal of Legal Studies* 8:49.

———. 1985. Why restrain alienation? *Columbia Law Review* 85:970.

———. 1989. The utilitarian foundations of natural law. *Harvard Journal of Law and Public Policy* 12:713.

———. 1993. *Bargaining with the state*. Princeton, NJ: Princeton University Press.

———. 1994. On the optimal mix of common and private property. *Social Philosophy and Policy* 11:17.

———. 1997. A clear view of the cathedral: The dominance of property rules. *Yale Law Journal* 106:2091.

———. 2000. The uneasy marriage of utilitarian and libertarian thought. *Quinnipiac Law Review* 19:783.

———. 2003. *Skepticism and freedom: A modern case for classical liberalism*. Chicago: University of Chicago Press.

———. 2006. Taking stock of takings: An author's retrospective. *William and Mary Bill of Rights Journal* 15:407.

———. 2007. Introduction. In *Economics of property law*, ed. Richard Epstein. Northampton, MA: Edward Elgar.

———. 2009. Florida's beach blues: When private rights collide with environmental protection. *Forbes*, December 1. http://www.forbes.com/2009/11/30/florida-beach-environment-politics -opinions-columnists-richard-a-epstein.html.

———. 2010. Carbon dioxide: Our newest pollutant. *Suffolk University Law Review* 43:797.

———. 2011a. *Design for liberty: Private property, public administration and the rule of law*. Cambridge, MA: Harvard University Press.

———. 2011b. Littoral rights under the takings law: The clash between the Ius Naturale and *Stop the Beach Renourishment v. Florida EPA*. *Duke Journal of Constitutional Law and Public Policy* 38:6.

———. 2011c. The natural law influences on the first generation of American constitutional law: Reflections on Philip Hamburger's law and judicial duty. *Journal of Law, Philosophy, and Culture* 6.

Farnham, Henry Philip. 1904. *Law of waters and water rights*. Rochester, NY: The Lawyers Co-Operative Publishing Company.

French, Susan F. 1994. Tradition and innovation in the new restatement of servitudes: A report from midpoint. *Connecticut Law Review* 27:119.

Gaius. 1932. Institutes of Gaius. In *The civil law*, vol. 1. Trans. Samuel P. Scott. Cincinnati, OH: The Central Trust Company.

Getzler, Joshua. 2006. *A history of water rights at common law*. Oxford: Oxford University Press.

Hamburger, Philip. 2008. *Law and judicial duty*. Cambridge, MA: Harvard University Press.

Honoré, A. M. 1961. Ownership. In *Oxford essays in jurisprudence*, ed. A. G. Guest, 107–147. Oxford: Oxford University Press.

Hume, David. 1739–1740. *A treatise of human nature*. Oxford.

Justinian. 2009. *Digest*, ed. Alan Watson. Philadelphia: University of Pennsylvania Press.

————. *Institutes*. http://faculty.cua.edu/Pennington/Law508/Roman%20Law/RomanLawTexts .htm.

Lewis, John. 1909. *A treatise on the law of eminent domain*. 3rd ed. Chicago: Callaghan.

Locke, John. 1980 [1690]. *Second treatise of government*, ed. C. B. MacPherson. Indianapolis: Hackett.

MacGrady, Glenn J. 1975. The navigability concept in the civil and common law. *Florida State University Law Review* 3:511.

Maloney, F. E., S. J. Plager, and F. N. Baldwin. 1968. *Water law and administration: The Florida experience*. Gainesville, FL: University of Florida Press.

Nicholas, Barry. 1962. *An introduction to Roman law*. Oxford: Clarendon Press.

Rose, Carol M. 1990. Energy and efficiency in the realignment of common-law water rights. *Journal of Legal Studies* 19:261.

Sened, Itai. 1997. *The political institution of private property*. Cambridge, U.K.: Cambridge University Press.

Simpson, A. W. Brian. 1995. Victorian judges and the problem of social cost: *Tipping v. St. Helens' Smelting Co*. In *Leading cases in the common law*. Oxford: Clarendon Press.

Thatcher, Oliver J., ed. 1907. The library of original sources: The Roman world. Milwaukee: University Research Extension Co. http://faculty.cua.edu/Pennington/Law508/InstitutesofJustinian .htm#Book%20I.

Commentary

HENRY E. SMITH

In law, both the relationship of the private and the public and the resemblance, if any, between water rights and real property in land have long preoccupied and confounded judges, commentators, and litigants, so it comes as some surprise that Richard Epstein counts the relationship of the public to the private as the key to unlocking the relationship of property in water and property in land. As Epstein sees it, a natural law grounded in utilitarianism points to basic parity between members of society and utilitarian adjustments, making public rights like the navigation servitude just an enormous compilation of private rights. Moreover, this parity-plus-adjustment procedure for thinking about resource conflicts provides, in his view, answers about the scope of rights to land and water, including the question of just compensation for public use. Although water by its topography differs from the prototypical situation with land, thus making parity more difficult and adjustment more necessary, Epstein argues that private rights based on parity plus adjustment scale up perfectly in both areas, thus making seemingly tricky questions of private and public rights in water much more straightforward than they have ever appeared before.

Grounding public rights in both land and water on similar basic private law baselines gets us surprisingly far, and pushing this idea as far as it will go is a real achievement, but the notions of parity and utilitarian-grounded natural law do not by themselves furnish workable baselines in the context of either the private law or the public law. And because of the special difficulties of a fugitive resource that runs downhill, the parity-plus-adjustment framework, despite its value as a theoretical baseline, falls especially short in the case of water.

The first part of this commentary makes a distinction between the interests people have in property and the devices property uses to serve them. People's interest in resources is primarily one of use, broadly conceived to include preservation values, but the law employs many shortcuts, such as rights to exclude that are implemented by trespass law, to serve those interests in a rough and wholesale fashion. In a world of zero transaction costs, rights might be more directly tailored to uses, but that is not our world.[1] Sometimes there is little choice but to focus on uses, as in nuisance and water law, but the need for shortcuts like trespass is grounded in transaction costs. By emphasizing theoretical baselines and not distinguishing between interests in use and the delineation of rights to serve those interests, Epstein's chapter

---

[1] Coase (1960) presupposed a bundle-of-rights theory, but property rights are lumpier than expected on the bundle theory precisely because of transaction costs (Merrill and Smith 2011).

minimizes the role of baselines that do not fit easily into the framework of parity plus adjustment. The second part of this commentary then turns to the notion of parity itself. Like equality, parity in Epstein's chapter begs an important question: parity of what? More particularly, a framework that approves some deviations from parity but not others must have a stable source of consensus on various matters, including the following: what is a baseline, and what constitutes a departure from it? What is a rule, and what constitutes an exception to it? And what distinguishes legitimate use of whatever system of rules we have from abuse of such a system? Utilitarian-based natural law, if such a thing is possible, does not furnish but rather presupposes such starting points.[2]

Finally, with regard to water, Epstein is correct that we must move more quickly away from exclusion than in the case of land and must develop a system of governance tailored closely to use. The operation of baselines and the scaling up of the private to the public do not work as simply as Epstein's chapter suggests, and not surprisingly, Epstein assumes a problematic baseline identified with common-law nuisance. The result is a gap between the parity-plus-adjustment framework and a full-blown theory of water law that can be filled only by a clearer sense of the baselines not just of interests, but also of delineation. Parity and adjustment get us surprisingly far, but not all the way.

Baselines and Delineation

For any project involving public versus private law—or, for that matter, property in land versus water—robust baselines are needed, because property involves both a set of interests and a set of modes of protection. Generally, property protects people's interests in the use of things, broadly taken to include aesthetic and other "uses" that require the preservation rather than the consumption of resources or the flows of services from them. Property serves these interests and allows owners and others to plan, invest, and transact by furnishing an array of protections, with their associated limitations. The first approximation is a set of rules of trespass that implements a right to exclude. But there is no interest in exclusion per se.[3] Rather, the ability or even the right to exclude is valuable for the wide range of uses that it enables a person to engage in without interference. Crucially, exclusion and trespass allow protection of these uses without the necessity of spelling them out or evaluating them (Smith 2004a; 2009b). But this basic setup does not serve people's purposes well enough, so the law shifts at some point to governance strategies, which prescribe proper use

---

[2] Whether it is possible is beyond the scope of this commentary. For the debate on this topic, see, e.g., Epstein (1989) and Posner (2004). Merrill and Smith (2007) have argued that considerations of information cost tend to bring rights-based and utilitarian theories of property closer together at the level of prescribed results, even if disagreement remains at a more foundational level. For present purposes, I am arguing only that property baselines may well require more of a surface moral consensus than courts, commentators, and law schools currently presuppose.

[3] What might broadly be called "exclusion theorists" disagree on this point. Compare Harris (1996, 30–32) (analyzing property as an "open ended set of use-privileges" protected by "trespassory rules"), Penner (1997, 68–74) (no interest in exclusion itself and formal right to exclude protects interests in use), Smith (2004b) (discussing how the right to exclude protects a broad and largely unspecified set of privileges to use), and Smith (2007) (interests are in use, not exclusion, but rights to exclude are devices for protecting interests in use) with Katz (2008) (grounding property in an interest in exclusive agenda setting for resources) and Merrill (1998) (attempting to reduce much of property to elaborations of the right to exclude).

(Smith 2002).[4] This can be achieved through off-the-rack common-law nuisance, through contract, or through regulations like zoning. Any of these devices may or may not be a good idea in a given instance, but their justification lies in dealing with use conflict in a more fine-grained way than is possible by giving the owner the simple right to repel invasions of a column of space or to disallow harmful touching of chattels.

Epstein's chapter conflates interests and the devices that serve them, which leads to a few anomalies. For example, he dismisses William Blackstone's definition of property as "that sole and despotic dominion which one man claims and exercises over the external things of the world, in total exclusion of the right of any other individual in the universe" (Blackstone 1979 [1766], 2). Blackstone never intended this definition to be the last word—it was his first on the subject—or to be taken literally.[5] The point is rather that in our actual world, exclusion looms large, and it does so for transaction-cost reasons. If delineation were cheaper, a use-by-use set of rights would be equally cheap and effective for the purposes to which property is put (Merrill and Smith 2011). Because he does not sufficiently distinguish interests and the formal rights that serve them, Epstein partially agrees with the conventional wisdom in disparaging Justice Marshall's opinion in *Loretto v. Teleprompter Manhattan CATV Corp.*, 458 U.S. 419 (1982), which held that a permanent physical invasion at the government's behest is a per se taking. If the right to exclude is viewed as an interest or as one stick among many in the bundle, protecting it by a per se rule against permanent physical invasions looks weird.[6] But if, because of delineation costs, exclusion is simply a lot clearer than other methods of protecting owners' interests in use, a per se rule in takings is more like the takings analogue to trespass, with its strict liability for invasions of the column of space defined by the *ad coelum* rule (Merrill and Smith 2007). Yes, it is over- and underinclusive, but that is what rough first approximations like trespass are.

More generally, Epstein's chapter ignores how delineation costs, and information costs in particular, shape property entitlements in ways that the parity-plus-adjustment framework leaves out. Consider the *numerus clausus*, the fixed and closed set of basic forms of property (Rudden 1987). In the face of arguments for the *numerus clausus* on information-cost grounds, including economies of scale and scope in government provisions of standardization in property (Merrill and Smith 2000), Epstein merely repeats arguments he made decades ago that land records solve all information-cost problems and that property can safely be as contractarian as contracts (Epstein 1982).[7] Whether he is right cannot ultimately be determined by a priori argument, as can be seen from areas in which standardized formats are required and "data dumps" do not solve information problems (Smith 2011). As Herbert Simon (1971) pointed out long ago, the scarcity is not of information but of human attention.

---

[4] See also Cheung (1970); Field (1989); and Rose (1991).

[5] See, e.g., Schorr (2009); see also Ellickson (1993) and Rose (1998).

[6] Heller and Krier call the per se rule for permanent physical invasions "passing strange" from the point of view of deterrence and distribution (1999, 1008).

[7] See also Conard (1942) (arguing that the enforcement of easements should not be objectionable on grounds of novelty as long as there is notice). Merrill and Smith have specifically addressed these points ever since their 2000 article, which refuted "notice cures all"; see also Smith (2011). Still no response from Epstein.

Are land records a substitute or a complement to standardization through devices like the *numerus clausus*? Suggestive evidence comes from Benito Arruñada's study (2003), which found that more definitive title records in registration systems are correlated with a stricter *numerus clausus*. The registrar stands in for the public (the set of *in rem* duty bearers) and cannot be expected to deal with contracting parties' idiosyncrasies. Likewise, Epstein simply assumes that trusts are contracts and are of no concern to anyone other than settlor, trustee, and beneficiary. Although trusts are a very clever device to allow for idiosyncrasy while minimizing third-party information costs,[8] the basic problem cannot be wished away. As long as beneficial interests sometimes bind third parties, the information-cost problem exists. Trust law solves the problem by holding third parties to equitable interests of which they had notice and by not placing on them a high burden of inquiry (Powell 1995, ¶ 513[3], at 41–142). Beneficiaries lose out sometimes precisely because of the information-cost problem.

Finally, central to Epstein's argument is the idea that the public baseline is merely a quantitative extension of the private law baselines. No room is left for qualitative differences between the public and the private that might stem from the inherently different problems that public rights are meant to solve. It is true that in some sense, the public is the composite of individuals, but to argue that public rights should share the qualities of private rights is to commit the fallacy of composition. More empirically, the types of network effects associated with some types of public property, including the navigation servitude discussed in Epstein's chapter, may call for devices that are not simply the sum of private easements. The whole category of "inherently public property" explored by Carol Rose (1986) is difficult to square with the reduction of public rights to private rights.[9] Even if this reduction of the public to the private is impossible only for transaction-cost reasons, those reasons are no less real.

The problem here is analogous to Epstein's lack of seriousness about the information-cost implication of *in rem* rights. Epstein implicitly treats *in rem* rights as a composite of *in personam* rights. They may be so in substance (in some sense), but *in personam* and *in rem* rights are very different in terms of delineation, including whether they should be standardized. That *in rem* rights are not congeries of *in personam* rights, as Hohfeld (1917) and the realists would have it,[10] does have substantive implications for the nature and scope of actual property rights. Likewise, Epstein would like to treat the public as a composite of the private. In some theoretical benchmark way this is true, but again, in our positive-transaction-cost world, they are treated differently in terms of their mechanisms, with implications for their scope.

Is the Notion of Parity Running on Empty?

The baseline Epstein proposes rests in the first instance on a notion of parity, or equal rights as between competing claimants and as between competing neighboring

---

[8] Merrill and Smith (2001a); see also Smith (2011).

[9] For an economically grounded taxonomy of public property doctrines, see Merrill (2011).

[10] See also Merrill and Smith (2001a; 2001b).

property owners in particular. This baseline is familiar from the natural rights tradition, although that tradition does not rest on utilitarian concerns alone (Claeys 2010).

For example, Locke would find a baseline in the set of reciprocal rights and duties that maximize the scope for each owner's productive labor.[11] Moreover, Locke and, more explicitly, Hume give a large role to accession in determining what the proper scope of a claim is: where the (productive) labor grossly predominates or is psychologically much larger than the material acted on, a first possessor or good-faith improver can make a claim to the whole (by paying compensation in the latter case).[12]

Whether the natural rights theorists succeed or fail depends on whether their substantive criterion for "maximizing" mutual freedom has content that is also morally appealing. Epstein's normative criteria are less clear. The parity condition itself does not necessarily maximize welfare. The question then becomes what constraints should be put on the utilitarian adjustments away from the baseline. Epstein clearly prefers Pareto improvements, but does everyone have to share equally in the benefits of every micro adjustment, or must it only be the case that everyone share at least a little in improvements, even if very little? Or are there situations in which disproportionate gains justify small sacrifices on the part of others? Epstein assumes that allowing airplanes to fly at cruising altitude over land without liability for trespass meets his criterion. But how do we know, especially when a landowner claims not to be benefited? Benefits in general are in the eye of the beholder.[13] Epstein presumably would not endorse the common claim that "this is for your own good," but in the realm of hypothetical rather than actual bargains, there is little defense against this siren call, and Epstein's baseline on its own provides an insufficient bulwark in this regard.

Epstein largely relies on common-law nuisance as a baseline. The problems here are familiar.[14] It is not hard to see why nuisance attracts Epstein (and Justice Scalia):

---

[11] Reciprocity grounds acquisition: "Whatsoever then he removes out of the State that Nature hath provided, and left it in, he hath mixed his Labour with, and joyned to it something that is his own, and thereby makes it his Property. It being by him removed from the common state Nature placed it in, it hath by this Labour something annexed to it, that excludes the common right of other Men" (Locke 1988 [1690], 288); see also Mossoff (2002), who argues that by "labor," Locke meant productive labor, and that this answers many critics of the Lockean theory as being absurd or incoherent.

[12] "This source of property can never be explain'd but from the imagination . . . From an object, that is related to us, we acquire a relation to every other object which is related to it, and so on, till the thought loses the chain by too long a progress . . . And this principle is of such force as to give rise to the right of *accession*, and causes us to acquire the property not only of such objects as we are immediately posses'd of, but also of such as are closely connected with them" (Hume 2000 [1739], 327 n. 75); in acquisition through mixing of labor, "labour makes the far greatest part of the value of [the asset]" (Locke 1937 [1689], 28). See also *Wetherbee v. Green*, 22 Mich. 311 (1871); Epstein (1979b); Merrill (2009); Newman (2010); and Smith (2007).

[13] A similar issue arises with using the provision of "public goods" as a limit on the legitimate function of government, as Epstein has advocated in the past. See Polsby's (1998) review of Epstein (1998), in which Polsby argues that the notion of a "public good" is too malleable to serve as the basis for an workable inherent limit on what the state may do and uses the subsidy for mohair producers as an example.

[14] *Lucas v. South Carolina Coastal Council*, 505 U.S. 1003, 1031–1032 (1992) (Scalia, J.) (holding that if a regulation prevents what would be a nuisance at common law, then the regulation is not a taking); but see also 1055 (Blackmun, J. dissenting) (criticizing nuisance exception and nuisance as too indeterminate as a source of a baseline); and 1068–1070 (Stevens, J., dissenting) (criticizing nuisance exception for artificially freezing the common law). Fisher comments, "What is most striking about the holding of *Lucas* is that it embeds in the already muddy law of takings . . . the even muddier law of nuisance" (1993, 1407); and Blumm and Ritchie (2005) note that contextual analysis in nuisance law is in tension with the categorical approach to takings in *Lucas*.

it is the closest the law comes to embodying the fine-grained controls that are needed to supplement the basic trespass regime (Smith 2009a). But although nuisance is not as fuzzy as is conventionally thought,[15] it still leaves a lot of questions potentially unanswered. Further, nuisance cannot be the only expression of the baseline, even one based on natural rights. Custom and doctrines, such as the conflagration rule,[16] also form important parts of the baseline package of rights.[17] The law of nuisance was not static either, and reliance on nuisance simply reintroduces some of the basic unavoidable questions in the area of baselines. Although one would like to find semiexogenous baselines, and although traditions, including nuisance, custom, and the like, form an important expression of them, more consensus is still needed.

Consensus on what? First, what is a modification of the baseline, and what is a departure from it? Thus, in nuisance, there may have been a time when lawyers and laypeople mostly converged on what counted as a nuisance and what counted as a legitimate dynamic development in nuisance law, on one hand, and what would be a surprising new turn in the law, on the other hand. It is harder to see the conditions for such a consensus in the skeptical postrealist era. For example, a principle like *sic utere tuo ut alienum non laedas* (use your property in such a way as not to injure another's), which used to form an important basis of the law of nuisance,[18] is now derided as circular,[19] and natural rights find fewer fans. Moreover, if legal professionals are taught that legal results should follow "all-things-considered" policy analysis, and legal materials should then be stretched to provide cover or decoration, it is hard to see where the consensus necessary for the baseline could be found, even if it could be reduced to the law of nuisance.

Relatedly, consensus is needed on what is a rule and what is an exception. It is not universally agreed that the right to exclude is central to property. Indeed, there are those who adamantly refuse to see any "core" or even starting point for delineation of property at all (Dagan 2011). If property has disintegrated or is maximally complex all the way through,[20] the baseline will be hopelessly indeterminate for Epstein's purposes.

The central question relating private and public law is how to compromise between stability and precommitment, on one hand, and dynamism and flexibility in the system itself, on the other hand (Merrill and Smith 2010). Strong property

---

[15] See Epstein (1979a); Penner (1993); and Smith (2004a).

[16] The conflagration rule denies compensation for emergency destruction of property in order to stop a spreading fire. Dana and Merrill (2002) note the similarity of the conflagration rule to the nuisance exception to the per se rule of *Lucas*.

[17] *Lucas*, 505 U.S. at 1029 n. 19 (making room in property baseline principally for conflagration rule, which "absolv[es] the State (or private parties) of liability for the destruction of 'real and personal property, in cases of actual necessity, to prevent the spreading of a fire' or to forestall other grave threats to the lives and property of others.").

[18] See, e.g., *Vill. of Euclid v. Ambler Realty Co.*, 272 U.S. 365, 387 (1926) ("In solving doubts, the maxim *sic utere tuo ut alienum non laedas*, which lies at the foundation of so much of the common law of nuisances, ordinarily will furnish a fairly helpful clew"); *Lussier v. San Lorenzo Valley Water Dist.*, 253 Cal. Rptr. 470, 473 (Cal. Ct. App. 1988) ("The basic concept underlying the law of nuisances is articulated in the ancient maxim *sic utere tuo ut alienum non laedas*, that is, so use your own as not to injure another's property").

[19] See *Lucas*, 505 U.S. at 1031 (Scalia, J.) (criticizing invocation of the *sic utere* maxim as conclusory); *Hale v. Farmers Elec. Membership Corp.*, 99 P.2d 454, 456 (N.M. 1940) (endorsing the view that although *sic utere* is a good moral precept, it is useless as a grounds for decision because it does not determine any right or obligation, and citing cases and commentary to this effect).

[20] See, e.g., Alexander (2009) and Grey (1980).

rights that cannot be changed except possibly with generous compensation will serve the purpose of precommitment and will encourage investment, planning, and peace of mind of owners. But pushing this further comes at the price of making more difficult any adjustments to the system because of changed circumstances. This dilemma shapes both private and public law and forms the basis for the partial deferral to owners by society. But it remains a mystery why the balance between precommitment and flexibility should be struck in the same fashion in the private and the public realm.

A classic debate about stability versus flexibility—the problem of government forbearance—can be found in the dueling opinions in *Charles River Bridge v. Warren Bridge*, 36 U.S. (11 Pet.) 420 (1837). The Massachusetts legislature granted and then extended the franchise for a bridge over the Charles River, which was very successful. Before the (extended) franchise ended, the legislature granted another franchise to another bridge close by, which would become public after covering its investment, with the effect of eliminating the value of the first franchise. The Supreme Court held that there was no constitutional violation, over a dissent by Justice Story. Chief Justice Taney's majority opinion emphasizes suspicion of monopolies and the need for flexibility in the face of rapid economic and technological change. Justice Story's dissent stresses the need for respect for contracts (and, by extension, property) and the need to precommit to an assured return to induce private parties to invest. Like Epstein, Story notes that government does not lose all flexibility, because it can condemn the bridge through eminent domain (with compensation).

It certainly is the case that precommitment versus flexibility is a theme that runs through private and public law and through property in land and water law. But the devices used in the public sphere are not necessarily scaled-up versions of those running between private parties. The whole point of antiretroactivity and the law of takings is that government precommitment may be wanted in contexts in which a simple government contract will not do (Logue 1996). For one thing, government may need to be disciplined more than private parties in light of its conflict of interest. A government strong enough to protect private property is, without additional safeguards, a government strong enough to take it away (Barzel 2002). Likewise, some public rules, like the navigation servitude and the conflagration rule, do not seem to be scaled-up versions of some private law easement or necessity doctrine but instead strike the stability-flexibility trade-off in a characteristically public way.

Fluid Property in Water

Where does this leave water? Epstein's chapter is correct in stating that we move away from exclusion more quickly in delineating rights to water than in the case of land. Smith (2008) made just this point, and more: even prior appropriation, which is often thought to furnish more parcel-like rights and to be more exclusionary than riparianism, is heavily based on governance strategies.[21] Because water is a fluid resource, it is costly to subject it to exclusion rules, and comparatively it has been

---

[21] See also Freyfogle (1989) and N. L. Johnson (2007).

easier, at least historically, to measure water in terms of use (Gould 1988; Rice and White 1987; Smith 2008).

The first limitation of the discussion in Epstein's chapter is that it explicitly restricts its domain to exclude prior appropriation, and likewise does not deal with hybrid systems (Kanazawa 1998), without saying why. The result is that the discussion is too Roman (based on Justinian), riparian, and even Blackstonian to generalize well. Moreover, some of the private-public issues that Epstein addresses are of even greater moment in western prior-appropriation water law. For one thing, property in land in the American West traces back to grants from the federal government. As it happens, federal law incorporates state water law,[22] which in turn grew out of miners' customs. Is Epstein claiming that there is a natural law constraint on how the federal government chose to integrate water law into these grants? At the state level, the Colorado Constitution, for example, declares that water is public property. Does this violate natural law? Or does it confirm the Blackstonian view (historically less than accurate) that property in water is always only usufructory? The problem is that all the history involved here is recent enough to make a more positivistic approach to the subject hard to resist.

More seriously, if historic practice, apart from the Supreme Court's opinion in *United States v. Cress*, 243 U.S. 316 (1917), which Epstein laments is almost unique in the twentieth century, has never required just compensation for actions like expanding a navigation servitude, then it would be hard to square such a requirement with natural law. Surely the natural law thinkers tended to take seriously patterns that were historical and widespread. If, in practice, public rights have not generally been treated as scaled-up versions of private rights, that might be of some significance for the natural law approach.

The problem noted earlier that parity by itself is an empty notion has severe implications for water. Again, a comparison with western prior-appropriation law is instructive. In the shift away from riparianism in states like Colorado, the miners and other early users wanted to avoid monopolization by riparians, but an open-ended set of users with full equality would tend to make water rights unusably small. Prior appropriation works to keep this from happening (Cardozo 1924; Schorr 2005).

Moreover, the central trade-off between flexibility and stability is especially dire in water law. In riparian states, the system is rather rigid in broad outlines, in that water cannot be used on nonriparian land, and reasonable use falls in a narrow band. Flexibility comes from the notion of "reasonableness" itself. In prior appropriation, greater scarcity makes it worthwhile to make the rights interlock very tightly: return flow can be appropriated by a downstream junior appropriator, and when the senior appropriator wants to change use or transfer the right to another, the change or transfer is subject to the no-injury rule (Gould 1988; Smith 2008). This makes changes and transfers quite costly (R. N. Johnson, Gisser, and Werner 1981). Full use of the water in a static sense with stability even for junior users comes at the price of dynamic rigidity. Whether the rigidity calls for public intervention to redefine rights is hotly contested, but it is far from clear that the solution would be a scaled-up version

---

[22] Mining Act of 1866, Ch. 262, § 9, 14 Stat. 251, 253 (codified as amended at 43 U.S.C. §661 [2006]).

of a private solution. If one were to move to a more consumption-based system (Lueck 1995),[23] would existing users need to be compensated? And if so, by whom?

Even riparianism has within it a set of priorities that are far from reciprocal. For example, in times of extreme scarcity, natural wants like drinking and watering animals take precedence over artificial wants like irrigation.[24] And if there is not enough water to go around, the natural wants of upstream users can be fully met before any water need be left for the natural wants of those downstream. This is a simple and workable system, especially in light of the fact that severe drought is rare in the East, but it is not based on parity and does not, as Epstein would require, equate the marginal value of the last drop for those upstream with the marginal value downstream. One could say that anyone would choose such a system behind the veil of ignorance, a device Epstein also endorses, but this proves too much. Any scheme that departs from parity and receives any utilitarian justification whatever can be said to be so wonderful that any rational person would pick it behind the veil of ignorance. But this is not the route to the kind of consensus that is needed to get things off the ground.

Epstein's chapter is cause for optimism and pessimism. That one can get as far as he does in explaining the public as an extension of the private is a reason for hope. Sometimes social contract theory does point in that direction. But some problems are so inherently public that the hypothetical aggregation of private rights and duties does not fully explain or justify the public aspect of property law. The public is not just quantitatively but sometimes also qualitatively different from the private. This is especially true in water, where, as Epstein notes, the problems with parity-based solutions become apparent early on.

Thus, Epstein succeeds in showing that private law baselines are quite useful as a first stage or first approximation for public law in both land and water. But the second stage or refinement can undermine the first stage unless some consensus exists about legitimate departures from these baselines, and the outlook for such consensus is not very bright. Parity and a utilitarian scaling up of private law solutions are interesting and fruitful benchmarks, but they have not been shown to be sufficient to justify the public rights and their limits and some basic features of water law itself.

Acknowledgments

For helpful comments, I would like to thank Robert Ellickson, Tom Merrill, Carol Rose, and participants at a meeting of the John and Jean De Nault Task Force on Property Rights, Freedom, and Prosperity at the Hoover Institution.

REFERENCES

Alexander, Gregory S. 2009. Reply: The complex core of property. *Cornell Law Review* 94:1063–1071.

---

[23] Meyers and Posner (1971) propose property rights to return flows.
[24] *Evans v. Merriweather*, 4 Ill. 492 (1842); *Restatement (Second) of Torts* 1979, § 850A.

Arruñada, Benito. 2003. Property enforcement as organized consent. *Journal of Law, Economics and Organization* 19:401–444.

Barzel, Yoram. 2002. *A theory of the state: Economic rights, legal rights, and the scope of the state.* Cambridge, U.K.: Cambridge University Press.

Blackstone, William. 1979 [1766]. *Commentaries on the Laws of England.* Vol. 2. Chicago: University of Chicago Press.

Blumm, Michael C., and Lucus Ritchie. 2005. *Lucas's* unlikely legacy: The rise of background principles as categorical takings defenses. *Harvard Environmental Law Review* 29:321–368.

Cardozo, Benjamin N. 1924. *The growth of the law.* New Haven: Yale University Press.

Cheung, Steven N. S. 1970. The structure of a contract and the theory of a non-exclusive resource. *Journal of Law and Economics* 13:49–70.

Claeys, Eric R. 2010. Jefferson meets Coase: Land-use torts, law and economics, and natural property rights. *Notre Dame Law Review* 85:1379–1446.

Coase, Ronald H. 1960. The problem of social cost. *Journal of Law and Economics* 3:1–44.

Conard, Alfred F. 1942. Easement novelties. *California Law Review* 30:125–150.

Dagan, Hanoch. 2011. *Property: Values and Institutions.* New York: Oxford University Press.

Dana, David A., and Thomas W. Merrill. 2002. *Property: Takings.* New York: Foundation Press.

Ellickson, Robert C. 1993. Property in land. *Yale Law Journal* 102:1315–1400.

Epstein, Richard A. 1979a. Nuisance law: Corrective justice and its utilitarian constraints. *Journal of Legal Studies* 8:49–102.

——. 1979b. Possession as the root of title. *Georgia Law Review* 13:1221–1243.

——. 1982. Notice and freedom of contract in the law of servitudes. *Southern California Law Review* 55:1353–1368.

——. 1989. The utilitarian foundations of natural law. *Harvard Journal of Law and Public Policy* 12:713–751.

——. 1998. *Principles for a free society: Reconciling individual liberty with the common good.* Reading, MA: Perseus Books.

Field, Barry C. 1989. The evolution of property rights. *Kyklos* 42:319–345.

Fisher, William W., III. 1993. The trouble with *Lucas. Stanford Law Review* 45:1393–1410.

Freyfogle, Eric T. 1989. Context and accommodation in modern property law. *Stanford Law Review* 41:1529–1556.

Gould, George A. 1988. Water rights transfers and third-party effects. *Land and Water Law Review* 23:1–41.

Grey, Thomas C. 1980. The disintegration of property. In *Property,* eds. J. Roland Pennock and John W. Chapman, 69–95. *Nomos* 22. New York: New York University Press.

Harris, J. W. 1996. *Property and justice.* Oxford: Clarendon Press.

Heller, Michael A., and James E. Krier. 1999. Deterrence and distribution in the law of takings. *Harvard Law Review* 112:997–1025.

Hohfeld, Wesley Newcomb. 1917. Fundamental legal conceptions as applied in judicial reasoning. *Yale Law Journal* 26:710–770.

Hume, David. 2000 [1739]. *A treatise of human nature.* Eds. David Fate Norton and Mary J. Norton. Oxford: Oxford University Press.

Johnson, Nicole L. 2007. Property without possession. *Yale Journal on Regulation* 24:205–251.

Johnson, Ronald N., Micha Gisser, and Michael Werner. 1981. The definition of a surface water right and transferability. *Journal of Law and Economics* 24:273–288.

Kanazawa, Mark T. 1998. Efficiency in western water law: The development of the California water doctrine, 1850–1911. *Journal of Legal Studies* 27:159–185.

Katz, Larissa. 2008. Exclusion and exclusivity in property law. *University of Toronto Law Journal* 58:275–316.

Locke, John. 1937 [1689]. *Treatise of civil government and A letter concerning toleration.* Ed. Charles L. Sherman. New York: D. Appleton-Century Co.

——. 1988 [1690]. *Two treatises of government,* ed. Peter Laslett. Cambridge, U.K.: Cambridge University Press.

Logue, Kyle D. 1996. Tax transitions, opportunistic retroactivity, and the benefits of govern-ment precommitment. *Michigan Law Review* 94:1129–1196.

Lueck, Dean. 1995. The rule of first possession and the design of the law. *Journal of Law and Economics* 38:393–436.

Merrill, Thomas W. 1998. Property and the right to exclude. *Nebraska Law Review* 77:730–755.

———. 2009. Accession and original ownership, *Journal of Legal Analysis* 1:459–510.

———. 2011. Private property and public rights. In *Research handbook on the economics of property law*, eds. Kenneth Ayotte and Henry E. Smith, 75–103. Cheltenham, U.K.: Edward Elgar.

Merrill, Thomas W., and Henry E. Smith. 2000. Optimal standardization in the law of property: The *numerus clausus* principle. *Yale Law Journal* 110:1–70.

———. 2001a. The property/contract interface. *Columbia Law Review* 101:773–852.

———. 2001b. What happened to property in law and economics? *Yale Law Journal* 111:357–398.

———. 2007. The morality of property. *William and Mary Law Review* 48:1849–1895.

———. 2010. *The Oxford introductions to U.S. law: Property.* New York: Oxford University Press.

———. 2011. Making Coasean property more Coasean. *Journal of Law and Economics* 54.

Meyers, Charles J., and Richard A. Posner. 1971. Market transfers of water rights: Toward an improved market in water resources. Legal Study No. 4, NTIS No. NWC-L-71-009 (July). National Water Commission. Springfield, VA: National Technical Information Service.

Mossoff, Adam. 2002. Locke's labor lost. *University of Chicago Law School Roundtable* 9:155–164.

Newman, Christopher M. 2010. Transformation in property and copyright. George Mason Law and Economics Research Paper No. 10–51 (October 6). http://ssrn.com/abstract=1688585.

Penner, J. E. 1993. Nuisance and the character of the neighbourhood. *Journal of Environmental Law* 5:1–29.

———. 1997. *The idea of property in law.* Oxford: Clarendon Press.

Polsby, Daniel D. 1998. What if this is as good as it gets? *Green Bag* 2:115–123.

Posner, Richard A. 2004. Pragmatic liberalism versus classical liberalism. *University of Chicago Law Review* 71:659–674.

Powell, Richard. 1995. *Powell on real property*, vol. 4., ed. Patrick J. Rohan. Newark, NJ: Matthew Bender.

Restatement (second) of torts. 1979. Philadelphia: American Law Institute.

Rice, Leonard, and Michael D. White. 1987. *Engineering aspects of water law.* New York: John Wiley & Sons.

Rose, Carol M. 1986. The comedy of the commons: Custom, commerce, and inherently public property. *University of Chicago Law Review* 53:711–781.

———. 1991. Rethinking environmental controls: Management strategies for common resources. *Duke Law Journal* 1991:1–38.

———. 1998. Canons of property talk; or, Blackstone's anxiety. *Yale Law Journal* 108:601–632.

Rudden, Bernard. 1987. Economic theory v. property law: The *numerus clausus* problem. In *Oxford essays in jurisprudence*, vol. 3, eds. John Eekelaar and John Bell, 239–263. Oxford: Clarendon Press.

Schorr, David B. 2005. Appropriation as agrarianism: Distributive justice in the creation of property rights. *Ecology Law Quarterly* 32:3–71.

———. 2009. How Blackstone became a Blackstonian. *Theoretical Inquiries in Law* 10:103–126.

Simon, Herbert A. 1971. Designing organizations for an information-rich world. In *Computers, communication, and the public interest*, ed. Martin Greenberger, 37–52. Baltimore: Johns Hopkins Press.

Smith, Henry E. 2002. Exclusion versus governance: Two strategies for delineating property rights. *Journal of Legal Studies* 31:S453–S487.

———. 2004a. Exclusion and property rules in the law of nuisance. *Virginia Law Review* 90:965–1049.

———. 2004b. Property and property rules. *New York University Law Review* 79:1719–1798.

———. 2007. Intellectual property as property: Delineating entitlements in information. *Yale Law Journal* 116:1742–1822.

———. 2008. Governing water: The semicommons of fluid property rights. *Arizona Law Review* 50:445–478.

———. 2009a. Community and custom in property. *Theoretical Inquiries in Law* 10:6–41.

———. 2009b. Mind the gap: The indirect relation between ends and means in American property law. *Cornell Law Review* 94:959–989.

———. 2011. Standardization in property law. In *Research handbook on the economics of property law*, eds. Kenneth Ayotte and Henry E. Smith, 148–173. Cheltenham, U.K.: Edward Elgar.

12

A Political Analysis of Property Rights

WILLIAM BLOMQUIST

Many previous treatments of property rights have been normative, in the Aristotelian or Lockean philosophical traditions. These accounts provide justifications for property rights. They are not empirical inquiries or explanations of how human beings have established property rights as social institutions (for an example, see chapter 11 by Epstein in this volume; for a critique, see Sened [1997]).

Other treatments of property rights have been in the economic styles of Anderson and Hill (1975), Davis and North (1971), Demsetz (1967), Libecap (1989; chapter 13 in this volume), and North (1981). In these accounts, scarcity conditions and/or the opportunity to realize net benefits induce rational individuals to experiment with and commit to the establishment of property rights. This economic analysis provides a view of why people may have established property rights, but less so of how property rights come into existence or how they change after they have been created. Rather, in these accounts, once scarcity rises to a level that makes the need for property rights apparent or the gains from establishing them exceed the costs of doing so, property rights just sort of appear.[1] They are born, but not made.

Political economists' and economic historians' accounts of the development or alteration of property rights display elements of both approaches. Such work has an empirical component, explaining why certain property rights came into being at a particular time and place (Kantor 1991; Sened 1997). The empirical component is typically combined with a normative critique showing why the property rights that were established were inefficient as a result of the corrupting influences of rent seeking, information asymmetries, and other such interferences that diverted individuals from creating the "right" kinds of rights.

These perspectives on property rights have contributed to and built a rich political economy literature on property rights. This chapter concerns a political analysis of property rights, as distinguishable from the more familiar political economy

---

[1] Eggertsson made this point: "The naïve model . . . postulates that exclusive control will replace open access when the (joint) benefits of doing so exceed the (joint) costs . . . In other words, in the naïve model control issues do not present a dilemma, property rights will adjust to maximize the joint value of resources—and economists need not be concerned with political processes" (1994, 11). Sened also characterizes this approach as naïve: "Analysts should not expect private property rights to come into existence just because they increase efficiency" (1997, 176).

of property rights.[2] Its focus is on how property rights rules are developed and changed in settings that involve multiple actors, multiple resource use values, and multiple rule-making arenas. This approach incorporates perspectives from broader depictions of natural resource uses and usage rights and from political science literature on the processes of policy making.

This chapter reflects the disciplinary bias of a political scientist. Political scientists are apt to be more concerned than philosophers or economists with the questions of how people create property rights and for what purposes, why and how they choose the types of property rights institutions they do, and how and why they change property rights over time. More plainly, a political analysis of property rights is explicitly and primarily concerned with (1) "who gets what, when, how," to quote Lasswell's (1958) famous characterization of politics; and (2) the even more intensely political questions of who decides who gets what, when, and how, and how that question is decided.[3]

These are especially pertinent questions in relation to property rights. Property rights are established and recognized by some form of authority—community consent, the decree of an official, or codification in some formal rule or instrument such as a constitution, statute, ordinance, or regulation. Mere usage or claim of right by an individual is insufficient to establish a property right, properly so called (Cole and Grossman 2002).[4] Rights may be established and/or recognized by various governmental bodies—legislative assemblies, courts, and agencies or officials of various kinds—as long as they have been invested with some legitimate rule-making authority. Community consent may be established less formally, via social conventions or norms, as long as those conventions or norms create a corresponding duty on the part of others to recognize the established right (Cole and Grossman 2002). Politics is necessarily entailed in the analysis of property rights because, and to the extent that, authoritative allocation is a part of the definition of property rights (Sened 1997). An alternative to Lasswell's plainer statement that politics is "who gets what, when, how" is Easton's more refined definition of politics as "the authoritative allocation of values" (1953, 146). Either phrasing expresses the connection between politics and property rights.

At least three other crucial characteristics of human political behavior must be incorporated into any political analysis. First, nothing is ever over. Even when an authoritative decision is made with respect to a particular issue, those whose preferences on that issue fail to carry the day rarely disappear or even capitulate. Rather, those who do not prevail in one decision-making arena at one time will search for ways to prevail on that issue at another time or in another forum or may reframe the

---

[2] Although this chapter departs from Sened (1997) on a point that will be highlighted, Sened's argument and mine coincide on this and several other points, as in his call for "a more realistic treatment of the role of politics in the evolution of private property and related individual rights" (1997, 7)

[3] Much of what is commonly characterized as "political" discussion, debate, or analysis may be more accurately labeled policy debate or analysis. "What should we do about problem X?" is a policy question. The political question, properly so called, is: who gets to decide what we will do about problem X, and how? When political scientists say that political science is the study of power, this is at the heart of what they mean. For example, how are authoritative decisions made, and who gets to participate and under what circumstances and constraints?

[4] For an alternative perspective, see the discussion of de facto versus de jure property rights in Schlager and Ostrom (1992).

issue itself (Baumgartner and Jones 2009; Schattschneider 1960; Stone 2002). Second, any valued thing (tangible or intangible) over which people contest can be divided, subdivided, recombined, and redefined, at least rhetorically. Such actions may be undertaken to gain strategic advantage, to resolve conflict through compromise (for instance, by allowing one interest to prevail or have control with respect to one aspect of the valued thing and another interest to prevail or have control with respect to some other aspect), or even for the sake of operating within constraints of available time and information.[5] Third, the values that are invoked in political or policy contests, such as efficiency, fairness, security, and community, are also contested in the political process. Political actors can and should be expected to pull any valued thing (and rights to that thing) into multiple pieces and then to search for ways and means to prevail in decision making over the allocation of rights to all or a piece of that valued thing. These crucial characteristics of human political behavior are as much a part of debates and decisions about property rights in natural resources as they are in any other realm of political decision making.[6]

These matters are not avoided or even necessarily ameliorated by the invocation or creation of markets. Because property rights are established and recognized through authoritative (political) institutions, the transaction costs of changing them are greater than zero. Economists who follow Coase have understood and emphasized that in the presence of positive transaction costs (that is, if rights cannot be traded freely and without cost until individuals' utilities cannot be improved by further adjustment), "it can make a great deal of difference—in terms of ultimate economic outcomes—who initially possesses the legal right *and* what that right *means*" (Cole and Grossman 2002, 326; emphasis in original; Bromley 1991).

The analysis of Schlager and Ostrom (1992) may be seen as focusing on the latter point: what that right means. They develop a property rights framework in the context of rights in relation to natural resources (Ostrom and Schlager 1996). This chapter incorporates their framework and combines a political analysis of institutional development and change with the following recognitions:

1. Both property rights and natural resources are typically multidimensional.
2. Human beings interact with natural resources in ways that reflect a multiplicity of values and a variety of uses.
3. These social and ecological interactions of humans and nature usually take place in settings where there are multiple potential decision makers and multiple potential decision forums within which choices about property rights institutions may proposed, discussed, debated, and decided (or not).

---

[5] Noncomprehensive policy making is rational. Time is limited, bargaining is costly, and there are always other issues and controversies vying for attention. Under these circumstances, rational individuals will tend to avoid or set aside issues that can at least conceptually and rhetorically be distinguished. There are incentives embedded in the structure of the action situation to decide only what needs to be decided for purposes of the controversy of the moment, and no more. Related issues, as well as new issues that arise as a consequence of past decisions, will come forward in time and find their way to one or more forums for resolution.

[6] All this political maneuvering and contestation cannot be swept under the term "rent seeking." That term implies or presumes that there is some objective definition of what constitutes an unearned or undeserved "rent," which merely begs the question.

Multiple Elements of Property Rights

Legal scholars, as well as practicing attorneys and judges, have long referred to property rights as actually consisting of a bundle of rights. The metaphor conveys the notion that property rights are to some extent decomposable into elements. With particular respect to the use of natural resources, Schlager and Ostrom (1992) disaggregated the overall term "property rights" into the following elements.

- *Rights of access*, also referred to as rights of entry, identify who has a recognizable claim to be "in" (and, by extension, who is "out") with respect to the resource. If the resource is present within a spatially delineated domain, such as a fishing ground, a forest, or a lake, those with rights of access have a cognizable and potentially enforceable claim to be able to be present within that domain.
- *Rights of withdrawal*, also referred to as rights of extraction or abstraction or use, are possessed by those who can legitimately take usable units (e.g., wildlife, timber, quantities of water) from the resource for their own use. Withdrawal rights often are conditional; that is, they include restrictions on when, where, and how much the rights holder may use the resource. Depending on the physical characteristics of the resource, an extension of the right of withdrawal may be a right of storage (a recognized right to leave one's temporal allocation of resource units in the resource for capture at a later time).
- *Rights of management*, which might also be thought of as a right to participate in decision making, identify those who can deliberate about and help decide the regulation of use patterns, the necessity and provision for improvements/repairs to facilities, and the like. Applying the concept of levels of action presented in Kiser and Ostrom's study (1982), Schlager and Ostrom (1992) distinguish between the operational-level rights of access or withdrawal and the collective-choice rights of management, exclusion, and alienation.
- *Rights of exclusion* identify those who have authority to determine—on their own or in concert with others—who cannot have access to or make withdrawals from the resource.
- *Rights of alienation*, also known as rights of transfer, are possessed by those who can legitimately confer their other property rights on someone else. Although rights of alienation may seem inherent in the other rights, they are distinct, and the distinction is very important. One may possess rights of access to a resource, for instance, by virtue of group membership, residence, or some other characteristic and thus be unable to transfer that access right to another person.[7]

As Schlager and Ostrom (1992) point out, these rights are independent of one another, on one hand, and related, on the other hand. In any particular circumstance, a person may possess some of these rights, but not all of them. The institutional rules

---

[7] Libecap (chapter 13 in this volume) has undertaken extensive research on the effects of alienation, studying what people do once they have the authority to sell or lease their water use rights, and what effects result (especially efficiency effects). From the discussion in his chapter, one can see that area-of-origin restrictions and compensation for third-party effects of transactions may also be viewed as rights claims.

conferring property rights in a resource constitute a system of rules identifying various aspects of property rights, and some property rights systems specify all of the elements in the list, while other property rights systems for other resources specify only some of those elements. On the other hand, the elements are related in the sense that they have a cumulative character, and possession of some rights is implied by or entailed in others. As one goes down the list from access through alienation, this cumulative character manifests itself. Rights of withdrawal imply that one has access to the resource. Rights of alienation are meaningful only if one has some other rights (e.g., access or withdrawal) to transfer.

This specification of the component elements of property rights in resources is useful in several ways (Ostrom and Schlager 1996; Schlager and Ostrom 1992). For theorists, it aids in unpacking the general concept of property rights and thus may help identify instances where theorists are calling different empirical referents by the same term, a step that is often vital to advancing theoretical debates and theory development. For researchers, it provides a means of comparing resource-management regimes, even when the resources themselves (not to mention their geographic, historic, and social settings) are divergent, which is a great advantage in being able to move beyond individual case studies to comparative qualitative and quantitative analyses. For resource users and those who may be prescribing improvements to resource-management practices, Schlager and Ostrom's framework provides a means of identifying the institutional arrangements that define the status quo and thus of considering in a more deliberate and systematic way what changes in resource use and/or conditions might follow from changing one or more elements of the users' rights. The multidimensionality of property rights also means that in their roles as political actors, resource users have five types or dimensions of property rights to fight over, not just one.

The relevance and significance of Schlager and Ostrom's property rights framework for a political analysis of property rights becomes even clearer as one adds other dimensions. One of these involves another process of disaggregation, this time with respect to the resource itself.

Multiple Properties and Uses of Resources

A number of resource economists, as well as some ecologists and planners, have referred to the multifunctionality of resources.[8] This term signifies that a particular resource yields more than one stream of value for people and for other species. For example, a forest may be simultaneously a source of timber, shade, open space, and habitat, a buffer between communities, a place of recreation, and a place of spiritual significance, as well as providing oxygen and consuming carbon dioxide.

Because this basic premise of multifunctionality has been well covered elsewhere, this chapter applies it directly in a way that relates to the discussion of property rights. The essential point is that property rights in a natural resource can be, and often are,

---

[8] Although the term has been in use since at least the 1990s, it gained wider currency after the Organisation for Economic Co-operation and Development promoted it in books by Maier and Shobayashi (2001) and Shobayashi (2003). For a recent application to policy, see Brouwer and van der Heide (2009).

defined or limited functionally. This point can be illustrated by considering water in a watershed.

A given watershed usually has both surface water and underground water. The surface water, flowing in watercourses such as streams or rivers or stored in bodies such as lakes or reservoirs, is subject to a variety of uses.[9] A first step toward categorizing the multiple uses of surface water in a watershed is to distinguish between in-channel and out-of-channel uses.

Values derived by people from in-channel uses of a surface water resource are associated with the following:

- Navigation: using the flow for shipment.
- Hydropower: using the flow for energy production.
- Recreation: using the water for exercise and entertainment.
- Waste conveyance and dilution: using the water for discharge and disposal.
- Aesthetics: using the water for scenic views, enhancing property along the shore, and the like.
- Spirituality: keeping natural or divine beings that are associated with the water undisturbed.
- Ecology: using or protecting the water for habitat.

It goes nearly without saying that these uses may conflict because one use may preclude or diminish the value of one or more other uses.

Values derived by people from out-of-channel uses of a surface water resource are associated with the following:

- Domestic uses: diverting water from the watercourse or water body for such purposes as drinking, cooking, and sanitation.
- Irrigation: diverting and using water for growing plants.
- Industry: diverting and using water for such purposes as cooling and manufacturing.
- Public safety: diverting and using water for fire suppression.

These out-of-channel uses can conflict not only with one another, but also with in-channel uses.

Groundwater in a watershed, which is hydrologically interconnected with surface water except in rare circumstances, also provides values for people that are associated with all the previous claims of right for out-of-channel uses of surface water, as well as the following uses:

- Ecology: claims of right for habitat.
- Storage: claims of right to use the capacity of the aquifer system to store and retrieve water.

---

[9] This point is made also in Epstein (chapter 11 in this volume), among others. He further notes that because of the multiple interests in any given body of water, the politics of water rights is always intense.

These groundwater uses may conflict with one another, and to the extent that groundwater in a watershed is hydrologically linked with surface water resources, these uses may conflict with in-channel or out-of-channel surface water uses as well.

Recognizing the multiplicity of uses and values is one step in the analysis, and recognizing the prospect of conflicts arising from multiple uses is another step. Both of these have been cited in the past in emphasizing the importance of water rights regimes that establish and define priorities among uses and can be employed by users to obviate or resolve conflicts. Combining the multiplicity of uses and values with Schlager and Ostrom's framework is another step, however.

Schlager and Ostrom's property rights framework does not align perfectly with the multiplicity of uses of water resources in a watershed. It is not clear, for example, that withdrawal rights are associated with uses of a surface water body for aesthetic or spiritual purposes. But the five categories of property rights in Schlager and Ostrom's framework can be associated with nearly all the water uses listed previously. Table 12.1 is a simple illustration of a mapping of Schlager and Ostrom's framework onto those water uses.

With the exception of a few less logical cases (like the example of withdrawal rights in connection with aesthetic uses), the cells in table 12.1 could be filled in with institutional arrangements specifying (1) who does or does not have that type of right in association with that particular use; (2) to what extent a person has that

TABLE 12.1

Elements of Property Rights in a Multifunctional Watershed

	Aspects of Property Rights				
	Access	Withdrawal	Storage	Management	Transfer
In-channel surface water uses					
Transportation/navigation					
Hydropower					
Recreation					
Waste disposal					
Aesthetic					
Spiritual					
Ecological					
Out-of-channel surface water uses					
Domestic use					
Irrigation					
Industry					
Public safety					
Groundwater					
Domestic use					
Irrigation					
Industry					
Public safety					
Ecological					

right; and (3) under what conditions (rights might vary according to the situation, e.g., when the resource is in drought or at risk of flooding).

By itself, Schlager and Ostrom's property rights framework demonstrated that users may (and in many cases do) have different degrees of right to the use of the same resource. In combination with the multifunctionality of resources, their framework produces an even more complex, but arguably more realistic, depiction of the actual circumstances of property rights systems, namely, that some users will have some rights to some uses of the resource, while other users will have other rights with respect to other uses of the resource. This critical point deserves additional emphasis by restatement: in the world we are trying to understand and explain, there is not a unique resource being used for a particular purpose by one set of users with one bundle of property rights. There are various resources with multiple valued uses, there are multiple and overlapping groups of users, and different users have different types of rights to different aspects of the valued uses of those resources.

In this more complicated reality, externalities take on differing types and gradations as well. What can be called reciprocal externalities may arise among rights holders who are engaged in the same use, such as irrigators. Conflicts arising from reciprocal externalities may be challenging, but they are at least potentially resolvable through marginal adjustments among claims of similar rights. In other words, irrigator A may have to divert and use a little less water in order for irrigator B to have a little more if B's right supersedes A's in some way that is recognized within that property rights system (seniority, for example). Nonreciprocal externalities arise between rights holders who are engaged in different uses. These conflicts are still at least potentially resolvable within a property rights system, but that system will have to include some sets of priorities among uses and not just among users. Thus, if the placement of a dam on a watercourse renders navigation beyond that location impossible, the property rights system will need to include some determination of whether navigation takes precedence over hydropower. Side payments among conflicting claimants may be possible, but the priority among uses established within the property rights system will determine who owes payment to whom.

In a social-ecological setting where there are rights of varying degree and uses of varying kinds, important questions arise that are critical to resource use and management. The questions that have often been raised and addressed through previous legal, economic, and policy analyses are as follows: Do some uses have priority over others? Within the same use, do some rights have priority over others? If so, on what basis?

To these more familiar questions, a political analysis of property rights adds the following: Who gets to decide? Can these priorities be changed? How, and by whom? Who is "in" and who is "out" of the "resource community," to use Barbanell's (2001, 67) term? Who has rights of participation?

The questions in the second group are harder to address merely by offering the hope of transferability of rights among rights holders. They are questions at the collective-choice level of action (Kiser and Ostrom 1982). And underneath those questions are questions at the constitutional-choice level: How do we decide who gets to decide over which domain of uses and resources, and who gets to participate in those decisions? Who can shift levels of action, and under what conditions?

Multiple Arenas and Strategies of Political Decision Making

Those questions carry us from the operational level of the resource itself to the collective-choice and constitutional-choice levels of the community. To assume that there is one decision maker for the community may be a useful abstraction for simple modeling, but it is nonetheless an abstraction and indeed a distraction for a political analysis of property rights.[10] In political situations, the number and nature of participants and the arenas in which participants will deliberate, negotiate, or fight are all at least potentially contestable. Political contestation is in large measure a matter of framing the issue at hand in a way that attempts to influence (1) the scope of the conflict so as to bring in or leave out certain participants and (2) which decision-making arenas will be used to reach decisions.

A great deal of work in political science has focused on these aspects of political contestation and how they enter into public policy making with respect to any topic, not only property rights. Kingdon (1995) highlighted the significance of molding the definitions of problems to fit one's preferred policy solutions—one view of energy shortage suggests the need to reduce consumption, while another view of energy shortage suggests the need to increase production. One can expect proponents of each solution to define the problem strategically. Stone (2002) and others have articulated and illustrated the malleability of issues and the strategic uses of rhetoric, as well as statistics, in political debate. These uses are often referred to as framing. Is water an instrumental economic commodity to be put to maximum beneficial use, or is it a part of the natural landscape and regional heritage to be preserved in its current state?

Closely related to framing is Schattschneider's emphasis on the importance of "managing the scope of conflict" (1960, 5). Political actors assess the relative balance of influence in any given conflict and then try either to bring in more people (enlarging the scope of conflict) in anticipation that a preponderance of them will come in on one's side or to keep people out (reducing the scope of conflict) in anticipation that a preponderance of them would come in on one's opponent's side. Part of managing the scope of conflict is the choice of decision arena, as Baumgartner and Jones (2009) and Kagan (2001; 2004), among others, have pointed out. In a community with more than one decision maker or decision-making arena—in other words, in most actual settings—there is also a strategic choice to be made about whether to press for policies (such as assignments of property rights) at a local or a larger scale and in a legislative body, a regulatory agency, a judicial forum, or some other structure.

If one incorporates these insights on policy making from the work of political scientists into a study of property rights, one may still rely on a presumption of rational actors, but those rational actors now are also political entrepreneurs from different constituencies associated with different uses of the resource. They contest for the establishment, recognition, and enforcement of their desired rights of access,

---

[10] On this point, the political analysis approach of this chapter diverges from the political economy analysis presented by Sened (1997). He retains the simplifying assumption of a unitary political actor. He acknowledges the existence of multiple governmental bodies and processes but decides that for purposes of his analysis, "government, its delegates or any decisive coalition in government, end up making decisions 'as if' they were unitary actors" (1997, 6).

withdrawal, management, exclusion, or alienation with respect to different uses of the resource—in the watershed example, to divert water for irrigation or to leave it in the stream for hydropower, recreation, or some other purpose. They also make calculations of the likelihood that their rights claims will prevail if the matters are decided in one type of decision-making forum or another, depending, among other things, on how they can frame the issues at stake and whether their cause will benefit from enlarging or reducing the scope of conflict. Thus, for example, in a hypothetical state in the western United States, irrigators might go to a state court to protect rights of withdrawal, rafters and fly fishermen might go to the state legislature seeking rights of access, the hydropower interests might go to the federal legislature seeking rights of exclusion, and an indigenous religious community or ecology advocates might go to the federal courts seeking rights of exclusion on other grounds.

Outcomes in any of these decision-making forums may be couched in definitive and formal language, but they are also inherently and unavoidably contingent. In the short run, they are liable to be contradicted by the actions of another forum or appealed to yet another; in the long run, they are vulnerable to being undermined or overridden by altered definitions of the problem or changes in the authority or jurisdiction of one or more of the decision-making forums. The implications of this understanding and approach are significant for the literature on property rights in natural resources. One implication is that it is highly unlikely in any actual setting that property rights in a natural resource will ever become "well defined" in the sense commonly used in the literature. Another is that even if a set of well-defined property rights in a natural resource were somehow to be arrived at, it would likely be a transitory state of affairs liable to be undone by the next entrepreneurial challenge.

Recent and Current Developments in Water Rights in Colorado

What does strategic political behavior regarding rights to a multifunctional resource in a multiple-venue policy-making arena look like? An in-depth study is beyond the scope of this chapter, but opportunities for illustration abound. Colorado provides a timely example. The story of the early development of water use rights in Colorado has been told often and well by others (Black 1960; Hutchins 2004; Jones and Cech 2009; Radosevich 1976; Wiel 2010 [1911]). There is no need here to attempt another comprehensive account of that institutional evolution from before statehood through the 1970s.[11] Recent and current controversies with respect to property rights in various water uses can more simply and directly illustrate how the approach described in the previous sections can shed light on actual cases.

In semiarid locations such as Colorado, stream flow tends to be highly variable within a year as well as across years, and arable land is often distant from surface

---

[11] Readers of this volume may find it difficult to relate the material in this section to the discussion of water rights in Epstein (chapter 11 in this volume). Colorado water rights doctrine is premised on prior appropriation rather than riparianism. Epstein focuses on riparianism and expressly sets aside the prior-appropriation doctrine. In the western United States, where water resource management problems have been most salient and complicated for the past 100 years or so, prior appropriation is a more common foundation of water rights law than riparianism.

streams. Since statehood in 1876, the foundation of Colorado water law has been, and remains, promoting and protecting the withdrawal of water from surface streams for use on lands near or far from the surface water source.[12] During the twentieth century, the basic emphasis in Colorado water law on withdrawing water from streams came under challenge as stream flows diminished, but also as the values (financial and other) of in-stream uses rose. Since the last decades of the twentieth century, Colorado water rights law has been changing and coping with competing claims of right to diverse water uses.

Appropriative rights (rights to divert or withdraw a specific amount of water from a specific source during a specified period of time) now account for essentially all expected water flows in Colorado. There is no "extra" water remaining. If all appropriative rights are exercised in an average year, many of the state's surface streams go dry. These appropriative rights are protected by seniority, but the state's economy and demography have changed significantly during the past half century. Colorado's population is overwhelmingly urban and suburban, and the state has attracted many residents and regular visitors who value recreation highly. Indeed, as an economic sector, recreation has outpaced and overtaken traditional agriculture in its contribution to the state's overall economy, as measured by jobs and income. Most (but not all) recreational uses involve leaving water flowing in the stream, rather than taking it out of the channel, which has been the principal emphasis of Colorado water law.

Of course, markets have been advocated as a means of addressing the pressures for adjustment in the state's water uses from traditional irrigated agriculture to municipal and especially recreational uses. Transfers of water rights have occurred in Colorado, and there is plenty of room for markets to continue to facilitate the transition from older to newer valued uses. The prerequisite for markets to play this role, however, is the actual and authoritative recognition of a use as a claim of right. Unless and until recreational in-stream uses gain legal recognition within Colorado law, markets cannot operate, at least not openly, to make those adjustments. An irrigator cannot sell or lease a water use right to a recreational outfitter, for example, unless and until the right to leave water in the stream and use it for recreation stands on a comparable legal footing with the irrigator's right to divert water and put it to use for crops or livestock. Much of the story of Colorado water law over the past half century has been the effort by advocates of nonconsumptive and in-channel water uses to gain a legal foothold in order to have a position from which to start transacting with holders of consumptive out-of-channel use rights.[13]

---

[12] Legally recognized water rights in Colorado are rights to the use of the water and not to ownership of the water itself. The Colorado Constitution declares that the waters of the state belong to the public and allows individuals to acquire rights to the use of those waters.

[13] Recreational uses of in-stream flows should not be confused with navigation. As Epstein (chapter 11 in this volume) and others point out, navigation of streams invokes federal law and its supremacy over any state's system of water use rights. The most popular recreational water uses in Colorado and in many other places are rafting, kayaking, canoeing, and tubing, which can be done on both nonnavigable and navigable streams. Colorado has very few stretches of river that would qualify as navigable and thus would be brought under federal law, but it has thousands of miles of streams on which people can engage in recreation in relatively small devices such as rafts. Recreational uses of those streams have spawned a rapidly growing economic sector of outfitters and tour companies. In addition, recreational fishing is an in-stream water use that does not require navigability, and fly fishing,

The question for advocates of recreational and other in-stream flow rights and protections in Colorado has been how to get the institutions governing Colorado water rights law to recognize and give priority to those claims of right. Colorado has a statewide system of local water courts that, in coordination with division offices of the state engineer, have recognized and adjudicated rights to divert and use water under the state's prior-appropriation doctrine. Questions or conflicts over the seniority, quantity, and timing of one user's diversion rights relative to others' have been handled and resolved in the water courts for decades. Both because of their legal mandate and their long relationships with the state's traditional water users, neither the water courts nor the State Engineer's Office have been seen by advocates of other water uses as receptive bodies in which to press for the recognition of new rights to other water uses.

Because of the growing economic importance of recreation and other in-stream water uses, however, the Colorado legislature has at times appeared to be a more promising body for enacting changes in state water law. The state's process for policy change through initiative and referendum is another available policy-making venue because with the demographic changes in the state, the voting population has become more receptive to appeals based on ecological and aesthetic values, as well as the popularity of recreation. Rule-making processes of both state and federal executive agencies charged with administering and enforcing environmental policies, including water conservation and habitat protection, or managing public lands are another prospective policy venue.

Changes in Colorado water rights law during the past half century have largely displayed the dynamics alluded to earlier in this chapter. Rights holders in the traditional and well-established areas of water use—agriculture and municipal/industrial supply—have tended to make their stand in the courts, relying on 150 years of precedent and practice from the Colorado Constitution and a body of case law composed of hundreds of thousands of rulings over those years. Rights claimants wishing to establish legal recognition of their uses at a minimum, and preferably legal parity with traditional uses, have taken their case to other policy venues, such as the legislature, referendum, and agency regulations.

In one of the most recent battles over what has come to be called the "right to float," commercial outfitters and other advocates of recreational stream uses found a legislative sponsor for a bill in 2009 that would have recognized their rights of access to streams that have historically been used for recreation. Furthermore, the proposed legislation would have given that access right superiority over the rights of adjacent landowners to exclude rafting on streams running through or adjacent to their lands by exempting the rafters from trespass actions by the landowners. Advocates of recreational uses also reached the Colorado secretary of state's office with four proposals for ballot initiatives to amend the state's constitution to recognize and give priority to the right to float. Landowners and irrigation interests countered with twenty constitutional initiative proposals of their own. The legislative proposal was changed in the Colorado House to a recommendation for study

---

which has become one of the most popular forms of recreational fishing during the past quarter century, basically requires nonnavigability.

of the issue by the Colorado Water Congress, a body composed of multiple representatives of water interests within the state, along with state government officials and staff.[14]

Related controversies have arisen and persist over the operation of reservoirs (Sibley 2010). Most reservoirs in Colorado were built to impound water flows during the wetter periods of the year for gradual release during the drier parts of the year to accommodate agricultural and municipal/industrial stream diversions. Once in-stream flow protections gained a legal foothold in Colorado in the 1970s, when the legislature charged the Colorado Water Conservation Board, an executive-branch agency, with determining in-stream flow needs for ecological as well as recreational uses, in-stream water use advocates (recreational interests, of course, but also wildlife and other conservation groups) began to challenge the traditional operation of reservoirs. The long-established method has ordinarily released just enough flow into streams during the summer and fall to accommodate diversion rights for out-of-channel uses recognized under the state's prior-appropriation system. In an average year, and certainly in a drier-than-average year, this practice has meant that as a practical matter, little or no flow remains in the stream once the out-of-channel diversions have been made. Proposed changes to reservoir operations in order to accommodate state-recognized in-stream flow uses are typically opposed by irrigators and other traditional users. These disagreements can also involve the federal government, both because some of the dams and reservoirs are operated by the U.S. Bureau of Reclamation and because Native American communities are among the irrigation users of the surface streams that the reservoirs regulate. State and federal legislative authority, state and federal courts, and state and federal executive-branch agencies are all potentially implicated in the resolution of controversies over reservoir operation and water use rights. This is a rich environment for the expected pattern in the recognition, protection, and enforcement of water use rights: advocates of certain types of rights seek out venues sympathetic to their claims and interests, while advocates of other types of rights try to divert action from those venues and pursue their interests in the forums they anticipate will be more favorable to them.

One other current controversy in Colorado is worth mentioning because it highlights the fact that conflicts over water use do not arise simply when competing users want the same water at the same time. Water uses can also conflict when those who engage in one use want water at a different time than other uses. A vital component of the Colorado recreational economy is snow skiing. Extending the skiing season and assuring the availability of snow even in drier years have led the Colorado skiing industry and its counterparts elsewhere to become increasingly dependent on snowmaking machinery. Artificial snowmaking is an example of a recreational, but out-of-channel, water use. Water is diverted from streams and transported to the snowmaking equipment. In semiarid Colorado, demand for water for snowmaking escalates in late fall, when water withdrawals for irrigation and municipal/industrial uses have largely exhausted stream flows over the summer and early fall. What remains in the stream is also needed in order to maintain

---

[14] See Smith (2010) for a very readable account of this and other controversies.

state-mandated minimum in-stream flows for environmental purposes, such as fish habitat. Thus far, negotiations among the various interests involved in particular locations (Sibley 2010) have prevented changes to policy that might place snowmaking water diversions on a legal par with irrigation, environmental, and other uses. Should policy change be sought or opposed by those interests, however, the thrust and parry are likely to take place in multiple arenas: the Colorado Water Conservation Board, the legislature, the courts, and possibly the referendum process.

These illustrations go beyond making the point that water rights law is complicated and dynamic. They show as well that (1) individuals contest not only over the same rights to a resource but over different rights; (2) a multifunctional resource multiplies the types of rights of use for which people may contest; and (3) a multiorganizational policy arena not only multiplies the number of decision points, but also changes the strategic assessments and behaviors of individuals and groups. The last point bears some further elaboration. As issues arise in connection with property rights in a multifunctional resource, and as governmental bodies address those issues in a noncomprehensive way (dealing with one claim of right to one use of the resource this time, another claim of right to the same or a different use of the resource the next time, and so on), individuals and groups gain information about which policy venues are more or less likely to be receptive to their interests and arguments. Individuals and groups pursue their interests in various venues as they calculate their relative likelihoods of success. Rather than being an "input" to the policy-making process—a problem to solve—divergent and conflicting property rights claims in a natural resource are the expected output of a policy-making process that features multiple policy-making venues.[15]

The considerations discussed in this chapter complicate the analysis of property rights immensely. Most people probably agree that simplicity is a desirable characteristic of analysis. On that basis, many scholars can be expected to continue to develop and refine analyses of property rights that eschew many or most of these complicating elements. One might therefore legitimately question the value of the discussion in this chapter.

The value of this discussion depends on the extent to which it accurately characterizes some of the factors and processes that go into the development and evolution of property rights institutions but have been disregarded in other approaches. It is worthwhile to ponder the likelihood of encountering actual situations where (1) resources have but one dimension and one use; (2) choices among alternative property rights arrangements are made by a single decision maker or in a single forum; and (3) those who take an interest in a resource have no inclination or ability to (re)frame the issues in question, alter the scope of conflict, and shift decision-making venues. Analytical approaches that explicitly or implicitly assume such

---

[15] Policy makers' political interests may be served by this dynamic as well. By deciding on, say, a right of access to one aspect of a natural resource in one venue at one time, and perhaps a right of management to that or some other aspect of the resource in another venue or at another time, policy makers multiply their opportunities to respond to many constituencies. "Solving" a problem comprehensively (but perhaps in a way that sends some interests home victorious and other interests home empty-handed) may well be less useful politically than being able to give one constituency after another a little bit of what it wants by addressing only one aspect of resource use at a time.

situations will be simpler to develop and refine, but they may turn out to be applicable to relatively limited sets of cases.

The more complicated approach sketched in this chapter constitutes the dynamics of a political analysis of property rights. Empirical applications of this approach should seek to determine the extent to which the analysis advances the explanation and understanding of how property rights have developed and changed over time in actual settings. If the results are promising, such a political analysis could represent an addition to the rich literature that has emerged over the past half century on property rights, primarily through the work of economists.

What remains to be done is to apply the kind of political analysis presented in this chapter to actual cases in depth and to determine whether it sheds light on the emergence of property rights institutions in those cases, the forms those institutions take, and how they change over time. This is a daunting task. But it may not suffice much longer to speculate about the presence or absence of property rights, or about the effects of one type of property right versus another, if we want to be able to speak about the world as it exists and as human beings have made it. Such work will be time consuming and painstaking, so one must hope that there will be a positive yield in the explanation and understanding of property rights that will warrant the effort.

REFERENCES

Anderson, Terry L., and Peter J. Hill. 1975. The evolution of property rights: A study of the American West. *Journal of Law and Economics* 18(1):163–179.

Barbanell, Edward M. 2001. *Common-property arrangements and scarce resources: Water in the American West.* Westport, CT: Praeger.

Baumgartner, Frank R., and Bryan D. Jones. 2009. *Agendas and instability in American politics.* 2nd ed. Chicago: University of Chicago Press.

Black, Peter E. 1960. *Colorado water law.* Fort Collins, CO: Colorado State University.

Bromley, Daniel W. 1991. *Environment and economy: Property rights and public policy.* Oxford: Blackwell.

Brouwer, Floor, and C. Martijn van der Heide, eds. 2009. *Multifunctional rural land management.* London: Earthscan.

Cole, Daniel H., and Peter Z. Grossman. 2002. The meaning of property rights: Law versus economics? *Land Economics* 78(3):317–330.

Davis, Lance, and Douglass C. North. 1971. *Institutional change and American economic growth.* New York: Cambridge University Press.

Demsetz, Harold. 1967. Toward a theory of property rights. *American Economic Review.* 57(2):347–359.

Easton, David. 1953. *The political system: An inquiry into the state of political science.* New York: Alfred A. Knopf.

Eggertsson, Thráinn. 1994. Property rights, economic analysis, and the information problem. Working Paper. Bloomington, Indiana: Workshop in Political Theory and Policy Analysis. http://de.scientificcommons.org/46556377.

Hutchins, Wells A. 2004. *Water rights laws in the nineteen western states.* 3 vols. Clark, NJ: Lawbook Exchange.

Jones, P. Andrew, and Tom Cech. 2009. *Colorado water law for non-lawyers.* Boulder: University Press of Colorado.

Kagan, Robert A. 2001. *Adversarial legalism: The American way of law.* Cambridge, MA: Harvard University Press.

———. 2004. American courts and the policy dialogue: The role of adversarial legalism. In *Making policy, making law: An interbranch perspective*, eds. Mark S. Miller and Jeb Barnes, 13–34. Washington, DC: Georgetown University Press.

Kantor, Shawn Everett. 1991. Razorbacks, ticky cows, and the closing of the Georgia open range: The dynamics of institutional change uncovered. *Journal of Economic History* 51(4):861–886.

Kingdon, John W. 1995. *Agendas, alternatives, and public policies*. 2nd ed. New York: Longman.

Kiser, Larry L., and Elinor Ostrom. 1982. The three worlds of action: A metatheoretical synthesis of institutional approaches. In *Strategies of political inquiry*, ed. Elinor Ostrom, 179–222. Beverly Hills, CA: Sage Publications.

Lasswell, Harold. 1958. *Politics: Who gets what, when, how*. New York: Meridian Books.

Libecap, Gary D. 1989. *Contracting for property rights*. New York: Cambridge University Press.

Maier, Leo, and Mikitaro Shobayashi. 2001. *Multifunctionality: Towards an analytical framework*. Paris: Organisation for Economic Co-operation and Development.

North, Douglass C. 1981. *Structure and change in economic history*. New York: Norton.

Ostrom, Elinor, and Edella Schlager. 1996. The formation of property rights. In *Rights to nature: Ecological, cultural, and political principles of institutions for the environment*, eds. Susan Hanna, Carl Folke, and Karl-Goran Maler, 127–156. Washington, DC: Island Press.

Radosevich, George E. 1976. *Evolution and administration of Colorado water law, 1876–1976*. Fort Collins, CO: Water Resources Publications.

Schattschneider, E. E. 1960. *The semisovereign people: A realist's view of democracy in America*. Hinsdale, IL: Dryden Press.

Schlager, Edella, and Elinor Ostrom. 1992. Property-rights regimes and natural resources: A conceptual analysis. *Land Economics* 68(3):249–262.

Sened, Itai. 1997. *The political institution of private property*. Cambridge, U.K.: Cambridge University Press.

Shobayashi, Mikitaro. 2003. *Multifunctionality: The policy implications*. Paris: Organisation for Economic Co-operation and Development.

Sibley, George. 2010. Going with the flow. *Headwaters*, Fall:18–21.

Smith, Jerd. 2010. Fighting for the right. *Headwaters*, Fall:11–17.

Stone, Deborah. 2002. *Policy paradox: The art of political decision making*. Rev. ed. New York: W. W. Norton and Co.

Wiel, Samuel C. 2010 [1911]. *Water rights in the western states*. 3rd ed. San Francisco, CA: Bancroft-Whitney Co.

Commentary

EDELLA C. SCHLAGER

I t would be a mistake, as Blomquist notes, to read his chapter and conclude only that natural resources and property rights systems are complex, perhaps even too complex to understand. Rather, if one reads the chapter carefully, what becomes apparent is that Blomquist draws on several tools to organize and embrace that complexity. Most notably, Blomquist implicitly draws on the notion of framework, as pioneered in the social sciences by Elinor Ostrom (Kiser and Ostrom 1982; Ostrom 2005; 2007; 2009; 2011). According to Ostrom (2005), frameworks are a means of systematically organizing inquiry about phenomena of interest. A framework consists of many elements and general relations among them. Blomquist calls on numerous elements, from a typology of rights (Schlager and Ostrom 1992) to levels of action (Kiser and Ostrom 1982; Ostrom 2005) and a typology of water uses. Each element either already appears or fits comfortably within Ostrom's social-ecological systems (SES) framework (Ostrom 2007; 2009). In fact, table 12.1 in Blomquist's chapter is a subset of the elements from the SES framework.

Frameworks serve many important purposes, but most important, frameworks support the accumulation of knowledge in several ways. The SES framework provides a common metatheoretical language that all scholars who study social-ecological systems, no matter what their disciplinary training is, may use. If a number of scholars are examining the relations among different kinds of natural resources and the property rights arrangements that govern use, they can rest assured that they are using a common language to describe and explain the same phenomena (Ostrom 2005). In addition, analysts use a framework to guide and structure diagnostic and prescriptive inquiry in support of theory development and testing (Ostrom 2005). That is precisely what Blomquist does in his chapter. He is diagnosing and drawing attention to many important elements that need to be considered in explaining how property rights are created and revised, with special emphasis on the collective-choice level of decision making. By using the social-ecological framework, analysts can embrace complexity without being overwhelmed by it (Ostrom 2007). Scholars can situate their analysis in a well-defined context by purposefully identifying the elements of the framework they will use to develop explanations of institutional change while recognizing the larger context in which those elements are situated. Blomquist's chapter illustrates how that may be done.

In addition to using the social-ecological framework, Blomquist points to important variables and the relationships among them that form the foundation of several theories of policy change (Cobb and Elder 1972; Jones and Baumgartner

2005; Kingdon 1995). Later in his chapter, Blomquist switches from framework to theory, focusing on resource users, public officials, and organizations' strategic use of collective-choice bodies and conflict to pursue or prevent changes in property rights. What makes Blomquist's analysis innovative is its focus on resource users—property rights holders and those who want to be property rights holders—and how they contest rights and values in diverse venues. Most theories of policy change focus on national-level policy-making processes and national laws. Blomquist's illustration of Colorado water rights dynamics suggests that applying the insights of these theories to local and state-level collective-choice processes is likely to produce numerous breakthroughs in explaining how and why property rights systems change over time.

Where I differ with Blomquist is over his suggestion for future research. He proposes that multiple case studies be developed using the elements he identifies in his chapter. Case studies that incorporate many interacting elements will allow scholars to determine whether more complex explanations better account for how and why property rights change. In other words, he proposes using the SES framework as a diagnostic tool. But Blomquist's chapter very ably covers diagnosis. Instead, future research should center on theory development, not framework application, by extending theories that account for either multiple interacting collective-choice processes or dynamic institutional change. For example, Blomquist's Colorado case study identifies different collective-choice bodies (courts, legislatures, regulatory agencies, and commissions) that have a say in defining and revising water rights. These bodies constitute a polycentric governance system. These collective-choice bodies may act independently of one another, but they nevertheless must take one another into account while making decisions. According to polycentric governance theories, rather than leading to chaos, such multiple, overlapping, but independent governments lead to enhanced information production, error detection, and opportunities for adaptation than do more centralized governance systems (Schlager and Blomquist 2008; Wilson 2002). Polycentric governance systems should generate property rights systems that are better adapted to the biophysical setting and more responsive to citizens' values than less complex governance systems. This is a theoretically grounded, empirical question that rests squarely in the embrace of the SES framework.

REFERENCES

Cobb, Roger W., and Charles D. Elder. 1972. *Participation in American politics: The dynamics of agenda setting.* Boston: Allyn and Bacon.

Jones, Bryan, and Frank Baumgartner. 2005. *The politics of attention.* Chicago: University of Chicago Press.

Kingdon, John W. 1995. *Agendas, alternatives, and public policies.* 2nd ed. New York: Longman.

Kiser, Larry L., and Elinor Ostrom. 1982. The three worlds of action: A metatheoretical synthesis of institutional approaches. In *Strategies of political inquiry,* ed. Elinor Ostrom, 179–222. Beverly Hills, CA: Sage Publications.

Ostrom, Elinor. 2005. *Understanding institutional diversity.* Princeton, NJ: Princeton University Press.

——. 2007. A diagnostic approach for going beyond panaceas. *Proceedings of the National Academy of Sciences* 104(39):15181–15187.

——. 2009. A general framework for analyzing sustainability of social-ecological systems. *Science* 325(5939):419–422.

——. 2011. Background on the institutional analysis and development framework. *Policy Studies Journal* 39(1):7–27.

Schlager, Edella, and William Blomquist. 2008. *Embracing watershed politics.* Boulder, CO: University Press of Colorado.

Schlager, Edella, and Elinor Ostrom. 1992. Property-rights regimes and natural resources: A conceptual analysis. *Land Economics* 68(3):249–262.

Wilson, James. 2002. Scientific uncertainty, complex systems, and the design of common pool resource systems. In *The drama of the commons*, eds. Elinor Ostrom, Thomas Dietz, Nives Dolšak, Paul Stern, Susan Stonich, and Elke U. Weber, 327–359. Washington, DC: National Academy Press.

Water Rights and Markets in the U.S. Semiarid West

Efficiency and Equity Issues

GARY D. LIBECAP

13

There is growing concern about the availability of fresh water worldwide. As per capita income rises and populations grow, demands for water for human consumption, agriculture, recreation, and environmental habitats are increasing.[1] At the same time, climate change is predicted to make precipitation more variable, with the possibility of longer drought periods (Barnett et al. 2008; World Water Assessment Programme 2009). As water values rise because of increasing demand and limited supply, one might expect that formal property rights to water would be made more precise and that water markets would become active to address allocation, management, and conservation pressures more effectively.

In a classic article, Harold Demsetz (1967) described a process of property rights development and market activity as asset values rise exogenously. Indeed, institutional arrangements for many resources, such as hard-rock minerals and oil and gas reservoirs in the United States, developed in a manner consistent with Demsetz's hypothesis (Libecap 1978; 2007; Libecap and Smith 2002). In a broader context, commodity markets adjust rapidly to price differentials and reallocate the assets so that price gaps narrow over time. However, this process of property rights formation and price convergence is not happening as quickly for fresh water in the western United States (Brewer et al. 2008; Young 1986).

There are both high resource and political costs of defining and enforcing property rights to water and of managing it with markets. This chapter examines these issues in 12 states in the semiarid U.S. West, where many of the intensifying demand and supply problems regarding fresh water are playing out.[2] To understand the problems of expanding water markets, it is critical to address the varying political, bureaucratic, and administrative incentives involved.

There are major differences in water prices across uses (agriculture, urban, environmental) in the western states that cannot be completely explained by differences in conveyance costs and water quality. Therefore, it appears that water markets have not developed fully enough to narrow the gaps. Moreover, the extent and

---

[1] The *Economist* (April 8, 2009, 52) speculates that no more than 20 percent of the available water can be "safely" withdrawn by humans on an ongoing basis without a negative impact on the natural environment.

[2] The states are Arizona, California, Colorado, Idaho, Montana, Nevada, New Mexico, Oregon, Utah, Texas, Washington, and Wyoming.

nature of water trading vary considerably across these states, most likely because of differences in water values and transaction costs of trade. This chapter's discussion of the resource and political costs of defining water rights and the use of markets shows that efficiency and equity issues often conflict. This tension reflects the social nature of the water resource.

Efficiency: The Extent of Water Trading

Water Price Differentials

Most western water markets are local. Trading is confined within water basins and sectors (among adjacent irrigators, for example). Typically, exchange outside a water basin is limited, and voluntary private transactions to move water from agriculture to urban use are often very costly and, in some cases, extremely contentious. There is virtually no private water trading across state boundaries.

Price differences across uses illustrate opportunities for exchange, but assembling data is difficult because of segmented markets, limited comparable observations of trades within and across sectors, high shipping or conveyance costs, diverse regulatory regimes, and variation in water quality. Accordingly, available price data must be examined with caution, but the patterns indicate the thinness of many water markets and of the efficiency gains from further reallocation.[3]

Data assembled by Clay Landry and reported in Libecap (2011) for two regional markets, the Reno/Truckee Basin, Nevada, and the South Platte Basin, Colorado, show significant price gaps between agriculture-to-urban and agriculture-to-agriculture transactions. For the Truckee Basin, the median price of 1,025 agriculture-to-urban water sales between 2002 and 2009 (2008 prices) was $17,685 per acre-foot (AF; an acre-foot is 325,851 gallons, about enough to meet the needs of four people for a year), whereas for 13 agriculture-to-agriculture sales during the same period the median price was $1,500/AF. For the South Platte, the median price for 138 agriculture-to-urban sales between 2002 and 2008 was $6,519/AF; for 110 agriculture-to-agriculture transactions, the median price was $5,309/AF.

Aggregating transactions across markets and time can compensate for limited comparable transactions within local markets and can give a sense of differences in value across sectors if one recognizes the qualifiers noted earlier. The data reported here are from a database of 4,220 observations from 1987 through 2008 compiled by the author.[4] The data set is not conclusive because some transactions are likely to be missed, especially those that take place within organizations, such as irrigation districts.

Of the 4,220 transactions in the database with information on the transacting parties, amounts, and nature of use, a smaller number, 2,765, have price data. Table 13.1 shows mean and median prices per acre-foot for leases and sales for agriculture-

---

[3] For additional discussion of western water markets, see Libecap (2011).

[4] The database currently includes 4,407 transactions through 2009. Because 2009 transactions continued to be indicated throughout 2010, the 2009 transactions currently in the database were excluded from the analysis. The full data set and the methodology are described at http://www.bren.ucsb.edu/news/water_transfers.htm. See also Brewer et al. (2008) for discussion of methodology.

TABLE 13.1

Water Transfer Prices by Sector, 1987–2008 (in 2008 dollars per committed acre-foot)

	Agriculture-to-Urban Leases	Agriculture-to-Agriculture Leases	Agriculture-to-Urban Sales	Agriculture-to-Agriculture Sales
Median price	$74	$19	$295	$144
Mean price	$190	$56	$437	$246
Number of observations	204	207	1,140	215

SOURCE: Author's calculations from database, http://www.bren.ucsb.edu/news/water_transfers.htm.

to-agriculture and agriculture-to-urban trades.[5] The prices for sales are given as the value per acre-foot of committed flow of water, which is analogous to a one-year lease price.[6] By discounting quantity flows, using the same methodology as for determining the present value of a perpetual bond, a single committed quantity is calculated. With this discounted quantity, the total sales price is converted into a price per acre-foot that is directly comparable to a one-year lease price per acre-foot. Multiyear lease prices are treated similarly, using the same method as that for finding the present value of a multiyear bond, and are combined with one-year leases in table 13.1. Historical use patterns indicate that as much as 90 percent of western water is consumed in agriculture, but most new demand is for urban and environmental uses.[7] Accordingly, the trades reported are for movements of water within and out of agriculture.

As shown, the annual mean and median sale and lease prices for agriculture-to-urban transactions are significantly higher than those for agriculture-to-agriculture trades (see the statistical discussion that follows). This condition in part indicates the benefits of out-of-sector water transfers. Other factors, such as more senior rights that may be associated with agriculture-to-urban transfers and higher wheeling or conveyance costs, also explain the higher prices. Further, because sales involve the transfer of water rights and a perpetual claim on water flows as compared with leases, which involve a shorter-term (often one-year) transfer of the right to use water, sale prices will be higher than lease prices.

Figure 13.1 shows the patterns of agriculture-to-agriculture and agriculture-to-urban median prices over time for sales and one-year leases. A Wilcoxon signed-rank test was performed,[8] and the yearly median price of agriculture-to-urban

---

[5] All prices were converted into dollars per acre-foot of water for comparison across time. Prices for one-year transactions were easily presented in acre-foot terms. For example, if 1,000 acre-feet of water were leased for one year for a total price of $100,000, then the price per acre-foot was $100.

[6] Consider a sale of 1,000 acre-feet of water for a total price of $2 million. The price per acre-foot is $2,000. This is the traditional method of showing sale prices. However, it is not directly comparable to the one-year lease price because the sale commits a flow of water to the buyer in perpetuity. In the example of a sale of 1,000 acre-feet of water for a total price of $2 million, discounting the quantity flows by 5 percent leads to a discounted sales price of $100 per acre-foot.

[7] http://www.ers.usda.gov/Briefing/wateruse/. U.S. Department of Agriculture, 22 Nov 2004.

[8] The Wilcoxon signed-rank test is similar to the standard difference-in-means t-test. However, its nonparametric nature allows additional flexibility because it does not require a priori assumptions about the distribution of its components. The statistical significance holds for the difference in means as well.

FIGURE 13.1

Prices over Time

Median Price of Sales

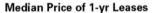

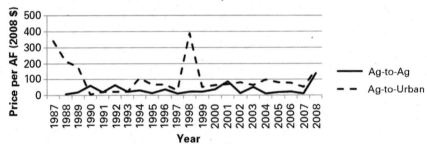

Median Price of 1-yr Leases

SOURCE: Author's calculations from database, http://www.bren.ucsb.edu/news/water_transfers.htm.

transfers is greater than that of agriculture-to-agriculture transfers at a 1 percent significance level.[9] In the database, agriculture-to-urban sales are dominated by transactions in Colorado on the Colorado–Big Thompson Project.[10] Although there are limited data on agriculture-to-agriculture sales outside Colorado, the median agriculture-to-urban sale price in the 11 western states excluding Colorado is much greater, $708/AF, than the median price of agriculture-to-agriculture sales, $251/AF.

There are two primary reasons that there are fewer observations for agriculture-to-agriculture sales outside Colorado.[11] One is that agriculture-to-agriculture sales can take place within irrigation districts, and these transactions are likely to be missed in the database used here. The entire 22-year database reports only 613 agriculture-to-agriculture trades for the 12 western states. Brozovic, Carey, and Sunding (2002) report that in the Westlands Water District alone, where active intradistrict trading takes place, 1,267 transactions occurred from 1993 to 1996. The

---

[9] W = 183, p-value = 0.0015.

[10] The Colorado–Big Thompson Project's institutional details are discussed later in this chapter.

[11] Of the 2,765 priced transactions used in this analysis, 215 were agriculture-to-agriculture sales, 32 of which were outside Colorado. In contrast, there were 1,140 agriculture-to-urban sales with price data, with 211 taking place outside Colorado.

second reason is that irrigators in western states often rely on leases instead of sales. Basically, leases are common because they involve low transaction costs with trades among neighboring irrigators. They typically do not require regulatory review. A Wilcoxon signed-rank test was performed on one-year lease prices for the 12 western states, of which Colorado represents a very small portion of transactions. The test shows that the yearly median price of agriculture-to-urban leases is greater than that of agriculture-to-agriculture transfers at a 1 percent significance level.[12]

Welfare Gains from Greater Market Trading

The differences in the prices of traded water in the two categories indicates that at the margin, there can be significant efficiency gains from reallocating some water from agriculture to urban and environmental uses. Here an attempt is made to model what some of these gains might look like. The obstacles to modeling the efficiency advantages of water trades fall into three broad categories. The first is the physical aspects of water trades. Water price depends not only on supply and demand generally, but also on local conditions, such as conveyance ability and water quality.[13] The second is the transaction costs associated with differing regulations and incomplete property rights regimes across jurisdictions. Regulations vary by state, and there can be county restrictions on transfers within states. The third is limited data. Water markets are local because of conveyance costs and regulatory restrictions. Therefore, they are thin, so there are limited observations of transfers and prices, and these data can be affected by observations that are not indicative of general patterns.

Figure 13.1 shows that agriculture-to-agriculture sales prices approximated agriculture-to-urban prices from 2006 to 2008. The high-priced agriculture-to-agriculture sales in these years, however, took place within the Colorado–Big Thompson Project, where administrative rules allow agriculture-to-agriculture and agriculture-to-urban transfers to occur freely, forcing agricultural users to pay the full opportunity cost of the water, which is the cost urban users are willing to pay. For example, the January 2007 issue of *Water Strategist* reported a number of trades from the Colorado–Big Thompson Project, among them a transfer from an irrigator to a developer for \$9,673/AF and from an irrigator to another irrigator for \$9,626/AF.

Given the observed differences in water values between agriculture and urban applications, it is interesting to estimate what the welfare gain might be under varying scenarios of a hypothetical increase in water trading from the agriculture to the urban sector. Two cases are considered: (1) transfer of just a small amount (1 percent) of current irrigation water or 10 percent of the current urban market, whichever is smaller, to urban use; and (2) transfer of 3 percent of irrigation water or 100 percent of the current urban market, whichever is smaller, to urban use. These constraints are designed to minimize any impact on agricultural or urban sector water prices

---

[12] $W = -158$, p-value $= 0.003$.

[13] Conveyance costs can be high. Water is heavy. An acre-foot of water weighs 2,719,226 pounds (325,851 gal/ AF × 8.435 pounds/gal), or 1,360 tons. Hansen, Howitt, and Williams (2007) report that 55 percent of the \$250/AF that the Metropolitan Water District of Southern California paid in 2002 for water from northern California was for the cost of conveying it.

and to reflect what might be feasible for an urban market to absorb.[14] Kenny et al. (2009) provide estimates of the total and irrigated use of water in the United States by state, and the Bren database, http://www.bren.ucsb.edu/news/water_transfers. htm, allows for trading estimates.

The state data are reported in table 13.2, which provides estimates of total surface water used and of water used in irrigation as of 2005, as well as the average committed volume of water transferred per year through all trades (sales, multi-year leases, and one-year leases) and that figure as a share of total use and irrigation use.[15] The final column lists the median price difference between agriculture-to-urban and agriculture-to-agriculture transfers.

Table 13.3 outlines the hypothetical transfers. Note that the volume of water in the proposed additional transfers is small compared with the water used for irriga-

TABLE 13.2

Surface Water Use (2005) and Average Water Trading Volume, Western United States, 1987–2008

State	Surface Water Use (2005) Total (AF)[b]	Irrigation (AF)	Current Total Water Transferred per Year (Committed)[a] Average Volume (AF)[c]	As % of Total Use	As % of Irrigation Use	Median Price Difference (Agriculture-to-Urban minus Agriculture-to-Agriculture)
AZ	3,154,970	2,540,000	1,056,749	33.5	41.6	$17
CA	22,087,390	15,700,000	1,939,336	8.8	12.4	$30
CO	10,984,830	10,000,000	779,478	7.1	7.8	$232
ID	15,169,140	12,700,000	491,005	3.2	3.9	N.A.
MT	9,736,660	9,530,000	28,698	0.3	0.3	$45
NV	1,374,870	828,000	118,677	8.6	14.3	$175
NM	1,611,860	1,550,000	221,979	13.8	14.3	$54
OR	5,077,910	3,780,000	442,625	8.7	11.7	$10
TX	6,695,160	1,680,000	1,735,658	25.9	103.3	$15
UT	4,117,390	3,610,000	228,932	5.6	6.3	$22
WA	3,765,180	2,890,000	183,402	4.9	6.3	$25
WY	3,663,120	3,570,000	48,835	1.3	1.4	$77
Total	87,438,480	68,378,000	7,275,374	8.3	10.6	

SOURCE: Author's calculations from database, http://www.bren.ucsb.edu/news/water_transfers.htm.

[a] Using committed amounts makes sense because they reflect the full amount of water obligated under the contract. Using the annual flow of the first year of the contract would understate the amount of water involved. See Brewer et al. (2008).

[b] Kenny et al. (2009) provide estimates of the total use and irrigated use of water in the United States by state, and the Bren dataset allows for trading estimates by author. This category excludes water used for thermoelectric cooling but includes surface water use for public consumption, agriculture (irrigation, livestock, and aquaculture), industry, and mining.

[c] Average volume is the sum of all committed flows transferred in each year, averaged over the 22-year period recorded in the database. Because transactions often are for multiple years, the data here are calculated by the author to reflect longer time horizons. If one says that 10,000 AF was transferred in 2008, the meaning is that the discounted sum of committed flows for the duration of the transaction was 10,000 AF in 2008 because some of the flows were actually transferred in later years. This allows for a consistent treatment of prices.

---

[14] The additional transfers are assumed to take place at the prevailing agriculture-to-urban market price. The net gain is this value less the opportunity cost of water in agriculture as approximated by the agriculture-to-agriculture price.

[15] As was discussed for table 13.1, all contracted amounts of water are converted to a similar committed flow.

TABLE 13.3
Potential Gains from Increased Agriculture-to-Urban Transactions

State	Current Average Annual Market Value (All Transfer Types and Sectors)[a]	Proposed new Agriculture-to-Urban Transfers (AF)[b]	Net Welfare Gain from Additional Transactions[c]	Net Welfare Gain as % of Current Market Value	Proposed Agriculture-to-Urban Transfers (AF)[d]	Net Welfare Gain	Net Welfare Gain as % of Current Market Value
AZ	$38,811,748	25,400	$440,362	1	76,200	$1,321,087	3
CA	$223,477,457	71,126	$2,135,504	1	471,000	$14,141,453	6
CO	$40,819,066	31,084	$7,224,465	18	300,000	$69,725,433	171
ID	$5,194,129	N.A.	N.A.	N.A.	40,710	$0	
MT	$294,998	1,186	$53,692	18	11,858	$536,920	182
NV	$4,191,448	2,185	$382,668	9	21,854	$3,826,683	91
NM	$36,334,302	14,570	$782,415	2	46,500	$2,497,023	7
OR	$10,014,045	151	$1,456	0	1,509	$14,562	0
TX	$39,093,722	16,800	$251,868	1	50,400	$755,604	2
UT	$6,328,674	17,820	$388,094	6	108,300	$2,358,663	37
WA	$1,097,697	9,016	$225,025	20	86,700	$2,163,814	197
WY	$267,649	772	$59,365	22	7,721	$593,651	222
Total	$405,924,936	190,110	$11,944,915	3	1,222,753	$97,934,893	24

NOTE: Differences that occur in the table are the result of rounding.

[a] This is the sum of the total price of every transaction from 1987 to 2008 in 2008 dollars divided by 22 years to arrive at a yearly average.

[b] One percent of surface irrigation water in AZ and TX and 10 percent of current agriculture to urban market for CA, CO, MT, NV, NM, OR, UT, WA, and WY.

[c] Net welfare gain is price difference (agriculture-to-urban minus agriculture-to-agriculture) multiplied by volume of additional transfers.

[d] Transfer minimum of 3 percent of irrigation volume or 100 percent of current urban market volume, whichever was smaller. The large welfare gain shown in Colorado likely reflects the difference in high prices paid for water within the Colorado–Big Thompson District discussed in the text.

tion or with total current transfers. Column two shows the value of current water transfers; column three the proposed increase under option (1); the associated welfare gains and its share of current transfers are in columns four and five, the increases under (2) are in column six, and the associated gains are in columns seven and eight.

The net welfare gain from moving a very small amount of water to urban users under (1) is estimated at $12 million per year and under (2) at $98 million per year. These figures represent gains of 3 percent and 24 percent, respectively, of the value of the yearly water market activity of almost $406 million. Even under the conservative conditions imposed in this exercise, there appear to be significant annual welfare gains from increased movement of water from agriculture to urban uses. Any increases in trading are constrained by the existing size (already small) of the urban market. The estimates are illustrative only, and some of the very large gains, such as in Colorado, Montana, Nevada, and Washington, may be partially due to limited observations of agriculture-to-agriculture trades in the database. Nevertheless, they indicate the potential benefits of a more active water market.

Water Transfers in 12 Western States, 1987–2008

All western states allow for transfers of water. There are three types of transfers: permanent sales of water rights, short-term leases (one year), and longer-term leases (up to thirty-five years or more). Transfers occur among those who use the water for the same purpose (e.g., irrigated agriculture) or for different purposes (agriculture-to-urban or environmental); they also occur within a water basin (where sources are interrelated geologically) or across basins (from one water region to another). Transfers by short-term leases within a basin among those who use water for the same purpose, such as farmers, typically have been the most common. Longer-term leases and sales of water rights often involve changes in the location and nature of the use of water.

Figure 13.2 illustrates the yearly path of all transfers in the 12 western states from 1987 through 2008, as well as those for agriculture-to-agriculture, agriculture-to-urban, and agriculture-to-environmental trades. The paths in the figure indicate that (1) the total number of water transfers is increasing (statistically significant); (2) agriculture-to-urban and agriculture-to-environmental trades are also rising (statistically significant); and (3) agriculture-to-agriculture trades show no discernible trend (statistically insignificant).[16]

Table 13.4 shows the nature of trades across states and by contract form from 1987 through 2008. Colorado dominates total market transactions, reflecting the institutional advantages of the Colorado–Big Thompson Project (CBT), which are described later and and within the CBT most of the transactions are sales. Other active market states are California, Texas, Arizona, and Nevada. Within California and Texas, short-term leases are the most prevalent contract, but multiyear leases and sales are also important. California's institutional and regulatory environments for water explain the focus on short-term leases. In Arizona and Nevada, which are

---

[16] Although Colorado dominates the number of transactions, the trends remain the same in direction and statistical significance when Colorado transactions are removed.

FIGURE 13.2

Number of Transfers in 12 Western States, 1987–2008

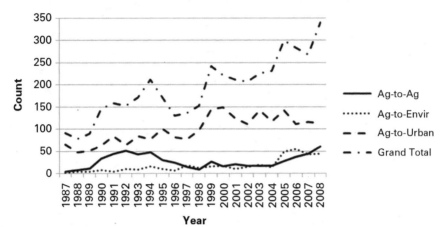

SOURCE: Author's calculations from database, http://www.bren.ucsb.edu/news/water_transfers.htm.

TABLE 13.4

Water Transactions by Type and State

	Number of All Transactions	Number of Sales	Number of Short-Term Leases	Number of Long-Term Leases
Arizona	233	158	46	12
California	656	108	317	77
Colorado	2,144	1,804	97	43
Idaho	148	31	107	3
Montana	46	3	14	26
New Mexico	153	73	59	15
Nevada	192	148	4	4
Oregon	125	24	56	25
Texas	320	91	141	71
Utah	84	61	15	7
Washington	57	24	23	9
Wyoming	62	6	41	5
Total	4,220	2,531	920	297

rapidly urbanizing, dry states, sales are common, but, not surprisingly, Montana and Wyoming, the least urban of the 12 western states, have the fewest water sales.

Table 13.5 breaks down the trading activity by state into the share that is within the agriculture or urban sectors and that which is from agriculture to urban. The differences between the annual flow and committed measures reflect the importance of sales and long-term leases in the committed amounts. Again, there are important differences across the states. Among the leading water-trading states, Arizona and California have relatively balanced transactions across sectors, but Colorado, Texas, Nevada, and Washington show considerable activity (a relatively high level of trades) to and within the urban sector.

TABLE 13.5

Share of Each Transfer's Classification in a State's Total Quantity Transferred

	Annual Flow				Committed			
	Agriculture-to-Urban (%)	Agriculture-to-Agriculture (%)	Urban-to-Urban (%)	Total (Million AF)	Agriculture-to-Urban (%)	Agriculture-to-Agriculture (%)	Urban-to-Urban (%)	Total (Million AF)
AZ	15	46	39	8.34	31	37	32	21.72
CA	41	32	27	5.04	37	32	31	12.60
CO	51	29	20	0.59	75	8	17	5.88
ID	39	55	6	1.59	29	67	5	2.36
MT	55	45	0	0.02	95	5	0	0.22
NM	15	78	7	0.10	36	55	10	0.91
NV	84	0	16	0.22	72	0	28	2.39
OR	0	100	0	0.10	0	100	0	0.29
TX	48	15	37	1.75	50	3	47	25.30
UT	38	32	29	0.31	53	3	44	4.05
WA	49	36	15	0.16	79	3	18	1.93
WY	37	63	0	0.10	38	62	0	0.41

SOURCE: Author's calculations from database, http://www.bren.ucsb.edu/news/water_transfers.htm.

It is clear that there is water market activity across the western states, and there are opportunities for more activity to address growing problems of scarcity and reallocation. The question is what measurement and equity issues will be encountered. The answer begins with an examination of water rights.

Institutions: Western Water Rights

Appropriative Surface Water Rights

In western states, individuals do not own water as they might own land. This in itself suggests the special nature of water. The state owns the water and holds it in trust for its citizens. Individuals hold usufruct rights to the water, subject to the requirement that the use be beneficial and reasonable, but the state has the authority to monitor use and water transfers to ensure that they are consistent with the public interest (Gould 1995; Simms 1995). Accordingly, there is a broad regulatory framework for water, and western water rights potentially have less protection and are more fragile than most other property rights (Gray 1994a; Sax 1990).

In most western states (Arizona, Colorado, Idaho, Montana, Nevada, New Mexico, Utah, and Wyoming), all surface water rights are based on the prior-appropriation doctrine that allows rights holders to withdraw a certain amount of water from a natural watercourse for beneficial purposes on land remote from the point of diversion (Getches 1997). The appropriative doctrine emerged in the nineteenth century in response to the development of mining and agriculture in the semiarid West, where growing numbers of people and economic activities were increasingly concentrated in areas where there was too little water (Kanazawa 1998). Prior appropriation allowed water to be separated from riparian land and moved via canals and ditches to new locations (Johnson, Gisser, and Werner 1981).

Appropriative rights are assigned through the rule of first possession or priority of claim. They grant rights to redirect a defined quantity of water from the source (surface water or groundwater), based on the time of the initial diversion. Those with the earliest water claims have the highest priority, and those with subsequent claims have lower-priority or junior claims. Therefore, there is a ladder of rights on a stream. This allocative mechanism ranks competing claimants by priority in order to ration water during times of drought. Transfers of water that change the point of diversion, timing, or nature of use generally are based on the amount of water consumed (MacDonnell 1990).[17]

Under prior appropriation, there is a critical interdependence among diverters from the same water source with different priority rights. Because as much as 50 percent of the original diversion may flow back to the stream or percolate down to the aquifer, it is available for subsequent users (Young 1986). During times of drought, when only senior appropriators may have their allotments fulfilled, junior appropriators are especially dependent on these return flows. They bear most of the downside risk of drought. Actions by senior rights holders that affect water consumption can influence the amount of water released downstream. Accordingly, water trading from agriculture to urban uses that involves export out of the basin can impair third parties and is subject to state regulation to ensure that no harm is inflicted on junior diverters (Getches 1997).

Riparian Surface Water Rights

In the eastern states, water rights are based on ownership of land appurtenant to water flows. Riparian landowners have rights to access the water adjacent to or passing through their properties for reasonable purposes, including fishing and navigation, and can use the water so long as doing so does not harm other riparian claimants downstream (Getches 1997). In cases of drought, all parties share in the reduced water flow. Riparian water rights are tied to the land and can be transferred only among adjacent properties.

Of the 12 western states examined in this chapter, the wettest states, California, Texas, Oregon, and Washington, have a hybrid of prior-appropriation and riparian systems, whereas the drier states have prior appropriation only (Getches 1997). When both systems operate, there can be questions of priority of claim when diversion under the prior-appropriation system seriously reduces the water available to riparian owners. Alternatively, riparian claims could prohibit diversion from streams as part of appropriative water claims. In western states, riparian claims have been limited, although they are given precedence in California in disputes with appropriative claimants under certain circumstances (Getches 1997).

---

[17] See Anderson and Johnson (1986) and Johnson, Gisser, and Werner (1981). Johnson, Gisser, and Werner describe how specifying a property right in water in terms of consumptive use with options for third-party grievances can be an effective method of promoting transfers. Howitt and Hansen (2005) and Smith (2008) discuss water rights and water regulation across the states.

Groundwater Rights

Groundwater rights vary across the western states, and most are less well defined than are surface water rights (Thompson 1993). Most groundwater rights allow owners of surface land access to a reasonable use of groundwater (Getches 1997). With multiple, fragmented surface properties and the vague standard of reasonable use, groundwater basins can be subject to competitive withdrawal and classic common-pool conditions (Glennon 2002; Provencher and Burt 1993).[18]

These are the basic water rights in the western United States. Their definition and enforcement are affected by the physical characteristics of water, regulatory standards, and the many parties that have a say in the exchange of any water right.

Efficiency and Equity

Because of water's fluid nature and the fact that many parties use it sequentially or simultaneously, there are significant resource and political costs in defining private water rights. To see the effects of its physical characteristics, it is useful to compare water with land, which is fixed and observable, and with mobile, wild-ocean fish stocks, which are mobile, like water, with regard to characteristics that affect the costs of defining and enforcing property rights.[19] Table 13.6 lists the three resources and their characteristics: ability to bound, partition, and exclude; ability to measure size and amount; variability of supply; and existence of simultaneous and sequential uses. The signs reported in each cell indicate how the characteristic affects the costs of definition of property rights for the resource; a plus sign indicates that it contributes to definition, while a negative sign indicates that it hinders definition. As can be seen, water is more like migratory fish stocks than it is like land with regard to the costs of bounding, exclusion, and measurement.

Costs of Bounding

Because surface water and groundwater are liquids, they cannot be bounded or partitioned easily across claimants and uses (Smith 2008). This characteristic is also generally true for fisheries, where numerous competing fishers can exploit the same mobile stock as an open-access resource (Hannesson 2004). Ownership of both resources is granted only upon extraction (diversion for water, harvest for fish) under the rule of capture. Stationary land is fixed and observable, so bounding costs are much lower. It is possible to fence and partition land to meet concurrent and sequential demands for farming, urban development, pastoral scenery, or other amenities, such as provision of wildlife habitat.

Costs of Measurement

Fluidity and, in the case of groundwater, the lack of observability also raise the costs of measuring a water right. For this reason, ownership is based on the amount diverted

---

[18] For similarities with oil pools, see Libecap (1989).

[19] For discussions of the bundle of property rights in land, ease of monitoring boundaries, and partitioning land across private and public uses, see Ellickson (1993).

TABLE 13.6

Resource Characteristics

Resource	Ability to Bound, Partition, Exclude	Ability to Measure Amount	Variability of Supply	Simultaneous Uses	Sequential Uses
Land	+	+	+	+	+
Fish stocks	−	−	−	−	−
Water	−	−	−	−	−

or pumped (Johnson, Gisser, and Werner 1981). The amount actually diverted, however, varies over time because of fluctuating precipitation that affects stream flow, reservoir size, and groundwater recharge. Seasonal precipitation patterns generally are predictable and can be incorporated into a water claim, but long-term variation due to drought is less predictable and adds uncertainty to water supply and diversion amounts associated with a water right.

Mobile, unobserved fish stocks have comparable measurement problems. The stock is affected by natural growth (recruitment), disease, ocean temperature, food supplies, pollution, and harvesting in ways that are often poorly understood. As a result, rights to fish or catch shares, such as individual transferable quotas, are based on the percentage of the annual allowable catch, not on a fixed amount of fish.[20] In contrast, there is no comparable problem for measuring fixed, observable land plots, where rights can be well defined with more certainty.

Interconnected Private and Public Goods Characteristics of Water

Because water diverters sequentially access the same (unconsumed) water and because associated amenity, riparian, and aquatic habitat values are often simultaneously supplied, private and public water uses are intertwined to an extent not found for land or fish stocks (Hanemann 2006; Smith 2008). The interconnected nature of water uses and values is a basis for state regulation of water rights and water trades. Although public goods or public interest claims have merit, these equity concepts can be so broad and elastic that they can be asserted in the political and judicial processes by special interests to weaken property rights and the efficiency benefits they can provide for incentives for wise use, conservation, and exchange.

Equity and Politics: Regulatory Constraints and Water Rights

Beneficial Use, Diversion Requirements, and Preferential Uses

Appropriative water rights are conditional on placing the water into beneficial use: the use-it-or-lose-it mandate and no injury to third parties. Beneficial use was included in the appropriative doctrine as a low-cost way of determining whether

---

[20] The New Zealand quota system began by assigning fixed amounts of fish but was changed to a percentage of allowable catch (Connor and Shallard 2010).

there was excess water to be assigned. Most western states define beneficial use generally as use for the benefit of the appropriator, other persons, or the public, with corresponding lists of what is considered beneficial use. Preferred applications vary somewhat across the states. Although irrigation was the dominant initial basis for diversion, the set of beneficial uses can be expanded or contracted as public values, judicial interpretations, and constituent-group politics change. For example, leaving water in-stream for habitat preservation recently has been accepted as a beneficial use across the states, although its exact definition differs among them (Getches 1997).[21]

The vague concept of beneficial use provides the basis for a potentially broad regulatory mandate (Getches 1997). Therefore, the determination of beneficial use and diversion requirements consistent with it makes water rights vulnerable to shifting legal and political interpretations and adds uncertainty to the water right. Historically, physical diversion and complete use of diverted water were deemed consistent with the doctrine and with maintenance of a water right, but this approach has motivated irrigators to place water into low-valued applications, even though its use elsewhere might have higher values. Further, until recent changes in state law recognized conserved water as consistent with beneficial use, irrigators avoided conservation. Any conserved water could be interpreted as evidence of a lack of beneficial use of the past allotment and therefore could be subject to claims by other diverters (Getches 1997).

The No-Injury Rule (Third-Party Effects) and Area-of-Origin Restrictions

Changes in the timing, location, and nature of use can affect the amount and quality of water consumed or released to the stream for subsequent users or uses. In this event, junior rights holders especially could be harmed. This is known as third-party impairment or a third-party effect. The prospect of third-party impairment has led western states to implement judicial or administrative procedures that must be followed before water use can be altered or water rights transferred. Although these procedures vary from state to state, they typically allow water use changes or water rights transfers only if there is no damage to other water rights holders, the "no injury rule" (Thompson 1993, 701). Water transfers that are unlikely to have these impacts, such as trades among adjacent irrigators, typically do not require state approval because any third-party impairment is minimal.

As a result, most trades that could affect release flows must be approved by state regulatory agencies. Petitions for trades must specify the amount of water involved, the duration of the contract, the timing of the exchange, the type of water right, the amount of consumptive use, and possibly hydraulic and other legal information. The agency evaluates the proposal to determine whether third-party effects are involved. Notice of the proposed change is published so that objections to the change may be filed. The burden of proof of no harm from the transfer usually rests with the applicant. The outcome of administrative review can be approval, approval

---

[21] See Anderson and Johnson (1986) and Scarborough (2010) for more discussion on in-stream flow rights.

subject to modification, or denial, as well as provision of opportunities for appeal (Colby 1995).[22]

Any objections by junior appropriators downstream or others may be resolved by adjustments in the amount of water, timing, or allowable uses in the exchange. Monetary payments or other forms of compensation also may be included. The resolution of other third-party complaints, however, may be less straightforward. If substantial amounts of farmland are fallowed, there could be a reduction in local demand for farm labor and in wholesale and retail trade within rural communities. Assessing the legitimacy, basis, and appropriate size of compensation to be paid for possible pecuniary impacts on farm labor and local merchants is complicated. There must be agreement on the damages, who should pay, and the terms and conditions of payment. All these issues are likely to be controversial, and they potentially weaken water rights and reduce the gains from water reallocation.[23]

Additional third-party claims are apt to be even more difficult to assess. Rural politicians may find their political base eroded if large water transfers lead to a decline in agricultural activities. Other local officials, including school-district administrators and county extension agents, may be similarly affected. Because these damages are hard to measure, monetary payments would be difficult to determine. More important, under current law and political practices, they would be illegal. Accordingly, local politicians and bureaucratic officials may have an incentive to oppose water trades in their own self-interest, as well as in the interest of other constituencies who may be harmed.

Despite these concerns, most studies suggest that third-party pecuniary effects will be small. Only limited amounts of water and fallowing are involved in most transactions. Water placed in low-valued uses is traded first, and as the amount of water involved increases, its marginal value rises. As water prices increase, alternative urban and environmental users demand less. There are also monetary and efficiency benefits from the sale and more efficient use of water (Hanak 2003; Howitt 1994). Hanak (2003) points out that fallowing irrigated farmland is likely to have no more than a 1 percent effect on overall county economic activity, even when payments for economic adjustments are not included.

Third-party impairment can be a legitimate concern, given the sequential uses of the same water by junior appropriative rights holders. At the same time, how it affects water rights and water transfers depends on how the problem is interpreted legally and on the range for objections. If third-party impairment is strictly defined and limited to downstream junior rights holders who would be directly affected, then regulatory review is consistent with efficiency. If the problem is broadly defined to include multiple other constituencies and claims of harm, then inefficient rent seeking becomes more probable, particularly given the high prices offered for water in some cases.

The regulatory process varies across the western states, in part because of the differential complexity of water supply and use and in part because of different supply

---

[22] See also Colby (1990) and Colby, McGinnis, and Rait (1989).

[23] For an examination of bargaining over pecuniary benefits of water transfers, see Libecap (2008).

and demand conditions. Two examples illustrate the process of regulation within the states.

California generally has protransfer legislation, but the regulatory and property rights environments are less supportive. These include mixed jurisdictions among state and federal agencies, a patchwork of county regulations of groundwater withdrawal and export, and a complex system of water rights with differential requirements for agency review (Gray 1994b). For example, only transfers of surface water rights acquired since 1914 require approval of the State Water Resources Control Board (SWRCB). Exchanges within the huge Central Valley Project (CVP), where the Federal Bureau of Reclamation has jurisdiction, usually involving short-term agricultural water trades, do not involve the SWRCB (Gray 1990; MacDonnell 1990). Because there are many irrigation districts and supply organizations within the CVP with interlaced claims to water, any transfer by one entity to outside buyers is apt to affect another claimant and trigger a regulatory review. The SWRCB also can deny a proposed water transfer if it would "unreasonably affect the overall economy of the area from which the water is being transferred" (California Water Code § 386). As a result, the administrative process of transferring water in California can be lengthy and complex, and the outcome can be uncertain.

Further, California counties are able to restrict extraction and export of groundwater out of county through area-of-origin restrictions. As of 2002, 22 of the 58 counties had done so (Gray 1994b; Hanak 2003; Hanak and Dyckman 2003). These county ordinances similarly can limit surface water transactions if they appear to diminish groundwater resources, either through lowered recharge or through greater farmer reliance on pumping. Although there are legitimate groundwater issues at stake, recent research by Hanak (2003) suggests that the overriding aim of the ordinances is to keep water within rural counties and limit reallocation to urban or environmental uses.

In Colorado the regulatory structure for the Northern Colorado Conservancy District that manages Colorado–Big Thompson (CBT) water differs from that for other parts of the state. In most of Colorado, water courts handle impairment claims for proposed water transactions. In the CBT, the courts do not have jurisdiction. Unlike more common appropriative water rights, within the CBT, each water right holder has the same priority and legal claim to a number of uniform water units that are tradable. The amount of water in each unit fluctuates annually with water supply. All shareholders are adjusted in the same manner. Return flows from any diversion are captured by the district so that all diversion effects are internalized districtwide. Because shares are homogeneous, transfers across users, especially across sectors, occur with minimal fees and paperwork (Carey and Sunding 2001; Thompson 1993). In effect, the CBT has a cap-and-trade framework and has by far the most active water market in the West in terms of numbers of trades. Sale prices for all uses are comparable, as they should be when opportunity costs are incorporated, water quality and right priority are the same, and transaction costs are low.[24]

---

[24] For example, sample agriculture-to-urban and agriculture-to-agriculture sales were priced at $9,350 and $9,300 per unit, respectively, as reported in the *Water Strategist* (October 2008, 7). The CBT also has the advantage

Public Resource, Public Interest, and Public Trust

For many persons, water is so critical and its uses are so complex that there are calls for it to be a public resource: "A hard look at water policy should seek distributional fairness . . . The public, through some acceptable process, must first decide which waters are for public use and which are available for private use within a market system . . . [Private] appropriation ought to be limited to the amount that is not needed by the whole community for the satisfaction of public values" (Bates et al. 1993, 185). Similarly, Dellapenna argues that the best option is to "treat water as inherently public property for which basic allocation decisions must be made by public agencies" (2005, 35).

To the extent that these equity demands are based on the public goods nature of water, they have to be weighed in the assignment and trade of private water rights. Indeed, most western states require administrative agencies to consider the public interest in reviewing applications for new water rights (Bretsen and Hill 2009). If, instead, they are used primarily by certain parties to constrain existing property rights and water trades in their behalf, there can be important efficiency implications. The broader the interpretation of the public interest in water, the weaker the private interest in it and the ability of property rights to avoid open-access conditions, to channel the resource to higher-valued uses through market exchange, and to encourage conservation and investment.[25]

As the public interest is expanded to include a broader array of uses and constituencies, many of which may be only loosely defined, more parties may assert a basis for disputing ownership and potential trades. As regulatory-based transaction costs rise, water will flow less easily to higher-valued uses, as is underscored by the persistent differences in water prices indicated in table 13.1 and figure 13.1.

It can be claimed legitimately that certain public goods values will not be reflected in market prices. Those claims require careful consideration, and there are techniques, such as contingent valuation, for assessing nonmarket values. Under those circumstances, water could be purchased by state agencies or nongovernmental organizations for public good applications. This practice occurs, for example, in purchases or leases of water for in-stream flows by organizations such as the Oregon Water Trust (Neuman 2004; Scarborough 2010). The value of such transactions is that the opportunity cost of water becomes clearer. This information affects the behavior of both current water rights holders as sellers (often irrigators) and in-stream purchasers, so that more water is smoothly transferred without costly controversy to higher-valued uses.

A broader public interest mandate also means that more allocative and management decisions necessarily will be made by the state and the political process. The record of state regulation of open-access fisheries is not one of success, and privatization of fisheries has resulted in significant rebounds of the stock (Costello, Gaines, and Lynham 2008). Whether the same result would apply for water remains to be

---

of using water stored in reservoirs, imported from elsewhere, a less complex case than when flowing streams are the water sources (Howitt and Hansen 2005, 60).

[25] Public access conflicts are examples of the efficiency/equity trade-offs that exist in the West. In one case, at least, the water resource appears to have suffered from judicial rulings upholding the right to access. See Mahan (2004).

seen, but the call for a wide interpretation of the public interest and, hence, greater state ownership and management should consider the conditions under which this institutional arrangement would be effective.

As part of this evaluation, more attention should be directed toward constituent-group politics and the determinants of political and bureaucratic decision making in the process of effective water management (Becker 1983; Peltzman 1976). In light of possible climate change and growing scarcity of water, the social losses of inefficient water management and allocation could be high.

A concept related to the public interest is the public trust doctrine, which is a common-law principle that creates the legal right of the public to use certain lands and waters, such as tidewaters or navigable rivers, and other waters and natural resources with high amenity or public goods values (Getches 1997). Under this doctrine, the rights of the public are vested in the state as owner of the resource and trustee of its proper use. In a far-reaching ruling by the California Supreme Court in 1983 in the Mono Lake case (*National Audubon Society v. Superior Court*, 685 P.2d 709, 712), the court stated that the "core of the public trust doctrine is the state's authority as sovereign to exercise a continuous supervision and control over the waters of the state." The doctrine can be applied retrospectively to roll back pre-existing appropriative rights that appear inconsistent with the public trust. There apparently is no constitutional basis for taking challenges of public trust restrictions of private water rights (Blumm and Schwartz 1995; Sax 1990; Simms 1995).

Because water is a mixed resource that provides private and public goods, there can be justifiable concerns about private water use that potentially harms public values. The benefits of public trust interventions, however, have to be weighed carefully against the value of the private uses to be restricted or prohibited. The doctrine is so elastic and potentially expansive that it can lead to extensive government intrusion in water rights. Such intrusion can add uncertainty to water ownership and weaken existing property rights and their ability to promote investment, trade, and efficient use of water.

Equity, Politics, and Bureaucratic Incentives: The Parties Involved in Water Transactions

Although water rights holders and prospective purchasers or lessees are key parties in any exchange, other institutions play key decision-making roles in the timing and extent of water trades. Their actions affect the transaction costs of exchange and the development of water markets. The institutional complexity surrounding water rights and marketing far exceeds anything comparable for land and even perhaps for fisheries with their myriad mixes of fishers, processors, and state, federal, and international management organizations.

State Regulatory Agencies, Water Supply Organizations, and Indian Tribes

The role of state regulatory agencies that must approve water transactions has already been discussed. Additionally, there are approximately 1,127 water supply organizations across 17 western states.[26] These institutions vary widely in governance structure, membership, decision-making authority, and water rights. Many hold water rights in trust for their members, whereas in some others the rights are held by the users. The organizations range from irrigation districts, mutual ditch and reservoir companies, water conservancy districts, and municipal water districts to water companies. This organizational complexity increases the number of decision rules and the transaction costs of defining clear property rights and of transferring water (Bretsen and Hill 2009).

For example, the governing boards of irrigation districts, the most common type of water supply institution, can be elected by district members (often land owners) or by broader community-wide voters. The voting rule can affect how the board responds to water transfer requests. Districts where members elect the governing board appear to respond more quickly to changes in water values and water market opportunities than do districts where the governing board is elected community-wide, where the interests are very heterogeneous and equity issues loom large.

The differential experiences of the Palo Verde Irrigation District (PVID) and the Imperial Irrigation District (IID) in negotiations to sell or lease water are illustrative. The PVID board is elected by members only, whereas the IID board is elected by community voters. In the case of publicly elected boards, members may be much less interested in selling or leasing water under their jurisdiction than are landowners (Eden et al. 2008; Rosen and Sexton 1993; Thompson 1993). The PVID board reached agreement to fallow land and transfer water for urban use with little controversy, whereas the IID board was mired in lengthy, complex negotiations.[27]

In addition to irrigation districts, the Federal Bureau of Reclamation is often involved in any water exchange. The Federal Bureau of Reclamation is the largest wholesaler of water in the United States and provides irrigation water for 140,000 farms covering 10,000,000 acres in 17 western states. It has more than 600 dams and reservoirs to capture and divert water, historically, mostly for irrigation.[28] The bureau provides water to irrigation districts through long-term service contracts. It can hold an appropriative right to the water within a reclamation project, and the water is distributed anywhere within the project. The agency historically has had uneven policies on water transfers (Thompson 1993). It also can arbitrarily adjust water deliveries to farmers in response to competing demands, such as those under the Endangered Species Act, without legal impairment to their perceived water rights. This weakens the security of any water rights that farmers thought they held and reduces their incentives for wise use and transfer (Bretsen and Hill 2009).[29]

The water held by Indian tribes potentially is a major source of water for marketing. Indian tribes have "reserved" water rights sufficient for the development of agriculture on their reservations. Their water rights date from the establishment of the reservation

---

[26] Water User's Organization Roster, U.S. Department of the Interior, Bureau of Reclamation, http://www.usbr .gov/uc/water/users/roster.pdf—as well as state agency Web sites; Leshy (1982).

[27] Glennon (2009), Haddad (2000), Hanak (2003), Northwest Economic Associates (2004), and Thompson (1993) discuss the Imperial Irrigation District's negotiations with San Diego and the Metropolitan Water District.

[28] U.S. Department of the Interior, Bureau of Reclamation, http://www.pvid.org/; http://www.usbr.gov/main/about/.

[29] Bretsen and Hill (2009) point out that in 1993, when the bureau cut deliveries to the Westlands Water District by 50 percent to meet environmental needs, the Ninth Circuit Court of Appeals ruled that the agency had not breached its contract with the district.

by treaty with the federal government, usually in the nineteenth century, and therefore generally supersede the priority of non-Indian claimants. Many of these treaty provisions have been enforced only recently, and Indian water rights have been adjudicated through litigation or confirmed by congressional statute. As water prices have risen, tribes have begun to be active participants in water markets.

Many parties, then, are involved in water transactions. Their differential interests raise the transaction costs of water trades and potentially weaken water rights.

Water Rights, Water Markets, Efficiency, and Equity Concerns

This chapter has outlined the complex nature of water as a mixed private/public resource and how that characteristic, as well as its physical qualities, complicate its management and allocation. Although the focus here has been on the U.S. West, similar conditions exist in other semiarid regions where increasing scarcity of fresh water is raising pressures for more efficient water use and management, as well as making greater equity demands.

Efficiency and equity demands often collide in a manner that inhibits action and maintains the status quo. This situation, however, is not sustainable as demands on a limited water resource grow. There is a greater need to facilitate the smooth reallocation of water from historical to new uses and to improve management of this all-important resource, as well as to provide for more environmental, amenity, and recreational uses. Firmer water rights and greater reliance on water markets can address efficiency concerns, and equity issues can be addressed in the allocation of water rights and in the regulatory process. But equity demands cannot dominate if the efficiency advantages of secure rights and markets are to be available for water. There are efficiency/equity trade-offs, and water policies must reflect this recognition.

Critics of appropriative water rights and water markets explicitly outline market failure. There is not, however, a similar level of precision in defining how the political, judicial, and administrative processes will function to manage and distribute water effectively, let alone address equity concerns, to meet growing challenges regarding this resource. These issues must be addressed before greater authority over water is shifted to the state as part of a public interest mandate. Comparative institutional analysis is necessary to determine how much decision making about water will be left optimally to private rights and (regulated) markets and how much will be delegated to the political, judicial, and administrative processes. Water demands no less.

Acknowledgments

I thank Lee Alston, Daniel Cole, Zack Donohew, Eric Edwards, and Elinor Ostrom for helpful comments, and Zack Donohew and Eric Edwards for superb research support.

REFERENCES

Anderson, Terry, and Ronald N. Johnson. 1986. The problem of instream flows. *Economic Inquiry* 24(4):535–553.

Barnett, Tim P., David W. Pierce, Hugo G. Halliday, Celine Bonfils, Benjamin D. Santer, Tapash Das, Govindasamy Bala, Andrew W. Wood, Toru Nozawa, Arthur A. Mirin, Daniel R. Caya, and Michael D. Dettinger. 2008. Human-induced changes in the hydrology of the western United States. *Science* 319:1080–1083.

Bates, Sarah F., David H. Getches, Lawrence J. MacDonnell, and Charles F. Wilkinson. 1993. *Searching out the headwaters: Change and rediscovery in western water policy.* Covelo, CA: Island Press.

Becker, Gary. 1983. A theory of competition among pressure groups for political influence. *Quarterly Journal of Economics* 98(3):371–400.

Blumm, Michael C., and Thea Schwartz. 1995. Mono Lake and the evolving public trust in western water. *Arizona Law Review* 37(3):701–738.

Bretsen, Stephen N., and Peter J. Hill. 2009. Water markets as a tragedy of the anticommons. *William and Mary Environmental Law and Policy Review* 33:723–783.

Brewer, Jedidiah R., Robert Glennon, Alan Ker, and Gary D. Libecap. 2008. Water markets in the West: Prices, trading, and contractual flows. *Economic Inquiry* 46(2):91–112.

Brozovic, Nicolas, Janis M. Carey, and David L. Sunding. 2002. Trading activity in an informal agricultural water market: An example from California. *Water Resources Update* 121(January): 3–16.

Carey, Janis M., and David L. Sunding. 2001. Emerging markets in water: A comparative analysis of the Central Valley and Colorado Big Thompson projects. *Natural Resources Journal* 41(Spring):283–328.

Colby, Bonnie G. 1990. Transaction costs and efficiency in western water allocation. *American Journal of Agricultural Economics* 72:1184–1192.

———. 1995. Water reallocation and valuation: Voluntary and involuntary transfers in the western United States. In *Water law: Trends, policies, and practice,* eds. Kathleen Marion Carr and James D. Crammond, 112–126. Chicago: American Bar Association.

Colby, Bonnie G., Mark A. McGinnis, and Ken Rait. 1989. Procedural aspects of state water law: Transferring water rights in the western states. *Arizona Law Review* 31(4): 697–720.

Connor, Robin, and Bruce Shallard. 2010. Evolving governance in New Zealand fisheries. In *Handbook of marine fisheries conservation and management,* eds. R. Quentin Grafton, Ray Hilborn, Dale Squires, Maree Tait, and Meryl J. Williams, 347–359. New York: Oxford University Press.

Costello, Christopher, Steven D. Gaines, and John Lynham. 2008. Can catch shares prevent fisheries collapse? *Science* 321(5896):1678–1681.

Dellapenna, Joseph W. 2005. Markets for water: Time to put the myth to rest? *Journal of Contemporary Water Research and Education* 131(1):33–41.

Demsetz, Harold. 1967. Toward a theory of property rights. *American Economic Review* 57(2):347–359.

Economist. 2009. Sin aqua non: Water shortages are a growing problem, but not for the reasons most people think. April 8, 52.

Eden, Susanna, Robert Glennon, Alan Ker, Gary Libecap, Sharon Megdal, and Taylor Shipman. 2008. Agricultural water to municipal use: The legal and institutional context for voluntary transactions in Arizona. *Water Report,* 9–20.

Ellickson, Robert. 1993. Property in land. *Yale Law Journal* 102:1315–1400.

Getches, David H. 1997. *Water law in a nutshell.* 3rd ed. St. Paul: West Publishing Co.

Glennon, Robert Jerome. 2002. *Water follies: Groundwater pumping and the fate of America's fresh waters.* Washington, DC: Island Press.

———. 2009. *Unquenchable: America's water crisis and what to do about it.* Washington, DC: Island Press.

Gould, George A. 1995. Recent developments in the transfer of water rights. In *Water law: Trends, policies, and practice,* eds. Kathleen Marion Carr and James D. Crammond, 93–103. Chicago: American Bar Association.

Gray, Brian E. 1990. Water transfers in California, 1981–89. In *The water transfer process as a management option for meeting changing water demands,* ed. Lawrence J. McDonnell, 2:3–13. Boulder: University of Colorado Law School, Natural Resources Law Center.

———. 1994a. The modern era in California water law. *Hastings Law Journal* 45(January):249–308.

———. 1994b. The role of laws and institutions in California's 1991 water bank. In *Sharing scarcity: Gainers and losers in water marketing*, eds. Harold O. Carter, Henry J. Vaux, Jr., and Ann F. Scheuring, 133–190. Davis, CA: Agricultural Issues Center.

Haddad, Brent M. 2000. *Rivers of gold: Designing markets to allocate water in California*. Washington, DC: Island Press.

Hanak, Ellen. 2003. *Who should be allowed to sell water in California? Third-party issues and the water market*. San Francisco: Public Policy Institute of California.

Hanak, Ellen, and Caitlin Dyckman. 2003. Counties wresting control: Local responses to California's statewide water market. *University of Denver Water Law Review* 6(Spring):490–518.

Hanemann, W. Michael. 2006. The economic conception of water. In *Water crisis: Myth or reality?* eds. Peter P. Rogers, M. Ramón Llamas, and Luis Martinez Cortina, 61–91. Abingdon, U.K.: Taylor and Francis.

Hannesson, Rögnvaldur. 2004. *The privatization of the oceans*. Cambridge, MA: MIT Press.

Hansen, Kristiana, Richard Howitt, and Jeffrey Williams. 2007. An econometric test of the endogeneity of market structure: Water markets in the western United States. Working Paper. Davis: Department of Agricultural and Resource Economics, University of California at Davis.

Howitt, Richard E. 1994. Effects of water marketing on the farm economy. In *Sharing scarcity: Gainers and losers in water marketing*, eds. Harold O. Carter, Henry J. Vaux, Jr., and Ann F. Scheuring, 97–132. Davis, CA: Agricultural Issues Center.

Howitt, Richard, and Kristiana Hansen. 2005. The evolving western water markets. *Choices* 20(1):59–63.

Johnson, Ronald N., Micha Gisser, and Michael Werner. 1981. The definition of a surface water right and transferability. *Journal of Law and Economics* 24(2):273–288.

Kanazawa, Mark T. 1998. Efficiency in western water law: The development of the California doctrine, 1850–1911. *Journal of Legal Studies* 27(1):159–185.

Kenny, Joan F., Nancy L. Barber, Susan S. Hutson, Kristin S. Linsey, John K. Lovelace, and Molly A. Maupin. 2009. Estimated use of water in the United States in 2005. U.S. Geological Survey Circular 1344. Washington, DC: U.S. Geological Survey.

Leshy, John D. 1982. Irrigation districts in a changing west—An overview. *Arizona State Law Journal* 345–376.

Libecap, Gary D. 1978. Economic variables and the development of the law: The case of western mineral rights. *Journal of Economic History* 38(2):338–362.

———. 1989. *Contracting for property rights*. New York: Cambridge University Press.

———. 2007. The assignment of property rights on the western frontier: Lessons for contemporary environmental and resource policy. *Journal of Economic History* 67(2):257–291.

———. 2008. Chinatown revisited: Owens Valley and Los Angeles—Bargaining costs and fairness perceptions of the first major water rights exchange. *Journal of Law, Economics and Organization* 25(2):311–338.

———. 2011. Institutional path dependence in adaptation to climate: Coman's "some unsettled problems of irrigation." *American Economic Review* 101 (February):64–80.

Libecap, Gary D., and James L. Smith. 2002. The economic evolution of petroleum property rights in the United States. *Journal of Legal Studies* 31(2, pt. 2):S589–S608.

MacDonnell, Lawrence J. 1990. *The water transfer process as a management option for meeting changing water demands*. Vol. 1. Boulder: University of Colorado Law School, Natural Resources Law Center.

Mahan, Josh, 2004. The battle for Mitchell Slough: When is a river not a river? *Missoula Independent*, January 8. http://missoulanews.bigskypress.com/missoula/the-battle-for-mitchell-slough/Content?oid=1135390.

Neuman, Janet C. 2004. The good, the bad, and the ugly: The first ten years of the Oregon water trust. *Nebraska Law Review* 83:432–484.

Northwest Economic Associates. 2004. *Third party impacts of the Palo Verde Land Management, Crop Rotation and Water Supply Program*. Draft Report (March 29). Sacramento: Northwest Economic Associates.

Peltzman, 1976. Toward a more general theory of regulation. *The Journal of Law and Economics* 19(2):211–240.

Provencher, Bill, and Oscar Burt. 1993. The externalities associated with the common property exploitation of groundwater. *Journal of Environmental Economics and Management* 24:139–158.

Rosen, Michael D., and Richard J. Sexton. 1993. Irrigation districts and water markets: An application of cooperative decision-making theory. *Land Economics* 69(1):39–53.

Sax, Joseph L. 1990. The Constitution, property rights and the future of water law. *University of Colorado Law Review* 61:257–282.

Scarborough, Brandon. 2010. *Environmental water markets: Restoring streams through trade.* Bozeman, MT: Property and Environment Research Center.

Simms, Richard A. 1995. A sketch of the aimless jurisprudence of western water law. In *Water law: Trends, policies, and practice*, eds. Kathleen Marion Carr and James D. Crammond, 320–329. Chicago: American Bar Association.

Smith, Henry E. 2008. Governing water: The semicommons of fluid property rights. *Arizona Law Review* 50(2):445–478.

Thompson, Barton H. 1993. Institutional perspectives on water policy and markets. *California Law Review* 81:673–764.

U.S. Department of Agriculture, Briefing/Wateruse? 22 November 2004. http://www.ers.usda .gov/Briefing/wateruse/.

U.S. Department of the Interior, Bureau of Reclamation, March 2011. http://www.usbr.gov/uc /water/users/roster.pdf

U.S. Department of the Interior, Bureau of Reclamation. http://www.pvid.org/; http://www.usbr .gov/main/about/.

World Water Assessment Programme. 2009. *Water in a changing world.* Paris: UNESCO.

Young, Robert A. 1986. Why are there so few transactions among water users? *American Journal of Agricultural Economics* 68(5):1143–1151.

Commentary

LEE J. ALSTON

> The reason that some activities are not the subject of contracts is exactly the same reason why some contracts are commonly unsatisfactory—it would cost too much to put the matter right.
>
> —Coase (1960, 39)

Gary Libecap makes a significant contribution to the literature on water by showing the huge potential economic welfare gains from more contracting for water, especially contracts from rural to urban uses. Moreover, Libecap shows the enormous variation in the potential gains across states. He estimates that transferring as little as 3 percent of irrigation water—which is equivalent to 100 percent of the current urban market—would represent a gain of $98 million a year, or 24 percent of the value of yearly market activity. Given these large welfare gains, there must be commensurate high costs to put the matter right. Libecap argues that water differs from contracting for land, and that because it is a fluid and many parties use it sequentially or simultaneously, there are significant resource and political costs in defining private water rights. This is undoubtedly true, but, as Libecap points out, although this is also the case for migratory fish, individual transferable quotas now exist for many fisheries.

A better understanding of the reasons for misallocation of water requires consideration of other differences between water and fish, or, more generally, the supply side of property rights. Curiously, Microeconomics 101 is about demand and supply, but with regard to property rights, economists have focused on demand-driven models such as that of Demsetz (1967). Demand-driven models explain well the initial specification and enforcement of property rights on frontiers.[1] Frontiers can be defined as regions where government specification and property rights are absent, so the initial settlers establish and enforce property rights. This can be either through first-party specification and enforcement (this is my land, and I will shoot you if you trespass) or through second-party specification and enforcement (the Libecap Livingston Livestock Association defines who has range rights and enforces them collectively through a semiannual roundup). There is evidence from the United States and elsewhere, for example, the Brazilian Amazon, that de facto

---

[1] Libecap has spent much of his career doing research on property rights on frontiers, so he is aware of the issues, but I encourage him to take some of the same issues from frontiers and apply them more rigorously to water markets and, in particular, the politics and norms behind the property rights associated with water. The following discussion draws on Alston, Harris, and Mueller (2009).

informal claims can be sufficient to support market transactions from lower-valued uses to higher-valued uses.

Demand models are sufficient to explain first-party specification and enforcement. But for second-party specification and enforcement, demand models are insufficient because of the collective-action problem. This does not mean that collective action never happens; indeed, as Ostrom and her collaborators have demonstrated, "commons" arrangements are fairly common. Ostrom and her colleagues have been working on a diagnostic for understanding the arrangements under which commons arrangements work better (Poteete, Janssen, and Ostrom 2010). Commons arrangements tend to work better where the claimants are homogeneous (although this is not universally true), have shared cultural endowments, and interact repeatedly. Conflict tends to emerge when the de facto property rights of the initial claimants have not just competing uses but competing types of usage, for example, ranchers in the semiarid West versus homesteaders, and the new claimants do not recognize the legitimacy of the de facto claims. For water, the conflict is between urban and agricultural users.

Indeed, it is conflict or potential conflict that tends to bring government into the property rights picture. Governments define and partially enforce de jure property rights.[2] We need to understand the objective function of the assignment and enforcement of property rights better. Scarcity value is one of the elements, but it is certainly not the only one. Because politicians rely on votes and money for electoral success, they consider how the assignment of property rights affects their constituents. In the case of water, its assignment is partially by law but there is an element of discretion in bureaucratic administrative agencies. We need to understand the motivation of administrative units and bureaucracies for building roadblocks to more efficient water markets. Libecap is well aware of these issues and he addresses differential decision making in irrigation districts in California. In his example of the voter-elected Imperial Irrigation District, the actions of community voters make perfect sense because if there is less irrigated land, there may be fewer jobs and revenue in the area, and this will affect them economically. These externalities need to be overcome in order for water contracting to be more pervasive. If we first understand the decision-making bodies and the benefits and costs that they perceive from water contracting, we may be in a position to compensate the political and economic losers from more water contracting. It is clear that decision making across states and within states must vary enormously because the differentials in the prices of water transfers are extremely large (see table 13.2).

Libecap makes an impressive contribution to the literature by compiling data illustrating the huge potential economic gains from transferring water rights from lower-valued to higher-valued users. He argues that the bottleneck in moving water to higher-valued users is the trade-off between equity and efficiency. Undoubtedly this plays a role. But making the potential economic gains a reality requires understanding the varying political, bureaucratic, and administrative incentives to constrain water markets. These incentives include economic, political, and social

---

[2] It would be too costly for governments to enforce property rights completely, so they leave some aspects of enforcement to individuals (many people lock the doors of their cars) and others to social norms (most people are not thieves because they believe that it is not right).

considerations. A better understanding of all three incentives for water use will help us decide whether we can "put the matter right" by making the necessary side payments to move water closer to its highest-valued economic use. We may realize that there are no feasible side payments that would be sufficient to compensate the decision makers because the political or social costs are too high. When this is the case, we move to a higher political economy game of rearranging the extant property rights to water.

REFERENCES

Alston, Lee J., Edwyna Harris, and Bernardo Mueller. 2009. De facto and de jure property rights: Land settlement and land conflict on the Australian, Brazilian and U.S. frontiers. NBER Working Paper 15264 (September). Cambridge, MA: National Bureau of Economic Research.

Coase, Ronald H. 1960. The problem of social cost. *Journal of Law and Economics* 3:1–44.

Demsetz, Harold. 1967. Toward a theory of property rights. *American Economic Review* 57(2):347–359.

Poteete, Amy R., Marco Janssen, and Elinor Ostrom. 2010. *Working together: Collective action, the commons, and multiple methods in practice.* Princeton, NJ: Princeton University Press.

Global Commons Issues

Climate Change

The Ultimate Tragedy of the Commons?

JOUNI PAAVOLA

T he dominant view among scholars and policy makers has been that climate change governance should be based on international agreements that involve most nations (Hare et al. 2010). The United Nations Framework Convention on Climate Change (UNFCCC) and the Kyoto Protocol (KP) are cornerstones of this approach. These kinds of governance strategies face two key hurdles. First, wide participation has to be secured for any agreement to come into force. Second, all agreements need to be implemented through national policies. But top-down solutions relying on the central role of the state have been a false panacea in the governance of many resources (E. Ostrom, Janssen, and Anderies 2007). It is no surprise, then, that progress in governing climate change has been slow and that only modest results have been obtained in curtailing greenhouse gas (GHG) emission reductions.

More recently, the debates on climate change governance have centered on the comprehensiveness of feasible agreements (Kuik et al. 2008). The proponents of comprehensive international agreements remain at one end of the continuum (Hare et al. 2010). At the other end are those who would not rely on international action (Rayner 2010). In between are those who consider that progress is best made through regional, sectoral, and other less comprehensive governance strategies (Barrett and Toman 2010; Falkner, Stephan, and Vogler 2010; Schmidt et al. 2008; Sugiyama and Sinton 2005). Within each strand, the relative merits of different policy instruments are still debated, although carbon markets have already gained a prominent position (Bernstein et al. 2010; Kuik et al. 2008; but see Spash 2010). Another strand of literature has examined voluntary governance solutions that do not centrally rely on the role of the state (Bäckstrand 2008; Bulkeley and Betsill 2003; Kern and Bulkeley 2009; Newell 2000). Much of the existing literature believes that a feasible strategy for climate change governance does exist, but opinions differ on what it is.

This chapter investigates the potential of institutional diversity and polycentric governance in the area of climate change. The new institutional literature (Dolšak and Ostrom 2003; E. Ostrom 1990; 2005; E. Ostrom et al. 2002; Young 2002) and governance literature in general (Rhodes 1996; Rosenau 1995) consider the absence of coercive state power as the hallmark of governance. But governance is what governments do. The apparent juxtaposition of "governance" and "government" hinges on the conception of government. But rather than being a monolithic external actor, the government can be understood as a set of arenas and instruments of collective action. This viewpoint helps construe governance as a continuum between state-based solutions and solutions that do not involve the state, with hybrid forms in between (Lemos and Agrawal 2006; Paavola 2007). That is, environmental governance can be understood broadly as the establishment, reaffirmation, or change of diverse institutions in order to manage the use of environmental resources.

New institutionalism has informed a significant body of research on local common-property arrangements and on international environmental conventions, but its potential is far from exhausted. Understanding the challenges of and solutions for governing large and complex environmental resources such as atmospheric sinks have been identified as key future tasks (Berkes 2008; Dietz, Ostrom, and Stern 2003; E. Ostrom et al. 1999). However, much of the literature still examines relatively simple single-level governance solutions, although the governance of large environmental resources is typically based on diverse solutions operating at multiple levels and across levels simultaneously. Thus, there is a need to develop analytic ways to address institutional diversity (E. Ostrom 2005; E. Ostrom et al. 1999).

In the related body of literature on polycentricity (E. Ostrom 2009; 2010a; 2010b; V. Ostrom 1972; V. Ostrom, Tiebout, and Warren 1961), polycentric order has been defined as "one where many elements are capable of making mutual adjustments for ordering their relationships with one another within a general system of rules where each element acts with independence of other elements" (V. Ostrom 1999, 57). Polycentric order is likely to emerge in a bottom-up way when diverse actors in a phenomenon like climate change seek to realize diverse benefits (or to avoid diverse costs) that accrue on different scales (E. Ostrom 2009). As Elinor Ostrom (2009) remarks, mitigation actions not only generate global benefits by reducing greenhouse gas emissions and the rate of climate change, but also create cobenefits such as better air quality, reduced reliance on fossil fuels, reduced exposure to their price fluctuations, and improved energy security. These benefits can be a sufficient motivation for mitigation actions, although perhaps not on a comprehensive scale.

Myriad voluntary climate change initiatives already exist. For example, the Cities for Climate Protection (CCP) program and the Cement Sustainability Initiative (CSI) attempt to address substantial GHG emissions, comparable to those of major emitting states. These initiatives have been successful in reducing GHG emissions or slowing their growth in comparison with business as usual. However, tentative evidence suggests that voluntary initiatives may do best at, or be limited to, realizing cost-saving emission reductions. Therefore, state-based and hybrid governance solutions may be needed to complement voluntary ones in order to stabilize the atmospheric concentrations of GHGs at a safe level. That is, institutional diversity is likely to characterize climate change governance, and it will emerge through both bottom-up and top-down processes.

Climate Change as a Problem

The Stern review considers climate change "the market failure on the greatest scale the world has seen" (Stern 2007, 27). The language of market failure and externalities is indeed widely applied to climate change. However, this chapter examines climate change as a problem in the sustainable use of atmospheric sinks for GHGs by drawing from the literature on the management of common-pool resources (Berkes 2008; E. Ostrom 1990; 2005; E. Ostrom et al. 2002; Poteete, Janssen, and Ostrom 2010).

Atmospheric sinks for GHGs can be understood as a common-pool resource (CPR) just like an aquifer or a fishery (Paavola 2008a). Sinks are stock resources that provide a flow of sink services. Aquifers and fisheries have a relatively well-understood capacity to generate a flow of resource units. Watercourses, air basins, and global atmospheric sinks have a comparable capacity to absorb pollutants that is replenished by natural processes. Atmospheric GHG sinks fulfill the first condition of being a CPR because the use of units of sink services is rival or subtractable: a unit used by one user is not available to others (E. Ostrom 1990). A key challenge in governing atmospheric sinks for GHGs is the same as with all other CPRs: to constrain their use so as to prevent their destruction. A derivative task is to distribute the sustainable capacity to provide sink services among the competing users.

Atmospheric GHG sinks also fulfill the second condition of being a CPR because it is difficult to exclude unauthorized users from using them (Paavola 2008a). The users of GHG sinks range from large coal-powered electricity-generation plants to families driving a car or keeping cattle. The size of the sink, the range of activities that make use of it, and the large number of users make it difficult to monitor the use of the sink and to exclude users. The perfect mixing of emissions of GHGs in the atmosphere and absence of clear borderlines contribute to the difficulty of exclusion (E. Ostrom 1990).

Because of these resource attributes, atmospheric sinks may experience the ultimate "tragedy of the commons" (Hardin 1968). Users have incentives to use sink service units before other users make them unavailable, and it is difficult to prevent them from doing so. When everybody acts in self-interest rather than exercising restraint to conserve global GHG sinks, the tragedy is nigh. Although Hardin (1998) later became optimistic about the emergence of restraint in the use of global atmospheric sinks, progress to date has been modest.

When exclusion costs are low, challenges of rival consumption are typically resolved by establishing private ownership and deciding who is entitled to what. Markets can then allocate resources to their most valuable uses. But private ownership is not feasible when exclusion costs are high, as is the case with global atmospheric sinks and other CPRs. Alternatives for governing global atmospheric sinks are the same as for other CPRs and include collective ownership and management (which may involve the use of markets), voluntary agreements to constrain the use of atmospheric sinks for GHGs, and widely shared values with associated individual behavior change to reduce GHG emissions. These alternatives may coexist as parts of a wider polycentric governance strategy for climate change.

The challenges of governing atmospheric GHG sinks are also shaped by the attributes of their users, which determine the starting point for collective action aimed at establishing or modifying governance institutions, affect the costs of acting collectively, and influence what governance solutions can be agreed on. Political-economic factors and current patterns in the use of atmospheric sinks for GHGs affect the prospects of collective action. One of the most important aspects of the global political-economic order is the role of states in representing users of global atmo-spheric sinks within their territories. The law on international relations treats states as equal, sovereign actors in international affairs. This formal equality contrasts with their unequal capacities and developmental attainments. Most developed countries have high levels of per capita income and strong, capable states. In the developing world, many states are weak and some are dysfunctional, and they have been unable to promote income growth and well-being among their citizens. Many developing-country states also have weaker capacity to advance their (and their citizens') interests in international negotiations.

States' economies exhibit different degrees of complexity, which affects their vul-nerability to climate change impacts. Most developed countries have complex econ-omies that offer many sources of income and are more resilient during periods of stress. The economies of many developing countries depend on primary production and are exposed to substantial climatic and economic risks. Because of underdevel-oped financial and insurance sectors in those countries, people cannot insure their assets and stand to lose them when disasters occur (Paavola 2008b; Paavola and Adger 2006). In developed countries, income is not sensitive to extreme weather events such as the European heat wave of 2003, although it caused substantial asset losses. In contrast, extreme weather events such as hurricanes can tax more than 10 percent of the gross domestic product (GDP) of a low-income country (Linnerooth-Bayer, Mechler, and Pflug 2005). The differences in vulnerability are even more sig-nificant with regard to loss of life. For example, Hurricane Andrew killed 23 people in Florida in 1992, but a comparable typhoon killed more than 100,000 people in Bangladesh a year earlier (Adger et al. 2005). Brooks, Adger, and Kelly (2005) suggest that educational attainment, health status, and quality of governance explain much of the difference in mortality due to natural disasters among countries.

Heterogeneities in the global community such as the ones just discussed make it difficult to agree on how to govern the use of atmospheric sinks for GHGs. Devel-oped countries have invested in energy-intensive lifestyles, technologies, and infra-structure, which make GHG reductions time consuming and expensive. But devel-oped countries also have the capability to avoid adverse consequences of climate change, as well as to recover from them. Furthermore, they form a relatively homo-geneous and powerful negotiation bloc that has experience from collective action in other contexts. Developing countries, particularly the least developed countries, have contributed little to climate change because of their limited energy use and reliance on renewable sources of energy, but their economic development requires increasing energy use and GHG emissions. They are also highly vulnerable to ad-verse climate change impacts. Finally, developing countries form a large and hetero-geneous negotiation bloc whose members range from oil-producing countries to small island states that are threatened with inundation by rising sea levels.

There are, of course, more coalitions in climate change negotiations than just de-veloped and developing countries, and the contours among and within the group-ings are far more complex than the preceding discussion suggests. But even this narrow account highlights that in the light of the literature on common-pool re-sources, there are significant obstacles to collective action to govern atmospheric sinks. The following account of progress to date in international climate change negotiations underscores this.

The Conventional View of Climate Change Governance and Its Record

Several lines of reasoning lead to the view that climate change governance has to be negotiated by states, codified as multilateral environmental agreements, and implemented through national legislation. First, research in environmental science has sought to understand phenomena such as climate change and the loss of biodiversity through lenses of global environmental change and earth systems science (Steffen et al. 2004; Vitousek et al. 1997). This kind of analytic globalization of environmental change easily leads to the view that feasible responses to global problems also must be global in nature.

Second, scholarship in international relations, particularly the realist tradition, provides a justification for "statism." Realism extends rational-choice reasoning to the "society of states." Other actors do not matter, and their involvement would be dubious anyway because it could violate the sovereignty of states. Self-interested states will agree to take collective action on an issue like climate change only if all parties to the agreement benefit either directly or via side payments or benefits made available by those who do directly benefit from an agreement (Barrett and Toman 2010; Sprinz and Vaahtoranta 1994). But all such international agreements lack mandatory power and need to be implemented through top-down processes that involve enactment and enforcement of national legislation.

Third, public finance reasoning supports "maximal multilateralism." From this viewpoint, internalization of an externality or the provision of a public good should take place at a scale encompassing all affected parties (Musgrave and Musgrave 1976; Tiebout 1956). In the case of climate change, the affected parties would be all who have to share the burden of mitigation, who benefit from mitigation actions, and who bear the burden of having to adapt to residual climate change impacts. That is, most, if not all, states should be involved in negotiations on climate change governance. There are, of course, counterarguments, which will be discussed later in this chapter.

Substantial mitigation of GHG emissions is possible. Technological solutions that are already known can deliver the GHG emission reductions needed to stabilize their atmospheric concentrations at 450 to 550 parts per million (ppm) (Pacala and Socolow 2004). These reductions can also be achieved at a reasonable cost. Stern (2007) argues that stabilizing the GHG concentrations at 500 to 550 ppm by 2050 would cost 1 percent of global GDP. In contrast, he estimates that "the overall costs and risks of climate change will be equivalent to losing at least 5% of global GDP each year, now and forever. If a wider range of risks and impacts is taken into account, the estimates of damage could rise to 20% of GDP or more" (Stern 2007, iv). About a third of the emission reductions needed to stabilize atmospheric concentration of GHGs at 450 to 550 ppm by 2030 would save rather than cost money (Enkvist, Nauclér, and Rosander 2007). But it has been difficult to reach an international agreement on GHG emission reductions.

The United Nations Framework Convention on Climate Change (UNFCCC) was adopted in 1992 as the key international response to climate change. The Kyoto Protocol (KP), adopted in 1997, established emission-reduction commitments for carbon dioxide, methane, nitrous oxide, hydrofluorocarbons, perfluorocarbons, and sulfur hexafluoride emissions for 37 industrialized countries and the European Community, or the so-called Annex 1 countries. Parties to the KP committed themselves to an overall 5 percent GHG emission reduction from 1990 levels during 2008–2012.

The GHG emissions of Germany, the United Kingdom, and Sweden were already 10 to 20 percent below those of the Kyoto base year in 2008 (EEA 2010). In the same year, GHG emissions of many countries of the former Soviet Union and of countries with economies in transition were 25 to 60 percent below their 1990 levels because of the collapse of their economies and manufacturing (EEA 2010). But GHG emissions were 32.2 and 42.3 percent higher in Portugal and Spain, respectively, in 2008 than they had been in 1990 (EEA 2010). Emissions also grew in Australia, Japan, and the United States by 15 to 25 percent from 1990 to 2004 (UNDP 2007). For comparison, carbon dioxide emissions of Brazil, India, and China, which were not parties to the KP, increased by 60 to 110 percent from 1990 to 2004 (UNDP 2007).

The "safe" level of below two degrees of global warming would require the stabilization of atmospheric GHG concentrations at 400 to 500 ppm (Mastrandrea and Schneider 2004), which would in turn require a reduction of 50 to 85 percent in GHG emissions by 2050 from 2000 levels (IPCC 2007). The KP cannot deliver this because too few countries participate in emissions reduction, because the targets of the countries that do participate are too lax (and are not complied with), and because too many sources of GHGs remain outside its scope. There have been calls to involve major developing economies in emissions reduction because of their substantial total emissions. But some major developing economies, such as China, Iran, and South Africa, also already have higher per capita GHG emissions than the globally available per capita emissions consistent with the stabilization of atmospheric GHG concentrations at a safe level (UNDP 2007). Land use and land use change, deforestation, aviation and marine bunker fuels, and carbon leakage associated with the consumption of imports from non–Annex 1 countries to Annex 1 countries are examples of issues that remain wholly or largely unaddressed by the current climate change regime.

Thus, the inclusive UNFCCC process has to date failed to generate solutions for tackling climate change. Barrett and Toman (2010), referring to research by Velders et al. (2007), suggest that the Montreal Protocol, which was adopted in 1987 to reverse the depletion of the ozone layer, has achieved GHG emission reductions four times greater than those of the KP. The Montreal Protocol was easier to negotiate because the depletion of the ozone layer involved fewer parties, mitigation costs were lower, and the same substances that deplete ozone layer are also greenhouse gases (Cole 2009).

Polycentric Climate Change Governance

Although climate change can usefully be understood as a problem of using a CPR, global atmospheric sinks for GHGs, the problem of the governance solution as a whole is distinct from decisions on the quality of CPRs. A stable climate is a public good (just like water or air quality, where pertinent sinks are also CPRs) because its use is not rival, and because it is difficult to exclude users from it once it is provided. Samuelson (1954) suggested that markets do not make available an optimal amount of public goods, and that they should be publicly provided. But public provision of a stable climate is not trivial; it should happen on a spatial scale that encompasses all affected parties (Musgrave and Musgrave 1976). That is, the provision of a stable climate should happen globally.

However, there is no world government, so the provision of a stable climate requires collective action. Olson (1971) argued that collective action is more likely to be unsuccessful in large groups where actors deem that their impact on collective-action outcomes is small and as a consequence have a stronger incentive to free ride. This argument applies to climate change if it is considered as a problem for humanity as a whole. When a large proportion of actors assess their situation in the way described here, collective action will be undermined.

One way to overcome the problem is to mobilize collective action on a smaller scale. This helps reduce the incentive to ride free because the impact of each individual on collective-action outcomes increases. At the same time, smaller groups may increase the homogeneity of involved actors, which should also facilitate collective action. Coordination among groups can be achieved by establishing larger-scale solutions in which the groups are represented. Representation treats collective-action groups as individuals and reduces the original large-numbers situation to one of small numbers. That is, multilevel governance solutions are likely to emerge as instruments for facilitating collective action in large groups.

The system of states representing their populations is one possible solution of this kind. However, it is not the only one, and state-based solutions are not necessarily one-size-fits-all. Ronald Coase's (1937) work on the nature of the firm suggests that the scope of any governance solution (in his case, the firm) is determined by the relative transaction costs of carrying out transactions internally and externally. Transaction costs do not favor comprehensiveness to the extreme. Subsequent work in transaction-cost economics highlights that different governance solutions create different incentives and have differential abilities to govern different kinds of transactions (Williamson 1999; 2000; 2005). The implications of this finding for climate change governance are that different rationales may exist for different governance solutions and that they may have different, albeit potentially coexisting, scopes. That is, multiple noncomprehensive solutions are a more likely outcome than one, all-encompassing governance solution.

Theoretical explanations of the emergence of multilevel governance also suggest that diverse institutional designs should exist for the provision of public goods such as a stable climate (Paavola 2008a). Different governance functions, such as provisioning, monitoring, and enforcement (Paavola 2007), may have different economies of scale or different optimal scales of operation (V. Ostrom, Tiebout, and Warren 1961). Collective environmental decisions may be best made at a higher level, while provision of the resource may best be undertaken at a lower level, for instance. This is the rationale for many comanagement arrangements. Important here is that the governance cost approach points to different kinds of multilevel solutions than the collective-action approach. The latter suggests nested governance solutions that are identical except for their different scale. The governance cost approach suggests that levels of governance may be functionally differentiated and complementary for a reason.

The literature on polycentricity offers additional insights for understanding institutional diversity in climate change governance. Vincent Ostrom and his colleagues originally proposed the notion of polycentricity to characterize complex metropolitan governance structures that had emerged after World War II for public service delivery in the United States (V. Ostrom 1972; V. Ostrom, Tiebout, and Warren 1961). These new complex structures did not have the single core that characterized conventional monocentric governmental arrangements. The scholarship on polycentricity sought to establish the rationale of such structures.

Until and even after Vincent Ostrom's seminal contributions and those of Buchanan (1965), Coase (1960; 1974), and Tiebout (1956), the government was considered the default provider of public goods and services. Market-failure reasoning provided the intellectual justification of this view. Against this background, the key interest of Vincent Ostrom was the horizontal dispersion of authority to govern. At that time, this was a novel phenomenon that the established notions of government and governance were not well equipped to account for. But vertical structuring of governance is also involved in the examples Ostrom and his colleagues discuss (V. Ostrom 1972; V. Ostrom, Tiebout, and Warren 1961).

The degree of horizontal dispersion of authority varies from monolithic governmental solutions to fragmentation of authority (figure 14.1). Hybrid solutions lie somewhere in between (Lemos and Agrawal 2006). Governance solutions range from those characterized by vertical symmetry to those that are vertically completely differentiated. Although individual governance solutions characterized by fragmentation of authority can be considered examples of polycentric governance, institutional diversity—the multitude of diverse governance solutions prevailing simultaneously—necessarily leads to polycentricity in a wider sense.

FIGURE 14.1
Horizontal Fragmentation and Vertical Differentiation as Dimensions of Polycentricity

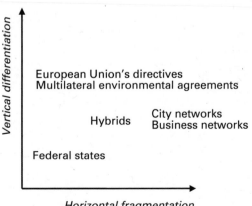

Another important attribute of governance solutions is the way in which they emerge: from the bottom up as a result of voluntary collective action or bargaining, or as a result of top-down, mandated processes. As previously noted, polycentric order may emerge in a bottom-up way when actors seek to realize benefits or to avoid costs that accrue on different scales (E. Ostrom 2009). Top-down processes create other governance solutions, which increases institutional diversity.

There is thus more to climate change governance than international negotiations and state-based climate change policies. Solutions based on or involving non-state actors also exist and are likely to be networks, rather than hierarchies or markets, and to exhibit the dispersion of authority and vertical differentiation simultaneously. Hooghe and Marks (2003) suggest that these governance solutions are likely to be voluntary (negotiated) and temporary rather than permanent and to have overlapping rather than exclusive membership. Hybrid governance solutions can involve states and partly rely on their mandatory powers, but they can also grant important roles to other actors and voluntary action. They play a role in the portfolio of governance solutions alongside state-based and voluntary solutions.

Voluntary Initiatives and Climate Change Governance

Polycentric climate change governance can involve a variety of actors, such as local governments and communities, nongovernmental and church-based organizations, businesses, and governmental organizations in different combinations and roles. Some solutions are limited to one area of activity, such as local governmental activities or an industry, while others can be more general in nature. Many of these solutions are voluntarily adopted and have voluntary membership, although the act of joining can create responsibilities. The Cities for Climate Protection (CCP) program and the Cement Sustainability Initiative (CSI) are examples.

Cities for Climate Protection

Local governments have actively developed and implemented governance solutions for reducing the emissions of greenhouse gases from their jurisdictions. The pioneer in this area has been the International Council for Local Environmental Initiatives (ICLEI) with its Cities for Climate Protection (CCP) program. Others include Climate Alliance, C40, and the U.S. Mayors' Climate Protection Agreement (Gore 2010; Kern and Bulkeley 2009; Linstroth and Bell 2007; Román 2010).

The ICLEI launched its CCP program in 1993. It aimed to enlist one hundred municipalities worldwide with joint emissions of one billion metric tons of CO_2 (ICLEI 1993). The program also sought to strengthen local commitments to GHG emission reduction, to develop and disseminate planning and management tools, to research and develop best practices, and to enhance national and international ties among municipalities.

The CCP program expects members to develop a local action plan to reduce GHG emissions, to undertake measures to reduce emissions from municipal building stock and vehicle fleets, to institute public awareness campaigns on climate change, and to join procurement initiatives that seek to create demand for climate-friendly products and services. Members are also expected to link with local governments in developing and emerging-economy countries to foster technological and financial transfers (ICLEI 1993).

The CCP progress report published in 2006 (ICLEI Local Governments for Sustainability 2006) highlighted that 550 local governments had joined the program since 1993. Their combined population was a quarter of a billion, or more than 4 percent of the global total. The combined GHG emissions from participating local governments were 1.85 billion tons of eCO_2 (carbon dioxide equivalent), or more than 6 percent of the global total (excluding emissions from land use and land use change). That is, GHG emissions of CCP members are comparable to those of large Annex 1 countries, such as Germany, Japan, and Russia. The participants reduced their joint emissions by 3 percent or 60 million tons of CO_2 between 1990 and 2006. These emission reductions brought substantial savings to participating cities that amounted to about $35 per reduced ton of CO_2 emissions (ICLEI Local Governments for Sustainability 2006).

Cement Sustainability Initiative

Another example of climate change governance is the Cement Sustainability Initiative (CSI), a program of the World Business Council for Sustainable Development (CSI 2002) that has been considered a model for the sectoral approach to climate change mitigation (Meckling and Chung 2009; Schmidt et al. 2008). The cement industry is a significant GHG emitter. Its worldwide CO_2 emissions are about 5 percent of the global total, comparable to those of Germany, Japan, and Russia in 2004 (CSI 2002; UNDP 2007).

The CSI was formed by 10 large cement manufacturers in 2002. Today, its members represent nearly two-thirds of the global cement-manufacturing capacity outside China (CSI 2009). The CSI aims to increase the cement industry's contribution to sustainable development and public understanding of that contribution. The agenda for action adopted in 2002 contained six key areas of work: (1) climate protection; (2) fuels and raw materials; (3) employee health and safety; (4) emissions reduction; (5) local impacts; and (6) international business processes (CSI 2002). The agenda invited other cement producers to join and committed to reporting on progress in three years' time.

GHG emissions of the cement industry originate from the chemical reactions of the key raw material, limestone (50 percent of the total), fuel used in the manufacturing processes (40 percent of the total), and electricity consumption, transport, and other sources (10 percent of the total). Thus, the industry's climate protection encompasses raw-material considerations, fuel mix (the use of renewable sources of energy or energy derived from waste), process technology and its efficiency, product quality (which influences the use of cement per output unit), logistics, and other factors (Damtoft et al. 2008).

The CSI developed a CO_2 protocol for use in defining and publicizing baseline emissions of involved companies. It facilitated the setting of targets by involved companies against their baseline emissions, as well as annual reporting of CO_2 emissions (CSI 2002). The data suggest that CO_2 emissions per produced ton of clinker decreased

6 percent between 1990 and 2006. Thermal energy efficiency improved by 14 percent over the same period. But the emissions of CSI members increased by 35 percent because their output grew by 50 percent in the same period.

The CSI data suggest that operational optimization has limited scope to influence CO_2 emissions because it is tied to the technological design of plants. Industry performance improves mainly through the addition of new, efficient plants and the decommissioning of old, inefficient plants. Alternative fossil fuels, waste, and biomass contribute to the fuel mix in different ways in different regions (CSI 2009). Raw-material mix, fuel mix, and product choices have substantial potential to reduce CO_2 emissions by the industry over the long run.

Key Observations

Climate change governance initiatives such as the CCP and the CSI can cover GHG emissions comparable to those of major Annex 1 countries. The CCP has also achieved GHG emission reductions comparable to those of major Annex 1 countries, and it has done so by providing cost savings to participants. The CSI has improved performance compared with business as usual in a period when the cement industry's output grew by 50 percent (CSI 2009). But voluntary initiatives such as the CCP and the CSI are most likely to be able to realize only those emission reductions that will yield cost savings. These are not insignificant—as Enkvist, Nauclér, and Rosander (2007) suggest, nearly a third of emission reductions needed by 2030 would actually provide a net benefit.

New forms of climate change governance may also have other, less tangible implications. The CCP and the CSI have established processes for assessing current performance and for setting targets and planning for their attainment. These processes make performance transparent and can create stakeholder pressure for further improvement. The CCP and the CSI have also identified and disseminated best practices and have pursued the creation of a market for new climate-friendly products and services. Over time, they may help bring down the marginal abatement costs of carbon and thus create new cost-effective measures for reduction of GHG emissions.

But because two-thirds of the GHG emission reductions needed by 2030 entail economic sacrifices, there clearly remains a role for conventional state-based solutions as part of a wider polycentric governance strategy. This raises the question: what should the division of labor among state-based, hybrid, and voluntary governance solutions be, and how do they interact? Voluntary industry initiatives such as the CSI are likely to benefit from the existence of political commitments because those commitments provide a basis for longer-term planning and investment. State-based governance solutions can also foster and facilitate the functioning of hybrid and voluntary climate change governance initiatives. For example, markets need backing by states, such as legal recognition and enforceability of contracts in courts, to be credible and to function.

From another viewpoint, hybrid and voluntary forms of climate change governance may play an important role in legitimizing and mainstreaming climate change to actors participating in them and to external political and economic decision makers. That is, they may lower the threshold of participating in mitigation activities and increase pressure to make progress in conventional state-based forms of climate change governance. At the same time, voluntary and hybrid forms of climate governance as part of a wider polycentric governance strategy offer a decentralized, flexible, and incentivized way to learn, innovate, and experiment with promising ways of reducing GHG emissions and targeting research and development investments.

In light of the foregoing conceptual and empirical discussion, what could a wider polycentric governance strategy for climate change look like? As already suggested, bottom-up and top-down processes are likely to generate a mosaic of institutional diversity that includes state-based, hybrid, and voluntary measures that operate at levels from local to international and across levels (table 14.1). The international cornerstones of climate change governance will continue to play a role and will gradually cover more GHG sources, include more ambitious emission-reduction targets, and address adaptation and its financing. However, this is likely to happen in a piecemeal and incremental way rather than comprehensively. National policies on climate change and related issues will also develop, both to implement international agreements and to pursue domestic goals. In light of the multiple-benefits origins of polycentric governance, voluntary initiatives focused on adaptation to climate change are likely to emerge when the adaptation agenda gains force. Insurance and risk-sharing arrangements for adaptation are likely to demand public-private cooperation and to be based on hybrid solutions. Public-private cooperation and hybrid solutions are also likely to underpin mitigation-focused activities, particularly those related to carbon markets and experimental technologies such as carbon capture and storage. Regional and local governments will also increasingly

TABLE 14.1

Institutional Diversity in Polycentric Climate Change Governance

Type and Level	Conventional	Hybrid	Voluntary
Global	Kyoto Protocol; post-Kyoto targets; adaptation funding	Carbon markets; REDD	Business sector initiatives
Regional	European Union's emissions trading scheme (EU-ETS)	Regional carbon markets; insurance provision and underwriting	Adaptation clearinghouses
National	Climate change; energy; and other legislation	Carbon markets; public-private partnerships in CCS; insurance provision and underwriting	Adaptation networks of local governments
Local	Climate-proofed zoning; property tax regimes; joint mitigation and adaptation	Public-private partnerships	Carbon-neutral communities

be involved in the delivery of mitigation and adaptation through planning, regulation, and public service provision.

Although the discussion here has focused on the potential and promises of hybrid and voluntary forms of climate change governance, they can also have problematic implications. Collaborative industry initiatives may not in reality be open to all and may result in restraints of competition. Voluntary initiatives in general are not representative, and their accountability remains unclear. These issues are increasingly drawing attention in research (Bäckstrand 2008; Unerman and O'Dwyer 2006).

Fostering Polycentric Climate Governance

The governance framework for climate change is still largely in the making, but both new institutional arguments about polycentricity and the emerging empirical evidence suggest that institutional diversity will characterize it. The governance framework will partly be based on the UNFCCC and the protocols and decisions of parties made under it. However, national policies and regulations, subnational and local policies and plans, and a variety of hybrid and voluntary initiatives will also play a role in climate change governance. Together, these institutional responses will create a wider polycentric governance strategy for climate change that will disperse authority and responsibility.

Although the dynamics of different kinds of institutional solutions as part of a wider polycentric governance strategy largely remain to be studied, something can be said about them. Voluntary and hybrid governance initiatives can clearly be comparable to major Annex 1 countries in terms of GHG emissions and emission-reduction achievements. These initiatives will be at their best in realizing emission reductions that save money, but they can also help create markets for carbon-friendly products and abatement technologies and bring down the marginal abatement cost of carbon over time. However, climate stabilization will also require emission reductions that will entail economic sacrifices. This means that state-based governance solutions will remain a part of the wider polycentric governance strategy.

The question is: how different governance solutions within the wider polycentric strategy will interact? Voluntary solutions may benefit from political commitment which can provide a basis for longer-term planning and investment. State-based governance solutions can also foster hybrid solutions involving markets. Voluntary initiatives may in turn play a role in mainstreaming and legitimizing climate change to actors participating in them and to external political and economic decision makers. They can lower the threshold of participating in voluntary climate change measures and create pressure for making progress in state-based forms of climate change governance. Voluntary and hybrid forms of climate change governance also offer a decentralized, flexible and incentivized way of learning about low-cost and promising ways of reducing greenhouse gas emissions and targeting R&D investments effectively.

There clearly is an urgent need to improve the evidence base on the performance of nonconventional forms of climate change governance and the interaction of different types of governance solutions that form parts of a wider polycentric governance strategy. The scholarship on common-pool resources and polycentricity is well placed to make a contribution in this area because it can draw on both a conceptual apparatus and comparable empirical evidence.

Acknowledgments

This chapter forms part of the work of the Centre for Climate Change Economics and Policy (CCCEP), a joint research center of the London School of Economics and the University of Leeds. I gratefully acknowledge the financial support of the United Kingdom Economic and Social Research Council to the CCCEP. I also thank Dan Cole, Tim Foxon, Andrew Gouldson, Lin Ostrom, Kerry Smith, and James van Alstine for their comments on earlier versions of this chapter.

REFERENCES

Adger, W. Neil, Terry P. Hughes, Carl Folke, Stephen R. Carpenter, and Johan Rockström. 2005. Social-ecological resilience to coastal disasters. *Science* 309:1036–1039.

Bäckstrand, Karin. 2008. Accountability of networked climate governance: Rise of transnational climate partnerships. *Global Environmental Politics* 8:74–102.

Barrett, Scott, and Michael Toman. 2010. Contrasting future paths for an evolving global climate regime. *Global Policy* 1:64–74.

Berkes, Fikret. 2008. Commons in a multi-level world. *International Journal of the Commons* 2(1):1–6.

Bernstein, Steven, Michele Betsill, Matthew Hoffmann, and Matthew Paterson. 2010. A tale of two Copenhagens: Carbon markets and climate governance. *Millennium: Journal of International Studies* 39(1):161–173.

Brooks, Nick, W. Neil Adger, and P. Mick Kelly. 2005. The determinants of vulnerability and adaptive capacity at the national level and the implications for adaptation. *Global Environmental Change* 15:151–163.

Buchanan, James M. 1965. An economic theory of clubs. *Economica* 32:1–14.

Bulkeley, Harriet, and Michele M. Betsill. 2003. *Cities and climate change: Urban sustainability and global environmental governance.* New York: Routledge.

Coase, Ronald H. 1937. The theory of the firm. *Economica* 4:386–405.

———. 1960. The problem of social cost. *Journal of Law and Economics* 3:1–44.

———. 1974. The lighthouse in economics. *Journal of Law and Economics* 17:357–376.

Cole, Daniel H. 2009. Climate change and collective action. *Current Legal Problems* 61:229–264.

CSI (Cement Sustainability Initiative). 2002. *The Cement Sustainability Initiative: Our agenda for action.* Geneva: World Business Council for Sustainable Development.

———. 2009. *Cement industry energy and CO_2 performance: Getting the numbers right.* Geneva: World Business Council for Sustainable Development.

Damtoft, Jesper Sand, Jacques Lukasik, Duncan Herfort, Danielle Sorrentino, and Ellis Martin Gartner. 2008. Sustainable development and climate change initiatives. *Cement and Concrete Research* 38:115–127.

Dietz, Thomas, Elinor Ostrom, and Paul C. Stern. 2003. The struggle to govern the commons. *Science* 302:1907–1912.

Dolšak, Nives, and Elinor Ostrom, eds. 2003. *The commons in the new millennium.* Cambridge, MA: MIT Press.

EEA (European Environmental Agency). 2010. *Annual European Union greenhouse gas inventory, 1990–2008, and inventory report, 2010.* Technical Report No 6/2010. Copenhagen, Denmark: European Environmental Agency. http://www.eea.europa.eu/publications/european-union -greenhouse-gas-inventory-2010.

Enkvist, Per-Anders, Tomas Nauclér, and Jerker Rosander. 2007. A cost curve for greenhouse gas reduction. *McKinsey Quarterly* 2007(1):35–45

Falkner, Robert, Hannes Stephan, and John Vogler. 2010. International climate policy after Copenhagen: Towards a "building blocks" approach. *Global Policy* 1:252–262.

Gore, Christopher D. 2010. The limits and opportunities of networks: Municipalities and Canadian climate change policy. *Review of Policy Research* 27:27–46.

Hare, William, Claire Stockwell, Christian Flachsland, and Sebastian Oberthür. 2010. The architecture of the global climate regime: A top-down perspective. *Climate Policy* 10:600–614.

Hardin Garrett. 1968. The tragedy of the commons. *Science* 162:1241–1248.

———. 1998. Extensions of "The tragedy of the commons." *Science* 380:682–683.

Hooghe, Liesbet, and Gary Marks. 2003. Unraveling the central state, but how? Types of multi-level governance. *American Political Science Review* 97:233–243.

ICLEI (International Council for Local Environmental Initiatives). 1993. *Cities for Climate Protection: An international campaign to reduce urban emissions of greenhouse gases.* http://www.iclei.org/index.php?id=10829.

ICLEI (International Council for Local Environmental Initiatives) Local Governments for Sustainability. 2006. *ICLEI international progress report—Cities for Climate Protection.* http://www.iclei.org/index.php?id=10829.

IPCC (Intergovernmental Panel on Climate Change). 2007. *Fourth assessment report.* 3 vols. Cambridge, U.K.: Cambridge University Press.

Kern, Kristine, and Harriet Bulkeley. 2009. Cities, Europeanization and multi-level governance: Governing climate change through transnational municipal networks. *Journal of Common Market Studies* 47:309–332.

Kuik, Onno, Jeroen Aerts, Frans Berkhout, Frank Biermann, Jos Bruggink, Joyeeta Gupta, and Richard S. J. Tol. 2008. Post-2012 climate policy dilemmas: A review of proposals. *Climate Policy* 8:317–336.

Lemos, Maria Carmen, and Arun Agrawal. 2006. Environmental governance. *Annual Review of Environmental Resources* 31:297–325.

Linnerooth-Bayer, Joanne, Reinhard Mechler, and Georg Pflug. 2005. Refocusing disaster aid. *Science* 309:1044–1046.

Linstroth, Tommy, and Ryan Bell. 2007. *Local action: The new paradigm in climate change policy.* Hanover, NH: University Press of New England.

Mastrandrea, Michael D., and Steven H. Schneider. 2004. Probabilistic integrated assessment of dangerous climate change. *Science* 304:571–575.

Meckling, Jonas O., and Gu Yoon Chung. 2009. Sectoral approaches for a post-2012 climate regime: A taxonomy. *Climate Policy* 9:652–668.

Musgrave, Richard A., and Peggy B. Musgrave. 1976. *Public finance in theory and practice.* 2nd ed. New York: McGraw-Hill.

Newell, Peter. 2000. *Climate for change: Non-state actors and the global politics of the greenhouse.* Cambridge, U.K.: Cambridge University Press.

Olson, Mancur. 1971. *The logic of collective action: Public goods and the theory of groups.* Cambridge, MA: Harvard University Press.

Ostrom, Elinor. 1990. *Governing the commons: The evolution of institutions for collective action.* Cambridge, U.K.: Cambridge University Press.

———. 2005. *Understanding institutional diversity.* Princeton, NJ: Princeton University Press.

———. 2009. A polycentric approach for coping with climate change. Policy Research Working Chapter 5095. World Bank.

———. 2010a. Beyond markets and states: Polycentric governance of complex economic systems. *American Economic Review* 100:641–672.

———. 2010b. A long polycentric journey. *Annual Review of Political Science* 13:1–23.

Ostrom, Elinor, Joanna Burger, Christopher B. Field, Richard B. Norgaard, and David Policansky. 1999. Revisiting the commons: Local lessons, global challenges. *Science* 284:278–282.

Ostrom, Elinor, Thomas Dietz, Nives Dolšak, Paul C. Stern, Susan Stonich, and Elke U. Weber, eds. 2002. *The drama of the commons.* Washington, DC: National Academy Press.

Ostrom, Elinor, Marco A. Janssen, and John M. Anderies. 2007. Going beyond panaceas. *Proceedings of the National Academy of Sciences* 104:15176–15178.

Ostrom, Vincent. 1972. Polycentricity. A paper presented at Workshop on Metropolitan Governance, the American Political Science Association, Washington, DC (September 5–9).

———. 1999. Polycentricity—Part 1. In *Polycentricity and local public economies*, ed. M. McGinnis, 52–74. Ann Arbor: University of Michigan Press.

Ostrom, Vincent, Charles M. Tiebout, and Robert Warren. 1961. The organization of government in metropolitan areas: A theoretical inquiry. *American Political Science Review* 55:831–842.

Paavola, Jouni. 2007. Institutions and environmental governance: A reconceptualization. *Ecological Economics* 63:93–103.

———. 2008a. Governing atmospheric sinks: The architecture of entitlements in the global commons. *International Journal of the Commons* 2:313–336.

———. 2008b. Livelihoods, vulnerability and adaptation to climate change: Lessons from Morogoro, Tanzania. *Environmental Science and Policy* 11:642–654.

Paavola, Jouni, and W. Neil Adger. 2006. Fair adaptation to climate change. *Ecological Economics* 56:594–609.

Pacala, Stephen, and Robert Socolow. 2004. Stabilization wedges: Solving the climate problem for the next 50 years with current technologies. *Science* 305:968–972.

Poteete, Amy R., Marco A. Janssen, and Elinor Ostrom. 2010. *Working together: Collective action, the commons, and multiple methods in practice.* Princeton, NJ: Princeton University Press.

Rayner, Steve. 2010. How to eat an elephant: A bottom up approach to climate policy. *Climate Policy* 10:615–621.

Rhodes, Roderick A. W. 1996. The new governance: Governing without government. *Political Studies* 44:652–667.

Román, Mikael. 2010. Governing from the middle: The C40 cities leadership group. *Corporate Governance* 10:73–84.

Rosenau, James N. 1995. Governance in the twenty-first century. *Global Governance* 1:13–43.

Samuelson, Paul A. 1954. The pure theory of public expenditure. *Review of Economics and Statistics* 36:387–390.

Schmidt J., N. Helme, J. Lee, M. Houdashelt, and N. Höhne. 2008. Sector-based approach to the post-2012 climate change policy architecture. *Climate Policy* 8: 494–515.

Spash C. L. 2010. The brave new world of carbon trading. *New Political Economy* 15: 169–195.

Sprinz D., and T. Vaahtoranta. 1994. The interest-based explanation of international environmental policy. *International Organization* 48: 77–105.

Steffen W., A. Sanderson, J. Jager, P.D. Tyson, B. Moore III, P. A. Matson, K. Richardson, F. Oldfield, H.-J. Schellnhuber, Billie L. Turner II, and Robert J. Wasson. 2004. *Global change and the earth system: A planet under pressure.* Heidelberg: Springer.

Stern, Nicholas. 2007. *The economics of climate change: The Stern review.* Cambridge, U.K.: Cambridge University Press.

Sugiyama, Taishi, and Jonathan Sinton. 2005. Orchestra of treaties: A future climate regime scenario with multiple treaties among likeminded countries. *International Environmental Agreements: Politics, Law and Economics* 5(1):65–88.

Tiebout, Charles M. 1956. A pure theory of local expenditures. *Journal of Political Economy* 64:416–424.

UNDP (United Nations Development Programme). 2007. *Human development report, 2007/2008: Fighting climate change; Human solidarity in a divided world.* Basingstoke, U.K.: Palgrave Macmillan.

Unerman, Jeffrey, and Brendan O'Dwyer. 2006. Theorising accountability for NGO advocacy. *Accounting, Auditing and Accountability Journal* 19:349–376.

Velders, Guus J. M., Stephen O. Anderson, John S. Daniel, David W. Fahey, and Mack McFarland. 2007. The importance of the Montreal Protocol in protecting climate. *Proceedings of the National Academy of Sciences* 104:4814–4819.

Vitousek, Peter M., Harold A. Mooney, Jane Lubchenko, and Jerry M. Melillo. 1997. Human domination of earth's ecosystems. *Science* 277:494–499.

Williamson, Oliver E. 1999. Public and private bureaucracies: A transaction cost economics perspective. *Journal of Law, Economics and Organization* 15:306–342.

———. 2000. The new institutional economics: Taking stock, looking ahead. *Journal of Economic Literature* 38:595–613.

———. 2005. The economics of governance. *American Economic Review* 95(2):1–18.

Young, Oran. 2002. *The institutional dimensions of environmental change: Fit, interplay, and scale.* Cambridge, MA: MIT Press.

Commentary

V. KERRY SMITH

Polycentric policies are unlikely to provide the first best level of climate services, especially when these services are viewed as global public goods. That is, we should not expect many independent centers of group decision making to succeed when the structure of the processes that produce climate services encourages free-riding (Barrett 2007; Sandler 1992). However, getting the ideal level of provision is not the point. Rather, it is about gaining greater acceptance for strategies that acknowledge decentralized actions may come reasonably close to the ideal. This is the essence of Paavola's argument for exploring climate change governance through the lens of polycentricity. In the end, an assessment of the relevance of his proposal must be based on empirical evidence and must consider the answers to a series of questions. For example, is there a sufficient set of areas for voluntary cooperation that will contribute to reducing greenhouse gases (or expanding the sinks for them)? Can the necessary set of actions be promoted by bundled policies and international agreements that can come reasonably close to a global ideal? Paavola seems optimistic, while I am agnostic. Neither of us can point to decisive evidence.

Institutional Design as Climate Policy

Barrett (2007) develops several themes related to the challenges faced by those seeking to design institutions to supply global public goods. One of the lessons that he argues must be considered in designing national policies in an interdependent world concerns the expectations of what can be accomplished. More specifically, Barrett notes that "the set of outcomes that every state is capable of realizing depends on the decisions of others. Moreover, the course set by every state helps to shape the decisions that others will make" (2007, 193).

My first concern with Paavola's argument is to ask whether we can formally describe conditions that would allow countries to internalize externalities voluntarily or, in this context, contribute to a global public good. The short answer is that there are such frameworks, but the formal details are a bit different than he describes. The framework developed by Carbone, Helm, and Rutherford (2009) is especially relevant to Paavola's discussion.

Their model relates to climate policy and concerns the feasibility of establishing permit trading systems that arise as part of voluntary agreements among countries. In this framework, the agreements are characterized as equilibria in which a country's decision to participate in the agreement and its independent decisions to issue a number of pollution permits for carbon emissions (as the mechanism to produce the global public good, climate services) are best responses to the actions of other countries. Thus, their model captures one of the elements that Barrett describes as central to realistic descriptions of problem solving in an interdependent world. In their model, firms in the countries that have agreed to be part of the group that trades permits may trade the permits with other firms in these countries. They also trade goods with all other countries in the world economy. The assumptions about the elasticities governing the structure of international trade are important parameters that influence the value of carbon leakage and the magnitude of terms-of-trade (TOT) effects. In the case of differentiated trade, TOT effects in goods are important, while those for permits among trading partners are relatively insensitive to the setting of these elasticities. Thus, the comparative influence of TOT effects in the goods market is not important as an incentive to form coalitions in the model. However, the TOT effects are important for the absolute level of emission reductions.

Carbone, Helm, and Rutherford's model is complex and considers a number of alternative international permit-trading coalitions. Their findings are also specific to how the model characterizes each economy's preferences and production possibilities. Nonetheless, it can be used to confirm part of Paavola's conjecture. Some voluntary international agreements achieve more than half the emission control that would be associated with a first best (centralized) choice.

Table C14.1 illustrates the results for three cases—homogeneous traded goods, homogeneous goods, and differentiated traded goods, with preexisting taxes. Each row corresponds to a different coalition or permit-trading zone that satisfies a weak external stability condition. That is, the coalition cannot be improved on in the sense that a new member (given each of the countries' choices of permits) is better off and the current members are also better off than in the absence of that new entrant. In all the trading structures considered there are coalitions that realize at least 50 percent of the first best emissions and we do not need top-down coordination. Thus, in principle the diversity in endowments, technologies, and preferences offers opportunities for subgroups to gain from trading permits by exploiting the opportunities for reducing the costs of controlling of CO_2 emissions through arbitrage.

Their model illustrates how voluntary institutions defining a trading zone for marketable permits (and thus the extent of one type of market) and another set of markets can work together without top-down coordination. It is an analytic example of Paavola's suggestion. However, there are a few differences from the real world, and at least one big issue is left unanswered. Each coalition member in their model recognizes that it does experience some benefits from controlling CO_2 emissions. It does not experience the full public good gain, but it does recognize that there are some "private" gains to its citizens. Equally important, it assumes that coalition proposals arise exogenously, "somehow." Getting started, of course, is a large part of the problem.

Reasons for Caution

In her Nobel lecture, Ostrom (2010) identifies a number of features of situations where locally generated institutions governing access to common-pool resources

TABLE C14.1

Carbone, Helm, and Rutherford's Analysis of International Climate Policy in Noncooperative Settings

	Emission Compared to First Best (%)	Global EV (%)
1. Relatively homogeneous goods trade (no taxes)		
EUR, CHN, FSU	65.4	1.0
EUR, CHN	64.9	1.0
JPN, CHN	59.3	0.8
USA, CHN	52.3	0.6
JPN, FSU	38.8	0.1
2. Relatively homogeneous goods trade (preexisting taxes)		
EUR, CHN, FSU	61.7	1.4
EUR, CHN	59.0	1.3
JPN, CHN	46.2	0.9
USA, CHN	47.1	0.9
JPN, FSU	28.2	0.1
3. Differentiated goods trade (no taxes)		
EUR, CHN, FSU	60.3	1.1
JPN, CHN, FSU	59.2	1.0
JPN, CHN	46.7	0.5
USA, CHN	57.8	1.0

SOURCES: Carbone, Helm, and Rutherford (2009) and online appendix, http://www2.econ.iastate.edu/jeem/res.asp?vol=58&num=3.

NOTE: The countries/regions are as follows:

EUR = Europe
CHN = China
FSU = Former Soviet Union
JPN = Japan
USA = United States

The model has six regions: USA, JPN, CHN, EUR, FSU, and the rest of the world. It has seven sectors: coal, crude oil, electricity, natural gas, refined oil, energy-intensive goods, and other manufacturers and services. There is no abatement technology. Produced goods can serve as inputs along with capital and labor. The first column compares the total carbon emission reduction with the first best solution's emission reduction. The second column shows the percentage change in equivalent variation (EV) when the solution for each coalition is compared with the no-trade Nash solution. The solution year is 2015.

are likely to survive. The principles that seem especially problematic for the case of managing the climate system include the following:

- There are clear boundaries between legitimate users and nonusers.
- The open-access or common-pool resource itself has a clear boundary.
- Provision rules assure that the distribution of costs of resource management is consistent with the distribution of benefits.
- People affected by the rules of use participate in deciding what the rules will be.
- Effects of users' activities and the condition of the resource being used are readily monitored.

It is hard to imagine how one would create the local activities needed to produce a stable climate system that would be consistent with these design principles. The examples Paavola provides do not help resolve these issues.

Consider the Cities for Climate Protection program. Even if the estimated CO_2 savings as reported (without a verification system) are accepted, they amount to less than 0.2 percent of annual global emissions. Moreover, the cost savings appear to be calculated incompletely, so one questions the ability to sustain or transfer these "successes." For example, one of the case studies cited in the report of ICLEI Local Governments for Sustainability (2006) notes a bus pass program that demonstrated a 10 percent reduction in downtown car use, with annual savings of $200,000 in fuel costs. The costs of subsidizing the bus pass system are omitted. Mandates that employers provide the passes and that the local governments provide cost shares for the system are omitted from the computation of the net costs of reducing CO_2 emissions. It is not clear that there are cost savings when everything is counted. Such practices in the original study call into question this group's conclusions concerning the cost savings for this initiative as they are cited by Paavola. They do not appear to include the costs of providing the alternative services.

Overall, then, Carbone, Helm, and Rutherford (2009) give us a "story" that suggests that there is a potential for progress without top-down, fully centralized systems. Moreover, it partially answers one of Barrett's concerns with countries providing global public goods: "If one group of countries supplies more of a global public good requiring aggregate efforts, other countries will not have an incentive to step up their efforts. Indeed, they may have an incentive to pare back. This is particularly true when trade leakage exacerbates free rider incentives" (2007, 101). Carbone, Helm, and Rutherford's formal analysis suggests that trade leakage may not be as important a disincentive as Barrett suggests. There are then two key concerns. First, their model avoids the issues associated with getting the coalitions started. Second, their model includes a reason for countries to do something. Independent permit supply decisions are based on recognizing the within-country benefits of controlling CO_2. These are taken into account by the countries involved. What is missed is the public nature of the benefits for all in the world economy.

Greater recognition of the public good nature of climate services offers a dimension that can be addressed and may well help in understanding how coalitions could get started as well. Measures of the benefits of maintaining current climate services are not explicitly recognized by those who are designing national policy and reacting to international proposals. Instead, they display skepticism and focus on costs. Whether the analysis is by Stern or Nordhaus, (Stern 2007; and Nordhaus 2008) the benefits of climate mitigation are the "poor relations" in their models.

Next Steps

The literature that attempts to estimate the trade-offs people would be willing to make for climate policy is underdeveloped. The small literature that does exist is very diverse. Johnson and Nemet (2010) reviewed 27 studies conducted between 1998 and 2010. The results are not comparable across studies because the things consumers (or respondents to surveys) were asked to evaluate as objects of choice were diverse. In some cases the choices were among policies such as a general climate-stabilizing initiative. In others it was a green energy program. Other studies linked climate change mitigation to policies that would increase gasoline prices to reduce temperature changes and food shortages. Other policies were described as promoting carbon sequestration. The list could be expanded further and the point is that in each many different things change, including the extent of climate change. We would not expect the measures of tradeoffs people would make to be the same because what they are getting is also different across the studies reviewed.

It would seem that efforts to understand these benefits and to use the resulting estimates to encourage leadership among policy makers in large economies would be a positive step forward. It is one way to use the insights from analytic models into how coalitions can act with bottom-up responses designed to reduce carbon emissions and improve the climate system. It may also help encourage leadership among large countries and, thus, the process of getting coalitions started.

Marketable permits need not be the only instrument. However, we need more analytic guidance to identify the ways other institutional mechanisms can be used with markets to enhance bottom-up responses when market and nonmarket responses are undertaken together.

Acknowledgments

This comment is based on work supported by the National Science Foundation under grant BCS-1026865, Central Arizona–Phoenix Long-Term Ecological Research.

REFERENCES

Barrett, Scott. 2007. *Why cooperate? The incentive to supply global public goods*. New York: Oxford University Press.

Carbone, Jared C., Carsten Helm, and Thomas F. Rutherford. 2009. The case for international emissions trade in the absence of cooperative climate policy. *Journal of Environmental Economics and Management* 58(November):266–281.

ICLEI (International Council for Local Environmental Initiatives) Local Governments for Sustainability. 2006. *ICLEI international progress report—Cities for climate protection*. http://www.iclei.org/index.php?id=10829.

Johnson, Evan, and Gregory F. Nemet. 2010. Willingness to pay for climate policy: A review of estimates. Working Paper No. 2010–011 (June). Madison: Robert M. La Follette School of Public Affairs, University of Wisconsin.

Nordhaus, William. 2008. *A question of balance: weighing the options on global warming policies*. New Haven: Yale University Press.

Ostrom, Elinor. 2010. Beyond markets and states: Polycentric governance of complex economic systems. *American Economic Review* 100(June): 641–672.

Sandler, Todd. 1992. *Collective action: Theory and applications*. Ann Arbor: University of Michigan Press.

Stern, Nicholas. 2007. *The economics of climate change: The Stern review*. Cambridge, U.K.: Cambridge University Press.

Sinking States

KATRINA MIRIAM WYMAN

In May 2009 the *New York Times Magazine* published an article about the efforts of the president of the Maldives to deal with the threats that climate change represents to his country (Schmidle 2009). These threats are serious. Like other small island states around the world, the Maldives may disappear because of the rise in sea levels due to climate change.[1] Facing the possible submergence of most of the country's land mass, President Mohamed Nasheed is not only trying to encourage leading greenhouse gas emitters such as the United States to reduce their emissions, but also is beginning to plan for the possibility that the residents of his country will have to relocate. The article reported that the president has "proposed moving all 300,000 Maldivians to safer territory, he named India, Sri Lanka and Australia as possible destinations and described a plan that would use tourism revenues from the present to establish a sovereign wealth fund with which he could buy a new country—or at least part of one—in the future" (Schmidle 2009, 40). At least one and possibly two other small island states also are seeking ways to resettle their residents because they similarly fear losing their territory to sea-level rise.[2]

Imagine that instead of seeking to buy land to resettle residents of the Maldives, the president claimed that his country's citizens have a right, for which they would not have to pay, to resettle on the land of one or more existing countries. This chapter considers whether the citizens of the Maldives and other states that may be submerged because of sea-level rise should have a legal right to resettle elsewhere.

At first glance, a claim of a right to resettle by the Maldives or any other island state threatened by climate change sounds highly fanciful. Even the president of the Maldives has only proposed buying land for his citizens in other countries; he has not suggested that the citizens of the Maldives have any right to resettle in the

---

[1] On other small island nations whose existence may be threatened by climate change, see e.g., Kristof (1997).

[2] Kiribati and possibly Tuvalu may be looking for ways to resettle their populations (Crouch 2008; Kolmannskog 2008; Schmidle 2009). However, in describing the policies that Kiribati and Tuvalu are pursuing to deal with climate change, McAdam (2011) does not suggest that either country currently is looking to purchase land in other countries. In addition to relocating, building floating facilities is another option sinking states might consider. In March 2010, the government of the Maldives and The Netherlands' Dutch Docklands signed an agreement under which the Dutch company would develop floating facilities, such as a convention center and golf courses, for the country. The Maldives indicated that it would try to develop "floating housing units" with the company in the future (President's Office 2010).

territory of another country. But the claim may not be as far-fetched as it initially appears. Climate change is already affecting coastlines in the Maldives and elsewhere. Warming is expected to continue, regardless of whether the major greenhouse gas-emitting countries agree to reduce their emissions in the near future, and there are estimates that it will require millions of persons to relocate.[3]

Moreover, there are historical precedents for the claim that a country has the right to establish settlements in other countries or territories. Western colonization of North and South America, Asia, and Africa from the late 1400s to the 1800s prompted scholarly debates about whether there was a right to establish settlements on the land of another people or state. Although there is a widespread perception that the westerners who considered the legitimacy of colonization universally justified settlement, this was not the case. In the late eighteenth century in particular, well-known scholars criticized Western imperialism.[4] The threatened disappearance of the Maldives and other small island states once again raises the question of whether there is a right to establish settlements in other countries. In a historical irony, the peoples who might seek to claim a right to establish settlements in our time are often the descendants of people colonized by the old European powers. For example, the Maldives was a British protected area and then a protectorate from 1796 until it gained independence in 1965, and earlier the islands were under the influence of the Portuguese and the Dutch (Metz 1994). Adding to the irony, the claimants this time theoretically might attempt to claim part of the land or territory of their ancestors' colonizers, although as mentioned above President Nasheed seems more interested in resettling closer to home in India, Sri Lanka, or Australia.

This chapter argues that the citizens of small island states such as the Maldives that are threatened by climate change should have a legal right under international law to resettle in other countries. To be clear, the chapter starts from the premise that people who are forced to resettle because of climate change are unlikely to have a right to resettle elsewhere under existing international law. They are not likely to be considered refugees under the Convention Relating to the Status of Refugees (United Nations 1951).[5] Nor are they likely to be able to claim a right to resettle under international human rights law.[6] In addition, the chapter argues that the citizens of

---

[3] On the prospects for continued warming, see IPCC (2007).

[4] Georg Cavallar explains that "the late eighteenth century produced a row of 'enlightened critics of empire' . . . and colonialism, among them Davenant, Raynal, Diderot, Gibbon, Condorcet and Herder" (2002, 257). See also Muthu (2003).

[5] Under the Refugee Convention, a refugee is defined as a person with a "well-founded fear of being persecuted for reasons of race, religion, nationality, membership of a particular social group or political opinion" (United Nations 1951, Article 1A[2], in conjunction with United Nations 1967, Article 1[2]). People displaced because of climate change are unlikely to satisfy this definition for several reasons. For example, they are unlikely to satisfy the persecution requirement or the requirement that persecution be on one of the five listed grounds. For legal analyses of the obstacles to bringing most climate refugees within the definition of the Refugee Convention, see, e.g., Docherty and Giannini (2009); McAdam (2009a; 2009b); McAdam and Saul (2010); Office of the United Nations High Commissioner for Refugees et al. (2009); and United Nations High Commissioner for Refugees (2008).

[6] For example, climate refugees probably could not rely on the non-refoulement principle, which is included or has been held to be provided in various human rights instruments (the European Convention for the Protection of Human Rights and Fundamental Freedoms, Article 3; International Covenant on Civil and Political Rights, Article 7; and Convention Against Torture and Other Cruel, Inhuman or Degrading Treatment or Punishment, Article 3) (Kolmannskog 2008). Climate refugees are unlikely to fall within the scope of the non-refoulement principle (McAdam and Saul 2010). Even if climate victims can invoke the principle, it is unlikely to meet the needs of most climate victims. It provides a right not to be returned, not the right to settle permanently in a for-

small island states should have an individual right to resettle. It sets to the side the fascinating question of whether a state or people should have a collective legal right to reconstitute itself elsewhere.[7] The possibility that a country threatened by climate change might disappear is difficult to contemplate. As Nauru's ambassador to the United Nations, Marlene Moses, explained in October 2009, "I think I speak for most Pacific Islanders when I say that I am quite happy where I am and have no desire to leave my island" (Mohrs 2009). The recognition of an individual right to resettle would be a second-best response, but it is nonetheless a place to start as we begin adapting to climate change.

In arguing that the citizens of sinking states should have a legal right to resettle, we may start by returning to the scholarly discussions from the age of discovery about when there is a right to settle areas that already belong to other peoples or states. Scholarly discussions from this period of what might be labeled a "right to safe haven" provide a basis for thinking about a right to resettle that citizens of sinking states could invoke.[8] It is often argued that the victims of climate change have rights against the countries that have historically emitted large quantities of greenhouse gases as a matter of corrective justice (Farber 2008; Penz 2010). However, the right to safe haven was discussed as a right (or a privilege) that displaced foreigners enjoyed against states generally and was therefore not rooted in corrective justice. Indeed the right to safe haven is likely preferable to claims rooted in corrective justice because it recognizes claims against many more countries and does not require claimants to prove that their current needs were caused by specific countries.[9]

There are several possible rationales for recognizing a right to safe haven in the twenty-first century. The chapter initially analyzes the option of grounding the right in a general moral theory that imposes obligations across national borders, such as utilitarianism or a cosmopolitan variant of liberal egalitarianism. Then it explores whether there might be a narrower, independent argument for the right that does not require accepting a general cosmopolitan moral theory. The independent argument that appears to be most promising is a rationale rooted in the natural law tradition recently secularized by Mathias Risse (2009) in an article in which he attempts to craft a right to relocate that could be invoked by islands that disappear because of climate change.[10] The advantages of the rationale he suggests are discussed in detail.

---

eign country (Docherty and Giannini 2009; Office of the United Nations High Commissioner for Refugees et al. 2009).

[7] For arguments that disappearing states may enjoy collective rights to sovereignty over territory, see Nine (2010). Meisels (2009) briefly sketches an argument for a collective right to sovereignty over territory based on egalitarian grounds. Gans (2008) offers a potentially relevant defense of ethnocultural nationalism and discusses the principles that should govern the allocation of territory among nations.

[8] The phrase "right to safe haven" is borrowed from Pauline Kleingeld (1998, 76), who uses the term in reference to Kant.

[9] Mathias Risse (2009) also distinguishes his recent effort to craft a right to relocate, which draws on the work of Hugo Grotius, from efforts on behalf of climate victims based on who caused climate change. Posner and Sunstein (2008) discuss the difficulties of invoking corrective justice in the climate change context in general.

[10] Risse's article was brought to my attention by my colleague Benedict Kingsbury after I started thinking about the rights of the citizens of sinking states to resettle. Tally Kritzman-Amir (2008) argues that a category of socioeconomic refugees warrants legal protection. To motivate her analysis, Kritzman-Amir uses the hypothetical example of the island state of Elbonia, which is about to become uninhabitable because of rising water levels. There also is a helpful emerging policy literature proposing mechanisms to assist persons dislocated by climate change (Baer 2010; Biermann and Boas 2008; Burkett 2009; Byravan and Rajan 2006; 2010; Docherty and Giannini

Finally, the chapter discusses how a right to safe haven might be implemented. In general, the right could be implemented similarly to international refugee rights, which arguably reflect the same concerns.[11] For example, as with refugee rights, individuals would be able to claim the right. A key difference is that international refugee law does not allocate responsibility for refugees among countries (Schuck 1997), as the proposal for the right to safe haven due to climate change does.

In suggesting that the right to safe haven could support claims by citizens of threatened states to resettle in other countries, this chapter hints that what is sauce for the goose could be sauce for the descendants of the gander. Centuries after the end of the age of discovery, the descendants of colonized peoples may have grounds for claiming rights elaborated in the West during the era of imperialism.

Rise in Sea Level

The rise in sea level is one of the most frequently mentioned signs that the climate is warming (IPCC 2007). According to the 2007 synthesis report of the Intergovernmental Panel on Climate Change (IPCC), "Global average sea level rose at an average rate of 1.8 [1.3 to 2.3] mm per year over 1961 to 2003 and at an average rate of about 3.1 [2.4 to 3.8] mm per year from 1993 and 2003," although the report cautions that "whether this faster rate for 1993 to 2003 reflects decadal variation or an increase in the longer-term trend is unclear" (IPCC 2007, 30). According to the synthesis report, "Sea level rise would continue for centuries due to the time scales associated with climate processes and feedbacks, even if GHG concentrations were to be stabilised" (IPCC 2007, 46).

Increases in sea levels are projected to have significant impacts. Milne et al. describe them as "one of the major socio-economic hazards associated with global warming," given that "about 200 million liv[e] . . . within coastal floodplains, and . . . two million square kilometres of land and one trillion dollars worth of assets [lie] . . . less than 1m above current sea level" (2009, 471). The synthesis report warns that "by the 2080s, many millions more people than today are projected to experience floods every year due to sea level rise. The numbers affected will be largest in the densely populated and low-lying megadeltas of Asia and Africa while small islands are especially vulnerable" (IPCC 2007, 48).

It is important to recognize the difficulties that plague scientific work about sea-level rise. First, there is considerable uncertainty about "global average sea-level rise" (Milne et al. 2009, 471). Complicating efforts to estimate the amount the seas will rise on average is uncertainty about "future changes in the Greenland and Antarctic ice sheet mass," which could lead to greater sea-level rise, and "uncertainty in the penetration of the heat into the oceans" (IPCC 2007, 73; Milne et al. 2009). Therefore, the synthesis report "does not assess the likelihood, nor provide a best estimate or an upper bound for sea level rise," opting instead for "model-based pro-

---

2009; Hodgkinson and Burton 2010; McAdam 2010; 2011; Penz 2010; Prieur et al. 2010). McAdam (2011) briefly reviews recent proposals for a treaty to protect victims of climate change.

[11] For the idea that modern refugee rights reflect Kant's concept of the right to safe haven, see Benhabib (2004) and Kleingeld (1998).

jections of global average sea level rise at the end of the 21st century (2090–2099)" (IPCC 2007, 45).

Second, predicting localized changes in sea levels is even more complicated than estimating the global rise (Milne et al. 2009). Noticeably absent from the synthesis report is any prediction that one or more specific small island states will disappear because of sea-level rise. Milne et al. explain, "Many different physical processes contribute to sea-level change . . . and none of these produce a spatially uniform signal. Indeed, one of the few statements that can be made with certainty is that future sea-level change will not be the same everywhere" (2009, 471). Satellite measurements of changes in sea-level rise since the 1990s provide evidence for this statement. Milne et al. explain that "over more than 14 years . . . the average is around 3 mm yr, [but] there are regions showing trends of over 10 mm yr and larger areas (notably the northeastern Pacific) where sea level has fallen over this period" (2009, 471). Indeed, there are scientists who doubt that the Maldives will disappear, despite the dire predictions about its fate.[12]

Still, the inability of scientists to predict whether the Maldives or other states will be submerged does not detract from the broader point that the impacts of climate change currently include and will continue to include sea-level rise that will affect the earth's geography and its people. According to one estimate, potentially "tens of millions of people" could be affected by rising sea levels caused by global warming (Representative of the Secretary General 2008, 1).[13] Most of the people who will be required to relocate because of climate change will probably relocate within their home countries, and the same is presumably true of the subset of individuals who will have to move because of rising sea levels caused by climate change.[14] The focus here is on whether the victims of sea-level rise in countries that become uninhabitable due to climate change should have a legal right in international law to a safe haven. The plight of citizens of sinking states starkly raises the obligations of other countries to climate victims, since the victims of sea-level rise in disappearing island nations would be unable to relocate within their national borders. A document from the United Nations High Commissioner for Refugees describes "the sinking island scenario whereby the inhabitants of island states such as the Maldives, Tuvalu, and Vanuatu may eventually be obliged to leave their own country as a result of rising sea levels and the flooding of low-lying areas" as "the potentially most dramatic manifestation of climate change" (United Nations High Commissioner for Refugees 2008, 5).

---

[12] Schmidle quotes Paul Kench, a coastal geomorphologist at the University of Auckland, who states that "the notion that the Maldives are going to disappear is a gross overexaggeration" (2009, 40). Webb and Kench (2010) suggest that the concerns that Pacific island nations will disappear as a result of sea-level rise may be exaggerated because historical data suggest that coral reef islands in the central Pacific have for the most part not eroded, but rather have changed their shape as sea levels have risen in recent decades. Zukerman (2010) reports on Webb and Kench's findings and reactions to them.

[13] There is considerable uncertainty about the number of persons who may be forced to relocate due to climate change. For discussions of the estimates and the uncertainty, see e.g., Biermann and Boas 2008; Brown 2008; Docherty and Giannini 2009; Guler 2009; Hulme 2008; McAdam 2009a.

[14] On the expectation that most people displaced by climate change will migrate internally within their home countries, see, e.g., McAdam 2011; Office of the United Nations High Commissioner for Refugees et al. 2009.

The Right to Safe Haven in Context

Writings on the rights of foreigners from the period of Western imperialism were authored by westerners who took divergent positions on the morality of Western imperialism. These writings are centrally concerned with the rights of powerful nations and individuals against weaker parties, but one may use them to attempt to formulate a right that could be claimed by the weak against the strong.

Western "discovery" of foreign lands from the late 1400s to the 1800s raised the question of when it would be just for citizens of Western countries to visit or settle in those lands (Pagden 1987). Hospitality rights were an important rubric under which these issues were considered. Immanuel Kant's doctrine of cosmopolitan right (or law), which consists solely of hospitality rights, is probably the best-known discussion today of the rights of foreigners to hospitality from the era of Western imperialism (Kleingeld 1998).[15] But hospitality rights antedate Kant (1724–1804). Duties to be hospitable to travelers were already recognized in many sources before the late 1400s, including Plato.[16] Indeed, Georg Cavallar (2002) suggests that there is little that is original in Kant's conception of the content of hospitality rights in light of the work of earlier scholars such as Samuel Pufendorf (1632–1694).[17]

The discussions of hospitality rights in Kant and earlier works tend to address different situations in which foreigners might present themselves to a state or a people other than their own without clearly distinguishing these situations. We can analyze discussions from the age of discovery of the rights of foreigners and the obligations of states in three types of situations: when foreigners attempt to interact with citizens of other states for trade or noneconomic reasons; when foreigners seek to settle permanently in another country, but not because they are imperiled; and when foreigners require a safe haven because they are imperiled. The last is the one most relevant to the victims of warming-induced sea-level rise.

Right to Interact

One situation considered during the period of colonization concerned the efforts of foreigners to initiate trade with or simply to visit other countries or their citizens, not to establish permanent settlements. Some writers, such as the Thomist theologian Francisco de Vitoria (1486–1546), take positions friendly to the Western powers, insisting that hospitality rights provide foreigners with rights to travel and trade provided they "do no harm" to the local population (1917 [1532], xxxvi).[18] Pufendorf's more moderate and nuanced view arguably sets the stage for Kant's discussion. In contrast to Vitoria, Pufendorf (1934 [1688]) insists that countries have the right to deny admission to foreign travelers and the right to refuse to trade. But Pufendorf

---

[15] For examples of contemporary discussions of Kant's cosmopolitan right, see Benhabib (2004); Kleingeld (1998); and Waldron (2000).

[16] In Pufendorf's enumeration of examples of discussions of duties of hospitality in *De jure naturae et gentium libri octo* (1934 [1688], 3.3.9), his sources include "Plato, *Laws*, Book XII, where he lists the duties owed strangers."

[17] Cavallar argues that "Kant offers a new justification of hospitality rights" by "revising the traditional argument from original ownership" (2002, 368).

[18] See also Cavallar (2002); Pagden (1987).

warns that it might be unwise to deny foreigners the right to visit if countries want their citizens to be welcome abroad. He also suggests that there is an exception to the right of a country to refuse trade: it cannot refuse to trade in goods that are "absolutely essential to human life" unless the exporting country itself may require the goods (1934 [1688], 3.3.11).

Kant maintains that there is "a right to visit" foreign lands, but he carefully limits the scope of this "right of foreign arrivals," arguing that it "pertains . . . only to conditions of the possibility of *attempting* interaction with the old inhabitants" (2006 [1795], 8:358). In other words, the right to visit is a right to offer to establish interactions with foreigners—not a right to establish such interactions, let alone to settle or conquer their lands.[19] The larger purpose behind granting foreigners the right to visit is to enable "remote parts of the world [to] . . . establish relations peacefully with one another, relations which ultimately become regulated by public laws and can thus finally bring the human species ever closer to a cosmopolitan constitution" (Kant 2006 [1795], 8:358). The right to visit is not an unqualified right. Visitors have to behave "peacefully" to enjoy the right (8:358). Countries can refuse to admit visitors or establish limits on their travels, perhaps even for no reason.[20] Kant approvingly describes China and Japan as "wisely" limiting the "interaction" of westerners with their citizens in light of the westerners' conduct in other parts of the world, such as "America, the negro countries, the Spice Islands [and] . . . the Cape" (8:358).[21]

In general, the rights to interact that Kant and others recognized have limited contemporary relevance for citizens of states facing loss of territory from sea-level rise. These citizens would not be seeking the right to visit or to trade with other countries, but rather the right to relocate. However, Pufendorf's argument that a state generally does not have the right to refuse to trade goods essential to human life provides a potentially useful precedent for areas of the world predicted to lose drinking water under climate change, whose residents could have to plead with water-rich regions for access to their resources. Aside from this type of narrow claim, though, it seems unlikely that the right to interact would enable victims of sea-level rise to achieve their ultimate objective of permanently relocating to safer territory. The discussions from the age of discovery of the right to settle and especially the right to safe haven may offer greater assistance.

---

[19] The scope of the right is further discussed in *The Metaphysics of Morals* (Kant 1996 [1797]). There Kant states "that all nations stand *originally* in a community of land, though not of *rightful* community of possession (*communio*) and so of use of it, or of property in it; instead they stand in a community of possible physical *interaction* (*commercium*), that is, in a thoroughgoing relation of each to all the others of *offering to engage in commerce* with any other, and each has a right to make this attempt without the other being authorized to behave toward it as an enemy because it has made this attempt" (1996 [1797], 6:352). A bit later Kant refers to "the right of citizens of the world *to try to* establish community with all and, to this end, to *visit* all regions of the earth. This is not, however, a right to *make a settlement* on the land of another nation (*ius incolatus*); for this, a specific contract is required" (1996 [1797], 6:353).

[20] Kleingeld argues that "a state has the right to deny a visit, as long as it does so non-violently" (1998, 75).

[21] China "allowed [foreigners] contact with, but not entrance to its territories," and Japan "allowed this contact to only one European people, the Dutch, yet while doing so it excludes them, as if they were prisoners, from associating with the native inhabitants" (Kant 2006 [1795], 8:359).

Right to Settle

A second situation discussed in the age of discovery is that of foreigners who seek to settle in another state for economic or other opportunities, not because they face danger or peril in their home countries. Some scholars from this period, such as Hugo Grotius (1583–1645), argue that foreigners have a robust right to settle without the consent of the peoples or states already in the territory. Anticipating John Locke's more famous agricultural argument for Western colonization, Grotius maintains that "if there be any waste or barren Land within our Dominions, that also is to be given to Strangers, at their Request, or may be lawfully possessed by them, because whatever remains uncultivated, is not to be esteemed a Property, only so far as concerns Jurisdiction, which always continues the Right of the antient People" (2005 [1625], II.2.XVII).[22]

On the other hand, there are Western scholars who object to the idea that land can be settled without the consent of the persons currently using it. For example, Kant argues that the right to hospitality does not include the right to settle without the consent of the affected people. He maintains that settlement "on the land of another nation" would require "a specific contract" (1996 [1797], 6:353).[23] In line with his insistence on consent for settlement, Kant was a forceful critic of Western colonialism.[24]

Ironically, the argument that settlement can be justified without the consent of the affected peoples represents an attractive position for countries facing loss of territory from sea-level rise, many of which were colonized during the age of discovery.[25] However, as a pragmatic matter, the argument that settlement of another country's territory does not require that country's consent seems unlikely to prevail in the twenty-first century, given the importance that international law now attaches to state sovereignty.[26] Moreover, as the critiques of colonization of Kant and others suggest, the idea that other states' or peoples' lands could be settled without their consent was controversial even during the age of discovery.

Right to Safe Haven

In assessing the right of persons to resettle, the most promising precedent in discussions during the age of discovery is situations in which individuals in peril seek

---

[22] Cavallar indicates that the passage embodies "an embryonic form of the agricultural argument" (2002, 259–260). Tuck offers the following explanation of the passage: "There is a general natural right to possess any waste land, but one must defer to the local political authorities, assuming they are willing to let one settle. If they are not, of course, then the situation is different, for the local authorities will have violated a principle of the law of nature and may be punished by war waged against them" (1999, 106).

[23] Kant also states: "It is not the *right of a guest* that the stranger has a claim to (which would require a special, charitable contract stipulating that he be made a member of the household for a certain period of time), but rather a right to visit, to which all human beings have a claim, to present oneself to society by virtue of the right of common possession of the surface of the earth" (2006 [1795], 8:358).

[24] See e.g., Kant (1996 [1797]; 2006 [1795]) for critiques of Western imperialism. Secondary sources discussing Kant's views on imperialism include Kleingeld (1998); Muthu (2003); and Waldron (2000).

[25] Walzer (1983) recognizes a related irony: the idea that foreigners have a right to settle unused land, which once provided a rationale for colonialization, now potentially could ground a right to immigrate from intensely populated developing countries to less densely populated countries such as the United States and Australia that were founded by colonists.

[26] For example, Ann Dummett argues that "belief in 'state sovereignty' is the objection most often advanced against free immigration" (1992, 174).

refuge in a foreign state. These discussions suggest an obligation on the part of countries to admit foreigners who are in peril and outside their home countries, and they imply that individuals enjoy what can be called a right to safe haven. This right is probably best understood as a counterpart in public international law to the private right of necessity. The right of private necessity concerns the right of individuals in imminent peril to take the property of others to preserve their own lives or property; the right to safe haven addresses the right of individuals to enter foreign countries when they are in peril outside their home countries and are unable to return there.

Grotius argues that "a fixed Abode ought not be refused to Strangers, who being expelled from their own Country, seek a Retreat elsewhere: Provided they submit to the Laws of the State, and refrain from every Thing that might give Occasion to Sedition" (2005 [1625], II.2.XVI). However, the right to permanent refuge does not necessarily include the right to acquire land on which to settle in the receiving state. Grotius explains that newcomers have the right to land in the host state only "if there be any waste or barren Land" in the state (2005 [1625], II.2.XVII).

Pufendorf also suggests that foreigners in peril have a right to settle in other countries, but this right is considerably more qualified than the one Grotius sketches. After referring to the duty Grotius envisions to grant "permanent settlement to strangers who have been driven from their former home, and seek entrance into another," Pufendorf argues that "it belongs, indeed, to humanity to receive a few strangers, who have not been driven from their homes for some crime, especially if they are industrious or wealthy, and will disturb neither our religious faith nor our institutions" (1934 [1688], 3.3.10). In contrast to Grotius, Pufendorf stresses the right of countries to take into account pragmatic considerations, such as the number of refugees and their potential impact, in deciding whether to allow refugees to resettle permanently, and if so, how many:

> But no one would be so bold as to assert that a great multitude, armed, and with hostile intent, should be received as if there were an obligation to do so, especially since it is hardly possible that the native inhabitants run no danger from such a host. Therefore, every state may decide after its own custom what privilege should be granted in such a situation. The state should consider well beforehand, whether it is to its advantage for the number of its inhabitants to be greatly increased; whether its soil is fertile enough to support all of them well; whether we will not be too crowded if they are admitted; whether the band that seeks admittance is competent or incompetent; whether the arrivals can be so distributed and settled that no danger to the state will arise from them. (1934 [1688], 3.3.10)

Moreover, Pufendorf envisions newcomers as enjoying more circumscribed rights to land than Grotius does. Pufendorf explains that the newcomers "cannot seize for themselves anything they may want or occupy . . . or any section of our land that may be unused, but they must be content with what we have assigned them" (1934 [1688], 3.3.10). According to Pufendorf, foreigners do not even have a right to barren lands.

For Pufendorf, the right to safe haven is a privilege or an imperfect right, and the decision to admit persons in peril is "an act of humanity" that "confer[s] a kindness"

(1934 [1688], 3.3.10). Although the considerations he identifies may sometimes favor denying entry, Pufendorf's insistence that there are pragmatic reasons for granting permanent refuge suggests that in general he might tilt the balance in favor of admission. He emphasizes that "we can observe that many states about us have grown immensely because they received foreigners and aliens with open arms, while others, who have repelled them, have been reduced to second-rate powers" (1934 [1688], 3.3.10). Cavallar speculates that Pufendorf might have been referring to the migration in the 1580s of more than 100,000 persons "from the Catholic south Netherlands . . . to the north," who are credited with "contributing to what has been called the economic 'miracle' at the onset of the Golden Age" (2002, 205).

Kant devotes much less attention to persons in peril than to foreigners who seek settlement or the right to visit. In a brief passage in the "Third Definitive Article of Perpetual Peace," he states: "If it can be done without causing his death, the stranger can be turned away, yet as long as the stranger behaves peacefully where he happens to be, his host may not treat him with hostility" (2006 [1795], 8:358).[27] According to Kleingeld, Kant elaborates on this statement in a draft of Perpetual Peace that indicates "that people who are forced by circumstances outside their control to arrive on another state's territory should be allowed to stay at least until the circumstances are favourable for their return. He gives the examples of shipwreck victims washed ashore and of sailors on a ship seeking refuge from a storm in a foreign harbour, thus in effect stating that cosmopolitan law implies the right to a safe haven" (1998, 76).[28]

Before Kant, Pufendorf similarly considered the rights of shipwreck victims to use the property of others to save themselves, but he did so in discussing the private right of necessity, not the right to safe haven. Just as Pufendorf maintained that refugees enjoy an imperfect right of refuge in foreign countries, he concluded that there is "an imperfect obligation" to assist persons in need, such as shipwreck victims, under the rubric of private necessity (1934 [1688], 2.6.5). In discussing private necessity, though, Pufendorf conceded that in cases of "supreme necessity," the imperfect obligation to assist persons in need could ripen into something resembling a perfect obligation (1934 [1688], 2.6.6).[29]

This brief survey of the views of Grotius, Pufendorf, and Kant emphasizes that they all conceive of countries as having some obligations to foreigners who are in peril outside their home countries. Their views imply that foreigners in this situa-

---

[27] "Death" is the translation in Kant (2006 [1795]), but Kleingeld translates Kant as stating "that a state may refuse a visitor only 'when it can happen without his destruction,'" rather than death (1998, 76). Kleingeld then argues that "'destruction' . . . could be interpreted more broadly than referring to death only. It could conceivably also include mental destruction or incapacitating physical harm, in which case the range of cases to which it applies would be much greater" (1998, 77). Benhabib (2004) also translates the passage as triggering a duty to allow the stranger to remain if destruction is the alternative. For the remainder of this chapter, I assume that the passage refers to "destruction" rather than "death."

[28] Benhabib implies that Kant gave more examples than the shipwreck where the right to safe haven would apply: "To refuse sojourn to victims of religious wars, to victims of piracy or ship-wreckage, when such refusal would lead to their demise, is untenable, Kant writes" (2004, 28).

[29] Salter (2005) also interprets Pufendorf as conceding that persons in extreme need have a perfect right to use the property of others, even though Pufendorf otherwise characterizes the property owner's duty to assist persons in need as an imperfect obligation. The rights of ships and sailors in distress to enter foreign ports and to receive assistance remain live issues today. For recent discussions of these rights, see Murray (2002); Oliver (2008–2009); and Whitehead (2009). Tully (2007) suggests that the existing state obligations to rescue persons in distress at sea offer a precedent for requiring states to provide at least temporary protections to the victims of sea-level rise.

tion enjoy some sort of right of safe haven in foreign nations. Although they differ in how they define the obligations of foreign countries and, consequently, the rights of foreigners, they seem to agree on a number of basic elements.

First, the obligation extends to individual foreigners, not groups of foreigners. Grotius refers to "Strangers" (2005 [1625], II.2.XVI), Pufendorf to "strangers" (1934 [1688], 3.3.10), and Kant to "the stranger" (2006 [1795], 8:358).

Second, the foreigners must meet certain criteria. Grotius, Pufendorf, and Kant seem to agree that foreigners must be seeking admission to a country other than their own and that they must be outside their home countries and unable to return to them, at least in the immediate future. These authors also identify additional qualifying criteria. Grotius indicates that the obligation is owed to "Strangers, who being expelled their own Country, seek a Retreat elsewhere: *Provided they submit to the Laws of the State, and refrain from every Thing that might give Occasion to Sedition*" (2005 [1625], II.2.XVI) (emphasis added). For Pufendorf, "[i]t belongs to . . . humanity to receive a few strangers, *who have not been driven from their homes for some crime, especially if they are industrious or wealthy, and will disturb neither our religious faith nor our institutions* (1934 [1688], 3.3.10) (emphasis added). According to the draft Kleingeld cites, the entitlement Kant sketches belongs to *"people who are forced by circumstances outside their control* to arrive on another state's territory" (1998, 76) (emphasis added). In the "Third Definitive Article of Perpetual Peace," Kant indicates that the stranger must be facing "'*destruction*'" if he is denied entry (Kleingeld 1998, 76) (emphasis added).[30]

Third, the obligation extends to all countries. None of the authors suggest that only countries that cause foreigners to be displaced are obligated to them or that foreigners have claims against a country only if they can prove that the country harmed them. In other words, the obligation toward foreigners is not rooted in corrective justice.

Fourth, the obligation that countries have is to admit qualifying foreigners, or at least some of them, potentially permanently. However, Grotius, Pufendorf, and Kant do not agree on the stringency of the obligation. Grotius most clearly articulates a right to enter and to obtain permanent refuge, stating that "a fixed Abode ought not to be refused to Strangers" provided they submit to the prevailing domestic authority (2005 [1625], II.2.XVI). According to the draft that Kleingeld cites, the beneficiaries of the right Kant sketches "should be allowed to stay at least until the circumstances are favourable for their return" (1998, 76). Although this wording does not explicitly refer to a permanent right to remain, it presumably would embrace such a right if the circumstances never become favorable for return, as in the case of a sinking state.[31] Pufendorf states that "it belongs, indeed, to humanity to receive a

---

[30] It is noteworthy that Kant is the only one of the three authors who mentions that the persons seeking refuge should be doing so through no fault of their own. Pufendorf's (1934 [1688]) failure to state this is striking because he insists that individuals seeking to use the property of another because of private necessity must be in need through no fault of their own. Indeed, he seems to fault Grotius for failing to insist that the need that triggers the private right of necessity must have arisen through no fault of the claimant. For more on Pufendorf's critique of the right of necessity in Grotius, see Salter (2005), whose interpretations of the role of fault in the Grotian right of necessity and of Pufendorf's critique of Grotius related to the role of fault differ from the interpretations presented here.

[31] Benhabib describes what is here termed the right to safe haven as "a claim to temporary residency which cannot be refused, if such refusal would involve the destruction—Kant's word here is *Untergang*—of the other" (2004, 28). Benhabib is ambiguous about the status of the claim to temporary residency (2004, 36 [suggesting the

few strangers," but he is much more willing to allow receiving countries to limit and potentially to refuse entry in accordance with domestic priorities (1934 [1688], 3.3.10).

For present purposes, the key point is that during the age of discovery, there was a concept of a right to safe haven. If residents of sinking states ultimately are driven from their homelands by rising sea levels, they would seem to meet the minimum requirements that Grotius, Pufendorf, and Kant agree are necessary to invoke this right: they are individuals, seeking admission to a foreign country, outside their home country and unable to return to it at least in the immediate future.

Justifications of the Right to Safe Haven

In the famous New York property case *Pierson v. Post*, 3 Cai. R. 175, 2 Am. Dec. 264 (1805), the dissent mocks the majority's references to treatises such as Pufendorf's and Grotius's. One might similarly ask why we should pay any attention today to Grotius's, Pufendorf's, and Kant's discussions of the right to safe haven. One reason is that the right to safe haven is justifiable in modern eyes.

Because the support of people from many different traditions will be necessary for the right to safe haven to be recognized in law and policy, an overlapping consensus of several different rationales supporting the right would be desirable.[32] We start by discussing the option of grounding the right to safe haven in a general moral theory, such as utilitarianism or a cosmopolitan variant of liberal egalitarianism. Then we explore the possibility of treating the right as an independent case for which a narrower, more focused argument could be made under the rescue principle or a resources argument rooted in the natural law tradition.

General Cosmopolitan Moral Theories

One option would be to ground a right to safe haven in a general moral theory. To be useful, the theory would have to suggest that we are obligated across national borders to citizens of other states. A cosmopolitan version of liberal egalitarianism and utilitarianism are two possible theories.

LIBERAL EGALITARIANISM

At first glance, it might seem that cosmopolitan liberal egalitarian theories provide a promising route for approaching a right to safe haven. Such theories generally suggest that we are obligated as a matter of justice to achieve a measure of socioeconomic equality globally, a task which likely would require transfers to people in other countries. Indeed, Kritzman-Amir (2008) argues for greater legal protection for socioeconomic refugees (a category she defines to include the citizens of sinking islands) primarily, although not exclusively, on the basis of cosmopolitan liberal egalitarian theories of justice.

---

duty to help persons whose life and limb are endangered is an "*imperfect moral duty*"]; 38 [referring to "the right of temporary sojourn" as "a right" rather than "a privilege"]).

[32] Appiah states that "the major advantage of instruments that are not framed as the working out of a metaphysical tradition is, obviously, that people from different metaphysical traditions can accept them" (2003, 105).

Consider, for example, Thomas Pogge's cosmopolitan extension of John Rawls's theory of justice. Pogge treats the world as a single unit in which persons are the morally significant actors, and he argues that "the social position of the globally least advantaged" should be "the touchstone for assessing our basic institutions" (1989, 242). He is sensitive to the global socioeconomic inequalities that arise from countries' different degrees of access to "natural assets (such as mineral resources, fertility, climate, etc.)" (1989, 250), and he suggests that it might be necessary to rearrange property rights in natural assets to reduce those inequalities.[33] Under Pogge's approach, then, the citizens of sinking states might have a claim to natural resources (perhaps including land) from other states as part of a general institutional reform.

The word "might" is deliberately used because Pogge seems to have limited himself to a relatively modest proposal for addressing the socioeconomic inequalities stemming from disparities in natural-resource endowments that would not reallocate ownership of identifiable natural resources among countries. His proposed "global resource dividend" would require countries to pay a small tax for using or selling their natural resources that would be channeled to assist the global poor, on the basis that "the global poor own an inalienable stake in all limited natural resources" (Pogge 2002, 196; see also Pogge [1994]).[34] To be consistent with his overriding concern for addressing global poverty, any proposal that Pogge might countenance for reallocating ownership of natural resources among countries presumably would have to aim to reduce the socioeconomic need of those who are worst off around the globe. Thus, even if Pogge contemplated reallocating resources among countries, the claims of the citizens of sinking states to resources would remain contingent on their socioeconomic need and not merely on the fact that they face the loss of their land mass and natural resources. The contingency of these claims would be particularly problematic for the wealthier citizens of sinking states because their financial assets might reduce the priority of their claims, even though they would be just as landless as their poorer compatriots.[35]

UTILITARIANISM

Utilitarianism provides a second possible ground for a right to safe haven. For utilitarians, the goal is to maximize overall well-being, and everyone's well-being is given the same weight, regardless of country of origin. There are many reasons that a right to safe haven might promote well-being. First, it would save lives and reduce suffering by providing persons driven from their homes with a place to resettle. As Pufendorf (1934 [1688]) mentions, receiving countries might benefit from the talents and diversity of the new arrivals and their offspring.[36] Wide recognition of the right also would provide persons who were safely ensconced in their home countries

---

[33] "A global difference principle may justify not merely a general adjustment of market prices but a different specification of property rights over natural assets–involving, for example, an international tax on (or international ownership and control of) natural assets" (Pogge 1989, 264).

[34] Pogge specifically states, "This idea does not require that we conceive of global resources as the common property of humankind, to be shared equally. My proposal is far more modest by leaving each government in control of the natural resources in its territory" (2002, 204–205).

[35] Recall that Pufendorf contemplated that "wealthy" persons might be admitted pursuant to what is here termed the right to safe haven (1934 [1688], 3.3.10).

[36] However, the economics of immigration are complex (Kritzman-Amir 2008).

with a form of insurance that they would be able to settle somewhere if they were ever driven away.[37] To be sure, the right would not be cost free. Implementation would require bureaucratic machinery, newcomers might need assistance in resettling, and, as with any form of insurance, there is a danger of moral hazard. If people know that they have a right to resettle elsewhere if they are driven from their homes, they might invest less in their home countries or exploit them unsustainably. The right also could have the unintended consequence of encouraging countries to drive some of their citizens or other countries' nationals from their homes because doing so would obligate other countries to accept the displaced individuals.[38] But overall, recognition of the right to safe haven probably would improve well-being compared with the status quo, especially if the number of people who seek to claim it is relatively low, a likely scenario because claimants would be unable to return to their home country and would experience dislocation from resettling in another country.

One problem with grounding the right to safe haven in a utilitarian framework is that although the right might improve well-being compared with the status quo, it may not be the measure that would most increase well-being compared with the status quo, and doing what would most increase well-being should be our priority if we are utilitarians.[39] Singer (2009) highlights another way of alleviating suffering that might increase well-being more than recognizing the right to safe haven: giving aid and development assistance to developing countries to reduce global poverty.[40]

One staggering statistic on world poverty is that 1.4 billion people live on less than $1.25 a day, the poverty line established by the World Bank (Singer 2009). If the 855 million people with "an income above the average income of Portugal . . . . each . . . gave $200 per year, that would total $171 billion" (Singer 2009, 143), almost the estimated $189 billion it would cost to achieve the poverty reduction and other objectives of the Millenium Development Goals. Singer argues that because "suffering and death from lack of food, shelter, and medical care are bad," we should be donating more to aid agencies because "it is in [our] . . . power to prevent something bad from happening, without sacrificing anything nearly as important" (2009, 15). However, Singer recognizes that the utilitarian principle that undergirds his argument—that we should give as much we can until giving would entail sacrificing something "nearly as important" as the additional lives that would be saved—requires the wealthy to donate considerably more than $200 a year and in fact to significantly change their lifestyles (2009). Thus, he offers a more modest proposal in the hope of making progress in reducing world poverty: people "who are financially comfortable" should give "roughly 5 percent of" their "annual income," and "the very rich" should give "rather more" (Singer 2009, 152).

---

[37] Carol Rose suggested that the right to safe haven could be justified as a form of insurance and reminded me of the functional discussion of group ownership of land in Ellickson (1992–1993), in which Ellickson mentions that insurance can be an alternative to group ownership of land to spread risks.

[38] Schuck provides examples of reasons that a country might encourage refugee outflows from neighboring states. The instigating country might wish "to use the refugees' flight to discredit or destabilize the source country regime . . . , or it may have revanchist designs on the source country" (1997, 273).

[39] I thank Liam Murphy for bringing this weakness of the utilitarian justification to my attention.

[40] See also Singer (1972).

Singer's proposal reminds us that we need to be cautious about grounding a right to safe haven in utilitarianism because there may be other measures, such as greater private and/or state aid to reduce poverty in developing countries, that might increase well-being even more and that should take priority under a utilitarian framework. Singer's proposal is not a substitute for the right to safe haven because he advocates greater private giving by individuals, not state action, which the recognition of the right would entail, although he is not opposed to state aid.[41] In fact, increasing aid to developing countries along the lines Singer recommends could be done as a complement to recognizing the right to safe haven.[42] But his proposal shows that utilitarianism offers at best a contingent case for the right to safe haven, because under the utilitarian framework, the strength of the argument for the right depends on how much recognizing the right would increase well-being compared with other possible options.

In addition to the specific difficulties with grounding the right to safe haven in utilitarianism or a cosmopolitan variant of liberal egalitarianism, there are broader reasons to resist grounding a right to safe haven in a general cosmopolitan moral theory. One is that rooting the right in a general theory requires endorsing that theory, as well as making a case that it would generate the right to safe haven. However, the notion that we are obligated to citizens of other states as a matter of justice is controversial (Nagel 2005), as are utilitarianism, Rawls's theory of justice, and probably any other general moral theory one might consider. If the right to safe haven has intuitive appeal, as it likely does for many people, it is probably not because they believe in a general moral theory of which that right is a part. It is more likely that there is something specifically compelling about people becoming homeless because the physical territory of their country disappears. It is possible that we can identify an independent rationale for the right that reflects this intuitive concern with the plight of the citizens of sinking states. We will consider two possibilities: the rescue principle and collective ownership of the earth.[43]

The Rescue Principle

The rescue principle is a potentially narrower rationale for the right to safe haven than the general theories discussed so far. As commonly understood, the rescue principle essentially holds that one has a positive duty to assist another person if that person is in urgent need and the first person can help him at little cost to himself. Even theorists who are reluctant to recognize obligations to citizens of other states as a matter of justice, or who outright reject this idea, claim that people sometimes should come to the assistance of citizens of other states on the basis of a humanitarian

---

[41] Point six of Singer's "seven-point plan" for individuals to help reduce global poverty is "Contact your national political representatives and tell them you want your country's foreign aid to be directed only to the world's poorest people" (2009, 169).

[42] Kritzman-Amir discusses "financial aid" as a "complementary measure" to the use of refugee law to assist socioeconomic refugees (2008, 170).

[43] In investigating ethical responsibilities to climate refugees, Penz (2010) similarly considers and quickly rejects cosmopolitan theories of justice as a basis for responsibilities to them. He prefers to ground such responsibilities in a version of corrective justice, an idea inconsistent with the right to safe haven elaborated in this chapter.

rescue principle. In arguing that people sometimes are obligated as a matter of humanity, but not justice, these theorists resemble Pufendorf when he argues that as "an act of humanity," people should admit those who are forced from their home countries even though they do not enjoy a legally enforceable right to help (1934 [1688], 3.3.10).

Consider, for example, the views of Thomas Nagel, who is skeptical of the idea that we are required to implement "global socioeconomic justice" (2005, 132). He argues that claims for distributive justice apply only to one's own state, because distributive justice "depends on . . . rights that arise only because we are joined together with certain others in a political society under strong centralized control" (2005, 127). Nonetheless, Nagel maintains that there is a "moral minimum" of basic rights and duties that "governs our relations with everyone in the world" (2005, 131). This moral minimum seems to include the rescue principle. Nagel explains that "this minimal humanitarian morality . . . does not require us to make [others'] . . . ends our own, but it does require us to pursue our ends within boundaries that leave them free to pursue theirs, and to relieve them from extreme threats and obstacles to such freedom if we can do so without serious sacrifice of our own ends" (2005, 131). Furthermore, Nagel mentions that "in extreme circumstances, denial of the right of immigration may constitute a failure to respect human rights or the universal duty of rescue. This is recognized in special provisions for political asylum, for example" (2005, 130). For Nagel, "minimal humanitarian morality" is "the consequence of the type of contractualist standard expressed by Kant's categorical imperative and developed in one version by Scanlon " (2005, 131). Adding further weight to the idea that Nagel's moral minimum includes the rescue principle, Scanlon specifically endorses "the Rescue Principle" on the basis that "it is difficult to see how it could reasonably be rejected" and argues that it "applies only in cases in which one can prevent something very bad from happening at only slight or moderate cost to oneself" (1998, 225).

Michael Walzer also subscribes to a narrow setting for distributive justice, but he claims that we have obligations that extend to foreigners outside this setting. Like Nagel, Walzer takes what he calls "the political community" rather than the globe as the setting for distributive justice (1983, 28), although Walzer counts not only countries, but also cities, as political communities. Nonetheless, Walzer, like Nagel, indicates that we may have obligations to persons outside our political communities, including potentially the obligation to allow them to enter our country.

Walzer discusses "the principle of mutual aid," a concept he borrows from John Rawls's book *A Theory of Justice* (Walzer 1983, 33). He initially describes this principle in individual terms that suggest that it resembles a positive duty to rescue:

> It is the absence of any cooperative arrangements that sets the context for mutual aid: two strangers meet at sea or in the desert or, as in the Good Samaritan story, by the side of the road. What precisely they owe one another is by no means clear, but we commonly say of such cases that positive assistance is required if (1) it is needed or urgently needed by one of the parties; and (2) if the risks and costs of giving it are relatively low for the other party. Given these conditions, I ought to

stop and help the injured stranger, wherever I meet him, whatever his membership or my own. (1983, 33)

Walzer then indicates that there is a collective analogue to the individual principle
of mutual aid:

> It is, moreover, an obligation that can be read out in roughly the same form at the
> collective level. Groups of people ought to help necessitous strangers whom they
> somehow discover in their midst or on their path. But the limit on risks and costs
> in these cases is sharply drawn. (1983, 33)

For Walzer, the collective version of mutual aid seems to be a modest constraint on
the right of countries to exclude persons. Walzer does not elaborate much on the
implications of the principle, but he suggests that it would obligate a country to accept refugees, although only if admission would not fundamentally transform the
country:

> The call "Give me . . . your huddled masses yearning to breathe free" is generous
> and noble; actually to take in large numbers of refugees is often morally necessary;
> but the right to restrain the flow remains a feature of communal self-determination.
> The principle of mutual aid can only modify and not transform admissions policies
> rooted in a particular community's understanding of itself. (1983, 51)[44]

In practice, Walzer's collective principle of mutual aid and Nagel's moral minimum suggest the possibility of grounding the right to safe haven in the rescue principle. The argument would be that the citizens of sinking states are persons urgently in
need, and host countries can alleviate this need at little cost to themselves by allowing these persons to resettle in their midst. Unfortunately, though, it is uncertain
that the rescue principle would provide a solid foundation for the right because the
idea that there is an obligation to rescue someone who is in urgent need when we
can do so at little cost to ourselves is indeterminate. Assume that the citizens of
sinking states would count as "necessitous" or "urgently" in need, to borrow Walzer's terms (1983, 33) because their lives are at stake due to the existential threat to
their countries. What would count as "risks" or "costs" in determining whether the
duty to rescue would apply, and how we are to know when these "risks" or "costs"
are sufficiently "low" to generate the duty on the part of host countries, are questions that remain unanswered. It seems that Walzer, at least, would count not only
the monetary costs of the rescue but also the noneconomic costs to the host country. These could be substantial even if the country is called on to admit only a small
number of people if the country has a history of limited or no immigration.[45] Scanlon
admits the indeterminacy problem underlying the rescue principle, warning that "I
would not say, for example, that we would be required to sacrifice an arm in order
to save the life of a stranger. But here a judgment is required, and I do not think

---

[44] Walzer is largely silent on the grounds for the principle of mutual aid, although he implies that mutual aid
might be a constraint derived from "justice" (1983, 61) or a "moral constraint" (1983, 62).

[45] Recall Walzer's statement that "The principle of mutual aid can only modify and not transform admissions
policies rooted in a particular community's understanding of itself" (1983, 51).

that any plausible theory could eliminate the need for judgments of this kind" (1998, 225).

The rescue principle may also be problematic because it is not clear that it reflects the intuitive appeal of the right of safe haven for citizens of sinking states. The rescue principle obligates us to "relieve" (Nagel 2005, 131) or to "help" (Walzer 1983, 33) others. These are both fairly general obligations that could require us to do many things quite apart from or in addition to allowing persons to resettle in our country. Pursuant to the rescue principle, for example, we might be required to send foreign aid in addition to or instead of admitting refugees. The rescue principle is narrower than a general moral theory, but the basis it provides for the right to safe haven still encompasses more than opening up a country's territory to persons whose home country has physically disappeared.

Collective Ownership of the Earth

Mathias Risse (2009) argues that Grotius offers a rationale for what Risse calls a right to relocation that would benefit states submerged by sea-level rise due to climate change. Risse's secularization of this rationale may offer the most promising ground for the right to safe haven elaborated in this chapter.

To understand Grotius's rationale, it is necessary to turn to his discussion of the private right of necessity because he hints at his rationale there, but not in his discussion of the right to safe haven. As mentioned earlier, the right of necessity can be regarded as an analogue in private law of the public international law right to safe haven. In both rights, the issue is whether a person's urgent needs override existing rights—a property owner's right to exclude in the case of private necessity, and a state's right to control entry in the case of the right to safe haven. But Grotius discusses the right to seek refuge in foreign nations separately from the right of persons in dire necessity to take the property of other individuals to save themselves.

Grotius argues that people facing "absolute Necessity" have a right to use the property of another (2005 [1625], II.2.VI.2).[46] However, there are limits on the right. The right that is granted is the right that according to Grotius existed before private property was established: a limited right to use resources that can be consumed, but not a right to accumulate resources.[47] Also, the necessitous person is entitled

---

[46] Grotius was by no means the first to argue for a right of necessity that overrides the owner's right to exclude. The idea that need trumps private property goes back at least to the twelfth century (Salter 2005). Aquinas's discussion (2002) of the idea that a person in need can take the property of another without being liable for theft is well known. For further discussion of Aquinas's views and their legacy, see e.g., Cavallar (2002); Hont and Ignatieff (1983); and Salter (2005).

[47] Grotius states that "in a Case of absolute Necessity, that antient Right of using Things, as if they still remained common, must revive" (2005 [1625], II.2.VI.2). He describes the primitive right to the use of things earlier in the chapter: "*All Things, as Justin has it, were at first common, and all the World had, as it were, but one Patrimony. From hence it was, that every Man converted what he would to his own Use, and consumed whatever was to be consumed; and such a Use of the Right common to all Men did at that Time supply the Place of Property, for no Man could justly take from another, what he had thus first taken to himself; which is well illustrated by that Simile of Cicero, Tho' the Theatre is common for any Body that comes, yet the Place that every one sits in is properly his own*" (2005 [1625], II.2.II.1). Buckle explains that "since the use-right arises precisely because of the person's needs, it extends no further than the satisfaction of those needs" (1991, 30). Salter (2005) argues that the original use right is even narrower and that it, and the right of necessity that mirrors the use right, are best understood as liberties or privileges, even though Grotius suggests that the right of necessity is a perfect right.

to take the property of another only after exercising "all other possible Means" of satisfying his own need (Grotius 2005 [1625], II.2.VII). For instance, Grotius suggests that the necessitous person must exhaust his own resources before taking the property of another.[48] In addition, the right cannot be exercised against an owner who is equally needy.[49] This implies an outer, albeit generous, limit on the right to take even the basic necessities: a person in urgent need must stop taking if he reduces the owner to an equal state of need. Moreover, the right to use the private property of another in case of necessity entails the obligation to make restitution to the property owner after the necessity ends and the user is "able to do it" (Grotius 2005 [1625], II.2.IX).[50]

What is interesting is the justification that Grotius hints at, but does not develop, for the private right of necessity:

> Even amongst the Divines, it is a received Opinion, that whoever shall take from another what is absolutely necessary for the Preservation of his own Life, is not from thence to be accounted guilty of Theft: That Sentiment is not founded on what some alledge, that the Proprietor is obliged by the Rules of Charity to give of his Substance to those that want it; but on this, that the Property of Goods is supposed to have been established with this favourable Exception, that in such Cases one might enter again upon the Rights of the primitive Community. For had those that made the first Division of common Goods been asked their Opinion in this Matter, they would have answered the same as we now assert. *Necessity*, says *Seneca* the Father, *that great Resource of human Frailty, breaks through the Ties of all Laws*; that is, all human laws, or Laws made after the Manner, and in the Spirit of human Laws. (2005 [1625], II.2.VI.4)

According to Risse (2009), Grotius's rationale for the right of necessity is that it would be inconsistent with the divine grant of the earth to humankind in common if the necessitous were deprived of the right to claim the basic necessaries by the human construct of private property.[51] According to Grotius, the earth was originally given

---

[48] In discussing when the right of private necessity entitles a person to take the property of another, Grotius states that "all other possible Means should be first used, by which such a Necessity may be avoided; either, for Instance, by applying to a Magistrate, to see how far he would relieve us, or by entreating the Owner to supply us with what we stand in Need of" (2005 [1625], II.2.VII). Through approving citations of several authorities, he then suggests that a person must first exhaust his own resources before appropriating for his own use the property of another. Grotius states that "*Plato* did not permit one Man to draw out of another's Well, 'till he had digged so far in his own Ground that there was no longer any Hopes or Expectation of Water. And *Solon* required, that a Man should first dig to the Depth of forty Cubits" (2005 [1625], II.2.VII).

[49] Grotius states that "this is no Ways to be allowed, if the right Owner be pressed by the like Necessity; for all Things being equal, the Possessor has the Advantage" (2005 [1625], II.2.VIII).

[50] This obligation to make restitution raises the question whether the person in need is exercising a right in using the property of the other. For instance, Pufendorf (1934 [1688]) suggests that it is inconsistent for Grotius to describe the right to use the property of another as a right and simultaneously insist on the obligation to make restitution after the necessity passes. Grotius (2005 [1625]) attempts to address the critique by arguing that the obligation to make restitution inheres in the right to use the property of another in a case of necessity.

[51] The following discussion of Grotius's rationale and its implications for the rights of citizens of sinking states closely follows Risse (2009). There are other interpretations of Grotius's rationale for the private right of necessity. For example, Buckle (1991) argues that the right of necessity exists to ensure that the reason for which private property was established is not undermined by the existence of private property. According to Buckle, private property exists for "the preservation of human beings in sophisticated societies" (1991, 45). "By excluding all but

458 KATRINA MIRIAM WYMAN

to humankind in common by God for humankind's use.[52] In the original community, everyone was given the right to use the resources granted by God, but not to accumulate more than he could use. The use right exists because "the preservation of life requires the using of natural resources" (Buckle 1991, 30). Human beings transitioned from the original community to private property by agreement, either express or tacit (Grotius 2005 [1625]). But the agreements establishing private property, Grotius insists, included an "Exception" (II.2.VI.4), perhaps analogous to an easement, to ensure that no one in dire straits was denied a right necessary for his survival to use the resources of the earth given by God to everyone in common.

Because of the similarity between the right of necessity and the right of safe haven, Grotius's justification for the right of necessity might also be used to justify an imperiled person's right to enter and remain in a foreign country.[53] The justification for the right to safe haven would run as follows: The earth was originally granted to humankind in common, and national borders are human constructs. People in urgent need of a physical territory have a right to ignore national borders and to enter and remain in foreign countries to exercise their right of self-preservation.

For nonbelievers, one potential problem with this justification is that it rests on the idea that God granted the earth to humankind. It is this original divine grant that triggers the right of individuals to override the rights of others to exercise the right of self-preservation. Risse recognizes the religious underpinnings of Grotius's thesis and attempts to "revitalize it nontheologically" (2009, 283). He does so by arguing that "all humans, no matter when and where they are born, must have *some* sort of symmetrical claim" to the earth because "the earth's resources and spaces are the accomplishment of no one, whereas they are needed by everyone" (286). Thus we might justify the right to safe haven on the basis that persons who require a refuge have a right to enter the territory of another country because everyone has an equal claim to the earth's resources, since none of us created them and each of us needs them to survive.

The Grotius-inspired collective ownership of the earth rationale is the strongest of the four rationales for the right to safe haven discussed in this chapter. This rationale has the benefit of justifying precisely what the right to safe haven provides: access to a portion of the earth's territory in situations where the claimant lacks a territory. The starting point for Grotius's rationale is humankind's collective claim to the earth, and that rationale justifies access to land under another's control, not sending foreign aid or any of the myriad other ways one might assist foreigners in need.

Another advantage of Grotius's rationale is that it suggests some limits on the circumstances in which countries would have to open their borders to admit persons. The import of the rationale is that it comes into force in extreme cases where persons lack access to land within their home countries sufficient to enable them to

---

the owner from free enjoyment of its product, however, systems of property, will, if applied indiscriminately, exclude even those in dire necessity" (Buckle 1991, 45).

[52] "Almighty GOD at the Creation, and again after the Deluge, gave to Mankind in general a Dominion over Things of this inferior World" (Grotius 2005 [1625], II.2.II.1)

[53] Indeed, Kant arguably attempts to ground cosmopolitan right in a metaphorical version of the common-ownership thesis that underpins Grotius's necessity-based justification (Benhabib 2004; Cavallar 2002).

exercise their right to self-preservation.[54] Citizens of sinking states would fall within this rationale because the disappearance of their islands would leave them without any land. Conceivably, the rationale might also apply to citizens of states whose territory is diminished through sea-level rise due to climate change, but these people would have to establish that they do not have enough remaining land within their home countries to exercise a right to self-preservation. Under this rationale, individuals could not claim the right to safe haven merely because their home states lacked enough territory to guarantee them a continued livelihood or to secure them a certain attractive standard of living.

The fact that Grotius's rationale suggests limits on the right to safe haven is important because the right will not be politically viable unless it has limits. One lesson from refugee law and politics under the existing Refugee Convention is that there is limited public tolerance in many potential host countries for admitting refugees, and that calls to admit larger numbers of refugees tend to create political backlashes (Martin 1991). Although the attitudes that give rise to backlashes might be criticized, they must be kept in mind in contemplating the creation of a new right to safe haven. One of the ways in which refugee law in the United States and elsewhere currently restrains the flow of refugees is the internal flight alternative doctrine (Martin et al. 2007). Under this doctrine, persons who otherwise might be considered refugees under the Refugee Convention are denied asylum in foreign countries when there is a part of their home country to which they could relocate and avoid persecution. The limit that Grotius's rationale suggests for the right to safe haven similarly would require potential claimants to draw first on the resources of their home country. As long as the home country retained sufficient land to enable persons to exercise their right to self-preservation, there would be no right to resettle elsewhere.

Implementation

Assume that individuals enjoy a right to safe haven on the basis of collective ownership of the earth. How might this right be implemented for the benefit of the victims of sea-level rise, the concern of this chapter? In reality, any right to safe haven is likely to be implemented through political discussions at both international and domestic levels. To provide a starting point for these political discussions, the principle that should guide the implementation of the right to a safe haven and possible mechanisms for implementing the right are discussed below.

Principle for Allocating Responsibility

There is an emerging policy literature that emphasizes the absence of any international law framework for dealing with the refugees whom climate change may

---

[54] Some evidence that Grotius envisions the right as coming into force when a person cannot turn to his home country is that he refers to an obligation to provide "a fixed Abode . . . to Strangers, who being expelled their own Country, seek a Retreat elsewhere" (2005 [1625], II.2.XVI). Framing the duty as owed to people "expelled" from their countries sets a high bar that leaves people who are living very poorly within their home countries unprotected. As mentioned earlier, Grotius's discussion of the right of private necessity similarly implies that a person in need is justified in using the property of another only after he has exhausted his own resources.

create. Various options have been proposed to avoid a crisis situation where countries fall back on ad hoc responses (Baer 2010; Biermann and Boas 2008; Burkett 2009; Byravan and Rajan 2006; 2010; Docherty and Giannini 2009; Hodgkinson and Burton 2010; McAdam 2010; 2011; Penz 2010; Prieur et al. 2010).[55] Under one intriguing proposal, "people living in areas that are likely to be obliterated or rendered uninhabitable would be provided the early option of migrating legally in numbers that are in some rough proportion to the host countries' cumulative greenhouse gas emissions" (Byravan and Rajan 2006, 249; Byravan and Rajan 2010). This proposal implicitly assumes that a sort of corrective justice should guide the allocation of responsibility for climate change migration. The term "corrective justice" is used loosely because the proposal allocates responsibility on the basis of country shares of overall emissions, not particular injuries caused by particular countries.[56]

As was implied earlier, there are drawbacks to allocating responsibility for climate change migration on the basis of corrective justice (Posner and Sunstein 2008). One is that corrective justice is a backward-looking approach that will limit victims to making claims against countries in proportion to their historical emissions, with the practical result that the relatively small number of countries with historically large emissions will bear most of the responsibility for climate migration. These emitters may not be the countries best suited to absorb newcomers or finance their relocation by the time citizens of sinking states migrate, given the potentially long time frame during which migration may occur. Moreover, if migration occurs decades or centuries in the future, it may be unjust to hold future citizens of historically large emitters responsible for emissions by their ancestors. One argument for holding future citizens responsible is that they are beneficiaries of the earlier wrongs. But future citizens of historically large emitters may not be net beneficiaries of their ancestors' emissions by the time migration occurs, because it is hoped that these large emitters will soon take significant actions to reduce their emissions. Some of those actions could be costly for present and future generations (Posner and Sunstein 2008). An important advantage of the collective ownership of the earth rationale for the right to safe haven is that this rationale offers a present or forward-looking basis for allocating responsibility for climate change migration. The collective ownership of the earth rationale focuses attention on what should be a more important principle than past wrongdoing in allocating responsibility: a country's resources to absorb or finance the absorption of newcomers.

Under this approach, the availability of resources, not historical wrongdoing, would be the basis for allocating responsibility for climate change migrants. Because the collective ownership of the earth rationale emphasizes everyone's equal entitlement to the resources of the earth, the remedy for a breach of the right to a safe haven should tend toward equalizing resource shares by imposing greater responsibilities for climate refugees on countries with greater resources. Thus, the availability

---

[55] Byravan and Rajan warn that "the international community . . . is probably inclined to treat the problem in the *ad hoc* manner in which refugee problems are otherwise managed" (2006, 248–249).

[56] In other words, Byravan and Rajan (2006; 2010) advocate a form of market share liability. See also Grimm (2007). Market share liability is not universally regarded as consistent with corrective justice.

of land, perhaps as measured by population density, should be a key consideration, given that the rationale for the right is the collective ownership of the earth. Less densely populated countries should incur more responsibility, while more densely populated countries should face less responsibility.

However, the availability of resources alone cannot be the sole basis for assigning responsibilities among countries. We live in a highly populated world that has been carved up among nations. There is no empty, surplus land available for settlement— or resettlement—that has not already been allocated among nations, as there arguably was in Grotius's day.[57] When we allocate responsibility for the citizens of sinking states among countries, we in effect are taking away land from citizens of existing states. In doing so, it makes sense to consider not just each country's available land mass, but also which countries can most afford to give up resources such as land. To do this, we need to look at more than population density. A country could have an expansive, relatively unpopulated land mass but be poorly positioned to take responsibility for resettling people because the country's land is of modest quality and the country has not developed other sources of wealth to support its existing population, let alone new people. Similarly, a country could be very densely populated but well positioned to accept newcomers because its land mass is extremely rich or because it has amassed economic wealth through other means. We should take account of measures of wealth, as well as population density, and thus use a basket of metrics.

Table 15.1 is a first step in thinking about the allocation of responsibility for climate migrants if a right to safe haven is grounded in the collective ownership of the earth. The table allocates responsibility for 300,000 persons, roughly the population of the Maldives, among the 34 current members of the Organisation for Economic Co-operation and Development (OECD) plus Brazil, Russia, China, and India. Three metrics are used. One metric is population density as of 2005, an indicator of the availability of land (United Nations 2008). Countries with lower population density are allocated responsibility for more newcomers. The other two metrics are 2005 gross domestic product (GDP) and 2005 GDP per capita, adjusted for purchasing power parity (International Monetary Fund 2010). GDP is a proxy for a country's total wealth, while GDP per capita is an indication of the average wealth of the country's citizens. The table displays the number of refugees for which a country would be responsible under the average of the three metrics and under each metric individually, as well as under a metric of country-specific cumulative emissions of carbon dioxide from energy for the period 1850 to 2005 (World Resources Institute 2010). Countries are listed in descending order of the number of refugees for which they would be responsible under the average of the three metrics. Table 15.2 highlights the implications of relying on the basket of metrics rather than historical emissions by comparing country shares under the two approaches. If countries agreed to assume responsibility for climate refugees on the basis of the basket of metrics, country allotments would need to be periodically updated to reflect changes in the availability of

---

[57] There may not have been much, if any, empty land available in Grotius's era if aboriginal use is given due respect.

TABLE 15.1

Allocation of Responsibility for 300,000 Climate Change Refugees Among 34 OECD Countries plus Brazil, Russia, India, and China

Country	Average	Per Capita GDP	Total GDP	Land per Person	Historical Emissions
United States	33,530	12,767	82,272	5,552	103,072
Canada	25,085	10,514	7,369	57,371	7,737
Australia	24,010	10,131	4,529	57,371	3,875
Iceland	22,663	10,551	69	57,371	29
China	12,356	1,216	34,595	1,256	29,656
Russia	12,036	3,539	11,053	21,514	28,777
Japan	11,597	9,068	25,211	511	13,585
Norway	9,997	14,214	1,433	14,343	567
Germany	8,738	9,115	16,353	745	25,028
United Kingdom	7,624	9,597	12,581	694	21,295
France	7,618	9,137	12,166	1,551	10,040
Luxembourg	7,428	21,108	214	962	209
Finland	6,967	9,104	1,041	10,757	750
Brazil	6,904	2,573	10,315	7,823	2,878
Sweden	6,775	9,793	1,926	8,606	1,332
Italy	6,644	8,414	10,635	883	5,780
New Zealand	6,529	7,443	671	11,474	408
Spain	5,987	8,229	7,707	2,025	3,265
India	5,491	624	15,349	500	8,258
Mexico	5,124	3,736	8,451	3,187	3,577
Ireland	5,123	11,468	1,032	2,869	507
The Netherlands	4,878	10,476	3,721	438	2,853
Korea	4,772	6,815	7,139	360	2,971
Austria	4,567	10,130	1,815	1,756	1,383
Switzerland	4,548	10,954	1,734	956	758
Chile	4,259	3,661	1,293	7,823	533
Denmark	4,192	10,029	1,181	1,366	1,089
Belgium	4,100	9,599	2,196	505	3,362
Greece	3,794	7,522	1,811	2,049	839
Estonia	3,618	4,971	146	5,737	360
Turkey	3,349	3,292	4,865	1,891	1,650
Slovenia	3,013	6,996	305	1,739	181
Poland	2,963	4,060	3,372	1,459	6,937
Israel	2,957	7,246	1,055	570	448
Portugal	2,953	5,989	1,372	1,497	556
Czech Republic	2,915	6,061	1,349	1,334	3,193
Hungary	2,592	5,069	1,114	1,594	1,304
Slovak Republic	2,306	4,792	562	1,565	959

SOURCE: Table 15.1 was prepared by Mark LeBel.

NOTE: The numbers in Table 15.1 are independently rounded. Due to rounding, the allocations for the average of per capita and total GDP and land per person may appear slightly off given the published numbers for each of these three metrics.

TABLE 15.2

Country Shares Under Average of Three Metrics and Historical
Emissions

Country	Percentage Under Average of Three Metrics	Percentage Under Historical Emissions
United States	11.2	34.4
Canada	8.4	2.6
Australia	8.0	1.3
Iceland	7.6	0.0
China	4.1	9.9
Russia	4.0	9.6
Japan	3.9	4.5
Norway	3.3	0.2
Germany	2.9	8.3
United Kingdom	2.5	7.1
France	2.5	3.3
Luxembourg	2.5	0.1
Finland	2.3	0.2
Brazil	2.3	1.0
Sweden	2.3	0.4
Italy	2.2	1.9
New Zealand	2.2	0.1
Spain	2.0	1.1
India	1.8	2.8
Mexico	1.7	1.2
Ireland	1.7	0.2
The Netherlands	1.6	1.0
Korea	1.6	1.0
Austria	1.5	0.5
Switzerland	1.5	0.3
Chile	1.4	0.2
Denmark	1.4	0.4
Belgium	1.4	1.1
Greece	1.3	0.3
Estonia	1.2	0.1
Turkey	1.1	0.6
Slovenia	1.0	0.1
Poland	1.0	2.3
Israel	1.0	0.1
Portugal	1.0	0.2
Czech Republic	1.0	1.1
Hungary	0.9	0.4
Slovak Republic	0.8	0.3

SOURCE: Table 15.2 was prepared by Mark LeBel.

NOTES: The percentages in Table 15.2 are based on underlying data prepared for Table 15.1, not the rounded data published in Table 15.1.

resources, such as land and economic wealth, as well as changes in information about the expected number of citizens of sinking states requiring refuge as the science of sea-level rise improves.

Implementation Mechanisms

Even if there is agreement that a country's resources, as well as its economic wealth, should determine the extent of the responsibilities that it owes the citizens of sinking states, it is still necessary to determine the mechanisms that countries could use to satisfy their obligations. Drawing partly on proposals for tradable quotas to deal with environmental problems such as greenhouse gases, Schuck (1997) proposes a tradable-quota regime for refugees in general, not specifically for climate refugees. Under Schuck's proposal, countries would agree to take quotas of refugees that they could meet either by accepting refugees or paying other countries to do so. Country allotments of climate refugees similarly could be made tradable.

Tradability would provide a way of mitigating the conflict between two rights at stake in the refugee context, the right of refugees to safe haven and the right of countries to control entry, because countries that did not want to admit refugees could pay others to resettle them. Although allowing countries to refuse entry to refugees might seem inconsistent with the idea that there is a right to safe haven, recall that there is nothing in Grotius, Pufendorf, Kant, or contemporary refugee law that gives refugees the right to choose their country of refuge. As Schuck explains with respect to modern refugee law, "Refugees are entitled only to basic protection from persecution, not residence in the society of their choice" (1997, 285).

Tradability could be achieved in two ways.[58] In a decentralized regime, countries would have quotas that they could honor either by accepting the requisite number of climate refugees or by paying other countries to take all or part of the quota. In a centralized regime, an international agency would, in effect, tax countries for the cost of resettling refugees on the basis of the quotas and then contract with countries to resettle the refugees. Schuck (1997) argues that a decentralized approach would be more likely to garner state support because it would have lower transaction costs and allow host countries to receive not only cash, but also other goods, such as trade benefits or political endorsement, for agreeing to accept refugees.

There are many possible objections to tradable quotas for climate refugees. One is that refugees could be required to settle in countries that lack the resources or the will to absorb newcomers. This concern could be addressed to some extent by restricting the countries to which quotas could be sold (in a decentralized regime) and the countries that could be contracted to resettle refugees (in a centralized regime) to countries with a certain level of resources and commitment to refugee protection, or potentially just to countries that received quotas in the first place.[59] Restricting

---

[58] The following discussion of tradable quotas for climate refugees draws heavily on Schuck's (1997) proposal for tradable quotas for refugees in general and his discussion of possible objections to the idea.

[59] Schuck proposes that refugee quotas should not be allotted "to a state that engages in systematic violations of human rights" (1997, 281) or to "states whose wealth falls below some minimal level" (1997, 282). He also suggests mechanisms for "minimizing" the "risk" that refugees will be treated poorly by countries that are paid to take them, although he acknowledges that the risk cannot be completely eliminated (294).

the market in these ways might reduce the gains from trade. By limiting the number of countries where refugees could be resettled, we might reduce the overall number of refugees who could be protected. But the costs of protecting refugees from inhospitable or dangerous circumstances almost certainly are worth incurring.

A second possible objection is that a tradable-quota regime would treat vulnerable people as commodities. Especially in a decentralized form, the tradable-quota regime would make countries with the resources and wealth to absorb newcomers the masters of the fate of refugees because these countries would determine through negotiations where refugees would be resettled. In doing so, the regime would fail to honor the suggestion from Nauru's ambassador to the United Nations that "the people who are most affected" should be asked what do about climate change (Mohrs 2009, 3). One way of allowing individuals from sinking states a voice in where they are resettled would be to adopt a centralized trading regime with an agency overseen by a board with representation from those states. The board could be given the task of approving any contracts to resettle individuals, and those states' representatives on the board would have an opportunity to influence the location of resettlement. Representation on the board would seem a small concession to make to people whose lives are being fundamentally uprooted through no fault of their own.[60]

In the United States and elsewhere, policy makers are mainly focusing on measures to mitigate climate change by reducing greenhouse gas emissions. This chapter draws attention to the need to start thinking about the adaptations that climate change may require. In particular, it is possible that sea-level rise caused by climate change may lead to the submergence of small island states and consequently the need to resettle their citizens. At the moment, the prospects seem slim that an international legal regime will soon emerge to address the adaptations that climate change will require. The small island states themselves apparently are divided about whether to raise the need for measures to facilitate relocation (McAdam 2011), and no politically powerful country is championing relocation assistance. But as Thomas Homer-Dixon (2010) argues, climate change is upon us, and it would be better not to wait until there is a crisis induced by climate change to think through the options for dealing with it.

Acknowledgments

I thank Ira Klein for bringing to my attention the statements of the president of the Maldives about resettling the citizens of his country and for triggering my interest in the rights of the citizens of the Maldives and other vulnerable small island states. For helpful comments, I thank Alexander Aleinikoff, Richard Barnes, Eric Biber, Peter Byrne, Daniel Cole, Ronald Dworkin, Daniel Farber, Stephen Holmes, Benedict Kingsbury, Janos Kis, Tally Kritzman-Amir, Liam Murphy, Thomas Nagel, Michael Oppenheimer, Elinor Ostrom, Peter Schuck, Richard Stewart, and Jeremy Waldron. Mark LeBel, New York University School of Law, candidate for J.D. 2012,

[60] Schuck (1997) has a series of different responses to the commodification objection to tradable quotas for refugees.

provided superb research assistance, including the preparation of the tables on the allocation of responsibility for 300,000 persons. Rachel Jones provided outstanding editorial assistance.

REFERENCES

Appiah, K. Anthony. 2003. Grounding human rights. In *Human rights as politics and idolatry*, eds. Amy Gutmann, Michael Ignatieff, K. Anthony Appiah, David A. Hollinger, Thomas W. Laqueur and Diane F. Orentlicher, 101–116. Princeton, NJ: Princeton University Press.

Aquinas, Thomas. 2002. *On law, morality, and politics*. 2nd ed. Trans. Richard J. Regan. Eds. William P. Baumgarth and Richard J. Regan. Indianapolis: Hackett Publishing Company.

Baer, Paul. 2010. Adaptation to climate change: Who pays whom? In *Climate ethics: Essential readings*, eds. Stephen Gardiner, Simon Caney, Dale Jamieson and Henry Shue, 247–262. New York: Oxford University Press.

Benhabib, Seyla. 2004. *The rights of others: Aliens, residents and citizens*. Cambridge, U.K.: Cambridge University Press.

Biermann, Frank, and Ingrid Boas. 2008. Protecting climate refugees: The case for a global protocol. *Environment* 50(6):8–16. http://www.environmentmagazine.org/Archives/Back%20Issues/November-December%202008/Biermann-Boas-full.html.

Brown, Oli. 2008. The numbers game. *Forced Migration Review* 31:8–9.

Buckle, Stephen. 1991. *Natural law and the theory of property: Grotius to Hume*. Oxford: Oxford University Press.

Burkett, Maxine. 2009. Climate reparations. *Melbourne Journal of International Law* 10:509–542.

Byravan, Sujatha, and Sudhir Chella Rajan. 2006. Providing new homes for climate change exiles. *Climate Policy* 6:247–252.

——. 2010. The ethical implications of sea-level rise due to climate change. *Ethics and International Affairs* 24(3):239–260.

Cavallar, Georg. 2002. *The rights of strangers*. Surrey, England: Ashgate Publishing.

Crouch, Brad. 2008. A road to nowhere. *Sunday Times*, October 5: 15.

Docherty, Bonnie, and Tyler Giannini. 2009. Confronting a rising tide: A proposal for a convention on climate change refugees. *Harvard Environmental Law Review* 33:349–403.

Dummett, Ann. 1992. Natural law and transnational migration. In *Free movement: Ethical issues in the transnational migration of people and of money*, eds. Brian Barry and Robert E. Goodin, 169–180. University Park: Pennsylvania State University Press.

Ellickson, Robert. 1992–1993. Property in land. *Yale Law Journal* 102:1315–1400.

Farber, Daniel. 2008. The case for climate compensation: Justice for climate change victims in a complex world. *Utah Law Review* 2008:377–413.

Gans, Chaim. 2008. *A just Zionism: On the morality of the Jewish state*. New York: Oxford University Press.

Grimm, Daniel. 2007. Global warming and market share liability: A proposed model for allocating tort damages among CO_2 producers. *Columbia Journal of Environmental Law* 32:209–250.

Grotius, Hugo. 2005 [1625]. *The rights of war and peace*, ed. Richard Tuck. 3 vols. Indianapolis: Liberty Fund. http://oll.libertyfund.org/title/1877.

Guler, Claudio. 2009. The climate refugee challenge. International Relations and Security Network (April 14). http://www.isn.ethz.ch/isn/Current-Affairs/Security-Watch/Detail/?ots591=4888CAA0-B3DB-1461-98B9-E20E7B9C13D4&lng=en&id=98861.

Hodgkinson, David, and Tess Burton. 2010. A convention for persons displaced by climate change. http://www.ccdpconvention.com/index.html.

Homer-Dixon, Thomas. 2010. Disaster at the top of the world. *New York Times*, August 22: A23.

Hont, Istvan, and Michael Ignatieff. 1983. Needs and justice in the *Wealth of Nations*: An introductory essay. In *Wealth and virtue: The shaping of political economy in the Scottish Enlight-*

enment, eds. Istvan Hont and Michael Ignatieff, 1–44. Cambridge, U.K.: Cambridge University Press.

Hulme, Mike. 2008. Commentary—Climate refugees: Cause for a new agreement? *Environment* 50(6):50–51. http://www.environmentmagazine.org/Archives/Back%20Issues/November-December%202008/hulme-full.html.

International Monetary Fund. 2010. World Economic Outlook database. April 2010. http://www.imf.org/external/pubs/ft/weo/2010/01/weodata/index.aspx.

IPCC (Intergovernmental Panel on Climate Change). 2007. *Climate change 2007: Synthesis report.* http://www.ipcc.ch/publications_and_data/publications_ipcc_fourth_assessment_report_synthesis_report.htm.

Kant, Immanuel. 1996 [1797]. *The metaphysics of morals.* Trans. and ed. Mary Gregor. Cambridge, U.K.: Cambridge University Press.

———. 2006 [1795]. Toward perpetual peace: A philosophical sketch. In *Toward perpetual peace and other writings on politics, peace, and history: Immanuel Kant*, ed. Pauline Kleingeld. Trans. David L. Colclasure. New Haven, CT: Yale University Press.

Kleingeld, Pauline. 1998. Kant's cosmopolitan law: World citizenship for a global order. *Kantian Review* 2:72–90.

Kolmannskog, Vikram Odedra. 2008. Future floods of refugees: A comment on climate change, conflict and forced migration. Norwegian Refugee Council. http://www.nrc.no/arch/_img/9268480.pdf.

Kristof, Nicholas D. 1997. Island nations fear sea could swamp them. *New York Times*, December 1: F9.

Kritzman-Amir, Tally. 2008. Socio-economic refugees. J.S.D. diss., Tel Aviv University Faculty of Law.

Martin, David A. 1991. The refugee concept: On definitions, politics, and the careful use of a scarce resource. In *Refugee policy: Canada and the United States*, ed. H. Adelman, 30–51. North York, Ont.: York Lanes Press.

Martin, David A., T. Alexander Aleinikoff, Hiroshi Motomura, and Maryellen Fullerton. 2007. *Forced migration: Law and policy.* St. Paul, MN: Thomson/West.

McAdam, Jane. 2009a. Environmental migration governance. University of New South Wales Faculty of Law Research Paper No. 2009-1. http://papers.ssrn.com/sol3/papers.cfm?abstract_id=1412002.

———. 2009b. From economic refugees to climate refugees? *Melbourne Journal of International Law* 10:579–595.

———. 2010. "Disappearing states," statelessness and the boundaries of international law. In *Climate change and displacement*, ed. Jane McAdam, 105–109. Oxford: Hart Publishing.

———. 2011. Swimming against the tide: Why a climate change displacement treaty is not *the* answer. *International Journal of Refugee Law* 23(1):2–27.

McAdam, Jane, and Ben Saul. 2010. An insecure climate for human security? Climate-induced displacement and international law. In *Human security and non-citizens: Law, policy and international affairs*, eds. Alice Edwards and Carla Fertsman, 357–403. Cambridge, U.K.: Cambridge University Press.

Meisels, Tamar. 2009. *Territorial rights.* 2nd ed. Breinigsville, PA: Springer.

Metz, Helen Chapin, ed. 1994. *Maldives: A country study.* Washington, DC: U.S. Government Printing Office for the Library of Congress. http://countrystudies.us/maldives/.

Milne, Glenn A., W. Roland Gehrels, Chris W. Hughes, and Mark E. Tamisiea. 2009. Identifying the causes of sea-level change. *Nature Geoscience* 2:471–478.

Mohrs, Falko. 2009. H. E. Ms. Moses makes a clear statement. October 16. http://www.unyouth.com/index.php?option=com_content&view=article&id=170:speech-ms-moses&catid=1:frontpage.

Murray, Christopher F. 2002. Note: Any port in a storm? The right of entry for reasons of *force majeure* or distress in the wake of the *Erika* and the *Castor. Ohio State Law Journal* 63:1465–1506.

Muthu, Sankar. 2003. *Enlightenment against empire.* Princeton, NJ: Princeton University Press.

Nagel, Thomas. 2005. The problem of global justice. *Philosophy and Public Affairs* 33(2):113–147.

Nine, Cara. 2010. Ecological refugees, states borders, and the Lockean proviso. *Journal of Applied Philosophy* 27(4):359–375.

Office of the United Nations High Commissioner for Refugees in cooperation with the Norwegian Refugee Council, the Representative of the Secretary General on the Human Rights of Internally Displaced Persons and the United Nations University. 2009. *Forced displacement in the context of climate change: Challenges for states under international law* (May 20). http://www.unhcr.org/4a1e4d8c2.html.

Oliver, John T. 2008–2009. Legal and policy factors governing the imposition of conditions on access to and jurisdiction over foreign-flag vessels in U.S. ports. *South Carolina Journal of International Law and Business* 5:209–345.

Pagden, Anthony. 1987. Dispossessing the barbarian: The language of Spanish Thomism and the debate over the property rights of the American Indians. In *The languages of political theory in early-modern Europe*, ed. Anthony Pagden, 79–98. Cambridge, U.K.: Cambridge University Press.

Penz, Peter. 2010. International ethical responsibilities to "climate change refugees." In *Climate change and displacement: Multidisciplinary perspectives*, ed. Jane McAdam, 151–173. Oxford: Hart Publishing.

Pogge, Thomas W. 1989. *Realizing Rawls*. Ithaca, NY: Cornell University Press.

———. 1994. An egalitarian law of peoples. *Philosophy and Public Affairs* 23(3):195–224.

———. 2002. Eradicating systemic poverty: Brief for a global resources dividend. In *World poverty and human rights: Cosmopolitan responsibilities and reforms*, ed. Thomas W. Pogge, 196–215. Cambridge, MA: Polity.

Posner, Eric A., and Cass R. Sunstein. 2008. Climate change justice. *Georgetown Law Journal* 96:1565–1612.

President's Office, Republic of Maldives. 2010. *Government and Dutch Docklands sign an agreement to develop floating facilities in the Maldives* (March 4). http://www.presidencymaldives.gov.mv/Index.aspx?lid=11&dcid=987.

Prieur, Michel, Jean-Pierre Marguénaud, Gérard Monédiaire, Julien Bétaille, Jean-François Dubost, Bernard Drobenko, Jean-Jacques Gouguet, Jean-Marc Lavieille, Séverine Nadaud and Damien Roets. 2010. *Draft Convention on the International Status of Environmentally-Dispaced Persons*. Second version (May). http://www.cidce.org/pdf/Draft%20Convention%20on%20the%20International%20Status%20on%20environmentally%20displaced%20persons%20%28second%20version%29.pdf.

Pufendorf, Samuel. 1934 [1688]. *De jure naturae et gentium libri octo*. Trans. C. H. Oldfather and W. A. Oldfather. Oxford: Clarendon Press; London: Humphrey Milford.

Rawls, John. 1971. *A theory of justice*. Cambridge, MA: Harvard University Press.

Representative of the Secretary General on the Human Rights of Internally Displaced Persons. 2008. *Displacement caused by the effects of climate change: Who will be affected and what are the gaps in the normative frameworks for their protection?* (October 10). http://www.brookings.edu/papers/2008/1016_climate_change_kalin.aspx.

Risse, Mathias. 2009. The right to relocation: Disappearing island nations and common ownership of the earth. *Ethics and International Affairs* 23:281–299.

Salter, John. 2005. Grotius and Pufendorf: On the right of necessity. *History of Political Thought* 26(2):284–302.

Scanlon, T. M. 1998. *What we owe to each other*. Cambridge, MA: Belknap Press of Harvard University Press.

Schmidle, Nicholas. 2009. Wanted: A new home for my country. *New York Times Magazine*, May 10:38.

Schuck, Peter H. 1997. Refugee burden-sharing: A modest proposal. *Yale Journal of International Law* 22:243–297.

Singer, Peter. 1972. Famine, affluence, and morality. *Philosophy and Public Affairs* 1(3):229–243.

———. 2009. *The life you can save: Acting now to end world poverty*. New York: Random House.

Tuck, Richard. 1999. *The rights of war and peace: Political thought and the international order from Grotius to Kant.* New York: Oxford University Press.

Tully, Stephen. 2007. The contribution of human rights as an additional perspective on climate change impacts within the Pacific. *New Zealand Journal of Public and International Law* 5:169–199.

United Nations. 1951. "Convention Relating to the Status of Refugees." Entered into force April 22, 1954. Treaty Series, vol. 189. http://www.unhcr.org/protect/PROTECTION/3b66c2aa10.pdf.

United Nations. 1967. "Protocol Relating to the Status of Refugees." Entered into force October 4, 1967. Treaty Series, vol. 606. http://www.unhcr.org/protect/PROTECTION/3b66c2aa10.pdf.

United Nations. 2008. Population Division. World population prospects: The 2008 Revision Population Database. http://esa.un.org/unpd/wpp/Other-Information/publications_2.htm.

United Nations High Commissioner for Refugees. 2008. *Climate change, natural disasters and human displacement: A UNHCR perspective* (October 23, 2008). http://www.unhcr.org/refworld/docid/492bb6b92.html.

Vitoria, Francisco de. 1917 [1532]. *De Indis.* Trans. John Bawley Pate. In *De Indis et de ivre belli relectiones,* ed. Ernest Nys. Washington, DC: Carnegie Institution of Washington. Reprint. 1934. In James Brown Scott, *The Spanish origin of international law: Francisco De Vitoria and his law of nations.* Oxford: Clarendon Press.

Waldron, Jeremy. 2000. What is cosmopolitanism? *Journal of Political Philosophy* 8:227–243.

Walzer, Michael. 1983. *Spheres of justice: A defense of pluralism and equality.* New York: Basic Books.

Webb, Arthur P., and Paul S. Kench. 2010. The dynamic response of reef islands to sea-level rise: Evidence from multi-decadal analysis of island change in the Central Pacific. *Global and Planetary Change* 72:234–246.

Whitehead, Lena E. 2009. No port in a storm—A review of recent history and legal concepts resulting in the extinction of ports of refuge. *Naval Law Review* 58:65–88.

World Resources Institute. 2010. Climate Analysis Indicators Tool. CAIT version 8.0. http://cait.wri.org/.

Zukerman, Wendy. 2010. Shape-shifting islands defy sea-level rise. *New Scientist* 206(2763):10.

Commentary

·RICHARD A. BARNES

In lay terms, property is about who gets what, why, and by what means. Although Katrina Wyman's chapter is concerned with the consequences of rising sea levels and seems at first glance somewhat remote from questions of property, more careful attention reveals that she is ultimately concerned with these basic elements of the function of property. Wyman provides a historically grounded, but radical vision of a moral basis for a right to safe haven. Although I do not agree entirely with all the points made, what is clear is that she demonstrates the great relevance of property concepts. A key impact of her chapter is that it serves as a reminder of the inadequacies of our legal institutions (including property) for servicing basic human needs. Although a property rights approach may not provide the easiest or politically acceptable basis for resolving these global problems, understanding the role and limitations of property is important.

There is at present no legal regime that allows displaced persons to resettle in the territory of another state. Wyman's exploration of the basis for such a right is important because without a compelling moral, political, or economic rationale for a legal right, a regime cannot be created to implement it. Wyman surveys several potential moral bases for a right, but her strongest case draws on the Grotian argument that conventional rules of property must give way to the preconventional universal use right that allows every person to use the resources of the earth to meet his preservation needs. Such a use right derives from the collective ownership of the earth, a position that preceded the development of conventional property rights.

When the Grotian use right is detached from unnecessary theological baggage and is presented as a means of sustaining life, it provides a compelling basis for a legal claim. Barnes (2009) has sought to present the same kind of argument. I also agree with Wyman that the interests of persons displaced because of climate change are best served by avoiding mechanisms based on retributive or corrective justice, which assign responsibility to those deemed to have contributed most to climate change. One difficulty with the use right approach is that the precise level of needs that ought to be satisfied under a basic use right is highly controversial. Assessing needs and meeting them also pose difficult practical questions, to which Wyman alludes in the final part of her chapter.

Displacement of persons due to climate change involves situations of necessity and people's access to the essentials for life. Therefore, the Grotian use right is immediately relevant. Necessity is a feature of many accounts of property and provides a key limit on the extent of property in most moral traditions. Examples are the duty not to accumulate beyond one's needs in the labor/desert account of property and the need to ensure that persons can assert sufficient material autonomy under liberal accounts of property. The difficulty is always translating these threshold limitations into positive rights and duties. If we consider how necessity manifests itself in law, especially at the level of international law with which Wyman is concerned, it is clear that it invariably falls short of the kind of positive right for which she is advocating. Under international law, necessity manifests itself in quite limited ways and typically operates as an immunity, rather than as a positive claim right. Thus, in the famous cases of *The Creole* (1853) and *The Rebecca* (1929), the courts were principally concerned with liability of the vessel owners for breaking local laws when the vessels entered the territory of the State, despite being in distress. The courts were clear that distress was a defense to liability and not the basis for a positive right to seek shelter. In recent times, states have vigorously defended their right to control entry into territory or even maritime zones (Barnes 2004). More generally, a strongly circumscribed notion of necessity is also treated as a defense in the law of state responsibility (ILC 2001, Article 25). So even if one accepts the moral basis of the right, transposition into a positive legal right remains highly questionable.

Wyman mentions the dissent in *Pierson v. Post* to show why moral and other historical claims should have some contemporary relevance. Although I would not want to discard the wisdom of these writers on whom our learned judges felt it appropriate to rely, I would still advise caution about how we treat such precedents. Grotius was a renowned scholar, but he is also noted for his pragmatism or advocacy (Perels 2010 [1882]). His treatises were in part polemics, used to underpin a notion of freedom of the high seas and to sustain Dutch trading interests. Therefore, we must beware of taking his arguments out of context. It is important to note that Wyman was careful to circumscribe the Grotian use right: it is a means of last resort, it is limited to consumables, and it is limited against the equally needy. Beyond those important limits, one might add that the use right was formulated at a time when there remained potentially considerable areas of *res nullius*, things and land that were not owned. Thus, there was scope for allowing the satisfaction of needs by acquiring such things. However, the modern world is characterized by the nearly complete subjugation of land territory and natural resources to the sovereignty (exclusive control) of states. This renders implementation of the use right immensely more difficult in practice. Furthermore, even if we accept necessity as permitting the taking of other's property to meet one's needs, it can be argued that what now remains of the use right has long since been absorbed into other institutions, such as the welfare system or public property. These institutions are designed to protect individual well-being and ensure that minimum needs can be met, and to guard against unilateral resort to takings. However, they are firmly grounded within domestic legal systems and are not readily applicable to the kind of international problems confronted in Wyman's chapter. In the international context, public or collective interests are far more difficult to secure because there is no state machinery capable of articulating and protecting them. To criticize Wyman's argument is really to criticize the lack of community and community machinery capable of preserving collective interests at the global level. In the case of rising sea levels, the problems arise out of our use of a common resource (the atmosphere). They affect another common resource (the oceans), and require a collective response. However, we lack institutions that are capable of handling these issues.

These difficulties pervade the final part of Wyman's chapter. The discussion of the mechanism for allocating responsibility to receive displaced persons is the most controversial part of the chapter because of the implications it has for political and social decision making. Indeed, before we can even address the question of what factors should guide the allocation of responsibility, we perhaps also need to ask who is to determine and operate this mechanism. If there is an individual right, then would the individual bear responsibility to advance the right, or would this responsibility have to be institutionalized? If collective institutional support at the interstate level is needed, but reasonably well-developed refugee law lacks the means to allocate responsibility for accepting persons who are fleeing persecution, why would the treatment of persons displaced by sea-level rise be any different, especially if this is a permanent rather than temporary state of affairs? There are also many questions about the values used. Of course, wealth and physical capacity to receive displaced persons may be useful factors in the equation, but what about other values, such as the cultural, religious, political, and social suitability of recipient states? The scale of the practical problems that require planning and negotiation is staggering. This short commentary is not the place to engage these important matters, but Wyman is to be applauded for taking steps to explore and define the parameters of this debate.

REFERENCES

Barnes, Richard. 2004. Refugee law at sea. *International and Comparative Law Quarterly* 53:47–77.
———. 2009. *Property rights and natural resources.* Oxford: Hart.
ILC (International Law Commission). 2001. *Articles on the responsibility of states for internationally wrongful acts.* Reproduced in *Report of the International Law Commission 53rd Session* (23 April–June and 2 July–10 August 2001). *United Nations General Assembly Official Records,* 56th Session, Supplement No. 10, at 43. UN Doc. A/56/10.
Perels, Ferdinand. 1882. *Das Offentlich Seerecht.* Berlin: Mittler und Sohn.

Contributors

Editors

DANIEL H. COLE
Professor
Maurer School of Law
School of Public and Environmental
    Affairs
Workshop in Political Theory
    and Policy Analysis
Indiana University
Bloomington, Indiana

ELINOR OSTROM
Senior Research Director
Workshop in Political Theory
    and Policy Analysis
Distinguished Professor and Arthur F.
    Bentley Professor of Political Science
Indiana University
Bloomington, Indiana
and
Founding Director
Center for the Study of Institutional
    Diversity
Arizona State University
Tempe, Arizona

Authors

C. LEIGH ANDERSON
Professor
Daniel J. Evans School of Public
    Affairs
Director
Marc Lindenberg Center
    for Humanitarian Action,
    International Development,
    and Global Citizenship
University of Washington
Seattle, Washington

WILLIAM BLOMQUIST
Dean and Professor
School of Liberal Arts
Indiana University–Purdue University
    Indianapolis
Indianapolis, Indiana

KAREN CLAY
Associate Professor of Economics
Heinz College
Carnegie Mellon University
Pittsburgh, Pennsylvania

NIVES DOLŠAK
Associate Professor
School of Marine and Environmental
    Affairs.
University of Washington
Seattle, Washington, and
Interdisciplinary Arts and Sciences
University of Washington
Bothell, Washington

THRÁINN EGGERTSSON
Professor
Institute of Economic Studies
University of Iceland
Reykjavik, Iceland
and
Hertie School of Governance
Berlin, Germany

RICHARD A. EPSTEIN
Lawrence A. Tisch Professor of Law
New York University School of Law
New York, New York
and
The Peter and Kirsten Bedford
    Senior Fellow
Hoover Institution and
Stanford University
Stanford, California
and
James Parker Hall Distinguished
    Service Professor Emeritus of Law and
    Senior Lecturer
University of Chicago Law School
Chicago, Illinois

WILLIAM A. FISCHEL
Professor of Economics and Hardy
    Professor of Legal Studies
Dartmouth College
Hanover, New Hampshire

GARY D. LIBECAP
Research Associate
National Bureau of Economic
    Research
Cambridge, Massachusetts
and
Sherm and Marge Telleen Research
    Fellow
Hoover Institution
Stanford University
Stanford, California
and
Distinguished Professor of Corporate
    Environmental Management
University of California
Santa Barbara, California

BONNIE J. MCCAY
Board of Governors Distinguished
    Service Professor
Department of Human Ecology
School of Environmental and Biological
    Sciences
Rutgers University
New Brunswick, New Jersey

ANDREA G. MCDOWELL
Professor of Law
Seton Hall Law School
Newark, New Jersey

JOUNI PAAVOLA
Professor
Deputy Director of the Centre
    for Climate Change Economics
    and Policy
Director of the Sustainability Research
    Institute
School of Earth and Environment
University of Leeds
Leeds, United Kingdom

GREGORY M. PARKHURST
Adjunct Professor
Weber State University
Ogden, Utah

JASON F. SHOGREN
Stroock Distinguished Professor
    of Natural Resource Conservation
    and Management
Chair of Department of Economics
    and Finance
University of Wyoming
Laramie, Wyoming

GAVIN WRIGHT
William Robertson
Co-Professor of American Economic
    History
Department of Economics
Stanford University
Stanford, California

KATRINA MIRIAM WYMAN
Professor of Law
New York University School of Law
New York, New York

RICHARD O. ZERBE
Daniel J. Evans Distinguished
    Professor and
Director of The Benefit-Cost Center
Evans School of Public Affairs
University of Washington
Seattle, Washington

Commentators

LEE J. ALSTON
Professor of Economics
Director
Program on Institutions
Institute of Behavioral Science
University of Colorado
Boulder, Colorado
and
Research Associate
National Bureau of Economic Research
Cambridge, Massachusetts

JOHN A. BADEN
Founder and Chairman
Foundation for Research on Economics
    and the Environment (FREE)
Bozeman, Montana

RICHARD A. BARNES
Reader
Law School
University of Hull
Hull, United Kingdom

ROBERT C. ELLICKSON
Walter E. Meyer Professor of Property
    and Urban Law
Yale Law School
New Haven, Connecticut

PETER Z. GROSSMAN
Clarence Efroymson Professor
    of Economics
College of Business
Butler University
Indianapolis, Indiana

SHI-LING HSU
Professor
Faculty of Law
University of British Columbia
Vancouver, British Columbia, Canada

MARK T. KANAZAWA
Ada M. Harrison Distinguished
  Teaching Professor of the
  Social Sciences
Director of Environmental Studies
Carleton College
Northfield, Minnesota

WALLACE E. OATES
Professor
Department of Economics
University of Maryland
College Park, Maryland
and
University Fellow
Resources for the Future
Washington, D.C.

EDELLA C. SCHLAGER
Professor
School of Government and Public Policy
University of Arizona
Tucson, Arizona

ANTHONY SCOTT
Emeritus Professor
Department of Economics
University of British Columbia
Vancouver, British Columbia, Canada

HENRY E. SMITH
Fessenden Professor of Law
Harvard Law School
Cambridge, Massachusetts

V. KERRY SMITH
Regent's Professor and W. P. Carey
  Professor of Economics
W. P. Carey School of Business
Arizona State University
Tempe, Arizona

JAMES WILSON
Professor of Marine Sciences and
  Economics
University of Maine
Orono, Maine

Index

Mayors' Climate Protection Agreement, U.S., 425

McCay, Bonnie J., 5, 252–255

McDowell, Andrea G., 3, 70, 73, 102, 119–120

McKinnon, R., 19

McNeil, Samuel, 113

Measure 37, 269

measurement: of air pollution, 175; committed, 397; cost, 400

Medicine Lodge treaty, 304

Mello-Roos bonds, 272

Meltzer, Rachel, 291

metallurgy, 85–86, 89

metropolitan federation, 264

Mexico, 243; law, 69

Michelman, Frank, 269, 278

Michigan, Lake, 342

microparadigm, 28, 33

microeconomics, 30

Mid-Atlantic Fishery Management Council, 221, 222

Middlesex Co. v. McCue, 329–330, 340

Mill, John Stuart, 196

Millennium Development Goals, 452

Miller v. Schoene, 128–130

mills, 339–340

Milne, Glenn A., 442–443

mineral lands, 113

minerals sector, 76–81; property rights, 89–92

Miners and Settlers of Spring Valley, 114

Miner's Ten Commandments, The, 100

Mines Alumni Association, 88

mining and miners, 96–97; adult males, 77; boundary disputes, 106, 108; camps, 1, 3; by census year, 77; claims, 91, 99–100, 103, 105, 110; code, 111–112; conventions, 110; of copper, 81, 85–87; district codes, 67, 70–75; early methods, 82; exclusion and, 114; foreign born, 79; forms, 104; higher education, 87–89; hydraulic, 83, 112; immigrants and, 78; monopolies, 101; partnerships, 101; patents, 91; power relationships, 112; quartz, 76, 83, 104, 112; riverbed, 104; rules, 113–116; of silver, 80–81; small-scale, 106; technology, 82–85; violence and, 106. *See also* gold rush

Ministry of Health, 24

misrule-by-variance, 275

mitigation, 418, 421, 428

Mobil Oil Corp. v. Superior Court of San Diego City, 140

mobile resource systems, 47

modernization, 17, 20

modified neoclassical approach, to institutions, 15

Mongolia, 102

monitoring, 56, 423; rules, 163

Mono Lake, 406

Monroe, Henry S., 87

Montana, 80

Montgomery, Ex parte, 279

Montreal Protocol, 178, 181, 188, 422

moral claim, 298, 301–302, 305–306

moral entitlement, 302

moral minimum, 454–455

moral theory, cosmopolitan, 441, 450

Moser, Petra, 90

Moses, Marlene, 441

Moses, Robert, 290

Motor Vehicle Air Pollution Control Act, 142–143

Mt. Kare, 108–109

Muckleshoot tribe, 307–308

Muir, John, 196

multicollinearity, 30

multifunctionality, of resources, 373, 376

multiyear leases, 396

Murphy's Diggings, 115

mutual aid, principle of, 454–455

Myers, Matthew S., 305–306

Nagel, Thomas, 454

naïve theory, 1–3, 37–38

nanny state, 140

Napoleonic Wars, 18

Nash equilibrium, 210

Nasheed, Mohamed, 9, 439

National Ambient Air Quality Standards (NAAQS), 159–160, 166, 172

National Oceanic and Atmospheric Administration (NOAA), 229

Native Americans, 295–296, 298, 302, 381; European Americans and, 303; land ownership by, 6–7; right to land, 308; treaties, 304–305; water rights, 406–408. *See also specific tribes*

natural law, 318–322

Natural Resource Conservation Service, 199

natural resources, 37–38; deterioration, 159; sustainability, 44–45

"Natural Resources and the Public Estate," 141

natural science, 25

Nature Conservancy, 240, 243, 244

Nauclér, Tomas, 427

Nauru, 441, 465

About the Lincoln Institute of Land Policy

The Lincoln Institute of Land Policy is a private operating foundation whose mission is to improve the quality of public debate and decisions in the areas of land policy and land-related taxation in the United States and around the world. The Institute's goals are to integrate theory and practice to better shape land policy and to provide a nonpartisan forum for discussion of the multidisciplinary forces that influence public policy. This focus on land derives from the Institute's founding objective—to address the links between land policy and social and economic progress—that was identified and analyzed by political economist and author Henry George.

The work of the Institute is organized in three departments: Valuation and Taxation, Planning and Urban Form, and International Studies, which includes programs on Latin America and China. We seek to inform decision making through education, research, policy evaluation, demonstration projects, and the dissemination of information through our publications, Web site, and other media. Our programs bring together scholars, practitioners, public officials, policy makers, journalists, and citizens in a collegial learning environment. The Institute does not take a particular point of view, but rather serves as a catalyst to facilitate analysis and discussion of land use and taxation issues—to make a difference today and to help policy makers plan for tomorrow.

The Lincoln Institute of Land Policy is an equal opportunity institution.

L LINCOLN INSTITUTE
OF LAND POLICY
CAMBRIDGE, MASSACHUSETTS

113 Brattle Street
Cambridge, MA 02138-3400 USA

Phone: 1-617-661-3016 or 1-800-526-3873
Fax: 1-617-661-7235 or 1-800-526-3944
E-mail: help@lincolninst.edu
Web: www.lincolninst.edu